Lecture Notes in Computer Science 3537

Commenced Publication in 1973
Founding and Former Series Editors:
Gerhard Goos, Juris Hartmanis, and Jan van Leeuwen

Alberto Apostolico   Maxime Crochemore
Kunsoo Park (Eds.)

Combinatorial
Pattern Matching

16th Annual Symposium, CPM 2005
Jeju Island, Korea, June 19-22, 2005
Proceedings

 Springer

Volume Editors

Alberto Apostolico
University of Padova, Department of Information Engineering
Via Gradenigo 6a, 35131 Padova, Italy
E-mail: axa@dei.unipd.it

Maxime Crochemore
King's College London
and University of Marne-la-Vallée, Institut Gaspard-Monge
77454 Marne-la-Vallée, France
E-mail: maxime.crochemore@univ-mlv.fr

Kunsoo Park
Seoul National University
School of Computer Science and Engineering
Seoul 151-744, Korea
E-mail: kpark@snu.ac.kr

Library of Congress Control Number: 2005927143

CR Subject Classification (1998): F.2.2, I.5.4, I.5.0, I.7.3, H.3.3, J.3, E.4, G.2.1, E.1

ISSN   0302-9743
ISBN-10   3-540-26201-6 Springer Berlin Heidelberg New York
ISBN-13   978-3-540-26201-5 Springer Berlin Heidelberg New York

Springer is a part of Springer Science+Business Media

springeronline.com

© Springer-Verlag Berlin Heidelberg 2005
Printed in Germany

Typesetting: Camera-ready by author, data conversion by Olgun Computergrafik
Printed on acid-free paper   SPIN: 11496656   06/3142   5 4 3 2 1 0

Preface

The 16th Annual Symposium on Combinatorial Pattern Matching was held on Jeju Island, Korea on June 19–22, 2005. Previous meetings were held in Paris, London, Tucson, Padova, Asilomar, Helsinki, Laguna Beach, Aarhus, Piscataway, Warwick, Montreal, Jerusalem, Fukuoka, Morelia, and Istanbul over the years 1990–2004.

In response to the call for papers, CPM 2005 received a record number of 129 papers. Each submission was reviewed by at least three Program Committee members with the assistance of external referees. Since there were many high-quality papers, the Program Committee's task was extremely difficult. Through an extensive discussion the Program Committee accepted 37 of the submissions to be presented at the conference. They constitute original research contributions in combinatorial pattern matching and its applications.

In addition to the selected papers, CPM 2005 had three invited presentations, by Esko Ukkonen from the University of Helsinki, Ming Li from the University of Waterloo, and Naftali Tishby from The Hebrew University of Jerusalem.

We would like to thank all Program Committee members and external referees for their excellent work, especially given the demanding time constraints; they gave the conference its distinctive character. We also thank all who submitted papers for consideration; they all contributed to the high quality of the conference.

Finally, we thank the Organizing Committee members and the graduate students who worked hard to put in place the logistical arrangements of the conference. It is their dedicated contribution that made the conference possible and enjoyable.

June 2005   Alberto Apostolico, Maxime Crochemore, and Kunsoo Park

Organization

Program Committee

Tatsuya Akutsu	Kyoto University
Alberto Apostolico	University of Padova and Purdue University
Setsuo Arikawa	Kyushu University
Maxime Crochemore	University of Marne la Vallée
Martin Farach-Colton	Rutgers University
Costas S. Iliopoulos	King's College London
Juha Karkkainen	University of Helsinki
Dong Kyue Kim	Pusan National University
Tak-Wah Lam	University of Hong Kong
Moshe Lewenstein	Bar Ilan University
Bin Ma	University of Western Ontario
Giovanni Manzini	University of Piemonte Orientale
S. Muthukrishnan	Rutgers University
Kunsoo Park	Seoul National University
Mathieu Raffinot	CNRS
Rajeev Raman	University of Leicester
Cenk Sahinalp	Simon Fraser University
Andrew C. Yao	Tsinghua University
Frances F. Yao	City University of Hong Kong
Nivio Ziviani	Federal University of Minas Gerais

Steering Committee

Alberto Apostolico	University of Padova and Purdue University
Maxime Crochemore	University of Marne la Vallée
Zvi Galil	Columbia University

Organizing Committee

Dong Kyue Kim	Pusan National University
Yoo-Jin Chung	Hankuk University of Foreign Studies
Sung-Ryul Kim	Konkuk University
Heejin Park	Hanyang University
Jeong Seop Sim	Inha University
Jin Wook Kim	Seoul National University

Sponsoring Institutions

Ministry of Science and Technology, Korea
Seoul National University
SIGTCS of the Korea Information Science Society

External Referees

Julien Allali
Marie-Pierre Béal
Anne Bergeron
Marshall Bern
Vincent Berry
Mathieu Blanchette
Dan Brown
Julien Clément
Fabien Coulon
Thierson Couto Rosa
Fabiano Cupertino Botelho
Artur Czumaj
Davi de Castro Reis
Fabien de Montgolfier
Funda Ergun
Paolo Ferragina
Guillaume Fertin
Dora Giammarresi
Sylvie Hamel

Tzvika Hartman
Patrice Koehl
Tsvi Kopelowitz
Gregory Kucherov
Thierry Lecroq
Veli Mäkinen
Wagner Meira, Jr.
Nadia Pisanti
Sven Rahman
Isidore Rigoutsos
Eric Rivals
Romeo Rizzi
Dominique Rossin
Kunihiko Sadakane
Jens Stoye
Jorma Tarhio
Stéphane Vialette
Hao-Chi Wong

Table of Contents

Sharper Upper and Lower Bounds for an Approximation Scheme for Consensus-Pattern

Broňa Brejová, Daniel G. Brown, Ian M. Harrower,
Alejandro López-Ortiz, and Tomáš Vinař

School of Computer Science, University of Waterloo
{bbrejova,browndg,imharrow,alopez-o,tvinar}@cs.uwaterloo.ca

Abstract. We present sharper upper and lower bounds for a known polynomial-time approximation scheme due to Li, Ma and Wang [7] for the Consensus-Pattern problem. This NP-hard problem is an abstraction of motif finding, a common bioinformatics discovery task. The PTAS due to Li *et al.* is simple, and a preliminary implementation [8] gave reasonable results in practice. However, the previously known bounds on its performance are useless when runtimes are actually manageable. Here, we present much sharper lower and upper bounds on the performance of this algorithm that partially explain why its behavior is so much better in practice than what was previously predicted in theory. We also give specific examples of instances of the problem for which the PTAS performs poorly in practice, and show that the asymptotic performance bound given in the original proof matches the behaviour of a simple variant of the algorithm on a particularly bad instance of the problem.

1 Introduction

Bioinformaticists often find themselves with several different DNA or protein sequences that are known to share a particular function, but where the origin of the function in the sequence is unknown. For example, suppose one has the DNA sequence of the region surrounding several genes, known to be regulated by a particular transcription factor. Here, the shared regulatory behavior may be caused by a sequence element common to all, to which the transcription factor binds. Discovering this experimentally is very expensive, so computational approaches can be helpful to limit searches.

The motif discovery problem is an abstraction of this problem. In it, we are given n sequences, all of length m, over an alphabet Σ. We seek a single motif, of length L that is found approximately as a substring of all sequences. Several variants of this problem exist. One can seek to minimize the maximum Hamming distance between the motif and its instances in all strings (*e.g.* [2, 10]), maximize the information content (minimize the entropy) of the chosen motif instances (*e.g.* [1, 3, 6]), or minimize the total of the Hamming distances between the motif and its instances [7]. This latter problem can be formally defined as follows:

A. Apostolico, M. Crochemore, and K. Park (Eds.): CPM 2005, LNCS 3537, pp. 1–10, 2005.

Definition 1 (CONSENSUS-PATTERN). *Given: n sequences $s_1, \ldots, s_n$, each of length m and over an alphabet of size A. Find a substring t_i of a given length L in each of the sequences and a median string s of length L so that the total Hamming distance $\sum_i d_H(s, t_i)$ is minimized.*

Li, Ma and Wang [7] give a very simple polynomial-time approximation scheme (PTAS) for this combinatorial motif problem. For a given value of r, consider all choices of r substrings of length L from the n sequences. We note explicitly here that the sampling is made with replacement, so that the same substring may occur multiple times. For each such collection $\mathcal{C}$ of substrings, we compute its consensus by identifying the most common letter in the first position of each chosen substring, the second position, and so on, producing a motif $M_{\mathcal{C}}$. It is easy to identify for a given motif $M_{\mathcal{C}}$ its closest match in each of the n sequences, and thus its score. We do this for all $n^r(m-L+1)^r$ possible collections of r substrings, and pick the collection with the best score. The algorithm has $O(L(nm)^{r+1})$ running time, and thus runs in polynomial time for any particular value of r. Li *et al.* also give an upper bound on the worst-case approximation ratio of this algorithm for $r \geq 3$:

$$1 + \frac{4A - 4}{\sqrt{e}\left(\sqrt{4r+1} - 3\right)}, \tag{1}$$

where A is the alphabet size. For example, if $r = 3$, this approach gives an algorithm that runs in $O(L(nm)^4)$ runtime, but whose approximation guarantee for DNA sequences (where $A = 4$) is approximately 13. To achieve a reasonable approximation ratio, 2, we would have to use $r \geq 8$ for DNA sequences, or $r \geq 27$ for protein sequences ($A = 20$), giving hopelessly large running times. The high value of the proven bound would seem to suggest that the algorithm will be useless in practice.

However, many successful combinatorial motif finders do work by generalizing from small samples in this way, such as SP-STAR [10] and CONSENSUS (samples of 1) [3], COMBINE (samples of 2 to 3) [9], COPIA (samples of arbitrary size) [8]. Here, focusing on Li *et al.*'s PTAS, we show tighter bounds on its performance that are much closer to reasonable numbers for practical values of r. We also provide the first substantial lower bounds on the PTAS's performance, by identifying specific examples of the problem for which the algorithm performs poorly. In the general case, for a binary alphabet, we find that the variant of the algorithm that works by sampling *without* replacement performs poorly on a particular bad example, and we conjecture that our example will also be difficult for the original Li *et al.* algorithm that samples *with* replacement.

Our results are summarized in Table 1.

2   Basic Observations

We begin our discussion of the algorithm by noting that it is sufficient to look at the performance of the PTAS when run on the actual instances of the motif (which are sequences of length L), rather than on the m-letter input strings.

Table 1. Overview of the results.

Condition	New results		Previous
	Lower bound	Upper bound	upper bound
$r = 1$	2	2	N/A
$r = 3$	1.5	≈ 1.528	$\approx 1 + 4.006 \cdot (A - 1)$
general r binary alphabet	$1 + \Theta(1/r^2)$ conjecture: $1 + \Theta(1/\sqrt{r})$ (proved for sampling without replacement)		$1 + \Theta(1/\sqrt{r})$
general r general alphabet	$1 + \Theta(1/r^2)$ conjecture: $1 + \Theta(1/\sqrt{r})$ (proved for sampling without replacement)		$1 + \Theta(A/\sqrt{r})$

Lemma 1. *Suppose that the PTAS of Li et al. achieves approximation ratio α for a given set $s_1 \ldots, s_n$ of input sequences, motif length L and sample motif size r. Suppose also that the instance of the optimal motif in sequence s_i is t_i. Then the PTAS, if run only on the sequences $t_1, \ldots, t_n$, would achieve approximation ratio at least α.*

Proof. We begin by noting that if $m = L$, the actual problem is trivial: the optimal motif s^* is the consensus of all of the input strings.

However, the PTAS still is well defined in this case, even though the actual optimization problem is trivial. It examines all sets $\mathcal{C}$ of r strings, including ones where the same string is chosen multiple times, and for each of them, computes its consensus $M_{\mathcal{C}}$. Then, the central motif $M_{\mathcal{C}*}$ with smallest total Hamming distance to all s_i is chosen as the motif center.

This motif center can be no better than the one found by the PTAS when run on the entire m-letter strings, because the set of substrings we have considered in the truncated problem is a subset of the set of substrings we would have examined in the full problem. As such, if the original algorithm would have found a solution whose approximation ratio is α, we can only have done as well or worse in the truncated problem.

This lemma is useful because if we can show that, for given values of L, n and r, and when run only on the optimal motif instances, the PTAS has approximation ratio at most β, then its approximation ratio on longer strings can still be no worse than β.

To simplify notation, we assume that the alphabet is $\{0, 1, \ldots, A - 1\}$. In the special case we focus on, where $m = L$, we also always renumber the characters in each column, so the consensus for that column is 0. This causes the overall optimal motif to be $s^* = 0^L$. This transformation only works when $m = L$; it does not work when $m > L$.

Finally, we can encounter the problem of ties, that is, a situation when the consensus string u of some collection $\mathcal{C}$ is not unique. Consider for example $r = 3$ and input strings 01, 02, 10, and 20. The optimal motif is 00, with cost 4. If $\mathcal{C}$

contains the first three strings, the consensus M_C can be any of the strings 00, 01, and 02. The first of them is optimal, but the latter two have cost 5.

It is not realistic to assume that the PTAS will always guess the best of all possible consensus strings; their number can be exponential in L. For simplicity, we assume that the PTAS will choose the worst consensus string, and study the performance of this "unlucky" motif finding algorithm, which in our example would choose either 01 or 02.

3   Upper Bounds

In this section, we give better worst-case bounds on the approximation guarantee of the algorithm in the cases where $r = 1$ or $r = 3$, corresponding to algorithms with quadratic or quartic bounds on their runtime.

Theorem 1. *The approximation ratio of the PTAS is at most 2 for all values of r, including $r = 1$, and for any alphabet size A.*

Proof. Let c be the cost of the optimal motif 0^L, that is, the total number of non-zero elements in all sequences. Let a_i be the number of non-zero elements in sequence s_i. If the PTAS chooses sequence s_i as the motif (which will happen when the r samples from the n sequences are all of s_i), the cost will increase by at most n for every column where s_i has non-zero element. Therefore the cost will be at most $c + na_i$. The sum of this quantity over all sequences s_i is $nc + n\sum_{i=1}^{n} a_i = 2nc$. Since the sum of costs for n different potential motifs s_i is at most $2nc$, at least one of these has cost at most $2c$, which means the approximation ratio is at most 2.

Theorem 2. *The approximation ratio of the PTAS for $r = 3$ is at most $(64 + 7\sqrt{7})/54 \approx 1.528$ regardless of the size of the alphabet.*

Proof. Let p be the proportion of zeroes and $q = (1 - p)$ be the proportion of non-zeroes in the input sequences. The optimal cost is therefore qnL. Let b_j be the number of non-zeroes in column j.

The algorithm will examine all possible samples consisting of 3 rows, choosing the one with the best consensus string. To get an upper bound, we will consider the expected cost of the consensus string obtained by sampling 3 rows uniformly at random.

For each column, we can estimate the expected cost of the column. The consensus in a particular column will only be non-zero if two or three of the chosen rows contain non-zero entries. If the column contains b non-zero entries, there are $b^3 + 3b^2(n - b)$ such samples. Each of these samples will incur cost of at most n in this column. The consensus will be zero for samples with two or three zeroes (their number is $(n - b)^3 + 3(n - b)^2b$). Each of these samples will incur cost b in this column.

Thus the expected cost $E(b)$ for a column with b non-zeroes is at most $C(b)/n^3$, where $C(b)$ is the sum of costs over all triples of rows:

$$C(b) = [b^3 + 3b^2(n - b)]n + [(n - b)^3 + 3(n - b)^2b]b = 2b^4 - 5b^3n + 3b^2n^2 + bn^3. \quad (2)$$

From linearity of expectation, the expected cost over all columns is

$$E(b_1, \ldots, b_L) = \sum_{j=1}^{L} E(b_j) = \frac{1}{n^3} \cdot \sum_{j=1}^{L} C(b_j). \tag{3}$$

There must exist a sample with cost at most $E(b_1, \ldots, b_L)$. Such a sample achieves approximation ratio $E(b_1, \ldots, b_L)/qnL$.

We will prove by induction on L that $E(b_1, \ldots, b_L) \leq HqnL$, where $H = (64 + 7\sqrt{7})/54$. This implies that $H \approx 1.528$ is an upper bound on the approximation ratio for $r = 3$.

For $L = 1$, the approximation ratio is

$$E(qn)/qnL = 2q^3 - 5q^2 + 3q + 1. \tag{4}$$

The maximum of this ratio, which is equal to H, is reached when $q = \frac{5-\sqrt{7}}{6}$.

Now, assume that the induction hypothesis is true for $L - 1$. We will prove that it is also true for L. The expected cost of the first column is $E(b_1)$, which can be computed with Equation 2 above. By our induction hypothesis, the expected cost of the remaining $L-1$ columns is at most $(qnL - b_1) \cdot H$. Note that $qnL - b_1$ is the optimal cost for the remaining $L - 1$ columns. Therefore:

$$\begin{aligned} E(b_1, \ldots, b_L) &\leq E(b_1) + (qnL - b_1) \cdot H \\ &= \underbrace{\frac{2b^4 - 5b^3n + 3b^2n^2 + (1 - H)bn^3}{n^3}}_{(*)} + HqnL \end{aligned} \tag{5}$$

We want to prove, that $(*)$ is never positive for b in the range $0 \leq b \leq n$. Indeed, $(*)$ can be simplified as $(b/(108n^3)) \cdot (6b - (5+2\sqrt{7})n) \cdot (6b - (5 - \sqrt{7})n)^2$. The first and third factors are always non-negative, and the second factor is non-positive for all $b < n$. Therefore the whole term $(*)$ is never positive on the interval.

It is, in fact, possible to easily characterize the "worst-case" scenario that maximizes $E(b_1, \ldots, b_L)$: this is achieved when the non-zero elements are distributed equally among a subset of the columns as follows.

Lemma 2. *For a given q, n, and L, $E(b_1, \ldots, b_L)$ is maximized, when for some $k \leq L$, $b_1, \ldots, b_k = 0$, and $b_{k+1} = b_{k+2} = \ldots = b_L \leq n$ (if we allow $b_1, \ldots, b_L$ to be non-integral).*

Proof. (by induction on L). For $L = 1$, the hypothesis holds trivially.

Let us assume that the hypothesis holds for all $L' < L$. Without loss of generality, we assume that the columns are sorted by b_j. If $b_1 = 0$, the hypothesis holds trivially from the induction hypothesis. Let $b_1 > 0$. Then, by the induction hypothesis, all the rest of the columns must by distributed equally (there are no columns with $b_i = 0$, since b_1 is the smallest). The cost will be therefore:

$$C(b_1) + (L - 1) \cdot C\left(\frac{qnL - b_1}{L - 1}\right), \tag{6}$$

where $nL(q-1)+n \leq b_1 \leq qn$, and $b_1 > 0$. This is indeed maximized for $b_1 = qn$, as can be shown by straightforward algebraic manipulation.

4   Lower Bounds

In this section, we present examples of inputs for which the Li *et al.* PTAS performs poorly. These examples give lower bounds on the approximation guarantee. For small values of r, we are able to give lower bounds which almost match our upper bounds the from previous section. For general values of r, we show an example where the PTAS has approximation ratio $1 + \Theta(1/r^2)$. Finally, we conjecture that lower bound on approximation ratio matches asymptotically the upper bound $1+\Theta(1/\sqrt{r})$ for a constant-size alphabet; to support this claim, we present an example for which a slightly modified algorithm has approximation ratio at least $1 + \Theta(1/\sqrt{r})$.

Theorem 3. *For $r = 1$, the approximation ratio is at least 2, even for binary inputs.*

Proof. We set $L = n$. The input will be the $n \times n$ identity matrix I_n, with ones on the diagonal and zeroes everywhere else. The cost of the optimal solution is n. The result of the PTAS for $r = 1$ will be one of the matrix rows, with cost $2n - 2$. The approximation ratio is therefore $2 - 2/n$, which converges to 2 as n grows without bound. This shows that the upper bound 2 is tight for $r = 1$.

Theorem 4. *For $r = 3$, the approximation ratio is at least $3/2$.*

Proof. For given k, consider the input with $n = 2k$, $L = 2$ containing for every $i = 1, 2, \ldots, k$ strings $0i$ and $i0$. For example for $k = 2$ the input will be the following:

$$
\begin{array}{c}
0\ 1 \\
0\ 2 \\
1\ 0 \\
2\ 0
\end{array}
$$

The optimal solution is 00, with cost $2k$. However, assuming that the PTAS breaks ties in the worst possible way, it will find motif $0x$ or $x0$, with cost $3k - 1$.

Theorem 5. *The approximation ratio of the PTAS is at least $1+\Theta(1/r^2)$.*

Proof. For any odd r, we create $n = r+2$ sequences, each of length $L = (r+5)/2$. The first $L - 1$ columns of the first $L - 1$ sequences will be an inverted identity matrix, with zeroes on the diagonal and ones everywhere else. The last column of these sequences contains zeroes. The remaining $n - L + 1$ sequences have zeroes in the first $L - 1$ columns and one in the last column. For example for $r = 5$ we have the following input:

```
0 1 1 1 0
1 0 1 1 0
1 1 0 1 0
1 1 1 0 0
0 0 0 0 1
0 0 0 0 1
0 0 0 0 1
```

The optimal solution 0^L has cost $c = (r+1)(r+5)/4$. Any solution that has a single one in it will have cost $c+1$, and it is clear that by choosing the last row r times, the algorithm will find a motif at least as good as $0^{L-1}1$. We show that the PTAS cannot find the optimal solution.

Assume that the PTAS can obtain the optimal solution 0^L. Then there must be some collection $\mathcal{C}$ of strings such that each column has more than $r/2$ zeroes. In particular, for the last column, more than half of these strings are chosen from the first $L - 1$ sequences of the input. Thus, to achieve more than $r/2$ zeroes in any other column $i < L$, we have to include at least one copy of sequence i (less than $r/2$ copies of the last $n - L + 1$ sequences are included). That means we need to include each of the first $L - 1$ sequences. But then all of the first $L - 1$ columns contain at least $L - 2 = (r+1)/2$ ones, and we will not find the correct motif. This is a contradiction. Therefore the PTAS cannot achieve the optimal solution.

Therefore the approximation ratio is $(c+1)/c = 1 + 4/[(r+1)(r+5)] = 1 + \Theta(1/r^2)$.

We were unable to obtain a lower bound matching the original upper bound of $1 + \Theta(A/\sqrt{r})$ of Li *et al.* [7]. However, we conjecture this upper bound is tight for a constant-size alphabet; to support this conjecture, we offer a lower bound of $1 + \Theta(1/\sqrt{r})$ for a modified algorithm.

In the original PTAS, the samples from which the possible motifs are generated are performed *with* replacement, so that a given substring can be chosen multiple times. Here, we will consider a variation of this, which requires that the same substring be chosen only once. In our context, where $L = m$, this means we will choose all subsets of size r of the n input strings, compute their consensus sequences, and take the best of these possible choices. Note that this modified algorithm will always give the same or worse results as the original PTAS.

We conjecture that this algorithm also forms a PTAS with similar bound to the original, and we conjecture that bad examples of the problem for this algorithm will also be bad examples of the problem for the Li *et al.* PTAS, with similar lower bounds.

Theorem 6. *Consider a modification of the PTAS, where we allow only a single sample from each input sequence. This modified algorithm has approximation ratio at least $1 + \Theta(1/\sqrt{r})$, even for a binary alphabet.*

Proof. We will give instances that give this bound in the limit as r goes to infinity. Let r be of the form $(2k + 1)^2$, and let $n = 2r$. Our problem instance will have $L = \binom{2r}{r+\sqrt{r}}$ columns: all possible columns with $r - \sqrt{r}$ ones and $r + \sqrt{r}$ zeros. The optimal solution 0^L will have score $L \cdot (r - \sqrt{r})$.

The modified PTAS will examine all possible subsets of r sequences (sampling without replacement). Note that in this particular example, any combination of r rows will give rise to a consensus string with the same cost. This is because any combination of r rows can be transformed to any other such combination by rearranging columns. Therefore every combination gives a consensus string with the same number of ones.

Since all samples are equivalent, we could as easily study a random sample of size r chosen from the $2r$ sequences, and identify the expected number of ones in the consensus string. Considering a single column, let p_r be the probability that the consensus for this column will is 1. That is, p_r is the probability that a random sample without replacement of size r from the population of $r - \sqrt{r}$ ones and $r + \sqrt{r}$ zeros will contain more than $r/2$ ones. By linearity of expectation, the expected number of ones in the consensus string will then be $L \cdot p_r$.

Since the symmetry argument shows that all solutions have the same value, all samples will identify a consensus string with $L \cdot p_r$ ones, and so will the algorithm. Thus, the modified PTAS will give a solution with value $L \cdot p_r \cdot (r + \sqrt{r}) + L \cdot (1 - p_r)(r - \sqrt{r})$. Since the optimum has value $L \cdot (r - \sqrt{r})$, the approximation ratio is $1 + \frac{2p_r\sqrt{r}}{r - \sqrt{r}} > 1 + 2p_r/\sqrt{r}$. Thus, if we can show that, as $r \to \infty$, p_r is greater than some constant ε, this will suffice to prove that the algorithm has approximation ratio at least $1 + \Theta(1/\sqrt{r})$.

We prove this by using the Central Limit Theorem for Finite Populations (e.g. [11, Section 3.4]). This is the variation on the Central Limit Theorem for sampling from finite populations without replacement. Specifically, it implies that if we sample r times from a population of $r + \sqrt{r}$ zeros and $r - \sqrt{r}$ ones, then as $r \to \infty$, the number of ones picked converges to a normal distribution, with mean $\mu = 1/2(r - \sqrt{r})$ and variance $\sigma^2 = r/8 - 1/8 \geq r/16$ [1].

We are interested in the probability p_r that the number of ones in the sample is at least $r/2$. Note, that in the normal distribution $N(\mu, \sigma)$, $r/2 \leq \mu + 2\sigma$, and therefore, for r above some threshold,

$$p_r \geq \Pr(N(\mu, \sigma) \geq \mu + 2\sigma) = \Pr(N(0, 1) \geq 2) \approx 0.023,$$

as $r \to \infty$. Therefore p_r has a constant lower bound, which is what we wanted to show.

The expected cost of the consensus can be computed using similar method for the original PTAS as well. However, the symmetry argument does not hold any more, and therefore there might be samples with cost lower than the expected

---

[1] There is a technical condition required for the theorem to hold, which is that

$$\lim_{N \to \infty} \frac{M(N - M)S(N - S)}{N^3} = \infty,$$

where N is the size of the population, M is the number of ones in the population, and S is the size of the sample. This condition holds trivially in our case.

cost. Thus the proof presented above cannot be directly extended to the original PTAS.

5 Conclusion and Open Problems

We have given lower and upper bounds for the performance of an extremely simple polynomial-time approximation scheme due to Li *et al.* [7] for the CONSENSUS-PATTERN problem, which is an abstraction of a common biological sequence motif detection problem. The PTAS examines all choices of r substrings of the input sequences, computes the consensus sequence of the substrings, and then finds the best matches to this consensus in all strings. After examining all possible choices, it chooses as the motif the consensus substring chosen with best overall performance.

Our bounds give a partial explanation for why algorithms based on sampling substrings of the input give good performance in practice. While they do not improve the upper bounds on the approximation ratio for large sample sizes, they do show that, for small sample sizes r, such as 3, the extremely simple PTAS can guarantee performance ratios of at most 1.528, as compared with bounds much larger with the original Li *et al.* proof.

We have also given new lower bounds on the best possible approximation ratio of the PTAS, by showing examples for which the PTAS has poor performance. In the case of 1-substring samples, our bad example gives an approximation ratio converging to 2, which matches our upper bound. In the case of 3-substring samples, we show that the best approximation ratio is at least 1.5, which is very close to our upper bound of 1.528. In the more general case of a binary input alphabet and arbitrary sample size r, we show an instance with lower bound $1 + \Theta(1/r^2)$. We also show that the slight variation on the PTAS that does not allow sampling with replacement, but only *without* replacement can only achieve ratios of at least $1 + \Theta(1/\sqrt{r})$, by applying limit theorems for samples of finite populations. We conjecture that this bound, which asymptotically matches the proven upper bound due to Li *et al.* for the original PTAS, also applies when sampling is allowed with replacement.

We should note that our worst-case bounds may have little applicability to real instances of motif-finding problems in practice. Indeed, in a quite different direction than we have gone in this work, many authors (*e.g.* [4, 5]) have focused on probabilistic models of sequences, and on the information content of subtle motifs, to identify the probability that a particular algorithm will correctly identify a motif implanted in them. In particular, these authors have focused on the probability of identifying weak motifs, whose score is not much higher than "decoys" in the sequence. Our results, which show that decoys are certain to be found by the PTAS, are for similarly weak motifs, but with no probabilistic basis.

Open problems. Numerous open problems still remain in this area. We would be interested in developing sharper bounds for the case of larger input alphabets. While our bounds on binary alphabets naturally carry to the case of larger alphabets, the upper bound grows with the size of the alphabet. It is possible that the true upper bound does not depend on the alphabet size, rather than that the current lower bound is too small. This is also supported by our upper bound for $r = 3$ of 1.528 regardless of the size of the alphabet (in fact, this upper bound also holds for all values of r greater than 4).

The other open problem we would suggest is to determine whether the algorithm based on sampling without replacement needed for the proof of Theorem 6 can be proven to be a PTAS with the same guarantee, or whether our bad example or one like it can be used to prove an analogous lower bound for the original PTAS.

Acknowledgements

All authors are supported by the National Science and Engineering Research Council of Canada. Additionally, the second author is supported by the Human Frontier Science Program. We would like to thank Christopher Small and Mary Thompson for pointing us to the presentation of the Central Limit Theorem for Finite Populations found in Dr. Thompson's book [11], which we used in the proof of Theorem 6.

References

1. T.L. Bailey and C. Elkan. Fitting a mixture model by expectation maximization to discover motifs in biopolymers. In *Proceedings of the 2nd International Conference on Intelligent Systems for Molecular Biology (ISMB 1994)*, pages 28–36. AAAI Press, 1994.
2. J. Buhler and M. Tompa. Finding motifs using random projections. In *Proceedings of the 5th Annual International Conference on Computational Molecular Biology (RECOMB 2001)*, pages 69–76, 2001.
3. G.Z. Hertz and G.D. Stormo. Identifying DNA and protein patterns with statistically significant alignments of multiple sequences. *Bioinformatics*, 15(7-8):563–577, 1999.
4. U. Keich and P.A. Pevzner. Finding motifs in the twilight zone. *Bioinformatics*, 18:1374–1381, 2002.
5. U. Keich and P.A. Pevzner. Subtle motifs: defining the limits of motif finding algorithms. *Bioinformatics*, 18:1382–1390, 2002.
6. C.E. Lawrence, S.F. Altschul, M.S. Boguski, J.S. Liu, A.F. Neuwald, and J.C. Wootton. Detecting subtle sequence signals: a Gibbs sampling strategy for multiple alignment. *Science*, 262(5131):208–214, 1993.
7. M. Li, B. Ma, and L. Wang. Finding similar regions in many strings. *Journal of Computer and System Sciences*, 65(1):73–96, 2002.
8. C. Liang. COPIA: A New Software for Finding Consensus Patterns in Unaligned Protein Sequences. Master's thesis, University of Waterloo, October 2001.
9. J. Liu. A Combinatorial Approach for Motif Discovery in Unaligned DNA Sequences. Master's thesis, University of Waterloo, March 2004.
10. P.A. Pevzner and S. Sze. Combinatorial approaches to finding subtle signals in DNA sequences. In *Proceedings of the 8th International Conference on Intelligent Systems for Molecular Biology (ISMB 2000)*, pages 269–278, 2000.
11. M.E. Thompson. *Theory of Sample Surveys*. Chapman and Hall, 1997.

On the Longest Common Rigid
Subsequence Problem

Bin Ma and Kaizhong Zhang

Department of Computer Science
University of Western Ontario
London, ON, Canada N6A 5B7
{bma,kzhang}@csd.uwo.ca

Abstract. The longest common subsequence problem (LCS) and the closest substring problem (CSP) are two models for the finding of common patterns in strings. The two problem have been studied extensively. The former was previously proved to be not polynomial-time approximable within ratio n^δ for a constant δ. The latter was previously proved to be **NP**-hard and have a PTAS. In this paper, the longest common rigid subsequence problem (LCRS) is studied. LCRS shares similarity with LCS and CSP and has an important application in motif finding in biological sequences. LCRS is proved to be **Max-SNP** hard in this paper. An exact algorithm with quasi-polynomial average running time is also provided.

1   Introduction

The finding of common patterns shared by many sequences is an important computational problem that has been extensively studied in the literature. In different applications, this problem has different versions.

Suppose m sequences $s_1, s_2, \ldots, s_m$ are given. Each s_i is of length n. The longest common subsequence problem (LCS) seeks for a sequence s that is a subsequence of each s_i. This problem was first shown to be **NP**-hard [10] and later shown to be hard to be approximated [3]. More specifically, Jiang and Li showed in their paper [3] that there exists a constant $\delta > 0$ such that, if longest common subsequence problem has a polynomial time approximation algorithm with performance ratio n^δ, then $\mathbf{P} = \mathbf{NP}$. In the same paper [3], they proved that a simple greedy algorithm can approximate LCS by an expected additive error $O(n^{\frac{1}{2}+\epsilon})$. Because the expected LCS length of n random sequences of length n is $\frac{n}{k} \pm n^{\frac{1}{2}+\epsilon}$ [3], this showed that the average performance of an approximation algorithm can be very good, despite that the worst case performance is bad.

Clearly, the difficulty of LCS comes from the exponential number of subsequences of a given string. If the subsequence is replaced by substring and the longest common substring of all s_i is sought for, the problem can be trivially solved by examining every substring of s_1. However, the problem of finding a string t of a given length L that matches a substring of every s_i *with the smallest errors* becomes **NP**-hard again under several different error measurements [5, 6].

A. Apostolico, M. Crochemore, and K. Park (Eds.): CPM 2005, LNCS 3537, pp. 11–20, 2005.

Approximation algorithms were also studied [5–9]. Specifically, when d_H is the Hamming distance, [8, 9] studied the *closest substring problem* (CSP), which is to find a length-L string t and a substring t_i of every s_i, so that $\max_i d_H(t, t_i)$ is minimized. The closest substring problem is **NP**-hard and polynomial time approximation schemes (PTAS) was provided in [8, 9]. Other error measurements were also studied in [5–9].

We note that both LCS and CSP are generalization of the trivial longest common substring problem. In LCS, substrings are generalized to subsequences. Whereas in CSP, an exact substring is generalized to be a substring with small errors. It was these two generalizations that changed the trivial longest common substring problem to be hard problems, respectively.

In this paper, we study another generalization of the longest common substring problem. We call the new problem *longest common rigid subsequence* (LCRS) and it is useful for motif findings in proteins.

Let Σ be an alphabet. Suppose $s = s[1]s[2] \ldots s[n]$ is a string over Σ. A *rigid subsequence* of s is a subsequence of s and the relative positions of the letters. More precisely, a rigid subsequence has the form $\langle t, P \rangle$, where $t = s[i_1]s[i_2] \ldots s[i_k]$ and $P = (i_2 - i_1, i_3 - i_1, \ldots, i_k - i_1)$ for $1 \le i_1 < i_2 < \ldots < i_k \le n$. We call P by the *shape* of this rigid subsequence. A *common rigid subsequence* of several strings $s_1, \ldots, s_m$ is a pair $\langle t, P \rangle$ that is a rigid subsequence of every s_i. The *longest common rigid subsequence problem* (LCRS) asks for the common rigid sequence $\langle t, P \rangle$ that maximizes the length of t.

Compared to LCS, LCRS is more restricted in the sense that the common subsequence now must appear in every s_i with the same shape. If compared with CSP, on one hand LCRS is more generalized because a shape needs to be computed; on the other hand LCRS is more restricted because it does not allow errors. Since the computational complexities of both LCS and CSP have been well-studied, it is of theoretical interest to ask about the complexity of LCRS.

In the context of computational biology and bioinformatics, LCRS has been used in the *motif* finding problem. In biochemistry, a *motif* is a recurring pattern in some DNA or protein sequences. Usually a motif is a short substring on the sequence but not all the positions on the substring are of the same importance. For example, by examining nine different protein sequences that bind to the SH3 domain, a consensus sequence, RPLPXXP, was revealed as the SH3 domain-binding motif [1]. The letter X in the sequence is a wildcard that can match any amino acids, which indicates that the amino acids at the two X-positions are not important to the biochemical function of the motif. Obviously, such a motif can be represented by a common rigid subsequence, $\langle \text{RPLPP}, (1,1,1,3) \rangle$.

Although different notations were used, for the finding of the motifs, [15] proposed a problem that is slightly more generalized than LCRS. Their problem requires to find the longest common rigid subsequences that occur in at least K of the n given sequences for a given number K. When $K = n$, this problem is exactly the LCRS problem. Exponential time algorithm was given in [15]. Later on, [13, 14] developed more efficient exponential time algorithms to the problem and variants. However, it was not shown in [13–15] whether this problem is **NP**-hard, though it was believed so.

In this paper, we answer the complexity of the LCRS problem by proving that LCRS is **Max-SNP** hard. In addition, we show that the problem can be solved with average quasi-polynomial running time $O(n^{O(\log_{|\Sigma|} n)})$, which is asymptotically better than the exponential time.

2 Hardness Result

In this section we prove that LCRS is **Max-SNP** hard. If a problem is **Max-SNP** hard, then there is a constant $\delta > 0$, such that the polynomial time approximation to that problem within ratio $1 + \delta$ will yield that **NP** = **P** [12]. It was shown that the Max-Cut problem, among other problems, is **Max-SNP** hard [12].

Max-Cut Given a graph $G = \langle V, E \rangle$. A cut of the graph is two disjoint vertex sets V_1 and V_2 such that $V_1 \cup V_2 = V$. The Max-Cut problem is to find the cut that maximizes the number of edges whose two vertices are in the two different sets V_1 and V_2.

We will prove that LCRS is also **Max-SNP** hard by an L-reduction from Max-Cut. More material about L-reduction can be found in [12].

Theorem 1. *LCRS is* **Max-SNP** *hard.*

Proof. The reduction is from Max-Cut. The alphabet used by our construction has four letters a, b, c, and d.

Suppose the instance of Max-Cut $G = \langle V, E \rangle$ has m vertices and n edges. In our construction, each vertex $v_i \in V$ $(i = 1, 2, \ldots, m)$ corresponds to a string s_i of the following form:

$$s_i = \text{xxx} \overbrace{\text{ccc}\ldots\text{c}}^{6(n^2+1)} \text{xxx} \overbrace{\text{ccc}\ldots\text{c}}^{6(n^2+2)} \text{xxx} \ldots \overbrace{\text{ccc}\ldots\text{c}}^{6(n^2+n-1)} \text{xxx}$$

where the xxx are three letters to be determined later in the proof. Let

$$s_0 = \text{aaa} \overbrace{\text{ddd}\ldots\text{d}}^{6(n^2+1)} \text{aaa} \overbrace{\text{ddd}\ldots\text{d}}^{6(n^2+2)} \text{aaa} \ldots \overbrace{\text{ddd}\ldots\text{d}}^{6(n^2+n-1)} \text{aaa}$$

For the presentation purpose we put $s_1, \ldots, s_m$ and s_0 together as follows

$$
\begin{array}{llll}
 & \overbrace{\phantom{\text{aaa}}}^{6(n^2+1)} & \overbrace{\phantom{\text{aaa}}}^{6(n^2+2)} & \overbrace{\phantom{\text{aaa}}}^{6(n^2+n-1)} \\
s_0: & \text{aaa ddd}\ldots\text{d aaa ddd}\ldots\text{d aaa} \ldots & \text{ddd}\ldots\text{d aaa} \\
s_1: & \text{xxx ccc}\ldots\text{c xxx ccc}\ldots\text{c xxx} \ldots & \text{ccc}\ldots\text{c xxx} \\
\vdots & \ddots & & \vdots \\
s_m: & \text{xxx ccc}\ldots\text{c xxx ccc}\ldots\text{c xxx} \ldots & \text{ccc}\ldots\text{c xxx}
\end{array}
$$

The letters c and d stand in our construction as delimiters. The other columns are separated by the delimiters into blocks of 3-columns. There are in total n such blocks, each corresponding to an edge in E. For the block corresponding to the edge $\langle v_i, v_j \rangle$ such that $i < j$, the three letters xxx in s_i is aba, the three letters in s_j is bab, and the three letters in the other strings are aaa, as follows:

$$
\begin{array}{ll}
s_0 & \ldots \text{aaa} \ldots \\
\ldots & \ldots \ldots \ldots \\
s_{i-1} & \ldots \text{aaa} \ldots \\
s_i & \ldots \text{aba} \ldots \\
s_{i+1} & \ldots \text{aaa} \ldots \\
\ldots & \ldots \ldots \ldots \\
s_{j-1} & \ldots \text{aaa} \ldots \\
s_j & \ldots \text{bab} \ldots \\
s_{j+1} & \ldots \text{aaa} \ldots \\
\ldots & \ldots \ldots \ldots \\
s_m & \ldots \text{aaa} \ldots
\end{array}
$$

Now we have an instance of LCRS. Next we prove that the solutions of this instance correspond to solutions of the Max-Cut.

Lemma 1. *A common rigid sequence of the instance constructed above does not contain any letter* c *and* d.

Proof. This is because s_0 does not have letter d and the other sequences do not have letter c. □

Lemma 2. *Suppose a common rigid subsequence z has length r, and the r letters are from $k_1, k_2, \ldots, k_r$ blocks of s_0, respectively ($k_1 \le k_2 \le \ldots \le k_r$). Then z uses letters from the $k_1, k_2, \ldots, k_r$ blocks of s_i for every i.*

Proof. Suppose z uses letters from the $k'_1, k'_2, \ldots, k'_r$ blocks of s_i for some i. Let d be the distance between letters j and $j+1$ of z. By a simple counting in s_0, we can get

$$
d - 6 < \sum_{k=k_j}^{k_{j+1}-1} 6(n^2 + k) + 3(k_{j+1} - k_j - 1) < d
$$

That is,

$$
d - 6 < 6n^2(k_{j+1} - k_j) + 3(k_{j+1} + k_j - 1)(k_{j+1} - k_j + 1) < d \qquad (1)
$$

Similarly, by counting in s_i, we get

$$
d - 6 < 6n^2(k'_{j+1} - k'_j) + 3(k'_{j+1} + k'_j - 1)(k'_{j+1} - k'_j + 1) < d \qquad (2)
$$

Because $k_j, k_{j+1}, k'_j, k'_{j+1}$ are all integers and $3(k_{j+1} + k_j - 1)(k_{j+1} - k_j + 1) = 3k_{j+1}^2 - 3(k_j - 1)^2 \le 3n^2$, by subtracting (2) from (1), we can first conclude that $k'_{j+1} - k'_j = k_{j+1} - k_j$ and then conclude that $k'_{j+1} + k'_j = k_{j+1} + k_j$. As a result, $k_j = k'_j$ and $k_{j+1} = k'_{j+1}$. □

Notice that the LCRS problem can be regarded as an equivalent problem which aligns the sequences s_i together by only adding gaps to the two ends of s_i. No insertion/deletion is allowed in the middle of the sequences. We call such an alignment an *ungapped alignment*. Then the a common rigid subsequence is equivalent to the columns where all the s_i have the same letter (the *consensus columns*). In such a view, Lemma 2 demonstrates that if the common rigid subsequence has more than one letters, then the corresponding blocks of all the strings are aligned together. Therefore, the shift (difference between the numbers of leading spaces in the two sequences) between two sequences can be at most two. The following lemma shows that the shift is actually smaller.

Lemma 3. *For each alignment, without reducing the number of consensus columns, we can modify the alignment so that the shift between any two sequences is at most one.*

Proof. The algorithm we use to modify the alignment is very simple, as follows. Let s_i and s_j be two sequences whose shift to each other is two. Without loss of generality, assume s_i has two more spaces at the left end than s_j. We simply add two more spaces at the left of s_j. This will reduce the shifts between s_i and s_j to 0.

Now we prove that this step of modification will not reduce the number of consensus columns. For each block, there are only three possible three-mer for each sequence. They are **aaa**, **aba**, and **bab**. Because there are always sequences with **aaa** in each block, if the block contains a consensus column, the consensus must not be letter **b**.

Furthermore, because s_i and s_j have shift 2, if one of s_i and s_j has **bab** at a block, it can be easily verified that the block does not contain a consensus column. Therefore, our modification will not reduce the consensus column at such a block. If none of s_i and s_j is **bab**, then there are only the following four cases (A), (B), (C), and (D).

$$
\begin{array}{lcccc}
s_i : & \texttt{ccaaa} & \texttt{ccaaa} & \texttt{ccaba} & \texttt{ccaba} \\
s_j : & \texttt{abacc} & \texttt{aaacc} & \texttt{aaacc} & \texttt{abacc} \\
 & \text{(A)} & \text{(B)} & \text{(C)} & \text{(D)}
\end{array}
$$

It is easy to see that in each of the four cases, the only possible consensus column is the column that has letter **a** in both s_i and s_j. Our modification will slide s_j to the right by two columns, which still preserve the match at that column. Therefore, our modification will not destroy any consensus column in the original alignment.

Let s_i be the sequence with the most leading spaces in the alignment. Applying the above mentioned modification to every s_j which has two-column shifts to s_i, we will get the desired alignment.   □

Because of Lemma 3, the sequences $s_1, \ldots, s_m$ are divided into two groups. One group of sequences have one more leading space than the other group. It is easy to see that in the block corresponding to an edge $\langle v_i, v_j \rangle$, a consensus column exists if and only if s_i and s_j are separated into the two groups. In this case, the letter a in bab matches one of the two a-letters in aba. All the other sequences are aaa in the same block and therefore they can always provide a letter a to the consensus column.

Thus, a cut of the vertices V corresponds to an alignment of $s_1, \ldots, s_m$. And the number of cut edges is equal to the number of consensus columns of the alignment, which is then equal to the length of the common rigid subsequence. So, Max-Cut is L-reduced to the LCRS problem. Because Max-Cut is **Max-SNP** hard, LCRS is **Max-SNP** hard too.   □

3   An Algorithm with Quasi-polynomial Average Running Time

In this section we present an algorithm with $O(n^{O(\log_{|\Sigma|} n)})$ average time complexity. We note that $n^{O(\log_{|\Sigma|} n)} = |\Sigma|^{O(\log_{|\Sigma|}^2 n)}$, which is better than exponential time.

The idea of the algorithm is simple. For a random instance, the probability of that a long rigid subsequence is common to all the input strings is small. Therefore, we do not expect to have too many long common rigid subsequences of the given strings. The question is how to enumerate these common rigid subsequences cleverly. A careless algorithm may spend too much time on eliminating the rigid subsequences that are not common in all the input strings.

Let S_i be the set of all the length-i common rigid subsequences of the input strings. Obviously, a rigid subsequence in S_i can be obtained by adding one more letter/position to some rigid subsequence in S_{i-1}. Our algorithm uses this idea to computes S_i from S_{i-1}, as in Figure 1.

Algorithm Grow.
1. Let $S_0 = \{$null string$\}$.
2. For i from 1 to n
3.   For the next rigid subsequence s in S_{i-1}
4.   For every rigid subsequence t that contains s but one letter longer
5.   if t is contained by all the strings
6.   add t to S_i.
7. Output the longest rigid subsequence in all S_i.

Fig. 1. Algorithm Grow.

Theorem 2. *For random instances, Algorithm Grow runs in $O(n^{O(\log_{|\Sigma|} n)})$ time on average.*

Proof. Without loss of generality, we assume that $m > 2\log_{|\Sigma|} n + 1$ because otherwise the problem can be solved in the desired time by trying all possible ungapped alignments of the m sequences.

In line 4, every rigid subsequence s has at most $O(n)$ ways to extend to a one-letter-longer subsequence t. And each such t takes $O(nmi)$ time to verify whether the condition in line 5 is true. Therefore, the time complexity of the algorithm is bounded by

$$O(n^2 m \times \sum_{i=1}^{n} i \times |S_i|).$$

In order to prove the theorem, we only need to prove that there are on average $O(n^{O(\log_{|\Sigma|} n)})$ elements in each S_i.

S_i contains all the length i common rigid subsequences. For each length-i rigid subsequence, the probability that it occurs at a given position of one random string is $|\Sigma|^{-i}$. Therefore, the probability that a length-n random string contains the rigid subsequence is less than $n \times |\Sigma|^{-i}$. The probability that the rigid subsequence is common to all of the m given strings is therefore no more than $\min\{1, (n \times |\Sigma|^{-i})^m\} = \min\{1, n^m \times |\Sigma|^{-im}\}$.

There are no more than $\binom{n}{i} \times |\Sigma|^i$ length-i rigid subsequences. Therefore, the expected number of subsequences in S_i is upper-bounded by

$$\binom{n}{i} \times |\Sigma|^i \times \min\{1, n^m \times |\Sigma|^{-im}\} \tag{3}$$

If $i \le 2\log_{|\Sigma|} n$, then

$$\binom{n}{i} \times |\Sigma|^i \times \min\{1, n^m \times |\Sigma|^{-im}\} \le n^i \times |\Sigma|^i \le n^{2+2\log_{|\Sigma|} n}$$

If $i > 2\log_{|\Sigma|} n$, because $m > 2\log_{|\Sigma|} n + 1$,

$$\binom{n}{i} \times |\Sigma|^i \times \min\{1, n^m \times |\Sigma|^{-im}\} \le n^i \times |\Sigma|^i \times n^m \times |\Sigma|^{-im}$$

$$= |\Sigma|^{(i\log_{|\Sigma|} n)+i+(m\log_{|\Sigma|} n)-im}$$

$$< 1.$$

The two cases discussed above indicate that there are at most $O(n^{O(\log_{|\Sigma|} n)})$ expected elements in each S_i. Therefore, the theorem is proved.   □

It is noteworthy that in the real motif finding situations, the input strings are not independent. They usually share a long motif. Let the length of the motif be L. Then S_i in Algorithm Grow will have at least $\binom{L}{i}$ elements, which can be an exponential number. To overcome this problem, we modify the algorithm a little bit by merging those elements that can form a longer rigid subsequence. By doing this, we eliminate the exponential number of shorter subsequences of a long rigid subsequence.

Let s be a rigid subsequence. As discussed in the proof of Theorem 1, the consensus columns of an ungapped alignment of the input strings correspond to

Algorithm Grow-Merge.
1. Let $S_i = \{\text{nullstring}\}$ for $i = 1 \ldots n$; $T = \emptyset$.
2. For k from 1 to n
3.   For the next rigid subsequence s in S_{k-1}
4.   If there are only several ungapped alignments that conform s
5.   For each of the s-conforming ungapped alignments A
6.   Put the rigid subsequence x corresponding to A in T
7.   Delete all the A-conforming subsequences from S_{k-1}.
8.   else
9.   For every spaced string t that contains s but one letter longer
10.   if t is contained by all the strings
11.   add t to S_k.
12. Output the longest substring in T.

Fig. 2. Algorithm Grow-Merge.

a rigid subsequence. If s is a part of the rigid subsequence of an ungapped alignment, we say that the ungapped alignment conforms s. Our modified algorithm is given in Figure 2.

Because of the existence of lines 4-7, the very long common rigid subsequence is more likely to be discovered in line 6, and its subsequences are deleted in line 7. Therefore, the exponential time as discussed above will less likely happen. It is also easy to see that the adding of lines 4-7 will not affect the asymptotical average time complexity of the algorithm on random instances. That is, Algorithm Grow-Merge still runs in average time $O(n^{O(\log_{|\Sigma|} n)})$.

4   Discussion

We proved that the longest common rigid subsequence problem (LCRS) is **Max-SNP** hard. LCRS is similar to the longest common subsequence problem and the closest substring problem. Because the complexities of the other two problems were well studied, it is of theoretical interest to study the complexity of LCRS.

Also, LCRS is useful in finding motifs in protein sequences. Although different notations were used, [13–15] modeled the motif finding problem into a problem that is very like LCRS. The only difference is that they only require the rigid subsequence to be common to K of the n input strings for a given K. When $K = n$, their problem is identical to LCRS. We note that our **Max-SNP** hardness result implies that their problem is also **Max-SNP** hard. Also, without giving the proofs, we note that Algorithm Grow and Algorithm Grow-Merge can be modified to solve their problem as well in $O(n^{\log_{|\Sigma|}(nm)})$ average running time. For example, the only necessary modifications to Algorithm Grow are to change the definition of S_i to be "the set of rigid sequences that are common in K of the n input strings", and to change line 5 of the algorithm accordingly.

Motifs in biological sequences often do not require exact matches. Small errors are allowed in the match between the motif and the sequences. The LCRS model of motif finding does not represent the errors. Researches that model the errors can be found, for example, in [2, 4, 7, 11, 16].

Acknowledgment

This research was undertaken, in part, thanks to funding from NSERC, PREA, and the Canada Research Chairs Program.

References

1. Identification of a src sh3 domain binding motif by screening a random phage display library. *Journal of Biological Chemistry*, 269:24034–24039, 1994.
2. E. F. Adebiyi and M. Kaufmann. Extracting common motifs under the levenshtein measure: theory and experimentation. In *Proceedings of the Workshop on Algorithms for Bioinformatics (WABI)*, pages 140–156, 2002.
3. T. Jiang and M. Li. On the approximation of shortest common supersequence and longest common subsequences. *SIAM Journal on Computing*, 24(5):1122–1139, 1995.
4. U. Keich and P.A.Pevzner. Finding motifs in the twilight zone. In *Proceedings of the sixth annual international conference on computational biology*, pages 195–204, 2002.
5. J. Kevin Lanctot, Ming Li, Bin Ma, Shaojiuc Wang, and Louxin Zhang. Distinguishing string selection problems. *Information and Computation*, 185(1):41–55, 2003. Early version appeared in SODA'99.
6. Ming Li, Bin Ma, and Lusheng Wang. Finding Similar Regions in Many Strings. In *Proceedings of the thirty-first annual ACM symposium on Theory of computing (STOC)*, pages 473–482, Atlanta, May 1999.
7. Ming Li, Bin Ma, and Lusheng Wang. Finding Similar Regions in Many Sequences. *Journal of Computer and System Sciences*, 65(1):73–96, 2002. Early version appeared in STOC'99.
8. Ming Li, Bin Ma, and Lusheng Wang. On the Closest String and Substring Problems. *Journal of the ACM*, 49(2):157–171, 2002. Early versions appeared in STOC'99 and CPM'00.
9. Bin Ma. A Polynomial Time Approximation Scheme for the Closest Substring Problem. In R. Giancarlo and D. Sankoff, editors, *Combinatorial Pattern Matching, 11th Annual Symposium (CPM)*, volume 1848 of *Lecture Notes in Computer Science*, pages 99–107, Montreal, Canada, June 21–23 2000. Springer.
10. D. Maier. The complexity of some problems on subsequences and supersequences. *Journal of the ACM*, 25:322–336, 1978.
11. M.S.Waterman, R. Arratia, and D.J.Galas. Pattern recognition in several sequences: consensus and alignment. *Bulletin of Mathematical Biology*, 46(4):515–527, 1984.
12. C.H. Papadimitriou and M. Yannakakis. Optimization, approximation, and complexity classes. *Journal of Computer and System Sciences*, 43:425–440.
13. S. Rajasekaran, S. Balla, and C. Huang. Exact algorithms for planted motif challenge problems. In *Proceedings of the 3rd Asia Pacific Bioinformatics Conference*, 2005.

14. S. Rajasekaran, S. Balla, C.-H. Huang, V. Thapar, M. Gryk, M. Maciejewski, and M. Schiller. Exact algorithms for motif search. In *Proceedings of the 3rd Asia Pacific Bioinformatics Conference*, 2005.
15. I. Rigoutsos and A. Floratos. Combinatorial pattern discovery in biological sequences: the teiresias algorithm. *Bioinformatics*, 14(1):55–67, 1998.
16. G. Stormo and G. W. Hartzell III. Identifying protein-binding sites from unaligned dna fragments. *Proc. Natl. Acad. Sci. USA*, 88:5699–5703, 1991.

Text Indexing with Errors

Moritz G. Maaß[*] and Johannes Nowak

Fakultät für Informatik, Technische Universität München
Boltzmannstraße 3, D-85748 Garching, Germany
{maass,nowakj}@informatik.tu-muenchen.de

Abstract. In this paper we address the problem of constructing an index for a text document or a collection of documents to answer various questions about the occurrences of a pattern when allowing a constant number of errors. In particular, our index can be built to report all occurrences, all positions, or all documents where a pattern occurs in time linear in the size of the query string and the number of results. This improves over previous work where the lookup time is not linear or depends upon the size of the document corpus. Our data structure has size $O(n \log^k n)$ on average and with high probability for input size n and queries with up to k errors. Additionally, we present a trade-off between query time and index complexity that achieves worst-case bounded index size and preprocessing time with linear lookup time on average.

1 Introduction

A text index is a data structure prepared for a document or a collection of documents that facilitates efficient queries for the occurrences of a pattern. Text indexing is becoming increasingly important. The amount of textual data available, e.g., in the Internet or in biological databases, is tremendous and growing. The sheer size of the textual data makes the use of indexes for efficient online queries vital. On the other hand, the nature of the data frequently calls for error-tolerant methods: data on the Internet is often less carefully revised and contains more typos than text published in classical media with professional editorial staff; biological data is often erroneous due to mistakes in its experimental generation. Moreover, in a biological context, matching with errors is useful even for immaculate data, e.g., for similarity searches. For online searches, where no preprocessing of the document corpus is done, there is a variety of algorithms available for many different error models (see, e.g., the survey [22]). Recently, some progress has been made towards the construction of error-tolerant text indexes [2, 6, 10], but in general the problem remains open.

When indexing a document (collection C of documents) of total size n and performing a query for a pattern of length m allowing k errors, the relevant parameters are the index size, the index construction time, the lookup time, and the error model. Usually, the least important of these parameters is the preprocessing time. Depending on the application, either size or query time dominates. We

[*] Research supported in part by DFG,grant Ma 870/5-1 (Leibnizpreis Ernst W. Mayr)

consider output-sensitive algorithms here, i.e., the complexity of the algorithms is allowed to depend on an additional parameter occ counting the number of occurrences of a pattern. The natural lower bound, linear $\Theta(n)$ size (preprocessing time) and linear $\Theta(m + occ)$ lookup time, can be reached[1] for exact matching (e.g., [19, 31, 32]). For edit or Hamming distance, no index with lookup time $O(m + occ)$ and size $O(n \log^l n)$ for $l = O(1)$ even for a small number of errors is known. In all reasonable-size indexes the lookup time depends on n or is not linear in m.

2   Our Results

There appear various definitions of approximate text indexing in the literature. The broader definition just requires the index to "speed up searches" [24], while a stricter approach requires to answer on-line queries "in time proportional to the pattern length and the number of occurrences" [2]. Our algorithm satisfies even the latter definition. We present and analyze a new index structure for approximate pattern matching problems allowing a constant number of $k = O(1)$ errors. The method works for various problem flavors, e.g., approximate text indexing (full text indexing), approximate dictionary lookup indexing (word based indexing), and approximate document collection indexing (see below). For all of these problems we achieve an optimal worst-case lookup time of $O(m + occ)$ employing an index that uses $O(n \log^k n)$ additional space and requires preprocessing time $O(n \log^{k+1} n)$, both on average and with high probability. For approximate dictionary lookup these bounds even improve to $O(|C| \log^k |C|)$ additional space and $O(|C| \log^{k+1} |C|)$ preprocessing time, where $|C|$ is the number of documents in the collection. Our data structure is based on a compact trie representation of the text corpus. This can either be a compact trie, a suffix tree, or a generalized suffix tree. From this tree further error trees are constructed. For the efficient retrieval of results, range queries are prepared on the leaves of the trees. The average case analysis is based on properties of mixing ergodic stationary sources which encompass a wide range of probabilistic models such as stationary ergodic Markov sources (see, e.g., [28]). To our knowledge, this yields the first reasonable sized indexes achieving optimal lookup time. Additionally, we present a trade-off between query time and index complexity, achieving worst-case bounded index size $O(n \log^k n)$ and preprocessing time $O(n \log^{k+1} n)$ while having linear lookup time $O(m + occ)$ on average.

3   Related Work

A survey on text indexing is given by Navarro et al. [24]. For the related nearest neighbor problem see the survey by Indyk [15]. For approximate dictionary indexing with a set of n strings of length m, one can construct a data structure that supports queries in $O(m)$ and has size $O(nm)$ [5]. For text indexing (on a single text of length n) we summarize the results in Table 1.

---

[1] We assume a uniform cost model throughout this work.

Table 1. Previous work on text indexing. (Results marked "avg" are achieved on average and results marked "whp" are achieved with high probability.)

Errors	Model	Query Time	Index Size and Preparation Time (if different)	Literature
none	exact	$O(m+\text{occ})$	$O(n)$	Weiner 1973 [32]
1	edit	$O(m \log n \log \log n + \text{occ})$	$O(n \log^2 n)$	Amir et al. 2000[2]
1	edit	$O(m \log \log n + \text{occ})$	$O(n \log n)$	Buchsbaum et al. 2000 [6]
1	Ham.	$O(m+\text{occ})$	$O(n \log n)$, $O(n \log^2 n)$ (avg,whp)	N 2004 [25]
1	edit	$O(m+\text{occ})$	$O(n \log n)$, $O(n \log^2 n)$ (avg,whp)	MN 2004 [18]
$O(1)$	edit	$O(m \min\{n, m^{k+1}\} + \text{occ})$	$O(\min\{n, m^{k+1}\} + n)$	Cobbs 1995 (Ukkonen 1993) [9, 30]
$O(1)$	edit	$O(kn^\epsilon \log n)$	$O(n)$	Myers 1994 [21]
$O(1)$	edit	$O(n^\epsilon)$	$O(n)$	Navarro et al. 2000 [23]
$O(1)$	edit	$O(m \log^2 n + m^2 + \text{occ})$ (avg)	$O(n \log n)$, $O(n \log^2 n)$ (avg)	Chávez et al. 2002 [8]
$O(1)$	edit	$O(m + \log^k n \log \log n + \text{occ})$	$O(n \log^k n)$	Cole et al. 2004 [10]
$O(1)$	Ham.	$O(\log^{k+1} n)$ (avg)	$O(n)$, $O(n)$	M 2004 [16]
$O(1)$	edit	$O(m+\text{occ})$	$O(n \log^k n)$, $O(n \log^{k+1} n)$ (avg,whp)	This paper
$O(1)$	edit	$O(m+\text{occ})$ (avg,whp)	$O(n \log^k n)$, $O(n \log^{k+1} n)$	This paper
k mismatches in a window of length r		$O(m+\text{occ})$ (avg)	$O(n \log^l n)$ (avg)	Gabriele et. al 2003 [13]

Due to the limited space, the most proofs are omitted. The interested reader is referred to [17] for more details and proofs.

4   Preliminaries

Let Σ be any finite alphabet and let $|\Sigma|$ denote its size. We consider $|\Sigma|$ to be constant. The set of all strings including the empty string ε is denoted by Σ^*. Let $t = t[1] \cdots t[n] \in \Sigma^n$ be a string of length $|t| = n$. If $t = uvw$ with $u, v, w \in \Sigma^*$, then u is a prefix, v a substring, and w a suffix of t. We define $t[i..j] = t[i]t[i+1] \cdots t[j]$, $\text{pref}_k(t) = t[1..k]$, and $\text{suff}_k(t) = t[k..n]$ (with $t[i..j] = \varepsilon$ for $i > j$). For $u, v \in \Sigma^*$ we let $u \sqsubseteq_{\text{pref}} v$ denote that $u = \text{pref}_{|u|}(v)$. For $S \subseteq \Sigma^*$ and $u \in \Sigma^*$ we let $u \in_{\text{pref}} S$ denote that there is $v \in S$ such that $u \sqsubseteq_{\text{pref}} v$. Let $u \in \Sigma^*$ be the longest common prefix of two strings $v, w \in S$. We define $\text{maxpref}(S) = |u|$. The size of S is defined as $\sum_{u \in S} |u|$.

We use the well-known *edit distance* (Levenshtein distance) to measure distances between strings. The edit distance of two strings u and v, $\text{d}(u, v)$, is defined as the minimum number of *edit operations* (*deletions, insertions,* and *substitutions*) that transform u into v. We restrict our attention to the unweighted model, i.e., every operation is assigned a cost of one. The edit distance between two strings $u, v \in \Sigma^*$ is easily computed using dynamic programming in $O(|u||v|)$. It can also be defined via the operators del, ins, and sub of type $\Sigma^* \to \Sigma^*$. If for two strings $u, v \in \Sigma^*$ we have distance $\text{d}(u, v) = k$, then there exist one or more sequences of operations $(op_1, op_2, \ldots, op_k)$, $op_i \in \{\text{del}, \text{ins}, \text{sub}\}$, such that $v = op_k(op_{k-1}(\cdots op_1(u) \cdots))$. We call a sequence $\rho(u, v) = (op_1, op_2, \ldots, op_k)$

of edit operations an *ordered edit sequence* if the operations are applied from left to right. In this light, *Hamming distance* is only a simplified version of edit distance, so we focus our attention on edit distance (Hamming distance is simpler and might help the intuition, especially for the next definition). The minimal prefix of a string u that contains all errors with respect to comparison to a string v plays an important role. For two strings $u, v \in \Sigma^*$ with $d(u,v) = k$, we define the k-minimal prefix length $\mathrm{minpref}_{k,u}(v)$ as the minimal value l for which $d(\mathrm{pref}_l(u), \mathrm{pref}_{l+|v|-|u|}(v)) = k$ and $\mathrm{suff}_{l+1}(u) = \mathrm{suff}_{l+1+|v|-|u|}(v)$. In other words, all errors between u and v are located in a prefix of length $\mathrm{minpref}_{k,u}(v)$ of u.

For fast lookup, strings can be stored in a *trie*. A trie $\mathcal{T}(S)$ for a set of strings $S \subset \Sigma^*$ is a rooted tree with edges labeled by characters from Σ. All outgoing edges of a node are labeled by different characters (unique branching criterion). Each path from the root to a leaf can be read as a string from S. Let u be the string constructed from concatenating the edge labels from the root to a node x. We define $\mathrm{path}(x) = u$. The string depth of node x is defined by $|\mathrm{path}(x)|$. The *word set* of $\mathcal{T}$ denoted $\mathrm{words}(\mathcal{T})$ is the set of all strings u, such that $u \sqsubseteq_{\mathsf{pref}} \mathrm{path}(x)$ for some $x \in \mathcal{T}$. For a node in $x \in \mathcal{T}$ we define $\mathcal{T}_x$ to be the subtrie rooted at x. For convenience we also denote $\mathcal{T}_u = \mathcal{T}_{\mathrm{path}(x)} = \mathcal{T}_x$. The string height of $\mathcal{T}$ is defined as $\mathrm{height}(\mathcal{T}) = \max\{|\mathrm{path}(x)| \mid x \text{ is an inner node of } \mathcal{T}\}$ which is the same as $\mathrm{maxpref}(\mathrm{words}(\mathcal{T}))$.

A *compact trie* is a trie where nodes with only one outgoing edge have been eliminated and edges are labeled by strings from Σ^+ (more precisely, they are labeled by pointers into the underlying strings). Eliminated nodes can be represented by *virtual nodes*, i.e., a base node, the character of the outgoing edge, and the length (compare the representation in [31]). Thus, all previous definitions for tries apply to compact tries as well, possibly using virtual instead of existing nodes. We only use compact tries, and we denote the compact trie for the string set S by $\mathcal{T}(S)$.

If a (compact) trie is never searched deeper than string depth l, i.e., below string depth l we only need to enumerate leaves, then we can drop the unique branching criterion on outgoing edges below this level. Weak tries are needed to bound the preprocessing time and space in the worst case in Section 7.

Definition 1 (Weak Trie). *For $l > 0$, the l-weak trie for a set of strings $S \subset \Sigma^*$ is a rooted tree with edges labeled by characters from Σ. For any node with a depth less than l, all outgoing edges are labeled by different characters, and there are no branching nodes with a depth of more than l. Each path from the root to a leaf can be read as a string from S.*

Up to level l, all previous definitions for (compact) tries carry over to (compact) weak tries. The remaining branches (in comparison to a compact trie) are all at level l. By $\mathcal{W}_l(S)$ we denote a compact l-weak trie for the set of strings S. Note that $\mathcal{W}_{\mathrm{maxpref}(S)}(S) = \mathcal{T}(S)$.

A basic tool needed for our algorithm are *range queries*. The following range queries are used to efficiently select the correct occurrences of a pattern depending on the problem type. The following range queries all operate on arrays containing integers. The goal is to preprocess these arrays in linear time so that the queries can be answered in constant time. Assume that A of size n is an array containing integer values (indexed 1 through n). A *bounded value range query* (BVR) for the range (i, j) with bound k on array A asks for the set of indices L in the given range where A contains values less than or equal to k. The set is given by $L = \{l \mid i \leq l \leq j \text{ and } A[l] \leq k\}$. A *colored range query* (CR) for the range (i, j) on array A asks for the set of distinct elements in the given range of A. These are given by $C = \{A[k] \mid i \leq k \leq j\}$. BVR queries can be answered with $O(n)$ preprocessing time and space and $O(|L|)$ query time [20], based on the well-known range minimum query (RMQ) problem which can be solved with $O(n)$ preprocessing and $O(1)$ query time [12]. CR queries can also be solved with $O(n)$ preprocessing time and space and $O(|C|)$ query time [20].

There are many different *text indexing* problems. We focus on the case where a single pattern P is to be found in a database consisting of a text T or a collection of texts C. The database is considered static and can be preprocessed to allow fast dynamic, on-line queries. When matching a pattern allowing k errors against the text database, we can report *occurrences* (i.e., the exact starting and ending points of a matching substring), *positions* (only the starting points), or – if we have more than one text – *documents* (in which the pattern can be matched). The number of outputs decreases from occurrence to position to document reporting. To ease further exposition, we take a unified view by considering our text database to be a set S of n strings, called the *base set*. The indexing problems handled by our approach are named by the structure of strings in the base set S. If S is the set of suffixes of a string T, we have the k-Approximate Text Indexing (k-ATI) problem. If S is a collection of independent strings, we have the k-Approximate Dictionary Indexing (k-ADI) problem. Finally, if S is the set of suffixes of a collection of documents, we have the k-Approximate Dictionary Indexing (k-ADI) problem. Note that in addition to the three types of reported outputs, for the (k-ADI) problem, it also makes sense to report only documents completely matched by the pattern, called *full hits*. Observe that in all instances in addition to the size of the (originally) given strings a (compact) trie for the underlying collection consumes $O(n)$ space by using pointers into strings instead of substrings.

5   The Basic Index Data Structure

In each of our indexing problems, in order to answer a query we have to find prefixes of strings in the base set S that match the search pattern P with k errors. We call $s \in S$ a *k-error, length-l occurrence* of P if $d(\text{pref}_l(s), P) = k$. We then also say that P "matches" s up to length l with k errors. To solve the various indexing problems defined in the previous section, we need to be able to find all k-error occurrences of P efficiently.

The basic idea of our index for k errors is to make $k + 1$ case distinctions on the position of the first i errors between the pattern P and a k-error match. If P matches a prefix $t \sqsubseteq_{\text{pref}} s$ of a string $s \in S$, we first look whether there is an exact match of a prefix of t and P that is larger than the height h_0 of the trie $\mathcal{T}$ for S. There can be at most one such string, and we check it in time $O(|P|)$ (we can check for an i-error match in time $O(i|P|)$, see, e.g., [29]). Otherwise, there is at least one error before h_0. We build a trie $\mathcal{T}'$ of all strings that contain one error before h_0 and search again for a prefix of P that extends above the height h_1 of $\mathcal{T}'$. If it exists, we check the corresponding string in time $O(|P|)$. Otherwise, there is at least another error before h_1, and we build the next trie $\mathcal{T}''$ by including the errors before h_1. We continue this case distinction until we have either reached the k-th trie or we can match the complete pattern. In the latter case, all leaves in the subtree below P are matches if all errors with the original string are in a prefix of the length of the pattern. We select the appropriate leaves using range queries on the i-minimal prefix lengths. Thus, we either check a single string in the i-th trie in time $O(i|P|)$, or we select a number of matches with range queries in time $O(|P| + \text{occ})$.

More generally, we use the parameters $h_0, \ldots, h_k$ to control the precomputing. The key property of the following inductively defined sets $W_0, \ldots, W_k$ is that we have at least one error before $h_0 + 1$, two errors before $h_1 + 1$, and so on until we have k errors before $h_{k-1} + 1$ in W_k. The partitioning into $k+1$ sets allows searching with different error bounds up to k and enables the efficient selection of occurrences.

Definition 2 (Error Sets). *For $0 \leq i \leq k$, the error set W_i are defined inductively. The first string set W_0 is defined by $W_0 = S$. The other sets are*

$$W_i = \Gamma_{h_{i-1}}(W_{i-1}) \cap S_i \ , \tag{1}$$

where the operator Γ_l is defined by $\Gamma_l(A) = \{op(u)v \mid uv \in A, |op(u)| \leq l + 1, op \in \{\text{del}, \text{ins}, \text{sub}\}\}$ on sets of strings $A \subset \Sigma^*$, S_i is defined as $S_i = \{r \mid \text{there exists } s \in S \text{ such that } d(s, r) = i\}$ (i.e., the strings within distance i of S), and h_i are integer parameters (that may depend on W_i).

The set W_i may consist of independent strings and of suffixes of independent strings. We assume that independent strings do not match prefixes of each other with $2k$ or less errors, i.e., for any $s \neq t \in S$ and any prefixes $u \sqsubseteq_{\text{pref}} s$ we have $d(u, t) > 2k$. This can be achieved by adding sentinels at the end of each string. Suffixes of the same strings can match each other, but there can be at most $2k + 1$ suffixes from the same string that match any string of length l.

Lemma 1 (String Set Sizes). *The size of the string sets W_i is bounded by $|W_i| = O(h_{i-1}|W_{i-1}|)$.*

To search the error sets efficiently, while not spending too much time in preprocessing, we use weak tries, which we call *error trees*.

Definition 3 (Error Trees). *The i-th error tree $\text{et}_i(S)$ is defined as $\text{et}_i(S) = \mathcal{W}_{h_i}(W_i)$. Each leaf x in $\text{et}_i(S)$ is labeled (id_s, l) if id_s is an identifier for $s \in S$, $d(s, \text{path}(x)) = i$, and $l = \text{minpref}_{i, \text{path}(x)}(s)$.*

The correctness of our approach derives from the proof of the following three key properties (assuming either $h_i > \text{maxpref}(W_i)$ or $P \leq h_i$):

1. Let t be a prefix of $s \in S$ and assume $l = \text{minpref}_{i,t}(P)$. If
   (i) t matches P with i errors, i.e., $d(t, P) = i$, and
   (ii) there exists an ordered edit sequence such that $\text{minpref}_{j,t_j}(t) \leq h_{i-1} +$
   1, where for all $0 \leq j \leq i$, $t_j = op_j(\cdots op_1(t) \cdots)$ are the edit stages,
   then there is a leaf x labeled (id_s, l) in $\text{et}_i(S)_P$. In other words, if the first i
   edit operations occur before the bounds $h_j + 1$, then the i-error occurrence
   is covered by precomputing.
2. Let x be a leaf in $\text{et}_i(S)_P$ with label (id_s, l) corresponding to a string $s \in S$.
   There exists $t \sqsubseteq_{\text{pref}} s$ with $d(t, P) = i$ if and only if $l \leq |P|$. Thus, not all
   leaves found in $\text{et}_i(S)_P$ correspond to i-error occurrences of P. To locate the
   correct leaves, we use range queries, see Section 6.
3. Finally, if P matches a prefix t of some string $s \in S$ with exactly i errors,
   then there is a dichotomy. Let $\rho(P, t) = (op_1, op_2, \ldots, op_i)$ be an ordered
   edit sequence.

   Case A Either P can be matched completely in the i-th error tree $\text{et}_i(S)$
   and a leaf x labeled (id_s, l) can be found in $\text{et}_i(S)_P$, or

   Case B there exists an edit operation in $\rho(P, t)$ that occurs after some h_j,
   i.e., a prefix $p \sqsubseteq_{\text{pref}} P$ of length $|p| > h_j$ is found in $\text{et}_j(S)$ and
   $\text{et}_j(S)_p$ contains a leaf x with label (id_s, l).

To capture the intuition first, it is easier to assume that we set $h_i = \text{maxpref}(W_i)$,
where the error trees become compact tries. Note that a leaf can have at most
$2k+1$ labels. The search algorithms are applications of these key properties. The
basic search data structure consists of the $k + 1$ error trees $\text{et}_0(S), \ldots, \text{et}_k(S)$.
The elementary step is to match P in each of the $k + 1$ error trees $\text{et}_i(S)$ for
$0 \leq i \leq k$. Property 3 gives two relevant cases that must be handled.

6   Text Indexing with Worst-Case Optimal Search-Time

To achieve worst-case optimal search-time, we set h_i in Definitions 2 and 3 to
the string height of the error tree $h_i = \text{maxpref}(W_i)$. It immediately follows
that Case B does not contribute to the main search complexity, since each leaf
represents at most $2k + 1$ different strings from the base set S. We have $k + 1$
error trees, thus, for constant k, the total search time spent for Case B is $O(m)$.

  The more difficult part is Case A. Some of the leaves in the subtree $\text{et}_i(S)_P$
may not correspond to i-error matches (i.e., not satisfying the second property
above), we cannot afford to traverse the complete subtree. Let n_i be the number
of leaf labels in $\text{et}_i(S)$. We create an array A_i of size n_i containing pointers to
the leaves of $\text{et}_i(S)$. At each inner node x we store pointers $\text{left}(x)$ and $\text{right}(x)$
to the left-most and right-most index in A_i of the leaves in the subtree rooted
at x. Depending on the desired output, we create additional arrays B_i from the
leaf labels of each error tree $\text{et}_i(S)$ and prepare them for CR or BVR queries to
select a desired subset in output optimal time. This takes time and space $O(n_i)$.

Theorem 1 (Worst-Case Search Times). *Let m be the length of the pattern P and* occ *be the number of outputs. Using $k + 1$ error trees and additional data structures linear in the size of the error trees, we can solve the problems k-ATI, k-ADI, k-ADCI with a worst-case lookup time of $O(m + \text{occ})$.*

Proof (Sketch). Case B takes time $O(m)$. Observe that for leaf label (id_s, l) in $et_i(S)_P$, a prefix of s matches P with at most i errors. Depending on the type of indexing problem we create the arrays B_i and prepare range queries on the array. For each indexing problem, we have different string identifiers, e.g., for k-ADCI id_s is a combination of the string number and the suffix number of the string. We use this and the annotated k-minimal prefix length l to prepare the range queries. For example, to report occurrences, we set $B_i[j] = l$ if the leaf stored in $A[j]$ has label (id_s, l). From the root x of $et_i(S)_P$ we then perform a BVRQ $(\text{left}(x), \text{right}(x), |P|)$ on B_i, which yields exactly the indexes of the leaves representing occurrences. Note that the structure of $et_i(S)_P$ (whether it is a trie or not) has no effect on the complexity. The pattern P is searched k times, and range queries are linear in their output, so the running time is $O(m + \text{occ})$.   □

Compact (weak) tries with n leaves can be implemented in size $O(n)$ plus the size of the underlying strings. The index size is bounded in the following theorem.

Theorem 2 (Data Structure Size and Preprocessing Time). *Let n be the number of strings in S, and let $h = \max_{0 \le i \le k} h_i$. Then, for constant k, the total size of the data structures is $O(nh^k)$ and the preprocessing time is $O(nh^{k+1})$.*

Proof (Sketch). By Lemma 1, the size of the k-th error tree dominates the total size. The total number of leaves of all error trees is $O(nh_0 \cdots h_{k-1})$, which also bounds the size of the range query data structures and time to build them. Each error tree is built naively, copying with errors from the preceding tree. To eliminate duplicates, strings are merged up to $h + k$ so that no errors occur in the remaining suffixes. Duplicates can than be eliminated using $O(|S|k)$ buckets to sort the strings with a common prefix of length $h + k$ in linear time by their string identifier in S and the suffix length in $\{h, \ldots, h + 2k\}$. In the error tree, strings are merged up to depth h_k only.   □

Note that in the worst-case $h_i = \Omega(n)$. The average-case is fortunately much better for a wide range of probabilistic models, and it occurs with high probability. The maximal string depth of any error tree is $O(\log n)$ on average and with high probability for a wide range of probabilistic models. For the analysis, we assume that all strings are generated independently and identically distributed at random by a stationary ergodic source satisfying the *mixing* condition (see, e.g., [28]). Let $\mathcal{F}_n^m$ be the σ-field generated by $\{X_k\}_{k=n}^m$ for $n < m$, then $\{X_k\}_{k=-\infty}^{\infty}$ satisfies the mixing condition, if there exist constants $c_1, c_2 \in \mathbb{R}$ and $d \in \mathbb{N}$ such that for all $-\infty \le m \le m + d \le n$ and for all $\mathcal{A} \in \mathcal{F}_{-\infty}^m$, $\mathcal{B} \in \mathcal{F}_{m+d}^\infty$, we have $c_1 \Pr\{\mathcal{A}\}\Pr\{\mathcal{B}\} \le \Pr\{\mathcal{A} \cap \mathcal{B}\} \le c_2 \Pr\{\mathcal{A}\}\Pr\{\mathcal{B}\}$. Note that this model includes independent trials and stationary ergodic Markov chains. In this model, one can prove that the probability that there is a repeated substring of length $(1 + \epsilon)\frac{\ln n}{r_2}$

in any string of length n is bounded by $cn^{-\epsilon}\ln n$ (where c and r_2 are constants with r_2 depending on the probability distribution) [27]. Using results from [26], it is possible to prove that the probability that there is a common substring of length $(1+\epsilon)\frac{l}{r_2}$ between the prefixes of length l' of any two strings in a set of n independent strings is bounded by $cn^2 l'^2 e^{-2(1+\epsilon)l}$. Thus, the probability of a repeated substring of length $(1+\epsilon)\frac{\ln n}{r_2}$ in a prefix of length $c'(1+\epsilon)\ln n$ is bounded by $c'n^{-2\epsilon}\ln^2 n$.

If the height of the k-th error tree is h, then there are two prefixes of strings in S within distance $2k$. Thus, there exists a common substring between this strings of length $\Omega(\frac{h}{2k})$. Therefore, if the strings are independent, we find that for constant k the expected height cannot exceed $O(\log n)$. To handle the case that both prefixes belong to suffixes of the same string, we have to prove that there is actually a repeated substring of length $\Omega(\frac{h}{2k})$. The idea for this proof is as follows: We assume that the height of the i-th error tree is larger than $ci \log n$ and prove that either there is such a substring, or that the size of the height of the $(i-1)$-th error tree is larger than $c(i-1)\log n$. Note that completely identical strings are joined since W_i are sets. Together this yields the following theorem.

Theorem 3 (Average Data Structure Size and Preprocessing Time). *Let n be the number of strings in S. Then, for any constant k, the average total size of the data structures used is $O(n \log^k n)$ and the average time for preprocessing is $O(n \log^{k+1} n)$. Furthermore, these complexities are achieved with high probability $1 - o(n^{-\epsilon})$ (for $\epsilon > 0$).*

7   Bounded Preprocessing Space

In the previous section, we achieved a worst-case guarantee for the search time. In this section, we describe how to bound the index size in the worst-case in trade-off to having an average-case lookup time. Therefore, we fix h_i in Definitions 2 and 3 to $h_i = h + 1 = c \log n + i$. By Theorem 2, the size of all trees is then $O(n \log^k n)$. For patterns P of length $|P| < h$, we use the same data structures and algorithms as described in the previous Section. Note that Case B never occurs. Since $|P| < h$, all errors must have occurred before h in the respective error tree and are thus accounted for. This yields the following corollary.

Corollary 1 (Small Patterns). *Let P be a pattern of length $m < c \log n$ for some constant c, and let occ be the number of outputs. The problems k-ATI, k-ADI, and k-ADCI can be solved with an index of size $O(n \log^k n)$ which is built in time $O(n \log^{k+1} n)$ and with lookup time $O(m + \text{occ})$.*

For larger patterns we need an auxiliary structure, which is a generalized suffix tree (see, e.g., [14]) for the complete input, i.e., all strings in S. The generalized suffix tree $\mathcal{G}(S)$ is linear in the input size and can be built in linear time (e.g., [19, 31]). We keep the suffix links that are used in the construction process. A suffix link is an auxiliary edge that points from a node x with $\text{path}(x) = av$ to a node y with $\text{path}(y) = v$, thus, allowing to "chop off" characters at the front of the current search string. For any pattern P of length m this allows to find all nodes x such that path(x) represents a right-maximal substring $P[i..j]$ of P in time $O(m)$ (see, e.g., the computation of matching statistics in [7]). The pattern P can match a string $s \in_{\text{pref}} S$ with k errors only if a substring $P[i..j]$ of length $\frac{m}{k+1} - 1$ matches a substring of s exactly. Thus, we find all positions of such substrings and check in time ckm^2 whether there is an occurrence within m characters of each position. Assuming that P is generated by an ergodic stationary source satisfying the mixing condition, we can prove that there are only very few positions and get the following theorem.

Theorem 4 (Large Patterns). *Let P be a pattern of length m and let* occ *be the number of outputs. Let n be the cardinality of S. The problems k-ATI, k-ADI, and k-ADCI can be solved with an index of size $O(n \log^k n)$ which is built in time $O(n \log^{k+1} n)$ and with lookup time $O(m + \text{occ})$ on average and with high probability.*

Proof (Sketch). We set h to $c(k + 1) \log n + 2k$ and handle all small pattern by Corollary 1. The probability that a substring of P of length at least l is found can be bounded by $nm^2 e^{-r_{max}l}$ (where r_{max} is a constant depending on the probability distribution [26]). Therefore, the probability to to perform any work is bounded by $m^2 n^{1-r_{max}(c)} = n^{-\epsilon}$ for suitably chosen c. Thus, the total expected work for large patterns is $O(1)$.   □

8   Conclusion and Open Problems

In the context of text indexing, our data structure and search algorithm works best for small patterns of length $O(\log n)$. The average-case analysis shows that these also contribute most. On the other hand, in the worst-case there are more efficient methods for larger strings. The method of Cole et al. [10] starts being useful for large strings of length $\omega(\log n)$ (the k-error neighborhood for strings of length $O(\log n)$ has size $O(\log^k n)$). The method is linear if $m = \Omega(\log^k n)$. For worst-case text indexing, significant progress depends upon the discovery of a linear-time-lookup method for medium to large patterns of size $\Omega(\log n) \cap O(\log^k n)$.

Our work together with [10] and [16] seems to indicate that – compared to exact searching – an additional complexity factor of $\log^k n$ is inherent. Regarding the index space, a linear lower bound has been proven for the exact indexing problem [11]. However, for the approximate indexing problem, lower bounds do not seem easy to achieve. Using asymmetric communication complexity some bounds for nearest neighbor search in the Hamming cube can be shown [3, 4], but these do not apply to the case where a linear number (in the size of the pattern) of probes to the index is allowed. The information theoretic method of [11] also seems to fall short because approximate lookup does not improve compression and there is no restriction on the lookup time.

Another direction for further research concerns the practical applicability. Although we believe that our approach is fairly easy to implement, we expect the constant factors to be rather large. Therefore, it seems very interesting to study whether the error sets can be thinned out by including less strings. For example, it is not necessary to include errors which "appear" on leaf edges of the preceding error tree. An even more practical question is, whether an efficient implementation without trees based on arrays is possible. Arrays with all leaves are needed anyway for the range minimum queries. Secondly, efficient array packing and searching is possible for suffix arrays [1]. For practical purposes a space efficient solution for $k \leq 3$ is already desirable.

Acknowledgements

We thank the anonymous referees for their insightful comments.

References

1. M. I. Abouelhoda, E. Ohlebusch, and S. Kurtz. Optimal exact string matching based on suffix arrays. In A. H. F. Laender and A. L. Oliveira, editors, *Proc. 9th Int. Symp. on String Processing and Information Retrieval (SPIRE)*, volume 2476 of *LNCS*, pages 31–43. Springer, 2002.
2. A. Amir, D. Keselman, G. M. Landau, M. Lewenstein, N. Lewenstein, and M. Rodeh. Indexing and dictionary matching with one error. *J. Algorithms*, 37:309–325, 2000.
3. O. Barkol and Y. Rabani. Tighter bounds for nearest neighbor search and related problems in the cell probe model. In *Proc. 32nd ACM Symp. on Theory of Computing (STOC)*, pages 388–396. ACM Press, 2000.
4. A. Borodin, R. Ostrovsky, and Y. Rabani. Lower bounds for high dimensional nearest neighbor search and related problems. In *Proc. 31st ACM Symp. on Theory of Computing (STOC)*, pages 312–321. ACM Press, 1999.
5. G. S. Brodal and L. Gąsieniec. Approximate dictionary queries. In *Proc. 7th Symp. on Combinatorial Pattern Matching (CPM)*, volume 1075 of *LNCS*, pages 65–74, 1996.
6. A. L. Buchsbaum, M. T. Goodrich, and J. Westbrook. Range searching over tree cross products. In *Proc. 8th European Symp. on Algorithms (ESA)*, volume 1879, pages 120–131, 2000.
7. W. I. Chang and E. L. Lawler. Sublinear approximate string matching and biological applications. *Algorithmica*, 12:327–344, 1994.
8. E. Chávez and G. Navarro. A metric index for approximate string matching. In *Proc. 5th Latin American Theoretical Informatics (LATIN)*, volume 2286 of *LNCS*, pages 181–195, 2002.
9. A. L. Cobbs. Fast approximate matching using suffix trees. In *Proc. 6th Symp. on Combinatorial Pattern Matching (CPM)*, volume 937 of *LNCS*, pages 41–54. Springer, 1995.
10. R. Cole, L.-A. Gottlieb, and M. Lewenstein. Dictionary matching and indexing with errors and don't cares. In *Proc. 36th ACM Symp. on Theory of Computing (STOC)*, pages 91–100, 2004.
11. E. D. Demaine and A. López-Ortiz. A linear lower bound on index size for text retrieval. In *Proc. 12th ACM-SIAM Symp. on Discrete Algorithms (SODA)*, pages 289–294. ACM, Jan. 2001.

12. H. N. Gabow, J. L. Bentely, and R. E. Tarjan. Scaling and related techniques for geometry problems. In *Proc. 16th ACM Symp. on Theory of Computing (STOC)*, pages 135–143. ACM, Apr. 1984.
13. A. Gabriele, F. Mignosi, A. Restivo, and M. Sciortino. Indexing structures for approximate string matching. In *Proc. 5th Italian Conference on Algorithms and Complexity (CIAC)*, volume 2653 of *LNCS*, pages 140–151, 2003.
14. D. Gusfield. *Algorithms on Strings, Trees, and Sequences: Comp. Science and Computational Biology*. Cambridge University Press, 1997.
15. P. Indyk. Nearest neighbors in high-dimensional spaces. In J. E. Goodman and J. O'Rourke, editors, *Handbook of Discrete and Computational Geometry*, chapter 39. CRC Press LLC, 2nd edition, 2004.
16. M. G. Maaß. Average-case analysis of approximate trie search. In *Proc. 15th Symp. on Combinatorial Pattern Matching (CPM)*, volume 3109 of *LNCS*, pages 472–484. Springer, July 2004.
17. M. G. Maaß and J. Nowak. Text indexing with errors. Technical Report TUM-I0503, Fakultät für Informatik, TU München, Mar. 2005.
18. M. G. Maaß and J. Nowak. A new method for approximate indexing and dictionary lookup with one error. *Information Processing Letters (IPL)*, To be published.
19. E. M. McCreight. A space-economical suffix tree construction algorithm. *J. ACM*, 23(2):262–272, Apr. 1976.
20. S. Muthukrishnan. Efficient algorithms for document retrieval problems. In *Proc. 13th ACM-SIAM Symp. on Discrete Algorithms (SODA)*. ACM/SIAM, 2002.
21. E. W. Myers. A sublinear algorithm for approximate keyword searching. *Algorithmica*, 12:345–374, 1994.
22. G. Navarro. A guided tour to approximate string matching. *ACM Computing Surveys*, 33(1):31–88, Mar. 2001.
23. G. Navarro and R. Baeza-Yates. A hybrid indexing method for approximate string matching. *J. Discrete Algorithms*, 1(1):205–209, 2000. Special issue on Matching Patterns.
24. G. Navarro, R. A. Baeza-Yates, E. Sutinen, and J. Tarhio. Indexing methods for approximate string matching. *IEEE Data Eng. Bull.*, 24(4):19–27, Dec. 2001.
25. J. Nowak. A new indexing method for approximate pattern matching with one mismatch. Master's thesis, Fakultät für Informatik, Technische Universität München, Boltzmannstr. 3, D-85748 Garching, Feb. 2004.
26. B. Pittel. Asymptotical growth of a class of random trees. *Annals of Probability*, 13(2):414–427, 1985.
27. W. Szpankowski. Asymptotic properties of data compression and suffix trees. *IEEE Transact. on Information Theory*, 39(5):1647–1659, Sept. 1993.
28. W. Szpankowski. *Average Case Analysis of Algorithms on Sequences*. Wiley-Interscience, 1st edition, 2000.
29. E. Ukkonen. Algorithms for approximate string matching. *Information and Control*, 64:100–118, 1985.
30. E. Ukkonen. Approximate string-matching over suffix trees. In *Proc. 4th Symp. on Combinatorial Pattern Matching (CPM)*, volume 684 of *LNCS*, pages 228–242. Springer, 1993.
31. E. Ukkonen. On-line construction of suffix trees. *Algorithmica*, 14:249–260, 1995.
32. P. Weiner. Linear pattern matching. In *Proc. 14th IEEE Symp. on Switching and Automata Theory*, pages 1–11. IEEE, 1973.

A New Compressed Suffix Tree Supporting Fast Search and Its Construction Algorithm Using Optimal Working Space[*]

Dong Kyue Kim[1] and Heejin Park[2,**]

[1] School of Electrical and Computer Engineering
Pusan National University, Busan 609-735, South Korea
[2] College of Information and Communications
Hanyang University, Seoul 133-791, South Korea
hjpark@hanyang.ac.kr

Abstract. The compressed suffix array and the compressed suffix tree for a given string S are full-text index data structures occupying $O(n \log |\Sigma|)$ bits where n is the length of S and Σ is the alphabet from which symbols of S are drawn. When they were first introduced, they were constructed from suffix arrays and suffix trees, which implies they were not constructed in optimal $O(n \log |\Sigma|)$-bit working space. Recently, several methods were developed for constructing compressed suffix arrays and compressed suffix trees in optimal working space. By these methods, one can construct compressed suffix trees supporting the pattern search in $O(m'|\Sigma|)$ time where $m' = m \log^\epsilon n$, m is the length of a pattern, and $\log^\epsilon n$ is the time to find the ith smallest suffix of S from the compressed suffix array for any fixed $0 < \epsilon \le 1$. However, compressed suffix trees supporting the pattern search in $O(m' \log |\Sigma|)$ time are not constructed by these methods.

In this paper, we present a new compressed suffix tree supporting $O(m' \log |\Sigma|)$-time pattern search and its construction algorithm using optimal working space. To obtain this result, we developed a new succinct representation of the suffix trees, which is different from the classic succinct representation of parentheses encoding of the suffix trees. Our succinct representation technique can be generally applicable to succinct representation of other search trees.

1 Introduction

A full-text index data structure for a text incorporates the indices for all the suffixes of the text. Two fundamental full-text index data structures are suffix trees [26, 31] and suffix arrays [10, 25], and many efficient algorithms have been developed for constructing suffix trees [6, 26, 31] and suffix arrays [18, 19, 22, 23]. They are used in numerous applications [14], which are exact string matching, computing matching statistics, finding maximal repeats, finding longest common substrings, and so on.

---

[*] This work was supported by Korea Research Foundation grant KRF-2003-03-D00343.
[**] Contact Author

A. Apostolico, M. Crochemore, and K. Park (Eds.): CPM 2005, LNCS 3537, pp. 33–44, 2005.
© Springer-Verlag Berlin Heidelberg 2005

There have been efforts to develop a full-text index data structure that has the capabilities of both suffix trees and suffix arrays without requiring much space. The enhanced suffix array due to Abouelhoda et al. [1, 2] is such an index data structure. It consists of a pos array (suffix array), an lcp array, and a child table. The child table stores the parent-child relationship between nodes in a given suffix tree. Thus, on the enhanced suffix array, every algorithm developed either on suffix trees or suffix arrays can be run with a small and systematic modification. The only drawback of the enhanced suffix array is that the child table supports $O(m|\Sigma|)$-time pattern search where m is the length of a pattern and Σ is an alphabet. Recently, Kim et al. [20, 21] developed a new child table supporting $O(m \log |\Sigma|)$-time pattern search. They called the enhanced suffix array with the new child table linearized suffix tree.

Although many useful full-text index data structures are developed, their space consumption ($O(n \log n)$ bits for a string of length n) motivates researchers to develop more space efficient one. Compressed suffix arrays and compressed suffix trees are space efficient full-text index data structures that consume $O(n \log |\Sigma|)$ bits. Munro et al. [28] developed a succinct representation of a suffix tree topology under the name of space efficient suffix trees. Grossi and Vitter [12, 13] developed compressed suffix arrays, which takes $O(\log^\epsilon n)$ time to find the ith lexicographically smallest suffix in the compressed suffix array for any fixed $0 < \epsilon \leq 1$. Ferragina and Manzini [7, 8] suggested opportunistic data structures under the name of FM-index. Sadakane [30] modified the compressed suffix array so that it acts as a self-indexing data structure. The compressed suffix array and the FM-index can be further compressed by using high-order empirical entropy of the text [9, 11].

When compressed suffix arrays and compressed suffix trees were first introduced, they were constructed from suffix arrays and suffix trees, which implies they were not constructed in optimal $O(n \log |\Sigma|)$-bit working space. For constructing compressed suffix arrays in optimal working space, Lam et al. [24] developed an $O(n \log n)$-time algorithm and Hon et al. [16] developed two algorithms one of which runs in $O(n \log \log |\Sigma|)$ time and the other runs in $O(n \log^\epsilon n)$ time. For constructing compressed suffix trees, Hon et al. [15, 16] proposed an $O(n \log^\epsilon n)$-time algorithm in optimal working space. By this method, one can construct a compressed suffix tree supporting pattern search in $O(m'|\Sigma|)$ time where $m' = m \log^\epsilon n$. However, compressed suffix trees supporting pattern search in $O(m' \log |\Sigma|)$ time cannot be constructed by this method.

In this paper, we present a new compressed suffix tree supporting $O(m' \log |\Sigma|)$-time pattern search and its construction algorithm running in $O(n \log^\epsilon n)$ time using optimal $O(n \log |\Sigma|)$-bit working space.

- Our compressed suffix tree consists of a compressed suffix array, a succinct representation of lcp information, and a succinct representation of a suffix tree topology. The compressed suffix array is the same as the one developed by Grossi and Vitter [13] and the succinct representation of lcp information is the same as the one developed by Sadakane [29, 30]. Our main contribution is to present a new succinct representation of a suffix tree topology which is different from the classic succinct representation of parentheses encoding of a suffix tree topology. The key idea of our succinct representation is to succinctly represent the child table presented by Kim et al. [20, 21] that stores the parent-child relationship between nodes in a suffix tree. The compressed child table can be generally applicable to succinct representation of other search trees.

- Our construction algorithm consists of procedures EXTLCP and CHILD. Procedure EXTLCP computes the depth array that plays an important role in constructing our compressed suffix trees. Procedure CHILD constructs the compressed suffix trees from the succinct representation of lcp information and the depth array.

2   Preliminaries

Consider a string S of length n over an alphabet Σ. Let $S[i]$ for $1 \le i \le n$ denote the ith symbol of S. We assume that $S[n]$ is a special symbol # which is lexicographically larger than any other symbol in Σ. We denote by $S[i..j]$ the substring of S that starts at the ith symbol and ends at the jth symbol. Accordingly, a prefix (resp. suffix) of S is denoted by $S[1..k]$ (resp. $S[k..n]$) for some $1 \le k \le n$. The suffix starting at the ith symbol, i.e., $S[i..n]$, is called the ith suffix of S.

The suffix array of S consists of a pos$[1..n]$ array and an lcp$[1..n]$ array. The pos$[1..n]$ array is basically a sorted list of all the suffixes of S. We store in pos$[i]$, $1 \le i \le n$, the starting position of the $i$the smallest suffix of S. The lcp$[1..n]$ array due to Kasai et al. [17] stores the lengths of the longest common prefix of two adjacent suffixes in the pos array. Specifically, we store in lcp$[i]$, $2 \le i \le n$, the length of the longest common prefix of pos$[i-1]$ and pos$[i]$, and we store -1 in lcp$[1]$ to indicate lcp$[1]$ is undefined. The suffix array of string $caggtcagtcacggtatca\#$ is shown in Fig. 1 (b).

Grossi and Vitter [13] developed the compressed suffix array that stores the same information as the pos array in $O(n)$ bits but it takes $O(\log^\epsilon n)$ time for any fixed $0 < \epsilon \le 1$ to get an element pos$[i]$ from the compressed suffix array. In addition, Sadakane [29] developed a succinct representation of the lcp array that requires $O(n)$ bits and from which we can get an element lcp$[i]$ in $O(\log^\epsilon n)$ time. The compressed suffix array and the succinct representation of the lcp array can be constructed in $O(n \log^\epsilon n)$ time using optimal $O(n \log |\Sigma|)$-bit working space due to Hon et al [16] and Hon and Sadakane [15], respectively.

The suffix tree of S is the compacted trie on the set of all suffixes of S. It has n leaves, each of which corresponds to a suffix of S. We denote the leaf corresponding to the ith suffix by leaf i. Figure 1 (c) shows the suffix tree of string $caggtcagtcacggtatca\#$. Each edge in the suffix tree of S has a label that is a substring of S, which is normally represented by the starting position and the ending position of the substring in S. Each node x also has a label, denoted by $label(x)$, that is the concatenation of the labels of the edges in the path from the root to the node.

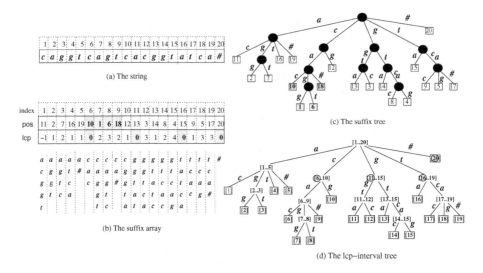

Fig. 1. The suffix array, the suffix tree, and the lcp-interval tree for *caggtcagtcac ggtatca#*.

The *lcp-interval tree* of S is a modification of the suffix tree of S such that each node x is replaced by the interval $[i..j]$ such that $\text{pos}[i..j]$ stores the suffixes in the subtree rooted at x. (Note that the suffixes in the subtree rooted at a node x are stored consecutively in the pos array because all of them have the same prefix.) The lcp-interval tree of string *caggtcagtcacggtatca#* is shown in Fig. 1 (d). Consider the node whose label is *ca* in Fig. 1 (c). The suffixes in the subtree of the node are stored in $\text{pos}[6..9]$ and thus the node is replaced by interval $[6..9]$ in Fig. 1 (d). The intervals in the lcp-interval tree are called *lcp-intervals*. We introduce a useful property of lcp-interval trees without proofs.

Lemma 1. *Let c_r, $1 \leq r \leq k$, denote the first index of the rth child of an lcp-interval $[i..j]$ where k is the number of children of $[i..j]$. The first indices $c_2, c_3, \ldots, c_k$ correspond to the indices of the smallest value in $\text{lcp}[i+1..j]$.*

Consider the lcp-interval $[1..20]$ in Fig. 1 (d). In $\text{lcp}[2..20]$, the smallest value 0 is stored in $\text{lcp}[6]$, $\text{lcp}[11]$, $\text{lcp}[16]$, and $\text{lcp}[20]$. The indices 6, 11, 16, and 20 correspond to the first indices of the children $[6..10]$, $[11..15]$, $[16..19]$ and $[20]$, respectively.

3   The Linearized Suffix Tree

The linearized suffix tree consists of a $\text{pos}[1..n]$ array, an $\text{lcp}[1..n]$ array and a child table $\text{cldtab}[1..n-1]$. Since we already introduced the pos and lcp arrays, we only describe the child table. The child table $\text{cldtab}[1..n-1]$ stores the parent-child relationship between the lcp-intervals in the *modified* lcp-interval tree whose data structure for node branching is the *complete binary tree*.

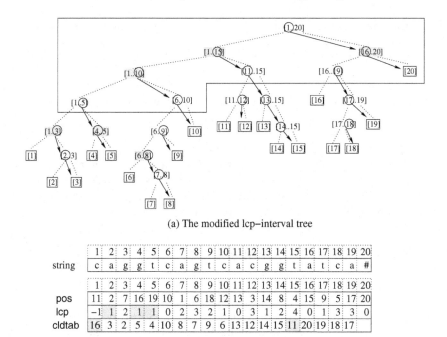

(a) The modified lcp–interval tree

	1	2	3	4	5	6	7	8	9	10	11	12	13	14	15	16	17	18	19	20
string	c	a	g	g	t	c	a	g	t	c	a	c	g	g	t	a	t	c	a	#

	1	2	3	4	5	6	7	8	9	10	11	12	13	14	15	16	17	18	19	20
pos	11	2	7	16	19	10	1	6	18	12	13	3	14	8	4	15	9	5	17	20
lcp	-1	1	2	1	1	0	2	3	2	1	0	3	1	2	4	0	1	3	3	0
cldtab	16	3	2	5	4	10	8	7	9	6	13	12	14	15	11	20	19	18	17	

(b) The linearized suffix tree

Fig. 2. The modified lcp-interval tree and the linearized suffix tree for *caggtcagtcac ggtatca#*. In Fig. 2 (a), for every index i in a circle, `cldtab[i]` stores the first index of the lcp-interval its arrow points to. Note that there are 19 circles and any two indices in circles are not the same and thus each entry of `cldtab[1..19]` stores only one element.

We first describe the shape of the complete binary tree for the children of an lcp-interval $[a..b]$. In this complete binary tree, the interval $[a..b]$ is the root, all the children of $[a..b]$ are leaves, and the other internal nodes are appropriately generated to form the complete binary tree. Let k denote the number of children of $[a..b]$. Let d and k' be integers such that $k = 2^d + k'$ for some $1 \leq k' \leq 2^d$. We generate a complete binary tree of depth $d + 1$ having $2k'$ leaves in level 0. Each ith $(1 \leq i \leq 2k')$ child of $[a..b]$ is the ith leftmost leaf in level 0 and the ith $(2k' + 1 \leq i \leq 2^d + k')$ child of $[a..b]$ is the $(i - k')$th leftmost node in level 1.

Example 1. Consider the lcp-interval $[1..20]$ in Fig. 1 (d). The lcp-interval $[1..20]$ has five children $[1..5]$, $[6..10]$, $[11..15]$, $[16..19]$, and $[20]$. Since $5 = 2^2 + 1$, we construct the complete binary tree of depth 3 (Fig. 2 (a)). The first two children $[1..5]$ and $[6..10]$ are the leaves in level 0. The other three children $[11..15]$, $[16..19]$, and $[20]$ are the leaves in level 1. Three internal nodes $[1..10]$, $[1..15]$, and $[16..20]$ are newly created.

We show how to store a modified lcp-interval tree in a child table. For each internal lcp-interval $[i..j]$, we store the first index of its right child in the child table. (Note that every internal lcp-interval in a modified lcp-interval tree has two children and we can enumerate the children of $[i..j]$ by storing the first index of its right child.) Let $\text{child}(i, j)$ denote the first index of the right child of $[i..j]$. The child table stores $\text{child}(i, j)$ in the following way.

– If $[i..j]$ is the right child or the root, we store $\text{child}(i, j)$ in cldtab[i].
– Otherwise, we store $\text{child}(i, j)$ in cldtab[j].

In Fig. 2, we store $\text{child}(1, 20)(= 16)$ in cldtab[1] because $[1..20]$ is the root, and we store $\text{child}(1, 15)(= 11)$ in cldtab[15] because $[1..15]$ is the left child. Since the number of internal lcp-intervals in the modified lcp-interval tree is $n-1$, we can store $\text{child}(i, j)$ for every internal lcp-interval $[i..j]$ in cldtab[$1..n - 1$] without conflicts. The formal proof is given in [21].

4   A New Compressed Suffix Tree

4.1   Definition

Our compressed suffix tree consists of a compressed suffix array due to Grossi and Vitter [13], a succinct representation of lcp information due to Sadakane [29, 30], and a compressed child table. We only describe the compressed child table. Before describing the compressed child table, we first introduce a difference child table. The difference child table differs from the child table in that it stores the minimum of $(\text{child}(i, j) - i)$ and $(j - \text{child}(i, j))$ instead of $\text{child}(i, j)$. The difference child table consists of a diff[$1..n - 1$] array and a sign[$1..n - 1$] array and it is defined as follows.

– Case 1: If $[i..j]$ is the right child or the root, we store $\min\{\text{child}(i, j) - i, j - \text{child}(i, j)\}$ in diff[i]. If $\text{child}(i, j) - i$ is stored in diff[i], we store 0 in sign[i] and we store 1, otherwise.
– Case 2: Otherwise, we store $\min\{\text{child}(i, j) - i, j - \text{child}(i, j)\}$ in diff[j]. We store 0 or 1 in sign[j], similarly.

Example 2. Recall that we store $\text{child}(1, 20)$ $(= 16)$ in cldtab[1] in Fig. 2 (b). For the case of difference child table, we first compute $\text{child}(1, 20) - 1 = 15$ and $20 - \text{child}(1, 20) = 4$. Since 4 is smaller than 15, we store 4 in diff[1] and 1 in sign[1] in Fig. 3.

	1	2	3	4	5	6	7	8	9	10	11	12	13	14	15	16	17	18	19	20
sign	1	1	0	1	1	1	1	0	1	1	0	1	0	1	1	1	1	1	1	0
diff	4	0	1	0	1	0	0	1	0	4	2	0	1	0	4	0	0	0	1	
C array	100	0	1	0	1	0	0	1	0	100	10	0	1	0	100	0	0	0	1	
D array	100	1	1	1	1	1	1	1	1	100	10	1	1	1	100	1	1	1	1	

Fig. 3. The difference child table and its succinct representation.

The compressed child table consists of a compressed `diff` array and a `sign` array. Let b_i denote the length of bits needed to represent `diff`$[i]$, i.e., if `diff`$[i] \neq 0$, $b_i = \lceil \log(\text{diff}[i] + 1) \rceil$ and $b_i = 1$ otherwise. The main idea of compressing the `diff` is that we only use b_i bits to store `diff`$[i]$. Let s_i denote $\Sigma_{k=1}^{i} b_k$. The compressed `diff` array is composed of two bit arrays C and D of length s_{n-1}. We denote the jth bits of the arrays by $C[j]$ and $D[j]$, respectively. The C array is basically a concatenated bit string of the integers stored in `diff`$[1..n-1]$ where each `diff`$[i]$ is represented by b_i bits. Specifically, $C[s_{i-1}+1..s_i]$ is the binary representation of `diff`$[i]$ using b_i bits. In Fig. 3 (c), the first 5 bits in the C array are 10001, which is the concatenation of the binary representation of 4, 0, and 1. We define the D array. All the bits in D are 0 except the $D[j]$ such that $j = s_k + 1$ for some k, $0 \leq k \leq n-2$, i.e., the $D[j]$ such that $C[j]$ is the most significant bit (MSB) of some integer `diff`$[k]$. In Fig. 3 (c), $D[1]$ is 1 because $C[1]$ is the MSB of 4 that is in `diff`$[1]$. The $D[2]$ and $D[3]$ are all 0's because they are not the MSB's of any integers in `diff`.

We can compute child(a, b) for an lcp-interval $[a..b]$ in $O(1)$ time from C, D, `sign` arrays, and a data structure for computing function $select$ in D [27]. We can compute child(a, b) from either `diff`$[a]$, `sign`$[a]$, a, and b, (Case 1) or `diff`$[b]$, `sign`$[b]$, a, and b, (Case 2). We have only to show how to obtain `diff`$[i]$, $1 \leq i \leq n-1$. we first compute $select(i)$ and $select(i+1)$ on D. Then `diff`$[i]$ is stored in $C[select(i)..select(i+1)-1]$ by definition of C and D arrays.

We show that C, D, and the `sign` arrays consume $5n$ or less bits. It is clear the `sign` array consumes $n-1$ bits. Since the length of C array is that of D array, we only show the length of C array is $2n$ or less bits. By definition of C array, the length $S(n)$ of C array for a string of length n can be represented by the recurrence relation below.

$$S(n) = \max\{\max_{k=1}^{n-1}\{S(k) + S(n-k) + \min\{\lceil \log(k+1) \rceil, \lceil \log(n-k+1) \rceil\}\},$$
$$S(n-1) + 1\}$$
$$= \max\{\max_{k=1}^{\lfloor n/2 \rfloor}\{S(k) + S(n-k) + \lceil \log(k+1) \rceil\}, S(n-1) + 1\}.$$

We can show that $S(n) < 2n$ using the fact that the right side of the equation is maximized when $k = n - 2^{d-1}$ such that $2^{d-1} < n \leq 2^d$. The proof of $S(n) < 2n$ is omitted. Since the data structure for $select$ consumes $o(n)$ bits, we get the following theorem.

Theorem 1. *The compressed child table consumes $5n + o(n)$ bits, and one can compute* `cldtab`$[i]$, $1 \leq i \leq n-1$, *in $O(1)$ time using the compressed child table.*

4.2   Pattern Search

We first describe the pattern search in a linearized suffix tree, which is the same as the pattern search in an lcp-interval tree except for finding the child of an lcp-interval $[i..j]$ whose incoming edge label starts with a symbol of a pattern. We find such child by traversing the complete binary tree rooted at $[i..j]$. We show how to obtain the first symbol of the incoming edge label of an lcp-interval $[a..b]$

in the complete binary tree when we are to compare it with the kth symbol of the pattern. Since we are traversing the modified lcp-interval tree from the root (of the modified lcp-interval tree) using the pattern, $S[\text{pos}[i] + (k-1)]$ stores the first symbol of the incoming edge label of $[a..b]$ by definition of the pos array.

Example 3. Consider finding the child of $[1..5]$ whose incoming edge label starts with g, when we search a pattern ag in the modified lcp-interval tree in Fig. 2 (a). First, we compare g with $S[\text{pos}[4]+1]$ that is t. Since g is smaller than t, we move to $[1..3]$. Then, we compare g with $S[\text{pos}[2]+1]$ that is g. Since g is the same as $S[\text{pos}[2]+1]$, we move to $[2..3]$.

It should be noted that we do not know the depth of the complete binary tree during the pattern search. Instead, we can determine whether we arrives a leaf or not using the lcp array. Let $[a..b]$ be an lcp-interval in the complete binary tree. If $[a..b]$ is the left child, it is not a leaf if $\text{lcp}[a] = \text{lcp}[\text{cldtab}[b]]$ and it is a leaf, otherwise. If $[a..b]$ is the right child, it is not a leaf if $\text{lcp}[\text{cldtab}[a]] = \text{lcp}[b]$ and it is a leaf, otherwise.

We consider finding a pattern P of length m in the linearized suffix tree. Since the complete binary tree is of depth $\log|\Sigma|$ in the worst case, we can find an lcp-interval $[p..q]$ that stores all the suffixes including P in $O(m\log|\Sigma|)$ time. Thus, we can count the number of occurrences of P (which is $q-p+1$) in $O(m\log|\Sigma|)$ time and enumerate all the occurrences in $O(m\log|\Sigma| + occ)$ time where occ is the number of occurrences.

The pattern search in the compressed suffix tree is the same as the pattern search in the linearized suffix tree except that each access to an element of pos, lcp, and cldtab ($O(1)$ time respectively) is replaced by an access to an element of a compressed suffix array ($O(\log^\epsilon n)$ time), a succinct representation of lcp information ($O(\log^\epsilon n)$ time), and our compressed suffix tree ($O(1)$ time). Hence, we get the following theorem.

Theorem 2. *Our compressed suffix tree can answer a counting query in $O(m'\log|\Sigma|)$ time and an enumeration query in $O(m'\log|\Sigma| + occ\log^\epsilon n)$ time for a pattern of length m where $m' = m\log^\epsilon n$.*

5   Construction of the Compressed Child Table

We show that we can construct the compressed suffix tree from the lcp array. We first introduce a depth array, which is a temporary array used to construct the compressed child table. The $\text{depth}[1..n-1]$ array is defined as follows. Consider the complete binary tree rooted at an interval $[a..b]$. Let $c_1, c_2, ..., c_k$ denote the first indices of the children of $[a..b]$. Then, we store in $\text{depth}[c_i]$ ($2 \leq i \leq k$) the depth of the lowest common ancestor of two adjacent child intervals $[c_{i-1}..c_i - 1]$ and $[c_i..c_{i+1} - 1]$ in the complete binary tree.

Example 4. In Fig. 4, the lowest common ancestor of $[2..3]$ and $[4]$ is $[1..5]$ whose depth is 0 and thus we store 0 in $\text{depth}[4]$. Similarly, we store 1 in $\text{depth}[2]$ and $\text{depth}[5]$.

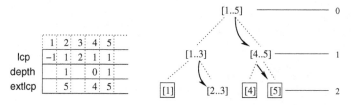

Fig. 4. The extended `lcp` array when $|\Sigma| = 16$.

Procedure EXTLCP
1:    $\text{ranking}[1..n-1] = 1$;
2:    $\text{numchild}[1..n-1] = 0$;
3:   $push(1)$;
4:   **for** $i := 2$ **to** n **do**
5:       **while** $\text{lcp}[i] < \text{lcp}[top()]$ **do**
6:             $lastIndex := pop()$;
7:             $\text{numchild}[lastIndex] := \text{ranking}[lastIndex] + 1$;
8:         **if** $\text{lcp}[i] = \text{lcp}[top()]$ **then**
9:           $\text{ranking}[i] := \text{ranking}[pop()] + 1$;
10:       $push(i)$
11:   $push(n)$;
12:   **for** $i := n - 1$ **downto** 1 **do**
13:       **while** $\text{lcp}[i] < \text{lcp}[top()]$ **do**
14:             $pop()$;
15:       **if** $\text{lcp}[i] = \text{lcp}[top()]$ **then**
17:           $\text{numchild}[i] := \text{numchild}[pop()]$;
18:           $ComputeDepth(\text{ranking}[i], \text{numchild}[i])$;
19:       $push(i)$
end

Fig. 5. Procedure EXTLCP.

Each element of the **depth** array can be stored in $\lceil \log \log |\Sigma| \rceil$ bits because the largest value that $\text{depth}[i]$, $1 \le i \le n$, may store is $\lceil \log |\Sigma| \rceil - 1$ due to the fact that a complete binary tree may have at most $|\Sigma|$ leaves. The extended `lcp` array (i.e., the `lcp` array and the **depth** array) reflects the structure of the modified lcp-interval tree. The child(i, j) of $[i..j]$ is the index k, $i + 1 \le k \le j$, minimizing $\text{lcp}[i] \| \text{depth}[i]$. We will denote $\text{lcp}[i] \| \text{depth}[i]$ by $\text{extlcp}[i]$. In Fig. 4, child$(1, 5)$ is 4 and 4 is the index that minimizing $\text{extlcp}[i]$ because $\text{extlcp}[4] = 4$ and $\text{extlcp}[2] = \text{extlcp}[5] = 5$.

Now, we show how to construct the compressed child table. Construction of the compressed child table consists of two following procedures.

1. Procedure EXTLCP (Fig. 5): For each lcp-interval $[a..b]$, we first compute the ranking of each child and the number k of children of $[a..b]$ (lines 1-10). Then, we compute $\text{depth}[c_i]$ for $2 \le i \le k$ (lines 11-19) where c_i is the first index of the ith child of $[a..b]$.

Procedure CHILD

```
1:    lastIndex := −1;
2:    C_F = C_B = D_F = D_B := NULL;
3:    push(1);
4:    for i := 2 to n + 1 do
5:        while extlcp[i] < extlcp[top()] do
6:            lastIndex := pop();
7:        if lastIndex ≠ −1 then
8:            diff = min{i − lastIndex, lastIndex − top()};
9:            C_F := C_F‖diff; // Append the bit representation of diff at the end of C_F.
10:           D_F := D_F‖10···0; // Append 1 followed by k − 1 number of 0's
11:           lastIndex := −1;      where k is the bit length of diff.
12:       else
13:           C_F := C_F‖00;   D_F := D_F‖10; // Append '00' to indicate diff is
14:       push(i)                                 not computed in this for loop.
15:   lastIndex := −1;                         Note that the bit representation
16:   push(n);                                  of diff cannot be '00'.
17:   for i := n − 1 downto −1 do
18:       while extlcp[i] < extlcp[top()] do
19:           lastIndex := pop();
20:       if lastIndex ≠ −1 then
21:           diff := min{lastIndex − i, top() − lastIndex};
22:           C_B := diff‖C_B;
23:           D_B := 10···0‖D_B; // Append 1 followed by k − 1 number of 0's
24:           lastIndex := −1;      where k is the bit length of diff.
25:       else
26:           C_B := 00‖C_B;   D_B := 10‖D_B;
27:       push(i)
28:   C = merge(C_F, C_B); D = merge(D_F, D_B);
end
```

Fig. 6. Procedure CHILD. Procedure CHILD assumes a sentinel value -2 is stored in lcp[0] and lcp[n + 1].

We describe how the function *ComputeDepth* computes depth[c_i], given i and k (ranking[i] and numchild[i] in line 18) when $k = 2^d$ for some d. (Computation of depth[c_i] when $k \neq 2^d$ for any d is slightly different.) Recall that depth[c_i] ($2 \leq i \leq k$) stores the depth of the lowest common ancestor of two adjacent child intervals [$c_{i-1}..c_i - 1$] and [$c_i..c_{i+1} - 1$]. Since the depth of the lowest common ancestor is $d - L_i$ where L_i is the level of the lowest common ancestor, we describe how to compute L_i. The L_i corresponds to the number of tailing 0's in the bit representation of i. For example, every odd numbered child has no tailing 0's and thus the level of it is 0.

We consider the running time of computing depth[c_i] for $2 \leq i \leq k$. To compute them, we have to scan the bit representation from the right until we reach the rightmost 1 for all integers $2, ..., k$. One can show this takes $O(k)$ time overall by resorting to the amortized analysis which is very similar to the one used to count the bit-flip operations of a binary counter [3]. Overall, this procedure takes $O(n \log^\epsilon n)$ time.

2. Procedure CHILD (Fig. 6): We first compute C_F and D_F for Case 2 of the difference child table (lines 3-14) and then C_B and D_B for Case 1 of the difference child table (lines 15-27). Then, we compute C by merging C_F and C_B and D by merging D_F and D_B. Overall, this procedure takes $O(n \log^\epsilon n)$ time.

We consider the working space of procedures EXTLCP and CHILD. Procedure EXTLCP uses ranking[$1..n$] and numchild[$1..n$] arrays. Since the largest value each element of them may store is $|\Sigma|$, they require $O(n \log |\Sigma|)$ bits. Procedure CHILD uses extlcp which is lcp||depth. The succinct representation of lcp requires $O(n)$ bits and depth[$1..n - 1$] requires $O(n \log \log |\Sigma|)$ bits. We consider the space required by stacks used by procedures EXTLCP and CHILD. Since the values in the stacks are monotone, we first encode them by the difference between adjacent numbers and then represent them by δ-code [4, 5]. Then, the space requirement of the stacks is $O(n)$ bits. Hence, we get the following theorem.

Theorem 3. *The compressed child table can be constructed in $O(n \log^\epsilon n)$ time using optimal $O(n \log |\Sigma|)$-bit working space.*

References

1. M.I. Abouelhoda, S. Kurtz, and E. Ohlebusch, Replacing suffix trees with enhanced suffix arrays, *J. of Discrete Algorithms* (2004), 53–86.
2. M. Abouelhoda, E. Ohlebusch, and S. Kurtz, Optimal exact string matching based on suffix arrays, *SPIRE* (2002), 31–43.
3. T.H. Cormen, C.E. Leiserson, R.L. Rivest, C. Stein, Introduction to Algorithms (Second Edition), *MIT Press* (2001).
4. P. Elias, Efficient storage and retrieval by content and address of static files, *J. Assoc. Comput. Mach.* 21 (1974), 246–260.
5. P. Elias, Universal codeword sets and representation of the integers, *IEEE. Trans. Inform. Theory* 21 (1975), 194–203.
6. M. Farach-Colton, P. Ferragina and S. Muthukrishnan, On the sorting-complexity of suffix tree construction, *J. Assoc. Comput. Mach.* 47 (2000), 987-1011.
7. P. Ferragina and G. Manzini, Opportunistic data structures with applications, *FOCS* (2001), 390–398.
8. P. Ferragina and G. Manzini, An experimental study of an opportunistic index, *SODA* (2001), 269–278.
9. P. Ferragina, G. Manzini, V. Makinen, and G. Navarro, An Alphabet-Friendly FM-index, *SPIRE* (2004), 150–160.
10. G. Gonnet, R. Baeza-Yates, and T. Snider, New indices for text: Pat trees and pat arrays. In W. B. Frakes and R. A. Baeza-Yates, editors, Information Retrieval: Data Structures & Algorithms, *Prentice Hall* (1992), 66–82.
11. R. Grossi, A. Gupta and J.S. Vitter, High-order entropy-compressed text indexes, *SODA* (2003), 841–850.
12. R. Grossi, A. Gupta and J.S. Vitter, When indexing equals compression: Experiments with compressing suffix arrays and applications, *SODA* (2004).

13. R. Grossi and J.S. Vitter, Compressed suffix arrays and suffix trees with applications to text indexing and string matching, *STOC* (2000), 397–406.

14. D. Gusfield, Algorithms on Strings, Trees, and Sequences, *Cambridge Univ. Press* (1997).

15. W.K. Hon and K. Sadakane, Space-economical algorithms for finding maximal unique matches, *CPM* (2002), 144–152.

16. W.K. Hon, K. Sadakane and W.K. Sung, Breaking a time-and-space barrier in constructing full-text indices, *FOCS* (2003), 251–260.

17. T. Kasai, G. Lee, H. Arimura, S. Arikawa, and K. Park, Linear-time longest-common-prefix computation in suffix arrays and its applications, *CPM* (2001), 181–192.

18. J. Kärkkäinen and P. Sanders, Simpler linear work suffix array construction, *ICALP* (2003), 943–955.

19. D.K. Kim, J. Jo, and H. Park, A fast algorithm for constructing suffix arrays for fixed-size alphabets, *WEA* (2004), 301–314.

20. D.K. Kim, J.E. Jeon, and H. Park, An efficient index data structre with the capabilities of suffix trees and suffix arrays for alphabets of non-negligible size, *SPIRE* (2004), 138–149.

21. D.K. Kim, M. Kim, and H. Park, Linearized suffix tree: an efficient index data structre with the capabilities of suffix trees and suffix arrays, *manuscript* (2004).

22. D.K. Kim, J.S. Sim, H. Park and K. Park, Linear-time construction of suffix arrays, *CPM* (2003), 186–199.

23. P. Ko and S. Aluru, Space-efficient linear time construction of suffix arrays, *CPM* (2003), 200–210.

24. T.K. Lam, K. Sadakane, W.K. Sung, and S.M. Yiu, A space and time efficient algorithm for constructing compressed suffix arrays, *Proc. of International Conference on Computing and Combinatorics*, (2002), 401–410.

25. U. Manber and G. Myers, Suffix arrays: A new method for on-line string searches, *SIAM J. Comput.* 22 (1993), 935–938.

26. E.M. McCreight, A space-economical suffix tree construction algorithm, *J. Assoc. Comput. Mach.* 23 (1976), 262–272.

27. J.I. Munro and V. Raman, Succinct representation of balanced parentheses and static trees, *SIAM J. on Comput.* 31 (2001), 762–776.

28. J.I. Munro, V. Raman and S.S. Rao, Space efficient suffix trees, *J. of Algorithms* 39 (2001), 205–222.

29. K. Sadakane, Succinct representations of lcp Information and improvements in the compressed suffix arrays, *SODA* (2002), 225–232.

30. K. Sadakane, New text indexing functionalities of the compressed suffix arrays, *J. of Algorithms* 48 (2003), 294–313.

31. E. Ukkonen, On-line construction of suffix trees, *Algorithmica* 14 (1995), 249–260.

32. P. Weiner, Linear pattern matching algorithms, *Proc. 14th IEEE Symp. Switching and Automata Theory* (1973), 1–11.

Succinct Suffix Arrays
Based on Run-Length Encoding

Veli Mäkinen[1,*] and Gonzalo Navarro[2,**]

[1] AG Genominformatik, Technische Fakultät
Universität Bielefeld, Germany
`veli@cebitec.uni-bielefeld.de`
[2] Center for Web Research
Dept. of Computer Science, University of Chile
`gnavarro@dcc.uchile.cl`

Abstract. A succinct full-text self-index is a data structure built on a text $T = t_1 t_2 \ldots t_n$, which takes little space (ideally close to that of the compressed text), permits efficient search for the occurrences of a pattern $P = p_1 p_2 \ldots p_m$ in T, and is able to reproduce any text substring, so the self-index replaces the text. Several remarkable self-indexes have been developed in recent years. They usually take $O(nH_0)$ or $O(nH_k)$ bits, being H_k the kth order empirical entropy of T. The time to count how many times does P occur in T ranges from $O(m)$ to $O(m \log n)$. We present a new self-index, called run-length FM-index (RLFM index), that counts the occurrences of P in T in $O(m)$ time when the alphabet size is $\sigma = O(\text{polylog}(n))$. The index requires $nH_k \log_2 \sigma + O(n)$ bits of space for small k. We then show how to implement the RLFM index in practice, and obtain in passing another implementation with different space-time tradeoffs. We empirically compare ours against the best existing implementations of other indexes and show that ours are fastest among indexes taking less space than the text.

1 Introduction

The classical problem in string matching is to determine the *occ* occurrences of a short pattern $P = p_1 p_2 \ldots p_m$ in a large text $T = t_1 t_2 \ldots t_n$. Text and pattern are sequences of characters over an alphabet Σ of size σ. Actually one may want to know the number *occ* of occurrences (this is called a *counting query*), the text positions of those *occ* occurrences (a *locating query*), or also a text context around them (a *context query*). When the same text is queried several times with different patterns, the text can be preprocessed to build an *index* structure that speeds up searches.

* Funded by the Deutsche Forschungsgemeinschaft (BO 1910/1-3) within the Computer Science Action Program.
** Funded by Millennium Nucleus Center for Web Research, Grant P01-029-F, Mideplan, Chile.

A. Apostolico, M. Crochemore, and K. Park (Eds.): CPM 2005, LNCS 3537, pp. 45–56, 2005.
© Springer-Verlag Berlin Heidelberg 2005

To allow fast searches for patterns of any size, the index must allow access to all *suffixes* of the text (the ith suffix of T is $t_i t_{i+1} \ldots t_n$). These kind of indexes are called *full-text indexes*. The *suffix tree* [24] is the best-known full-text index, requiring $O(m)$ time for counting and $O(occ)$ for locating.

The suffix tree, unfortunately, takes $O(n \log n)$ bits of space, while the text takes $n \log \sigma$ bits[1]. In practice the suffix tree requires about 20 times the text size. A smaller constant factor, close to 4 in practice, is achieved by the *suffix array* [16]. Yet, the space complexity is still $O(n \log n)$ bits.

Many efforts to reduce these space requirements have been pursued. This has evolved into the concept of a *self-index*, a succinct index that contains enough information to reproduce any text substring. Hence a self-index *replaces* the text. Several self-indexes that require space proportional to the *compressed* text have been proposed recently [3, 5, 8, 10, 19, 22].

Some structures [5, 8] need only $nH_k + o(n)$ bits of space, which is currently the lowest asymptotic space requirement that has been achieved. Here H_k stands for the *kth order entropy* of T [17]. Using a recent sequence representation technique [6], the structure in [5] supports counting queries in $O(m)$ time on alphabets of size $O(\text{polylog}(n))$. Other self-indexes require either more time for counting [5, 8, 19, 22], or $O(nH_0)$ bits of space [23].

In this paper we describe how run-length encoding of Burrows-Wheeler transformed text [1], together with the backward search idea [3], can be used to obtain a self-index, called RLFM index for "run-length FM-index", requiring $nH_k \log \sigma + O(n)$ bits of space, which answers counting queries in $O(m)$ time on alphabets of size $O(\text{polylog}(n))$. Just as for other indexes [5, 8], the space formula is valid for any $k \leq \alpha \log_\sigma n$, for any constant $0 < \alpha < 1$. The index is interesting in practice as well. We give several considerations to implement the RLFM index, which are of interest by themselves and also yield an implementation for a simpler index, which we call SSA for "succinct suffix array". We show experimentally on an English text collection that the RLFM index and the SSA take less space than the text, and among such indexes, they are the fastest in counting queries.

The RLFM index motivated the work in [5, 6]. The latter supersedes our original idea [15] in theory, yet in practice the RLFM index is still appealing.

2   Basic Concepts

We denote by $T = t_1 t_2 \ldots t_n$ our *text* string. We assume that a special *endmarker* $t_n = \$$ has been appended to T, such that "$\$$" is smaller than any other text character. We denote by $P = p_1 p_2 \ldots p_n$ our *pattern* string, and seek to find the occurrences of P in T. For clarity, we assume that P and T are drawn over alphabet $\Sigma = \{\$, 1, \ldots, \sigma\}$.

Empirical kth Order Entropy. Let n_c denote the number of occurrences in T of character $c \in \Sigma$. The zero-order empirical entropy of string T is $H_0(T) =$

---

[1] By log we mean $\log_2$ in this paper.

$-\sum_{c\in\Sigma}\frac{n_c}{n}\log\frac{n_c}{n}$, where $0\log 0 = 0$. If we use a fixed codeword for each character in the alphabet, then $nH_0(T)$ bits is the smallest encoding we can achieve for T. If the codeword is not fixed, but it depends on the k characters that precede the character in T, then the smallest encoding one can achieve for T is $nH_k(T)$ bits, where $H_k(T)$ is the kth order empirical entropy of T. This is defined [17] as

$$H_k(T) = \frac{1}{n}\sum_{W\in\Sigma^k}|W_T|H_0(W_T),$$

where W_T is the concatenation of all characters t_j such that Wt_j is a substring of T. String W is the k-context of each such t_j. We use H_0 and H_k as shorthands for $H_0(T)$ and $H_k(T)$.

The Burrows-Wheeler Transform (BWT). The BWT [1] of a text T produces a permutation of T, denoted by T^{bwt}. Recall that T is assumed to be terminated by the endmarker "$\$$". String T^{bwt} is the result of the following transformation: (1) Form a *conceptual* matrix $\mathcal{M}$ whose rows are the cyclic shifts $t_i t_{i+1}\ldots t_n t_1 t_2 \ldots t_{i-1}$ of the string T, call F its first column and L its last column; (2) sort the rows of $\mathcal{M}$ in lexicographic order; (3) the transformed text is $T^{bwt} = L$.

The main step to reverse the BWT is to compute the *LF mapping*, so that $LF(i)$ is the position of character $L[i]$ in F. This is computed as $LF(i) = C[L[i]] + Occ(L, L[i], i)$, where $C[c]$ is the number of occurrences of characters $\{\$, 1, \ldots, c-1\}$ in T, and $Occ(L, c, i)$ is the number of occurrences of character c in the prefix $L[1, i]$. Then T can be obtained backwards from T^{bwt} by successive applications of LF.

We note that matrix $\mathcal{M}$ is essentially the *suffix array* $\mathcal{A}[1, n]$ of T, as sorting the cyclic shifts of T is the same as sorting its suffixes, given the endmarker "$\$$": $\mathcal{A}[i] = j$ if and only if $\mathcal{M}[i] = t_j t_{j+1}\ldots t_{n-1}\$t_1 \ldots t_{j-1}$.

The FM-Index. The FM-index [3, 4] is a self-index based on the Burrows-Wheeler transform. It solves counting queries by finding the interval of $\mathcal{A}$ that contains the occurrences of pattern P. The FM-index uses the array C and function $Occ(L, c, i)$ defined before. Figure 1 shows the counting algorithm. It maintains the invariant that, at the ith phase, variables sp and ep point, respectively, to the first and last row of $\mathcal{M}$ prefixed by $P[i, m]$.

Note that while array C can be explicitly stored in little space, implementing $Occ(T^{bwt}, c, i)$ is problematic. The first solution [3] implemented $Occ(T^{bwt}, c, i)$ by storing a compressed representation of T^{bwt} plus some additional tables. With this representation, $Occ(T^{bwt}, c, i)$ could be computed in constant time and therefore the counting algorithm required $O(m)$ time.

The representation of T^{bwt} required $O(nH_k)$ bits of space, while the additional tables required space exponential in σ. Assuming that σ is constant, the space requirement of the FM-index is $5nH_k + o(n)$. In a practical implementation [4] this exponential dependence on σ was avoided, but the constant time guarantee for answering $Occ(T^{bwt}, c, i)$ was no longer valid.

Algorithm FMcount($P[1, m]$,$T^{bwt}[1, n]$)
(1) $i \leftarrow m$;
(2) $sp \leftarrow 1$; $ep \leftarrow n$;
(3)   **while** ($sp \leq ep$) **and** ($i \geq 1$) **do**
(4) $c \leftarrow P[i]$;
(5) $sp \leftarrow C[c] + Occ(T^{bwt}, c, sp - 1){+}1$;
(6) $ep \leftarrow C[c] + Occ(T^{bwt}, c, ep)$;
(7) $i \leftarrow i - 1$;
(8)   **if** ($ep < sp$) **then return** "not found"
                  else return "found ($ep - sp + 1$) occurrences".

Fig. 1. FM-index algorithm for counting the occurrences of P in T.

The method to locate pattern occurrences or to show contexts around them also employs the $Occ()$ function, but we omit the details here.

Succinct Data Structures for Binary Sequences. Given a binary sequence $B = b_1 b_2 \ldots b_n$, we denote by $rank_b(B, i)$ the number of times bit b appears in the prefix $B[1, i]$, and by $select_b(B, i)$ the position in B of the ith occurrence of bit b. By default we assume $rank(B, i) = rank_1(B, i)$ and $select(B, i) = select_1(B, i)$. There are several results [2, 12, 18] that show how B can be represented using $n + o(n)$ bits so as to answer *rank* and *select* queries in constant time. The best current results [20, 21] answer those queries in constant time using only $nH_0(B) + o(n)$ bits of space.

Wavelet Trees. Sequences $S = s_1 s_2 \ldots s_n$ on general alphabets of size σ can also be represented using $nH_0(S) + o(n \log \sigma)$ bits by using a *wavelet tree* [8]. This tree retrieves any s_i in $O(\log \sigma)$ time. Within the same time bounds, it also answers generalized *rank* and *select* queries.

The wavelet tree is a perfectly balanced binary tree where each node corresponds to a subset of the alphabet. The children of each node partition the node subset into two. A bitmap B_v at the node v indicates to which children does each sequence position belong. Each child then handles the subsequence of the parent's sequence corresponding to its alphabet subset. The leaves of the tree handle single alphabet characters and require no space.

To answer query $rank_c(S, i)$, we first determine to which branch of the root does c belong. If it belongs to the left, then we recursively continue at the left subtree with $i \leftarrow rank_0(B_{root}, i)$. Otherwise we recursively continue at the right subtree with $i \leftarrow rank_1(B_{root}, i)$. The value reached by i when we arrive at the leaf that corresponds to c is $rank_c(S, i)$. The character s_i is obtained similarly, this time going left or right depending on whether $B_v[i] = 0$ or 1 at each level, and finding out which leaf we arrived at. Query $select_c(S, i)$ is answered by traversing the tree bottom-up.

If every bitmap in the wavelet tree is represented using a data structure that takes space proportional to its zero-order entropy, then it can be shown that the whole wavelet tree requires $nH_0(S) + o(n \log \sigma)$ bits of space [8]. When $\sigma = O(\text{polylog}(n))$, a generalization of wavelet trees takes $nH_0(S) + o(n)$ bits and answers all those queries in constant time [6].

3   RLFM: A Run-Length-Based FM-Index

We studied in [14] the relationship between the runs in the Burrows-Wheeler transformed text and the kth order entropy. We summarize the main result in the following.

Theorem 1. *The length n_{bw} of the run-length encoded Burrows-Wheeler transformed text $T^{bwt}[1, n]$ is at most $n \min(H_k(T), 1) + \sigma^k$, for any $k \geq 0$. In particular, this is $nH_k(T) + o(n)$ for any $k \leq \alpha \log_\sigma n$, for any constant $0 < \alpha < 1$* [2].

We aim in this section at indexing only the runs of T^{bwt}, so as to obtain an index, called *run-length FM-index (RLFM)*, whose space is proportional to nH_k. We exploit run-length compression to represent T^{bwt} as follows. An array S contains one character per run in T^{bwt}, while an array B contains n bits and marks the beginnings of the runs.

Definition 1. *Let string $T^{bwt} = c_1^{\ell_1} c_2^{\ell_2} \ldots c_{n_{bw}}^{\ell_{n_{bw}}}$ consist of n_{bw} runs, so that the ith run consists of ℓ_i repetitions of character c_i. Our representation of T^{bwt} consists of the string $S = c_1 c_2 \ldots c_{n_{bw}}$ of length n_{bw}, and of the bit array $B = 10^{\ell_1 - 1} 10^{\ell_2 - 1} \ldots 10^{\ell_{n_{bw}} - 1}$.*

It is clear that S and B contain enough information to reconstruct T^{bwt}: $T^{bwt}[i] = S[rank(B, i)]$. Since there is no useful entropy bound on B, we assume that *rank* is implemented in constant time using some succinct structure that requires $n + o(n)$ bits [2, 18]. Hence, S and B give us a representation of T^{bwt} that permit us accessing any character in constant time.

The problem, however, is not only how to access T^{bwt}, but also how to compute $C[c] + Occ(T^{bwt}, c, i)$ for any c and i (recall Figure 1). This is not immediate, because we want to add up all the run lengths corresponding to character c up to position i.

In the following we show that the above can be computed by means of a bit array B', obtained by reordering the runs of B in lexicographic order of the characters of each run. Runs of the same character are left in their original order. The use of B' will add other $n + o(n)$ bits to our scheme. We also use C_S, which plays the same role of C, but it refers to string S.

---

[2] The original analysis [14] has constant 2 multiplying $nH_k(T)$. We later noticed that the analysis can be tightened to give constant 1. This comes from showing that $-(x/(x + y)) \log(x/(x + y)) - (y/(x + y)) \log(y/(x + y)) \geq 2x/(x + y)$ for any $x, y \geq 0$, while in Eq. (4) of [14] the expression at the right of the inequality was $x/(x + y)$.

Definition 2. *Let* $S = c_1 c_2 \ldots c_{n_{bw}}$ *of length* n_{bw}, *and* $B = 10^{\ell_1-1} 10^{\ell_2-1} \ldots$ $10^{\ell_{n_{bw}}-1}$. *Let* $d_1 d_2 \ldots d_{n_{bw}}$ *be the permutation of* $[1, n_{bw}]$ *such that, for all* $1 \leq i < n_{bw}$, *either* $c_{d_i} < c_{d_{i+1}}$, *or* $c_{d_i} = c_{d_{i+1}}$ *and* $d_i < d_{i+1}$. *Then, bit array* B' *is defined as* $B' = 10^{\ell_{d_1}-1} 10^{\ell_{d_2}-1} \ldots 10^{\ell_{d_{n_{bw}}}-1}$. *Let also* $C_S[c] = |\{i, \ c_i < c, \ 1 \leq i \leq n_{bw}\}|$.

We now prove our main results. We start with two general lemmas.

Lemma 1. *Let* S *and* B' *be defined for a string* T^{bwt}. *Then, for any* $c \in \Sigma$ *it holds*

$$C[c] + 1 \ = \ select(B', C_S[c] + 1). \quad \cdot$$

Proof. $C_S[c]$ is the number of runs in T^{bwt} that represent characters smaller than c. Since in B' the runs of T^{bwt} are sorted in lexicographic order, $select(B', C_S[c] + 1)$ indicates the position in B' of the first run belonging to character c, if any. Therefore, $select(B', C_S[c]+1)-1$ is the sum of the run lengths for all characters smaller than c. This is, in turn, the number of occurrences of characters smaller than c in T^{bwt}, $C[c]$. Hence $select(B', C_S[c] + 1) - 1 = C[c]$.

Lemma 2. *Let* S, B, *and* B' *be defined for a string* T^{bwt}. *Then, for any* $c \in \Sigma$ *and* $1 \leq i \leq n$, *such that* i *is the final position of a run in* B, *it holds*

$$C[c] + Occ(T^{bwt}, c, i) \ = \ select(B', C_S[c] + 1 + Occ(S, c, rank(B, i))) - 1.$$

Proof. Note that $rank(B, i)$ gives the position in S of the run that finishes at i. Therefore, $Occ(S, c, rank(B, i))$ is the number of runs in $T^{bwt}[1, i]$ that represent repetitions of character c. Hence it is clear that $C_S[c] < C_S[c] + 1 + Occ(S, c, rank(B, i)) \leq C_S[c+1] + 1$, from which follows that $select(B', C_S[c] + 1 + Occ(S, c, rank(B, i)))$ points to an area in B' belonging to character c, or to the character just following that area. Inside this area, the runs are ordered as in B because the reordering in B' is stable. Hence $select(B', C_S[c] + 1 + Occ(S, c, rank(B, i)))$ is $select(B', C_S[c] + 1)$ plus the sum of the run lengths representing character c in $T^{bwt}[1, i]$. That sum of run lengths is $Occ(T^{bwt}, c, i)$. The argument holds also if $T^{bwt}[i] = c$, because i is the last position of its run and therefore counting the whole run $T^{bwt}[i]$ belongs to is correct. Hence $select(B', C_S[c] + 1 + Occ(S, c, rank(B, i))) = select(B', C_S[c] + 1) + Occ(T^{bwt}, c, i)$, and then, by Lemma 1, $select(B', C_S[c] + 1 + Occ(S, c, rank(B, i))) - 1 = C[c] + Occ(T^{bwt}, c, i)$.

We now prove our two fundamental lemmas that cover different cases in the computation of $C[c] + Occ(T^{bwt}, c, i)$.

Lemma 3. *Let* S, B, *and* B' *be defined for a string* T^{bwt}. *Then, for any* $c \in \Sigma$ *and* $1 \leq i \leq n$, *such that* $T^{bwt}[i] \neq c$, *it holds*

$$C[c] + Occ(T^{bwt}, c, i) \ = \ select(B', C_S[c] + 1 + Occ(S, c, rank(B, i))) - 1.$$

Proof. Let i' be the last position of the run that precedes that of i. Since $T^{bwt}[i] \neq c$ in the run i belongs to, we have $Occ(T^{bwt}, c, i) = Occ(T^{bwt}, c, i')$ and also $Occ(S, c, rank(B, i)) = Occ(S, c, rank(B, i'))$. Then the lemma follows trivially by applying Lemma 2 to i'.

Lemma 4. *Let S, B, and B' be defined for a string T^{bwt}. Then, for any $c \in \Sigma$ and $1 \leq i \leq n$, such that $T^{bwt}[i] = c$, it holds*

$$C[c] + Occ(T^{bwt}, c, i) = select(B', C_S[c] + Occ(S, c, rank(B, i)))$$
$$+ i - select(B, rank(B, i)).$$

Proof. Let i' be the last position of the run that precedes that of i. Then, by Lemma 2, $C[c] + Occ(T^{bwt}, c, i') = select(B', C_S[c] + 1 + Occ(S, c, rank(B, i')))$ -1. Now, $rank(B, i') = rank(B, i) - 1$, and since $T^{bwt}[i] = c$, it follows that $S[rank(B, i)] = c$. Therefore, $Occ(S, c, rank(B, i')) = Occ(S, c, rank(B, i) - 1) = Occ(S, c, rank(B, i)) - 1$. On the other hand, since $T^{bwt}[i''] = c$ for $i' < i'' \leq i$, we have $Occ(T^{bwt}, c, i) = Occ(T^{bwt}, c, i') + (i - i')$. Thus, the outcome of Lemma 2 can now be rewritten as $C[c] + Occ(T^{bwt}, c, i) - (i - i') = select(B', C_S[c] + Occ(S, c, rank(B, i))) - 1$. The only remaining piece to prove the lemma is that $i - i' - 1 = i - select(B, rank(B, i))$, that is, $select(B, rank(B, i)) = i' + 1$. But this is clear, since the left term is the position of the first run i belongs to and i' is the last position of the run preceding that of i.

Since functions *rank* and *select* can be computed in constant time, the only obstacle to complete the RLFM using Lemmas 3 and 4 is the computation of *Occ* over string S. This can be done in constant time using a new sequence representation technique [6], when the alphabet size is $O(\text{polylog}(n))$. This needs a structure of size $|S|H_0(S) + o(|S|)$. Using Theorem 1, this is no more than $nH_kH_0(S) + o(n)$ for $k \leq \alpha \log_\sigma n$, for constant $0 < \alpha < 1$ [3].

The representation of our index needs the bit arrays B and B', plus the sublinear structures to perform *rank* and/or *select* over them, and finally the small array C_S. These add $2n + o(n)$ bits, for a grand total of $n(H_k(H_0(S) + o(1)) + 2) + o(n)$ bits. As H_k actually stands for $\min(1, H_k)$, and $H_0(S) \leq \log \sigma$, we can simplify the space complexity to $nH_k \log \sigma + O(n)$ bits.

Theorem 2. *The RLFM index, of size $n \min(H_k, 1) \log \sigma + 2n + o(n) = nH_k \log \sigma + O(n)$ bits for any $k \leq \alpha \log_\sigma n$, for any constant $0 < \alpha < 1$, can be built on a text $T[1, n]$ with alphabet size $\sigma = O(\text{polylog}(n))$, so that the occurrences of any pattern $P[1, m]$ in T can be counted in time $O(m)$.*

The RLFM index can easily be extended to support reporting and context queries. We defer the details to the journal version of this paper.

---

[3] This can also be solved in $nH_kH_0(S) + O(n)$ space, with the same restrictions, using older techniques [23]. The final complexity changes only in small details.

4   Practical Considerations

The most problematic aspect to implement our proposal is the use of a technique to represent sequences in a space proportional to its zero-order entropy [6]. This technique has not yet been implemented, and this will require considerable additional effort. The same is true with the alternative technique that could be used [23] to obtain similar time and space complexity.

Yet, previous structures supporting *rank* on binary sequences in $n + o(n)$ bits [2, 18] are very simple to implement. So an alternative is to use a wavelet tree built on the S string of the RLFM index (that is, the run heads). The wavelet tree is simple to implement, and if it uses structures of $n + o(n)$ bits to represent its binary sequences, it requires overall $|S| \log \sigma (1 + o(1)) = nH_k \log \sigma (1 + o(1))$ bits of space to represent S. This is essentially the same space we achieved using the theoretical approach.

With the wavelet tree, the $O(1)$ time to compute $Occ(S, c, i) = rank_c(S, i)$, becomes $O(\log \sigma)$. Therefore, a RLFM index implementation based on wavelet trees counts in $O(m \log \sigma)$ time.

The same idea can also be applied *without* run-length encoding. Let us call SSA (for "succinct suffix array") this implementation. We notice that the SSA can be considered as a practical implementation of a previous proposal [23]. It has also been explicitly mentioned as a simplified version in previous work [5], with the same $O(m \log \sigma)$ time complexity.

We propose now another simple wavelet tree variant that permits us representing the SSA using $n(H_0 + 1)(1 + o(1))$ bits of space, and obtains on average $O(H_0)$ rather than $O(\log \sigma)$ time for the queries on the wavelet tree. Instead of a balanced binary tree, we use the *Huffman tree* of T to define the shape of the wavelet tree. Then, every character $c \in \Sigma$, of frequency n_c, will have its corresponding leaf at depth h_c, so that $\sum_{c \in \Sigma} h_c n_c \leq n(H_0 + 1)$ is the number of bits of the Huffman compression of T.

Consider the size of this tree. Note that each text occurrence of each character $c \in \Sigma$ appears exactly in h_c bit arrays (those found from the root to the leaf that corresponds to c), and thus it takes h_c bits spread over the different bit arrays. Summed over all the occurrences of all the characters we obtain the very same length of the Huffman-compressed text, $\sum_{c \in \Sigma} h_c n_c$. Hence the overall space is $n(H_0 + 1)(1 + o(1))$ bits.

Note that the time to retrieve $T^{bwt}[i]$ is proportional to the length of the Huffman code for $T^{bwt}[i]$, which is $O(H_0)$ if i is chosen at random. In the case of $Occ(T^{bwt}, c, i) = rank_c(T^{bwt}, i)$, the time corresponds again to $T^{bwt}[i]$ and is independent of c. Under reasonable assumptions, one can say that on average this version of the SSA counts in $O(H_0 m)$ time.

Finally, we note that the Huffman-shaped wavelet tree can be used for the RLFM index. This lowers its space requirement again to $nH_k H_0(S)$, just like the theoretical version. It also reduces the average time to compute $rank_c(S, i)$ or $S[i]$ to $O(H_0(S))$, which is no worse than $O(\log \sigma)$.

5   Experiments

We compare our SSA and RLFM implementations against others. We used an 87 MB text file (ZIFF collection from TREC-3) and randomly chose 10,000 patterns of each length from it. We compared counting times against the following indexes/implementations: FM [4] (0.36), Navarro's implementation of FM-index, FM-Nav [19] (1.07), CSA [22] (0.39-1.16), LZ [19] (1.49), CompactSA [13] (2.73), CCSA [14] (1.65), our $n\lceil\log n\rceil$-bits implementation of the suffix array, SA [16] (4.37), and our implementation of a sequential search algorithm, BMH [11] (1.0). The last three, not being self-indexes, are included to test the value of compressed indexing. The values in parentheses tell the space usage of each index as a fraction of the text size. Our indexes take SSA (0.87) and RLFM (0.67). We applied the ideas of Section 4, and also optimized rank/select implementations [7] for all the indexes. The codes for FM-Nav, CSA, and LZ indexes are available at http://www.dcc.uchile.cl/~gnavarro/software and the codes for the other indexes at http://www.cs.helsinki.fi/u/vmakinen/software.

Only the CSA has a tradeoff in counting time and space usage. We denote by CSAX the tradeoffs (X is the sampling rate for absolute Ψ-values). The sizes of CSA10, CSA16, CSA32, and CSA256, are 1.16, 0.86, 0.61, and 0.39, respectively. Figure 2 shows the times to count pattern occurrences of length $m = 5$ to $m = 60$. We omit CSA10 and CSA16, whose performance is very similar to CSA32. It can be seen that FM-Nav is the fastest self-index, but it is closely followed by our SSA, which needs 20% less space (0.87 times the text size). The next group is formed by our RLFM and the CSA, both needing space around 0.6. Actually RLFM is faster, and to reach its performance we need CSA10, which takes space 1.16. For long patterns CCSA becomes competitive

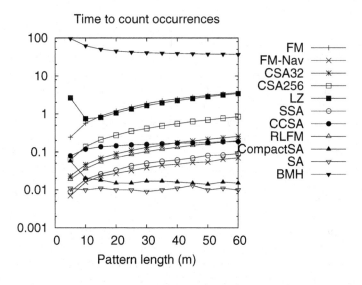

Fig. 2. Query times (msec) for counting the number of occurrences.

in this group, yet it needs as much space as 1.65 times the text size. Compared to non-self-indexes (that take much more space), we see that self-indexes are considerably fast for counting, especially for short patterns. For longer ones, their small space consumption is paid in a 10X slowdown for counting. Yet, this is orders of magnitude faster than a sequential search, which still needs more space as the text has to be in uncompressed form for reasonable performance. Figure 3 illustrates the space/time tradeoff, for $m = 30$.

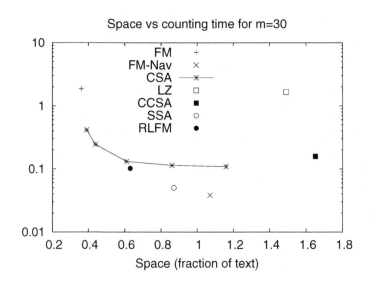

Fig. 3. Space/time tradeoff for counting the number of occurrences.

Finally, we notice that SSA gives a good estimate for the efficiency obtainable with the more succinct index in [5]. That index has potential to be significantly more space-efficient, but needs a more careful wavelet tree implementation (in terms of constant terms in space usage) than what we have currently in SSA. This is needed in order to gain advantage of the compression boosting mechanism. Also, implementing the sequence representation developed in [6] will probably improve in practice the performance of the index in [5], as well as that of the SSA and RLFM index.

6   Conclusions

Inspired by the relationship between the kth order empirical entropy of a text and the runs of equal characters in its Burrows-Wheeler transform, we have designed a new index, the RLFM index, that answers counting queries in time linear in the pattern length for any alphabet whose size is polylogarithmic on the text length. The RLFM index was the first in achieving this.

We have also considered practical issues of implementing the RLFM index, obtaining an efficient implementation. We have in passing presented another index, the SSA, that is larger and faster than the RLFM index. We have compared both indexes against the existing implementations, showing that ours are competitive and obtain practical space-time tradeoffs that are not reached by any other implementation.

References

1. M. Burrows and D. Wheeler. A block sorting lossless data compression algorithm. Technical Report 124, Digital Equipment Corporation, 1994.
2. D. Clark. *Compact Pat Trees*. PhD thesis, University of Waterloo, 1996.
3. P. Ferragina and G. Manzini. Opportunistic data structures with applications. In *Proc. FOCS'00*, pp. 390–398, 2000.
4. P. Ferragina and G. Manzini. An experimental study of an opportunistic index. In *Proc. SODA'01*, pp. 269–278, 2001.
5. P. Ferragina, G. Manzini, V. Mäkinen, and G. Navarro. An alphabet-friendly FM-index. In *Proc. SPIRE'04*, pp. 150–160, 2004.
6. P. Ferragina, G. Manzini, V. Mäkinen, and G. Navarro. Succinct representation of sequences. Technical Report TR/DCC-2004-5, Dept. of CS, Univ. Chile, Aug. 2004.
7. R. González, Sz. Grabowski, V. Mäkinen, and G. Navarro. Practical implementation of rank and select queries. To appear in *Proc. WEA'05* (poster).
8. R. Grossi, A. Gupta, and J. Vitter. High-order entropy-compressed text indexes. In *Proc. SODA'03*, pp. 841–850, 2003.
9. R. Grossi, A. Gupta, and J. Vitter. When indexing equals compression: Experiments with compressing suffix arrays and applications. In *Proc. SODA'04*, pp. 636–645, 2004.
10. R. Grossi and J.S. Vitter. Compressed suffix arrays and suffix trees with applications to text indexing and string matching. In *Proc. STOC'00*, pp. 397–406, 2000.
11. R. N. Horspool. Practical fast searching in strings. *Softw. Pract. Exp.*, 10(6):501–506, 1980.
12. G. Jacobson. Space-efficient static trees and graphs. In *Proc. FOCS'89*, pp. 549–554, 1989.
13. V. Mäkinen. Compact suffix array — a space-efficient full-text index. *Fundamenta Informaticae*, 56(1–2):191–210, 2003.
14. V. Mäkinen and G. Navarro. Compressed compact suffix arrays. In *Proc. CPM'04*, pp. 420–433, 2004.
15. V. Mäkinen and G. Navarro. Run-length FM-index. In *Proc. DIMACS Workshop: "The Burrows-Wheeler Transform: Ten Years Later"*, pp. 17–19, Aug. 2004. Also in *New Search Algorithms and Time/Space Tradeoffs for Succinct Suffix Arrays*, Tech. Report. C-2004-20, Univ. Helsinki, Apr. 2004.
16. U. Manber and G. Myers. Suffix arrays: a new method for on-line string searches. *SIAM Journal on Computing*, 22(5):935–948, 1993.
17. G. Manzini. An analysis of the Burrows-Wheeler transform. *Journal of the ACM*, 48(3):407–430, 2001.
18. I. Munro. Tables. In *Proc. FSTTCS'96*, pp. 37–42, 1996.

19. G. Navarro. Indexing text using the Ziv-Lempel trie. *Journal of Discrete Algorithms*, 2(1):87–114, 2004.
20. R. Pagh. Low redundancy in dictionaries with $O(1)$ worst case lookup time. In *Proc. ICALP'99*, pp. 595–604, 1999.
21. R. Raman, V. Raman, and S. Srinivasa Rao. Succinct indexable dictionaries with applications to encoding k-ary trees and multisets. In *Proc. SODA'02*, pp. 233–242, 2002.
22. K. Sadakane. Compressed text databases with efficient query algorithms based on the compressed suffix array. In *Proc. ISAAC'00*, pp. 410–421, 2000.
23. K. Sadakane. Succinct representations of *lcp* information and improvements in the compressed suffix arrays. In *Proc. SODA'02*, pp. 225–232, 2002.
24. P. Weiner. Linear pattern matching algorithm. In *Proc. IEEE Symposium on Switching and Automata Theory*, pages 1–11, 1973.

Linear-Time Construction of Compressed Suffix Arrays Using $o(n \log n)$-Bit Working Space for Large Alphabets[*]

Joong Chae Na

School of Computer Science and Engineering, Seoul National University
jcna@theory.snu.ac.kr

Abstract. The *suffix array* is a fundamental index data structure in string algorithms and bioinformatics, and the *compressed suffix array (CSA)* and the *FM-index* are its compressed versions. Many algorithms for constructing these index data structures have been developed. Recently, Hon et al. [11] proposed a construction algorithm using $O(n \cdot \log \log |\Sigma|)$ time and $O(n \log |\Sigma|)$-bit working space, which is the fastest algorithm using $O(n \log |\Sigma|)$-bit working space.

In this paper we give an efficient algorithm to construct the index data structures for large alphabets. Our algorithm constructs the suffix array, the CSA, and the FM-index using $O(n)$ time and $O(n \log |\Sigma| \log_{|\Sigma|}^{\alpha} n)$-bit working space, where $\alpha = \log_3 2$. Our algorithm takes less time and more space than Hon et al.'s algorithm. Our algorithm uses least working space among alphabet-independent linear-time algorithms.

1 Introduction

Given a string T of length n over an alphabet Σ, the suffix array due to Manber and Myers [16] and independently due to Gonnet et al. [6] is basically a sorted list of all the suffixes of T. The suffix array requires $O(n \log n)$-bit space. Manber and Myers [16] and Gusfield [9] proposed $O(n \log n)$-time algorithms for constructing the suffix array. Recently, almost at the same time, Kim et al. [13], Kärkkäinen and Sanders [12], and Ko and Aluru [14] developed algorithms to directly construct the suffix array in $O(n)$ time and $O(n \log n)$-bit space. These algorithms are based on similar recursive divide-and-conquer schemes.

As the size of data such as DNA sequences increases, compressed versions of the suffix array such as the *compressed suffix array (CSA)* [7, 8] and the *FM-index* [5] were proposed to reduce the space requirement of suffix arrays. Lam et al. [15] first developed an algorithm to directly construct the CSA, which uses $O(|\Sigma|n \log n)$ time and $O(n \log |\Sigma|)$ bits. Hon et al. [10] improved the construction time to $O(n \log n)$, while maintaining the $O(n \log |\Sigma|)$-bit space complexity.

It had been an open problem whether the index data structures such as the suffix array, the CSA, and the FM-index, can be constructed in $o(n \log n)$ time *and* $o(n \log n)$-bit working space. Recently, it was solved by Hon et al. [11].

---

[*] This work was supported by the MOST Grant M6-0203-00-0039.

A. Apostolico, M. Crochemore, and K. Park (Eds.): CPM 2005, LNCS 3537, pp. 57–67, 2005.
© Springer-Verlag Berlin Heidelberg 2005

They proposed an algorithm for constructing the index data structures using $O(n \log \log |\Sigma|)$ time and $O(n \log |\Sigma|)$-bit working space. This algorithm followed the *odd-even scheme* (i.e., $\frac{1}{2}$-recursion), which was used in Farach's algorithm [3, 4] and Kim et al.'s algorithm [13].

In this paper we give another algorithm for constructing the index data structures in $o(n \log n)$ time and $o(n \log n)$-bit working space. Our algorithm constructs the suffix array, the CSA, and FM-index using $O(n)$ time and $O(n \log |\Sigma| \cdot \log_{|\Sigma|}^{\alpha} n)$-bit space, where $\alpha = \log_3 2$. The time complexity of our algorithm is independent of the alphabet size. Hence, our algorithm is the first alphabet-independent linear-time algorithm for constructing the index data structures using $o(n \log n)$-bit space.

The framework of our algorithm follows Kärkkäinen and Sanders's *skew scheme* [12] (i.e., $\frac{2}{3}$-recursion). The merit of our algorithm due to the skew scheme [12] is that the *merging step* is simple compared with Hon et al.'s algorithm [11]. As in Hon et al.'s algorithm [11], moreover, our algorithm don't need the *encoding step*, which is the most complex and time-consuming step in the skew scheme.

It remains an open problem to construct the suffix array, the CSA, and the FM-index *optimally*, i.e., using $O(n)$ time and $O(n \log |\Sigma|)$-bit working space.

2   Preliminaries

In this section we give some basic notations and definitions including the Ψ function of the Compressed Suffix Array (CSA) [7], the array C of the Burrows-Wheeler Transformation (BWT) [1], and the Ψ' function, which is similar to Ψ and the core of our algorithm.

Let T be a string of length n over an alphabet Σ. For simplicity, we assume that n is a multiple of 3. We denote the ith character by $T[i]$ and the substring $T[i]T[i+1]\cdots T[j]$ by $T[i..j]$. We assume that $T[n] = \$$ is a unique terminator which is lexicographically smaller than any other character in Σ. For $1 \le i \le n$, $T[i..n]$ is a *suffix* of T and $T[i..n]T[1..i-1]$ is a *circular string* of T. We denote circular string $T[i..n]T[1..i-1]$ by $T\langle i \rangle$.

For $1 \le i \le n/3$, a suffix $T[3 \cdot i - 2..n]$, a suffix $T[3 \cdot i - 1..n]$, and $T[3 \cdot i..n]$ are called a *residue-1* suffix, a *residue-2* suffix, and a *residue-3* suffix of T, respectively. Let $T[i..n]$ be lexicographically the kth smallest suffix of T. Then, the *rank* of $T[i..n]$ in the suffixes of T is k. The suffix array of T is a lexicographically sorted array of the suffixes of T. Formally, the suffix array $SA[1..n]$ of T is an array of integers such that $SA[k] = i$, where k is the rank of $T[i..n]$ in the suffixes of T. See Figure 1 for an example.

2.1 Ψ Function and C Array

We define the Ψ_T function [7, 11], or simply Ψ. Let $T[k..n]$ be the suffix stored in the ith entry of SA. Then, $\Psi[i]$ is a position in SA where $T[k+1..n]$ are stored.

i	$C[i]$	$SA[i]$	$\Psi[i]$	
1	a	9	8	\$
2	b	8	1	a\$
3	b	4	5	aabba\$
4	b	2	7	abaabba\$
5	a	5	9	abba\$
6	b	7	2	ba\$
7	a	3	3	baabba\$
8	\$	1	4	babaabba\$
9	a	6	6	bba\$

Fig. 1. The suffix array SA, Ψ function, and C array of S = babaabba\$.

More formally,

$$\Psi[i] = \begin{cases} SA^{-1}[SA[i] + 1] & \text{(if } SA[i] \neq n) \\ SA^{-1}[1] & \text{(if } SA[i] = n) \end{cases}$$

See Figure 1 for an example. The Ψ function is piece-wise increasing. Thus, the Ψ function can be encoded using $O(n \log |\Sigma|)$ bits in the form $T[SA[i]] \times n + \Psi[i] - 1$, which is an increasing sequence, so that each $\Psi[i]$ can be retrieved in constant time [2, 8, 17].

Lemma 1. [11] *Given T and the Ψ function, the suffix array and the compressed suffix array can be constructed in $O(n)$ time and $O(n \log |\Sigma|)$-bit working space.*

The $C[1..n]$ array is defined as

$$C[i] = \begin{cases} T[SA[i] - 1] & \text{(if } SA[i] \neq 1) \\ T[n] & \text{(if } SA[i] = 1) \end{cases}$$

See Figure 1 for an example.

Lemma 2. [11] *Given the C array of T, the FM-index can be constructed in $O(n)$ time and $O(n \log |\Sigma|)$-bit working space.*

It is known that Ψ and C are one-to-one corresponding and the transformation between them can be done in linear time using $O(n \log |\Sigma|)$ bits.

Lemma 3. [11] *Given $C[1..n]$, we can compute $\Psi[1..n]$ in $O(n)$ time and $O(n \log |\Sigma|)$ bits.*

Lemma 4. [11] *Given $\Psi[1..n]$ and T, we can construct $C[1..n]$ in $O(n)$ time and $O(n \log |\Sigma|)$ bits.*

2.2 Ψ' Function

Let T_1, T_2 and T_3 be the strings of length $n/3$ over the alphabet Σ^3, which are formed by merging every 3 characters in $T\langle 1 \rangle$, $T\langle 2 \rangle$ and $T\langle 3 \rangle$, respectively.

S_{12} = bab aab ba\$ aba abb a\$b S_3 = baa bba \$ba

i	P	C'_{12}	SA_{12}	$\Psi'_{S_{12}}$	F_{12}	
1	0	b	6	1	a	\$b
2	1	b	2	4	a	ab ba\$
3	0	b	4	2	a	ba abb a\$b
4	0	a	5	3	a	bb a\$b
5	1	b	3	1	b	a\$
6	1	\$	1	3	b	ab aab ba\$

(a) P, SA_{12}, $\Psi'_{S_{12}}$, F_{12} and C'_{12}

i	C'_3	SA_3	Ψ'_{S_3}	F_3	
1	a	3	6	\$	ba
2	a	1	2	b	aa bba \$ba
3	a	2	5	b	ba \$ba

(b) SA_3, Ψ'_{S_3}, F_3 and C'_3

Fig. 2. P array, Ψ' function, F array and C' array for S = babaabba\$. F and C' are defined in Section 5.

Then, the residue-1, residue-2, and residue-3 suffixes of T correspond one-to-one to the suffixes of T_1, T_2 and T_3, respectively. Note that the last characters of T_1, T_2, and T_3 is unique. We denote the concatenation T_1 and T_2 by T_{12}. Let SA_{12} and SA_3 be the suffix array of T_{12} and T_3, respectively.

Fact 1 *Consider a suffix $T_{12}[i..2n/3]$ ($= T[3i-2..n]T[2..n]T[1]$) for $1 \leq i \leq n/3$. Because the last character of T_1 is unique, the rank of this suffix is determined by $T[3i-2..n]$. Thus, $T[3i-2..n]$ can be regarded as the suffix stored in the kth entry of SA_{12}, where $k = SA_{12}^{-1}[i]$.*

We divide SA_{12} into two parts. Part 1 and 2 store the suffixes of T_1 and T_2, respectively. Formally, the ith entry of SA_{12} belongs to Part 1 if $1 \leq SA_{12}[i] \leq n/3$, and it belongs to Part 2 otherwise. The *part array* $P[1..2n/3]$ of SA_{12} is a bit-array representing which part the ith entry of SA_{12} belongs to. We set $P[i] = 1$ if the ith entry of SA_{12} belongs to Part 1, and $P[i] = 0$ otherwise.

Lemma 5. *Given T, $\Psi_{T_{12}}$, and $SA_{12}^{-1}[1]$, we can construct $P[1..2n/3]$ in $O(n)$ time and $O(n)$ bits.*

Proof. For simplicity of notations, we denote $\Psi_{T_{12}}$ by Ψ. Let $t = SA_{12}^{-1}[1]$. For $1 \leq i < 2n/3$, $SA_{12}[\Psi^i[t]] = i+1$. By definition, $SA_{12}[\Psi[i]] = SA[i] + 1$. Thus, $SA_{12}[\Psi^i[t]] = SA_{12}[\Psi^{i-1}[t]] + 1 = \cdots = SA_{12}[\Psi[t]] + i - 1 = SA_{12}[t] + i = i+1$.

Hence, we have $P[t] = P[\Psi^i[t]] = 1$ for $1 \leq i < n/3$. We set $P[t] = 1$ and initialize $P[j] = 0$ for $j \neq t$. And we iteratively compute $\Psi^i[t]$ and set $P[\Psi^i[t]] = 1$ for $1 \leq i < n/3$. The total time required is $O(n)$, and the space is $O(n)$ bits for P.

We define Ψ' of T which plays a central role in our algorithm. Intuitively, the Ψ' function is just like Ψ, but Ψ' is defined in SA_{12} and SA_3. The Ψ' function consists of Part 1 and Part 2 of $\Psi'_{T_{12}}$, and Ψ'_{T_3}. The definition of Ψ' is as follows:

- Part 1 of $\Psi'_{T_{12}}[i]$:
  Let $T[3k-2..n]$ be a suffix stored in the ith entry of SA_{12}, which belongs to Part 1. Then, $\Psi'_{T_{12}}[i]$ is the position in SA_{12} (which belongs to Part 2) where $T[3k-1..n]T[1]$ is stored.

For example, consider $\Psi'_{T_{12}}[2]$ in Figure 2. The suffix stored in the 2nd entry of SA_{12} is $T[4..9]$ (=aabba\$). $T[5..9]T[1]$ (=abba\$b) is stored in the 4th entry of SA_{12}. Therefore, $\Psi'_{T_{12}}[2] = 4$.

- Part 2 of $\Psi'_{T_{12}}[i]$:
  Let $T[3k - 1..n]T[1]$ be a suffix stored in the ith entry of SA_{12}, which belongs to Part 2. Then, $\Psi'_{T_{12}}[i]$ is the position in SA_3 where $T[3k..n]T[1..2]$ is stored. For example, consider $\Psi'_{T_{12}}[4]$ in Figure 2. The suffix stored in the 4th entry of SA_{12} is $T[5..9]T[1]$ (=abba\$b). $T[6..9]T[1..2]$ (=bba\$ba) is stored in the 3rd entry of SA_3. Therefore, $\Psi'_{T_{12}}[4] = 3$.

- $\Psi'_{T_3}[i]$:
  Let $T[3k..n]T[1..2]$ be a suffix stored in the ith entry of SA_3. Then, $\Psi'_{T_3}[i]$ is a position in SA_{12} (which belongs to Part 1) where $T[3k + 1..n]$ is stored (we assume that when $3k = n$, $T[3k + 1..n]$ is $T[1..n]$).
  For example, consider $\Psi'_{T_3}[3]$ in Figure 2. The suffix stored in the 3rd entry of SA_3 is $T[6..9]T[1..2]$ (=bba\$ba). $T[7..9]$ (=ba\$) is stored in the 5th entry of SA_{12}. Therefore, $\Psi'_{T_3}[3] = 5$.

More formally,

$$\Psi'_{T_{12}}[i] = \begin{cases} SA_{12}^{-1}[SA_{12}[i] + n/3] \text{ if } 1 \le SA_{12}[i] \le n/3 \ (\text{Part 1}) \\ SA_3^{-1}[SA_{12}[i] - n/3] \text{ if } n/3 < SA_{12}[i] \le 2n/3 \ (\text{Part 2}) \end{cases}$$

$$\Psi'_{T_3}[i] = \begin{cases} SA_{12}^{-1}[1] \qquad \text{if } SA_3[i] = 3/n \\ SA_{12}^{-1}[SA_3[i] + 1] \text{ othersiwe.} \end{cases}$$

Similarly to Ψ, the Ψ' function can be encoded in $O(n \log |\Sigma|)$ bits, so that each $\Psi'_{T_{12}}[i]$ and $\Psi'_{T_3}[i]$ can be retrieved in constant time. Part 1 of $\Psi'_{T_{12}}$ is piece-wise increasing. Thus, we encode Part 1 of the $\Psi'_{T_{12}}$ function in the form $T[3SA_{12}[i] - 2] \cdot n + \Psi'_{T_{12}}[i] - 1$, which is an increasing sequence. Similarly, we can encode Part 2 of $\Psi'_{T_{12}}$ and Ψ'_{T_3}.

3 Framework

We will describe how to construct the Ψ function and the C array of T in $O(n)$ time. Then, we can construct the suffix array, the compressed suffix array, and the FM-index in $O(n)$ time and $O(n \log |\Sigma|)$-bit working space using T, the Ψ function, and the C array by Lemmas 1 and 2.

For simplicity, we assume that the length of T is a multiple of $3^{\lceil \log_3 \log_{|\Sigma|} n \rceil + 1}$. Let h be $\lceil \log_3 \log_{|\Sigma|} n \rceil$. We denote $T\langle a_1, \ldots, a_p \rangle$ to be the string formed by concatenating circular strings $T\langle a_1 \rangle, \ldots, T\langle a_p \rangle$ in order. For any string S over Σ, we define $S^{(k)}$ to be the string over the alphabet Σ^{3^k}, which is formed by concatenating every 3^k characters in S to make one character. By definition, $S^{(0)} = S$. For $1 \le k \le h$, we recursively define a string T^k over Σ^{3^k} as follows. We define T^0 as $T\langle 1 \rangle^{(0)}$ ($= T$). Let $T^{k-1} = T\langle a_1, \ldots, a_{2^{k-1}} \rangle^{(k-1)}$. Then,

$$T^k = T\langle a_1, \ldots, a_{2^{k-1}}, a_{2^{k-1}+1}, \ldots, a_{2^k} \rangle^{(k)}$$
$$= T\langle a_1 \rangle^{(k)} \ldots T\langle a_{2^k} \rangle^{(k)},$$

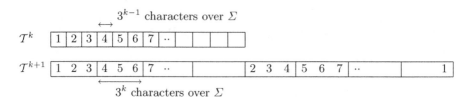

Fig. 3. The relationship between T^k and T^{k+1}.

where $a_{2^{k-1}+i} = a_i + 3^{k-1}$ for $1 \le i \le 2^{k-1}$. That is, $T^1 = T\langle 1, 2\rangle^{(1)}$, $T^2 = T\langle 1, 2, 4, 5\rangle^{(2)}$, $T^3 = T\langle 1, 2, 4, 5, 10, 11, 13, 14\rangle^{(3)}$, and so on. The length of T^k is $(2/3)^k n$.

Fact 2 *For $1 \le i < j \le 2^k$, $a_i < a_j$.*

Lemma 6. *For $1 \le i \le 2^k$, the last character of $T\langle a_i\rangle^{(k)}$ is unique in T^k.*

Proof. We first prove that $a_{2^k} \le 3^k$ by induction. When $k = 0$, $a_{2^0} = 1 = 3^0$. Supposing that $a_{2^{k-1}} \le 3^{k-1}$, $a_{2^k} = a_{2^{k-1}} + 3^{k-1} \le 3^{k-1} + 3^{k-1} < 3^k$.

Because $T\langle a_i\rangle[n - a_i + 1] = \$$ and $a_i \le 3^k$, $\$$ is contained only in the last character of $T\langle a_i\rangle^{(k)}$. By Observation 2, the position of $\$$ in $T\langle a_i\rangle$ is different from that in $T\langle a_j\rangle$ for any $j \ne i$. Therefore, the last character of $T\langle a_i\rangle^{(k)}$ is unique in T^k. ∎

Consider the relationship between T^k and T^{k+1}. See Figure 3. Let $S[1..m]$ be string T^k. Roughly speaking, T^{k+1} is the string of length $2m/3$, which is formed by merging every 3 characters in $S\langle 1\rangle S\langle 2\rangle$ ($= T^k\langle 1, 2\rangle^{(1)}$). In other words, the suffixes of T^{k+1} correspond to the residue-1 and residue-2 suffixes of T^k, i.e., T^k's are essentially the same as the strings made by Kärkkäinen and Sanders's $\frac{2}{3}$-recursion [12].

Lemma 7. *The suffix array of T^{k+1} is the same as the suffix array of $T^k\langle 1, 2\rangle^{(1)}$.*

Proof. We compare the characters of T^{k+1} and $T^k\langle 1, 2\rangle^{(1)}$. Let $m = 2^k$ and $X_i[1..p] = T\langle a_i\rangle^{(k)}$, where p must be a multiple of 3. Let X be $X_1[1..p]X_2[1..p]$ $\ldots X_m[1..p]$, i.e., $T^k = X$. Let

$$P = X_1[2..p] \ X_1[1] \ X_2[2..p] \ X_2[1] \ldots X_m[2..p] \ X_m[1], \quad \text{and}$$
$$Q = X_1[2..p] \ X_2[1] \ X_2[2..p] \ X_3[1] \ldots X_m[2..p] \ X_1[1].$$

Then, $T^{k+1} = X^{(1)} \cdot P^{(1)}$ and $T^k\langle 1, 2\rangle^{(1)} = X^{(1)} \cdot Q^{(1)}$.

Consider the $(\frac{p}{3} \cdot i)$th characters of $P^{(1)}$ and $Q^{(1)}$, for $1 \le i \le m$.

$$P^{(1)}[p \cdot i/3] = X_i[p-1] \ X_i[p] \ X_i[1] \quad \text{and}$$
$$Q^{(1)}[p \cdot i/3] = X_i[p-1] \ X_i[p] \ X_{i+1}[1].$$

That is, only the 3rd components of these characters are different. However, the 3rd components of these characters don't affect the order of suffixes of T^{k+1} and $T^k\langle 1,2\rangle^{(1)}$ because $X_i[p]$ is unique by Lemma 6. The other characters of T^{k+1} and $T^k\langle 1,2\rangle^{(1)}$ are the same. Therefore, we get the lemma.

Corollary 1. *The Ψ function of T^{k+1} is the same as the Ψ function of $T^k\langle 1,2\rangle^{(1)}$.*

The basic framework to construct Ψ_T $(=\Psi_{T^0})$ goes bottom-up. That is, we construct Ψ_{T^k} for $k=h$ down to 0. The algorithm is divided into two phases. Phase 1 consists of step h and Phase 2 consists of the remaining h steps. The details of each phase are as follows.

For Phase 1, we construct Ψ_{T^h} by first building the suffix array of T^h using any linear-time construction algorithm [4, 12–14], and then converting it to Ψ_{T^h}.

In step k of Phase 2, we construct Ψ_{T^k} from $\Psi_{T^{k+1}}$. Recall that $T^k\langle 1,2\rangle^{(1)}$ and $T^k\langle 3\rangle^{(1)}$ are denoted by T^k_{12} and T^k_3, respectively. We first compute $\Psi'_{T^k_{12}}$ and $\Psi'_{T^k_3}$ using T^k and $\Psi_{T^{k+1}}$. Then, we construct Ψ_{T^k} by merging $\Psi'_{T^k_{12}}$ and $\Psi'_{T^k_3}$.

In Sections 4 we describe how to compute $\Psi'_{T^k_{12}}$ and $\Psi'_{T^k_3}$ from T^k and $\Psi_{T^{k+1}}$ ($= \Psi_{T^k_{12}}$ by Corollary 1) in $O(|T^k|+|\Delta|)$ time and $O(|T^k|\log|\Delta|+|\Delta|)$-bit space, where Δ is the alphabet of T^k. In Sections 5 we describe how to merge $\Psi'_{T^k_{12}}$ and $\Psi'_{T^k_3}$ in $O(|T^k|)$ time and $O(|T^k|\log|\Delta|)$-bit space.

Theorem 1. *The Ψ function of T can be constructed in $O(n)$ time and $O(n\log|\Sigma|\cdot\log^{\alpha}_{|\Sigma|} n)$-bit space, where $\alpha = \log_3 2$.*

Proof. For Phase 1, we first construct the suffix array for T^h whose size is $n(2/3)^{\log_3\log_{|\Sigma|} n} \le n(\log_{|\Sigma|} n)^{\alpha-1}$. This requires $O(n)$ time and $O(n\log|\Sigma|\cdot\log^{\alpha}_{|\Sigma|} n)$-bit space by using any linear-time construction algorithm [4, 12–14]. Then Ψ_{T^h} can be constructed in $O(n)$ time and $O(n\log|\Sigma|\cdot\log^{\alpha}_{|\Sigma|} n)$-bit space. Thus, Phase 1 takes $O(n)$ time and $O(n\log|\Sigma|\cdot\log^{\alpha}_{|\Sigma|} n)$-bit space.

For every step i in Phase 2, we construct Ψ_{T^i}. Let Δ_i be the alphabet of T^i. For the space, each step requires $O(|T^i|\log|\Delta_i| + |\Delta_i|)$ bits. Note that $|T^i| = (2/3)^i n$ and $|\Delta_i| \le |\Sigma|^{3^i} \le n$, so $|T^i|\log|\Delta_i| = (2/3)^i n\log|\Sigma|^{3^i} = 2^i n\log|\Sigma| \le n\log|\Sigma|\cdot\log^{\alpha}_{|\Sigma|} n$. Therefore, the space for Phase 2 is $O(n\log|\Sigma|\cdot\log^{\alpha}_{|\Sigma|} n)$ bits. The time of each step is $O((|T^i| + |\Delta_i|))$. The total time of Phase 2 is

$$\sum_{i=1}^{\lceil\log_3\log_{|\Sigma|} n\rceil-1} O\left(n\left(\frac{2}{3}\right)^i + |\Sigma|^{3^i}\right) = O(n).$$

Finally, consider the space storing $T^i = T\langle a_1,\ldots,a_{2^i}\rangle^{(i)}$. We don't store T^i explicitly but the values of a_j $(1 \le j \le 2^i)$. We can get a character of T^i in constant time using the values of a_j and T. The circular strings of T which compose T^h include all those which compose T^i. Therefore, we just store 2^h integers of size $\log n$ for the whole algorithm. The space is $\log n\cdot\log^{\alpha}_{|\Sigma|} n$ bits.

| i | P | X_i | | |
		$x[i]$	$S_{12}[SA_{12}[i]..m/3]$	$S[1..2]$
1	0	·	·	·
2	1	b	aa bba \$	ba
3	0	·	·	·
4	0	·	·	·
5	1	b	ba \$	ba
6	1	\$		ba

k	sorted x	$i \to \Psi'_{S_3}$
1	\$	6
2	b	2
3	b	5

(a) $x[i]$ and X_i (b) $x[i]$ and index i after stable sorting on x

Fig. 4. Consider S = babaabba\$. For comparison, see Figure 2.

4   Constructing Ψ'

Let $S[1..m]$ be T^k. We define S_{12} and S_3 just as T^k_{12} and T^k_3, respectively. We denote the suffix arrays of S_{12} and S_3 by SA_{12} and SA_3, respectively. Let Δ be the alphabet of S, and P be the part array of SA_{12}. We assume $S[0] = S[m]$.

Given $S[1..m]$, $\Psi_{S_{12}}$, and $SA^{-1}_{12}[1]$, we will describe how to construct $\Psi'_{S_{12}}$ and Ψ'_{S_3}. The algorithm consists of three parts: Constructing Ψ'_{S_3} using Part 1 of $\Psi_{S_{12}}$, constructing Part 2 of $\Psi'_{S_{12}}$ using Ψ'_{S_3}, and constructing Part 1 of $\Psi'_{S_{12}}$ using Part 2 of $\Psi'_{S_{12}}$. We describe only how to construct Ψ'_{S_3} using Part 1 of $\Psi_{S_{12}}$. Part 1 and 2 of $\Psi'_{S_{12}}$ can be constructed similarly.

We define $x[1..2m/3]$ as an array of characters such that $x[i] = S[3SA_{12}[i]-3]$ if $P[i] = 1$, and $x[i]$ isn't defined otherwise. For i with $P[i] = 1$, let X_i be the string $x[i]S_{12}[SA_{12}[i]..m/3]S[1..2]$ if $SA_{12}[i] \neq 1$, and the string $x[i]S[1..2]$ ($= S[n]S[1..2]$) otherwise. For i with $P[i] = 0$, X_i isn't defined. See Figure 4 (a) for an example. From now on, we consider only $x[i]$'s and X_i's such that $P[i] = 1$. Let X be the set $\{X_i \mid P[i] = 1, 1 \le i \le 2m/3\}$. Then, X_i is a suffix of S_3 and X is the same as the set of suffixes of S_3.

Lemma 8. *The stable sorting order of $x[i]$ is equal to the rank of X_i in X.*

Proof. Let X_p be the element of X such that $SA_{12}[i] = 1$. By omitting the first characters of every X_k's except X_p, they are of the form $S_{12}[SA_{12}[i]..m/3]S[1..2]$, which are already sorted in SA_{12} (note that $S[1..2]$ does not affect the order because $S_{12}[m/3]$ is unique). The first character of X_p ($= S[m]$) is unique. Thus, the rank of X_i is equal to the stable sorting order of $x[i]$.

Lemma 9. *Let k be the stable sorting order of $x[i]$ with $P[i] = 1$. Then $\Psi'_{S_3}[k] = i$.*

Proof. Let $S[p..n]$ be the suffix stored in the ith entry of SA_{12}. Then, $x[i]$ is $S[p-1]$ and the rank of X_i ($= S[p-1..n]S[1..2]$) is k in X by Lemma 8. By definition, $\Psi'_{S_3}[k]$ is a position in SA_{12} where $S[p..n]$ is stored. Therefore, $\Psi'_{S_3}[k] = i$. See Figure 4 (b).

Lemma 10. *Given S, $\Psi_{S_{12}}$, and $SA^{-1}_{12}[1]$, Ψ'_{S_3} can be constructed in $O(m+|\Delta|)$ time and $O(m \log |\Delta| + |\Delta|)$-bit space.*

Procedure Const_C_array
begin
  $i \leftarrow 1; j \leftarrow 1$;
  for $k = 1$ to m
    $rval \leftarrow$ Compare_suffix(i, j);
    if $rval > 0$ then
      $C[k] \leftarrow C'_{12}[i]$;
      $i \leftarrow i + 1$;
    else
      $C[k] \leftarrow C'_3[j]$;
      $j \leftarrow j + 1$;
end

Function Compare_suffix(i, j)
begin
  if $P[i] = 1$ then
    $x \leftarrow (F_{12}[i], \Psi'_{S_{12}}[i])$;
    $y \leftarrow (F_3[j], \Psi'_{S_3}[j])$;
  else
    $x \leftarrow (F_{12}[i], F_3[\Psi'_{S_{12}}[i]], \Psi'_{S_3}[\Psi'_{S_{12}}[i]])$;
    $y \leftarrow (F_3[j], F_{12}[\Psi'_{S_3}[j]], \Psi'_{S_{12}}[\Psi'_{S_3}[j]])$;
  if $x < y$ then
    return 1;
  else return -1;
end

Fig. 5. Constructing the C array of S.

Proof. Given S, $\Psi_{S_{12}}$, and $SA_{12}^{-1}[1]$, we first construct x in $O(m)$ time and $O(m \log |\Delta|)$ bits using a method similar to that in Lemma 5.

Then, for $i = 1$ to $2m/3$ with $P[i] = 1$, we iteratively compute the stable sorting order k of $x[i]$ and set $\Psi'_{S_3}[k] = i$. The total iteration of the stable sorting can be performed in $O(m + |\Delta|)$ time using $O(m \log |\Delta| + |\Delta|)$ bits [11].

Similarly, we can construct Part 2 of $\Psi'_{S_{12}}$ using Ψ'_{S_3} and Part 1 of $\Psi'_{S_{12}}$ using Part 2 of $\Psi_{S_{12}}$. Thus, we get the following lemma.

Lemma 11. *Given S, $\Psi_{S_{12}}$, and $SA_{12}^{-1}[1]$, we can construct $\Psi'_{S_{12}}$ and Ψ'_{S_3} in $O(m + |\Delta|)$ time and $O(m \log |\Delta| + |\Delta|)$-bit space.*

5 Merging $\Psi'_{S_{12}}$ and Ψ'_{S_3}

In this section we will describe how to construct Ψ_S by merging $\Psi'_{S_{12}}$ and Ψ'_{S_3}. We first construct the C array of S by merging $\Psi'_{S_{12}}$ and Ψ'_{S_3}. Merging $\Psi'_{S_{12}}$ and Ψ'_{S_3} is similar to Kärkkäinen and Sanders's algorithm [12], which merge SA_{12} and SA_3 in $O(m)$ time. Then, we convert C to Ψ_S by Lemma 3.

Let $F_{12}[1..2m/3]$ and $F_3[1..m/3]$ be arrays of the first characters, over Δ, of the suffixes in SA_{12} and S_3, respectively. That is, $F_{12}[i] = S[3SA_{12}[i] - 2]$ if $P[i] = 1$, and $F_{12}[i] = S[3(SA_{12}[i] - m/3) - 1]$ otherwise, and $F_3[i] = S[3SA_3[i]]$. Similarly, let $C'_{12}[1..2m/3]$ and $C'_3[1..m/3]$ be arrays of the characters preceding F_{12} and F_3 in S, respectively. That is, $C'_{12}[i] = S[3SA_{12}[i] - 3]$ if $P[i] = 1$, and $C'_{12}[i] = S[3(SA_{12}[i] - m/3) - 2]$ otherwise, and $C'_3[i] = S[3SA_3[i] - 1]$. Note that characters in C'_{12} and C'_3 compose C. See Figure 2 for an example. We can construct these arrays in $O(m)$ time and $O(m \log |\Delta|)$ bits as in Lemma 5.

We construct the C array by merging SA_{12} and SA_3. This merging is similar to merging two sorted arrays of integers. Figure 5 shows Procedure Const_C_array, which constructs the C array. Procedure Const_C_array consists of m iterations. Let $S[p..m]$ be the suffix in the ith entry of SA_{12} and $S[q..m]$ be the suffix in the jth entry of SA_3 (note that we ignore characters following $S[m]$

in SA_{12} and S_3 because these characters do not affect the order of suffixes). In the kth iteration, we determine which suffix is lexicographically the kth smallest by comparing $S[p..m]$ with $S[q..m]$, and thus we can compute $C[k]$. During the merging stage, we can get $SA^{-1}[1]$ which will be used in the next step.

Function Compare_suffix(i, j) compares $S[p..m]$ and $S[q..m]$ using the Ψ' function and arrays F_{12} and F_3. We have two cases according to the values of $P[i]$. Consider the case of $P[i] = 1$. Then, $S[p..m]$ is a residue-1 suffix and $S[q..m]$ is a residue-3 suffix. We first compare $S[p]$ ($= F_{12}[i]$) with $S[q]$ ($= F_3[j]$). If $S[p] = S[q]$, we compare $S[p+1..m]$ with $S[q+1..m]$. Because $S[p+1..m]$ and $S[q+1..m]$ are residue-2 and residue-1 suffixes, respectively, $\Psi'_{S_{12}}[i]$ and $\Psi'_{S_3}[j]$ represent the ranks of $S[p+1..m]$ and $S[q+1..m]$ in SA_{12}, respectively. Therefore, we can determine which suffix is smaller by comparing one pair of characters and one pair of integers. Similarly, we can do by comparing two pairs of characters and one pair of integers in case of $P[i] = 0$.

Function Compare_suffix(i, j) takes constant time and so Procedure Const_C_array takes $O(m)$ time. The space for arrays and Ψ' function is $O(m \log |\Delta|)$ bits. By Lemma 3, we convert C to Ψ_S in $O(m)$ time and $O(m \log |\Delta|)$ bits. Hence, we get the following lemma.

Lemma 12. *Given S, $\Psi'_{S_{12}}$, Ψ'_{S_3}, and $SA_{12}^{-1}[1]$, we can compute Ψ_S and $SA^{-1}[1]$ in $O(m)$ time and $O(m \log |\Delta|)$-bit space.*

References

1. M. Burrows and D. J. Wheeler. A block-sorting lossless data compression algorithm. Technical Report 124, Digital Equipment Corporation, Paolo Alto, California, 1994.
2. D. R. Clark. *Compact Pat Trees*. PhD thesis, University of Waterloo, Waterloo, 1988.
3. M. Farach. Optimal suffix tree construction with large alphabets. In *Proceedings of the 38th Annual IEEE Symposium on Foundations of Computer Science*, pages 137–143, 1997.
4. M. Farach-Colton, P. Ferragina, and S. Muthukrishnan. On the sorting-complexity of suffix tree construction. *Journal of the ACM*, 47(6):987–1011, 2000.
5. P. Ferragina and G. Manzini. Opportunistic data structures with applications. In *Proceedings of the 41st Annual IEEE Symposium on Foundations of Computer Science*, pages 390–398, 2000.
6. G. H. Gonnet, R. Baeza-Yates, and T. Snider. New indices for text: Pat trees and pat arrays. In W. B Frakes and R. Baeza-Yates, editors, *Information Retrieval: Data Structures & Algorithms*, pages 66–82. Prentice Hall, 1992.
7. R. Grossi and J. S. Vitter. Compressed suffix arrays and suffix trees with applications to text indexing and string matching. In *Proceedings of the 32nd Annual ACM Symposium on Theory of Computing*, pages 397–406, 2000.
8. R. Grossi and J. S. Vitter. Compressed suffix arrays and suffix trees with applications to text indexing and string matching. Technical Report Submitted for publication, 2001.

9. D. Gusfield. An "Increment-by-one" approach to suffix arrays and trees. manuscript, 1990.

10. W. K. Hon, T. W. Lam, K. Sadakane, and W. K. Sung. Constructing compressed suffix arrays with large alphabets. In *Proceedings of the 14th International Symposium on Algorithms and Computation*, pages 240–249, 2003.

11. W. K. Hon, K. Sadakane, and W. K. Sung. Breaking a time-and-space barrier in constructing full-text indices. In *Proceedings of the 44th Annual IEEE Symposium on Foundations of Computer Science*, pages 251–260, 2003.

12. J. Kärkkäinen and P. Sanders. Simple linear work suffix array construction. In *Proceedings of the 30th International Colloquium on Automata, Languages, and Programming*, pages 943–955, 2003.

13. D.K. Kim, J. Sim, H. Park, and K. Park. Linear-time construction of suffix arrays. In *Proceedings of the 14th Symposium on Combinatorial Pattern Matching*, pages 186–199, 2003.

14. P. Ko and S. Aluru. Space-efficient linear time construction of suffix arrays. In *Proceedings of the 14th Symposium on Combinatorial Pattern Matching*, pages 200–210, 2003.

15. T. W. Lam, K. Sadakane, W. K. Sung, and S. M. Yiu. A space and time efficient algorithm for constructing compressed suffix arrays. In *Proceedings of the 9th International Computing and Combinatorics Conference*, pages 401–410, 2002.

16. U. Manber and G. Myers. Suffix arrays: A new method for on-line string searches. *SIAM Journal on Computing*, 22(5):935–948, 1993.

17. J. I. Munro. Tables. In *Proceedings of Conference on Foundations of Software Technology and Theoretical Computer Science*, pages 37–42, 1996.

Faster Algorithms for δ,γ-Matching and Related Problems

Peter Clifford[1], Raphaël Clifford[2,*], and Costas Iliopoulos[2]

[1] Department of Statistics, 1 South Parks Road, Oxford, UK
[2] Algorithm Design Group, Department of Computer Science,
King's College London, London, UK
raph@dcs.kcl.ac.uk

Abstract. We present new faster algorithms for the problems of δ and (δ, γ)-matching on numeric strings. In both cases the running time of the proposed algorithms is shown to be $O(\delta n \log m)$, where m is the pattern length, n is the text length and δ a given integer. Our approach makes use of Fourier transform methods and the running times are independent of the alphabet size. $O(n\sqrt{m \log m})$ algorithms for the γ-matching and total-difference problems are also given. In all the above cases, we improve existing running time bounds in the literature.

1 Introduction

This paper focuses on a set of string pattern-matching problems that arise in musical analysis, and especially in musical information retrieval. A musical score can be viewed as a string: at a very rudimentary level, the alphabet could simply be the set of notes in the chromatic or diatonic notation, or the set of intervals that appear between notes (e.g. pitch may be represented as MIDI numbers and pitch intervals as number of semitones). Approximate repetitions in one or more musical works play a crucial role in discovering similarities between different musical entities and may be used for establishing "characteristic signatures" (see [12]). Such algorithms can be particularly useful for melody identification and musical retrieval.

Both exact and approximate matching techniques have been used for a variety of musical applications (see overviews in [5, 6, 12, 16]). The specific problem studied in this paper is pattern-matching for numeric strings where a certain tolerance is allowed during the matching procedure. This type of pattern-matching has been considered necessary for various musical applications and has been used by some researchers (see e.g. [10]). A number of efficient algorithms will be presented in this paper that tackle various aspects of this problem.

Most computer-aided musical applications adopt an absolute numeric pitch representation (most commonly MIDI pitch and pitch intervals in semitones; duration is also encoded in a numeric form). The absolute pitch encoding, however,

---

* Corresponding author

A. Apostolico, M. Crochemore, and K. Park (Eds.): CPM 2005, LNCS 3537, pp. 68–78, 2005.

may be insufficient for applications in tonal music as it disregards tonal quali-
ties of pitches and pitch-intervals (e.g. a tonal transposition from a major to a
minor key results in a different encoding of the musical passage and thus exact
matching cannot detect the similarity between the two passages). One way to
account for similarity between closely related but non-identical musical strings
is to use what will be referred to as δ-matching. In δ-matching, equal-length
patterns consisting of integers match, if each corresponding integer differs by
not more than δ, e.g. a C-major $\{60, 64, 65, 67\}$ and a C-minor $\{60, 63, 65, 67\}$
sequence can be matched if a tolerance $\delta = 1$ is allowed in the matching process.

An important class of problems can be specified in terms of a text string
$t = t_1 \cdots t_n$ and a pattern string $p = p_1 \cdots p_m$ over an alphabet Σ. The classical
string-matching problem is to find all occurrences of the pattern p in the text
t, in other words to find all indices i such that p and the substring $t[i, m] :=
t_i \cdots t_{i+m-1}$ are identical. In the case of the δ-matching, γ-matching and (δ, γ)
matching problems, the input is a pattern p, the text t and integers δ and γ, while
the alphabet is assumed to be an interval of integers. Informally, the *δ-matching*
problem is to find all indices i such that the maximum of $|p_j - t_{i+j-1}|$ over all j's
is no larger than δ. For *γ-matching* the problem is to find all indices i such that
the sum of $|p_j - t_{i+j-1}|$ is no larger than γ. The (δ, γ)-*matching* problem is to
find all indices i such that the maximum of $|p_j - t_{i+j-1}|$ over all j's is bounded
by δ and that the sum of the absolute differences is no larger than γ. Other
natural measures of dissimilarity are the *total difference*, $\sum_{j=1}^{m} |p_j - t_j|$; the *total
squared difference*, $\sum_{j=1}^{m} (p_j - t_j)^2$; and the *maximum difference*, $\max_{j=1}^{m} |p_j - t_j|$.
These are respectively the L_1 distance, the square of the L_2 distance and the
L_∞ distance between two vectors $p[1, m]$ and $t[1, m]$.

1.1   Previous Work

An $o(nm)$ solution for δ-matching can be derived by a reduction to the *less-than-
matching problem* [3]. In less-than-matching the task is to find all i such that
every value in p is less than or equal to its corresponding value in $t[i, m]$. The
problem of δ-matching can be solved using two instances of less-than-matching
giving an overall time complexity of $O(n\sqrt{m \log m})$ using FFTs [2]. An alternative approach is given in [9], where an instance of δ matching is reduced to at
most $2\delta + 1$ instances of exact matching with wild cards. Using FFTs again, the
total time required is therefore $O(\delta n \log m)$. For many applications, including
musical ones, δ does not depend on the size of the input and can be assumed
to be small. A number of heuristics and bit-parallel techniques have also been
developed for δ, γ and (δ, γ)-matching but all have worst case time complexity
of $O(nm)$ (see e.g. [6, 12]). Very recently it has been shown that for integer
alphabets only, γ-matching can be performed in $O(n\sqrt{\gamma \log (\gamma)})$ time [4]. The
observation that L_2 matching can be performed simply in $O(n \log m)$ time was
made at least as early as 2001 [15]. There have also been recent improved results
on the related problem of finding the closest pair in very high dimensions using
the L_1 and L_∞ norms [14].

1.2 Our Results

We present a different and direct $O(\delta n \log m)$ solution to δ-matching on integer valued data. This method is asymptotically faster than a reduction to less-than matching, when δ is $o(\sqrt{m/\log m})$. For (δ, γ)-matching, we give a similar $O(\delta n \log m)$ solution which is faster than the current known $O(nm)$ bound, if δ is $o(m/\log m)$.

An $o(nm)$ solution for γ-matching, for arbitrary γ, can be derived from the total-difference problem. We will show that the total-difference problem can be solved in $O(n\sqrt{m \log m})$ running time for integer and real valued data. Our method is based on the divide and conquer approach introduced by Abrahamson and developed by Amir [1, 3].

The paper is organized as follows. In Section 2 we give a simple illustration of our approach to δ-matching for the case $\delta = 1$. In Sections 3 and 4 we solve the δ-matching and (δ, γ)-matching problems in $O(\delta n \log m)$ time. In Section 5, we show that Abrahamson's method can be used to calculate γ-matches for arbitrary values of γ in $O(n\sqrt{m \log m})$ time. Finally, in Section 6 we conclude and state some open problems.

2   Fast Fourier Transform and 1-Matching

Fast Fourier transforms (FFT) were first applied to string matching by Fischer and Paterson in 1974 [13]. Since then FFTs have been the basis of several fast algorithms for different forms of approximate matching. The most important property of the FFT is that, for numerical strings, all the inner-products,

$$p \cdot t[i, m] \stackrel{\text{def}}{=} \sum_{j=1}^{m} p_j t_{i+j-1}, \ \ 1 \le i \le n - m + 1,$$

can be calculated accurately and efficiently in $O(n \log m)$ time (see e.g. [11], Chapter 32).

The basic idea when using FFTs to tackle approximate matching problems is to express the dissimilarity measure in terms of an inner-product. For example, since $(x - y)^2 = x^2 - 2xy + y^2$, we can express the total squared difference between p and $t[i, m]$ as

$$\sum_{j=1}^{m} (p_j - t_{i+j-1})^2 = \sum_{j=1}^{m} p_j^2 - 2p \cdot t[i, m] + \sum_{j=1}^{m} t_{i+j-1}^2 .$$

The first and last terms can be calculated in $O(n + m)$ time and the middle terms can be calculated in $O(n \log m)$ time using the FFT. The exact matching problem is then solved immediately since there is an exact match at all values of i where the total squared difference is zero. Of course a similar argument can be made for any dissimilarity measure which is zero when there is an exact match and bounded away from zero otherwise. By using a score of $x/y + y/x - 2 = (x -$

$y)^2/xy$, Cole and Hariharan [7] show that FFT methods can also solve the exact matching problem with wild cards in $O(n \log m)$ time, effectively independent of $|\Sigma|$.

Our algorithms for δ-matching and (δ, γ)-matching build on the ideas in [7]. We construct a function that is zero when there is a match between two symbols and larger than some fixed positive value otherwise. We then show how the function can be computed efficiently using FFTs. The main innovation is in the use of even periodic functions and their discrete cosine expansions to achieve this goal.

As a simple illustration, consider the δ-matching problem, with $\delta = 1$. First notice that the periodic function $\frac{1}{2} - \frac{1}{2}(-1)^x$ takes the value 0, when x is even, and 1 when it is odd. If we define $g(x) = x^2 + \frac{1}{2}(-1)^x - \frac{1}{2}$, it follows that $g(x - y) = 0$ when $|x - y| \leq 1$ and $g(x - y) \geq 4$ otherwise. But we can write

$$g(x - y) = x^2 - 2xy + y^2 + \tfrac{1}{2}(-1)^x(-1)^y - \tfrac{1}{2},$$

since $x + y$ has the same parity as $x - y$. This is the key idea. We now define new strings $\epsilon(t)$ and $\epsilon(p)$ where the jth element of $\epsilon(t)$ is 1 if t_j is even and -1 otherwise and similarly for $\epsilon(p)$. It follows that $\sum_{j=1}^{m} g(p_j - t_{i+j-1})$ can be expressed in terms of two inner-products $p \cdot t[i, m]$ and $\epsilon(p) \cdot \epsilon(t[i, m])$, both of which can be calculated in $O(n \log m)$ time, plus other terms that are calculable in $O(n + m)$ time. The δ-matching problem is then solved since, provided that the FFT is carried out to sufficient precision, we can identify indices where $\sum_{j=1}^{m} g(p_j - t_{i+j-1}) = 0$. In this case and the ones to follow, we need only enough precision to be able to distinguish 0 from any number greater than or equal to 1. The relative error of the Cooley-Tukey FFT method, for example, is $\lambda \log n$ where λ is the machine floating-point precision (the smallest positive number such that $1 + \lambda$ is distinguishable from unity in the floating point representation employed). Therefore, for any realistic size of input, non integer values resulting from the FFT calculation can simply be rounded to the nearest whole number without fear of mistake. See [17] for a more in depth discussion of FFT accuracy under different measures of error.

3   An Algorithm for δ-Matching

Given a text t of length n, a pattern p of length m and an integer δ, the δ-matching problem is to determine $\mathcal{I}_\delta$, where

$$\mathcal{I}_\delta = \{i : \max_{j=1..m} |p_j - t_{i+j-1}| \leq \delta\}. \tag{3.1}$$

In other words, the problem is to find all indices i in t such that the maximum difference between p_j and t_{i+j-1} is no larger than δ for all j. We say that we have a δ-*match* at each $i \in \mathcal{I}_\delta$.

We start by generalising the arguments that were used in Section 2 to tackle the δ-matching problem for the special case $\delta = 1$. The idea is essentially the same, namely to modify the squared difference by subtracting a periodic function thereby obtaining a function that is zero over a range of differences. We start with a few definitions and basic results about vector spaces.

A real-valued function $f(x)$ defined on $\mathbb{Z}$, the set of integers, is even and periodic with period 2δ, if

$$f(x) = f(-x) \text{ and } f(x) = f(x + k2\delta) \text{ for all } x, k \in \mathbb{Z}$$

Using standard properties of the discrete cosine transform [11] a convenient basis for the space of these functions is the set of functions

$$h_k(x) = r(k)\cos(xk\pi/\delta), \ k = 0, \ldots, \delta,$$

where $r(k) = 1/\sqrt{2\delta}$, if $k \bmod \delta = 0$ and $r(k) = 1/\sqrt{\delta}$, otherwise. These functions are orthonormal in the sense that $\sum_{x=1-\delta}^{\delta} h_j(x)h_k(x) = 0$ when $j \neq k$ and $\sum_{x=1-\delta}^{\delta} h_k^2(x) = 1$. Consequently, any even function $f(x)$ with period 2δ can be written as

$$f(x) = \sum_{k=0}^{\delta} \alpha_k h_k(x),$$

where the coefficients are given by

$$\alpha_k = \sum_{x=1-\delta}^{\delta} f(x)h_k(x).$$

We will be interested in two special cases of such functions, $f^{[1]}$ and $f^{[2]}$, where

$$f^{[1]}(x) = |x| \text{ and } f^{[2]}(x) = x^2 \text{ for } |x| \leq \delta.$$

Both $f^{[1]}(x)$ and $f^{[2]}(x)$ are even and periodic and so defined over the whole of $\mathbb{Z}$. We denote the coefficients of these functions by $\{\alpha_k^{[1]}\}$ and $\{\alpha_k^{[2]}\}$, respectively.

To tackle the δ-matching problem, consider the function

$$g(x) = x^2 - f^{[2]}(x).$$

By construction, this is an even function with the property that $g(x) = 0$ for $|x| \leq \delta$ and $g(x) \geq 1$, otherwise. Figure 1 shows the functions x^2 and $f^{[2]}$ and the result after subtraction. The following lemma follows immediately.

Lemma 1. *There is a δ-match of pattern p at position i of t, for some $i \in \{1..n - m + 1\}$, if and only if*

$$\sum_{j=1}^{m} g(p_j - t_{i+j-1}) = 0$$

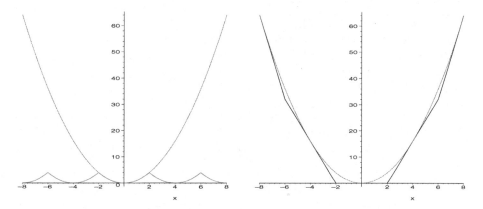

Fig. 1. The functions x^2, $f^{[2]}(x)$ and $g(x) = x^2 - f^{[2]}(x)$: $\delta = 2$

The important point is that

$$g(x - y) = x^2 + y^2 - 2xy - \alpha_0^{[2]}r(0)$$

$$- \sum_{k=1}^{\delta} \alpha_k^{[2]}r(k)c_k(x)c_k(y)$$

$$- \sum_{k=1}^{\delta-1} \alpha_k^{[2]}r(k)s_k(x)s_k(y)$$

where

$$c_k(x) = \cos(xk\pi/\delta)$$
$$s_k(x) = \sin(xk\pi/\delta),$$

and we have used the fact that $s_0(x) = s_\delta(x) = 0$ and $c_0(x) = 1$. In other words, $g(x - y)$ involves a total of 2δ product terms, so the dissimilarity measure based on g can be expressed in terms of 2δ inner-products.

Theorem 1. *Given a text t of length n, a pattern p of length m and an integer δ, we can compute all δ-matches in $O(\delta n \log m)$ time following the steps in Algorithm 1.*

Proof. The $\alpha_k^{[2]}$ need only be computed once for the particular value of δ that is of interest since they do not depend on the input pattern or text. Each coefficient requires $O(\delta)$ multiplications and additions to compute and so the total time to compute all $\alpha_k^{[2]}$ for a given δ is $O(\delta^2)$. The arrays A and B can be calculated simply in linear time. C can be calculated with a single inner-product calculation in $O(n \log m)$ time using FFTs. The arrays D and E require δ and $\delta - 1$ inner-product calculations respectively taking a total of $O(\delta n \log m)$ time to compute. It follows that δ-matching can be carried out with 2δ inner product calculations in $O(\delta n \log m)$ time. □

Algorithm 1: The δ-matching algorithm

Data: Numeric strings p and t and an integer δ

Result: Array $G_i = \sum_{j=1}^m g(p_j - t_{i+j-1})$ for $1 \le i \le n - m + 1$

$\alpha_k^{[2]} = \sum_{x=1-\delta}^{\delta} x^2 h_k(x)$;

$A = \sum_{j=1}^m p_j^2$ and $B_i = \sum_{j=1}^m t_{i+j-1}^2$ for $1 \le i \le n - m + 1$;

$C_i = p \cdot t[i, m]$ for $1 \le i \le n - m + 1$;

for $k \in \{1, \dots, \delta\}$ **do**

    Construct a pair of arrays $p'_j = \alpha_k^{[2]} r(k) c_k(p_j)$ and $t'_j = c_k(t_j)$;

    Construct an array $D_i(k) = p' \cdot t'[i, m]$ for $1 \le i \le n - m + 1$;

end

for $k \in \{1, \dots, \delta - 1\}$ **do**

    Construct a pair of arrays $p'_j = \alpha_k^{[2]} r(k) s_k(p_j)$ and $t'_j = s_k(t_j)$;

    Construct an array $E_i(k) = p' \cdot t'[i, m]$ for $1 \le i \le n - m + 1$;

end

$G_i = A + B_i - 2C_i - \alpha_0 r(0) m - \sum_{k=1}^{\delta} D_i(k) - \sum_{k=1}^{\delta-1} E_i(k)$;

---

4   An Algorithm for (δ, γ)-Matching

Given a text t of length n, a pattern p of length m and integers δ, γ, the (δ, γ)-matching problem is to determine $\mathcal{I}_{\delta, \gamma}$, where

$$\mathcal{I}_{\delta,\gamma} = \{i : \max_{j=1..m} |p_j - t_{i+j-1}| \le \delta \quad \text{and} \quad \Sigma_{j=1}^m |p_j - t_{i+j-1}| \le \gamma\}.$$

In other words, for (δ, γ)-matching, we require both that the maximum difference between p_j and t_{i+j-1} over all j's is bounded by δ and that the sum of differences is no larger than γ. We say that we have a (δ, γ)-*match* at each $i \in \mathcal{I}_{\delta,\gamma}$.

For (δ, γ)-matching, we make use of the set of locations $\mathcal{I}_\delta$, where the δ-matches occur (see (3.1))

Now consider the even periodic function $f^{[1]}(x)$. Recall that this is the same as $|x|$ when $|x| \le \delta$. We define the periodic total difference between p and $t[i, m]$ to be

$$\Delta_i = \sum_{j=1}^m f^{[1]}(p_j - t_{i+j-1}),$$

for $i = 1, \dots, n - m + 1$.

Since $f^{[1]}(x - y)$ can expressed as a linear combination of $2\delta - 1$ product terms, i.e.

$$f^{[1]}(x - y) = \alpha_0^{[1]} r(0)$$

$$+ \sum_{k=1}^{\delta} \alpha_k^{[1]} r(k) c_k(x) c_k(y)$$

$$+ \sum_{k=1}^{\delta-1} \alpha_k^{[1]} r(x) s_k(y) s_k(y),$$

it follows that all the periodic differences can be calculated in $(2\delta - 1)O(n \log m)$ time using FFTs. In particular, we can identify

$$\mathcal{J}_\gamma^* = \{i : \Delta_i \leq \gamma\},$$

the set of locations where the periodic total difference is no larger than γ.

The (δ, γ)-matching problem is now solved. Locations that are in the intersection $\mathcal{I}_\delta \cap \mathcal{J}_\gamma^*$ will meet both the δ-matching and γ-matching criteria since total differences are correctly calculated for all locations in $\mathcal{I}_\delta$. The final algorithm requires $4\delta - 1$ inner-product calculations and takes $O(\delta n \log m)$ time overall.

Theorem 2. *Given a text t of length n, a pattern p of length m and integers δ, γ we can compute all (δ, γ)-matches in $O(\delta n \log m)$ time.*

5   Total-Difference and γ-Matching

Given a text t of length n, a pattern p of length m, the problem of *total-difference* is to determine the sum of differences

$$M_i = \sum_{j=1}^m |p_j - t_{i+j-1}|, \quad \text{for } 1 \leq i \leq n - m + 1.$$

A naive algorithm for the total difference problem involves $O(n)$ successive calculations each of length $O(m)$ and therefore runs in $O(nm)$ time. For the canonical case, $n = 2m$, this implies that the running time is quadratic in m. In [8] the question of whether the problem can be solved in subquadratic time is raised. We will give a subquadratic algorithm, running in $O(m\sqrt{m \log m})$ time for the canonical problem and hence by the usual argument in time $O(n\sqrt{m \log m})$ for text of length n.

Given a text t of length n, a pattern p of length m, the problem of γ-matching is to determine $\mathcal{J}_\gamma$, where

$$\mathcal{J}_\gamma = \{i : \sum_{j=1}^m |p_j - t_{i+j-1}| \leq \gamma\}.$$

For γ-matching, the problem is to find all indices i such that the total difference between p and $t[i, m]$ is no larger than γ. A solution to the total difference problem immediately gives a solution to the γ-matching problem.

The essence of the method is firstly to solve an incomplete version of the problem using FFTs and then tidy up loose ends afterwards by straightforward calculations.

We start by observing that the difference between two numbers x and y can be calculated as the sum of four products

$$|x - y| = xI_xJ_y - I_xyJ_y + J_xyI_y - xJ_xI_y,$$

where $I_a = 1$ if $a > \theta$ and $I_a = 0$ otherwise and $J_a = 1 - I_a$, provided x and y are on opposite sides of some arbitrary value θ. When this is not the case the right hand side is 0. This observation forms the basis of the algorithm. In other words contributions to M_i from pairs of values (p_j, t_{i+j-1}) on opposite sides of specific thresholds are accumulated first. The remaining terms are collected in the second stage of the algorithm.

The total-Difference Algorithm

Assume $n = 2m$.

1. PARTITION
Sort the values in the set $\{p_1, p_2, \ldots, p_m\}$ in increasing order and let A be the associated array of indices of the sorted p-values. Now partition A from left to right into b successive arrays each of length m/b. Denote the kth of these arrays by A_k and let θ_k be its largest element. For notational convenience define $\theta_0 = -\infty$.

Next consider the set $\{t_1, t_2, \ldots, t_{2m}\}$. By sorting this set in increasing order, obtain a corresponding collection of arrays $\{B_k : k = 1, 2, \ldots, b\}$, where B_b contains all the indices j, such that $t_j > \theta_{b-1}$ and B_k contains all the indices j, such that $\theta_{k-1} < t_j \le \theta_k$ for $k < b$. The end result is that we can associate each entry t_j in the text with m/b entries in the pattern, since j must belong to one of the arrays B_k and there are m/b members of the array A_k.

2. FAST FOURIER TRANSFORM
For $k = 1, \ldots, b$ and x a real number define two functions:

$$I_k(x) = \begin{cases} 1 & \text{if } x > \theta_k \\ 0 & \text{otherwise,} \end{cases} \quad \text{and} \quad J_k(x) = \begin{cases} 1 & \text{if } \theta_{k-1} < x \le \theta_k \\ 0 & \text{otherwise.} \end{cases}$$

For each k, create four new text strings $\epsilon_{k1}(t), \epsilon_{k2}(t), \epsilon_{k3}(t)$ and $\epsilon_{k4}(t)$ with jth elements that are respectively $t_j I_k(t_j), I_k(t_j), J_k(t_j)$ and $t_j J_k(t_j)$. Correspondingly, create four new pattern strings $\nu_{k1}(p), \nu_{k2}(p), \nu_{k3}(p)$ and $\nu_{k4}(p)$ with jth elements that are respectively $J_k(p_j), -p_j J_k(p_j), p_j I_k(p_j)$ and $-I_k(p_j)$. With this construction

$$\sum_{j=1}^{m} |p_j - t_{i+j-1}| = \sum_{k=1}^{b} \sum_{\ell=1}^{4} \nu_{k\ell}(p) \cdot \epsilon_{k\ell}(t[i, m]) + \quad \text{remainder},$$

where the remainder contains terms from pairs of values (p_j, t_{i+j-1}) where $p_j \in A_k$ and $t_{i+j-1} \in B_k$ for some k.

3. THE REMAINING CASES
Now deal with the omitted cases, i.e. pairs of text and pattern elements that lie in associated arrays (A_k, B_k) for some k. Working through each of the arrays B_k, for each element of the text the number of associated elements in the pattern is m/b. The total number of such pairs considered is then $2m \times m/b$. For these cases, the contributions to the total differences can be calculated in the straightforward manner in $O(m^2/b)$ time.

Theorem 3. *Given a text t of length n and a pattern p of length m, we can compute all sums of differences in $O(n\sqrt{m \log m})$ time.*

Proof. The running time for Step 1 is $O(m \log m)$. The running time for Step 2 is $4bO(m \log m)$, since $4b$ FFTs have to be calculated. The running time for Step 3 is $O(m^2/b)$, so the total time is $O(m^2/b + 4bm \log m)$. Taking $b = \sqrt{m/\log m}$, the running time is then $O(m\sqrt{m \log m})$ for the case $n = 2m$ and hence $O(n\sqrt{m \log m})$ in general. $\square$

6   Conclusion and Open Problems

We have given new faster solutions to approximate matching problems on numerical strings. In particular, we have presented an algorithm for computing L_1 distances in $O(n\sqrt{m \log m})$ time (the total difference problem) and an $O(\delta n \log m)$ for δ and (δ, γ)-matching. A number of questions remain unresolved. For example, is it possible to calculate all L_∞ distances in $o(nm)$ time? Can Abrahamson's method be extended to the general L_p class of vector norms? Finally, our methods for δ and (δ, γ)-matching rely on the data being integer valued. Is it possible to find $o(nm)$ algorithms for these problems for real valued data?

References

1. K. Abrahamson. Generalized string matching. *SIAM journal on Computing*, 16(6):1039–1051, 1987.
2. A. Amir. Private communication. 2004.
3. A. Amir and M. Farach. Efficient 2-dimensional approximate matching of half-rectangular figures. *Information and Computation*, 118(1):1–11, 1995.
4. A. Amir, O. Lipsky, E. Porat, and J. Umanski. Approximate matching in the L_1 metric. In *Proceedings of the 16th Annual Symposium on Combinatorial Pattern Matching (CPM'05)*. Springer, 2005. This volume.
5. E. Cambouropoulos, M. Crochemore, C. S. Iliopoulos, L. Mouchard, and Y. J. Pinzon. Computing approximate repetitions in musical sequences. *International Journal of Computer Mathematics*, 79(11):1135–1148, 2002.
6. R. Clifford, T. Crawford, C. Iliopoulos, and D. Meredith. String matching techniques for music analysis. In *String Algorithmics*, NATO book series. KCL Press, 2004.
7. R. Cole and R. Hariharan. Verifying candidate matches in sparse and wildcard matching. In *Proceedings of the Annual ACM Symposium on Theory of Computing*, pages 592–601, 2002.
8. R. Cole, R. Hariharan, and P. Indyk. Fast algorithms for subset matching and tree pattern matching. Preprint.
9. R. Cole, C. Iliopoulos, T. Lecroq, W. Plandowski, and W. Rytter. On special families of morphisms related to δ-matching and don't care symbols. *Information Processing Letters*, 85(5):227–233, 2003.
10. D. Cope. Pattern-matching as an engine for the computer simulation of musical style. In *Proceedings of the International Computer Music Conference*, pages 288–291, 1990.

11. T. H. Cormen, C. E. Leiserson, and R. L. Rivest. *Introduction to Algorithms*. MIT Press, 1990.
12. T. Crawford, C. S. Iliopoulos, and R. Raman. String-matching techniques for musical similarity and melodic recognition. In *Computing in Musicology*, volume 11, pages 73–100. MIT-Press, 1998.
13. M. Fischer and M. Paterson. String matching and other products. In R. Karp, editor, *Proceedings of the 7th SIAM-AMS Complexity of Computation*, pages 113–125, 1974.
14. P. Indyk, M. Lewenstein, O. Lipsky, and E. Porat. Closest pair problems in very high dimensions. In *Automata, Languages and Programming: 31st International Colloquium, ICALP 2004*, pages 782–792, Turku, Finland, July 2004.
15. E. Porat. Private communication. 2004.
16. P. Y. Rolland and J. G. Ganascia. Musical pattern extraction and similarity assessment. In E. Miranda, editor, *Readings in Music and Artificial Intelligence*, pages 115–144. Harwood Academic Publishers, 2000.
17. J. C. Schatzman. Accuracy of the discrete Fourier transform and the fast Fourier transform. *SIAM Journal of Scientific Computing*, 17(5):1150–1166, 1996.

A Fast Algorithm for Approximate String Matching on Gene Sequences

Zheng Liu[1], Xin Chen[1], James Borneman[2], and Tao Jiang[1]

[1] Department of Computer Science, University of California, Riverside
[2] Department of Plant Pathology, University of California, Riverside

Abstract. Approximate string matching is a fundamental and challenging problem in computer science, for which a fast algorithm is highly demanded in many applications including text processing and DNA sequence analysis. In this paper, we present a fast algorithm for approximate string matching, called FAAST. It aims at solving a popular variant of the approximate string matching problem, the *k-mismatch problem*, whose objective is to find all occurrences of a short pattern in a long text string with at most k mismatches. FAAST generalizes the well-known Tarhio-Ukkonen algorithm by requiring two or more matches when calculating shift distances, which makes the approximate string matching process significantly faster than the Tarhio-Ukkonen algorithm. Theoretically, we prove that FAAST on average skips more characters than the Tarhio-Ukkonen algorithm in a single shift, and makes fewer character comparisons in an entire matching process. Experiments on both simulated data sets and real gene sequences also demonstrate that FAAST runs several times faster than the Tarhio-Ukkonen algorithm in all the cases that we tested.

1 Introduction

Approximate string matching is a fundamental and challenging problem in computer science. It is an operation that usually costs a large amount of computational resources. Therefore, a fast algorithm for approximate string matching is highly demanded in many applications including text processing and gene sequence analysis. There are two important variants of the approximate string matching problem: the k-mismatch problem and the k-difference problem. In both, we are given a short *pattern* string $P = p_1 p_2 \cdots p_m$ and a long *text* string $T = t_1 t_2 \cdots t_n$ over an alphabet Σ, and an integer k. The k-mismatch problem is to find all occurrences of the pattern P in the text T with at most k mismatches (*i.e.*, substitutions) allowed, whereas the k-difference problem finds all substrings of T with *edit distance* at most k to P. We are interested in the former problem in this paper.

There are many various algorithms dealing with the k-mismatch problem in the string matching literature. In 1992, Baeza-Yates and Gonnet [1] first proposed the Shift-Add algorithm for exact string matching, and then naturally generalized it to handle mismatches. El-Mabrouk and Crochemore [5] tackled

A. Apostolico, M. Crochemore, and K. Park (Eds.): CPM 2005, LNCS 3537, pp. 79–90, 2005.

the k-mismatch problem by incorporating the Boyer-Moore technique [3] into the Shift-Add algorithm. Two algorithms that are the most relevant to ours are those proposed by Tarhio and Ukkonen [9] and by Baeza-Yates and Gonnet [2]. Both can be considered as generalizations of the Boyer-Moore algorithm [3] for exact string matching, but they employ different methods to calculate shift distances. A basic principle of these algorithms is to skip as many characters as possible while not missing any pattern occurrence. The Baeza-Yates-Gonnet algorithm takes advantage of *the good suffix rule*. If the shifted pattern matches the pattern of the previous alignment with at most $2k$ mismatches, further comparisons are needed to check a possible match at the shifted position. Therefore, the shift distance is the minimum distance (> 0) so that the shifted pattern matches this pattern at the previous alignment with at most $2k$ mismatches. The Tarhio-Ukkonen algorithm instead takes advantage of *the bad character rule*. When more than k mismatches occur, the last $k + 1$ characters of the text in the current alignment need have at least one match after the pattern is shifted to the right. The shift distance is thus calculated as the minimum distance (> 0) so that the shifted pattern has at least one match to the last $k + 1$ characters of the text in the previous alignment.

In this paper, we present a fast approximate string matching algorithm, called FAAST, which further generalizes the Tarhio-Ukkonen algorithm. Instead of requiring at least one match in the last $k + 1$ characters of the text in the previous alignment, the new algorithm requires at least x matches in the last $k + x$ characters when calculating shift distances, where x is a small integer value (typically 2 or 3 in our experiments). Apparently, the new algorithm will be the Tarhio-Ukkonen algorithm if we define $x = 1$. Although it seems a trivial modification, FAAST could run significantly faster than the Tarhio-Ukkonen algorithm, as demonstrated in our experiments.

In the ongoing *Oligonucleotide Fingerprinting Ribosomal Genes* (OFRG) project [10], we have applied the FAAST algorithm to the *gene sequence acquisition problem*. The problem of gene sequence acquisition is, given a collection of gene DNA sequences and a primer, how to extract all the gene sequences that contain the primer sequence (allowing a few mismatches). From the computational point of view, it is equivalent to the k-mismatch problem. In some cases, however, there are degenerate characters (*i.e.*, representing more than one character in an alphabet) in the primer sequence. This problem has traditionally been tackled by constructing a *nondeterministic finite automata* (NFA) [7, 8], which unfortunately requires a long preprocessing time and a large amount of memory space. In this paper, we will propose a simple approach to deal with degenerate characters based on the FAAST algorithm.

The rest of the paper is organized as follows. The next section reviews the Tarhio-Ukkonen algorithm. In Section 3, we focus on discussing our new algorithm FAAST. Experiments on simulated data and real gene sequences are presented in Section 4, and some concluding remarks are given in Section 5.

2   The Tarhio-Ukkonen Algorithm

Based on the Boyer-Moore-Horspool (BMH) algorithm [6], the Tarhio-Ukkonen algorithm [9] generalizes both the right-to-left scanning of the pattern and the computation of shift distances to allow string matching with k-mismatches. The BMH algorithm always tries to match the text character above the rightmost character of the pattern no matter where a mismatch occurs during an alignment. Similarly, when there are more than k mismatches occur, the Tarhio-Ukkonen algorithm shifts the pattern to a position such that the rightmost $k + 1$ text characters in the previous alignment have at least one match. The shift distance is defined as the minimum one that satisfies the above condition.

Assume a substring $t_{j-k}...t_j$ of the text is aligned with the rightmost $k + 1$ characters $p_{m-k}...p_m$ of P, and a shift is needed. For each $i \in [m - k, m]$ and each $a \in \Sigma$, we denote by $d_k[i, a]$ the minimum distance between p_l and p_i such that $p_l = a$ and $l < i$. Precisely, for a given i, $d_k[i, a]$ is initially set as $m - k$ and then updated if a smaller distance value is found, that is

$$d_k[i, a] = min\{\{m - k\} \cup \{s | p_{i-s} = a, s \in [1, i - 1], a \in \Sigma\}\} \qquad (1)$$

Similarly, denote by $d[t_{j-k}...t_j]$ the minimum distance to shift the pattern to a position so that there is at least one match in the text substring above $p_{m-k}...p_m$. Then, we have

$$d_k[t_{j-k}, t_{j-k+1}, ..., t_j] = min\{d_k[m - i, t_{j-i}], i \in [0, k]\} \qquad (2)$$

The Tarhio-Ukkonen algorithm can solve the k-mismatch problem in expected time $O(kn(1/m - k + k/c))$, where c is the alphabet size [9]. In the following, we give a simple example to illustrate, how the Tarhio-Ukkonen works in an approximate string matching process. The example uses pattern $P = $ AAGTCG-TAAC and text $T = $ AACTGTTAACTTGCGACTAG, with $k = 2$. The Tarhio-Ukkonen algorithm constructs a shift table of $d_k[i, a]$ for P by (1), as shown in Table 1. The first two shifts in the approximate matching process is detailed in Table 2.

3   Our Algorithm

FAAST – a fast algorithm for approximate string match – can find all occurrences of a pattern $P = p_1...p_m$ in a text string $T = t_1...t_n$ with up to k mismatches. In this section, we first describe the idea and implementation of the FAAST

Table 1. A shift table of $d_k[i, a]$ $(k = 2, m = 10, n = 20)$

position	A	C	G	T
8	6	3	2	1
9	1	4	3	2
10	1	5	4	3

Table 2. An example of running Tarhio-Ukkonen algorithm($k = 2, m = 10, n = 20$)

Text:	AACTGTTAACTTGCGACTAG
Pattern:	AAGTCGTAAC (Shift 1)
	AAGTCGTAAC (Shift 2)
	AAGTCGTAAC
Shift 1:	The 3rd mismatch occurs at the 3rd position of the pattern string. The shift distance is calculated based on the last 3 characters of the aligned text, *i.e.*, AAC. $d_k[AAC] = min\{d_k[8, A], d_k[9, A], d_k[10, C]\} = 1$
Shift 2:	The 3rd mismatch occurs at the 7th position of the pattern string. The shift distance is calculated based on the last 3 characters of the aligned text, *i.e.*, ACT. $d_k[ACT] = min\{d_k[8, A], d_k[9, C], d_k[10, T]\} = 3$

algorithm. Then, its correctness and efficiency are proved and analyzed. Finally, a special consideration is taken in FAAST to enable it to work for patterns with degenerate characters.

3.1   Algorithm Description

Note that, in the Tarhio-Ukkonen algorithm, the shift distance is calculated as the minimum one such that there exists at least one match when aligning the rightmost $k + 1$ text characters in the current alignment with the pattern after a shift. In order to achieve faster matching process, FAAST instead calculates the shift distance as the minimum one such that the rightmost $k + x$ characters of the current aligned text will have at least x matches after the shift. Here, x generally takes a small integer value, *e.g.*, two or three. An example will be given at the end of this subsection to demonstrate that FAAST generally skips more characters than the Tarhio-Ukkonen algorithm in a shift.

FAAST consists of a preprocessing step and a matching step, as the Tarhio-Ukkonen does. In the preprocessing step, FAAST will calculate the shift distances of all possible strings of length $k + x$ in the alphabet Σ and tabulate them in a table d_{kx}, as follows. First, given a pattern string $P = p_1p_2 \cdots p_m$ and a position i ($i \in [m - k - x + 1, m]$), we denote by $\mathcal{U}_{kx}[i, a]$ a set of distances between p_i and all occurrences of the character a to the left of p_i in P. That is,

$$\mathcal{U}_{kx}[i, a] = \{s|p_{i-s} = a, s \in [1, i - 1], a \in \Sigma\} \quad (3)$$

Then, given a string $t_{j-k-x+1} \cdots t_j$ of length $k + x$ and a shift distance l ($l \in [1, m - k]$), we define a set as

$$\mathcal{V}_{kx}[t_{j-k-x+1} \cdots t_j, l] = \{i|l \in \mathcal{U}_{kx}[m - i, t_{j-i}], i \in [0, k + x - 1]\} \quad (4)$$

In $\mathcal{V}_{kx}[t_{j-k-x+1} \cdots t_j, l]$, we store the position offsets (relative to t_j) of all characters in $t_{j-k-x+1} \cdots t_j$ that will be matched after shifting the pattern to the right by l characters. For example, if only t_j and t_{j-2} are matched after shifting

Algorithm 1: Computation of table d_{kx}

1.	for a in Σ
2.	for $i := m$ downto $m - k - x + 1$
3.	$\mathcal{U}_{kx}[i, a] := \{m - k\};$ {Set initialization}
4.	for $i := m$ downto $m - k - x + 1$
5.	for $s := i - 1$ downto 1
6.	if $i - s < m - k$ then
7.	$\mathcal{U}_{kx}[i, p_s] := \mathcal{U}_{kx}[i, p_s] \cup \{i - s\};$ {Set union}
8.	for each string $t_{j-k-x+1} \cdots t_j$ in Σ
9.	for $l := 1$ to $m - k$
10.	$|\mathcal{V}_{kx}[t_{j-k-x+1} \cdots t_j, l]| := 0;$ {Set size initialization}
11.	for $l := 1$ to $m - k$
12.	for $i := m$ downto $m - k - x + 1$
13.	if $l \in \mathcal{U}_{kx}[i, t_{j-m+i}]$ then
14.	$|\mathcal{V}_{kx}[t_{j-k-x+1} \cdots t_j, l]| := |\mathcal{V}_{kx}[t_{j-k-x+1} \cdots t_j, l]| + 1;$
15.	if $|\mathcal{V}_{kx}[t_{j-k-x+1} \cdots t_j, l]| \geq min[x, m - k - l]$
16.	$d_{kx}[t_{j-k-x+1} \cdots t_j] := l;$
17.	break; {Go to step 8}

the pattern to the right by l characters, the value of $\mathcal{V}_{kx}[t_{j-k-x+1} \cdots t_j, l]$ would be $\{0, 2\}$. Finally, the shift distance $d_{kx}[t_{j-k-x+1} \cdots t_j]$ can be calculated using the following formula, where $|\cdot|$ is the size of a set:

$$d_{kx}[t_{j-k-x+1} \cdots t_j]$$

$$= min\{l \mid |\mathcal{V}_{kx}[t_{j-k-x+1} \cdots t_j, l]| \geq min\{x, m - k - l\}, l \in [1, m - k]\} \qquad (5)$$

This formula guarantees that the minimum l distance is made such that either the current aligned rightmost $k+x$ text characters have at least x matches in the next alignment when all these text characters are aligned with the pattern after the shift, or the current aligned rightmost $k + x$ text characters have at least $m - l - k$ ($< x$) matches in the next alignment when only $m - l$ ($< k + x$) text characters are aligned with the pattern after the shift. Both cases requires no more than k mismatches in the new alignment between the $k + x$ text characters and the shifted pattern.

The details of the preprocessing algorithm are provided in pseudocode as Algorithm 1: Step 1-7 describes the construction of set $\mathcal{U}_{kx}[i, a]$. The details of the size calculation for set $\mathcal{V}_{kx}[t_{j-k-x+1} \cdots t_j, l]$ is covered in step 9-14, and the rest part of Algorithm 1 fills out the table $d_{kx}[t_{j-k-x+1} \cdots t_j]$. Note that the calculation of d_{kx} uses a pattern as input, but does not depend on any text.

In the matching step, we compare a pattern P with a text string T. We denote by h the index of a character that is currently scanned in T and by i the index of the corresponding character in P. $t_{j-k-x+1} \ldots t_j$ refers to the text string that is aligned above $p_{m-k-x+1} \ldots p_m$. The matching process remains similar to that in the Tarhio-Ukkonen algorithm except that, when there are more than k

mismatches occur, we look up a different table for shift distances. The details of this step are provided in pseudocode as Algorithm 2:

Algorithm 2: Approximate string matching

1.	$j := m$;
2.	while $j \leq n$ do begin
3.	$h := j$; $i := m$; $e := 0$; {e: the number of mismatches}
4.	while $i > 0$ and $e \leq k$ do begin
8.	if $t_h \neq p_i$ then
9.	$e := e + 1$;
9.	$i := i - 1$; $h := h - 1$;
10.	end of while
11.	if $e \leq k$ then
12.	record the occurrence position j;
13.	$j := j + d_{kx}[t_{j-k-x+1} \cdots t_j]$;
14.	end of while.

An example is given to illustrate how a shift table d_{kx} is calculated and how an approximate string matching proceeds. We use the same pattern and text as those used in the previous section for the Tarhio-Ukkonen algorithm. The set of shift distances, i.e., $\mathcal{U}_{kx}$, is listed in Table 3 and a part of the table $\mathcal{V}_{kx}[t_{j-k-x+1} \cdots t_j, l]$ is listed in Table 4. The first two shifts in the approximate matching process is detailed in Table 5. As we have seen earlier, distances of the first two shifts made by the Tarhio-Ukkonen algorithm are 1 and 3, whereas they are 7 and 7 by FAAST, respectively. Therefore, our algorithm FAAST can generally skip many more characters than the Tarhio-Ukkonen algorithm in a single shift. As a result, FAAST could significantly speed up the approximate string matching process, as proved theoretically in the next subsection.

Table 3. A set of shift distances of $\mathcal{U}_{kx}$ ($k = 2, x = 3, m = 10, n = 20$)

position	A	C	G	T
6	4,5	1	3	2
7	5,6	2	1,4	3
8	6,7	3	2,5	1,4
9	1,7,8	4	3,6	2,5
10	1,2,8,9	5	4,7	3,6

3.2   Algorithm Analysis

In this section, we discuss in detail the correctness of FAAST, its time and space complexity, the average shift distance, and the total character comparisons.

Correctness. We establish the correctness of FAAST by the following theorem.

Table 4. An example of $\mathcal{V}_{kx}[t_{j-k-x+1}\cdots t_j, l]$ ($k = 2, x = 3, m = 10, n = 20, l = [1..8]$)

l	1	2	3	4	5	6	7	8
AAAAA	0,1	0		4	3,4	2,3	1,2	0,1
...								
GCGAC	1	2,3	4		0,2		1	1
...								
GTCGT			0,1,2,3,4			0,1		
...								
TTAAC	0	4	3		0	2	1,2	1
...								
TTTTT	2	1,4	0,3	2	1	0		

Table 5. An example of running FAAST($k = 2, x = 3, m = 10, n = 20$)

Text:	AACTGTTAACTTGCGACTAG	
Pattern:	AAGTCGTAAC	(Shift 1)
	AAGTCGTAAC	(Shift 2)
	AAGTCGTAAC	

Shift 1: The 3rd mismatch occurs at the 3rd position of the pattern string. The shift distance is calculated based on the last 5 characters of the aligned text, *i.e.*, TTAAC. $d_{kx}[TTAAC] = 7$

Shift 2: The 3rd mismatch occurs at the 5th position of the pattern string. The shift distance is calculated based on the last 5 characters of the aligned text, *i.e.*, GCGAC. $d_{kx}[GCGAC] = 7$

Theorem 1. *Given any alignment between P and $t_{j-m+1}...t_j$ in T, P can be shifted by $d_{kx}[t_{j-k-x+1}\cdots t_j]$ characters to the right without passing by any approximate occurrences of P in T.*

Proof. Denote by $p_{i-k-x+1}...p_i$ the substring of P that is aligned below $t_{j-k-x+1}$ $...t_j$ after shifting $d_{kx}[t_{j-k-x+1}\cdots t_j]$ characters to the right. Note that P may be aligned with only a part of $t_{j-k-x+1}...t_j$, and we omit such cases in our proof just for simplicity. Assume that an occurrence of P is passed by during the shift. When aligning this occurrence with P, we have a substring of P, denoted by $p_{i'-k-x+1}...p_{i'}$, that is aligned below $t_{j-k-x+1}...t_j$, such that there are at most k mismatches in the alignment of $p_{i'-k-x+1}...p_{i'}$ with $t_{j-k-x+1}...t_j$, and $i < i'$. These lead to a contradiction to the definition of $d_{kx}[t_{j-k-x+1}\cdots t_j]$, and the theorem thus follows. □

Time and space complexity. In the preprocessing part, calculation of $\mathcal{U}_{kx}$ takes time $O(m(k + x))$ and space $O((m - k)(k + x)c)$, where c is the alphabet size of Σ, which is 4 for DNA sequences. Meanwhile, it takes time $O(c^{k+x}(m - k)(k + x))$ and space $O(c^{k+x})$ to tabulate d_{kx}. Therefore, the total time spent on preprocessing is $O((k + x)((m - k)c^{k+x} + m))$ and space is $O(c^{k+x} + c(m - k)$

$(k+x)))$. In the matching part, it needs $O(mn)$ time in the worst case. Instead, we are more interested in its performance in the average case.

Average shift distance. The average shift distance refers to the number of characters in the text that the pattern is expected to skip in one shift. Intuitively, the larger the average shift distance is, the faster the approximate matching, and thus the better the algorithm performs.

We use the *random string assumption* in our analysis. It assumes that each character in P and T is independently chosen at random from the alphabet set Σ. Also, we assume that the probability that two characters give rise to a match is p. Under this assumption, we have

Lemma 1. *The probability P_{kx} for the last $k+x$ characters of P to have at least x matches in an alignment with T is $P_{kx} = 1 - \sum_{i=0}^{x-1} C_{k+x}^i (1-p)^{k+x-i} p^i$.*

Proof. Note that the probability, denoted as $P_{kx,i}$, of $k+x$ characters having exactly i matches in an alignment forms a binomial distribution, *i.e.*,

$$P_{kx,i} = C_{k+x}^i (1-p)^{k+x-i} p^i \tag{6}$$

By summing up $P_{k+x,i}$ with i from 0 to $x-1$, we obtain

$$P_{kx} = 1 - \sum_{i=0}^{x-1} C_{k+x}^i (1-p)^{k+x-i} p^i \tag{7}$$

$\square$

We simplify the calculation of the average shift distance, without taking into account the effect of the limit length of a pattern. Therefore, the shift distance can take a value up to the infinity in the calculation, which provides an approximation to the real average shift distance.

Theorem 2. *The average shift distance E_{kx}^d of the algorithm is $E_{kx}^d \approx 1/P_{kx}$.*

Proof. We denote by $P_{s,kx}$ the probability that the shift distance s is taken. Then,

$$P_{s,kx} = (1 - P_{kx})^{s-1} P_{kx}, \quad s > 0 \tag{8}$$

Therefore, we have

$$E_{kx}^d \approx \sum_{s=1}^{\infty} s P_{s,kx} = \sum_{s=1}^{\infty} s(1 - P_{kx})^{s-1} P_{kx} \quad = 1/P_{kx} \tag{9}$$

$\square$

In the following, k is set to be 3, as used in our gene sequence analysis application [10]. We plot the curves of the average shift distances against the character matching probability p, in Fig. 1(a). Different values of x are employed, including one, which is used in the Tarhio-Ukkonen algorithm. As shown in the figure, the average shift distances become much larger as we increase x from 1 to 3, for small values of p. Therefore, FAAST can provide a very fast approximate matching process, in particular for gene DNA sequences where p is about 0.25 (the alphabet size is 4).

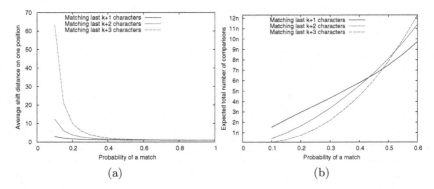

Fig. 1. (a) Comparison of average shift distances under different numbers of matches in the last $k + x$ characters, where $k = 3$. (b) The expected total number of character comparisons under different numbers of matches in the last $k + x$ characters, where $k = 3$

Total character comparisons. The total number of character comparisons made in an entire matching process is proportional to the running time of the program. Therefore, it is a very useful criterion to measure the performance of a string matching algorithm. Here, we again use the random string assumption and ignore the effect of the limit length of a pattern, as discussed above, to simplify our calculations.

Lemma 2. *The expected number E^c_{kx} of comparisons made between two successive shifts, is $E^c_{kx} \approx (k + x)/(1 - p)$.*

Proof. Note that the matching process between two successive shifts does not terminate until we find the $(k + 1)^{th}$ mismatch in an alignment. As discussed in [9], the distribution of $E^c_{kx} - (k + x)$ converges to a negative binomial distribution when the pattern size increases to infinity. The expected value of $E^c_{kx} - (k + x)$ under this distribution is $(k+x)p/(1-p)$. That is, $E^c_{kx} - (k+x) \approx (k+x)p/(1-p)$, and thus the lemma follows.   □

By the above lemma and Theorem 3, we can easily obtain

Theorem 3. *The expected total number TE^c_{kx} of character comparisons made for a text of length n is $TE^c_{kx} \approx nP_{kx}(k + x)/(1 - p)$.*

Fig. 1(b) shows the expected total number of comparisons TE^c_{kx} made under different values of x and p. We can see that, if more matches are required in the calculation of shift distances and if the character matching probability is $p < 0.5$, a large amount of comparisons could be saved in a string matching process. For example, given a gene DNA sequence of length n and $p = 0.25$, a total of $2.29n$ character comparisons will be saved as x increases from 1 to 3.

3.3 Degenerate Characters

In many applications, we need to find in a text all occurrences of a pattern string that contains degenerate characters. For example, in the gene sequence acquisition problem, degeneracy in a DNA sequence refers to the phenomenon that one character may represent several nucleotide bases. In the official IUPAC-IUB single-letter base codes [4], R stands for G/A, Y for T/C, and H for A/C/T, *etc.* A naive method treats the pattern string with degeneracy as a set of multiple patterns, which makes string matching several times slower.

Degeneracy brings up two new issues for the FAAST algorithm. One is the new definition of match, and the other occurs in the calculation of shift distances. We consider two degenerate characters as a match if they share a common non-degenerate character, *e.g.*, R and H is a match when aligning them. When calculating shift distances, FAAST treats a degenerate character as any of its corresponding non-degenerate characters, and takes the minimum shift distance given by these non-degenerate characters as the shift distance of the degenerate character. The procedure in the matching step of FAAST remains unchanged. We notice that, in this way, FAAST will not miss any occurrence of pattern with at most k mismatches. Experiments on strings with degenerate characters are presented in the next section.

4   Experimental Results

We have tested FAAST on both simulated data sets and real DNA gene sequence data on a PC with Intel Pentium CPU (2.8GHz and 1G memory), and compared its performance with that of the Tarhio-Ukkonen algorithm [9].

To produce simulated data sets, we used a random generator to select four DNA bases {A, C, G, T} randomly with equal probabilities. Text sequences we tested are $2M$ (*i.e.*, two millions) bases long, and a pattern with 39 bases. We listed in Table 6 the average shift distances, total numbers of character comparisons, preprocessing time, and the total running time. The results show a clear tendency that, as x increases from one to seven, FAAST can shift by larger distances on average and make fewer comparisons. Though the preprocessing time is increasing, the total running time is consistently decreasing. For example, FAAST needs only 11.2 seconds with $x = 5$, whereas the Tarhio-Ukkonen algorithm (*i.e.*, $x = 1$) takes 210.2 seconds, which is about 18 times slower.

Table 6. The average shift distances, total character comparisons, preprocessing time, and total running time of FAAST on simulated DNA sequences of $2M$ bases. The pattern size is 39, and $k = 3$

x	1	2	3	4	5	6	7
Average shift distance	1.41	2.76	5.59	16.38	31.31	37.77	38.87
Total Comparisons($\times 2M$)	6.70	3.68	1.86	0.65	0.34	0.28	0.27
Total running time(sec)	210.2	114.4	58.1	20.6	11.2	10.8	16.7
Preprocessing time(sec)	0.01	0.01	0.03	0.08	0.36	1.58	6.90

To test the performance of our algorithm on real gene DNA sequence data, we downloaded 18,491 18S ribosomal fungal DNA sequences and 81,343 16S ribosomal bacterial DNA sequences from the NCBI DNA sequence database. We randomly picked 150 sequences to form a test set and compared the preprocessing time, string matching time and total running time of the Tarhio-Ukkonen algorithm with our generalized algorithm FAAST. This was repeated 5 times and the average result was reported. The bacterial sequence set includes totally 170K bases and the fungal sequence set includes 179K bases. The detailed results are shown in Table 7 and Table 8 for bacterial sequences and fungal sequences, respectively. For 150 random bacterial sequences, if we choose x as 5, our algorithm needs a total running time of 2.63 seconds whereas the Tarhio-Ukkonen algorithm (*i.e.*, $x = 1$) needs 18.78 seconds. Similarly, for 150 random fungal sequences, our algorithm needs only 5.62 seconds but the Tarhio-Ukkonen algorithm needs 16.45 seconds. Therefore, our algorithm with $x = 5$ runs about 7 times and 3 times faster than the Tarhio-Ukkonen algorithm on the bacterial and fungal sequences that we tested, respectively.

Table 7. The total running time, preprocessing time, and string matching time of FAAST on 150 bacterial DNA sequences with different x values and $k = 3$. The pattern used is AGRRTTTGATYHTGGYTCAG

x	1	2	3	4	5	6	7
Total running time(sec)	18.78	13.05	7.74	3.84	2.63	3.21	8.55
Preprocessing time(sec)	0.01	0.01	0.02	0.09	0.35	1.57	6.96
String matching time(sec)	18.77	13.04	7.72	3.75	2.28	1.64	1.59

Table 8. The total running time, preprocessing time, and string matching time of FAAST on 150 fungal DNA sequences with different x values and $k = 3$. The pattern used is TTAGCATGGAATAATRRAATAGGA

x	1	2	3	4	5	6	7
Running time(sec)	16.45	11.43	9.24	6.78	5.62	8.24	26.48
Preprocessing time(sec)	0.02	0.03	0.08	0.32	1.34	5.77	23.86
String matching time(sec)	16.43	11.40	9.16	6.46	4.28	2.47	2.62

5   Conclusion

FAAST has been embedded in a web-based system to enable biologists to build their own gene sequence databases. The whole system has been successfully used in the OFRG project [10]. The algorithm is designed especially for gene DNA sequences with an alphabet of size 4, to solve the gene sequence acquisition problem. As the alphabet size and the x value get large, we notice that the time and memory required for the shift distance calculation increase quickly, which in turn deteriorates the performance of FAAST. We plan to look into this problem in the future.

Acknowledgements

The research was supported in part by NSF grants DBI-0133265 and CCR-0309902, and National Key Project for Basic Research (973) grant 2002CB512801.

References

1. Baeza-Yates, R., Gonnet, G.H. (1992) A New Approach to Text Searching. *Communication of the ACM*, Vol. 35, No.10.
2. Baeza-Yates, R.A., Gonnet, G.H. (1994) Fast String Matching with Mismatches. *Information and Computation* 108, pp. 187-199.
3. Boyer, R.S., Moore, J.S. (1977) A fast string searching algorithm. *Communications of the ACM*, 10(20), pp. 762-772.
4. Cornish-Bowden, A. (1985) Nomenclature for incompletely specified bases in nucleic acid sequences: recommendations 1984, *Nucl. Acids Res*, 13, pp. 3021-3030.
5. El-Mabrouk, N., Crochemore, M. (1996) Boyer-Moore strategy to efficient approximate string matching. *LNCS*, Vol. 1075, Combinatorial Pattern Matching, pp. 24-38.
6. Horspool, R.N. (1980) Practical fast searching in strings. *Software - Practice and experience*, 10, 501-506.
7. Navarro, G. and Raffinot, M. (1999) Fast Regular Expression Search. *LNCS*, Vol. 1668, Proceedings of the 3rd International Workshop on Algorithm Engineering, pp. 198-212.
8. Navarro, G. (2003) Approximate Regular Expression Searching with Arbitrary Integer Weights. *LNCS*, Vol. 2906, Proceedings of ISAAC'03, pp. 230-239.
9. Tarhio, J., Ukkonen, E. (1993) Approximate Boyer-Moore String Matching. *SIAM J. Comput.*, 22, pp. 243-260.
10. Valinsky L., Scupham A., Vedova G.D., Liu Z., Figueroa A., Jampachaisri K., Yin B., Bent E., Mancini-Jones, R., Press J., Jiang T., and Borneman J. (2004) Oligonucleotide Fingerprinting of Ribosomal RNA Genes (OFRG), pp. 569-585. In G. A. Kowalchuk, F. J. de Bruijn, I. M. Head, A. D. L. Akkermans, J. D.van Elsas (ed.) Molecular Microbial Ecology Manual (2nd ed). Kluwer Academic Publishers, Dordrecht, The Netherlands.

Approximate Matching in the L_1 Metric

Amihood Amir[1,*], Ohad Lipsky[2], Ely Porat[3,**], and Julia Umanski[2]

[1] Department of Computer Science,
Bar-Ilan University, 52900 Ramat-Gan, Israel
and Georgia Tech
Tel. (972-3)531-8770
amir@cs.biu.ac.il
[2] Department of Computer Science,
Bar-Ilan University, 52900 Ramat-Gan, Israel
Tel. (972-3)531-8408
ohadlipsky@yahoo.com, julia_um@hotmail.com
[3] Department of Computer Science,
Bar-Ilan University, 52900 Ramat-Gan, Israel
Tel. (972-3)531-7620
porately@cs.biu.ac.il

Abstract. *Approximate matching* is one of the fundamental problems in pattern matching, and a ubiquitous problem in real applications. The Hamming distance is a simple and well studied example of approximate matching, motivated by typing, or noisy channels. Biological and image processing applications assign a different value to mismatches of different symbols.

We consider the problem of approximate matching in the L_1 metric – the k-L_1-*distance problem*. Given text $T = t_0, ..., t_{n-1}$ and pattern $P = p_0, ..., p_{m-1}$ strings of natural number, and a natural number k, we seek all text locations i where the L_1 distance of the pattern from the length m substring of text starting at i is not greater than k, i.e. $\sum_{j=0}^{m-1} |t_{i+j} - p_j| \leq k$.

We provide an algorithm that solves the k-L_1-distance problem in time $O(n\sqrt{k \log k})$. The algorithm applies a bounded divide-and-conquer approach and makes novel uses of non-boolean convolutions.

1   Introduction

One of the famous "open problems in stringology" [11] was the *k-mismatches problem* whose input is a text string $T = t_0, ..., t_{n-1}$, pattern string $P = p_0, ...,$ $p_{-1}m$, where $p_i, t_j \in \Sigma$, $i = 0, ..., m - 1$; $j = 0, ..., n - 1$, and natural number k. The required output is all locations in T where the pattern matches with no more than k mismatches. A year later, Landau and Vishkin [15] developed an algorithm that solved the problem in time $O(kn)$. That result was achieved via a different algorithm by Galil and Giancarlo [12]. Amir, Lewenstein and Porat [6]

* Partly supported by NSF grant CCR-01-04494 and ISF grant 282/01.
** Partially supported by GIF Young Scientists Program grant 2055-1168.6/2002.

A. Apostolico, M. Crochemore, and K. Park (Eds.): CPM 2005, LNCS 3537, pp. 91–103, 2005.
© Springer-Verlag Berlin Heidelberg 2005

showed an algorithm whose time bounds are $O(n\sqrt{k \log k})$. Karloff [14] showed that the Hamming distance (the number of mismatches at every text location) can be approximately computed in time $O(n \log m)$.

The number of mismatches was an important measure as part of an *edit distance* between typed strings. Advances in Multimedia, Digital Libraries and Computational Biology have shown that a much more generalized theoretical basis of string matching could be of tremendous benefit [20, 21]. To this end, string matching has had to adapt itself to increasingly broader definitions of "matching", as well as different distance measures.

In computer vision, for example, it does not make sense to say that a pattern pixel with a close grey level to the text pixel should generate the same error penalty as, say, a white pattern pixel being matched to a black text pixel. Similarly in biology, the energy level for bonding different proteins is different, suggesting that not all "mismatches" should be counted equally. In various other applications, such as earthquake prediction [18], stock market analysis [17], and music retrieval [22], the distance measure used is the Minkowsky L_1 norm. The L_1 norm is of particular importance also due to the fact that strings can be embedded in the L_1 space and the distance between their associated vectors approximates the *edit distance with moves* of the strings [9].

We also show some results on computing the distance between the pattern and every text location under different metrics [16]. In this paper we are concerned with text and pattern composed of natural numbers. We seek all text locations where the L_1 distance between the pattern and text is bounded by an input value. Formally, our problem is the following.

Definition 1.

1. *Let $X = x_0 x_1 ... x_{n-1}$ and $Y = y_0 y_1 ... y_{n-1}$ be two strings over alphabet Σ. Then the L_1 distance between X and Y ($d_1(X,Y)$) is defined as*

$$d_1(X,Y) =^{def} \sum_{i=0}^{n-1} |x_i - y_i|.$$

2. *The k-L_1-distance problem is defined as follows.*
   INPUT: Text string $T = t_0, ..., t_{n-1}$, pattern string $P = p_0, ..., p_{m-1}$, where $p_i, t_j \in \mathbb{N}$, $i = 0, ..., m - 1$; $j = 0, ..., n - 1$, and natural number k.
   OUTPUT: All text locations i where $d_1(P, T^{(i)}) \leq k$, where $T^{(i)} = t_i t_{i+1} ... t_{i+m-1}$ (i.e. $\sum_{j=0}^{m} |t_{i+j} - p_j| \leq k$).

Lipsky [16] showed that the L_1-distance between the pattern and all text locations can be computed in time $O(n\sqrt{m \log m})$. There is no algorithm that solves the k-L_1-distance problem faster than that, when k is smaller, the equivalent version to Galil's problem for k-mismatches. We show a $O(n\sqrt{k \log k})$ algorithm for the k-L_1-distance problem. Our algorithm employs the *bounded divide-and-conquer* approach, that has proven successful in solving a number of pattern matching problems (e.g. [1, 5, 6]). However, a non-trivial divide-and-conquer approach was necessary. In addition, we make use of non-boolean convolutions, a technique that was pioneered only in the last few year. This technique has proven useful in surprising solutions to some interesting problems in the recent past [2–4, 8]. We also use *counting* arguments for filtration. For the sake of completeness we include the algorithms for L_1, L_p (for even p) and L_∞ matching.

The paper is constructed as follows. In Section 2 we present the algorithms for L_1, L_2 and L_∞ matching. Section 3 gives an immediate and easy $O(nk)$ algorithm, that will serve as a building block for our more efficient algorithm. In section 4 we give an efficient algorithm for a special case, where the pattern has a small alphabet. This will also serve as a subroutine for one of our cases. In section 5 we present the bounded divide-and-conquer algorithm. We conclude with a short discussion and open problems.

2   Matching Algorithms for the L_1, L_2 and L_∞ Metrics

2.1   An L_1 Matching Algorithm

We present here an $O(n\sqrt{m \log m})$-time algorithm that solves the L_1 Matching problem. In fact, we design an $O(n\sqrt{n \log n})$-time algorithm, but we can cut the text into n/m overlapping segments of length $2m$, run the algorithm for each of this segments, and concatenate the results to be the result of our problem, thus achieve an $O(\frac{n}{m} m \sqrt{m \log m}) = O(n\sqrt{m \log m})$-time algorithm. since we use this method of cutting the text, we can assume in our algorithm that $n \leq 2m$. Our algorithm is based on the "high/low-frequency" pattern matching technique of Abrahamson [1]. This technique was introduced in the context of counting mismatches (also known as the *String matching with mismatches* problem). The technique consists of three steps: First, the alphabet is divided into frequent and non-frequent symbols where non-frequent symbols are grouped together and replaced by "frequent" representatives. Next, an $O(n|\Sigma| \log m)$ algorithm is used. Finally corrections are done for the error caused by using representatives instead of original symbols. We will further extend this technique to adapt the L_1 matching problem. Note that instead of alphabet symbols, we now have numbers, since $\Sigma \subset \Re$.

Algorithm Stages
Let $n = |t|$, $m = |p|$ and $k = \sqrt{m/\log m}$ (we can assume $n \leq 2m$).

1. Dividing the alphabet numbers into $O(k)$ intervals.
2. Computing distances of numbers of different intervals.
3. Computing distances of numbers within the same interval.

We discuss each stage in details.

The alphabet numbers are divided into $O(k)$ intervals in the following way: we start by sorting the numbers of both text and pattern into one sorted sequence s. Next we mark each subsequence of a "frequent" number f as an interval $[f, f]$, where *frequent* defined to be a number that appears in s at least $(n+m)/k$ times. Now, we are left with only non-frequent numbers unmarked. Since there are at most k frequent elements, the unmarked numbers are scattered into, at most, $k+1$ sorted continuous pieces of s. We divide each such piece as follows: as long as there are more than $(n+m)/k$ unmarked numbers in this piece, we mark the smallest $(n+m)/k$ numbers as an interval $[min, max]$ (where min and max are the smallest and largest numbers of those $(n+m)/k$ numbers, respectively), and we mark all other instances of max to belong this interval as well. After iterating this step on a continuous piece, either all numbers in this piece are marked into intervals, or at most $(n+m)/k$ numbers are left unmarked. in the latter case we mark those numbers into one interval $[min, max]$, similarly to the others.

Our algorithm analysis is a result of the following claims. Their proofs will be presented in the journal version of this paper and can also be found in [16].

Claim 1 *At the end of the above described process we have the alphabet numbers divided into $O(k)$ disjoint intervals.*

Claim 2 *After dividing the alphabet numbers into $O(k)$ intervals as described above, for each interval which is not of the form $[x, x]$, there are at most $O(m/k)$ numbers which belong to this interval.*

The purpose is to compute $L_1[i] = \sum_{j=1}^{m} |t_{i+j-1} - p_j|$ for every $i = 1, 2, \ldots, n - m+1$. In the second stage we compute a part of it. We ignore all the cases where t_{i+j-1} and p_j are in the same interval and compute the L_1 distance only for numbers from different intervals. Formally, we compute $\forall i \in \{1, \ldots, n - m + 1\} Stage_2[i] = \sum_{j=1}^{m} |t_{i+j-1} - p_j| \overline{\chi_{interval}(t_{i+j-1}, p_j)}$, where $\chi_{interval}(x, y) = 1$ if x and y are within the same interval, and 0 otherwise. This computation is done by two simple convolutions for each interval. In the first convolution we add the p numbers, each as negative ,zero or positive (dependent on its being smaller than the interval numbers, within the interval or greater, respectively), and in the second convolution we do similarly with the text numbers. This is done by $O(k)$ convolutions, one for each interval.

Claim 3 *At the end of the second stage,*

$$Stage_2[i] = \sum_{j=1}^{m} |t_{i+j-1} - p_j| \overline{\chi_{interval}(t_{i+j-1}, p_j)}.$$

Now, we only need to add to the results of $Stage_2$ the distances caused by numbers from the same interval. This is done in a straight forward way. The steps are as follows:

1. Initialize $Stage_3[i] = 0$ for $i = 1, 2, \ldots, n - m + 1$.
2. For every interval I_r (which is not of the form of $[x, x]$)
   (a) For every $t_i, p_j \in I_r$,
       if $j \le i \le n$ then $Stage_3[i - j + 1] \leftarrow Stage_3[i - j + 1] + |t_i - p_j|$.

Claim 4 *At the end of the third stage*

$$Stage_3[i] = \sum_{j=1}^{m} |t_{i+j-1} - p_j| \chi_{interval}(t_{i+j-1}, p_j).$$

Finally, from claim 3 and claim 4 it follows that summing up $Stage_2$ and $Stage_3$ vectors will give us the solution.

Time: Note that we have $n \leq 2m$. The time that is needed for the first stage is the time needed to sort the numbers, $O(m \log m)$, and linear time steps. Next, the second stage consists of $2k$ convolutions; thus taking $O(km \log m)$ time. Finally, the third stage, that runs for each of the $O(k)$ intervals in quadratic time. Now, using claim 2 this stage is bounded by $O(k(\frac{m}{k})^2) = O(m^2/k)$. combining all those bounds, and choosing $k = \sqrt{m/\log m}$ yields an $O(m\sqrt{m \log m})$-time algorithm. If $n > 2m$ we use the technique of cutting the problem into n/m problem instances of text size $2m$, and concatenate the results. The total time, therefore, is $O(\frac{n}{m}m\sqrt{m \log m}) = O(n\sqrt{m \log m})$.

2.2 L_2 Matching and Convolution Equivalence

We show here that the time needed for the convolution computation of the text string with the pattern string is equal to the time needed to solve the L_2 matching problem. The current best time for this convolution computation is $O(n \log n)$, using FFT as described in [10]. Thus, this is also the time needed to compute the L_2 matching. We can slightly improve the L_2 matching time by using the trick of cutting the text into $2m$ consecutive overlapping pieces in order to obtain $O(n \log m)$ instead of $O(n \log n)$.

Observation 1 *Let $L_2[1, \ldots, n-m+1]$ be the result vector of the L_2 matching computation. we observe that:*

$$L_2[i]^2 = \sum_{j=1}^{m} |t_{i+j-1} - p_j|^2 = \underbrace{\sum_{j=1}^{m} t_{i+j-1}^2}_{(1)} + \underbrace{\sum_{j=1}^{m} p_j^2}_{(2)} - \underbrace{2t \otimes p[i]}_{(3)}$$

It is clear that (for all $i's$) computing (1) and (2) elements can be done in linear time. (3) is one convolution that can be computed in time $O(n \log m)$. Then if the values of $L_2[i]$ are computed we can extract (in linear time) the values of $t \otimes p$ and vice versa.

2.3 String Matching with L_∞ Distance

This problem differs from the problems of L_1 and L_2 Matching in the fact that here the distance function defined between strings is not the sum of distances between symbols, but defined on all pairs of symbols. We first construct an $O(n|\Sigma| \log n)$ time algorithm, and then construct an algorithm that approximates L_∞ Matching up to a factor of $1 + \varepsilon$ and works in time of $O(\frac{1}{\varepsilon}n \log m \log |\Sigma|)$.

$O(n|\Sigma| \log(m + |\Sigma|))$ Algorithm:

The method in this algorithm is encoding the text and the pattern in such a way that in one convolution, and linear time pass on the convolution result we find the results.

Key Idea: If we look at one text number, t, and one pattern number p. We encode both of them to a $|\Sigma|$ long binary strings. The encoding of t is all 0's except the t-th bit which is 1, and similarly with p, which is encoded to all 0's except the p-th bit. Let $c(i)$ denote the encoded i. Now, we start by $c(p)$ aligned below $c(t)$ and start at position $-|\Sigma|$ (where $c(t)$ fixed to start at position 1). We move $c(p)$ to the right till both 1-bits are one below the other. At this position, the distance between the starting position of $c(t)$ and the starting position of $c(p)$ equals to the difference $|t-p|$, an example is given in Figure 1. If we look at $r = c(t) \otimes c(p)$ we will have either $r[-|t-p|] = 1$ or $r[|t-p|] = 1$. Extending this idea to encoding strings of numbers requires adding leading (or tracing) zeros between the encoded numbers.

Algorithm Steps

1. Construct $c^t(T) = c^t(t_1) \cdots c^t(t_n)$
2. Construct $c^p(P) = c^p(p_1) \cdots c^p(p_m)$
3. Compute $R = c^t(T) \otimes c^p(P)$
4. For $i = 1, \ldots, n - m + 1$

$$O[i] \leftarrow \max_{s=-|\Sigma|}^{|\Sigma|} \chi_{\neq 0}(R[(2i-1)|\Sigma| + 1 + s]) |s|$$

Claim 5 *At the end of the algorithm* $O[i] = \max_{j=1}^{m} |t_{i+j-1} - p_j|$.

Time: The time needed to convolve 2 strings of size $n|\Sigma|$ and $m|\Sigma|$ is $O(n|\Sigma| \log n)$. The computation of $O[i]$ takes $2|\Sigma|$ steps , and $i = 1, 2, \ldots, n - m + 1$ so this step takes $O(n|\Sigma|)$. Both steps together take $O(n|\Sigma| \log n)$. We can slightly improve the time by using the technique of cutting the text into n/m overlapping segments, each of length $2m$ to a total time of $O(n|\Sigma| \log(m + |\Sigma|))$.

In [16] an algorithm is presented that approximates the L_∞ Matching up to a factor of $1 + \varepsilon$. If ε is taken to be 1 then we can mark all locations where the error is greater than $2k$ and then reduce the alphabet to a cyclic alphabet of size $4k$. Using the above algorithm we get an $O(nk \log m)$ algorithm.

3   The Constant-Time Jump Algorithm

We begin by reviewing the Landau-Vishkin k-mismatches algorithm.

1. Let $a, b \in \Sigma$. Define

$$neq(a, b) =^{def} \begin{cases} 1, & \text{if } a \neq b; \\ 0, & \text{if } a = b. \end{cases}$$

2. Let $X = x_0x_1...x_{n-1}$ and $Y = y_0y_1...y_{n-1}$ be two strings over alphabet Σ. Then the *hamming distance* between X and Y ($ham(X,Y)$) is defined as

$$ham(X,Y) =^{def} \sum_{i=0}^{n-1} neq(x_i, y_i).$$

3. The *The String Matching with k Mismatches* Problem is defined as follows:

   INPUT: Text $T = t_0...t_{n-1}$, pattern $P = p_0...p_{m-1}$, where $t_i, p_j \in \Sigma$, $i = 0,...n-1$; $j = 0,...,m-1$, and a natural number k.

   OUTPUT: All pairs $\langle i, ham(P, T^{(i)}) \rangle$, where i is a text location for which $ham(P, T^{(i)}) \leq k$, where $T^{(i)} = t_i t_{i+1}...t_{i+m-1}$.

Landau and Vishkin [15] introduced a method of using suffix trees (see e.g. [19, 23]) and Lowest Common Ancestor (see e.g. [7, 13]) in order to allow constant-time "jumps" over equal substrings in the text and pattern. Since we are interested only in locations with at most k errors, we can simply start at each text location, and check how many mismatches there are. Every mismatch takes time $O(1)$, since we cover the longest equal substring and land on the next mismatch. If a location has more than k mismatches, we stop. Thus, verification of every location takes time $O(k)$ for a total of $O(nk)$.

The following observation is crucial to our algorithm.

Observation 2 $ham(P, S) \leq d_1(P, S)$.

Proof: Since the alphabet of our strings is $\mathbb{N}$, any two elements p_i, s_j that are not equal have $|p_i - s_j| \geq 1$. $\square$

The above observation, coupled with Landau and Vishkin's method of allowing, for every text location, an $O(1)$ time jump from mismatch to mismatch, gives the following simple algorithm for computing the k-L_1-distance problem. Call it the *Constant-Time Jump Algorithm*. The idea is to add the absolute values of the difference between text and pattern symbol at all mismatches, until the value of k is exceeded (no match) or the pattern is covered (match).

```
C.1.  for every text location i:
          initialize D ← 0.
          while D < k do:
              jump to next mismatch location i + ℓ
              if i + ℓ = i + m + 1 {no mismatches till end of pattern} then end while-loop
              D ← D + |t_{i+ℓ} − p_ℓ|
          endwhile
      endfor
```

Time: Observation 2 guarantees that there will be at most $k + 1$ necessary jumps, and a "jump" takes time $O(1)$, thus the while-loop takes time $O(k)$ per text location i. The for-loop is the length of the text $O(n)$. The total time is, therefore, $O(nk)$.

The Constant-Time Jump Algorithm can prove very useful if we succeed in quickly filtering out locations where there can be no pattern match and leaving for verification a relatively small number of potential candidates. Suppose that number is s. Then the total verification time becomes $O(sk)$. We will show a case where $s = O(\frac{n}{\sqrt{k}})$. The total verification time is then $O(n\sqrt{k})$.

4   The Small Alphabet Case

We now consider the case where P has a very *small* alphabet, e.g. less than u different alphabet symbols. We will use convolutions, as introduced by Fischer and Paterson [10]. We need some definitions first.

Define

$$\chi_\sigma(x) = \begin{cases} 1 \text{ if } x = \sigma \\ 0 \text{ if } x \neq \sigma \end{cases}$$

If $X = x_0 \ldots x_{n-1}$ then $\chi_\sigma(X) = \chi_\sigma(x_0) \ldots \chi_\sigma(x_{n-1})$. For string $S = s_0 \ldots s_{n-1}$, S^R is the reversal of the string, i.e. $s_{n-1} \ldots s_0$.

Define $D_\sigma^1(x) = |x - \sigma|$, and for $X = x_0 \ldots x_{n-1}$, $D_\sigma^1(X) = D_\sigma^1(x_0) \ldots D_\sigma^1(x_{n-1})$.

We return to the L_1 distance problem for small alphabets. The product $D_\sigma^1(T)$ by $\chi_\sigma(P^R)$ is an array where the number in each location is the part of the L_1 distance contributed by the symbol σ in the pattern, i.e. the sum of the absolute value of the difference between every σ in the pattern and its corresponding text element. If we multiply $D_\sigma^1(T)$ by $\chi_\sigma(P)^R$, for every $\sigma \in \Sigma$, and add the results, we get the total L_1 distance. Since polynomial multiplication can be done in time $O(n \log m)$ using FFT, and we do $|\Sigma| = u$ multiplications, the total time for finding all mismatches using this scheme is $O(un \log m)$.

In our divide-and-conquer algorithm, we will reduce to a case where the alphabet size is $O(\sqrt{k/\log m})$, so the problem will be solved in time $O(n\sqrt{k \log m})$.

5   The Algorithm

We are now ready to present the general algorithm.

Definition 2. *A symbol that appears in the pattern at least $2\sqrt{k \log m}$ times is called frequent. A symbol that is not frequent is called rare.*

We consider two cases, where there exist at least $\sqrt{k/\log m}$ frequent symbols, and where the number of frequent symbols is smaller than $\sqrt{k}$. We begin with the large number of frequent symbols.

5.1   Many Frequent Symbols

Lemma 1. *Let $\{a_1, \ldots, a_{\sqrt{k/\log m}}\}$ be frequent symbols. Then there exist in the text at most $\frac{2n\sqrt{\log m}}{\sqrt{k}}$ locations where there is a pattern occurrence with no more than k mismatch errors.*

Proof: By counting. Choose $2\sqrt{k\log m}$ occurrences of every frequent symbol and call them the *relevant* occurrences. For every text element t_i, mark all locations where a pattern occurrence would match t_i, in case t_i is one of the frequent symbols $\{a_1, ..., a_{\sqrt{k/\log m}}\}$ and the match is one of the relevant occurrences. In other words, we mark all locations $i - j$ where $t_i = p_j$, $t_i \in \{a_1, ..., a_{\sqrt{k/\log m}}\}$, and p_j is a relevant occurrence of t_i.

The total number of marks we made is at most $n2\sqrt{k\log m}$. The only cases that interest us are those where no more than k errors occur. Consider a fixed text location as a start of a pattern occurrence. If more than k of our $\sqrt{k/\log m}$ frequent symbols and their $2\sqrt{k\log m}$ relevant occurrences are mismatches, then there clearly does not exist a pattern occurrence with less than k mismatches. Thus, any text location with less than k marks, can not be a pattern occurrence.

Since the total number of marks is $n2\sqrt{k\log m}$ and each potential pattern occurrence must have at least k marks, it leaves us with at most $\frac{n2\sqrt{k\log m}}{k} = \frac{2\sqrt{\log m}\,n}{\sqrt{k}}$ candidates.   □

Because of Observation 2, we know that every location that has been discarded for having more than k mismatch errors, can certainly not have L_1 distance less than k. Thus we only need to verify the remaining $O(\frac{n\sqrt{\log m}}{\sqrt{k}})$ locations.

Verification: Each of the remaining $O(\frac{n\sqrt{\log m}}{\sqrt{k}})$ potential locations can be verified in time $O(k)$ per location by the Constant-Time Jump Algorithm described in section 3 for a total $O(n\sqrt{k\log m})$ time.

Finding the Potential Locations: The $\frac{2n\sqrt{\log m}}{\sqrt{k}}$ potential pattern starts can be found in time $O(n\sqrt{k\log m})$ as shown in [6].

5.2   Few Frequent Symbols

We are left with the case of few frequent symbols (less than $O(\sqrt{k/\log m})$). We show how to count the L_1 distance contributed by the frequent symbols, and how to count the L_1 distance contributed by the rare symbols.

The L_1 distance of the frequent symbols can be computed using the algorithm in Section 4. The only remaining task is to show that the total L_1 distance contribution of all the rare symbols can be computed fast.

We handle the rare cases differently depending on the following two situations:

1. The total number of occurrences of rare symbols in the pattern is not greater than $2k$.
2. The total number of occurrances of rare symbols in the pattern is greater than $2k$.

Few Rare Symbols. We show a reduction of the k-L_1 distance problem to convolutions. Recall that the case we are considering is where we have at most $2k$

occurrences of rare numbers, where each rare number occurrs at most $2\sqrt{k \log m}$ times.

Algorithm Outline:
Sort all $2k$ occurrences of rare elements, and divide them into $O(\sqrt{k/\log m})$ consecutive blocks, each of size between $2\sqrt{k \log m}$ and $4\sqrt{k \log m}$, such that all occurrences of every symbol appear in a single block. We are guaranteed that such a division can be achieved since no symbol appears more than $2\sqrt{k \log m}$ times.

For every one of the $O(\sqrt{k/\log m})$ blocks two convolutions. These convolutions compute the L_1 distance of the elements of the block with all text elements **greater** than the elements in the block, as well as the L_1 distance of the elements of the block with all text elements **smaller** than the block symbols.

Adding the L_1 distances of all blocks provides the L_1 distance of the pattern at every text location.

We now compute the L_1 distance of every text element with all block symbols in whose range it is.

Adding the above two values we get the L_1 distance of the block symbols with the text.

Algorithm Time: Each convolution takes $O(n \log m)$ time. Two convolutions are done for each of the $O(\sqrt{k/\log m})$ blocks, for a total of $O(n\sqrt{k \log m})$ time. We will show that the L_1 distance of the block with all text elements whose range is the same as the block symbols can be done in time $O(n\sqrt{k \log m})$ for a total time of $O(n\sqrt{k \log m})$

Details of Convolutions:
Consider block B whose smallest number is a and whose largest number is b. Define
$$\chi_B(x) = \begin{cases} 1 \text{ if } a \leq x \leq b \\ 0 \text{ otherwise} \end{cases}$$

For $X = x_0 \ldots x_{n-1}$, let $\chi_B(X) = \chi_B(x_0) \ldots \chi_B(x_{n-1})$.
Let
$$Diff_B(x) = \begin{cases} -x & \text{if } x < a \\ 0 & \text{if } a \leq x \leq b \\ x & \text{if } x > b \end{cases}$$

For $X = x_0 \ldots x_{n-1}$, let $Diff_B(X) = Diff_B(x_0) \ldots Diff_B(x_{n-1})$.

The convolution $Diff_B(T) \otimes \chi_B(P^R)$ adds the correct contribution of the text element to the absolute value of the difference with the corresponding pattern symbol, since we subtract the text number if it is smaller than the pattern number, and add it if it is bigger. We now need to add the appropriate pattern part (add if it is bigger than the corresponding text number and subtract, otherwose). This is done by the following convolution:
Define
$$I_B(x) = \begin{cases} x \text{ if } a \leq x \leq b \\ 0 \text{ otherwise} \end{cases}$$

For $X = x_0 \ldots x_{n-1}$, let $I_B(X) = I_B(x_0) \ldots I_B(x_{n-1})$.

Let

$$Sign_B(x) = \begin{cases} 1 & \text{if } x < a \\ 0 & \text{if } a \leq x \leq b \\ -1 & \text{if } x > b \end{cases}$$

For $X = x_0 \ldots x_{n-1}$, let $Sign_B(X) = Sign_B(x_0) \ldots Sign_B(x_{n-1})$.

The convolution $Sign_B(T) \otimes I_B(P^R)$ adds the correct contribution of the pattern element to the absolute value of the difference with the corresponding text symbol, since we subtract the pattern number if it is smaller than the text number, and add it if it is bigger.

Details of the Block Distance to Text Numbers in its Range:
We have not computed the L_1 distance of the numbers in block B, with any text number x within its range, i.e. $a < x < b$, where a is the smallest and b is the largest number in block B.

This can be computed simultaneously for all blocks if we view the problem from the text side. Simply scan all text elements and for each one compute the appropriate L_1 distance with **all** pattern numbers in block B. Since the block size is $O(\sqrt{k \log m})$, the total time for this step is $O(n\sqrt{k \log m})$.

Many Rare Symbols. The final case we need to consider is where we have more than $2k$ occurrences of rare numbers, where each rare number occurrs at most $2\sqrt{k \log m}$ times.

We construct a new pattern, where we choose $2k$ occurrences of rare numbers in the pattern, and ignore all others. For these occurrences we compute the L_1 distance using the algorithm in Subsection 5.2. Any text location whose computed (partial) L_1 distance exceeds k can be discareded immediately. For each of the remaining candidate locations, we employ the Constant-Time Jump Algorithm of section 3. The following lemma shows that the number of locations where the L_1 distance is less than k is small.

Lemma 2. *Assume the partial L_1 distance was computed for the $2k$ rare symbols in the pattern. Then there exist in the text at most $\frac{2n\sqrt{\log m}}{\sqrt{k}}$ locations where the L_1 distance is less than k.*

Proof: By counting. Assume that for every text element t_i, we had marked all locations where a pattern occurrence would match t_i. In other words, we mark all locations $i - j$ where $t_i = p_j$, where p_j is one of the considered $2k$ pattern symbols.

For reason similar to those in Lemma 1, there are at most $\frac{2n\sqrt{\log m}}{\sqrt{k}}$ locations where there are more than k matches. However, every location where there are not k matches has more than k mismatches and, by Observation 2, has L_1 distance greater than k. Consequently, every location with L_1 distance less than k has at least k matches. So the total number of locations with L_1 distance less than k does not exceed $\frac{2n\sqrt{\log m}}{\sqrt{k}}$. $\qquad\square$

Verification: Each of the remaining $O(\frac{n\sqrt{\log m}}{\sqrt{k}})$ potential locations can be verified in time $O(k)$ per location by the Constant-Time Jump Algorithm described in section 3 for a total $O(n\sqrt{k \log m})$ time.

6   Discussion and Open Problems

It should be remarked that for $k > m$ the algorithm to be used is that of Lipsky [16] for a time of $O(n\sqrt{m \log m})$. We should also explain the discrepancy between our promissed time of $O(n\sqrt{k \log k})$ and delivered time of $O(n\sqrt{k \log m})$. The reason is that our algorithm is intended for use only in case of $m^{1/3} < k < m$, where $\log m = O(\log k)$. For smaller k, we can adapt the algorithm of [6] to find the L_1 distance in time $O((n + \frac{nk^3}{m}) \log k)$. Details of this adaptation are left for the journal version of this paper.

We believe that it is important to develop efficient algorithms for approximate matching using various Minkowsky metrics as distance functions. We showed here and algorithm for the L_1 metric. A challenge would be an approximate matching algorithm for the L_∞ metric.

References

1. K. Abrahamson. Generalized string matching. *SIAM J. Comp.*, 16(6):1039–1051, 1987.
2. A. Amir, A. Aumann, R. Cole, M. Lewenstein, and E. Porat. Function matching: Algorithms, applications, and a lower bound. In *Proc. 30th ICALP*, pages 929–942, 2003.
3. A. Amir, R. Cole, R. Hariharan, M. Lewenstein, and E. Porat. Overlap matching. *Information and Computation*, 181(1):57–74, 2003.
4. A. Amir, E. Eisenberg, and E. Porat. Swap and mismatch edit distance. In *Proc. 12th Annual European Symposium on Algorithms (ESA)*, pages 16–27, 2004.
5. A. Amir and M. Farach. Efficient 2-dimensional approximate matching of half-rectangular figures. *Information and Computation*, 118(1):1–11, April 1995.
6. A. Amir, M. Lewenstein, and E. Porat. Faster algorithms for string matching with k mismatches. *J. Algorithms*, 2004.
7. O. Berkman, D. Breslauer, Z. Galil, B. Schieber, and U. Vishkin. Highly parallelizable problems. *Proc. 21st ACM Symposium on Theory of Computation*, pages 309–319, 1989.
8. R. Cole and R. Hariharan. Verifying candidate matches in sparse and wildcard matching. In *Proc. 34st Annual Symposium on the Theory of Computing (STOC)*, pages 592–601, 2002.
9. G. Cormode and S. Muthukrishnan. The string edit distance matching problem with moves. In *Proc. 13th annual ACM-SIAM Symposium on Discrete Algorithms (SODA)*, pages 667–676. Society for Industrial and Applied Mathematics, 2002.
10. M.J. Fischer and M.S. Paterson. String matching and other products. *Complexity of Computation, R.M. Karp (editor), SIAM-AMS Proceedings*, 7:113–125, 1974.
11. Z. Galil. Open problems in stringology. In Z. Galil A. Apostolico, editor, *Combinatorial Algorithms on Words*, volume 12, pages 1–8. NATO ASI Series F, 1985.
12. Z. Galil and R. Giancarlo. Improved string matching with k mismatches. *SIGACT News*, 17(4):52–54, 1986.
13. D. Harel and R.E. Tarjan. Fast algorithms for finding nearest common ancestor. *Computer and System Science*, 13:338–355, 1984.
14. H. Karloff. Fast algorithms for approximately counting mismatches. *Information Processing Letters*, 48(2):53–60, 1993.

15. G. M. Landau and U. Vishkin. Efficient string matching with k mismatches. *Theoretical Computer Science*, 43:239–249, 1986.

16. O. Lipsky. Efficient distance computations. Master's thesis, Bar-Ilan University, Department of Computer Science, Ramat-Gan 52900, ISRAEL, 2003.

17. E. Maasoumi and J. Racine. Entropy and predictability of stock market returns. *Journal of Econometrics*, 107(1):291–312, 3 2002. available at http://ideas.repec.org/a/eee/econom/v107y2002i1-2p291-312.html.

18. L. Malagnini, R.B. Herman, and M. Di Bona. Ground motion scaling in the apennines (italy). *Bull. Seism. Soc. Am.*, 90:1062–1081, 2000.

19. E. M. McCreight. A space-economical suffix tree construction algorithm. *J. of the ACM*, 23:262–272, 1976.

20. M. V. Olson. A time to sequence. *Science*, 270:394–396, 1995.

21. A. Pentland. Invited talk. NSF Institutional Infrastructure Workshop, 1992.

22. I. Shmulevich, O. Yli-Harja, E. Coyle, D. Povel, and K. Lemstrom. Perceptual issues in music pattern recognition — complexity of rhythm and key finding, April 1999.

23. P. Weiner. Linear pattern matching algorithm. *Proc. 14 IEEE Symposium on Switching and Automata Theory*, pages 1–11, 1973.

An Efficient Algorithm
for Generating Super Condensed Neighborhoods

Luís M.S. Russo* and Arlindo L. Oliveira

IST / INESC-ID, R. Alves Redol 9, 1000 Lisboa, Portugal
aml@inesc-id.pt, lsr@algos.inesc-id.pt

Abstract. Indexing methods for the approximate string matching problem spend a considerable effort generating condensed neighborhoods. Here, we point out that condensed neighborhoods are not a minimal representation of a pattern neighborhood. We show that we can restrict our attention to super condensed neighborhoods which are minimal. We then present an algorithm for generating Super Condensed Neighborhoods. The algorithm runs in $O(m\lceil m/w\rceil s)$, where m is the pattern size, s is the size of the super condensed neighborhood and w the size of the processor word. Previous algorithms took $O(m\lceil m/w\rceil c)$ time, where c is the size of the condensed neighborhood. We further improve this algorithm by using Bit-Parallelism and Increased Bit-Parallelism techniques. Our experimental results show that the resulting algorithm is very fast.

1 Introduction

Approximate string matching is useful in areas of computer science as text searching, pattern recognition, signal processing and computational biology. The problem is to retrieve all segments, of a large text string whose *edit distance* to a shorter pattern string is at most k. If the text is large enough, an efficient algorithm must preprocess the text. This approach has been actively researched in recent years [1, 3, 8, 10, 14, 16, 17]. Hybrid algorithms that divide their time into a *neighborhood generation* phase and a *filtration* phase are the current state of the art.

In this paper we focus our attention on improving the *neighborhood generation* phase of such algorithms.

2 Basic Concepts and Notation

2.1 Strings

Definition 1. *A string is a finite sequence of symbols taken from a finite alphabet Σ. The empty string is denoted by ϵ. The size of a string S is denoted by $|S|$.*

---

* Supported by the Portuguese Science and Technology Foundation through program POCTI and project POSI/EEI/10204/2001 and Project BIOGRID POSI/SRI/ 47778/2002

A. Apostolico, M. Crochemore, and K. Park (Eds.): CPM 2005, LNCS 3537, pp. 104–115, 2005.

By $S[i]$ we denote the symbol at position i of S and by $S[i..j]$ the substring from position i to position j or ϵ if $i > j$. Also we denote by $S\langle i \rangle$ the point[1] in between letters $S[i-1]$ and $S[i]$. $S\langle 0 \rangle$ represents the first point and $S\langle i-1..j \rangle$ denotes $S[i..j]$.

2.2 Computing Edit Distance

Definition 2. *The* edit *or* Levenshtein *distance between two strings* ed(S, S') *is the smallest number of edit operations that transform S into S'. We consider as operations insertions (I), deletions (D) and substitutions (S).*

For example: D S I

                                          abcd

$ed(abcd, bedf) = 3$ bedf

The edit distance between strings S and S' is computed by filling up a dynamic programming table $D[i,j] = ed(S\langle 0..i \rangle, S'\langle 0..j \rangle)$, constructed as follows:

$$D[i,0] = i, \qquad D[0,j] = j$$
$$D[i+1,j+1] = D[i,j], \text{ if } S[i+1] = S'[j+1]$$
$$1 + \min\{D[i+1,j], D[i,j+1], D[i,j]\}, \text{otherwise}$$

Table 1 is an example of the dynamic programming table D. According to the definition,
$$ed(abbaa, ababaac) = ed(S, S') = D[|S|, |S'|] = D[5,7] = 2.$$

Table 1. Table $D[i,j]$ for *abbaa* and *ababaac*.

col		0	1	2	3	4	5	6	7
row			a	b	a	b	a	a	c
0		0	1	2	3	4	5	6	7
1	a	1	0	1	2	3	4	5	6
2	b	2	1	0	1	2	3	4	5
3	b	3	2	1	1	1	2	3	4
4	a	4	3	2	1	2	1	2	3
5	a	5	4	3	2	2	2	1	2

2.3 Finding Approximate Matches

For the purpose of finding matches, a useful variation of this table is table $D'[i,j] = \min_{0 \leq l \leq j}\{ed(S\langle 0..i \rangle, S'\langle l \; .. \; j \rangle)\}$, computed as table D but setting $D[0,j] = 0$, as shown in table 2.

According to the definition, line $D'[|S|, j]$ stores the smallest edit distance between S and a substring of S' starting at some point l and ending at j. Suppose

---

[1] The notion of point is superfluous but it helps in the definition of a simple and coherent notation.

Table 2. (Left)Table $D'[i, j]$ for *abbaa* and *ababaac*. (Section 3) Improper canonical paths are indicated by arrows, (Section 4) improper cell bits are indicated on tracebacks. (Right) Binary representation of column 1.

col	0	1	2	3	4	5	6	7	VAL
row		a	b	a	b	a	a	c	2 1 0
0	0	0	0	0	0	0	0	0	
a 1	↑0 1	↖0 0	1 ⋰1	⋰1 0	1 ⋰1	⋰1 0	⋰1 0	1 ⋰1	0 0 0
b 2	↑0 2	0 ↑ 1	↖0 0	1 ⋰1	⋰1 0	1 ⋰1	1 ⋰1	⋰1 1	0 0 1
b 3	↑0 3	0 ↑ 2	0 ↑ 1	↖0 1	1 ⋰1	⋰1 1	1 ⋰1	1 ⋰2	0 1 0
a 4	↑0 4	0 ↑ 3	0 ↑ 2	↖0 1	1 ⋰2	⋰1 1	⋰1 1	1 ⋯2	0 1 1
a 5	↑0 5	0 ↑ 4	0 ↑ 3	0 ↑ 2	↖0 2	1 ⋰2	⋰1 1	⋰1 2	1 0 0

we want to find all occurrences of *abbaa* in *ababaac* with at most one error. By looking at row $D'[5, j]$ we find out that such occurrences can end only in point 6. In particular there are two such occurrences *ababaa* and *abaa*.

Definition 3. *A cell in D or D' is active iff its value is smaller than k.*

Take $k = 1$ for our example. In tables 1 and 2 inactive cells are shaded.

A complete up to date survey on this problem has been presented by Navarro [12].

3   Indexed Approximate Pattern Matching

3.1   Overview

If we wish to find the occurrences of P in T in sub-linear time, i.e. $O(|T|^{\alpha})$ for $\alpha < 1$, we can use an index structure for T. Suffix arrays [13] and q-grams have been proposed in the literature [8, 10].

These algorithms are hybrid in the sense that they find a tradeoff between neighborhood generation and filtration techniques.

3.2   Neighborhood Generation

A first and simple-minded approach to the problem consists in generating all the words at distance k from P and looking them up in the index.

Definition 4. *The* k-neighborhood *of S is* $U_k(S) = \{S' \in \Sigma^* : ed(S, S') \leq k\}$

Since $U_k(S)$ turns out to be quite large ($|U_k(S)| = O(|S|^k|\Sigma|^k)$) [15], we restrict our attention to the *condensed k-neighborhood*.

Definition 5. *The* condensed k-neighborhood *of S, $CU_k(S)$ is the largest subset of $U_k(S)$ whose elements S' verify the following property: if S'' is a proper prefix of S' then $ed(S, S'') > k$.*

Algorithm 1 generates $CU_k(P)$ [2]².

Algorithm 1 Condensed Neighborhood Generator Algorithm.

```
1:  procedure SEARCH(Search State s, Current String v)
2:      if IS_MATCH_STATE(s) then
3:          REPORT(v)
4:      else if EXTENDS_TO_MATCH_STATE(s) then
5:          for z ∈ Σ do
6:              s' ← UPDATE(s, z)
7:              SEARCH(s', v.z)
8:          end for
9:      end if
10: end procedure
11: SEARCH(⟨0, 1, ..., |P|⟩, ε)
```

The search state (s) is a dynamic programming column of D associated to P. The IS_MATCH_STATE predicate checks whether the last cell is active. The EXTENDS_TO_MATCH_STATE predicate checks whether there are active cells in s. The UPDATE procedure computes the dynamic programming column that results from applying a to s.

For example, if s is column 5 of table 1, then the IS_MATCH_STATE predicate returns false, since cell $D[5, 5]$ is inactive. The EXTENDS_TO_MATCH_STATE, on the other hand, returns true, since cell $D[4, 5]$ is active. The UPDATE procedure computes column 6 from column 5 and a. When s is column 6, the IS_MATCH_STATE evaluates to true and the algorithm reports *ababaa* as being at distance 1 from *abbaa*. This way column 7 never gets evaluated. Let us skip line 5 for $z = b$. If $z = c$ and s is column 5 then the UPDATE procedure returns $\langle 6, 5, 4, 3, 2, 2 \rangle$. In this case both the IS_MATCH_STATE and the EXTENDS_TO_MATCH_STATE predicates fail and the search backtracks.

The reason why the *condensed neighborhood* is important is that it represents the *k-neighborhood*.

Lemma 1. *If $S \in U_k(S')$ then some prefix of S is in $CU_k(S')$.*

---

² We can shortcut the generate and search cycle by running algorithm 1 on the index structure. For example in the suffix tree this can be done by using a tree node instead of v.

We can generalize the idea and think of representing U_k by substrings instead of only by prefixes. This leads to the notion of *super condensed neighborhood*.

Definition 6. *The* super condensed k-neighborhood *of* S, $SCU_k(S)$ *is the largest subset of* $U_k(S)$ *whose elements* S' *verify the following property: if* S'' *is a proper substring of* S' *then* $ed(S, S'') > k$.

The *super condensed neighborhood* represents the *k-neighborhood* as follows:

Lemma 2. *If* $S \in U_k(S')$ *then some substring of* S *is in* $SCU_k(S')$.

In our example $ababaa$ and $abaa$ are in the *condensed neighborhood* of $abbaa$, but only $abaa$ is in the *super condensed neighborhood*.

It is easy to see that the *Super Condensed k-neighborhood* is minimal, since any subset of $U_k(P)$ that represents it (as in lemma 2) must contain $SCU_k(P)$, for a word in $SCU_k(P)$ can only be represented by itself.

Definition 7. *A traceback is a pointer from cell* $D'[i, j]$ *to a predecessor neighbor cell, given by the following conditions:*

vertical $D'[i + 1, j] \to D'[i, j]$ *iff* $D'[i + 1, j] = 1 + D'[i, j]$
diagonal $D'[i + 1, j + 1] \to D'[i, j]$ *iff*
$\quad D'[i + 1, j + 1] = 1 + D'[i, j]$ *or* $S[i + 1] = S'[j + 1]$
horizontal $D'[i, j + 1] \to D'[i, j]$ *iff* $D'[1, j + 1] = 1 + D'[i, j]$

A canonical traceback for $D'[i, j]$ *is the first traceback that* $D'[i, j]$ *has in the ordering above.*

A canonical path is a path in D' made of canonical tracebacks. We refer to a canonical path as improper if it ends in $D[0, 0]$ (see table 2). The idea behind canonical paths is that they always show the rightmost position of a minimal match between S and a substring of S'.

Definition 8. *A cell* $D'[i, j]$ *is improper iff its canonical path is improper.*

The denomination improper is motivated by the following lemma.

Lemma 3. *If* $D'[i, j]$ *is an improper cell then* $D[i, j] = D'[i, j]$.

This is a a direct consequence from the observation that improper cells start matching from point 0 just like the cells in D. In fact the converse of the lemma is also true.

Computing the *super condensed neighborhood* can also be done by algorithm 1 but we change our states to columns of D' and restrict our attention to improper active cells.

Observe that, in this version of the algorithm, the string $ababaa$ is no longer reported. In fact it can be seen that in column 4 of table 2 there are no active improper cells and hence neither column 5 nor column 6 get evaluated.

A theoretical time analysis shows that this new algorithm runs in $O(m^2 |SCU_k(P)|)$, while the previous algorithm takes $O(m^2 |CU_k(P)|)$.

In [10] Myers proved that $|CU_k(P)| = O(|P|^{pow(|P|/k)})$, where:

$$pow(\alpha) = \log_{|\Sigma|} \frac{(\alpha^{-1} + \sqrt{1+\alpha^{-2}})+1}{(\alpha^{-1} + \sqrt{1+\alpha^{-2}})-1} + \alpha \log_{|\Sigma|}(\alpha^{-1} + \sqrt{1+\alpha^{-2}}) + \alpha$$

It is hard to improve on this bound for the *super condensed neighborhood* so $|SCU_k(P)| = O(|P|^{pow(|P|/k)})$. However there is a clear practical improvement, as we show in the results section.

4   Bit Parallel Implementation

Myers presented a way to parallelize the computation of D and D' [11] that reduces the complexity of computing a dynamic programming table to $O(m\lceil m/w \rceil)$ were w is the size of the computer word. In our aplication the $\lceil m/w \rceil$ tipicaly takes the value 1 since $m = \Theta(\log_\sigma n)$ for hybrid algorithms.This leads to a complexity of $O(m)$.

Heikki Hyrrö presented a modification of Myers algorithm [5] that we will now describe and extend to solve our problem.

Ukkonen was the first to notice the following properties of D and D' [15]:

Diagonal Property $D[i+1, j+1] - D[i, j] = 0$ or 1
Vertical Adjacency Property $D[i+1, j] - D[i, j] = $ -1, 0 or 1
Horizontal Adjacency Property $D[i, j+1] - D[i, j] = $ -1, 0 or 1

The following bit-vectors can then be used to represent and compute columns of D'.

Vertical Positive $VP[i+1, j] = 1$ iff $D[i+1, j] - D[i, j] = 1$
Vertical Negative $VN[i+1, j] = 1$ iff $D[i+1, j] - D[i, j] = -1$
Horizontal Positive $HP[i, j+1] = 1$ iff $D[i, j+1] - D[i, j] = 1$
Horizontal Negative $HN[i, j+1] = 1$ iff $D[i, j+1] - D[i, j] = -1$
Diagonal Zero $D0[i+1, j+1] = 1$ iff $D[i+1, j+1] = D[i, j]$
Pattern Match Vectors $PM_z[i] = 1$ iff $P[i] = z$, for each $z \in \Sigma$

The above bit-vectors are packed in computer words along i, i.e. by columns. In algorithm 2 we show how to compute a column of D'.

The procedure UPDATE of algorithm 2 is essentially the algorithm explained in the original work on bit parallelism [5, 11].

We will now show how the UPDATE_PROPER_CELLS procedure works. We define an improper cell vector $CP1$ to account for improper cells.

Improper Cells $CP1[i, j] = 1$ iff $D'[i, j]$ is a proper cell.

Table 2 shows an example of this computaion. Since we assume the bit vectors are of size m we can't store this information for the cells in row 0. This is not a big problem since apart, except for cell $D'[0, 0]$, all other $D'[0, j]$ cells are inactive. Special care must hence be taken to update the proper cells of column 1. This can be done by suffices changing the 1 in line 26 for $VP \& 1$.

The single purpose of line 23 is to discover whether the first improper cell in a column will became proper in the next column. For example, in table 2, the first

---

Algorithm 2 Bit-Parallel Algorithm, bitwise operations in C-style.

1: **procedure** INITIALIZE(Pattern P)
2:     $VP \leftarrow (1^m)_2$
3:     $VN \leftarrow (0^m)_2$
4:     **For** $z \in \Sigma$ **Do** $PM_z \leftarrow (0^m)_2$
5:     **For** $1 \leq i \leq m$ **Do** $PM_{P[i]}| \leftarrow 2^{i-1}$
6:     $CP1 \leftarrow 0$
7:     $VAL_0 \leftarrow (10101010 \ldots)_2$
8:     $VAL_1 \leftarrow (01100110 \ldots)_2$
9:     $\vdots$
10:     **return** $VP, VN, CP1, VAL_0, \ldots, VAL_{\lceil \log m \rceil - 1}$
11: **end procedure**
12: **procedure** UPDATE(Previous Column (VP, VN, $CP1$, VAL_0, $\ldots$, $VAL_{\lceil \log m \rceil - 1}$), Letter z)
13:     $D0 \leftarrow (((PM_z \ \& \ VP) + VP)^\wedge VP)|PM_z|VN$
14:     $HP \leftarrow VN| \sim (D0|VP)$
15:     $HN \leftarrow VP \ \& \ D0$
16:     $VAL_0, \ldots, VAL_{\lceil \log m \rceil} \leftarrow$ CARRY_EFFECT(HP, HN, VAL_0, $\ldots$, $VAL_{\lceil \log m \rceil - 1}$)
17:     $VP \leftarrow (HN << 1)| \sim (D0|(HP << 1))$
18:     $VN \leftarrow (HP << 1) \ \& \ D0$
19:     $CP1 \leftarrow$ UPDATE_PROPER_CELLS($CP1$, PM_z, HN, VN, VP)
20:     **return** VP, VN, $CP1$, VAL_0, $\ldots$, $VAL_{\lceil \log m \rceil - 1}$
21: **end procedure**
22: **procedure** UPDATE_PROPER_CELLS($CP1$, PM, HN, VN, VP)
23:     $CP1 \leftarrow ((PM|HN| \sim VN) \ \& \ ((CP1 << 1)|1))|CP1$
24:     $CP1| \leftarrow VP$
25:     $CP1 \leftarrow (CP1 >> 1)$
26:     $CP1 \leftarrow (CP1 + 1)^\wedge CP1$
27:     **return** $CP1$
28: **end procedure**
29: **procedure** CARRY_EFFECT(HP, HN, VAL_0, $\ldots$, $VAL_{\lceil \log m \rceil - 1}$)
30:     $carry \leftarrow HP \mid HN$
31:     $VAL_0 \leftarrow carry^\wedge VAL_0$
32:     $carry \ \& \leftarrow HN^\wedge VAL_0$
33:     $VAL_1 \leftarrow carry^\wedge VAL_1$
34:     $carry \ \& \leftarrow HN^\wedge VAL_1$
35:     $\vdots$
36:     $VAL_{\lceil \log m \rceil - 1} \leftarrow carry^\wedge VAL_{\lceil \log m \rceil - 1}$
37: **end procedure**

---

improper cell of column 3 is $D'[3,3]$. What line 1 does is to check whether the canonical traceback of $D'[3,4]$ is non-horizontal. An horizontal canonical traceback respects the condition $\sim PM\& \sim HN\&VN$, (see cells $D'[3,6]$, $D'[3,7]$, $D'[4,6]$ and $D'[4,7]$).

Line 24 of algorithm 2 adds the vertical dependences to the list of improper cells since, if a cell has a vertical canonical traceback to a proper cell, then it is also proper. By introducing vertical dependencies line 24 also activates some unnecessary bits. In order to determine which bits actually represent improper cells we shift $CP1$ (line 25) and send a carry through it (line 26). The carry stops in the last improper cell. Finally we clean up the unnecessary bits and restore the ones eliminated by the carry by doing a xor with the previous $CP1$ (line 26). The $\sim CP1$ provides a mask of improper cells.

Keeping track of which cells are active can be done in several ways.

WHILE Keeping a pointer to the lowest active cell and moving upwards.

NFA Using a bit parallel implementation of an NFA for approximate pattern matching [17] similar to [13].

CARRY Storing the values of D' in computer words.

The pointer solution is as far as we know the standard solution to this problem. If k is small the NFA solution becomes viable since it uses k state vectors, i.e. computer words.

The idea of the CARRY solution is to store the values of D' in an unorthodox way. Values are stored across computer words instead of in a single one. This solution requires $\lceil \log |P| \rceil$ computer words, the VAL vectors. We define $VAL_k[i, j]$ as the $(k + 1)$ digit in the binary representation of $D'[i, j]$. For an example, see table 2.

Updating the VAL vectors is a matter of simulating the carry effect of the ALU. This is implemented in the CARRY_EFFECT procedure. We propagate the addition and subtraction carries in the same word.

It is enough to identify active cells whose value is k. In our example this can be done by evaluating $\sim \text{VAL}_0$ & VAL_1 & $\sim \text{VAL}_2$.

A final improvement is to adapt the previous algorithm so that it works in an increased bit-parallelism fashion [7]. The idea of increased bit parallelism is to tile the computer word with more than one D' column and compute more than one D' column per instruction. In this approach the algorithm that is used is essentially the same but one must redefine the "+", ">>", "<<" operations to respect the column boundaries. The 1's must also be replaced accordingly.

Our approach was to move the instruction 6 of algorithm 1 to the exterior of the for cycle (instruction 5). In this case we had to make the UPDATE procedure update the column for all the letters of Σ. This was done by concatenating all the PM_z vectors into a single PM vector. We also had to copy the values of the D' column $|\Sigma|$ times into the computer word just before instruction 7. This was done by $>>$ and $|$ operations.

5 Experimental Results

We investigated the ratio between the average size of the condensed neighborhood versus the size of super condensed neighborhood (figure 1). This was done by generating the neighborhoods of 50 random patterns.

Next we verified that this ratio among averages translated into the time performance of the algorithm for patterns of size 16 where no partition occurs (table 3). This was done by comparing Myers implementation with ours. For this we tested 1000 random patterns on random text. These implementations do not yet resort to bit-parallelism.

These tests were performed in a 2.40 Ghz Intel Xeon processor, 4 GB RAM, Linux OS 2.4.20-28.7smp and gcc 2.96.

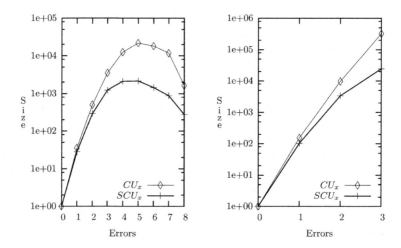

Fig. 1. Average size of the condensed neighborhood versus the super condensed neighborhood for $|P| = 16$ and $|\Sigma| = 2$ (left), $|P| = 6$ and $|\Sigma| = 16$ (right).

Table 3. Average time of Myers algorithm for $|P| = 16$ and $|\Sigma| = 2$.

Errors	1	2	3	4	5	6	7	8
$CU - time(ms)$	1.31	1.59	3.24	7.95	13.15	11.71	7.15	4.21
$SCU - time(ms)$	1.28	1.54	2.38	3.28	3.59	3.27	2.98	2.41

Finally we tested the bit-parallel version and the increased bit-parallel version for patterns of size 8 using a 800MHz PowerPC G3 processor with 512K level 2 cache 640MB SDRAM, Mac Os X 10.2.8 and gcc 3.3. The results are shown in Table 4[3].

The first row shows the times needed to generate *Condensed Neighborhoods* while the next three rows show the times needed to generate *Super Condensed Neighborhoods* with our three alternatives. The three final rows show the times

---

[3] Please note that some of the results in table 4 are out of the sub-linear region of the index. This will be corrected by extending our prototype to larger $|\Sigma|$. The graphics in figure 1 show that this should produce even better results.

Table 4. Bit-parallel and increased bit-parallel algorithms in milliseconds.

	$|\Sigma| = 2$		$|\Sigma| = 4$	
	$k = 2$	$k = 4$	$k = 2$	$k = 4$
CU_k	0.036	0.013	1.038	20.459
SCU_k-WHILE	0.013	0.005	0.378	0.356
SCU_k-NFA	0.012	0.008	0.293	0.566
SCU_k-CARRY	0.012	0.004	0.297	0.312
SCU_k-INC-WHILE	0.011	0.004	0.254	0.225
SCU_k-INC-NFA	0.009	0.006	0.132	0.249
SCU_k-INC-CARRY	0.009	0.003	0.125	0.142

needed to generate *Super Condensed Neighborhoods* using increased bit paral-lelism.

Tables 4,3 and the graphics in Figure 1 show clearly the advantages of the techniques described in this work, both in terms of the neighborhood size and the speedup obtained by the bit parallel algorithms.

6   Conclusions and Future Work

In this work, we propose to address the problem of indexed approximate pattern matching by restricting our attention to super condensed neighborhoods. We have shown that this entailed a significant time improvement that was verified by experimental results.

Arguments of the same nature have been used before. In fact an early exploit of the Super Condensed Neighborhood idea was an heuristic used in [13]. The idea was that it is enough to find those matches to P that begin by matching one of its first $k + 1$ characters. The condition obviously guarantees that in column 1 there will be no improper active cells. A refinement of this idea has also been presented in [6]. Our algorithm generalizes all these cases.

More recently the authors of [8] presented the notion of artificial *prefix-stripped length-q* neighborhood, that modifies the condensed neighborhood in a way that adapts to Myers algorithm but that it not minimal. The notion of *super condensed neighborhood* had in fact been considered by the previous authors[4] and also in [4].

We proposed an algorithm for generating *super condensed neighborhoods* that adapts very well to a bit-parallel and increased bit-parallel approaches. To achieve this we proposed a new way of managing the active cells that clearly outperformed previous methods and adapted much better to increased bit-par-allelism.

The results show that the use of *Super Condensed Neighborhood* speeds up the generation of the neighborhood by a significant factor that increases with the alphabet size and the error level.

---

[4] Personal communication.

Finally we would like to point out that this work is by no means finished. Our prototype must be extended to deal with larger $|\Sigma|$ and tested on the hybrid index [13]. The algorithm should also benefit greatly from an improvement like the one proposed in [9], specially since our binary representation is suitable for the necessary test predicates and this reduces the theoretical complexity truly to $O(ms)$. This would minimize the effect of the copy phase. Additionally our approach to increased bit-parallelism is still a bit naive. In particular we believe that there should be a way to squeeze more bits into the computer word, eventually by altering the copy phase.

Acknowledgments

We are grateful to Eugene Myers for providing us access to his prototype. We also thank Gonzalo Navarro and Heikki Hyyrö for their suggestions and remarks.

References

1. R. Baeza-Yates. Text retrieval: Theory and practice. volume I, pages 465–476. 12th IFIP World Computer Congress, Elsevier Science, 1992.
2. R. Baeza-Yates and G. Gonnet. A new approach to text searching. *Communications of the ACM*, (35(10)):74–82, 1992.
3. A.L. Cobbs. Fast approximate matching using suffix trees. In *Proceedings of the 6th Annual Symposium on Combinatorial Pattern Matching (CPM95)*, LNCS 937, pages 41–54. Springer, 1995.
4. Dan Gusfield. *Algorithms on Strings, Trees, and Sequences*. Cambridge University Press, 1999.
5. H. Hyyrö. Explaining and extending the bit-parallel approximate string matching algorithm of myers. Technical Report A-2001-10, Dept. of Computer and Information Sciences, University of Tampere, Tampere, Finland, 2001.
6. H. Hyyrö. *Practical Methods for Approximate String Matching*. PhD thesis, University of Tampere, 2003.
7. H. Hyyrö, K. Fredriksson, and G. Navarro. Increased bit-parallelism for approximate string matching. In *Proc. 3rd Workshop on Efficient and Experimental Algorithms (WEA'04)*, LNCS 3059, pages 285–298, 2004.
8. H. Hyyrö and G. Navarro. A practical index for genome searching. In *Proceedings of the 10th International Symposium on String Processing and Information Retrieval (SPIRE 2003)*, LNCS 2857, pages 341–349. Springer, 2003.
9. Heikki Hyyrö. An improvement and an extension on the hybrid index for approximate string matching. In *Proceedings of the 11th International Symposium on String Processing and Information Retrieval (SPIRE 2003)*, LNCS 3246, pages 208–209. Springer, 2004.
10. E. Myers. A sublinear algorithm for approximate keyword matching. *Algorithmica*, (12):345–374, 1994.
11. G. Myers. A fast bit-vector algorithm for approximate pattern matching based on dynamic programming. In *Proceedings of the 9th Annual Symposium on Combinatorial Pattern Matching (CPM98)*, LNCS 1448, pages 1–13. Springer-Verlag, 1998.

12. G. Navarro. A guided tour to approximate string matching. *ACM Computing Surveys*, 33(1):31–88, 2001.
13. G. Navarro and R. Baeza-Yates. A hybrid indexing method for approximate string matching. *Journal of Discrete Algorithms*, 1(1):205–239, 2000.
14. G. Navarro, R. Baeza-Yates, E. Sutinen, and J. Tarhio. Indexing methods for approximate string matching. *IEEE Data Engineering Bulletin*, 24(4):19–27, 2001.
15. E. Ukkonen. Finding approximate patterns in strings. *Journal of Algorithms*, pages 132–137, 1985.
16. E. Ukkonen. Approximate string matching over suffix trees. volume 684 of *LNCS 2857*, pages 228–242. Procedings of the 4th Annual Symposium on Combinatorical Pattern Matching (CPM93), Springer, 1993.
17. S. Wu and U. Manber. Fast text searching allowing errors. *Communications of the ACM*, (35(10)):83–91, 1992.

The Median Problem for the Reversal Distance in Circular Bacterial Genomes

Enno Ohlebusch, Mohamed Ibrahim Abouelhoda,
Kathrin Hockel, and Jan Stallkamp

Faculty of Computer Science, University of Ulm, 89069 Ulm, Germany
eo@informatik.uni-ulm.de

Abstract. In the median problem, we are given a distance or dissimilarity measure d, three genomes G_1, G_2, and G_3, and we want to find a genome G (a median) such that the sum $\sum_{i=1}^{3} d(G, G_i)$ is minimized. The median problem is a special case of the multiple genome rearrangement problem, where one wants to find a phylogenetic tree describing the most "plausible" rearrangement scenario for multiple species. The median problem is NP-hard for both the breakpoint and the reversal distance [5, 14]. To the best of our knowledge, there is no approach yet that takes biological constraints on genome rearrangements into account. In this paper, we make use of the fact that in circular bacterial genomes the predominant mechanism of rearrangement are inversions that are centered around the origin or the terminus of replication [8, 10, 18]. This constraint simplifies the median problem significantly. More precisely, we show that the median problem for the reversal distance can be solved in linear time for circular bacterial genomes.

1 Introduction

During evolution, the genomic DNA sequences of organisms are subject to genome rearrangements such as *transpositions* (where a section of the genome is excised and inserted at a new position in the genome, without changing orientation) and *inversions* (where a section of the genome is excised, reversed in orientation, and re-inserted). In unichromosomal genomes, the most common rearrangements are inversions, which are usually called *reversals* in bioinformatics. In the following, we will focus on unichromosomal genomes and use the terms "inversion" and "reversal" synonymously. The study of genome rearrangements started more than 65 years ago [7], but interest on the subject has flourished in the last decade because of the progress in large-scale sequencing. In the context of genome rearrangement, a genome G is typically viewed as a *signed permutation*, where each integer corresponds to a unique gene and the sign corresponds to its orientation. A $+$ $(-)$ sign means that the gene lies on the leading (lagging) DNA strand.

Consider two genomes $G_1 = (\pi_1, \ldots, \pi_n)$ and $G_2 = (\gamma_1, \ldots, \gamma_n)$ on the same set of genes $\{1, \ldots, n\}$. Two adjacent genes π_i and π_{i+1} in G_1 determine a *breakpoint* in G_1 w.r.t. G_2 if and only if neither π_i precedes π_{i+1} in G_2 nor

A. Apostolico, M. Crochemore, and K. Park (Eds.): CPM 2005, LNCS 3537, pp. 116–127, 2005.

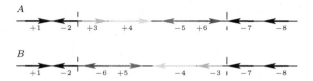

Fig. 1. Genome $(+1, -2, +3, +4, -5, +6, -7, -8)$ before and after the inversion $\rho(3, 6)$.

$-\pi_{i+1}$ precedes $-\pi_i$ in G_2. The *breakpoint distance* $bd(G_1, G_2)$ between G_1 and G_2 is defined as the number of breakpoints in G_1 w.r.t. G_2 [13, 19]. This is clearly equal to the number of breakpoints in G_2 w.r.t. G_1. In other words, the breakpoint distance between G_1 and G_2 is the smallest number of places where one genome must be broken so that the pieces can be rearranged to form the other genome.

Given a genome $G = (\pi_1, \ldots, \pi_{i-1}, \pi_i \ldots, \pi_j, \pi_{j+1}, \ldots, \pi_n)$, a *reversal* $\rho(i, j)$ applied to G reverses the segment $\pi_i, \ldots, \pi_j$ and produces the permutation $G\rho(i, j) = (\pi_1, \ldots, \pi_{i-1}, -\pi_j, -\pi_{j-1}, \ldots, -\pi_{i+1}, -\pi_i, \pi_j, \pi_{j+1}, \ldots, \pi_n)$ (see Figure 1 for an illustration). Given two genomes G_1 and G_2, the *reversal distance* $rd(G_1, G_2)$ between them is defined as the minimum number of reversals required to convert one genome into the other. (The phrase *sorting by reversals* refers to the equivalent problem of finding the minimum number of reversals required to convert a permutation π into the identity permutation.) The study of the reversal distance was pioneered by Sankoff [15] and has received increasing attention in recent years. There are dozens of papers on the subject; see e.g. [1, 2, 9, 11] and the references therein.

As already mentioned, the median problem is NP-hard for both the breakpoint and the reversal distance [5, 14]. That is the reason why researchers developed heuristics to solve the median and the multiple genome rearrangement problem. For the breakpoint-based multiple genome rearrangement problems very good heuristics exist [3, 16]. These rely on the ability to solve the breakpoint median problem by reducing it to the Traveling Salesman Problem. Solutions to the reversal median problem can be found in [4, 6, 12, 17]. There is a dispute about the "right" distance in multiple genome rearrangement problems. While [3, 16] argue that the breakpoint distance is the better choice, [12] conjecture that the usage of the reversal distance yields better phylogenetic reconstructions. Furthermore, [4] discusses some advantages of the reversal distance approach over the breakpoint distance approach.

2   Inversions Around the Origin of Replication

In this paper, we study the median problem (unless stated otherwise, the term median problem refers to the reversal median problem) for circular bacterial genomes. As mentioned earlier, it has been observed [8, 10, 18] that inversions within circular bacterial genomes are centered around the origin or the terminus of replication. That is, the genes keep their distance to the origin O and the

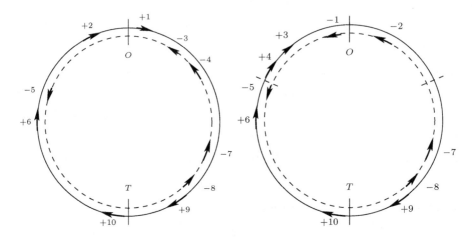

Fig. 2. Left: A cartoon representation of a circular bacterial genome. Of course, bacteria have hundreds, or even thousands, of genes. Moreover, a bacterial genome does not have long stretches of DNA without genes. Right: The same genome after the inversion $\bar{\rho}(4)$.

terminus T of replication under a reversal, but they are translocated to the opposite DNA strand and thus change their orientation.

As usual in the comparison of genomes on the gene level, we assume that the genomes have the same set $\{1, \ldots, n\}$ of unique genes and that inversions do not cut genes. As a consequence, genes may neither overlap on the same DNA strand nor on different DNA strands. In our model, in which inversions around the origin/terminus of replication are the predominant mechanism of rearrangement, it is further assumed that in each genome, these n genes occur in the same order w.r.t. the distance to the origin of replication.

Because the genes keep their distance to O, we enumerate them in increasing distance to the origin. That is, starting with the origin of replication, we simultaneously traverse both DNA strands of the circular genome in clockwise and counterclockwise order. This process ends when the terminus of replication is reached and it divides the circular genome into two halves. The clockwise traversal yields the right half and the counterclockwise traversal yields the left half. A gene encountered gets the next number (the first gene gets number 1). If this gene is lying on the leading strand, it is labeled with a $+$ sign, otherwise it gets a $-$ sign. If it was encountered in the clockwise (resp. counterclockwise) direction, its labeled number is put to the right (resp. left) of the origin O and a 0 to the left (resp. right) of O, which for better readability will be denoted by the symbol $|$. For example, if the first gene is encountered in the counterclockwise direction and is lying on the leading strand, then this yields $(+1 \mid 0)$.

$(+10, 0, 0, 0, +6, -5, 0, 0, +2, 0 \mid +1, 0, -3, -4, 0, 0, -7, -8, +9, 0)$ is a more complex example, which is shown in Figure 2.

In what follows, $\bar{\rho}(i)$ denotes an inversion centered around the origin of replication that acts on the ith nearest genes of O. Furthermore, we will use postfix notation to denote the application of a reversal to a genome. For example,

$$(+10, 0, 0, 0, +6, -5, 0, 0, +2, 0 \mid +1, 0, -3, -4, 0, 0, -7, -8, +9, 0)\, \overline{\rho}(4)$$
$$= (+10, 0, 0, 0, +6, -5, +4, +3, 0, -1 \mid 0, -2, 0, 0, 0, 0, -7, -8, +9, 0)$$

Similarly, $\underline{\rho}(i)$ denotes an inversion centered around the terminus of replication that acts on the ith nearest genes of T. As an example consider

$$(+10, 0, 0, 0, +6, -5, 0, 0, +2, 0 \mid +1, 0, -3, -4, 0, 0, -7, -8, +9, 0)\, \overline{\rho}(2)$$
$$= (0, -9, 0, 0, +6, -5, 0, 0, +2, 0 \mid +1, 0, -3, -4, 0, 0, -7, -8, 0, -10)$$

Next, we will simplify the above representation without loosing any information. $(+10, 0, 0, 0, +6, -5, 0, 0, +2, 0 \mid +1, 0, -3, -4, 0, 0, -7, -8, +9, 0)$, for example, will be represented by the bit vector $(1, 0, 1, 1, 0, 0, 1, 1, 1, 0)$ and the orientation vector $(+, -, -, -, +, -, -, -, +, -)$. In the bit vector, a 1 (resp. 0) at position p means that the gene with number p is located in the right (resp. left) half of the circular bacterial genome. Furthermore, a $+$ (resp. $-$) sign in the orientation vector at position p means that the gene lies on the leading (resp. legging) strand if it is in the right half (i.e., if there is a 1 at position p in the bit vector). Otherwise, if the gene is in the left half (i.e., there is a 0 at position p in the bit vector), a $+$ (resp. $-$) sign at position p means that the gene lies on the legging (resp. leading) strand. With this definition, the orientation vector is invariant (i.e., it does not change) under inversions around O and T. In the following, the orientation vector will hence not be mentioned explicitly. Therefore, the preceding inversions are modeled by

$$(1, 0, 1, 1, 0, 0, 1, 1, 1, 0)\, \overline{\rho}(4) = (0, 1, 0, 0, 0, 0, 1, 1, 1, 0)$$

$$(1, 0, 1, 1, 0, 0, 1, 1, 1, 0)\, \underline{\rho}(2) = (1, 0, 1, 1, 0, 0, 1, 1, 0, 1)$$

Lemma 1. *The composition of inversions is commutative and associative.*

Proof. Let ρ_1, ρ_2, and ρ_3 be inversions. We have $\rho_1 \cdot \rho_2 = \rho_2 \cdot \rho_1$ (commutativity) and $(\rho_1 \cdot \rho_2) \cdot \rho_3 = \rho_1 \cdot (\rho_2 \cdot \rho_3)$ (associativity) because every gene is inverted the same amount of times on either side of the respective equation.

An important consequence of the preceding lemma is that reordering any sequence of inversions does not change the result.

Note that every reversal ρ has an inverse, viz. ρ itself because $\rho \cdot \rho = id$.

Lemma 2. *Let $\rho_1, \rho_2, \ldots, \rho_k$ be reversals. Then $G\rho_1 \cdot \rho_2 \cdots \rho_k = G'$ if and only if $G'\rho_1 \cdot \rho_2 \cdots \rho_k = G$.*

Proof. For $k = 1$, this follows from $G\rho_1 = G' \Leftrightarrow G\rho_1 \cdot \rho_1 = G'\rho_1 \Leftrightarrow G = G'\rho_1$. Now the claim follows by induction on k in conjunction with Lemma 1.

The inverse $inv(G)$ of a genome G is defined by $inv(G) := G\rho(n)$, where $\rho(n) := \overline{\rho}(n) = \underline{\rho}(n)$. Given reversal ρ, a reversal σ satisfying $\rho(n) \cdot \rho = \sigma$ is called the *complementary reversal* of ρ.

Lemma 3. *Every reversal ρ has a (unique) complementary reversal σ.*

Proof. If $\rho = \overline{\rho}(i)$, then $\sigma = \underline{\rho}(n - i)$ because $\rho(n) \cdot \overline{\rho}(i) = \underline{\rho}(n - i)$. Otherwise, if $\rho = \underline{\rho}(i)$, then $\sigma = \overline{\rho}(n - i)$ because $\rho(n) \cdot \underline{\rho}(i) = \overline{\rho}(n - i)$.

$$1\!:\!1110\!:\!110\!:\!1$$
$$1\!:\!0001\!:\!110\!:\!0$$

Fig. 3. Breakpoints between two genomes, here depicted by colons.

3   The Reversal Distance

Let $(b_1, b_2, b_3, \ldots, b_n)$ be the bit vector representation of a circular bacterial genome G. In the rest of the paper, we will just speak of genome G, that is, we omit the phrase "circular bacterial". Furthermore, we will use the following notations for $1 \le i \le j \le n$: $G[i] = b_i$ and $G[i..j] = (b_i, \ldots, b_j)$.

Given two genomes G and G', we fix one of the genomes, say G', and try to transform G into G' by as few inversions as possible.

Definition 4. *Let $G = (b_1, b_2, b_3, \ldots, b_n)$ and $G' = (b'_1, b'_2, b'_3, \ldots, b'_n)$ be two circular genomes.*

1. *An interval $[i..j]$ of indices (where $1 \le i \le j \le n$) is called a strip if $b_k = b'_k$ for all $i \le k \le j$, $b_{i-1} \ne b'_{i-1}$ if $i \ne 1$, and $b_{j+1} \ne b'_{j+1}$ if $j \ne n$.*
2. *If $[i..j]$ is a strip, then $(i-1, i)$ (if $i \ne 1$) and $(j, j+1)$ (if $j \ne n$) are breakpoints between G and G'.*

Figure 3 shows two genomes G and G' with three breakpoints. Note that if $G = inv(G')$, then there is no strip, hence no breakpoint between them. Thus, if there is no breakpoint between G and G', then either $G = G'$ or $G = inv(G')$.

Lemma 5. *Let G, G' and $\overline{\rho}(i)$ with $1 \le i \le n - 1$ be given.*

1. *For all $(j, j+1)$ with either $1 \le j < i$ or $i < j < n$ we have: $(j, j+1)$ is a breakpoint between G and G' if and only if $(j, j+1)$ is a breakpoint between $G\overline{\rho}(i)$ and G'.*
2. *$(i, i+1)$ is a breakpoint between G and G' if and only if $(i, i+1)$ is not a breakpoint between $G\overline{\rho}(i)$ and G'.*

Proof. (1) If $i < j < n$, then there is nothing to show because $\overline{\rho}(i)$ has no effect on the genes j and $j + 1$. Suppose $1 \le j < i$. The following equivalences hold:

$(j, j+1)$ is a breakpoint between G and G'
$\Leftrightarrow$ either $(b_j = b'_j$ and $b_{j+1} \ne b'_{j+1})$ or $(b_j \ne b'_j$ and $b_{j+1} = b'_{j+1})$
$\Leftrightarrow$ either $(inv(b_j) \ne b'_j$ and $inv(b_{j+1}) = b'_{j+1})$
    or $(inv(b_j) = b'_j$ and $inv(b_{j+1}) \ne b'_{j+1})$
$\Leftrightarrow (j, j+1)$ is a breakpoint between $G\overline{\rho}(i)$ and G'

(2) This case follows by a similar reasoning as in (1).

Of course, a similar statement holds when $\overline{\rho}(i)$ is replaced with $\underline{\rho}(i)$. This is also true for the following corollary, which follows from the preceding lemma.

Corollary 6. *Let G, G' and $\overline{\rho}(i)$ with $1 \leq i \leq n-1$ be given.*

1. *If $(i, i+1)$ is a breakpoint between G and G', then the number of breakpoints between $G\overline{\rho}(i)$ and G' is one less than the number of breakpoints between G and G'.*
2. *If $(i, i+1)$ is not a breakpoint between G and G', then the number of breakpoints between $G\overline{\rho}(i)$ and G' is one more than the number of breakpoints between G and G'.*

First, we consider the case in which only inversions around the origin of replication are allowed. The following simple procedure $rd\_O(G, G')$ returns the reversal distance between two genomes G and G', using inversions around O only. (The procedure $rd\_T(G, G')$ that returns the reversal distance between G and G' using inversions around T only is defined similarly.)

procedure $rd\_O(G, G')$
    determine the breakpoints $(i_1, i_1 + 1), \ldots, (i_k, i_k + 1)$ between G and G'
    if $G\overline{\rho}(i_1) \cdots \overline{\rho}(i_k) = G'$ **then** return k **else** return $k + 1$

The correctness of procedure $rd\_O(G, G')$ is a direct consequence of Corollary 6. Each reversal $\overline{\rho}(i_1), \ldots, \overline{\rho}(i_k)$ removes one breakpoint, so that there is no breakpoint between $G\overline{\rho}(i_1) \cdots \overline{\rho}(i_k)$ and G'. Hence, we have $G\overline{\rho}(i_1) \cdots \overline{\rho}(i_k) = G'$ or $G\overline{\rho}(i_1) \cdots \overline{\rho}(i_k) = inv(G')$. In the latter case, k must be incremented by 1 because $\rho(n)$ has to be applied to make the genomes equal. It is easy to see that in both cases the algorithm returns the minimum number of inversions needed to transform G into G'.

Since the breakpoints $(i_1, i_1 + 1), \ldots, (i_k, i_k + 1)$ between G and G' can be determined in $O(n)$ time and also the test as to whether two genomes are equal requires $O(n)$ time, the worst case running time of the procedure is $O(n)$.

Next, we consider the general case in which both inversions around the origin and the terminus of replication are allowed.

procedure $rd(G, G')$
    if G and G' do not have a breakpoint **then**
        if $G = G'$ **then** return 0 **else** return 1
    else
        choose a strip $[i..j]$
        $k_l := rd\_O(G[1..i-1], G'[1..i-1])$
        $k_r := rd\_T(G[j+1..n], G'[j+1..n])$
        return $(k_l + k_r)$

Procedure $rd(G, G')$ returns the minimum number of inversions needed to transform G into G' because each inversion removes one breakpoint. The transformed genome must be equal to G' (i.e., it cannot be $inv(G')$) because the chosen strip is not changed by the inversions. Furthermore, procedure $rd(G, G')$ runs in linear time because the procedures rd_O and rd_T do so.

4   The Median Problem for the Reversal Distance

Recall that in the median problem we want to find a genome G (a median) such that $\sum_{i=1}^{3} rd(G, G_i)$ is minimized. In the following, let $d_m(G_1, G_2, G_3) = \min\{\sum_{i=1}^{3} rd(G, G_i) \mid G \text{ is a genome}\}$. Furthermore, for $b^1, b^2, b^3 \in \{0, 1\}$ let

$$majority(b^1, b^2, b^3) = \begin{cases} 1 \text{ if } \sum_{j=1}^{3} b^j \geq 2 \\ 0 \text{ otherwise} \end{cases}$$

Again, we first consider the case in which only inversions around the origin of replication are allowed. In this case, the following procedure $median\_O$ returns a median, as shown in Theorem 7. (The procedure $median\_T$ that returns a median using inversions around T only is defined analogously.)

procedure $median\_O(G_1, G_2, G_3)$ $/ \star$ where $G_j = (b_1^j, b_2^j, b_3^j, \ldots, b_n^j) \star /$
    $d := 0$
    for $i := n$ **downto** 1 **do**
      $b := majority(b_i^1, b_i^2, b_i^3)$
      if there is a j, $1 \leq j \leq 3$, such that $b_i^j \neq b$ **then**
        $G_j := G_j \bar{\rho}(i)$
        $d := d + 1$
    return (G_1, d)

If we would really apply the reversals to the genomes (in line 5 of the procedure), then $median\_O(G_1, G_2, G_3)$ would take quadratic time. However, a linear time implementation is possible by simply counting the number of times a gene i was inverted in genome G_j. If it was flipped an even number of times giving G'_j, then $G'_j[1..i] = G_j[1..i]$. Otherwise, if it was flipped an odd number of times, then $G'_j[1..i] = inv(G_j[1..i])$.

Theorem 7. *If procedure* $median\_O(G_1, G_2, G_3)$ *returns the pair* (G, d), *then G is a median of the three genomes* $G_j = (b_1^j, b_2^j, b_3^j, \ldots, b_n^j)$, $1 \leq j \leq 3$, *using inversions around O only, and d is the number of required reversals.*

Proof. We proceed by induction on the length n of the genomes. The case $n = 1$ is trivial. According to the inductive hypothesis, procedure $median\_O$ returns a median of three genomes of size $n - 1$. For $1 \leq j \leq 3$, let $G'_j = (b_1^j, b_2^j, b_3^j, \ldots, b_{n-1}^j)$. If $b_n^1 = b_n^2 = b_n^3$, then an application of the inductive hypothesis to G'_1, G'_2, and G'_3 proves the theorem. Otherwise, there is a bit, say b_n^3, such that $b_n^1 = b_n^2 \neq b_n^3$. Hence procedure $median\_O$ first applies $\rho(n)$ to G_3, i.e., it inverts G_3, and then computes a median $G' = (\hat{b}_1^j, \hat{b}_2^j, \hat{b}_3^j, \ldots, \hat{b}_{n-1}^j)$ of G'_1, G'_2, and $inv(G'_3)$. Let $d' = rd(G', G'_1) + rd(G', G'_2) + rd(G', inv(G'_3))$ and $G = (\hat{b}_1^j, \hat{b}_2^j, \hat{b}_3^j, \ldots, \hat{b}_{n-1}^j, b_n^1)$. Clearly, $\sum_{j=1}^{3} rd(G, G_j) = d' + 1$.
     In order to prove that G is a median of G_1, G_2, and G_3, it suffices to show that the bit representation of nth gene of a median cannot be b_n^3. For an indirect proof, suppose the contrary. Then, in an optimal sequence of inversions that

transforms G_1 (G_2) into a median, there must be one that inverts the whole genome. According to Lemma 1, we may assume that this inversion is the first in the sequence. Procedure $median\_O$ applied to $inv(G_1'), inv(G_2')$, and G_3' gives a median $\tilde{G}' = (\tilde{b}_1^j, \tilde{b}_2^j, \tilde{b}_3^j, \ldots, \tilde{b}_{n-1}^j)$ of these. It is not difficult to see that

$$rd(\tilde{G}', inv(G_1')) + rd(\tilde{G}', inv(G_1')) + rd(\tilde{G}', G_3') = d'$$

because the two problems under consideration are equivalent (inverting all genes in one problem yields the other problem). $\tilde{G} = (\tilde{b}_1^j, \tilde{b}_2^j, \tilde{b}_3^j, \ldots, \tilde{b}_{n-1}^j, b_n^3)$ cannot be a median of G_1, G_2, and G_3 because $\sum_{j=1}^{3} rd(\tilde{G}, G_j) = d' + 2 > d' + 1 = \sum_{j=1}^{3} rd(G, G_j)$. This contradiction shows that the bit representation of the nth gene of a median cannot be b_n^3.

Next, we consider the median problem in which both inversions around the origin and the terminus of replication are allowed. We distinguish between two cases: (a) G_1, G_2, and G_3 have a common bit and (b) G_1, G_2, and G_3 do not have a common bit.

Definition 8. *We say that i is a* common bit *of the genomes G_1, G_2, and G_3 if $G_1[i] = G_2[i] = G_3[i]$.*

Lemma 9. *Suppose $G'\rho_1 \cdot \rho_2 \cdots \rho_k = G$ and $G'[i] = G[i]$, that is, i is a common bit of G and G'. Then there are inversions $\rho_1' \cdot \rho_2' \cdots \rho_k'$ such that $G'\rho_1' \cdot \rho_2' \cdots \rho_k' = G$ and each ρ_j' does not invert the ith gene.*

Proof. If there is an inversion that inverts the ith gene, then there must be an inversion that inverts it back. If both are inversions around O (a similar statement holds if both act around T), say $\bar{p}(p)$ and $\bar{p}(q)$, then they can be replaced by the inversions $\underline{p}(n - p)$ and $\underline{p}(n - q)$ around T. These do not invert the ith gene; see Figure 4.

If one is an inversion around O, say $\bar{p}(q)$, and the other is an inversion around T, say $\underline{p}(p)$, then they can be replaced with the inversions $\bar{p}(n - p)$ and $\underline{p}(n - q)$. These do not invert the ith gene; see Figure 4. Now the lemma follows by induction on the number of inversions in $\rho_1 \cdot \rho_2 \cdots \rho_k$ that invert the ith gene.

If G_1, G_2, and G_3 have a common bit, the following procedure computes a median; see Theorem 10.

procedure $median\_cb(G_1, G_2, G_3)$
    determine a common bit i of G_1, G_2, and G_3
    $(G_l, d_l) := median\_O(G_1[1..i - 1], G_2[1..i - 1], G_3[1..i - 1])$
    $(G_r, d_r) := median\_T(G_1[i + 1..n], G_2[i + 1..n], G_3[i + 1..n])$
    return $(G_l G_1[i] G_r, d_l + d_r)$

Procedure $median\_cb(G_1, G_2, G_3)$ runs in linear time because the procedures $median\_O$ and $median\_T$ do so.

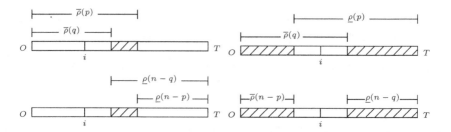

Fig. 4. Left: Two inversions around the origin of replication inverting the same gene i can be replaced by two inversions around the terminus, both not changing gene i. Right: Two inversions (one around the origin and the other around the terminus) that both invert the same gene i can be replaced by two different inversions (again one around the origin and the other around the terminus) that both do not invert gene i.

Theorem 10. *If G_1, G_2, and G_3 have a common bit, then median_cb(G_1, G_2, G_3) returns a pair (G, d) such that G is a median of the three genomes and $d = d_m(G_1, G_2, G_3)$.*

Proof. We claim that if there is a median G' of G_1, G_2, and G_3, such that $G'[i] \neq G_1[i] = G_2[i] = G_3[i]$, then there is another median G such that $G[i] = G_1[i] = G_2[i] = G_3[i]$.

Let G' be such a median of G_1, G_2, and G_3. Then, for $1 \leq j \leq 3$, there are inversions such that $G_j \rho_1^j \cdot \rho_2^j \cdots \rho_{\ell_j}^j = G'$ and $\ell_1 + \ell_2 + \ell_2$ is minimal. Because $G'[i] \neq G_1[i] = G_2[i] = G_3[i]$, in each $G_j \rho_1^j \cdot \rho_2^j \cdots \rho_{\ell_j}^j = G'$, $1 \leq j \leq 3$, the ith gene must have been inverted. By Lemma 1, we may assume that $\rho_{\ell_j}^j$ inverts the ith gene. Moreover, according to Lemma 9, we may assume that none of the other inversions inverts the ith gene.

(a) Suppose that $\rho_{\ell_1}^1$, $\rho_{\ell_2}^2$, and $\rho_{\ell_3}^3$ all act around O, say $\rho_{\ell_j}^j = \overline{\rho}(l_j)$ (for T, the reasoning is verbatim the same). Then inverting the complementary regions yields a median G with $G[i] = G_1[i] = G_2[i] = G_3[i]$; see Figure 5. To be precise, $G = G_j \rho_1^j \cdot \rho_2^j \cdots \rho_{\ell_j - 1}^j \cdot \underline{\rho}(n - l_j)$ for every j with $1 \leq j \leq 3$.

(b) Suppose that $\rho_{\ell_1}^1$, $\rho_{\ell_2}^2$, and $\rho_{\ell_3}^3$ do not act around the same spot, say $\rho_{\ell_1}^1 = \overline{\rho}(l_1)$ and $\rho_{\ell_2}^2 = \overline{\rho}(l_2)$ act around O, but $\rho_{\ell_3}^3 = \underline{\rho}(r_3)$ acts around T. Again, inverting the complementary regions yields a median G with $G[i] = G_1[i] = G_2[i] = G_3[i]$; see Figure 5. More precisely, $G = G_j \rho_1^j \cdot \rho_2^j \cdots \rho_{\ell_j - 1}^j \cdot \underline{\rho}(n - l_j)$ for $1 \leq j \leq 2$ and $G = G_3 \rho_1^3 \cdot \rho_2^3 \cdots \rho_{\ell_3 - 1}^3 \cdot \overline{\rho}(n - r_3)$.

Thus, there is also a median G of G_1, G_2, and G_3 such that $G[i] = G_1[i] = G_2[i] = G_3[i]$. Then, according to Lemma 9, G_j can be converted to G by (the same number of) inversions that do not invert the ith gene. That is, some of the inversions act only on the genes left to index i, while the others act only on the genes right to index i. In other words, $G = G_l G_1[i] G_r$, where G_l (G_r) is a median of $G_1[1..i - 1]$, $G_2[1..i - 1]$, and $G_3[1..i - 1]$ obtained by inversions around O $(G_1[i + 1..n]$, $G_2[i + 1..n]$, and $G_3[i + 1..n]$ obtained by inversions

Fig. 5. Left: Case (a) of the proof of Theorem 10. Right: Case (b) of that proof.

around T). Therefore, the correctness of procedure *median_cb* is a consequence of the correctness of the procedures *median_O* and *median_T*.

Now we consider the last case, in which G_1, G_2, and G_3 do not have a common bit. It can be shown (see Theorem 13) that in this case the following procedure *median_ncb*(G_1, G_2, G_3) returns a median of the three genomes. Moreover, the procedure runs in linear time because the procedures *median_cb* and *rd* do so.

procedure *median_ncb*(G_1, G_2, G_3)
    if two genomes coincide, say $G_i = G_j$ with $i \neq j$ **then** return $(G_i, 1)$
    else if one of the genomes is the inverse of another, say $G_i = inv(G_j)$ with $i \neq j$
        then return $(G_i, 1 + rd(G_i, G_k))$ where $k \in \{1, 2, 3\} \setminus \{i, j\}$
    else   / $\star$ $G_i \neq G_j$ and $G_i \neq inv(G_j)$ for all $i \neq j$ $\star$ /
        $(G', d') := median\_cb(inv(G_1), G_2, G_3)$
        $d_1' := rd(inv(G_1), G_2) + rd(inv(G_1), G_3)$
        if $d_1' = d'$ **then** return (G_1, d')
        else return (G', d')

Due to space limitations, the proofs of the following lemmata are omitted.

Lemma 11. *If G and G' are two genomes such that neither $G = G'$ nor $inv(G) = G'$, then $rd(G, G') = rd(inv(G), G')$.*

Lemma 12. *Let G_1, G_2, and G_3 be genomes such that $G_i \neq G_j$ and $G_i \neq inv(G_j)$ for all $i \neq j$. Then the following statements are equivalent for $\{i, j, k\} = \{1, 2, 3\}$:*

1. $d_m(inv(G_i), G_j, G_k) = rd(inv(G_i), G_j) + rd(inv(G_i), G_k)$
2. *$inv(G_i)$ is a median of $inv(G_i)$, G_j, and G_k.*
3. *G_i is a median of G_i, G_j, and G_k.*

Theorem 13. *If the three genomes G_1, G_2, G_3 do not have a common bit, then procedure median_ncb(G_1, G_2, G_3) returns a pair (G, d) such that G is a median of the three genomes and $d = d_m(G_1, G_2, G_3)$.*

Proof. As in the procedure, we proceed by case analysis.

if-statement: If two genomes coincide, say $G_i = G_j$ with $i \neq j$, then it follows $G_i = inv(G_k)$ where $k \in \{1, 2, 3\} \setminus \{i, j\}$. Clearly, inverting G_k yields the median G_i.

else if-statement: Suppose G_1, G_2, and G_3 are pairwise distinct but one of the genomes is the inverse of another, say $G_i = inv(G_j)$ with $i \neq j$. Let $k \in \{1, 2, 3\} \setminus \{i, j\}$. Because G_i, G_j, and G_k are pairwise distinct and $G_i = inv(G_j)$, Lemma 11 implies that $rd(G_i, G_k) = rd(G_j, G_k)$. Thus, for $d_i := rd(G_i, G_i) + rd(G_i, G_j) + rd(G_i, G_k)$, we have $d_i = 1 + rd(G_j, G_k)$.

We must show that G_i is a median of the three genomes. For an indirect proof, suppose that G_i is not a median. Let G be a median of G_i, G_j, and G_k, i.e., there are reversals such that

$$G_i\rho_1^i \cdot \rho_2^i \cdots \rho_{\ell_i}^i = G, \quad G_j\rho_1^j \cdot \rho_2^j \cdots \rho_{\ell_j}^j = G, \text{ and } G_k\rho_1^k \cdot \rho_2^k \cdots \rho_{\ell_k}^k = G$$

It follows from the last two equations in combination with Lemma 2 that $G_j\rho_1^j \cdot \rho_2^j \cdots \rho_{\ell_j}^j \cdot \rho_1^k \cdot \rho_2^k \cdots \rho_{\ell_k}^k = G_k$. Consequently, $rd(G_j, G_k) \leq \ell_j + \ell_k$. On the other hand, since G is a median and G_i is not, we have $\ell_i + \ell_j + \ell_k < d_i = 1 + rd(G_j, G_k)$ and hence $\ell_i + \ell_j + \ell_k < 1 + \ell_j + \ell_k$. We conclude that $\ell_i = 0$, that is, $G = G_i$. This contradiction proves that G_i is a median of the three genomes.

else-statement: We have $G_i \neq G_j$ and $G_i \neq inv(G_j)$ for all $i \neq j$. This implies that $inv(G_1)$, G_2, G_3 have a common bit, as can be seen as follows. If both G_1, G_2, G_3 and $inv(G_1)$, G_2, G_3 would not have a common bit, then it would follow that $G_2[\ell] = G_3[\ell]$ for all $1 \leq \ell \leq n$. In other words, $G_2 = inv(G_3)$. This contradiction shows that $inv(G_1)$, G_2, G_3 must have a common bit. Therefore, we can apply procedure *median_cb* to compute a median G' of $inv(G_1)$, G_2, and G_3. Let $d_1' = rd(inv(G_1), G_2) + rd(inv(G_1), G_3)$. If $d_1' = d'$, then G_1 is a median of G_1, G_2, and G_3 by Lemma 12. We will show that $d_1' \neq d'$ (or, equivalently, $d_1' > d'$) implies that G' is also a median of G_1, G_2, and G_3. According to Lemma 12, neither is G_1 a median of G_1, G_2, and G_3 nor is $inv(G_1)$ a median of $inv(G_1)$, G_2, and G_3. Since G' is a median of $inv(G_1)$, G_2, and G_3, there are reversals such that $inv(G_1)\rho_1'^1 \cdot \rho_2'^1 \cdots \rho_{\ell_1'}'^1 = G'$, $G_2\rho_1'^2 \cdot \rho_2'^2 \cdots \rho_{\ell_2'}'^2 = G'$, $G_3\rho_1'^3 \cdot \rho_2'^3 \cdots \rho_{\ell_3'}'^3 = G'$, and $d' = \ell_1' + \ell_2' + \ell_3'$. Moreover, $\ell_1' > 0$ because $inv(G_1) \neq G'$. It follows from $inv(G_1)\rho_1'^1 \cdot \rho_2'^1 \cdots \rho_{\ell_1'}'^1 = G_1\rho(n)\rho_1'^1 \cdot \rho_2'^1 \cdots \rho_{\ell_1'}'^1$ in conjunction with Lemma 3 that there is an inversion σ^1 such that $G_1\sigma^1 \cdot \rho_2'^1 \cdots \rho_{\ell_1'}'^1 = G'$. Therefore, $d \leq d'$, where $d := d_m(G_1, G_2, G_3)$. We show that $d < d'$ is impossible. For an indirect proof, suppose that $d < d'$ holds. Let G be a median of G_1, G_2, and G_3, i.e., there are reversals such that $G_1\rho_1^1 \cdot \rho_2^1 \cdots \rho_{\ell_1}^1 = G$, $G_2\rho_1^2 \cdot \rho_2^2 \cdots \rho_{\ell_2}^2 = G$, $G_3\rho_1^3 \cdot \rho_2^3 \cdots \rho_{\ell_3}^3 = G$, and $d = \ell_1 + \ell_2 + \ell_3$. Since $G \neq G_1$, we have $\ell_1 > 0$. It follows from $inv(G_1)\rho(n) \cdot \rho_1^1 \cdot \rho_2^1 \cdots \rho_{\ell_1}^1 = G_1\rho_1^1 \cdot \rho_2^1 \cdots \rho_{\ell_1}^1 = G$ that there is an inversion σ such that $inv(G_1)\sigma \cdot \rho_2^1 \cdots \rho_{\ell_1}^1 = G$. Thus, $rd(G, inv(G_1)) + rd(G, G_2) + rd(G, G_3) \leq \ell_1 + \ell_2 + \ell_3 = d < d'$. This contradicts the definition of $d' = \min\{rd(G, inv(G_1)) + rd(G, G_2) + rd(G, G_3) \mid G \text{ is a genome}\}$. In conclusion, $d' = d$, i.e., G' is a median of G_1, G_2, and G_3.

References

1. D.A. Bader, B.M.E. Moret, and M. Yan. A linear-time algorithm for computing inversion distance between signed permutations with an experimental study. *Journal of Computational Biology*, 8:483–491, 2001.

2. A. Bergeron, J. Mixtacki, and J. Stoye. Reversal distance without hurdles and fortresses. In *Proc. 15th Annual Symposium on Combinatorial Pattern Matching*, volume 3109 of *Lecture Notes in Computer Science*, pages 388–399. Springer-Verlag, 2004.
3. M. Blanchette, G. Bourque, and D. Sankoff. Breakpoint phylogenies. In *Proc. Genome Informatics Workshop*, pages 25–34. Univ. Academy Press, 1997.
4. B. Bourque and P.A. Pevzner. Genome-scale evolution: Reconstructing gene orders in the ancestral species. *Genome Research*, 12(1):26–36, 2002.
5. A. Caprara. Formulations and hardness of multiple sorting by reversals. In *Proc. 3rd Annual International Conference on Research in Computational Molecular Biology*, pages 84–94. ACM Press, 1999.
6. A. Caprara. On the practical solution of the reversal median problem. In *Proc. 1st International Workshop on Algorithms in Bioinformatics*, volume 2149 of *Lecture Notes in Computer Science*, pages 238–251. Springer-Verlag, 2001.
7. T. Dobzhansky and A.H. Sturtevant. Inversions in the chromosomes of *Drosophila pseudoobscura*. *Genetics*, 23:28–64, 1938.
8. J.A. Eisen, J.F. Heidelberg, O. White, and S.L. Salzberg. Evidence for symmetric chromosomal inversions around the replication origin in bacteria. *Genome Biology*, 1(6):1–9, 2000.
9. S. Hannenhalli and P.A. Pevzner. Transforming cabbage into turnip (polynomial algorithm for sorting signed permutations by reversals). *Journal of the ACM*, 48:1–27, 1999.
10. D. Hughes. Evaluating genome dynamics: The constraints on rearrangements within bacterial genomes. *Genome Biology*, 1(6):1–8, 2000.
11. H. Kaplan, R. Shamir, and R.E. Tarjan. A faster and simpler algorithm for sorting signed permutations by reversals. *SIAM J. Comput.*, 29(3):880–892, 1999.
12. B.M.E. Moret, A.C. Siepel, J. Tang, and T. Liu. Inversion medians outperform breakpoint medians in phylogeny reconstruction from gene-order data. In *Proc. 2nd International Workshop on Algorithms in Bioinformatics*, volume 2542 of *Lecture Notes in Computer Science*, pages 521–536. Springer-Verlag, 2002.
13. J.H. Nadeau and B.A. Taylor. Lengths of chromosomal segments conserved since divergence of man and mouse. *Proceedings of the National Academy of Sciences of the United States of America*, 81(3):814–818, 1984.
14. I. Pe'er and R. Shamir. The median problems for breakpoints are NP-complete. Technical Report TR98-071, Electronic Colloquium on Computational Complexity, 1998.
15. D. Sankoff. Edit distance for genome comparison based on non-local operations. In *Proc. 3rd Annual Symposium on Combinatorial Pattern Matching, 3rd Annual Symposium*, volume 644 of *Lecture Notes in Computer Science*, pages 121–135. Springer-Verlag, 1992.
16. D. Sankoff and M. Blanchette. Multiple genome rearrangement and breakpoint phylogeny. *Journal of Computational Biology*, 5(3):555–570, 1998.
17. A.C. Siepel and B.M.E. Moret. Finding an optimal inversion median: Experimental results. In *Proc. 1st International Workshop on Algorithms in Bioinformatics*, volume 2149 of *Lecture Notes in Computer Science*, pages 189–203. Springer-Verlag, 2001.
18. E.R.M. Tiller and R. Collins. Genome rearrangement by replication-directed translocation. *Nature Genetics*, 26:195–197, 2000.
19. G.A. Watterson, W.J. Ewens, T.E. Hall, and A. Morgan. The chromosome inversion problem. *Journal of Theoretical Biology*, 99:1–7, 1982.

Using PQ Trees for Comparative Genomics

Gad M. Landau[1,2,*], Laxmi Parida[3], and Oren Weimann[1,**]

[1] Department of Computer Science, University of Haifa
Mount Carmel, Haifa 31905, Israel
{landau,oweimann}@cs.haifa.ac.il
[2] Department of Computer and Information Science, Polytechnic University
Six MetroTech Center, Brooklyn, NY 11201-3840, USA
landau@poly.edu
[3] Computational Biology Center, IBM TJ Watson Research Center
Yorktown Heights, New York 10598, USA
parida@us.ibm.com

Abstract. Permutations on strings representing gene clusters on genomes have been studied earlier in [3, 12, 14, 17, 18] and the idea of a maximal permutation pattern was introduced in [12]. In this paper, we present a new tool for representation and detection of gene clusters in multiple genomes, using PQ trees [6]: this describes the inner structure and the relations between clusters succinctly, aids in filtering meaningful from apparently meaningless clusters and also gives a natural and meaningful way of visualizing complex clusters. We identify a minimal consensus PQ tree and prove that it is equivalent to a maximal πpattern [12] and each subgraph of the PQ tree corresponds to a non-maximal permutation pattern. We present a general scheme to handle multiplicity in permutations and also give a linear time algorithm to construct the minimal consensus PQ tree. Further, we demonstrate the results on whole genome data sets. In our analysis of the whole genomes of human and rat we found about 1.5 million common gene clusters but only about 500 minimal consensus PQ trees, and, with *E Coli K-12* and *B Subtilis* genomes we found only about 450 minimal consensus PQ trees out of about 15,000 gene clusters. Further, we show specific instances of functionally related genes in the two cases.

Keywords: Pattern discovery, data mining, clusters, patterns, motifs, permutation patterns, PQ trees, comparative genomics, whole genome analysis, evolutionary analysis.

1 Introduction

Given two permutations of n distinct characters, Uno and Yagiura [18] defined a *common interval* to be a pair of intervals of these permutations consisting of the same set of characters, and devised an $\mathcal{O}(n + K)$ time algorithm for

---

* Partially supported by NSF grant CCR-0104307, by the Israel Science Foundation grant 282/01, and by IBM Faculty Partnership Award.
** Partially supported by the Israel Science Foundation grant 282/01.

extracting all common intervals of two permutations, where $K(\leq \binom{n}{2})$ is the number of common intervals. Heber and Stoye [14] extended this result to k sequences and presented an $\mathcal{O}(nk+K)$ time algorithm for extracting all common intervals of k permutations. The characters here represent genes and the string of characters represent the genome. Bergeron, Corteel and Raffinot [3] relaxed the "consecutive" constraint by introducing *gene teams* - allowing genes in a cluster to be separated by gaps that do not exceed a fixed threshold, and presented an $\mathcal{O}(kn \log^2 n)$ time algorithm for finding all gene teams.

A common technique of deciding whether two genes are similar is using the biological concept of orthologs and paralogs. Two genes are matched if they are either orthologous (appear in different organisms, but have the same evolutionary origin and are generated during speciation) or paralogous (appear in the same organism and caused by the duplication of ancestor genes). A slightly modified model of a genome sequence, that allows paralogs, was introduced by Schmidt and Stoye [17]. They extended the previous model of [14] by representing genomes as sequences rather then permutations, and devised a $\Theta(n^2)$ algorithm for extracting all common intervals of two sequences. He and Goldwasser [13] extended the notion of gene teams [3] to COG teams by allowing any number of paralogs and orthologs, and devised an $\mathcal{O}(mn)$ time algorithm to find such COG teams for *pairwise* chromosome comparison (where m and n are the number of orthologous genes in the two chromosomes).

In [12], pattern discovery was formalized as the $\pi pattern$ problem. Let the pattern $P=p_1, p_2, \ldots, p_m$ and the string $S=s_1, s_2, \ldots, s_n$ be both sequences of characters (with possible repeats) over a given alphabet Σ (in our case genes). P *appears* in location i in S iff $(p_1, p_2, \ldots, p_m)$ is a permutation of $(s_i, \ldots, s_{i+m-1})$. P is a πpattern if it appears at least K times in S for a given K. A notation for *maximal $\pi patterns$* was introduced as a model to filter meaningful from apparently meaningless clusters. A πpattern p_1 is non-maximal with respect to πpattern p_2, if each occurrence of p_1 is covered by an occurrence of p_2 and each occurrence of p_2 covers an occurrence of p_1. The algorithm presented in [12] works in two stages: In stage 1, all πpatterns of sizes $\leq L$ are found in $\mathcal{O}(Ln \log|\Sigma| \log n)$ time, where n is the total length of all the sequences. For every πpattern found the algorithm stores a list of all the locations where the pattern appears, i.e, *location list*. In stage 2, a straightforward comparison of every two location lists is used to extract the maximal πpatterns out of all the πpatterns found in stage 1. Assume stage 1 outputs p πpatterns, and the maximum length of a location list is ℓ, stage 2 runs in $\mathcal{O}(p^2 \ell)$ time. Integrating the two stages to produce only the maximal πpatterns was introduced as an open problem.

The common approach in practice is to output all the found patterns as sets of genes. This approach provides no knowledge of the ordering of the genes in each appearance of the pattern, and also outputs meaningless clusters. In this paper we use the PQ tree data structure [6] to devise a new tool for obtaining the *maximal notation* of the appearances of a pattern in linear time. A formal definition of the maximal notation is given in [12]:

Definition 1. *Maximal notation:* *Given k permutations on an alphabet Σ, representing k occurrences of a pattern. The maximal notation is obtained by using a '-' between two groups of one or more genes to denote that these groups appear as immediate neighbors in all the k permutations, and using a ',' otherwise.*

Example. Consider the pattern $\{a, b, c, d, e, f\}$ appearing once as $abcdef$ and once as $bdacfe$, then the maximal notation of this pattern is $((a, b, c, d) - (e - f))$.

There are two main reasons for obtaining the maximal notation: (1). This notation provides knowledge of the inner structure of a pattern. $((a, b, c, d) - (e - f))$ shows that e appears always adjacent to f, and they both appear always adjacent to the group $\{a, b, c, d\}$. (2) This notation provides knowledge of the non-maximal relations between patterns, and can be used to filter meaningful from apparently meaningless clusters (non-maximal). $((a, b, c, d) - (e - f))$ shows that the patterns $\pi_1 = \{e, f\}$ and $\pi_2 = \{a, b, c, d\}$ are non-maximal w.r.t the pattern $\pi_3 = \{a, b, c, d, e, f\}$. Thus $((a, b, c, d) - (e - f))$ holds all the information of patterns π_1, π_2 and π_3.

Results. Our main theoretical results are: (a) we prove that a minimal consensus PQ tree is equivalent to a maximal πpattern [12] and each subgraph of the PQ tree corresponds to a non-maximal permutation pattern, and (b) give an algorithm that obtains the maximal notation of a πpattern p in $\mathcal{O}(nk)$ time, where k is the number of appearances of p and n is the number of characters in p (we assume all the characters in p are distinct. In section 5 we suggest a solution for patterns containing repeats of characters). We present several uses of this algorithm: (1) In the genome model that allows only orthologous genes (all k sequences are permutations of $\{1, 2, \ldots, n\}$), we can use this algorithm to obtain the maximal notation of the entire πpattern $\{1, 2, \ldots, n\}$. (2) In the most general genome model that allows orthologous and paralogous genes (a gene may appear any number of times in a sequence, and may appear in only some of the sequences) we assume some other gene clustering algorithm found the πpattern p. We use our tool to obtain the maximal notation of p. (3) We modify this algorithm to an $\mathcal{O}(nk^2)$ time algorithm that finds all maximal πpatterns in the genome model that allows orthologous genes as well as genes that do not appear in all the sequences. We present experimental results for the various types of data (Section 6). Our main practical results are the use of the tool on whole genome data sets: (1) human and rat genomes and (2) *E Coli K-12* and *B Subtilis* genomes. In both we show that the PQ trees help reduce the number of clusters to be analyzed as well as help in visualizing the internal structures of the clusters. We also hypothesize the function of an unknown gene in *E Coli* based on the permutation pattern.

Roadmap. We begin with an introduction to the PQ tree data structure in Section 2 and show that the minimal consensus PQ tree is indeed the maximal notation of a permutation pattern in Section 3. We present an $\mathcal{O}(kn)$ time algorithm to obtain the minimal consensus PQ tree in Section 4 and present variations of this algorithm for the different genome models in Section 5. We conclude with experimental results in Section 6. The proofs of the theorems and lemmas are omitted and will appear in the full version of this paper.

2 Preliminaries – PQ Tree

In this section we present the PQ tree data structure and definitions as introduced by Booth and Leuker [6], as a tool to solve the general consecutive arrangement problem. The general consecutive arrangement problem is the following: *Given a finite set X and a collection $\mathcal{I}$ of subsets of X, does there exist a permutation π of X in which the members of each subset $I \in \mathcal{I}$ appear as a consecutive substring of π?* Booth and Leuker introduced an efficient algorithm (linear in the length of the input, $\mathcal{O}(n^2)$ in our terms) that solves this problem using a PQ tree. A PQ tree is a rooted tree whose internal nodes are of two types: P and Q. The children of a P-node occur in no particular order while those of a Q-node appear in a left to right or right to left order. We designate a P-node by a circle and a Q-node by a rectangle. The leaves of T are labeled bijectively by the elements of X. The *frontier* of a tree T, denoted by $F(T)$, is the permutation of X obtained by reading the labels of the leaves from left to right.

Definition 2. *Equivalent PQ trees:* *Two PQ trees T and T' are equivalent, denoted $T \equiv T'$, if one can be obtained from the other by applying a sequence of the following transformation rules: (1) Arbitrarily permute the children of a P-node, and (2) Reverse the children of a Q-node.*

Any frontier obtainable from a tree equivalent with T is considered *consistent* with T, and $\mathcal{C}(T)$ is defined as follows: $\mathcal{C}(T) = \{F(T')|T' \equiv T\}$. These last definitions are illustrated in Figure 1. We accordingly define the number of frontiers obtainable from a tree equivalent with T to be $|\mathcal{C}(T)|$. Clearly the equivalence relation is reflexive, symmetric and transitive. To make it computationally straightforward, we use a slightly stricter version of a PQ tree called the *canonical PQ tree*.

Definition 3. *Canonical PQ tree:* *A PQ tree that has no node with only one child and no P node with only two children.*

X = { a,b,c,d,e }

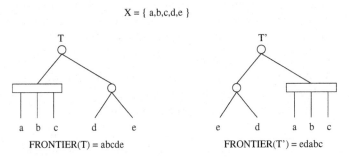

Fig. 1. Two equivalent PQ trees, $T' \equiv T$ and their frontiers. Note that $\mathcal{C}(T) = \mathcal{C}(T') = \{abcde, abced, cbade, cbaed, deabc, decba, edabc, edcba\}$.

Note that it is straightforward to convert any PQ tree to its canonical form: a node with a single child is merged with its immediate predecessor. This process is continued until no such node remains. Further, any P node with exactly two children is changed to a Q node. Through the rest of the paper, we assume a PQ tree is a canonical PQ tree. Some PQ trees are given special names: Given a finite set X, the PQ tree consisting of a single P node with $|X|$ children that are all leaves is called the *universal PQ tree*. We denote the universal tree as T_U. Another important PQ tree is the *null tree*, which has no nodes at all. By convention the null tree has no frontier and it's set of consistent permutations is empty. The most important contribution of [6] is an efficient algorithm for the *REDUCE*() function defined below.

Definition 4. *REDUCE($\mathcal{I}$,T')*: *Given a collection $\mathcal{I}$ of subsets of $N = \{1, 2, \ldots, n\}$ and a PQ tree T' whose leaves are $\{1, 2, \ldots, n\}$, the function* REDUCE*($\mathcal{I}$,T') builds a PQ tree T such that $f \in \mathcal{C}(T)$ iff $f \in \mathcal{C}(T')$ and every $i \in \mathcal{I}$ appears as a consecutive substring of f.*

The procedure $REDUCE(\mathcal{I},T')$ will return the null tree if no frontier $f \in \mathcal{C}(T')$ is such that every $i \in \mathcal{I}$ appears as a consecutive substring of f. Note that if T_U is the universal PQ tree, then $REDUCE(\mathcal{I},T_U)$ builds a PQ tree T such that $f \in \mathcal{C}(T)$ iff every $i \in \mathcal{I}$ appears as a consecutive substring of f. By [6], if the number of subsets in $\mathcal{I} \leq n$, as in our case (see Section 4), then the time complexity of $REDUCE(\mathcal{I},T_U)$ is $\mathcal{O}(n^2)$. In Section 4.1 we present an $\mathcal{O}(n)$ time complexity algorithm for the *REDUCE* function when $\mathcal{I}$ is a set of at most n intervals, based on a data structure presented in [14].

The following observation is immediate from the definition of the *REDUCE*() function. Informally, it says that if T is the PQ tree returned by $REDUCE(\mathcal{I},T_U)$ then if we add more subsets of N to $\mathcal{I}$ then $|\mathcal{C}(T)|$ gets smaller.

Observation 1. *Given two collections $\mathcal{I}_1$, $\mathcal{I}_2$ of subsets of N, if $\mathcal{I}_1 \subseteq \mathcal{I}_2$ and T_1=*REDUCE*($\mathcal{I}_1$,T_U) and T_2=*REDUCE*($\mathcal{I}_2$,T_U) then $\mathcal{C}(T_2) \subseteq \mathcal{C}(T_1)$.*

3   The Minimal Consensus PQ Tree

In this section we define a minimal consensus PQ tree as a representation of the maximal notation of the k occurrences of a πpattern. Through the rest of this paper we define Π to be a set of k permutations $\pi_1, \pi_2, \ldots, \pi_k$ representing k occurrences of a πpattern $N = \{1, 2, \ldots, n\}$.

Definition 5. *Notation of a PQ tree:* *The notation of a PQ tree is obtained by writing the PQ tree as a parenthesized string with different symbols encoding P (comma separators) and Q (dash separators) nodes.*

For example in Figure 1, T is denoted as $((a - b - c), (d, e))$ and the PQ tree in Figure 2 is denoted as $(g - (e - (a - b - c) - d) - f)$. Given Π, our main goal is to construct a PQ tree T from Π, such that the notation of T is the maximal notation of Π. We would like to construct a PQ tree T such that $\mathcal{C}(T) = \{\pi_1, \pi_2, \ldots, \pi_k\}$

however, this is not always possible. Consider a πpattern $\{a, b, c, d, e\}$ appearing four times as $abcde, abced, cbade, edabc$, the PQ tree T in Figure 1 is the one that best describes these appearances. However, $edcba \in \mathcal{C}(T)$ although the πpattern never appeared as $edcba$. On the other hand, notice that the universal PQ tree over Σ, T_U ,is such that $\{\pi_1, \pi_2, \ldots, \pi_k\} \subseteq \mathcal{C}(T_U)$. Hence the idea of *minimal* is introduced. In section 3.2 we suggest a way of reducing the redundant frontiers from the minimal consensus PQ tree. We next present a way of relating a set of permutations to a PQ tree.

Definition 6. *Minimal consensus PQ tree: Given Π, A consensus PQ tree T of Π is such that $\Pi \subseteq \mathcal{C}(T)$ and the consensus PQ tree is minimal when there exists no $T' \not\equiv T$ such that $\Pi \subseteq \mathcal{C}(T')$ and $|\mathcal{C}(T')| < |\mathcal{C}(T)|$.*

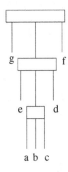

(1) Consensus Trees: If T_U is the universal PQ tree, note that $\pi_1, \pi_2 \in \mathcal{C}(T) \subseteq \mathcal{C}(T_U)$. Thus the consensus of two strings need not give rise to a unique PQ tree.

(2) PQ tree expression power: Consider $\pi_3 = gdcbaef$, clearly $\pi_3 \neq \pi_1$ and $\pi_3 \neq \pi_2$, however $\pi_3 \in \mathcal{C}(T)$.

(3) Height of the PQ tree: A consensus PQ tree of only two strings (permutations) of length L can possibly be of height $\mathcal{O}(L)$.

Fig. 2. Let $\pi_1 = geabcdf$ and $\pi_2 = fecbadg$. The PQ tree T in the figure is a minimal consensus PQ tree of $\{\pi_1, \pi_2\}$. We use this example to illustrate three different ideas as shown on the right.

Figure 2 illustrates the motivation for the definition of minimal consensus. By defining the minimal consensus PQ tree, the problem now is to devise a method to construct the minimal consensus PQ tree given Π. Later we show that the notation of the minimal consensus PQ tree of Π is the maximal notation of Π. We use the following definition from [18]:

Definition 7. *Common Interval (C_Π): Given Π, w.l.o.g we assume that $\pi_1 = id_n := (1, 2, \ldots, n)$. An interval $[i, j]$ $(1 \leq i < j \leq n)$ is called a common interval of Π iff the elements of the set $\{i, i + 1, \ldots, j\}$ appear as a consecutive substring in every $\pi_i \in \Pi$ $(i = 1, 2, \ldots, k)$. The set of all common intervals of Π is denoted C_Π.*

See Figure 3 for an example of common intervals and a minimal consensus PQ tree. Next we state some theorems leading up to the uniqueness of a minimal consensus tree.

Theorem 2. *Given Π, T_C=REDUCE(C_Π,T_U) is a minimal consensus PQ tree of Π.*

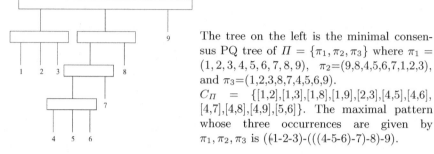

The tree on the left is the minimal consensus PQ tree of $\Pi = \{\pi_1, \pi_2, \pi_3\}$ where $\pi_1 = (1, 2, 3, 4, 5, 6, 7, 8, 9)$, $\pi_2 = (9,8,4,5,6,7,1,2,3)$, and $\pi_3 = (1,2,3,8,7,4,5,6,9)$. $C_\Pi = \{[1,2],[1,3],[1,8],[1,9],[2,3],[4,5],[4,6], [4,7],[4,8],[4,9],[5,6]\}$. The maximal pattern whose three occurrences are given by π_1, π_2, π_3 is ((1-2-3)-(((4-5-6)-7)-8)-9).

Fig. 3. Maximal notation of a πpattern and the corresponding minimal consensus PQ tree.

The following corollary is immediate from the proof of Theorem 2.

Corollary 1. *If T_1 and T_2 are two minimal consensus PQ trees of Π, then $C(T_1) = C(T_2)$.*

Theorem 3. *For two PQ trees T_1 and T_2', if $C(T_1) = C(T_2')$, then $T_1 \equiv T_2'$.*

The following lemma is straightforward to verify.

Lemma 1. *Given Π, the minimal consensus PQ tree T of Π is unique (up to equivalence).*

The minimal consensus PQ tree is not necessarily unique when a character can appear more than once in a πpattern. We handle this problem in Section 5.

3.1   Identifying Maximal πpatterns in the Minimal Consensus PQ Tree

In this section we describe a PQ subtree as a method for identifying non-maximal permutation patterns, and we make the simplifying assumption that there are no multiplicities in the πpatterns, this problem is addressed in Section 5.

Definition 8. PQ subtree: *Given a PQ tree T, the variant v' of a node v is defined as follows: (1) If v is a P node then it's only variant v' is the P node itself. (2) If v is a Q node with k children, then a variant v' of v is a Q node with any $k' \le k$ consecutive children of v. A PQ subtree is rooted at a variant v' of node v and includes all its descendants in the PQ tree T.*

Let $L(v')$ denote the set of the labels of the leafnodes reachable from v'. Further, given the leafnode labels $p = \{\alpha_1, \alpha_2, \ldots, \alpha_n\}$, the least common ancestor (LCA) of p is that variant v' of a node v satisfying the following: (1) $p \subseteq L(v')$ and (2) there exists no variant v'' of v or any other node such that $p \subseteq L(v'')$ and $|L(v'')| < |L(v')|$.

Recall that a πpattern p_1 is non-maximal with respect to πpattern p_2, if each occurrence of p_1 is covered by an occurrence of p_2 and each occurrence of p_2 covers an occurrence of p_1 (notice that $p_1 \subseteq p_2$). Through the rest of this section we assume $p_1 = \{\alpha_1, \alpha_2, \ldots, \alpha_n\}$ and p_2 are πpatterns such that p_1 is non-maximal with respect to p_2. We denote T_i as the minimal consensus PQ tree of the appearances of πpattern p_i, and C_{Π_i} as the set of all common intervals of the occurrences of p_i. The following definition will aid in describing the connection between PQ subtrees and non-maximal πpatterns (Theorem 4).

Definition 9. $T_i^{p_j}$: *Given a PQ tree T_i, and $p_j = \{\alpha_1, \alpha_2, \ldots, \alpha_n\}$, let v' be the LCA of p_j in T_i. Then $T_i^{p_j}$ is the PQ subtree rooted at v'.*

Theorem 4. *Given πpatterns p_1, p_2 on some S, if p_1 is non-maximal w.r.t p_2 then $T_2^{p_1} \equiv T_1$.*

Notice that the converse of Theorem 4 is true only if every occurrence of p_1 is covered by an occurrence of p_2. The following theorem proves that given Π, the problem of obtaining the maximal notation of Π is equivalent to the problem of constructing the minimal consensus PQ tree of Π.

Theorem 5. *The notation of the minimal consensus PQ tree of a πpattern is the maximal notation of the πpattern.*

3.2 Specializing the PQ Tree

Given Π, we would like to construct a PQ tree T such that $\mathcal{C}(T) = \Pi$. However, as shown earlier this is not always possible using a PQ tree. This requires more precise definitions of the P and the Q node. Adding restrictions to the PQ tree will help solve the problem. We suggest the following: (1) Assigning a bi-directional annotation to the Q node as $\Leftrightarrow$ only when the children appear in both directions in the strings and un-annotated otherwise. (2) The exact permutations appearing in the strings for the P node. For example if a P node has 7 children and the annotation is (3162574,5142736), then this implies that the P node has three possible permutations on it's children as 1234567, 3162574 and 5142736. Note that the children are not necessarily leaf nodes. See Figure 4 for an example. The advantage of this is that the PQ tree remains the same and the annotations simply help remove the extra frontiers, $\mathcal{C}(T) \setminus \Pi$, where T is the un-annotated PQ tree.

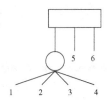

Consider $\Pi = \{123456, 241356\}$. The PQ tree on the left is the minimal consensus PQ tree of Π. Consider the following restrictions: (1) The Q node is un-annotated (2) The exact permutations of the P node is (2413). The restricted PQ tree is such that $\mathcal{C}(T) = \Pi$.

Fig. 4. The restricted PQ tree.

4   Constructing a Minimal Consensus PQ Tree in $\mathcal{O}(kn)$ Time

In this section we devise new algorithms for computing the minimal consensus PQ tree. The first algorithm runs in $\mathcal{O}(kn + n^2)$ time. We then improve this algorithm to $\mathcal{O}(kn)$ time, which is optimal since the length of the input is kn.

We first find a subset of C_Π of size $\mathcal{O}(n)$ that holds sufficient information about the k permutations. For example, consider the πpattern $\{1, 2, 3\}$ appearing twice as $\Pi = \{123, 321\}$, then $C_\Pi = \{[1, 2], [2, 3], [1, 3]\}$. In Theorem 2 we proved that the minimal consensus PQ tree T is such that in every $f \in \mathcal{C}(T)$ the sets $\{1, 2\}$, $\{2, 3\}$ and $\{1, 2, 3\}$ appear as a consecutive substring. Notice that the common interval $[1, 3]$ is redundant in the sense that if the sets $\{1, 2\}$ and $\{2, 3\}$ appear as a consecutive substring in every $f \in \mathcal{C}(T)$, then $\{1, 2, 3\}$ must also appear as a consecutive substring in every $f \in \mathcal{C}(T)$. The common interval $[1, 3]$, which is the union of $[1, 2]$ and $[2, 3]$, is therefore not necessary for constructing T. We next show that the set of common intervals that are necessary for constructing T is the set of *irreducible intervals* as defined in [14]: Given Π, without loss of generality, we assume that $\pi_1 = id_n := (1, 2, \ldots, n)$. Two common intervals $c_1, c_2 \in C_\Pi$ have a non-trivial overlap if $c_1 \cap c_2 \neq \emptyset$ and they do not include each other. A list $p = (c_1, c_2, \ldots, c_{\ell_{(p)}})$ of common intervals $c_1, c_2, \ldots, c_{\ell_{(p)}} \in C_\Pi$ is a chain (of length $\ell_{(p)}$) if every two successive intervals in p have a non-trivial overlap. A chain of length one is called a trivial chain. A common interval I is called *reducible* if there is a non-trivial chain that generates it (I is the union of all elements in all the intervals of the chain), otherwise it is called *irreducible*. This partitions the set of common intervals C_Π into the set of reducible intervals and the set of irreducible intervals, denoted I_Π. Obviously, $1 \leq |I_\Pi| \leq |C_\Pi| \leq \binom{n}{2}$ [14]. The set of irreducible common intervals of Π from the example in Figure 3 is: $I_\Pi = \{[1, 2], [1, 8], [2, 3], [4, 5], [4, 7], [4, 8], [4, 9], [5, 6]\}$ and their chains are illustrated in Figure 5.

The Algorithm. The following algorithm takes advantage of the fact that the irreducible intervals hold as much information as C_Π.

Algorithm PQ-Construct:
Input: Π.
Output: The minimal consensus PQ tree T of Π.

1. Compute I_Π using the algorithm described in [14].
2. Compute T=REDUCE(I_Π, T_U) using the algorithm described in [6].
3. Return T.

In Theorem 2 we proved that T_C=REDUCE(C_Π, T_U) is the minimal consensus PQ tree of Π. In the following lemma we prove that if T_I=REDUCE(I_Π, T_U) then T_C=T_I, thus proving the correctness of the algorithm.

Lemma 2. *Given Π, $T_I = REDUCE(I_\Pi, T_U)$ is the minimal consensus PQ tree of Π.*

Time complexity of the algorithm. Given k permutations each of length n, by [14], $|I_\Pi| < n$ and further, I_Π can be computed in $\mathcal{O}(kn)$ time. By [6], computing $T = REDUCE(I_\Pi, T_U)$ takes $\mathcal{O}(n^2)$ time. The minimal consensus PQ tree can therefore be computed in $\mathcal{O}(kn + n^2)$ time.

4.1   Computing REDUCE(I_Π,T_U) in Linear Time

In this section we modify step 2 of the PQ-Construct algorithm to run in $\mathcal{O}(n)$ time. In [14] a data structure $\mathcal{S}$ was used to obtain the irreducible intervals. For each chain of non-trivially overlapping irreducible intervals, $\mathcal{S}$ contains a doubly-linked list that holds the intervals of that chain in left-to-right order. Moreover, intervals from different lists with the same left or right end are connected by *vertical pointers* yielding for each index $x \in N$ a doubly-linked *vertical list*. The final data structure $\mathcal{S}$ of the example in Figure 3 is shown in Figure 5. We next describe a new algorithm called *REPLACE* that transform $\mathcal{S}$ to the minimal consensus PQ tree. The general idea is to replace every chain by a Q node where the children of the Q node are the roots of subtrees with leaves induced by the intersection between the intervals of the chain. For example, in Figure 5 the chain ($[1, 8], [4, 9]$) is replaced by a Q node of three children where each child is the root of a subtree containing the leaves $\{1, 2, 3\}$, $\{4, 5, 6, 7, 8\}$ and $\{9\}$ respectively. Then, every element that is not a leaf or a Q node and is pointed by a vertical link is replaced with a P node. For example, in Figure 5 the vertical links from $[4, 8]$ to $[4, 7]$ and 8 implies that $[4, 8]$ is replaced by a P node with two children where each child is the root of a subtree containing the leaves $\{4, 5, 6, 7\}$ and $\{8\}$ respectively. Finally, a P node with 2 children is replaced by a Q node. The PQ tree obtained by REPLACE on $\mathcal{S}$ is illustrated in Figure 3.

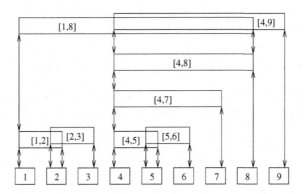

Fig. 5.   Sketch of the data structure $\mathcal{S}$ of the example in Figure 3. The chains of non-trivially overlapping irreducible intervals are: ($[1, 2], [2, 3]$), ($[4, 5], [5, 6]$) and ($[1, 8], [4, 9]$).

A similar idea, for the case of *conserved intervals* [2] (as opposed to irreducible intervals) is discussed in [2, 4, 5].

The following theorem proves that we obtain the minimal consensus PQ tree using REPLACE.

Theorem 6. *If T' is the PQ tree obtained from $\mathcal{S}$ by REPLACE and $T = REDUCE(I_\Pi, T_U)$ then $T \equiv T'$.*

Time complexity of the algorithm. By [14], I_Π and $\mathcal{S}$ can be computed in $\mathcal{O}(kn)$ time. REPLACE can be performed by a simple bottom up traversal of $\mathcal{S}$, therefore in $\mathcal{O}(n)$ time. The minimal consensus PQ tree can therefore be computed in $\mathcal{O}(kn)$ time.

5   Algorithms for Various Genome Models

We next present three different genome models that use the PQ tree tool to detect and represent the maximal patterns as PQ trees. The first model allows only orthologous genes [18] (all the k sequences are permutations of the same n genes, thus, every gene appears exactly once in every sequence). The second model allows both orthologous and paralogous genes (a gene may appear any number of times in a sequence, and may appear in only some of the sequences). The third allows orthologous genes as well as genes that do not appear in all the sequences (a gene can appear at most once in a sequence).

(1) Genomes as Permutations with No Multiplicity. This model is ideal for our tool. Since the k sequences are permutations of Σ with no multiplicity, Σ is a πpattern (common interval) of size n. Furthermore, it is the only maximal πpattern in the sequences. We construct the minimal consensus PQ tree, T, of the set of sequences and obtain the maximal notation of the only maximal πpattern in $\mathcal{O}(kn)$ time. Notice that by traversing T we can output all the πpatterns (common intervals) of the sequences (every subtree of T is a πpattern) in $\mathcal{O}(K)$ time, where $K (\leq \binom{n}{2})$ is the number of πpatterns. Therefore, in $\mathcal{O}(nk + K)$ time we can output all the non-maximal πpatterns, exactly like Heber and Stoye [14] do, but we also present the maximal notation of every πpattern found, and present the non-maximal relations between them. We introduce experimental results of human and rat whole genome comparison for this type of data in Section 6.

(2) Genomes as Strings with Multiplicity. In this case the input is a set of k sequences of n genes, where a gene can appear $K \geq 0$ times.

A string that has at least one character that appears more than once is termed as a string with *multiplicity*. For example if $p_1 = abcegd$ and $p_2 = acgcab$, then p_1 has no multiplicity. However that is not the case with p_2 where a and c each appear more than once.

Consider a pattern p with occurrences as $acbdefc$ and $cdabfec$. Clearly p has a unique minimal consensus PQ tree corresponding to $acbdefc'$ and $cdabfec'$ and treating c' as a distinct character. However, the minimal consensus PQ tree is not necessarily unique when a character can appear more than once in a πpattern.

This is illustrated in an example in Figure 6. We handle multiplicity by reporting the multiple minimal consensus PQ trees. This is explained using the example of Figure 6. Each character is labeled with a distinct integer in the reference sequence and the remaining sequences are treated as multi-sets (strings of sets of characters). In the example, $p_1 = deabcxc = 1234567$ and, $p_2 = cdeabxc =$ $[57]12346[57]$ and $p_3 = cxcbaed = [57]6[57]4321$. If Π_1 and Π_2 are two choices such that $C_{\Pi_2} \subset C_{\Pi_1}$, then clearly the choice of Π_1 is made over Π_2. Continuing the example, the two choices for p_2 are (1) $p_2 = 5123467$, hence $p_3 = 5674321$ or $p_3 = 7654321$ so that $[6,7] \in C_{\Pi}$ and (2) $p_2 = 7123465$, hence $p_3 = 5674321$ or $p_3 = 7654321$ so that $[5,6] \in C_{\Pi}$. See Figure 6 for the corresponding PQ trees. We present an experimental result for this type of data, of a pairwise comparison between the genomes of E $Coli$ K-12 and B $Subtilis$ in Section 6. We used the algorithm described in [12] to find the πpatterns and our tool to present the maximal patterns as PQ trees (thus automatically filtering out the non-maximal patterns).

(3) Genomes as Strings with No Multiplicity. In this case the input is a set of k sequences of n genes, where a gene can appear $K \leq 1$ times. We present

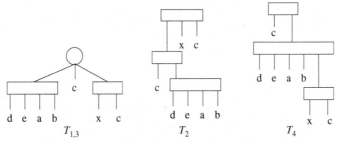

Let $p_1=deabcxc$, $p_2=cdeabxc$ and $p_3=cxcbaed$. Then $p_1 = deabcxc = 1234567$ and, $p_2 = cdeabxc = [57]12346[57]$ and $p_3 = cxcbaed = [57]6[57]4321$. The two choices for p_2 are (1) $p_2 = 5123467$, hence $p_3 = 5674321$ or $p_3 = 7654321$ and (2) $p_2 = 7123465$, hence $p_3 = 5674321$ or $p_3 = 7654321$. Thus the four cases are

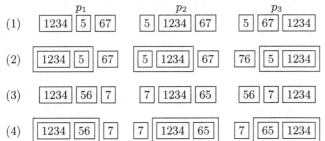

The trees above represent the four cases: $T_{1,3}$ represents the first and third cases, T_2 and T_4 represent the second and fourth cases respectfully. Notice that T_2 and T_4 are both minimal consensus PQ trees of $\{p_1, p_2, p_3\}$ since $|\mathcal{C}(T_2)| = |\mathcal{C}(T_4)| = 8$.

Fig. 6. πpatterns with multiplicity.

an $\mathcal{O}(nk^2)$ time algorithm that finds all maximal πpatterns in the sequences (notice that there can now be more then one maximal πpattern). The idea is to transform the sequences into permutations of the same set, and then build the minimal consensus PQ tree of these permutations. Consider the following example where there are two sequences, 1234567 and 1824376. First we go over the sequences and tag the genes that do not appear in all the sequences, we get 12345'67 and 18'24376. Then, for every tagged gene g' we replace it with $g'g''$ in the sequences where g' appears, and in the sequences where g' doesn't appear we add g' in the beginning of the sequence and g'' in the end of the sequence. After doing that we get 8'12345'5''678'' and 5'18'8''243765''. Now the tagged sequences are permutations of the same set, and furthermore, every πpattern that appeared in all the original sequences, appears in the tagged sequences, and every πpattern that appears in the tagged sequences but doesn't appear in the original sequences must contain a tagged element (this is achieved by splitting the tagged and double tagged elements). Next we construct the minimal consensus PQ tree T, of the tagged sequences. Notice that if a subtree T_i of T has no tagged leaves and there is no subtree T_j of T such that T_i is a subtree of T_j and T_j has no tagged leaves, then T_i represents a maximal πpattern. The minimal consensus PQ tree of the set of tagged sequences created from our example is shown in Figure 7.

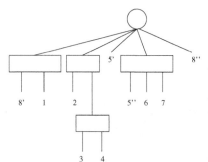

Consider two sequences 1234567 and 1824376, after tagging and adding characters as explained we get the two permutations 8'12345'5''678'' and 5'18'8''243765'', their minimal consensus PQ tree is illustrated above. The subtrees that have no tagged elements (notated $(2 - (3 - 4))$ and $(6 - 7))$ are the only maximal πpatterns of the original sequences.

Fig. 7. An example illustrating the use of tagged sequences.

Time complexity of the algorithm. There are initially k sequences of length n each. It takes $\mathcal{O}(nk^2)$ time to tag and add the elements as needed and we get k tagged sequences of the same length (which is at most $2nk$ if every gene appears in only one sequence, which rarely happens). The minimal consensus PQ tree construction of the tagged sequences takes $\mathcal{O}(nk^2)$ time using the $\mathcal{O}(nk)$ algorithm presented in Section 4. Therefore, the algorithm takes $\mathcal{O}(nk^2)$ time.

We present an experimental result for this type of data, of a comparison between eight *chloroplast* genomes in the full version of this paper.

6   Experimental Results

Human and Rat Genomes. In order to build a PQ tree for human and rat whole genome comparisons we used the output of a program called SLAM [1,

7, 8], SLAM is a comparative-based annotation and alignment tool for syntenic genomic sequences that performs gene finding and alignment simultaneously and predicts in both sequences symmetrically. When comparing two sequences, SLAM works as follows: Orthologous regions from the two genomes as specified by a homology map are used as input, and for each gene prediction made in the human genome there is a corresponding gene prediction in the rat genome with identical exon structure. We used the results from SLAM of comparing human (NCBI Build 31, November 2002) and rat (RGSC v2, November 2002) genomes, sorted by human chromosomes. The data in every chromosome is presented as a table containing columns: *Gene name, rat coords, human coords, rat coding length, human coding length* and *# Exons*.

There were 25,422 genes predicted by SLAM, each gene appears exactly once in each of the genomes. We mapped every one of the 25,422 genes to an integer, thus, the human genome becomes the identity permutation $(1, 2, 3, \ldots, 25422)$, and the rat genome becomes a permutation of $\{1, 2, 3, \ldots, 25422\}$ obtained from the SLAM output table. The full mapping can be found in our web page: http://crilx2.hevra.haifa.ac.il/∼orenw/MappingTable.ps.

Ignoring the trivial permutation pattern involving all the genes, there were only 504 interesting maximal ones out of 1,574,312 permutation patterns in this data set (we only consider patterns that do not cross chromosomes). In Figure 8 we present a subtree of the Human-Rat whole genome PQ tree. This tree corresponds to a section of 129 genes in human chromosome 1 and in rat chromosome 13. By our mapping, these genes appear in the human genome as the permutation: (1997-2125) and in the rat genome as the permutation: (2043-2041, 2025-2018, 2123-2125, 2122-2044, 2040-2026, 2017-1997). Figure 8 is the minimal consensus PQ tree of these two permutations.

Another subtree of the Human-Rat whole genome PQ tree, corresponding to a section of 156 genes in human chromosome 17 and in rat chromosome 10 is ((21028-21061)-(21019-21027)- (21018-20906)). The neighboring genes PMP22 and TEKTIN3 (corresponding to 21014 and 12015) are functionally related genes as explained in [10].

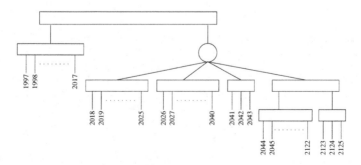

Fig. 8. A PQ subtree of the minimal consensus PQ tree of the human and rat orthologous genes, as predicted by SLAM.

E Coli K-12 and B Subtilis Genomes. Here we present a simple, yet interesting PQ tree obtained from a pairwise comparison between the genomes of *E Coli K-12* and *B Subtilis*. The input data was obtained from NCBI GenBank, in the form of the order of COGs (Clusters Of Orthologous Groups) and their location in each genome.

The data can be found in http://euler.slu.edu/~goldwasser/cogteams/data as part of an experiment discussed by He and Goldwasser in [13], whose goal was to find COG teams. They extracted all clusters of genes appearing in both sequences, such that two genes are considered neighboring if the distance between their starting position on the chromosome (in bps) is smaller than a chosen parameter $\delta > 0$. One of their experimental results, for $\delta = 1900$ was the detection of a cluster of only two genes: COG0718, whose product is an uncharacterized protein conserved in bacteria, and COG0353, whose product is a recombinational DNA repair protein. They conjecture that the function of COG0353 might give some clues as to the function of COG0718 (which is undetermined).

In our experiment we built PQ trees of clusters of genes appearing in both sequences, such that two genes are considered neighboring if they are consecutive in the input data irrespective of the distance between them. There were 450 maximal permutation patterns out of 15,000 patterns discovered by our tool. Here we mention a particularly interesting cluster: (COG2812-COG0718-COG0353). The product of COG2812 is DNA polymerase III, which according to [9] is also related to DNA repair. The PQ tree clearly shows that COG0718, whose function is undetermined is located between two genes whose function is related to DNA repair. This observation further contributes to the conjecture that the function of COG0718 might be also related to DNA repair. Note that the reason that COG2812 was not clustered with COG0718 and COG0353 in [13] is because the distance between COG2812 and COG0718 is 1984 ($> \delta = 1900$).

Acknowledgments

We would like to thank Jens Stoye, Mathieu Raffinot and Ross McConnell for fruitful discussions.

References

1. M. Alexandersson, S. Cawley and L. Pachter. SLAM- Cross-species gene finding and alignment with a generalized pair hidden Markov model. In *Genome Research*, 13(3):496–502, 2003.
2. A. Bergeron, M. Blanchette, A. Chateau and C. Chauve. Reconstructing ancestral gene orders using conserved intervals. In *Proceedings of the Fourth Workshop on Algorithms in Bioinformatics (WABI)*, 14–25, 2004.
3. A. Bergeron, S. Corteel and M. Raffinot. The algorithmic of gene teams. In *Proceedings of the Second Workshop on Algorithms in Bioinformatics (WABI)*, 464–476, 2002.
4. A. Bergeron, J. Mixtacki and J. Stoye. Reversal Distance without Hurdles and Fortresses. In *Proceedings of the 15th Annual Symposium on Combinatorial Pattern Matching (CPM)*, 388–399, 2004.

5. A. Bergeron and J. Stoye. On the similarity of sets of permutations and its applications to genome comparison. In *Proceedings of the ninth Annual International Conference on Computing and Combinatorics (COCOON)*, 68–79, 2003.

6. K. Booth and G. Leuker. Testing for the consecutive ones property, interval graphs, and graph planarity using pq-tree algorithms. In *Journal of Computer and System Sciences*, 13:335–379, 1976.

7. N. Bray, O. Couronne, I. Dubchak, T. Ishkhanov, L. Pachter, A. Poliakov, E. Rubin and D. Ryaboy. Strategies and Tools for Whole-Genome Alignments. In *Genome Research*, 13(1):73–80, 2003.

8. N. Bray, I. Dubchak and L. Pachter. AVID: A Global Alignment Program. In *Genome Research*, 13(1):97–102, 2003.

9. S. K. Bryan, M. E. Hagensee and R. E. Moses. DNA Polymerase III Requirement for Repair of DNA Damage Caused by Methyl Methanesulfonate and Hydrogen Peroxide. In *Journal of Bacteriology*, 16(10):4608–4613, 1987.

10. K.H. Burns, M.M. Matzuk, A. Roy and W. Yan. Tektin3 encodes an evolutionarily conserved putative testicular micro tubules-related protein expressed preferentially in male germ cells. In *Molecular Reproduction and Development*, 67:295–302, 2004.

11. G. Didier. Common intervals of two sequences. In *Proceedings of the Third Workshop on Algorithms in Bioinformatics (WABI)*, 17–24, 2003.

12. R. Eres, L. Parida and G.M. Landau. A combinatorial approach to automatic discovery of cluster-patterns. In *Proceedings of the Third Workshop on Algorithms in Bioinformatics (WABI)*, *Lecture Notes in Bioinformatics*, 2812:139–150, 2003.

13. X. He and M.H. Goldwasser. Identifying conserved gene clusters in the presence of orthologous groups. In *Proceedings of the Eighth Annual International Conferences on Research in Computational Molecular Biology (RECOMB)*, 272–280, 2004.

14. S. Heber and J. Stoye. Finding all common intervals of k permutations. In *Proceedings of the 12th Annual Symposium on Combinatorial Pattern Matching (CPM)*, 207–218, 2001.

15. R.M. McConnell. A certifying algorithm for the consecutive-ones property. In *Proceedings of the Fifteenth Annual ACM-SIAM Symposium on Discrete Algorithms (SODA)*, 15:761–770, 2004.

16. J. Mulley, P. Holland. Small genome, big insights. In *Nature*, 431:916-917, 2004.

17. T. Schmidt and J. Stoye. Quadratic time algorithms for finding common intervals in two and more sequences. In *Proceedings of the 15th Annual Symposium on Combinatorial Pattern Matching (CPM)*, 347–358, 2004.

18. T. Uno and M. Yagiura. Fast algorithms to enumerate all common intervals of two permutations. In *Algorithmica*, 26(2):290–309, 2000.

Hardness of Optimal Spaced Seed Design

François Nicolas and Eric Rivals

L.I.R.M.M.
University of Montpellier II, CNRS U.M.R. 5506
161 rue Ada, F-34392 Montpellier Cedex 5, France
{nicolas,rivals}@lirmm.fr

Abstract. Speeding up approximate pattern matching is a line of research in stringology since the 80's. Practically fast approaches belong to the class of filtration algorithms, in which text regions dissimilar to the pattern are excluded (filtered out) in a first step, and remaining regions are compared to the pattern by dynamic programming in a second step. Among the necessary conditions used to test similarity between the regions and the pattern, many require a minimum number of common substrings between them. When only substitutions are taken into account for measuring dissimilarity, it was shown recently that counting spaced subwords instead of substrings improve the filtration efficiency. However, a preprocessing step is required to design one or more patterns, called gapped seeds, for the subwords, depending on the search parameters. The seed design problems proposed up to now differ by the way the similarities to detect are given: either a set of similarities is given *in extenso* (this is a "region specific" problem), or one wishes to detect all similar regions having at most k substitutions (general detection problem). Several articles exhibit exponential algorithms for these problems. In this work, we provide hardness and inapproximability results for both the region specific and general seed design problems, thereby justifying the exponential complexity of known algorithms. Moreover, we introduce a new formulation of the region specific seed design problem, in which the weight of the seed (*i.e.*, number of characters in the subwords) has to be maximized, and show it is as difficult to approximate than MAXIMUM INDEPENDENT SET.

1 Introduction

A routine task in computational genomics is to search among all known sequences those being similar to a sequence of interest. "Similar" means that can be aligned over reasonably long portions. The similarity in sequence helps in the annotation of the sequence of interest as it may reveal, *e.g.*, if it is a gene, a similarity in function, in regulation, in its interaction with other molecules, in three dimensional structure of the protein product, or a common origin. This task is known as sequence similarity search. Since the 90's, heuristic algorithms [1] are preferred to the direct application of dynamic programming schemes, which require quadratic time. In practice, as the size of the sequence databases

A. Apostolico, M. Crochemore, and K. Park (Eds.): CPM 2005, LNCS 3537, pp. 144–155, 2005.

grows exponentially, efficiency is achieved by *filtration*. The underlying principle of filtration is to exclude in a first step regions of the sequence database that are surely not similar to the query sequence by testing a simple necessary condition. The second step performs an alignment procedure by dynamic programming with the few remaining regions. Application of filtration occurs in software like FLASH [5] or QUASAR [3].

Usual necessary conditions rely on counting common contiguous subwords to the query and the database sequence. Recently, several authors research have emphasized that the shape of the subwords plays a key role in filtration efficiency, and proposed to use "carefully chosen arbitrary shapes" for the subwords [4, 11–14]. The shape of the subwords is given by a gapped seed, *e.g.*, a pattern like ##-##--# where the # symbol indicates which position should match between the query's and database sequence's subword, and the - are don't care positions. One central problem is to choose such a seed to optimize the filtration efficiency. Given a set of similarities (alignments) of interest, the goal is to find the best seed or family of seeds. The problem has been declined in several formulations, either as a decision or a maximization problem. In the former, one searches for a seed that detects all similarities, in the latter for a seed that detects all similarities and maximizes, *e.g.*, the number of # (its weight). Several algorithms whose complexity depends exponentially on the length of the seed have been proposed to solve these problems, but it is not known to which complexity class the simplest forms of the seed design problem belong. Our article answer these questions by showing these problems are NP-hard, or even worse, difficult to approximate.

In [12], the case of lossy filtration is investigated. The authors show that computing the hit probability of set of seeds is NP-hard, but can be approximated (admits a PTAS). They also prove the NP-hardness and the inapproximability of a region specific multiple seeds design problem, where both the set of similarities and the weight of the seeds are constrained (see problem RSOS below).

In this abstract, we consider both lossy and lossless filtrations. We improve on the results of [12] by showing the inapproximability of RSOS even in the case of a single seed (Section 4). Moreover, we prove the hardness of a general seed design problem: NON DETECTION as defined in [11] (Section 2). In this problem, one considers the set of all similarities at a given Hamming distance from the query (this is independent on the query). The problem is more general than RSOS. As by-product of our proof, we introduce and classify a tiling problem (SSC). Several works [4, 7, 11] give empirical and theoretical evidences that support the correlation between the weight of the seed and filtration efficiency. Building on this idea, we propose an optimization problem MWLS in which the weight of the designed seed has to be maximized. We provide a proof of NP-hardness and of inapproximability for MWLS (Section 3).

In the remaining of this section, we introduce a notation, define the investigated problems, and survey known results. Sections 2, 3, and 4 are each dedicated to a problem as listed above and are independent of each other.

1.1   Definitions and Problems

Let $\mathbb{Z}$ denote the set of all integers and for any a, $b \in \mathbb{Z}$, let $[a, b]$ be the set of all $x \in \mathbb{Z}$ satisfying $a \leq x \leq b$. For any finite set X, we denote by $\#X$ the *cardinality* of X. An *alphabet* Σ is a finite set of *letters*. A *word* or *string* over Σ is a finite sequence of elements of Σ. The set of all words over Σ is denoted by $\Sigma^\star$. For a word x, $|x|$ denotes the *length* of x. Given two words x and y, we denote by xy the *concatenation* of x and y. For every $1 \leq i \leq j \leq |x|$, $x[i]$ denotes the i-th letter of x, and $x[i \ ; j]$ denotes the *substring* $x[i]x[i + 1] \ldots x[j]$. For every letter a, $|x|_a := \# \{i \in [1, |x|] : x[i] = a\}$ denotes the number of *occurrences* of the letter a in x. For every integer $n \geq 0$, x^n denotes the concatenation of n copies of x.

Definition 1 (Weight, seed). *The* weight *of a word $w \in \{\#, \text{-}\}^\star$, denoted $\|w\|$, is the number of occurrences of the symbol # in w. A* seed *is a non empty word over the alphabet $\{\#, \text{-}\}$ and whose first and last letter is a # (i.e., an element of $\# \{\#, \text{-}\}^\star \# \cup \{\#\}$).*

Definition 2 (Similarity). *A* similarity *is a word over $\{0, 1\}$. Let m, k be two integers such that $0 \leq k \leq m$. An (m, k)-similarity is a similarity of length m with k occurrences of the symbol 0 and $m - k$ occurrences of the symbol 1 (i.e., an element of $\{s \in \{0, 1\}^m : |s|_0 = k\}$).*

Definition 3 (Detection). *Let g be a word over $\{\#, \text{-}\}$, Γ a set of words over $\{\#, \text{-}\}$, and s a similarity. Let $i \in [0, |s| - |g|]$. We say that g detects s at position i if, for all $j \in [1, |g|]$, $s[i + j] = 1$ whenever $g[j] = \#$. We say that g detects s whenever there exists $i \in [0, |s| - |g|]$ such that g detects s at position i. Moreover, Γ detects s if there is $g \in \Gamma$ that detects s.*

Note that in the previous definition, g (resp. Γ) may be a seed (resp. a set of seeds). In the sequel, ϵ denotes an arbitrarily small positive real number.

We study the complexity of three problems. In Section 2, we consider the decision problem [11]:

> **Name:** Non Detection
> **Instance:** A seed g, two integers m and k satisfying $0 \leq k \leq m$.
> **Question:** Does it exist an (m, k)-similarity not detected by g?

We show that Non Detection is NP-complete (Theorem 2). Note that we assume that any instance (g, m, k) has size $O(|g| + m)$, *i.e.*, that the integers m and k are encoded in unary. If encoded in binary (as usual), (g, m, k) would have size only $O(|g| + \log m)$. In other words, we demonstrate that Non Detection is *strongly* NP-complete.

In Section 3, we investigate the difficulty to approximate the maximization problem:

> **Name:** region specific Maximum Weight Lossless Seed (MWLS)
> **Instance:** A finite set S of similarities.

Solution: A seed g that detects all similarities of S.

Measure: The weight of g.

Theorem 3 proves it does not exist a polynomial time approximation algorithm for MWLS with bound $(\#S)^{0.25-\epsilon}$ unless $\mathrm{P} = \mathrm{NP}$.

In Section 4, we study the maximization problem [12]:

Name: REGION SPECIFIC OPTIMAL SEEDS (RSOS)

Instance: Two integers d and p, a finite set S of similarities.

Solution: A set Γ of seeds satisfying $\#\Gamma = d$ and $\|g\| = p$ for any $g \in \Gamma$.

Measure: The number of similarities in S detected by Γ.

Theorem 4 states that, even when restricted to instances (d, p, S) such that $d = 1$, it does not exist a polynomial time approximation algorithm for RSOS with bound $\frac{e}{e-1} - \epsilon$.

We need additional definitions on hypergraphs. A *hypergraph* is a pair $H := (V, \mathcal{E})$ where V is a finite set of *vertices* and $\mathcal{E}$ is a set of subsets of V. The elements of $\mathcal{E}$ are called *hyperedges*. An *independent set* I of H is a subset of V such that for any $E \in \mathcal{E}$, one has $E \not\subseteq I$. Let $r \geq 2$ be an integer. H is said to be *r-uniform* when for any $E \in \mathcal{E}$, $\#E = r$. A 2-uniform hypergraph is a *graph* and its hyperedges are simply called *edges*.

1.2 Related Works

Concerning NON DETECTION. Let m and k be two integers such that $0 \leq k \leq m$. Let us denote by

- $\mathrm{U}(\Gamma, m, k)$ the number of (m, k)-similarities left undetected by the set of seeds Γ,
- $\mathrm{T}(\Gamma, m, k)$ the largest integer $t \geq 0$ satisfying: for any (m, k)-similarity s, there are t distinct pairs (i_1, g_1), (i_2, g_2), $\ldots$, (i_t, g_t) such that for any $j \in [1, t]$ one has $g_j \in \Gamma$, $i_j \in [0, |s| - |g_j|]$ and g_j detects s at position i_j. Informally, $\mathrm{T}(\Gamma, m, k)$ is the minimal number of positions at which any (m, k)-similarity is detected by Γ.

In [11], one finds dynamic programming algorithms to compute $\mathrm{U}(\Gamma, m, k)$ and $\mathrm{T}(\Gamma, m, k)$ in time proportional to

$$m \times \sum_{j=0}^{k} \binom{\lambda}{j}(k - j + 1) + (\#\Gamma) \times \sum_{j=0}^{k} \binom{\lambda}{j} \quad \text{with} \quad \lambda := \max_{g \in \Gamma} |g| \ .$$

A simple bound [4] guarantees that these algorithms have complexities in $O(2^{\lambda} \times (mk + \#\Gamma))$, and are thus Fixed Parameter Tractable (FPT) for parameter λ (see [6] for details on parameterized complexity). The algorithm that computes $\mathrm{T}(\Gamma, m, k)$ described in [11] generalizes to a family of seeds the one for the case of a single seed given in [4, Section 4].

Solving NON DETECTION for an instance (g, m, k) means to decide whether $U(\{g\}, m, k)$ differs from zero (resp. if $T(\{g\}, m, k)$ equals zero). Theorem 2 implies that, even if we restrict ourselves to the case of a single seed ($\#\Gamma = 1$), any algorithm computing $U(\Gamma, m, k)$ (resp. $T(\Gamma, m, k)$) requires in the worst case exponential time. Thus, the algorithms given in [4, 11] have the best time complexities one can hope for.

Concerning MWLS **and** RSOS. It is shown in [12] that the decision version of RSOS is NP-hard, even when searching for a single seed instead of a family of seeds. The authors of [12] also prove that RSOS does not admit a polynomial time approximation algorithm with bound $\frac{e}{e-1} - \epsilon$ unless P = NP. Theorems 3 and 4 improve on these results.

2   Hardness of NON DETECTION

To show the hardness of NON DETECTION, we introduce an intermediate problem:

> **Name:** SOAPY SET COVER (SSC)
> **Instance:** A finite subset $G \subseteq \mathbb{Z}$, two non-negative integers N and q.
> **Question:** Does it exist a subset $T \subseteq \mathbb{Z}$ of cardinality q such that $G + T$ contains at least N consecutive integers?

It is related to tiling problems. We assume that any instance (G, N, q) of SSC has size $O(\max G - \min G + N + q)$. In other words, we assume that the integers N and q are encoded in unary, and that the set G is encoded by a bit-vector.

First in Theorem 1, we reduce EXACT COVER BY 3-SETS (X3C) to SSC. In X3C, we are given a 3-uniform hypergraph $(V, \mathcal{E})$ and search for a subset of $\mathcal{E}$ that partitions V. X3C is NP-hard [9] (it can be seen as a generalization of 3D-MATCHING). Then, in Theorem 2 we reduce SSC to NON DETECTION.

Theorem 1. SSC *is* NP-*complete.*

Proof. SSC is in NP, since for any positive instance (G, N, q) of SSC, a subset $T \subseteq [1 - \max G, N - \min G]$ of cardinality at most q satisfying $[1, N] \subseteq G + T$ is a polynomial certificate for SSC on (G, N, q). Let us now reduce X3C to SSC.

Let $(V, \mathcal{E})$ be an instance of X3C. If 3 does not divide $\#V$ then $(V, \mathcal{E})$ is a negative instance of X3C that we transform into $(\emptyset, 1, 0)$, a negative instance of SSC. Without loss of generality, we can now suppose that after numbering the elements of V, $V = [q + 1, 4q]$ where $q := \frac{\#V}{3}$. Let us also number the elements of $\mathcal{E}$: set $m := \#\mathcal{E}$ and write $\mathcal{E} = \{E_1, E_2, \ldots, E_m\}$.

Let $N := 2q^2 + 4q$. For any $i \in [1, m]$ and any $j \in [1, q]$, let:

$$F_j := [(j - 1)(2q - 1) + 4q + 1, j(2q - 1) + 4q],$$
$$G_{i,j} := \{j\} \cup E_i \cup F_j \cup \{N - j + 1\}, \qquad \tau_{i,j} := 2N((i-1)q + j - 1),$$

and set $G := \bigcup_{i=1}^{m} \bigcup_{j=1}^{q} (G_{i,j} + \tau_{i,j})$.

We obtain an instance (G, N, q) of SSC. One can easily check that this transformation takes polynomial time.

Let us first explain the gadget of the proof. The sets $G_{i,j}$ (for $(i, j) \in [1, m] \times [1, q]$) are subsets of $[1, N]$, and the $\tau_{i,j}$'s are the mq multiples of $2N$ comprised between 0 and $2N(mq - 1)$. Thus, G is a subset of $[1, 2Nmq]$. Moreover, each of the mq intervals of length $2N$ partitioning $[1, 2Nmq]$ (that is to say, the $[2N(k-1) + 1, 2Nk]$'s for $k \in [1, mq]$) contain a unique $G_{i,j} + \tau_{i,j}$ in their left half and no element of G in their right half.

Let us now dwell on the $G_{i,j}$: the cardinality of $G_{i,j}$ is $2q + 4$ since $G_{i,j}$ is the disjoint union of the hyperedge E_i whose cardinal is 3, of the segment F_j whose cardinality equals $2q - 1$, and of two singletons.

Let $F := [4q + 1, N - q] = [4q + 1, 2q^2 + 3q]$. The four segments $[1, q]$, $[q + 1, 4q]$, F, and $[N - q + 1, N]$ have length q, $3q$, $2q^2 - q$, and q, respectively. They form a partition of $[1, N]$. Each contributes to $G_{i,j}$: the singleton $\{j\}$ is included in $[1, q]$, the hyperedge E_j is included in $[q + 1, 4q] = V$, F_j is included in F, and the singleton $\{N - j + 1\}$ in $[N - q + 1, N]$. Besides, $\{F_1, F_2, \ldots, F_q\}$ is the unique partition of F in segments of length $2q - 1$.

Lemma 11. *If $(V, \mathcal{E})$ is a positive instance of* X3C *then (G, N, q) is a positive instance of* SSC.

Proof. Suppose there exists $\mathcal{C} \subseteq \mathcal{E}$ that is a partition of V. Then, $\mathcal{C}$ has cardinality $\#V/3 = q$ and thus, there are $i_1, i_2, \ldots, i_q \in [1, m]$ such that $\mathcal{C} = \{E_{i_1}, E_{i_2}, \ldots, E_{i_q}\}$. Let us set $T := \{-\tau_{i_1,1}, -\tau_{i_2,2}, \ldots, -\tau_{i_q,q}\}$.

By construction, T has cardinality q and for any $j \in [1, q]$, one has

$$G_{i_j,j} = (G_{i_j,j} + \tau_{i_j,j}) - \tau_{i_j,j} \subseteq G - \tau_{i_j,j} \subseteq G + T$$

therefore $G + T$ includes

$$\bigcup_{j=1}^{q} G_{i_j,j} = \bigcup_{j=1}^{q} \{j\} \cup \bigcup_{j=1}^{q} E_{i_j} \cup \bigcup_{j=1}^{q} F_j \cup \bigcup_{j=1}^{q} \{N - j + 1\}$$
$$= [1, q] \quad \cup \quad V \quad \cup \quad F \quad \cup [N - q + 1, N] \ = [1, N] \,.$$

It follows that (G, N, q) is a positive instance of SSC. $\square$

It remains to show that whenever (G, N, q) is a positive instance of SSC, $(V, \mathcal{E})$ is a positive instance of X3C. For this, we need the following lemma.

Lemma 12.

$$\forall t \in \mathbb{Z} \quad \exists (i, j) \in [1, m] \times [1, q] \qquad (G + t) \cap [1, N] \subseteq G_{i,j} + \tau_{i,j} + t \,.$$

Proof. Let $t \in \mathbb{Z}$. $G + t$ can be written as the union of the sets $G_{i,j} + \tau_{i,j} + t$ with $(i, j) \in [1, m] \times [1, q]$. Now by construction, the $G_{i,j} + \tau_{i,j}$'s, and thus, the $G_{i,j} + \tau_{i,j} + t$'s, are distant from each other of at least N positions. It follows that the intersection of $G + t$ with $[1, N]$ cannot contain some elements of two distinct $G_{i,j} + \tau_{i,j} + t$'s. $\square$

Now assume that (G, N, q) is a positive instance of SSC. There is $T \subseteq \mathbb{Z}$ satisfying $\#T = q$ and $[1, N] \subseteq G + T$.

Lemma 13. *There are (i_1, j_1, u_1), (i_2, j_2, u_2), ..., $(i_q, j_q, u_q) \in [1, m] \times [1, q] \times \mathbb{Z}$ such that the sets $G_{i_1, j_1} + u_1$, $G_{i_2, j_2} + u_2$, ..., $G_{i_q, j_q} + u_q$ are pairwise distinct and form a partition of $[1, N]$.*

Proof. Let us number arbitrarily the elements of T: $T := \{t_1, t_2, \ldots, t_q\}$. Lemma 12 guarantees that, for each $k \in [1, q]$, there are $i_k \in [1, m]$ and $j_k \in [1, q]$ satisfying $(G + t_k) \cap [1, N] \subseteq G_{i_k, j_k} + \tau_{i_k, j_k} + t_k$.

Let $u_k := \tau_{i_k, j_k} + t_k$. Since $[1, N] \subseteq G + T = \bigcup_{k=1}^{q} (G + t_k)$, it follows that $[1, N] \subseteq \bigcup_{k=1}^{q} (G + t_k) \cap [1, N] \subseteq \bigcup_{k=1}^{q} (G_{i_k, j_k} + u_k)$. So, $[1, N]$, whose cardinality is $N = q \times (2q + 4)$, is covered by the $G_{i_k, j_k} + u_k$'s (for $k \in [1, q]$), which are at most q and have each cardinality $2q + 4$. This requires that the $G_{i_k, j_k} + u_k$'s are pairwise distinct and partition $[1, N]$. □

Proving that $u_1 = u_2 = \cdots = u_q = 0$ will enable us to deduce from Lemma 13 that the G_{i_k, j_k}'s (for $k \in [1, q]$) are pairwise disjoint, and so will the q hyperedges E_{i_1}, E_{i_2}, ..., E_{i_q} (be pairwise disjoint). This will mean that $\{E_{i_1}, E_{i_2}, \ldots, E_{i_q}\}$ is a partition of V, and $(V, \mathcal{E})$ a positive instance of X3C.

Let us first show that

$$\forall k \in [1, q] \qquad -q < u_k < q. \tag{1}$$

The integers j and $N - j + 1$ are respectively the smallest and largest elements of $G_{i, j}$. Then for any $k \in [1, q]$, one has:

$$\min(G_{i_k, j_k} + u_k) = j_k + u_k \quad \text{and} \quad \max(G_{i_k, j_k} + u_k) = N - j_k + 1 + u_k.$$

As $G_{i_k, j_k} + u_k$ is included in $[1, N]$ (Lemma 13), it yields $1 \leq j_k + u_k$ and $N - j_k + 1 + u_k \leq N$, which implies $1 - j_k \leq u_k \leq j_k - 1$. As j_k is at most q, one gets $1 - q \leq u_k \leq q - 1$, what we wanted.

Second, let us prove

$$\{j_1, j_2, \ldots, j_q\} = [1, q]. \tag{2}$$

By definition of j_k (Lemma 13), one has $\{j_1, j_2, \ldots, j_q\} \subseteq [1, q]$. Thus, it suffices to show that the j_k's ($k \in [1, q]$) are pairwise distinct. The proof relies on the following claim:

Claim 11. *If S is a segment of length $2q - 1$ and if u is an integer satisfying $-q < u < q$ then the center of S (i.e., $(\max S + \min S)/2$) belongs to $S + u$.*

Assume there are $k, l \in [1, q]$ satisfying $k \neq l$ and $j_k = j_l$. By (1), one has $-q < u_k, u_l < q$, and so, by Claim 11, both $F_{j_k} + u_k$ and $F_{j_l} + u_l$ contain the center of $F_{j_k} = F_{j_l}$. This contradicts the fact that $G_{i_k, j_k} + u_k$ and $G_{i_l, j_l} + u_l$ are disjoint (by Lemma 13) and thus, we have shown (2).

Equation (2) allows to renumber the triples (i_k, j_k, u_k) (for $k \in [1, q]$) in such a way that $j_k = k$ for all $k \in [1, q]$.

Now, assume the set $K := \{k \in [1, q] : u_k \neq 0\}$ is non-empty, and set $\kappa := \min K$. The following claim will lead to a contradiction.

Claim 12. *Let* $S \subseteq \mathbb{Z}$ *and* $X \subseteq S$ *such that* $\min X = \min S$ *and* $\max X = \max S$. *Then* X *is the unique translate of* X *included in* S *(i.e., for any* $u \in \mathbb{Z}$, $X + u \subseteq S$ *implies* $u = 0$).

For any $j \in [1, \kappa - 1]$, the set $G_{i_j, j} + u_j$

  - contains j and $N - j + 1$ (since $j \notin K$ requires $u_j = 0$ and $G_{i_j, j} = G_{i_j, j} + u_j$)
  - and, has an empty intersection with $G_{i_\kappa, \kappa} + u_\kappa$ (by Lemma 13).

Thus, none of j and $N - j + 1$ belongs to $G_{i_\kappa, \kappa} + u_\kappa$. As by Lemma 13, $G_{i_\kappa, \kappa} + u_\kappa$ is a subset of $[1, N]$, one gets $G_{i_\kappa, \kappa} + u_\kappa \subseteq [\kappa, N - \kappa + 1]$. Applying Claim 12 with $X := G_{i_\kappa, \kappa}$ and $S := [\kappa, N - \kappa + 1]$ yields $u_\kappa = 0$, which contradicts $\kappa \in K$.

We have then demonstrated that $K = \emptyset$, *i.e.*, that $u_1 = u_2 = \cdots = u_k = 0$. This concludes the proof of Theorem 1. $\qquad\square$

Theorem 2. NON DETECTION *is* NP-*complete.*

Proof. NON DETECTION is in NP, since for any positive instance (g, m, k) of NON DETECTION, an (m, k)-similarity not detected by g is a polynomial certificate for NON DETECTION on (g, m, k). Hence, to obtain the NP-completeness of NON DETECTION, it suffices to reduce SSC to NON DETECTION (Theorem 1).

Let (G, N, q) be an instance of SSC. If needed, we may translate G such that $\min G = 0$; from now on we make this assumption. Thus, we have $G \subseteq [0, \max G]$. Let g be the word over $\{\#, \text{-}\}$ of length $\max G + 1$ defined by: for all j in $[1, |g|]$, $g[j] = \#$ iff $|g| - j \in G$.

One has $|g| - 1 = \max G \in G$ and $|g| - |g| = 0 \in G$; thus, $g[1] = g[|g|] = \#$, *i.e.*, the first and last letters of g are $\#$. Let $m := N - 1 + |g|$ and $k := \min\{m, q\}$. We obtain an instance (g, m, k) of NON DETECTION in a time polynomial in function of (G, N, q).

Additionally, one has $N - 1 = m - |g|$ and thus,

$$[0, N - 1] = [0, m - |g|] . \tag{3}$$

• Assume (g, m, k) is a positive instance of NON DETECTION.

There is an (m, k)-similarity s that is not detected by g. Let us set $T := \{j \in [1, m] : s[j] = 0\} - |g|$. On one hand, T is a translate of a set of cardinality k (by Definition 2) and has itself cardinality $k \leq q$. Let $i \in [0, N - 1]$. On the other hand by Equation (3), one has $i \in [0, m - |g|]$ and then, by hypothesis, g does not detect s at position i. Therefore, there exists $j \in [1, |g|]$ satisfying $g[j] = \#$ and $s[i + j] = 0$. So, one gets $|g| - j \in G$ and $i + j - |g| \in T$, and this yields $i = (|g| - j) + (i + j - |g|) \in G + T$. We have thus shown that $G + T$ includes $[0, N - 1]$, from which we deduce that (G, N, q) is a positive instance of SSC.

• Conversely, let (G, N, q) be a positive instance of SSC.

Then, there exists $T \subseteq \mathbb{Z}$ having cardinality q and such that $[0, N - 1] \subseteq G + T$. Let $s \in \{0, 1\}^m$ be defined by: for all $i \in [1, m]$, $s[i] = 0$ iff $i \in T + |g|$.

Let $i \in [0, m - |g|]$. By Equation (3), one has $i \in [0, N - 1]$ and then, by hypothesis, there are $\gamma \in G$ and $t \in T$ such that $i = \gamma + t$. Setting $j := |g| - \gamma$, one gets $g[j] = \#$ since $|g| - j = \gamma \in G$. It follows that

$$i + j = (\gamma + t) + (|g| - \gamma) = t + |g| \in T + |g|$$

and thus, that $s[i + j] = 0$. It implies that g cannot detect s at position i. As i can be chosen arbitrarily in $[0, m - |g|]$, g does not detect s.

Now, it is true that $|s|_0 \leq |s| = m$ and $|s|_0 \leq \#(T + |g|) = \#T = q$, and so $|s|_0 \leq \min\{m, q\} = k$. By replacing enough 1 in s by 0's, one obtains an (m, k)-similarity that is undetected by g. It follows that (g, m, k) is a positive instance of NON DETECTION and this concludes the proof of Theorem 2.   □

3   Hardness and Inapproximability of MWLS

In order to demonstrate the inapproximability of MWLS, we reduce MAXIMUM INDEPENDENT SET (MIS) to it. In MIS, given a graph $G = (V, \mathcal{E})$, one searches for the largest independent set I of G. It is known [10] that MIS cannot be approximated within bound $(\#V)^{0.5-\epsilon}$ unless P = NP.

Let $n \geq 1$ be an integer. Let us set $\delta_i^n := (i - 1)n^2 + i^2$ for any $i \in [1, n]$. Recall that a Golomb ruler is a set of integers such that the difference between any two distinct points in this set characterizes these two points [2].

Lemma 1. *The set* $\{\delta_1^n, \delta_2^n, \ldots, \delta_n^n\}$ *is a Golomb ruler with n marks computable in polynomial time in n.*

Proof. It is clear that the set $\{\delta_1^n, \delta_2^n, \ldots, \delta_n^n\}$ is computable in polynomial time in n. Let $i_1, j_1, i_2, j_2 \in [1, n]$ satisfying $i_1 < j_1$ and $i_2 < j_2$. It remains to show that our set is a Golomb ruler, *i.e.*, that $\delta_{j_1}^n - \delta_{i_1}^n = \delta_{j_2}^n - \delta_{i_2}^n$ implies $i_1 = i_2$ and $j_1 = j_2$.

For any $\alpha \in \{1, 2\}$, set $N_\alpha := \delta_{j_\alpha}^n - \delta_{i_\alpha}^n$, $q_\alpha := j_\alpha - i_\alpha$, and $r_\alpha := j_\alpha^2 - i_\alpha^2$. One has $N_\alpha = q_\alpha n^2 + r_\alpha$ and $0 \leq r_\alpha < n^2$, and so q_α and r_α are respectively the quotient and the remainder of the Euclidean division of N_α by n^2. Moreover, i_α and j_α can be written in function of q_α and r_α:

$$i_\alpha = \left(r_\alpha q_\alpha^{-1} - q_\alpha \right) / 2 \qquad \text{and} \qquad j_\alpha = \left(r_\alpha q_\alpha^{-1} + q_\alpha \right) / 2. \qquad (4)$$

Assume $\delta_{i_1}^n - \delta_{j_1}^n = \delta_{i_2}^n - \delta_{j_2}^n$. One gets $N_1 = N_2$, and by the uniqueness of the quotient and remainder of a division, one obtains $q_1 = q_2$ and $r_1 = r_2$. So, one deduces from (4) that $i_1 = i_2$ and $j_1 = j_2$.   □

Definition 4 (Gadgets). *Let $X \subseteq [1, n]$. Let w_X^n denote the word over $\{\#, -\}$ satisfying: $|w_X^n| = n^3 + n^2$, $\|w_X^n\| = \#X$, and $w_X^n[\delta_x^n] = \#$ for any $x \in X$. Let g_X^n denote the seed obtained from w_X^n by deleting the leading and trailing $-$ symbols.*

Next Lemma means that the g_X^n (for $X \subseteq [1, n]$) are in one-to-one correspondence with the subsets of $[1, n]$. It builds on Lemma 1.

Lemma 2. *Let X_1 and X_2 be two subsets of $[1, n]$ having cardinality at least 2. Then, $g_{X_1}^n = g_{X_2}^n$ if and only if $X_1 = X_2$.*

Proof. For any $\alpha \in \{1, 2\}$, let us set $g_\alpha := g_{X_\alpha}^n$ and $w_\alpha := w_{X_\alpha}^n$. There exists $p_\alpha \in [0, n^3 + n^2 - |g_\alpha|]$ such that $w_\alpha = (\text{-})^{p_\alpha} g_\alpha (\text{-})^{n^3 + n^2 - |g_\alpha| - p_\alpha}$.

Assume $g_1 = g_2$ and let us show that $X_1 = X_2$. Notice that $X_\alpha = \{x \in [1, n] : w_\alpha[\delta_x^n] = \#\}$, so X_α is completely determined by w_α; therefore, it suffices to show that $w_1 = w_2$ or equivalently that $p_1 = p_2$.

One has $|g_\alpha| \geq \|g_\alpha\| = \#X_\alpha \geq 2$, and for any $i \in [1, |g_\alpha|]$, $w_\alpha[p_\alpha + i] = g_\alpha[i]$. Especially, if $i = 1$, one gets $w_\alpha[p_\alpha + 1] = g_\alpha[1] = \#$; so, there exists $i_\alpha \in X_\alpha$ such that $p_\alpha + 1 = \delta_{i_\alpha}^n$. Also, if $i = |g_\alpha|$, one obtains $w_\alpha[p_\alpha + |g_\alpha|] = g_\alpha[|g_\alpha|] = \#$ and thus, there is $j_\alpha \in X_\alpha$ satisfying $p_\alpha + |g_\alpha| = \delta_{j_\alpha}^n$.

On one hand, one has $\delta_{j_\alpha}^n = p_\alpha + |g_\alpha| \geq p_\alpha + 2 > p_\alpha + 1 = \delta_{i_\alpha}^n$. On the other hand, one also has $\delta_{j_1}^n - \delta_{i_1}^n = |g_1| - 1 = |g_2| - 1 = \delta_{j_2}^n - \delta_{i_2}^n$. Then Lemma 1 ensures that $\delta_{i_1}^n = \delta_{i_2}^n$, from which we deduce $p_1 = \delta_{i_1}^n - 1 = \delta_{i_2}^n - 1 = p_2$. $\square$

Definition 5 (Some more gadgets). *Let $v \in [1, n]$. Let σ_v^n denote the similarity satisfying: $|\sigma_v^n| = n^3 + n^2$, $|\sigma_v^n|_1 = n - 1$, and $\sigma_v^n[\delta_x^n] = 1$ for any $x \in [1, n]$ such that $x \neq v$.*

Next Lemma explains the role of the σ_v^n's (for $v \in [1, n]$). Combined with the preceding lemma, it implies that the seeds detecting σ_v^n are in one-to-one correspondence with the g_X^n's (for $X \subseteq [1, n]$, $v \notin X$), as well as with the subsets of $[1, n]$ that do not contain v.

Lemma 3. *Let $v \in [1, n]$ and let g be a seed. Then, g detects σ_v^n if and only if there exists $X \subseteq [1, n]$ such that $v \notin X$ and $g = g_X^n$.*

Proof. • Assume there is $X \subseteq [1, n]$ such that $v \notin X$ and $g = g_X^n$. As g_X^n is a substring of w_X^n, it is enough to show that w_X^n detects σ_v^n at position 0. Let $i \in [1, n^3 + n^2]$ such that $w_X^n[i] = \#$. There exists $x \in X$ such that $i = \delta_x^n$. Since $v \notin X$, one has $x \neq v$ so, $\sigma_v^n[i] = \sigma_v^n[\delta_x^n] = 1$, what we wanted.

• Conversely, suppose g detects σ_v^n. Let $p \in [0, |\sigma_v^n| - |g|]$ such that g detects σ_v^n at position p. Then, $w := (\text{-})^p g(\text{-})^{n^3 + n^2 - |g| - p}$ detects σ_v^n at position 0. Let us set $X := \{x \in [1, n] : w[\delta_x^n] = \#\}$. First, note that $\sigma_v^n[\delta_v^n] = 0$; consequently, $w[\delta_v^n] = \text{-}$ and thus, $v \notin X$. Moreover, since w detects σ_v^n and has the same length as σ_v^n, it is easy to see that $w = w_X^n$ and thus, $g = g_X^n$. $\square$

Theorem 3. *MWLS is NP-hard. Moreover, if MWLS admits a polynomial time approximation algorithm with bound $(\#S)^{0.25 - \epsilon}$ then P $=$ NP.*

Proof. We reduce MIS to MWLS in such a way that it preserves the approximation properties. Let $G = (V, \mathcal{E})$ be a graph; G is an instance of MIS. Let $n := \#V$. After numbering the vertices of G, we can assume $V = [1, n]$ and thus, for any edge $E \in \mathcal{E}$, we have $E = \{\min E, \max E\}$. We build the set of similarities $S_G := \{1^{n^3 + n^2}\} \cup \{s_E^n : E \in \mathcal{E}\}$ where $s_E^n := \sigma_{\min E}^n 0^{n^3 + n^2} \sigma_{\max E}^n$ for any egde $E \in \mathcal{E}$. S_G is an instance of MWLS that can be constructed from G in polynomial time. Next two Lemmas guarantee that our reduction preserves the approximation.

Lemma 31. *For any independent set I of G, there is a seed of weight $\#I$ that detects all similarties in S_G.*

Proof. Let I be an independent set of G. Clearly, g_I^n is a seed of weight $\#I$ detecting $1^{n^3+n^2}$. Moreover, any edge $E \in \mathcal{E}$ admits an extremity v such that $v \notin I$. Hence, by Lemma 3, g_I^n detects σ_v^n and, all the more reason for g_I^n to detect its superstring s_E^n. □

Lemma 32. *For any seed g of weight at least 2 detecting all similarities in S_G, there is an independent set I of G whose cardinality equals $\|g\|$. Moreover, I is computable in polynomial time in function of g.*

Proof. Let $E \in \mathcal{E}$. Let f_E be a substring of s_E^n detected by g with the same length as g. Since g starts and ends by a #, f_E starts and ends by a 1. Moreover, the presence of $1^{n^3+n^2}$ in S_G implies $|f_E| = |g| \le n^3 + n^2$. Hence, the block $0^{n^3+n^2}$ that lies between $\sigma_{\min E}^n$ and $\sigma_{\max E}^n$ in s_E^n is longer than f_E. This requires f_E to be fully included in $\sigma_{\min E}^n$ or $\sigma_{\max E}^n$. Thus, there exists $v_E \in \{\min E, \max E\}$ such that g detects $\sigma_{v_E}^n$ and, by Lemma 3, this garantees the existence of $X_E \subseteq [1, n]$ such that $g = g_{X_E}^n$ and $v_E \notin X_E$.

Since $\#X_E = \|g\| \ge 2$, Lemma 2 implies that the X_E's (with $E \in \mathcal{E}$) are all equal to each other, and thus, their common value, denoted I, is an independent set of G of cardinality $\|g\|$. Besides, it is easy to see that $I = \{x \in [1, n] : g[\delta_x^n] = \#\}$ can be computed in polynomial time from g. □

One has $\#S_G = \#\mathcal{E} + 1 \le (\#V)^2$; so, if there exists an approximation algorithm for MWLS with bound $(\#S)^{0.25-\epsilon}$, Lemmas 31 and 32 would allow to design an approximation algorithm for MIS whose bound is $(\#S_G)^{0.25-\epsilon} \le ((\#V)^2)^{0.25-\epsilon} = (\#V)^{0.5-2\epsilon}$. But, this is possible only if P = NP [10]. This concludes the proof of Theorem 3. □

4   Hardness and Inapproximability of RSOS

We obtain the result on the hardness to approximate RSOS by reducing MAXIMUM COVERAGE (MC) to RSOS. Our reduction is different than the one in [12] since it works even for a single seed. We use an alternative formulation of MC: given a hypergraph $(V, \mathcal{E})$ and an integer $k \ge 0$, search for a subset $C \subseteq V$ of cardinality k that maximizes the number of hyperedges $E \in \mathcal{E}$ satisfying $C \cap E \ne \emptyset$. This problem is not approximable within $\frac{e}{e-1} - \epsilon$ unless P = NP [8]. Actually, we obtain a stronger result that is the pendant to the one of Feige [8] for MC: unless P = NP, it does not exist a polynomial algorithm that, for any instance of RSOS, returns not a solution, but only an approximate value of the optimal solution within bound $\frac{e}{e-1} - \epsilon$ of the optimal.

Theorem 4. *Even if restricted to instances (d, p, S) such that $d = 1$, RSOS does not admit a polynomial time approximation algorithm with bound $\frac{e}{e-1} - \epsilon$ unless P = NP.*

Due to lack of space, the proof of Theorem 4 is not included in this extended abstract.

Acknowledgments

This work is supported by the CNRS STIC Specific Action #185 and the ACI IMPBio "REPEVOL". We thank G. Kucherov and L. Noé for introducing us to the problem NON DETECTION.

References

1. S. F. Altschul, W. Gish, W. Miller, E. W. Meyers, and D. J. Lipman. Basic local alignment search tool. *Journal of Molecular Biology*, 215(3):403–410, 1990.
2. W. C. Babcock. Intermodulation interference in radio systems. *Bell System Technical Journal*, 32(1):63–73, 1953.
3. S. Burkhardt, A. Crauser, P. Ferragina, H.-P. Lenhof, E. Rivals, and M. Vingron. q-gram Based Database Searching Using a Suffix Array (QUASAR). In *Third Annual International Conference on Computational Molecular Biology*, pages 77–83, Lyon, France, 11–14 April 1999. ACM Press.
4. S. Burkhardt and J. Kärkkäinen. Better filtering with gapped q-grams. *Fundamenta Informaticae*, 56(1–2):51–70, 2003.
5. A. Califano and I. Rigoutsos. FLASH: A fast look-up algorithm for string homology. In L. Hunter, D. Searls, and J. Shavlik, editors, *Proceedings of the 1st International Conference on Intelligent Systems for Molecular Biology*, pages 56–64, Menlo Park, CA, USA, July 1993. AAAI Press.
6. R. G. Downey and M. R. Fellows. *Parameterized Complexity*. Monographs in Computer Science. Springer, 1999.
7. M. Farach-Colton, G. M. Landau, S. Cenk Sahinalp, and D. Tsur. Optimal spaced seeds that avoid false negatives. url: http://cs.haifa.ac.il/~landau/gadi/seeds.ps.
8. U. Feige. A threshold of $\ln n$ for approximating set cover. *Journal of the Association for Computing Machinery*, 45(4):634–652, 1998.
9. M. R. Garey and D. S. Johnson. *Computers and Intractability: A Guide to the Theory of NP-Completeness*. W. H. Freeman and Co., 1979.
10. J. Håstad. Clique is hard to approximate within $n^{1-\epsilon}$. *Acta Mathematica*, 182:105–142, 1999.
11. G. Kucherov, L. Noé, and M. Roytberg. Multi-seed lossless filtration. In *Proceedings of the 15h Annual Symposium on Combinatorial Pattern Matching (CPM'04)*, volume 3109, pages 297–310. Lecture Notes in Computer Science, 2004.
12. M. Li, B. Ma, D. Kisman, and J. Tromp. PatternHunter II: Highly sensitive and fast homology search. *Journal of Bioinformatics and Computational Biology*, 2(3):417–439, 2004.
13. B. Ma, J. Tromp, and M. Li. Patternhunter: faster and more sensitive homology search. *Bioinformatics*, 18(3):440–445, 2002.
14. L. Noé and G. Kucherov. Improved hit criteria for DNA local alignment. *BMC Bioinformatics*, 5(149), 2004. doi:10.1186/1471-2105-5-149.

Weighted Directed Word Graph*

Meng Zhang, Liang Hu, Qiang Li, and Jiubin Ju

College of Computer Science and Technology, Jilin University,
Changchun 130012, China
zm@mail.edu.cn

Abstract. Weighted Directed Word Graph is a new text-indexing structure which is based on a new compaction method on DAWG. WDWGs are basically cyclic, means that they may accept infinite strings. But by assigning weights to the edges, the acceptable strings are limited only to the substrings of input strings. The size of WDWGs is smaller than that of DAWGs both in theory and practice. A linear-time on-line construction algorithm for WDWGs is also presented.

1 Introduction

Index structures, such as Directed Acyclic Word Graph (DAWG)[1, 4], suffix trees[5], play an important role in many applications such as pattern matching, intrusion detection systems and computational biology. A major drawback that limits the applicability of indexes is their space complexity. In this paper, we introduce the Weighted Directed Word Graph (WDWG), a new index structure that is as efficient as the DAWG, but more space economical. We compact the DAWG in a new way that merges states to fewer state sets and the edges that emit from state set to fewer weighted edges. As a result, we obtain a family of weighted automata that can be seen as an alternative to suffix trees and DAWGs. We demonstrate that for a given word w, the WDWG of w has at most $|w| + 1$ states and $2|w| - 1$ transition edges. On-line algorithm to build WDWG from input word in liner time is also given.

2 Basic Definitions

Let Σ be a nonempty alphabet and Σ^* the set of words over Σ, with ε as the empty word. Let w be a word in Σ^*, $|w|$ denotes its length, $w[i]$ its ith letter, and $w[i : j]$ its factor(subword) that begins at position i and ends at position j. If $w = xyz$ with $x, y, z \in \Sigma^*$, then x, y and z denotes some subwords of w, x is a prefix of w, and z is a suffix of w. Denote w^r the reverse word of w. $Pref(w)$ denotes the set of all prefixes of w, $Suff(w)$ denotes the set of all suffixes of w and $Fact(w)$ the set of its factors. Let $S \subset \Sigma^*$. For any string $u \in \Sigma^*$,

---

* Supported by National Natural Science Foundation of China No.90204014 and Natural Science Foundation of Science and Technology Department of Jilin Province No.20030516

A. Apostolico, M. Crochemore, and K. Park (Eds.): CPM 2005, LNCS 3537, pp. 156–167, 2005.

let $u^{-1}S = \{x|ux \in S\}$. The syntactic congruence associated with $Suff(w)$ is denoted by $\equiv_{Suff(w)}$ and is defined, for $x, y, w \in \Sigma^*$, by

$$x \equiv_{Suff(w)} y \Longleftrightarrow x^{-1}Suff(w) = y^{-1}Suff(w).$$

We call classes of factors the congruence classes of the relation $\equiv_{Suff(w)}$. Let $[u]_w$ denote the congruence class of $u \in \Sigma^*$ under $\equiv_{Suff(w)}$. The longest element in the equivalence class $[u]_w$ is called its *representative*.

Definition 1 *The **DAWG** of w is a directed acyclic graph with set of states $\{[u]_w|u \in Fact(w)\}$ and set of edges $\{([u]_w, a, [ua]_w)|u, ua \in Fact(w), a \in \Sigma\}$. Denoted by $DAWG(w)$. The state $[\varepsilon]_w$ is called the **root** of $DAWG(w)$.*

Denote the state set of $DAWG(w)$ by $SD(w)$, the edge set by $ED(w)$. An edge labeled by a is called an a-edge. The edges of the DAWG are divided into two categories. The edge $([u]_w, a, [ua]_w)$ is called soild if ua is the representative of $[ua]_w$, otherwise it is called secondary. With each node $[u]_w$ we associate a number $depth([u]_w)$ defined as the depth of $[u]_w$ in the tree of solid edges. Let p be a state of $DAWG(w)$, different from root, and u be the representative of p. The suffix link of p, denoted by $fail(p)$, is the state whose representative v is the longest suffix of u such that v not $\equiv_{Suff(w)} u$. Then the sequence $(p, fail(p), fail^2(p), \ldots)$ is finite and ends at the root of $DAWG(w)$. This sequence is called the *suffix chain* of p, denoted by $SC(p)$.

Definition 2 *Let $w \in \Sigma^*$, ε is a prime prefix of w; Let t be a prefix of w, if t is not a suffix of any prefix of w, then t is a prime prefix of w. The set of prime prefixes of w is denoted by $pp(w)$.*

Prime prefixes of w are in one to one correspondence with the leaves of implicit suffix tree [5] of w^r. It is clear that w is a prime prefix of itself. For wa, any prime prefix of w, which is not a suffix of wa, is a prime prefix of wa.

3   Weighted Directed Word Graph

The nodes and suffix links of $DAWG(w)$ form the suffix tree of reverse string of w [1]. Let p be a prime prefix of w, $SC([p]_w) = (s_1, s_2, \ldots, s_m)$ where $s_1 = [p]_w, s_m = [\varepsilon]_w$. Let s_i be the first state in $SC([p]_w)$ that has an a-edge, then all the states in $SC(s_i)$ have an edge labeled by a. Let the destinations of these edges be $d_1, d_2, \ldots, d_{m-i+1}$, then by deleting reduplicate states this sequence is the suffix chain of d_1 omitted $[\varepsilon]_w$. For $j \geq i$, let the subword set $I(p, j) = s_1 \cup s_2 \cup \ldots \cup s_j$, $J = d_1 \cup d_2 \cup \ldots \cup d_j$. For $\forall t \in I(p, j)$, if $|t| \leq depth(s_i)$, then $ta \in J$. This implies that the set $I(p, j), j \geq i$, has an edge $(I(p, j), J, a, L)$ labeled by a with a *weight* $L = depth(s_i)$ which demarcates $I(p, j)$.

Through the observation above, we find, by certain rules, we can merge the states along suffix chains into a series of state sets. And the states, which are destinations of edges labeled by the same letter emitted from states in one set, are just merged into one set. The sets and the weight edges form a new index structure with less states and edges. An example of WDWG is displayed in Fig.1.

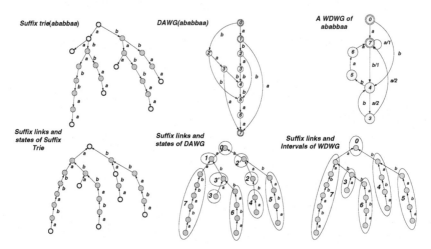

Fig. 1. $w = ababbaa$. Graphics upset are suffix trie for w, $DAWG(w)$ and a possible WDWG for w. Undersides are corresponding trees formed by suffix links and nodes of each structure upset. The digital after the letter on some WDWG edges is the *weight* of the edge, weight of the edge with no digital is the depth of the state emits the edge.

We now give some important notions that are bases of the new structure. For state s of $DAWG(w)$, denote $Fs(s)$ the set of states whose suffix links are s, called *fail set* of s. Give function $min\colon SD(w) \to SD(w)$, for state s, if $Fs(s) = \varPhi$ or $s = [\varepsilon]_w$, then $min(s)$ is undefined; else $min(s)$ is a state selected from $Fs(s)$. Function min is called an order function of $DAWG(w)$ and $min(s)$ is called the *electee child* of s.

Definition 3 *Let M be an order function of $DAWG(w)$. A partial order $\leq_M$ can be derived from M as follow: for $t \in Fs(s)$, if $t \neq M(s)$, then $M(s) \leq_M t$; for state r, t, if there exists $r' \in SC(r)$ and $t' \in SC(t)$, such that $r' \leq_M t'$, then $r \leq_M t$. The partial order $\leq_M$ is called a backdating order of w.*

We define the interval and partition by backdating order as following:

Definition 4 *Let $p \in pp(w)$, $\leq_M$ be a backdating order of w. The state s_c, which is the first state in $SC([p]_w)$ such that $s_c \neq M(fail(s_c))$ or $fail(s_c) = [\varepsilon]_w$, is called the **terminal point** of backdating path of p under $\leq_M$. The set, includes all the subwords belong to the states in suffix chain from $[p]_w$ to s_c, is denoted by $[p]_w^M$, called the **interval** of p under M. The interval set $I_M(w) = \{[p]_w^M \,|\, p \in pp(w)\}$ is called a **partition** of $Fact(w)$ by M.*

For a partition of $Fact(w)$, it is clear that any subword of w belongs to just one interval. For an interval I of a partition, any subword in I is a suffix of the longest subword in I. Denote the longest subword u in I by $end(I)$, the shortest one v by $short(I)$, and denote I by $[v, u]$. $short(I)$ is called the *starting position* of I. Denote the length of I by $length(I) = |u| - |v| + 1$. Let v' be the suffix of v that $|v'| = |v| - 1$, then I can also be denoted by $(v', u]$. Denote the set $Ia \cap Fact(w)$ by Ia/w.

An interval may contain several states of $DAWG(w)$. The new index structure ensures that the states, which are destinations of edges emitted from states in an interval, are merged into one interval. This property is defined as follow.

Definition 5 *The pair* $(I, \alpha) \in I_M(w) \times \Sigma$ *is called a **consistent pair**, if there is one and only one interval in* $I_M(w)$, *say* J, *that* $I\alpha/w \subseteq J$. *If any* $(I, \alpha) \in I_M(w) \times \Sigma$ *is consistent pair, then* $I_M(w)$ *is called a **consistent partition** of* w. *The partition order* $\leq_M$ *is called a **consistent partial order** of* w.

For an order function M of $DAWG(w)$, $I_M(w)$ is not always a consistent partition. Fig.2 illustrates an inconsistent partition and a consistent one.

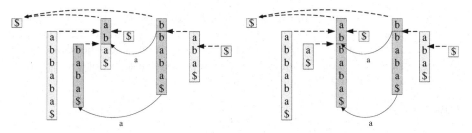

Fig. 2. The left figure is an inconsistent partition of $Fact(ababbaa)$ and the right is a consistent one. Dotted edges are suffix links of intervals, that will be defined later. The set $[b, ababb]a$ is scattered to $[a, aba]$ and $[bba, ababba]$ in left figure, but keeps integrity in the right figure.

Taking advantage of consistent partition, we define the new index structure.

Definition 6 *The **Weighted Directed Word Graph** (WDWG) for* w *under a consistant partition* $I_M(w)$ *is a weighted directed graph with node(state) set* $I_M(w)$, *and edge set* $\{(I, J, a, L)|I, J \in I_M(w), Ia/w \neq \Phi$ *and* $Ia/w \subseteq J, \forall t \in I$, *if* $|t| \leq L$, *then* $ta \in J$, *else* ta *is not a subword of* $w\}$. *Denoted by* $WDWG_M(w)$. $[\varepsilon]_w^M$ *is called the root of* $WDWG_M(w)$.

WDWGs is not always acyclic as DAWGs. In some cases, the source and destination of an edge may be the same interval. So we delete "acyclic" from the name of the structure. For an edge $e = (p, q, a, L)$ of a WDWG, we say that p has an edge emits from L. According to L, the interval p is divided into two parts: $A = \{t|t \in p \text{ and } |t| \leq L\}$; $B = \{t|t \in p \text{ and } |t| > L\}$. Any subword t in A, ta is a subword of w. Any subword t in B, ta is not a subword of w. As in DAWG, edges in WDWG are divided into two groups: solid edges and non-solid edges. If $end(q) = L + 1$, an edge (p, q, a, L) is solid, otherwise it is non-solid. Define the *suffix link* of an interval I as follow: $fail(I) = J$, where the suffix of $short(I)$ with length $|short(I)| - 1$ is in J. The suffix links of WDWG are also weighted. The weight of suffix link (I, J) is $|short(I)|$. $|short(I)|$ is called the attach point of I on $fail(I)$. The sequence $(I, fail(I), fail^2(I), \ldots, [\varepsilon]_w^M)$ is called the suffix chain of I, denoted by $SC(I)$. For each interval I of $WDWG_M(w)$, denote the set of intervals whose fail links are I by $Fs(I)$. The intervals and suffix links of

WDWG of w form a structure similar to *suffix cactus* [6] of w^r. The relationship between WDWG of w and suffix cactus of w^r has an analogy with that between *factor automaton* [1] and suffix tree of w^r.

Define automaton $ST(Q, E, T, i)$ based on $WDWG_M(w)$ as following: $Q = \{(q, l)|q \in S(WDWG_M(w)), |short(q)| \leq l \leq |end(q)|\}$, $E = \{(p, l), a, (q, l + 1)|(p, l), (q, l + 1) \in Q, a \in \Sigma, \exists(p, q, a, L) \in E(WDWG_M(w)), l \leq L\}$, $T = Q$ and $i = ([\varepsilon]_w^M, 0)$. Apparently, the automaton is equivalent to suffix trie of w. By this automaton, $WDWG_M(w)$ provides an index on $Fact(w)$.

4   Size of WDWG

The bounds on the maximum number of states and edges in $WDWG_M(w)$ in terms of the length of w are derived in this section. According to the definition of WDWG, the states in $WDWG_M(w)$ are in one to one correspondence with prime prefixes of w. For the number of prime prefixes of w is not greater than $|w| + 1$, the bound on the number of states is:

Lemma 1 *For $w \in \Sigma^*$, $WDWG_M(w)$ has at most $|w| + 1$ states.*

For the bound on the number of edges, we have:

Lemma 2 *For $w \in \Sigma^*$, $WDWG_M(w)$ has at most $2|w| - 1$ edges.*

Proof. Each edge of $DAWG(w)$ can be mapped to an edge of $WDWG_M(w)$ through the mapping σ defined as following:

$$\sigma((s, a, t)) = (I, J, a, L)$$

where (s, a, t) is an edge of $DAWG(w)$, (I, J, a, L) is an edge of $WDWG_M(w)$, $s \subseteq I, t \subseteq J$. According to the definition of WDWG, for any edge e of $DAWG(w)$, $\sigma(e)$ is unique. Edges labeled by a, which emit from DAWG states that belong to I, are mapped to (I, J, a, L). So σ is an injective mapping.

Let $p \neq \varepsilon$ be a prime prefix, $nc(p)$ denote the number of $DAWG(w)$ states in $[p]_w^M$, $(s_1 = [p]_w, \ldots, s_{nc(p)})$ is the backdating path of p under $\leq_M$. For p occurs in w just once, this means for $p \neq w$, $[p]_w$ has only one edge. For $p \neq w$, if the only solid edge of $[p]_w$ is labeled by a, then all the states on suffix chain of $[p]_w$ have an edge labeled by a. So the $nc(p)$ edges labeled by a emitted from $s_1, \ldots, s_{nc(p)}$ are mapped to one weighted edge. If $p = w$, $[w]_w$ has no edge.

If $fail([w]_w) = [\varepsilon]_w$, then $nc(w) = 1$ and 0 edge is mapped to 0 weighted edge. Let E_D denote the number of edges of $DAWG(w)$ and E_R denote that of $WDWG_M(w)$, S_D denote the number of states of $DAWG(w)$ and S_R denote that of $WDWG_M(w)$. For σ is an injective mapping, we have $E_D - E_R \geq (\Sigma_{p \in pp(w)} nc(p) - 1) - (S_R - 1)$. Therefore $E_D - E_R \geq S_D - S_R$ and

$$E_R \leq E_D - S_D + S_R.$$

By lemma 1.6 in [1], there is: $E_D - S_D \leq |w| - 2$. By lemma1, there is $S_R \leq |w| + 1$, so:

$$E_R \leq 2|w| - 1.$$

If $fail([w]_w) \neq [\varepsilon]_w$, then states on suffix chain of $fail([w]_w)$ have edges labeled by a which one of edges of $fail([w]_w)$ is labeled by. So the $nc(w) - 1$ edges labeled by a emitted from $s_1 = [w]_w, \ldots, s_{nc(w)}$ are mapped to one weighted edge. For σ is an injective mapping, we have $E_D - E_R \geq (\Sigma_{p \in pp(w)} nc(p) - 2) - (S_R - 1)$. Therefore $E_R \leq E_D - S_D + S_R + 1$. By lemma 1 and lemma 1.6 in [1], we have

$$E_R \leq 2|w|.$$

For $E_D - S_D$ is the number of non-solid edges, if $E_D - S_D$ reaches its maximum, there are maximum number of non-solid edges. In this case, each non-solid edge (p, a, q) is associated with the suffix uav of w as follows: u is the label of the longest path from initial state to p, and v is the label of the longest path from q to a terminal state [1, 3]. If $fail([w]_w) \neq [\varepsilon]_w$, then any suffix of w that belongs to $fail([w]_w)$ will not be associated with any non-solid edges, because those suffixes that are not included in terminal state. So $E_D - S_D < |w| - 2$. Therefore we have $E_R \leq 2|w| - 1$. So in both cases, $E_R \leq 2|w| - 1$.□

The following theorem is the direct consequence of Lemma 1 and Lemma 2.

Theorem 1 *For $w \in \Sigma^*$, a Weighted Directed Word Graph for w has at most $|w| + 1$ states and $2|w| - 1$ edges.*

5   On-Line Construction of WDWG

The on-line construction algorithm of WDWG processes the letters of w from left to right. At each step of construction, a WDWG of the prefix of w that has been processed is created correctly. The main works of the algorithm are to convert the current partition to a new consistence partition.

w and a consistent order function M of w are the only two parameters that determine the $WDWG_M(w)$. When a letter, say a, is inputted, the algorithm selects a consistent order function of wa, say M', based on M. In this process, there is at most one $DAWG(w)$ state whose electee child is changed. Now we demonstrate how the process works. First, define $tail(w)$ as the longest suffix of w that occurs more than once in w. In the construction of DAWG, during the process of converting $DAWG(w)$ to $DAWG(wa)$, there are two cases:

(a) If the state represented by $tail(wa)$ already exists in $DAWG(w)$, then the DAWG construction creates a new state $[wa]_{wa}$;

(b) Else two states are created: $[wa]_{wa}$, $[tail(wa)]_{wa}$.

In (a), the state, whose electee child is likely to be changed by the WDWG construction algorithm, is $[tail(wa)]_w = [tail(wa)]_{wa}$. In case (b), let x be a substring such that $x \in [tail(wa)]_w$ and $x \notin [tail(wa)]_{wa}$. Then, $[tail(wa)]_w$ is split to two state: $[tail(wa)]_{wa}$ and $[x]_{wa}$. $Fs([tail(wa)]_{wa}) = \{[x]_{wa}, [wa]_{wa}\}$. A state in $Fs([tail(wa)]_{wa})$ is selected as the electee child of $[tail(wa)]_{wa}$. Electee children of all the states of $DAWG(w)$ are hold fixed. In both cases, the only state whose electee child is likely to be changed is $[tail(wa)]_{wa}$.

In case(a), if $tail(wa) = \varepsilon$, then letter a doesn't occur in w, the interval of wa is set to $[a, wa]$. For $Fs([wa]_{wa}) = \Phi$, so $M'([wa]_{wa})$ is undefined and $M' = M$. Let the interval set $S = \{I \in I_{M'}(wa) | Ia/wa \neq \Phi\}$. Intervals in S are in one to one correspondence with the intervals on $SC([w]_w^M)$, and for any $I \in S$, there is $Ia/wa \subseteq [wa]_{wa}^{M'}$. For I_M is a consistent partition of $DAWG(w)$, so $I_{M'} = I_M \cup [a, wa]$ is a consistent partition too. Then we get:

Lemma 3 *Let $I_M(w)$ be a consistent partition of w. If $tail(wa) = \varepsilon$, then $I_{M'}(wa) = I_M(w) \cup [a, wa]$ is a consistent partition.*

In case (a), if $tail(wa) \neq \varepsilon$, then the algorithm selects the electee child of $[tail(wa)]_{wa}$ from $[wa]_{wa}$ and $M([tail(wa)]_w)$. In case (b), the algorithm selects the electee child of $[tail(wa)]_{wa}$ from $[wa]_{wa}$ and $q = [r, t]$ which is the $WDWG_M(w)$ interval that $tail(wa)$ belongs to. According to the electee child selected, there are three operations to convert a partition of w to that of wa.

If $[wa]_{wa}$ is selected as $M'([tail(wa)]_{wa})$, then there are

- **split**(q, wa) creates $[wa]_{wa}^{M'} = [r, wa]$, sets $q = (tail(wa), t]$, holds other intervals fixed, that is $I_{M'}(wa) = I_M(w) \cup \{[r, wa]\} \cup \{(tail(wa), t]\} - \{q\}$;
- **prolong**(q, wa) if $t = tail(wa)$, then it sets q to $[r, wa]$, $[wa]_{wa}^{M'} = q$, holds other intervals fixed, that is $I_{M'}(wa) = I_M(w) \cup \{[r, wa]\} - \{q\}$.

If q is selected as $M'([tail(wa)]_{wa})$, then there is

- **attach**(q, wa) creates $[wa]_{wa}^{M'} = (tail(wa), wa]$, holds other intervals fixed, that is $I_{M'}(wa) = I_M(w) \cup \{(tail(wa), wa]\}$.

The first interval I in $SC([w]_w^M)$ that $Ia/w \neq \Phi$ is denoted by $fail([w]_w^M, a)$, which is the first interval in $SC([w]_w^M)$ that has an a-edge. The following lemma summarizes the modification that must be made to update a consistent partition of w to that of wa.

Lemma 4 *Let $I_M(w)$ be a consistent partition of w and $tail(wa) \neq \varepsilon$, v be the longest suffix of w in $p = fail([w]_w^M, a)$, u be the longest word in p that ua is a factor of w, and $q = [r, t]$ be the interval that $tail(wa)$ belongs to. Transform $I_M(w)$ to $I_{M'}(wa)$ as the following:*

- (i) *if $|v| > |u|$, then set $M'([tail(wa)]_{wa}) = [wa]_{wa}$,*
  - a) *if $pa/w = q$, then $I_{M'}(wa) = I_M(w) \cup \{[r, wa]\} - \{q\}$,*
  - b) *else $I_{M'}(wa) = I_M(w) \cup \{[r, wa]\} \cup \{(tail(wa), t]\} - \{q\}$;*
- (ii) *if $|v| < |u|$, then select the state in $Fs([tail(wa)]_{wa})$ which is not $[wa]_{wa}$ as the electee child of $[tail(wa)]_{wa}$, $I_{M'}(wa) = I_M(w) \cup (tail(wa), wa]$;*
- (iii) *if $|v| = |u|$, then set the electee child of $[tail(wa)]_{wa}$ optionally, that transform $I_M(w)$ to $I_{M'}(wa)$ according to (i) or (ii) optionally.*

Then the partition $I_{M'}(wa)$ is a consistent partition of wa.

Proof. Let $p = fail([w]_w^M, a) = [x, y]$, $[w]_w^M$ be the current *active* state.

(i) $|v| > |u|$

In $I_M(w)$, $[x, u]a$ is a sub-interval of q, but $(u, v]a$ is not. To ensure the consistence of $I_{M'}(wa)$, the interval $pa/wa = [x, v]a$ should be in one interval in $I_{M'}(wa)$. Then the operation $split(q, wa)$ is employed to reach this goal. We get $I_{M'}(wa)$, in which $[wa]_{wa}^{M'} = [r, wa]$, $q = (tail(wa), t]$, and $pa/wa \subseteq [wa]_{wa}^{M'}$.

Now we check the consistency of $I_{M'}(wa)$. Let set $Sp = \{I \in I_M(w)|Ia/w = \Phi$ and $Ia/wa \neq \Phi\}$. For each $I \in Sp$, $Ia/wa \in (va, wa]$, because $(va, wa] \subseteq [wa]_{wa}^{M'}$, therefore (I, a) is a consistent pair. Let $IP \in I_{M'}(wa)$, that $[x, v] \subseteq IP$, then $IPa/wa = [x, v]a \subseteq [wa]_{wa}^{M'}$, therefore (IP, a) is a consistent pair. Let interval set $S1 = \{I \in I_M(w)|Ia/w \neq \Phi$ and $Ia/w \subseteq q$ and $|short(I)| > |short(IP)|\}$. For each $I \in S1$, $Ia/wa \in (tail(wa), t] = q$. Therefore, any pair (I, a) where $Ia/wa \subseteq q$ or $Ia/wa \subseteq [wa]_{wa}^{M'}$ is consistent. So all the pair $(I, a) \in I_{M'}(wa) \times \Sigma$ where $Ia/wa \neq \phi$ are consistent, then $I_{M'}(wa)$ is a consistent partition of wa. If $t = tail(wa)$, then $prolong(q, wa)$ is employed, $q = [r, wa]$, $[wa]_{wa}^{M'} = q$, other intervals are held fixed. It is clear that $I_{M'}(wa)$ is consistent. Case(i) is illustrated in Fig.3.

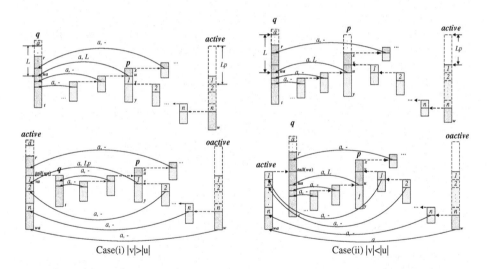

Case(i) $|v|>|u|$ Case(ii) $|v|<|u|$

Fig. 3. Two cases in updating $I_M(w)$ to $I_{M'}(wa)$. The figures upset are sketches of $I_M(w)$, undersides are sketches of $I_{M'}(wa)$. Dashed edges are suffix links, the solids are edges of WDWG. In the figures, $|v| = Lp$ and $|u| = L$.

(ii) $|v| < |u|$

$[x, u]$ is the longest sub-interval of p that $[x, a] \subseteq Fact(w)$. To ensure the consistence of $I_{M'}(wa)$, the interval $[x, u]a$ should be in one interval in $I_{M'}(wa)$, then the operation $attach(q, wa)$ is employed to reach this goal. For $\forall(I, a) \in I_M(w) \times \Sigma, Ia/w \neq \Phi$, because all the intervals in $I_M(w)$ are preserved in $I_{M'}(wa)$, then (I, a) is a consistent pair in $I_{M'}(wa)$. Let set $Sp = \{I \in I_M(w)|Ia/w = \Phi$ and

$Ia/wa \neq \Phi\}$, which is the suffix chain of $[w]_w^M$ ended at interval whose suffix link is p. For each $I \in Sp$, there is $Ia/wa \subseteq (tail(wa), wa]$, therefore (I, a) is a consistent pair. So any pair $(I, a) \in I_{M'}(wa) \times \Sigma$ that $Ia/wa \neq \Phi$ is consistent pair, then $I_{M'}(wa)$ is a consistent partition of wa. This is illustrated in Fig. 3.

(iii) $|v| = |u|$

This case is the degenerate case of (i) or (ii). So either employ the $split(q, wa)$ or $attach(q, wa)$, the $I_{M'}(wa)$ generated is a consistent partition of wa. $\square$

The operations on set Fs of each interval are critical in proving the linear time of construction of WDWG. To achieve the linear time, we implement the set $Fs(q)$ by adjacency lists, named *fail list* of q. First, attach to each interval q a fail list node, named *shadow* of q, denoted by $sh(q)$. q is called the *master* of $sh(q)$. Intervals in $Fs(q)$ are put into several groups according to starting position. Within each group, the intervals have the same starting position and an interval's shadow is selected as the *representative* of the group. Fail list of q is the list of representatives of groups in $Fs(q)$ ordered by the starting position in incremental order. The next group pointer of representative points to the next representative in fail list, while the next group pointer of non-representative shadow points to the representative of the group it belongs to.

Array FS is employed to store the header of each interval's fail list. Array $SHORT$ is employed to store the length of the shortest word in each interval, array $Fail$ stores the fail values of intervals. Function $Insert(h, q)$ inserts the shadow of interval q into a fail list h. Function $Divide\&Redirect(h, L, q)$ divides fail list h into two fail lists, the first includes groups of h, whose starting positions are not less than L, the second is the list of other groups. Function $Divide\&Redirect$ also redirects suffix link of master of each shadow in first list to q. Function $CrtState(L, q)$ creates a new interval p with $SHORT[p] = L$, $Fail[p] = q$. In construction, only the $Fail$ value of representative's master interval is correct, to get the other interval's suffix link, we must fetch the $Fail$ of representative interval.

The construction algorithm includes three procedures: $Build\_WDWG$, $Update$, and $split$. $Build\_WDWG$ is the main procedure. For a new letter, $Build\_WDWG$ updates the current WDWG by calling $Update$.

x is input word with length len.
$Build\_WDWG(x, len)$

1 $root \leftarrow CrtState(0, NULL)$
2 $active \leftarrow root; i \leftarrow 0$
3 **while** $i < len$ **do**
4     $active \leftarrow Update(x, i, active)$
5     $i \leftarrow i + 1$
6 **end while**

Let $w = x[0 : i - 1]$, $x[i] = a$, $Update$ transforms the $WDWG_M(w)$ to $WDWG_{M'}(wa)$. The main works of $Update$ include three parts: (1) Creating $I_{M'}(wa)$ from $I_M(w)$ according to lemma 3 and lemma 4; (2) Inserting new edges; Redirecting edges; (3) Adjusting suffix links. First, $Update$ backdates the suffix chain of $active = [w]_w^M$, until a state that already has an a-edge is found. Let the state be $p = [x, y]$ and the state the a-edge leads to be q, the length of the longest common suffix of w and y be Lp, the length of a-edge be L.

If $Lp \leq L$ and the a-edge is solid, then $active$ is set to q, the a-edge is marked as non-solid; else procedure $split$ is called to deal this case. If $Lp > L$, then $Update$ creates partition $qn = [wa]_{wa}^{M'} = (tail(wa), wa]$, holds other intervals fixed and sets $Fail[qn] = q$, adds qn to $FS[q]$. If no state with an a-edge is encountered, then according to lemma 3, create $qn = [wa]_{wa}^{M'} = [a, wa]$, set $Fail[qn] = fail(qn) = root$. At last, $Update$ traverse the $SC([w]_w^M)$ not include p and the subsequent and puts new a-edges from each state to $[wa]_{wa}^{M'}$. The length of each new edge $([u]_{wa}^{M'}, [wa]_{wa}^{M'}, a, L)$ is set to the length of longest common suffix of u and w. For the address of new active state is not predictable, $Update$ doesn't add new a-edges in walking up the $SC([w]_w^M)$ for the first time .

$Update(x, i, active)$

1 $a \leftarrow x[i]$	17 **break**
2 $p \leftarrow r \leftarrow oactive \leftarrow active$	18 **else**
3 $fl \leftarrow L \leftarrow Lp \leftarrow i$	19 $Lp \leftarrow SHORT[p] - 1$
4 **while** TRUE **do**	20 $p \leftarrow \boldsymbol{fail}(p)$
5 **if** p has an a-edge $e = (p, q, a, L)$ **then**	21 **if** $p = NULL$ **then**
6 **if** $L < Lp$ **then**	22 $active \leftarrow \boldsymbol{CrtState}(1, root)$
7 **if** e is solid **and** $L = Lp$ **then**	23 $\boldsymbol{Insert}(FS[root], active)$
8 $active \leftarrow q$	24 **break**
9 Mark e as non-solid	25 **end if**
10 **else**	26 **end if**
11 $(qn, p, q, active) \leftarrow \boldsymbol{split}(p, q, L, a)$	27 **end while**
12 **end if**	28 **while** $r \neq p$ do **do**
13 **else**	29 $E \leftarrow E + \{(oactive, active, a, fl)\}$
14 $active \leftarrow \boldsymbol{CrtState}(Lp + 2, q)$	30 **if** $r = oactive$ **then**
15 $\boldsymbol{Insert}(FS[q], active)$	31 Mark $(r, active, a, fl)$ as solid
16 **end if**	32 **end if**
	33 $fl \leftarrow SHORT[r] - 1$
	34 $r \leftarrow \boldsymbol{fail}(r)$
	35 **end while**
	36 **return** $active$

Procedure split creates $qn = [wa]_{wa}^{M'} = [short(q), wa]$, sets $q = (tail(wa), t]$, holds other intervals fixed and adjusts all affected suffix links and edges. First, let qn inherit all edges of q, set the length of edges whose length are greater than $|tail(wa)|$ to $|tail(wa)|$ and delete the edges that no longer belong to q. Second, by the aid of table $FS[q]$, suffix links that point to q, which emit from intervals whose attach point on q is greater than $|tail(wa)|$, are redirected to qn. During the redirection, $FS[q]$, $FS[fail(q)]$ and $FS[qn]$ are updated simultaneously. Third, all a-edges, emit from $SC(p)$, that points to q are redirected to qn.

$split(p, q, lim, a)$

1	$qn \leftarrow CrtState(SHORT[q], fail(q))$	15	**if** r has a-edge (r, r', a, x) **then**
2	$Insert(FS[fail(q)], qn)$	16	**if** $r' = q$ **then**
3	$r \leftarrow p$	17	$E \leftarrow E + \{(r, qn, a, x)\} - \{(r, r', a, x)\}$
4	**for** each edge (q, q', a, x) of q **do**	18	**else**
5	**if** $x \leq lim + 1$ **then**	19	**break**
6	$E \leftarrow E + \{(qn, q', a, x)\} - \{(q, q', a, x)\}$	20	**end if**
7	**else**	21	**else**
8	$E \leftarrow E + (qn, q', a, lim + 1)$	22	$r \leftarrow fail(r)$
9	**end if**	23	**end if**
10	**end for**	24	**end while**
11	$SHORT[q] \leftarrow lim + 2$	25	**if** $p = q$ **then**
12	$(FS[qn], FS[q]) \leftarrow Divide\&Redirect\ (FS[q], SHORT[q], qn)$	26	$\mathbf{return}(qn, fail(p), qn, qn)$
13	$Insert(FS[qn], q)$	27	**else**
14	**while** $r \neq NULL$ **do**	28	$\mathbf{return}(qn, p, q, qn)$
		29	**end if**

Theorem 2 *Let $w \in \Sigma^*$, the WDWG for w under a consistent order function M can be built in linear time in the length of w.*

The proof of liner time complexity of construction of WDWG can be found in [8]. For every prefix of $\$x$ is a prime prefix of $\$x$, there are no prolong operations during the construction of WDWG of $\$x$. Therefore the appending of new edges and searching for a-edge can be done simultaneity, for the new active is always the interval newly created. The construction of $\$x$ is neater than that of x. The relationship between WDWG of x and that of $\$x$ has an analogy with that between *factor automaton* [1] and DAWG.

6   Implement and Experiments

During the construction, WDWG can be implemented by data structures such as adjacency list. After construction, by processing the WDWG constructed, we implement WDWG in a more space-economical way. In this implementation intervals are stored in continuous memory. Each interval I includes three parts: the number of its edges, the last letter of $end(I)$ and the edge set of I which is stored in continuous memory ordered by label of edge. Each edge includes two part: address of destination interval and weight. Only the non-solid edges need to be stored, for solid edges are in the form of $([x[0 : i]]_x^M, [x[0 : i+1]]_x^M, x[i+1], i+1)$. The label of edge needs not be stored. For edges that point to interval I, the label of these edges is the last letter of $end(I)$. In the implementation, the number of edges takes 1 byte, weight and address take 4 bytes, character take 1 byte.

Table 1 compares the size of WDWGs and DAWGs for different sequences. DNA sequences are segments from Homo sapiens chromosome 21. English texts are excerpted from "*Liberty and Liberalism*" (www.econlib.org). Chinese texts are from essays of Steven Cheung, that are read in byte by byte.

Table 1. Size Statistic of DAWG and WDWG.

source	$|\Sigma|$	$|x|$	DAWG Number of states	DAWG Number of edges	WDWG Number of states	WDWG Number of edges	Bytes per character
DNA1	4	500000	844244	1235805	499978	792996	6.68
DNA2	4	500000	829619	1259255	499993	797433	6.75
Random	4	500000	881696	1181151	499910	729621	5.68
English1	71	100000	153044	214086	99996	155982	6.68
English2	71	100000	152753	215485	99995	157529	6.60
Chinese	256	20000	25445	45417	19998	39511	9.81
Chinese	256	30000	37795	67760	29998	59173	9.78

7 Conclusions and Further Researches

We have described the WDWG and its on-line linear construction in this paper. There are still many interesting issues, such as finding the consistent orders that yield WDWGs with minimum number of edges. The combination of merging and compaction of suffix trie implies a new kind of index structures that are smaller than CDAWGs [2, 4, 7]. There are works to be done to reveal this structure and its construction.

References

1. A.Blumer,J.Blumer, D.Haussler, A.Ehrenfeucht, M.T.Chen, and J.Seiferas. The smallest automation recognizing the subwords of a text. Theoretical Computer Science, 40:31-55, 1985.
2. A. Blumer, J. Blumer, D. Haussler, R. McConnell, and A. Ehrenfeucht. Complete inverted files for effcient text retrieval and analysis. Journal of the ACM, 34(3):578–C595, 1987.
3. Maxime Crochemore and Christophe Hancart. Automata for matching patterns. In G. Rozenberg and A. Salomaa, editors, *Handbook of Formal Languages*, volume 2, Linear Modeling: Background and Application, chapter 9, pages 399–462. Springer-Verlag, 1997.
4. Maxime Crochemore and Renaud Vérin. Direct construction of compact directed acyclic word graphs. In A Apostolico and J. Hein, editors, *Combinatorial Pattern Matching (Aarhus, 1997)*, volume 1264 of *LNCS*, pages 116–129. Springer-Verlag, 1997.
5. D. Gusfeld. Algorithms on Strings Trees and Sequences. Cambridge UniversityPress, New York, New York, 1997.
6. J. Kärkkäinen. Suffix cactus: a cross between suffix tree and suffix array. Combinatorial Pattern Matching, 937:191-204, July 1995.
7. Shunsuke Inenaga, Hiromasa Hoshino, Ayumi Shinohara, Masayuki Takeda, Setsuo Arikawa, Giancarlo Mauri, and Giulio Pavesi, On-Line Construction of Compact Directed Acyclic Word Graphs, Discrete Applied Mathematics, 146(2): 156-179 (special issue for CPM'01), March 2005.
8. Meng Zhang. Linerity of Weighted Directed Word Graph,Technical Report of Jilin University, College of Computer Science and Technology, 2005.

Construction of Aho Corasick Automaton in Linear Time for Integer Alphabets

Shiri Dori[1] and Gad M. Landau[1,2,*]

[1] Department of Computer Science, University of Haifa,
Mount Carmel, Haifa 31905, Israel
landau@cs.haifa.ac.il, shiri@cri.haifa.ac.il
[2] Department of Computer and Information Science, Polytechnic University,
Six MetroTech Center, Brooklyn, NY 11201-3840, USA
landau@poly.edu

Abstract. We present a new simple algorithm that constructs an Aho Corasick automaton for a set of patterns, P, of total length n, in $O(n)$ time and space for integer alphabets. Processing a text of size m over an alphabet Σ with the automaton costs $O(m \log |\Sigma| + k)$, where there are k occurrences of patterns in the text.

1 Introduction

The *exact set matching* problem [7] is defined as finding all occurrences in a text T of size m, of any pattern in a set of patterns, $P = \{P_1, P_2, ..., P_q\}$, of cumulative size n over an alphabet Σ. The classic data structure solving this problem is the automaton proposed by Aho and Corasick [2], which is constructed in $O(n \log |\Sigma|)$ preprocessing time and $O(m \log |\Sigma| + k)$ search time, where k represents the number of occurrences of patterns in the text. This solution is suitable especially for applications in which a large number of patterns is known and fixed in advance, while the text varies. We will explain the data structure in detail in Section 2.

The suffix tree of a string is a compact trie of all the suffixes of the string. Several algorithms construct it in linear time for a constant alphabet size [14, 16, 17]. Farach [5] presented a linear time algorithm for integer alphabets. Generalized suffix trees for a set of strings, as defined in [7], are also constructed in time linear to the cumulative length of the strings. Lately, much attention has been paid to the suffix array [6, 13], a sorted enumeration of all the suffixes of a string. The algorithm in [13] constructed this space-efficient alternative to suffix trees in $O(n \log n)$ time, but recently a few $O(n)$ algorithms were suggested [8, 10, 12]. New developments suggest further refinements; the enhanced suffix array can entirely replace the suffix tree [1] with the same incurred complexities [9]. In [9], a history of the evolution of suffix trees and arrays was relayed.

The linear time construction of the suffix tree and suffix array for integer alphabets was achieved after years of research. It is only natural to extend this

---

* Partially supported by the Israel Science Foundation grant 282/01.

A. Apostolico, M. Crochemore, and K. Park (Eds.): CPM 2005, LNCS 3537, pp. 168–177, 2005.
© Springer-Verlag Berlin Heidelberg 2005

development to the third "member" of this data structure family – the Aho Corasick automaton. We answer this challenge and present a new algorithm which constructs the Aho Corasick automaton in $O(n)$ preprocessing time for integer alphabets. The search time remains as it was, $O(m \log |\Sigma| + k)$.

At the heart of our algorithm lies the observation of a close connection between the Aho Corasick Failure function and the index structure of the reversed patterns, be it a suffix tree or an enhanced suffix array. This connection is explained in detail in Section 3.2.

Our algorithm uses the new linear time algorithms to construct suffix arrays and suffix trees for integer alphabets. In this paper, we handle three issues: constructing the Goto trie for all patterns, using the linear time construction of suffix arrays; constructing the Failure function for all pattern prefixes by building a generalized suffix tree, using the linear time construction of suffix trees; and finally, keeping logarithmic search time in each node, using conventional methods.

The paper is organized as follows: in Section 2 we define the Aho Corasick automaton. In Section 3 we describe the construction of the automaton in several steps: the Goto function (Section 3.1), the Failure function (Section 3.2), and the combination of the two (Section 3.3). The original Output function, which we have not changed, is mentioned briefly in Section 3.4, and the entire algorithm is outlined in Section 3.5. We show how to maintain the $O(m \log |\Sigma| + k)$ bound on query processing in Section 4, and summarize our results in Section 5.

2   Preliminaries

The *exact set matching* problem [7] is defined as finding all occurrences in a text, T, of any pattern in a set of patterns, $P = \{P_1, P_2, ..., P_q\}$. This problem was first solved by Aho and Corasick [2] by creating a finite state machine to match the patterns with the text in one pass. In other words, their method defined the following functions (slightly redefined in [7]):

- Goto function: an uncompressed trie representation of the set of patterns. Let $L(v)$ denote the label along the path from the root to node v. Then, for each node v, $L(v)$ represents the prefix of one or more patterns; for each leaf u, $L(u)$ represents a pattern. The Goto function is also known as a keyword tree [2, 7].
- Failure function: based on a generalization of the Knuth-Morris-Pratt algorithm [11], the function is defined in two parts:
  - The Failure function of a string s (which is a prefix of a pattern) is the longest proper suffix of s that is also a prefix of some pattern [2, 7].
  - The Failure link, $v_1 \mapsto v_2$, between two nodes in the Goto trie, links v_1 to a (unique) node v_2 such that the Failure function of $L(v_1)$ is $L(v_2)$ [7].
- Output function: for a node v, the Output function is defined as all patterns which are suffixes of $L(v)$, i.e., end at this node. As shown in the original article [2] and embellished in [7], the Output function for each node v_1 consists of two parts:

- $L(v_1)$, if it equals a pattern.
- $Output(v_2)$, where $v_1 \mapsto v_2$ is a Failure link. Note that this is a recursive construction.

These three functions, Goto, Failure and Output, completely define an Aho Corasick automaton, which is no longer an automaton or a state machine in the classic sense. When a text is processed, we attempt to traverse the trie using the Goto function. For a given character, if no appropriate child exists in the current node, the Failure links are traversed instead, until we find such a node or reach the root. Whenever a node with a non-empty output is reached, all output words must be found. Figure 1 shows an example of an Aho Corasick automaton for a set P.

3   Building the Aho Corasick Automaton

Our algorithm to construct the Aho Corasick automaton consists of three main steps: constructing the Goto function, constructing the Failure function and links, and merging the two. We will now explain each step in detail. We will often use a notation S_P for the concatenation of the patterns in P, with unique endmarkers separating them: $S_P = \$_0 \ P_1 \ \$_1 \ P_2 \ \$_2... \ \$_{q-1} \ P_q \ \$_q$.

3.1   Building the Goto Function

The Goto function is constructed in two steps: sorting the patterns in P and building the trie that represents them.

The patterns can be sorted using suffix arrays, by constructing the suffix array for S_P, thus sorting all suffixes of S_P; out of these, we can filter only the complete words and receive their sorted order. Alternatively, a two-pass radix sort can be employed to sort the strings [3, 15].

Once the patterns are sorted, the trie is built simply by traversing and extending it for each pattern in the sorted order. We keep a list of children for each node, with the invariant that they are ordered alphabetically. For each pattern in turn, we will attempt to traverse the trie, knowing that if the next character exists, it will be at the tail of the list of children in the current node. If not, we may create it and insert it to the tail, thus keeping the invariant. Once a character was not found, we can extend the trie for the rest of the pattern from this point on. This is nearly identical to the original method employed by Aho and Corasick [2], with the sole difference that they kept arrays in each node, whereas we keep sorted lists.

Time Complexity. Sorting takes $O(n)$ time for integer alphabets using a suffix array for S_P [8]. As for the trie, the work for each character is either traversing a link at a known position or creating a new node; both take up $O(1)$. The work for each pattern is proportional to its length, so for the entire set it will be $O(n)$.

3.2   Building the Failure Function

Having constructed the trie representing the Goto function for P, we turn to construct the Failure links on top of it. We chose to describe the algorithm using a suffix tree for simplicity, but an enhanced suffix array can easily replace it [1, 9].

We have defined S_P as the string representing the patterns in P. We define T^R to be the suffix tree of the reverse of this string, that is, the suffix tree of $(S_P)^R$. The properties of trees for reverse strings were discussed in [4]. Also, Gusfield [7] has discussed generalized suffix trees for a set of strings. In Section 6.4 of [7], he showed how to construct this tree without creating synthetic suffixes that combine two or more patterns. Therefore, $ signs never appear in the middle of edges of the suffix tree, and only mark the end of a label.

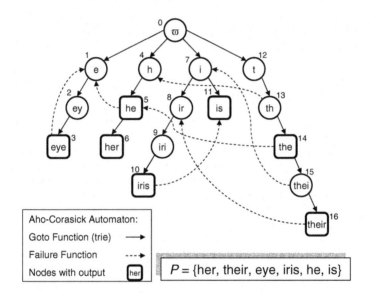

Fig. 1. An Aho Corasick automaton for the set P. The dotted arrows represent Failure links. For brevity's sake, we did not include Failure links that point to the root. Nodes that have a non-empty output are emphasized.

Observe the tree in Figure 2. This is T^R for the same patterns seen in Figure 1. The following properties of T^R are relevant to our discussion:

– For each node v in the trie representing the Goto function, there exists a unique node u in T^R which represents its reverse label, that is, $L(v) = L(u)^R$. For example, in Figure 1, node 16, labeled "their", has its match in Figure 2, with node m, labeled "rieht".
– When considering a node u_1 and its ancestor u_2 in T^R, the label of u_2 is a prefix of the label of u_1. Since these are reverse labels of the original string, the original label of u_2 is a suffix of the original label of u_1.

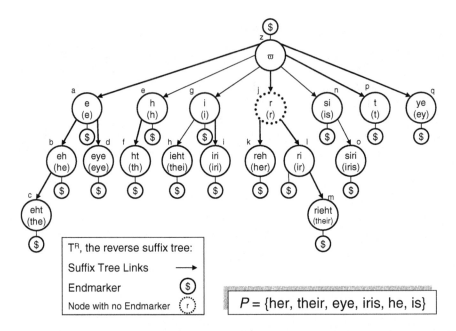

Fig. 2. T^R for the patterns of Figure 1. Since the labels are reversed, we included the original label in parenthesis. For example, node c representing "eht" in T^R corresponds to node 14 representing "the" in the trie of Figure 1. The endmarker, $, marks one of two options: for a leaf, its label ends with a $; for an internal node, it has a son which represents this label ending with a $. If we treat an internal node as marked by a $, this is actually shorthand for noting the second case.

- When a node u in T^R is marked by a $, this means that its original label begins with a $; i.e., the reverse label of u is a prefix of some pattern in P.
- In Lemma 1 we will show that all nodes in T^R which are marked by a $, and only those, have a corresponding node in the trie.

Observe the Failure links in Figure 1. For example, the Failure function of node 10, "iris", is node 11, "is", as seen by the dotted arrow between the two nodes. Now, let us turn our attention to their corresponding nodes in T^R. Here, node n, "si" (the reverse of "is"), is the nearest ancestor of node o, "siri" (the reverse of "iris"), and it is also marked by a $. In other words, "is" is the longest proper suffix of "iris" which is also a prefix of some pattern: exactly the definition of the Failure function. Also, notice node 8, labeled "ir", which corresponds to node l, "ri", in T^R. The Failure function of "ir" is not "r", since "r" is not a prefix of any pattern. Indeed, node j representing "r" in T^R is not marked by a $ sign, and additionally, there is no node in the original trie representing "r". Therefore the Failure function of "ir" is ϕ (node z), its nearest ancestor in T^R with a $ sign.

Definition 1. *Consider node u_1 in T^R. We define the proper ancestor of u_1, $u_2 = PA(u_1)$, as the closest ancestor of u_1 in T_R which is marked by a $.*

PA can be computed for every node in T^R by a simple preorder traversal of T^R.

Now, consider nodes v_1 and v_2 in the trie, so that there exists a Failure link $v_1 \mapsto v_2$. Let u_1, u_2 be the corresponding nodes in T^R. Then $u_2 = PA(u_1)$. Our algorithm is based on this property. Now that we've found this information in T^R, we would like to relay it to the nodes in the trie. Each node in the trie must be connected to its corresponding node in T^R, and we will handle this in Section 3.3.

Time Complexity. The suffix tree T^R built in this step can be constructed in linear time, either using Farach's algorithm [5], or indirectly using suffix arrays and Longest Common Prefix values [5, 8]. The tree is then traversed once in order to find PA, but in a preorder fashion and not as a search, therefore the traversal is also linear.

3.3 Integrating Failure with Goto

We have shown how to obtain $PA(x)$ for each node in T^R, but we must integrate this information with the trie representing the Goto function. We do this once, during construction, recording the Failure links in the trie nodes, so that the trie is a self-contained Aho Corasick automaton. The integration is based upon the ability to infer, for each node in the trie, its corresponding \$-marked node in T^R, and vice versa. This is achieved through the actual string S_P, in the following steps:

- During or after construction of the Goto function, we compute the following: for each character in S_P, we will keep a pointer to its representative node in the trie – the one visited or constructed when this character was dealt with. An example of this is shown in Figure 3(a).
- As part of the construction of any suffix tree, and so of T^R, each node records the first and last indices of one of the appearances of its label in the string, $(S_P)^R$ in our case. From these indices we can compute the corresponding appearance of the original label in S_P: for \$-marked nodes, the label's last index in S_P represents a prefix of some pattern. An example of this appears in Figure 3(b) and (c).
- Combining the information we have about S_P, we map a trie node for each \$-marked node in T^R and vice versa. Lemma 1 below shows that this is a one-to-one mapping, as shown also in Figure 3(d).
- We use this mapping to record the information of PA, garnered from T^R, among nodes in the trie as Failure links. For each node v_1 in the trie, we:
  - Find node u_1 in T^R which corresponds to v_1.
  - Find $u_2 = PA(u_1)$.
  - Find node v_2 in the trie which corresponds to u_2.
  - Create a Failure link, $v_1 \mapsto v_2$, among the trie nodes.

Lemma 1. *There exists a one-to-one mapping between \$-marked nodes in T^R and nodes in the trie.*

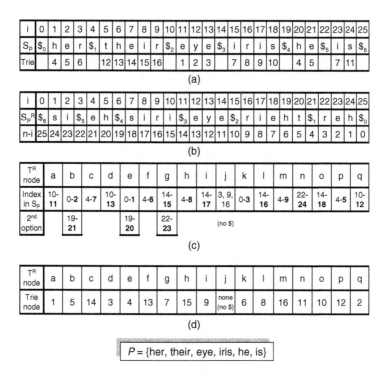

(a)

i	0	1	2	3	4	5	6	7	8	9	10	11	12	13	14	15	16	17	18	19	20	21	22	23	24	25
S_P	$\$_0$	h	e	r	$\$_1$	t	h	e	i	r	$\$_2$	e	y	e	$\$_3$	i	r	i	s	$\$_4$	h	e	$\$_5$	i	s	$\$_6$
Trie		4	5	6		12	13	14	15	16		1	2	3		7	8	9	10		4	5		7	11	

(b)

i	0	1	2	3	4	5	6	7	8	9	10	11	12	13	14	15	16	17	18	19	20	21	22	23	24	25
S_P^R	$\$_6$	s	i	$\$_5$	e	h	$\$_4$	s	i	r	i	$\$_3$	e	y	e	$\$_2$	r	i	e	h	t	$\$_1$	r	e	h	$\$_0$
n-i	25	24	23	22	21	20	19	18	17	16	15	14	13	12	11	10	9	8	7	6	5	4	3	2	1	0

(c)

T^R node	a	b	c	d	e	f	g	h	i	j	k	l	m	n	o	p	q
Index in S_P	10-11	0-2	4-7	10-13	0-1	4-6	14-15	4-8	14-17	3, 9, 16	0-3	14-16	4-9	22-24	14-18	4-5	10-12
2nd option		19-21			19-20		22-23			(no $)							

(d)

T^R node	a	b	c	d	e	f	g	h	i	j	k	l	m	n	o	p	q
Trie node	1	5	14	3	4	13	7	15	9	none (no $)	6	8	16	11	10	12	2

P = {her, their, eye, iris, he, is}

Fig. 3. Integrating the Goto and Failure functions shown in Figures 1 and 2. **(a)** S_P and the trie nodes corresponding to each character. **(b)** $(S_P)^R$ and corresponding indices in S_P. **(c)** T^R nodes and the indices in S_P corresponding to their labels. The first index is always a $, and the last index (in bold) is the relevant one. A label may appear more than once in the string, e.g. node b representing "he" has two possible mappings to the string. **(d)** T^R nodes and their corresponding trie nodes, computed from parts (a) and (c) combined. For example, the label "thei", which is a prefix of the pattern "their", spans indices 4-8 in S_P (including $); its last index, 8, maps to trie node 15 as shown in (a). Its reverse label, "ieht", is represented by node h, as shown in (c); combining these, we map node 15 to node h in (d). Note that even if several options exist in (c), they all map to the same trie node. Also note that node j, which is not marked by a $, has no corresponding node in the trie.

Proof. Any $-marked node u in T^R represents a prefix of some pattern in S_P, and thus has a unique corresponding node v in the trie. Now we prove the other direction: a label of any node v in the trie represents a prefix of a pattern. Hence, in S_P the label is preceded by a $, meaning that its reversed label in $(S_P)^R$ is followed by a $. Therefore, there is a single $-marked node u in T^R corresponding to v. Note that there can be $ signs only at the end of a node's label in a generalized suffix tree [7].

Time Complexity. Constructing the mapping takes constant time for each node, and the creation of Failure links consists of a traversal of the trie. The entire phase takes $O(n)$ time.

3.4   Building the Output Function

The Output function can be computed, just as in [2], during the computation of the Goto and Failure functions, with a traversal on the trie. Gusfield refines these computations and explains them in detail in Section 3.4.6 of [7]. The recursive manner of the Output function is exemplified in Figure 1, where node 14 labeled "the" has an output of "he", due to its Failure link to node 5.

Time Complexity. Computing the Output function consists of some constant-time processing during the construction of the Goto function, and a traversal of the trie with the Failure links, so it costs $O(n)$ time.

3.5   Algorithm: Constructing an Aho Corasick Automaton

The complete algorithm for constructing an Aho Corasick automaton in linear time is outlined below, along with the sections in which each part was described. As mentioned earlier, the suffix tree T^R can be entirely replaced by an enhanced suffix array E^R with the same complexity [1, 9].

1. Construct the Goto function (a trie) for P:
   (a) Sort the patterns using a suffix array for S_P. (Section 3.1)
   (b) Construct a trie for the sorted patterns, in which each node will hold its sons in a sorted list. (3.1)
   (c) Connect the Goto function to S_P. (3.3)
2. Construct the Failure function for P:
   (a) Construct T^R, the suffix tree of $(S_P)^R$. (3.2)
   (b) Compute PA for each \$-marked node. (3.2)
   (c) Connect the Failure function to S_P. (3.3)
3. Combine the Failure and Goto functions:
   (a) Through S_P, connect each node in the trie with its corresponding \$-marked node in T^R. (3.3)
   (b) Transfer the information from PA in T^R to the trie nodes and construct all Failure links. (3.3)
4. Construct the Output function. (3.4)

Once these steps are completed, one can discard T^R entirely. The ensuing data structure will hold any information needed for query processing on an Aho Corasick automaton.

4   Processing Queries

It is a generally accepted fact that, for non-negligible alphabets, there exists a tradeoff between the space consumed and the time required to search in each node, depending on the branching method in the nodes [7, 9]. If an array of size $|\Sigma|$ is used in each node, the time to search will be constant. If only a list of actual sons is held, the cumulative space for the tree will be proportional to the number of nodes, but search time in each node will rise to $O(|\Sigma|)$. Finally, the generally accepted, heavy-duty solution, is to hold a balanced search tree in each node, thus limiting the space needed in the tree overall, but increasing both insertions and search time to the tree by a factor of $\log |\Sigma|$.

Constructing the Goto trie as described above will yield a linked list of sons in each node, allowing for $O(|\Sigma|)$ search time spent in each node in the worst case. But notice that this list is alphabetically ordered, and its size is known. Hence, one of several simple procedures known in folklore can be applied at any time after the trie's construction to reduce the query time to $O(\log |\Sigma|)$ at each node.

We visit every node and allocate an array in size proportional to the number of its sons, then transfer the list of sorted sons to this array, in $O(n)$ total time. The array of sons can then be searched in $O(\log(\#of\,sons)) = O(\log |\Sigma|)$. This step can be further augmented, if needed, to create a balanced search tree in each node, still with $O(n)$ time and $O(\log |\Sigma|)$ search in each node.

The Output function allows a constant time spent for each occurrence of any pattern in the text.

Time Complexity. Traversing the automaton costs $O(m \log |\Sigma|)$ time for a text of length m. Finding the output patterns will cost $O(k)$, where k denotes the number of occurrences of patterns from P in the text. Hence, the entire complexity of query processing is $O(m \log |\Sigma| + k)$.

5   Summary

We have presented a new algorithm, which is simple to understand and implement, that constructs the Aho Corasick automaton in $O(n)$ time. This algorithm is the third addition to a growing group of linear algorithms for string problems over integer alphabets.

In addition, we have brought forth an interesting observation regarding the Failure function of the Knuth-Morris-Pratt algorithm [11], generalized to a set of patterns in the Aho Corasick automaton [2]. This Failure function is intimately connected with the generalized suffix tree of the patterns, and this has provided the basis for our algorithm.

Acknowledgments

We are grateful to Maxime Crochemore, Raffaele Giancarlo, Moshe Lewenstein, Kunsoo Park and Pierre Peterlongo for helpful discussions.

References

1. Abouelhoda, M.I., S. Kurtz and E. Ohlebusch. Replacing suffix trees with enhanced suffix arrays. *J. Discrete Algorithms*, 2(1):53–86, 2004.

2. Aho, A.V. and M.J. Corasick. Efficient string matching. *Comm. ACM*, 18(6):333–340, 1975.
3. Andersson, A. and S. Nilsson. A New Efficient Radix Sort. *Proc. 35th IEEE Symposium on Foundations of Computer Science*, pp. 714–721, 1994.
4. Chen, M.T. and J. Seiferas. Efficient and Elegant Subword-Tree Construction. In A. Apostolico and Z. Galil, editors, *Combinatorial Algorithms on Words*, pp. 97–107. Springer-Verlag, 1985.
5. Farach, M. Optimal suffix tree construction with large alphabets. *Proc. 38th IEEE Symposium on Foundations of Computer Science*, pp. 137–143, 1997.
6. Gonnet, G., R. Baeza-Yates and T. Sinder. New Indices for text: PAT trees and PAT arrays. In W.B. Frakes and R. Baeza-Yates (Eds.), *Information Retrieval: Data Structures and Algorithms*. Prentice Hall, 1992.
7. Gusfield, D. Algorithms on strings, trees, and sequences. Cambridge University Press, 1997.
8. Kärkkäinen, J. and P. Sanders. Simple linear work suffix array construction. In *Proc. 30th International Colloquium on Automata, Languages and Programming (ICALP 03)*, pp. 943–955, 2003. LNCS 2719.
9. Kim, D.K., J.E. Jeon and H. Park. Efficient Index Data Structure with the Capabilities of Suffix Trees and Suffix Arrays for Alphabets of Non-negligble Size. In A. Apostolico and A. Melucci (Eds.), *String Processing and Information Retrieval (SPIRE 04)*, pp. 138–149, 2004. LNCS 3246.
10. Kim, D.K., J.S. Sim, H. Park and K. Park. Linear-time construction of suffix arrays. *Symp. Combinatorial Pattern Matching (CPM 03)*, pp. 186–199, 2003. LNCS 2676.
11. Knuth, D.E., J.H. Morris, Jr. and V.R. Pratt. Fast pattern matching in strings. *SIAM J. Comput.*, 6:323–350, 1977.
12. Ko, P. and S. Aluru. Space-efficient linear-time construction of suffix arrays. *Symp. Combinatorial Pattern Matching (CPM 03)*, pp. 200–210, 2003. LNCS 2676.
13. Manber, U. and G. Myers. Suffix arrays: A new method for on-line string searches. *SIAM J. Comput.*, 22(5):935–948, 1993.
14. McCreight, E.M. A space-economical suffix tree construction algorithm. *J. of the ACM*, 23(2):262–272, 1976.
15. Paige, R. and R.E. Tarjan. Three Partition Refinement Algorithms. *SIAM J. Comput.*, 16(6): 973–989, 1987.
16. Ukkonen, E. On-line construction of suffix trees. *Algorithmica*, 14:249–260, 1995.
17. Weiner, P. Linear pattern matching algorithm. *Proc. 14 IEEE Symposium on Switching and Automata Theory*, pp. 1–11, 1973.

An Extension of the Burrows Wheeler Transform and Applications to Sequence Comparison and Data Compression

Sabrina Mantaci, Antonio Restivo, G. Rosone, and Marinella Sciortino

University of Palermo, Dipartimento di Matematica ed Application,
Via Archirafi 34, 90123 Palermo, Italy
{sabrina,restivo}@math.unipa.it,
giovyros@virgilio.it, mari@math.unipa.it

Abstract. We introduce a generalization of the Burrows-Wheeler Transform (BWT) that can be applied to a multiset of words. The extended transformation, denoted by E, is reversible, but, differently from BWT, it is also surjective. The E transformation allows to give a definition of distance between two sequences, that we apply here to the problem of the whole mitochondrial genome phylogeny. Moreover we give some consideration about compressing a set of words by using the E transformation as preprocessing.

1 Introduction

Michael Burrows and David Wheeler introduced in 1994 (cf. [1]) a reversible transformation on words (BWT from now on) that arouses considerable interest and curiosity in the field of Data Compression.

Very recently some combinatorial aspects of this transform have been investigated (cf. [11, 12]). For instance, by using the Burrows-Wheeler transform, one can derive a further characterization of Standard words, that are very important objects in the field of Combinatorics on Words (cf. [11]).

Moreover it has been remarked (cf. [4]) that there exists a close relation between BWT and a technique, used by Gessel and Reutenauer in [6] for stating a correspondence between finite words and a set of permutations with a given cyclic structure and a given descent set (cf. also Chapter 11 of [9]).

The main contribution of this paper consists in defining an extension of the Burrows-Wheeler transform (denoted by E) applied to a multiset of words, that is inspired by the Gessel and Reutenauer result. This transformation involves a new order relation between words, different from the lexicographic one. In the sorting process derived from such an order relation we make use of the Fine and Wilf Theorem.

We apply our transformation in order to define a new method for comparing sequences. In particular, we introduce a new distance between two sequences (or between two set of sequences) that, intuitively, takes into account that the more similar two sequences are, the more symbols coming form each sequence are

A. Apostolico, M. Crochemore, and K. Park (Eds.): CPM 2005, LNCS 3537, pp. 178–189, 2005.

shuffled in the output of E. Moreover we report the results obtained by applying our method to the problem of the whole mitochondrial genome phylogeny.

We also show another application of the extended transformation to text compression. We observe that the simultaneous compression of a set of k words $\{x_1, \ldots, x_k\}$ by using the transformation E as preprocessing, is better than compressing each word x_i separately. In particular, most BWT-based compressors divide the text into blocks, compress each block separately and then concatenate the compressed blocks. We experimentally verify that our method provides an improvement of such a technique.

2   Preliminaries

The Burrows-Wheeler transform represents an extremely useful tool for textual lossless data compression. The idea is to apply a reversible transformation in order to produce a permutation $BWT(w)$ of an input word w, defined over an alphabet A, so that the word becomes easier to compress. Actually the transformation leads to group characters together so that the probability of finding a character close to another instance of the same character is substantially increased. BWT transforms a word $w = w_0 w_1 \cdots w_n$ by constructing all n cyclic rotations of w, sorting them lexicographically and extracting the last character of each rotation. The word $BWT(w)$ consists of the sequence of these characters. Moreover the transformation computes the index I, that is the row containing the original word in the sorted list of rotations.

For instance, suppose we want to compute $BWT(w)$ where $w = abraca$. In Figure 1 we show the matrix that consists of all cyclic shifts of w, lexicographically sorted.

$$
\begin{array}{c}
\quad\quad F \quad\quad\quad L \\
\quad\quad \downarrow \quad\quad\quad \downarrow \\
\begin{array}{rl}
1 & a\ a\ b\ r\ a\ c \\
I \rightarrow 2 & a\ b\ r\ a\ c\ a \\
3 & a\ c\ a\ a\ b\ r \\
4 & b\ r\ a\ c\ a\ a \\
5 & c\ a\ a\ b\ r\ a \\
6 & r\ a\ c\ a\ a\ b
\end{array}
\end{array}
$$

Fig. 1. The matrix of all cyclic rotations of the word $w = abraca$.

The last column L of the matrix represents $BWT(w) = caraab$ and $I = 2$ since the original word w appears in row 2. The first column F, instead, contains the sequence of the characters of w lexicographically sorted.

Remark 1. Recall that the Burrows-Wheeler transform is reversible, in the sense that given $BWT(w)$ and the index I, it is possible to recover the original word w. Notice however that the BWT, considered as an application from A^* to itself, is not surjective, that is, there exist some words in A^* that are not image

of any word by the Burrows-Wheeler transform. For instance, let us consider
the word $u = bccaaab$. It is easy to see that there exists no word w such that
$BWT(w) = u$.

3   An Extension of the BWT to k Words

In a recent paper ([4]), Crochemore, Désarménien and Perrin remarked that the
Burrows-Wheeler transform is closely related to a special case of a result on
combinatorics on permutations, given by Gessel and Reutenauer (cf. [6]). In this
section we define a transformation, denoted by E, inspired by the Gessel and
Reutenauer work, that extends the BWT to k words, with $k \geq 1$.

As we remarked in the previous section, the BWT is not surjective over A^*.
On the contrary, the new extended transformation, that we are going to define,
establishes a bijective correspondence between the multisets of conjugacy classes
of primitive words in A^* and the set of all words over an alphabet A.

In order to define the new transformation we need to introduce a new order
relation between words that differs from the usual lexicographical order when
one word is a prefix of the other one.

3.1   A New Order Relation Between Words

Let A be a finite ordered alphabet. We denote by A^* the set of words over A.
We say that two words $x, y \in A^*$ are *conjugate* if $x = uv$ and $y = vu$ for some
$u, v \in A^*$. A word $v \in A^*$ is *primitive* if $v = u^n$ implies $v = u$ and $n = 1$.
Recall that (cf. [8]) every word $v \in A^*$ can be written in a unique way as a
power of a primitive word, i.e. there exists a unique primitive word w and a
unique integer k such that $v = w^k$. We denote w by $root(v)$ and k by $exp(v)$.
If u is a word in A^*, we denote by u^ω the infinite word obtained by infinitely
iterating u, i.e. $u^\omega = uuuuu \ldots$. Remark that $u^\omega = v^\omega$ if and only if u and v are
power of the same word. On infinite words is naturally defined the lexicographic
ordering, that is, taken two infinite words $x = x_1 x_2 \ldots$ and $y = y_1 y_2 \ldots$, with
$x_i, y_i \in A$, we say that $x <_{lex} y$ if there exists an index $j \in \mathbb{N}$ such that $x_i = y_i$
for $i = 1, 2, \ldots, j - 1$ and $x_j < y_j$. Note that if $x = y$, the relation $<_{lex}$ is not
defined. Remark that $u^\omega = v^\omega$ if and only if $root(u) = root(v)$.

Definition 1. *Let u, v be two words over a finite alphabet A. We say that*

$$u \preceq_\omega v \Longleftrightarrow \begin{cases} exp(u) \leq exp(v) & \text{if } root(u) = root(v) \\ u^\omega <_{lex} v^\omega & \text{otherwise} \end{cases}$$

It is easy to verify that $\preceq_\omega$ is a total order. We also remark that this order
relation is different from the lexicographic one. In fact for instance $ab <_{lex} aba$
but $aba \preceq_\omega ab$. Although when $root(u) \neq root(v)$ the $\preceq_\omega$ order of u and v
is defined by using infinite words, the following proposition shows that it is
possible to decide their mutual $\preceq_\omega$-ordering by extending them up to the length
$|u| + |v| - \gcd(|u|, |v|)$. Such a bound is a consequence of a well known result of

Periodicity on Words, the Fine and Wilf theorem. For a given finite or infinite word w, we denote by $pref_k(w)$ the prefix of w of length k.

Proposition 1. *Given two words u and v, with $root(u) \neq root(v)$,*

$$u \preceq_\omega v \iff pref_k(u^\omega) <_{lex} pref_k(v^\omega),$$

where $k = |u| + |v| - \gcd(|u|, |v|)$.

The bound given in Proposition 1 is tight: this is a consequence of the tightness of such a bound in the Fine and Wilf Theorem.

Example 1. We can consider the words $u = abaab$ and $v = abaababa$. One can see that $v \preceq_\omega u$ and u^ω and v^ω differ for the character in position 12=5+8-1. However remark that $u <_{lex} v$.

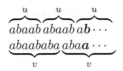

3.2   The Extended Transformation

In this subsection, the transformation E is introduced under the hypothesis that the words considered are primitive. This is not actually a restrictive hypothesis, since in practice almost all the processed texts are primitive (or become primitive by adding an end-of-string symbol). Let $S = \{u_1, \ldots u_k\}$ be a multiset of k primitive words of A^*. We define the transformation $E(u_1, \ldots, u_k)$ as follows:

- Let $w_1, w_2, \ldots, w_m$ be the sequence of conjugates of elements of S, sorted according to the order $\preceq_\omega$, that is $w_i \preceq_\omega w_j$ for $1 \leq i < j \leq m$.
- We denote by $\mathcal{I}$ the set of indices representing the positions in the sequence $\{w_i\}_{i=1}^m$ of the original words in S.
- We denote by $L[i]$ (resp. $F[i]$) the last (resp. first) character of the word w_i, for $i = 1, \ldots, m$. Then we define

$$L = L[1]L[2]\ldots L[m], \qquad F = F[1]F[2]\ldots F[m].$$

- The output of $E(u_1, \ldots u_k)$ is the couple $(L, \mathcal{I})$,

If we arrange the sorted sequence of the conjugates of elements of S in a table, the word L is obtained by concatenating the last elements of each row in the table.

Notice that in case of $k = 1$, that is $S = \{u\}$ the output of $E(S)$ is equal to the $BWT(u)$.

Example 2. Let $S = \{abac, cbab, bca, cba\}$. We represent in Figure 2 on the left side the $<_{lex}$-ordered list of all w^ω, where the w's are the conjugates of elements in S, and on the right side the final table with the $\preceq_\omega$-ordered rows:

$a\,b\,a\,c\,a\,b\cdots$	1 $a\,b\,a\,\mathbf{c}$
$a\,b\,c\,a\,b\,c\cdots$	2 $a\,b\,\mathbf{c}$
$a\,b\,c\,b\,a\,b\cdots$	3 $a\,b\,c\,\mathbf{b}$
$a\,c\,a\,b\,a\,c\cdots$	4 $a\,c\,a\,\mathbf{b}$
$a\,c\,b\,a\,c\,b\cdots$	5 $a\,c\,\mathbf{b}$
$b\,a\,b\,c\,b\,a\cdots$	6 $b\,a\,b\,\mathbf{c}$
$b\,a\,c\,a\,b\,a\cdots \;\Longrightarrow$	7 $b\,a\,c\,\mathbf{a}$
$b\,a\,c\,b\,a\,c\cdots$	8 $b\,a\,\mathbf{c}$
$b\,c\,a\,b\,c\,a\cdots$	9 $b\,c\,\mathbf{a}$
$b\,c\,b\,a\,b\,c\cdots$	10 $b\,c\,b\,\mathbf{a}$
$c\,a\,b\,a\,c\,a\cdots$	11 $c\,a\,b\,\mathbf{a}$
$c\,a\,b\,c\,a\,b\cdots$	12 $c\,a\,\mathbf{b}$
$c\,b\,a\,b\,c\,b\cdots$	13 $c\,b\,a\,\mathbf{b}$
$c\,b\,a\,c\,b\,a\cdots$	14 $c\,b\,\mathbf{a}$

Fig. 2. The output of $E(S)$ is the couple $(L,\mathcal{I})$ where $L = ccbbbcacaaabba$ and $\mathcal{I} = \{1,9,13,14\}$.

Proposition 2. *Let S be a multiset of primitive words and let $(L,\mathcal{I}) = E(S)$. The following properties hold:*

1. *For every $i \notin \mathcal{I}$, $F[i]$ follows $L[i]$ in one of the words in S.*
2. *For a given character a, its occurrences in F appear in the same order as in L, i.e. its i-th instance in F corresponds to its i-th instance in L.*

We show that the transformation described above is reversible. Let $(L,\mathcal{I}) = E(S)$ be the extended transform of a multiset of some primitive words S. We can obtain F by alphabetically sorting the characters of L. It is possible to define a permutation θ on $\{1,\ldots,|L|\}$ as follows: $\theta(i) = j$ if $F[i]$ and $L[j]$ correspond to the same character in a word of S, according to Item 2 of Proposition 2. In other words, if $F[i]z$ is a conjugate of a word $u \in S$, for some $z \in A^*$, then the permutation θ associates it to the other conjugate $zF[i] = zL[j]$.

Example 3. Given the word $L = ccbbbcacaaabba$ obtained in Example 2, one can construct F

$$F = aaaaabbbbbcccc$$
$$L = ccbbbcacaaabba$$

and define the permutation

$$\theta = \begin{pmatrix} 1 & 2 & 3 & 4 & 5 & 6 & 7 & 8 & 9 & 10 & 11 & 12 & 13 & 14 \\ 7 & 9 & 10 & 11 & 14 & 3 & 4 & 5 & 12 & 13 & 1 & 2 & 6 & 8 \end{pmatrix}.$$

We can consider the decomposition of θ into disjoint cycles, $\theta = \sigma_1\sigma_2\cdots\sigma_k$. From Item 1 of Proposition 2 one can derive that k is equal to the cardinality of S and each σ_i corresponds to a conjugacy class of a word in S. Moreover, because of primitivity of words in S, for every $j = 1,\ldots,k$, there exists a unique index, say I_j, that is moved by σ_j. So, one can reconstruct each word in S by using Item 2 of Proposition 2:

$$w_1 = F[I_1]F[\theta(I_1)]F[\theta^2(I_1)] \cdots F[\theta^{l_1}(I_1)],$$
$$w_2 = F[I_2]F[\theta(I_2)]F[\theta^2(I_2)] \cdots F[\theta^{l_2}(I_2)],$$
$$\cdots$$
$$w_k = F[I_k]F[\theta(I_k)]F[\theta^2(I_k)] \cdots F[\theta^{l_k}(I_k)],$$

where $l_1, l_2, \ldots, l_k$ are the length of the cycles $\sigma_1, \sigma_2, \ldots, \sigma_k$, respectively.

Example 4. Given the permutation found in Example 3, its cyclic decomposition is the following:

$$\theta = (1\ 7\ 4\ 11)(2\ 9\ 12)(3\ 10\ 13\ 6)(5\ 14\ 8).$$

By starting from the indices $1, 9, 13, 14$, we get respectively the words

$$w_1 = F[1]F[7]F[4]F[11] = abac, \qquad w_2 = F[9]F[12]F[2] = bca,$$
$$w_3 = F[13]F[6]F[3]F[10] = cbab, \qquad w_4 = F[14]F[8]F[5] = cba.$$

From above considerations the following theorem holds:

Theorem 1. *Let $\mathcal{M}$ be the family of finite multisets of primitive words over A^* and let $\mathcal{N}$ the family of finite subsets of $\mathbb{N}$. The transformation $E : \mathcal{M} \to A^* \times \mathcal{N}$ such that $S \mapsto (L, \mathcal{I})$, is injective.*

Differently from what we observed in Remark 1, for any word $L \in A^*$, there exists a multiset S of primitive words and a set $\mathcal{I}$ of indices such that $E(S) = (L, \mathcal{I})$. Moreover if we don't care about the indices, we can associate to each word $L \in A^*$ a unique multiset of conjugacy classes of primitive words in A^* (see next Example 5). This result, that plays an important role both in Combinatorics on Words and in the study of Free Lie Algebras, was firstly synthesized in a theorem, due to Gessel and Reutenauer (cf [6]), and reported below.

Theorem 2. *There exists a bijection between A^* and the family of multisets of conjugacy classes of primitive words in A^*.*

Example 5. Let $w = bccaaab$ as in Remark 1. It is easy to verify that w is the word obtained by applying E to the conjugacy classes of ab and $abcac$.

4   Comparing Sequences by the Extended Transformation

In this section we apply our transformation in order to introduce a new method for comparing sequences. The new distance between words here defined is simple and efficient to compute, and it is particularly advantageous in the case of multiple sequences comparison. We remark that our distance is not based on sequence alignment. Several alignment-free distance measures have recently been introduced (see for instance [5, 7, 14, 15] and references therein) since they better fit with the problem of comparing genomic sequences than the methods based on sequence alignment. In fact, such methods compare sequences by considering only local edit operations on their fragments. Instead, the recent developments in genome sequences technologies have allowed to handle the complete genome of many different species, and have highlighted that, in order to capture evolutionary and functional mechanisms of different species, we need to consider a new set of sequence modifications, that involve recombination or shuffling of segments of genome. The distance we define takes into account such kind of modifications and therefore it can be successfully applied to compare genomic sequences, as shown in Subsection 4.3.

4.1   A New Distance Between Two Sequences

We define a new notion of distance between two sequences. Such a notion is based on the following intuitive idea. Given two sequences u and v, we consider the sorted list $w_1, w_2, \ldots, w_m$ of the conjugates of u and v, obtained in the first step of the computation of $E(\{u, v\})$. If the same segment s appears both in u and v, then the conjugates of u and v starting with s are likely to be close in the above list. The greater is the number of segments shared by the two sequences u and v, the greater is the number of alternations in the above list between the elements coming from u and those coming from v. Thus, we define a distance that takes into account the alternation of the symbols coming from different sequences in the output of the transformation E.

More formally, let $S = \{u, v\}$ and let $w_1, w_2, \ldots, w_m$ be the sorted list of conjugates of u and v obtained in the first step of the computation of $E(\{u, v\})$. Consider the new alphabet $\Sigma = \{U, V\}$ and the map γ that associates to each sequence w_i in the list, a symbol of Σ as follows:

$$\gamma(w_i) = \begin{cases} U \text{ if } w_i \text{ is a conjugate of } u \\ V \text{ if } w_i \text{ is a conjugate of } v \end{cases}$$

Denote by $\Gamma(u, v)$ the sequence $\gamma(w_1)\gamma(w_2)\cdots\gamma(w_m)$.

Example 6. Let us consider the sequences $u = bcaa$ and $v = ccbab$. The sorted list of conjugates of u and v is the following.

$$\begin{array}{ll} a\ a\ b\ c & U \\ a\ b\ c\ a & U \\ a\ b\ c\ c\ b & V \\ b\ a\ b\ c\ c & V \\ b\ c\ a\ a & U \\ b\ c\ c\ b\ a & V \\ c\ a\ a\ b & U \\ c\ b\ a\ b\ c & V \\ c\ c\ b\ a\ b & V \end{array}$$

In this case $\Gamma(u, v) = U^2 V^2 U V U V^2$.

Definition 2. *Let $u, v \in A^*$ be two sequences and $\Gamma(u, v) = U^{n_1} V^{n_2} U^{n_3} \cdots V^{n_k}$. We define the measure $\delta(u, v)$ as follows:*

$$\delta(u, v) = \sum_{\substack{i=1, \\ n_i \neq 0}}^{k} (n_i - 1)$$

Example 6 (continued). It is easy to compute that $\delta(u, v) = 3$.

Remark 2. One can verify that

1. $\delta(u, v) = \delta(v, u)$, i.e. the distance measure δ is symmetric.
2. If u and v are conjugate then $\delta(u, v) = 0$. In fact in this case $\Gamma(u, v) = (UV)^{|u|}$, hence for every $i = 1, \ldots, k$ one has that $n_i = 1$.
3. If u' is a conjugate of u and v' is a conjugate of v, then $\delta(u, v) = \delta(u', v')$. Therefore δ is a distance measure for conjugacy classes.
4. $\delta(u, v) = 0$ does not imply that u and v are conjugates, as shown in next example.

Example 7. Let $u = aabc$ and $v = abbc$. Although the two sequences are not conjugate, $\delta(u, v) = 0$ since $\Gamma(u, v) = (UV)^4$.

As common usage, we refer to δ as a "distance" when in fact neither it has to obey the triangle inequality (see Example 8) nor the condition $\delta(u, v) = 0 \Rightarrow u = v$ holds.

4.2 Multiple Sequence Comparison

A particular feature of our method is that it can also be applied to a set of k different sequences, with $k > 2$. More formally, let $S = \{u_1, u_2, \ldots, u_k\}$ be a set of sequences and let $w_1, w_2, \ldots, w_m$ be the sorted list of the conjugates of the elements of S obtained in the first step of the computation of $E(S)$. Consider the new alphabet $\Sigma = \{U_1, U_2, \ldots, U_k\}$ and the map γ that associates to each sequence w_i in the list, a symbol of Σ as follows:

$$\gamma(w_i) = U_j \text{ if } w_i \text{ is a conjugate of } u_j$$

Denote by $\Gamma(u_1, u_2, \ldots, u_k)$ the sequence $\gamma(w_1)\gamma(w_2)\cdots\gamma(w_m)$.

It is easy to see that for each pair $i, j = 1, \ldots, k$, $\Gamma(u_i, u_j)$ can be obtained from $\Gamma(u_1, u_2, \ldots, u_k)$ by deleting all symbols U_h with $h \neq i, j$. Conversely it is possible to prove ([8, Lemma 6.2.19]) that $\Gamma(u_1, u_2, \ldots, u_k)$ can be uniquely recovered from the set $\{\Gamma(u_i, u_j) \mid i, j = 1, \ldots, k\}$.

Example 8. Consider the set of sequences $S = \{u_1 = abaab, u_2 = babab, u_3 = abbba\}$. We have that:

$$\Gamma(u_1, u_2, u_3) = U_1 U_3 U_1^2 U_2^2 U_3 U_1 U_3 U_1 U_2^2 U_3 U_2 U_3$$

From previous remark, we can get from $\Gamma(u_1, u_2, u_3)$ the following:

$$\Gamma(u_1, u_2) = U_1^3 U_2^2 U_1^2 U_2^3,$$
$$\Gamma(u_2, u_3) = U_3 U_2^2 U_3^2 U_2^2 U_3 U_2 U_3,$$
$$\Gamma(u_1, u_3) = U_1 U_3 U_1^2 U_3 U_1 U_3 U_1 U_3^2.$$

Such sequences show that δ does not satisfy the triangle inequality. In fact $\delta(u_1, u_2) = 6$, $\delta(u_2, u_3) = 3$ and $\delta(u_1, u_3) = 2$.

Previous example shows how we can compute the distance δ of all pairs taken out of a set S of k sequences of length n by simultaneously applying the transformation E to the entire set S. Such a technique is very useful from a computational point of view for instance in order to construct phylogenetic trees (see Subsection 4.3). Actually, in order to obtain the $k \times k$ distance matrix, we can compute $\Gamma(S)$ by performing a single sorting of $k \times n$ sequences of length n instead of $O(k^2)$ sortings of $2n$ sequences of length n.

From a theoretical point of view, such a method allows to define, in a natural way, a notion of distance between sets of sequences. Actually, given two sets S and T, we denote by $w_1, w_2, \ldots, w_m$ the sorted list of the conjugates of the elements of S and T obtained in the first step of the computation of $E(S \cup T)$. We can consider the new alphabet $\Sigma = \{U, V\}$ and the map γ that associates to each sequence w_i in the list, a symbol of Σ as follows:

$$\gamma(w_i) = \begin{cases} U \text{ if } w_i \text{ is a conjugate of an element of } S \\ V \text{ if } w_i \text{ is a conjugate of an element of } T \end{cases}$$

Denote by $\Gamma(S, T)$ the sequence $\gamma(w_1)\gamma(w_2)\cdots\gamma(w_m)$.

If $\Gamma(u, v) = U^{n_1} V^{n_2} U^{n_3} \cdots V^{n_h}$, we can define the distance between S and T as follows:

$$\delta(S, T) = \sum_{\substack{i=1, \\ n_i \neq 0}}^{h} (n_i - 1)$$

Such a measure provides a further tool for cluster analysis and data classification.

4.3 Experimental Validation on Biological Sequences

The distance introduced in this paper measures the dissimilarity between two cyclic sequences (cf. Point 3 of Remark 2)[1]. So, in order to test our method, in this subsection we describe the results of the application of the normalized version of our distance to the whole mitochondrial genome phylogeny, since the mitochondrial DNA can be considered as a cyclic sequence. Actually, in the experiment of this subsection we construct a phylogeny of the Eutherian orders using complete unaligned mitochondrial genomes. We choose our group of sequences by using the mtDNA genomes of 20 mammals from *GenBank*, as listed in Figure 3. Such a set of species contains placental mammals, marsupials and monotremes. As shown in the dendrogram obtained by using a single linkage clustering (see Figure 3), our method allows to classify the analyzed species into Primates, Ferungulates, Rodents, Marsupial and Monotremes. Moreover we obtain a phylogeny that is very close to the ones described in most of the papers in which the species considered are almost the same (cf. [2, 3, 7, 14]). Our resulting phylogeny proposes the following grouping of the placental mammals: (Primates,

---

[1] Recall that in order to consider not cyclic sequences, it suffices to add an end-of-string symbol # to the sequences.

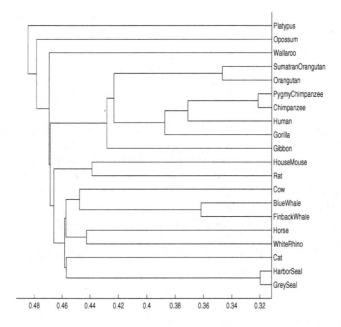

Fig. 3. The evolutionary tree built from complete mammalian mtDNA sequences of the 20 species analyzed in (Cao et al., 1998).

(Ferungulates, Rodents)). A more detailed analysis and further experiments can be found in [10].

Nevertheless, the goal of this experiment is not to confirm or refute previous phylogenetic studies but rather to show that the method here introduced can be a helpful tool for the comparative genomics research community.

5   Simultaneous Compression of a Set of k Texts

Recall that the Burrows Wheeler transform has been introduced as a tool to preprocess a word to be compressed, in order to get a word easier to compress. Actually the transformation leads to group characters together so that the probability of finding a character close to another instances of the same character is substantially increased. Moreover the reversibility of the BWT allows to recover the original word. We have introduced a transformation that extends the BWT to a (multi)set of k primitive words having similar features than BWT. So one can think to use the transformation E as a preprocessing for the simultaneous compression of k different texts. We denote by $\mathcal{C}$ a compressor that uses the transformation E as preprocessing. If $x_1, \ldots, x_k$ is a multiset of words, we denote by $\mathcal{C}(x_1, \ldots, x_k)$ the word obtained by applying the compressor $\mathcal{C}$ to the output of the transformation E over the set $\{x_1, \ldots, x_k\}$. Since E is a transformation that acts on multisets of words, it is easy to see that if π is a permutation on $\{1, \ldots, k\}$, then $\mathcal{C}(x_1, \ldots, x_k) = \mathcal{C}(x_{\pi(1)}, \ldots, x_{\pi(k)})$. The interest of our approach is based on the intuitive idea that the more similar two texts x and y are, the more effective is their simultaneous compression with respect to compressing each text separately.

Such a fact has several interesting application. For example, most BWT-based compressors process the input file x of length n by parsing it into blocks of size M. A single block is read, compressed and written to the output file before the next one is considered (cf. [13] and references therein). In this section we use the notion of simultaneous compression in order to define an E-based compressor that divides the input text into blocks of length M and then compress them simultaneously. Some preliminary experiments (see the Table 1) show that our method gives a better compression ratio than BWT-based method mentioned above, when applied to the same blocks. Moreover our method allows to compress the files with an asymptotically comparable time complexity and smaller memory requirement than the ones required for compressing the whole text at once with a BWT-based compressor.

Indeed we can note that the transformation of the whole text x involves a sorting of n words of length n; our method involves a sorting of n words of length M. This requires still an $O(n)$ time complexity, but reduces the size of the memory used to $O(n)$ instead of $O(n^2)$.

We test our method on some files of the Calgary Corpus. We use a compressor C that divides the text of size N into blocks of size M, preprocesses such a set of blocks by the transformation E and then applies to the output of E the Move to Front algorithm (MTF) followed by the Huffman Coding. Recall that MTF encodes an instance of the character x by an integer that counts the number of distinct symbols seen after the latest occurrence of x.

The results of our experiment, synthesized in Table 1, show that our method is more effective than the technique used by a BWT-based compressor (here denoted by $\mathcal{A}$) that divides the text into blocks of size M, preprocesses by BWT and compresses (by MTF and the Huffman Coding) each block separately, and finally concatenates the outputs. In particular, in the Table 1, for each

Table 1. The effect of varying the block size on compression of some files from the Calgary Corpus.

File	Size (in bytes)	Alg.	$M = 16K$	$M = 64K$	$M = N$
bib	111261	C	2.547	2.461	2.425
		$\mathcal{A}$	3.204	2.634	
obj1	21504	C	4.743	–	4.740
		$\mathcal{A}$	5.076	–	
paper2	82199	C	2.805	2.786	2.779
		$\mathcal{A}$	3.330	2.917	
progl	71646	C	2.145	2.138	2.131
		$\mathcal{A}$	2.440	2.200	
trans	93695	C	2.064	1.978	1.950
		$\mathcal{A}$	2.667	2.123	

input block size M and for each file of the considered dataset, we compare the compression ratios (expressed as output bits per input character) obtained by applying the compressor C and A, respectively.

We remark that, in order to decompress the text, we need to encode also, during the compression step, the set $\mathcal{I}$ of indices produced by transformation E, according to the order in which the blocks of length M appear in the original text.

References

1. M. Burrows and D.J. Wheeler. A block sorting data compression algorithm. Technical report, DIGITAL System Research Center, 1994.
2. Y. Cao, A. Janke, P. J. Waddell, M. Westerman, O. Takenaka, S. Murata, N. Okada, S. Pääbo, and M. Hasegawa. Conflict among individual mitochondrial proteins in resolving the phylogeny of eutherian orders. *J. Mol. Evol.*, 47:307–322, 1998.
3. R. Cilibrasi and P. Vitányi. Clustering by compression. *IEEE Trans. Information Theory (submitted)*, 2005.
4. M. Crochemore, J. Désarménien, and D. Perrin. A note on the Burrows-Wheeler transformation. *Theoret. Comput. Sci.* to appear.
5. F. Ergun, S. Muthukrishnan, and C. Sahinalp. Comparing sequences with segment rearrangements. *Lecture Notes in Comput. Sci*, pages 183–194, 2003. Proc. of the FSTTCS'03, Bombay, India.
6. I. M. Gessel and C. Reutenauer. Counting permutations with given cycle structure and descent set. *J. Combin. Theory Ser. A*, 64(2):189–215, 1993.
7. M. Li, X. Chen, X. Li, B. Ma, and P. Vitányi. The similarity metric. *IEEE Trans. Inform. Th.*, 12(5):3250–3264, 2004.
8. M. Lothaire. *Combinatorics on Words*, volume 17 of *Encyclopedia of Mathematics*. Addison-Wesley, Reading, Mass., 1983. Reprinted in the *Cambridge Mathematical Library*, Cambridge University Press, 1997.
9. M. Lothaire. *Algebraic Combinatorics on Words.* Cambridge University Press, 2002.
10. S. Mantaci, A. Restivo, G. Rosone, and M. Sciortino. A new sequence distance measure based on the Burrows-Wheeler transform. Technical Report 268, University of Palermo, Dipartimento di Matematica ed Appl., December 2004.
11. S. Mantaci, A. Restivo, and M. Sciortino. Burrows-Wheeler transform and Sturmian words. *Informat. Proc. Lett.*, 86:241–246, 2003.
12. S. Mantaci, A. Restivo, and M. Sciortino. Combinatorial aspects of the Burrows-Wheeler transform. *TUCS (Turku Center for Computer Science) General Pubblication*, 25:292–297, 2003. proc. WORDS 2003.
13. G. Manzini. The Burrows-Wheeler transform: Theory and practice. In *Proc. of the 24th International Symposium on Mathematical Foundations of Computer Science (MFCS '99)*, pages 34–47. Springer-Verlag LNCS n. 1672, 1999.
14. H.H. Otu and K. Sayood. A new sequence distance measure for phylogenetic tree construction. *Bioinformatics*, 19(16):2122–2130, 2003.
15. S. Vinga and J. Almeida. Alignment-free sequence comparison – a review. *Bioinformatics*, 19(4):513–523, 2003.

DNA Compression Challenge Revisited: A Dynamic Programming Approach

Behshad Behzadi and Fabrice Le Fessant

LIX, Ecole Polytechnique, Palaiseau cedex 91128, France
{Behzadi,Lefessan}@lix.polytechnique.fr

Abstract. Standard compression algorithms are not able to compress DNA sequences. Recently, new algorithms have been introduced specifically for this purpose, often using detection of long approximate repeats. In this paper, we present another algorithm, *DNAPack*, based on dynamic programming. In comparison with former existing programs, it compresses DNA slightly better, while the cost of dynamic programming is almost negligible.

1 Introduction

DNA sequences contain only four bases $\{A, C, T, G\}$. Thus, each base (symbol) can be represented by two bits. However, the standard text compression tools, such as `compress`, `gzip` and `bzip2`, cannot compress these DNA sequences; the size of the files encoded with these tools is larger than two bits per symbol. Consequently, DNA sequences compression has recently become a challenge.

Some characteristics of DNA sequences show that they are not random sequences. If these sequences were totally random, the most efficient and logical way to store them would be using two bits per base. However, DNA is used for the expression of proteins in living organisms, and thus must contain some logical organization. Moreover, approximate repeats (repeats with mutations) and complementary palindromes (reversed repeats, where A and C are respectively replaced by T and G, and reciprocally) are well-known to frequently appear inside long DNA sequences.

Based on these characteristics, several algorithms have been proposed for the compression of DNA sequences. However, even if these algorithms obtain much better results than standard universal compression algorithms, the compression ratios are not very high. We briefly discuss some of the existing algorithms in the order of their introduction (from the oldest to the most recent ones):

Biocompress [7], and its second version *Biocompress-2* [8], were the first DNA-specific compression algorithms. They are similar to the Ziv-Lampel data compression method. *Biocompress-2* detects exact repeats and complementary palindromes located in the already encoded sequence, and then encodes them by the repeat length and the position of a previous repeat occurrence. When no significant repetition is found, *Biocompress-2* uses order-2 arithmetic coding (Arith-2).

A. Apostolico, M. Crochemore, and K. Park (Eds.): CPM 2005, LNCS 3537, pp. 190–200, 2005.

The *Cfact* algorithm [13] looks for the longest exact matching repeat. For this purpose, it uses a suffix tree on the entire sequence. Using two passes, repetitions are encoded this way when the gain is guaranteed, otherwise the two-bits-per-base (2-Bits) encoding is used.

The *GenCompress* algorithm [3, 4, 9] yields to a significantly better compression ratio than the previous algorithms. The idea is to use approximate (and not exact) repetitions. It exists in two variants: *GenCompress-1* uses the Hamming distance (only substitutions) for the repeats while *GenCompress-2* uses the edition distance (deletion, insertion and substitution) for the encoding of the repeats.

CTW+LZ [10] is another algorithm, based on the context tree weighting method. It combines a LZ-77 type method like *GenCompress* and the *CTW* algorithm. Long exact/appoximate repeats are encoded by LZ77-type algorithm, while short repeats are encoded by *CTW*. Although they obtain good compression ratios, its execution time is too high to be used for long sequences.

DNACompress [5] is a DNA compression tool, which employs the Ziv-Lampel compression scheme as *Biocompress-2* and *GenCompress*. It consists of two phases: during the first phase, it finds all approximate repeats including complementary palindromes, using a specific software, *PatternHunter* [11]. Then the approximate repeats and the non-repeat regions are encoded. In practice, the execution time of *DNACompress* is much less than *GenCompress*.

DNAC [6] is another DNA compression tool, working in four phases: during the first phase, it builds a suffix tree to locate exact repeats. During the second phase, all the exact repeats are extended into approximate repeats by dynamic programming. In the third phase, it extracts the optimal non-overlapping repeats from the overlapping ones, and in the last phase, it encodes all the repeats.

DNASequitur is a grammar-based compression algorithm for DNA sequences which infers a context-free grammar to represent the input data. Even if the algorithm is elegant, the practical results show that other methods achieve better compression ratios.

Some DNA compression methods are based only on the exact matches [2, 12]. However the exection times stated in [12] are better than other compressors but the compression ratios are generally worse than the best existing compressors.

In this paper, we propose a new algorithm, *DNAPack*, which uses Hamming distance for the repeats and complementary palindromes, and either CTW or Arith-2 compression for the non-repeat regions. Unlike the above algorithms, *DNAPack* does not choose the repeats by a greedy algorithm, but uses a dynamic programming approach instead.

The content of the paper is organized as follows: in section 2, we describe the different techniques and concepts used in our algorithm. In section 3, we present the algorithm we use to find a semi-optimal decomposition of the file, and the encoding of the compressed file is presented in section 4. Finally, in section 5, we compare our results on a standard set of DNA sequences with results published for the other algorithms.

2   Useful Techniques

Our algorithm like all of the other DNA-oriented algorithms is based on partitioning the sequence into two kinds of segments: the *repeat* segments (or copied) and the *non-repeat* segments. The repeat segments are either *approximate direct* repeats (repeats with some substitutions) or the *approximate complementary palindrome* repeats (reversed repeats where bases are replaced by their complementary base). In order to achieve the best results in compression, several techniques are used for encoding the different kinds of segments. In this section, we describe a set of techniques and methods which we use in our algorithm.

2.1   Encoding of Non-repeat Regions

For the encoding of the non-repeat regions, we need to compress arbitrary sequences of bases without long repeats. Two different techniques have been shown to be efficient on these regions:

Order-2 Arithmetic Coding. In comparison to the Huffman Coding algorithm, Arithmetic Coding overcomes the constraint that the symbol to be encoded has to be coded by a round number of bits. This leads to higher efficiency and a better compression ratio in general. The adaptive arithmetic coding of order 2 has the best compression ratio on the DNA sequences; in this arithmetic encoding the adaptive probability of a symbol is computed from the context after which it appears. The best ratio for DNA is obtained for order-2 (contexts are the last two symbols), which seems to correspond to the amino-acid codons, i. e. groups of three bases coding an amino-acid in a protein.

Context Tree Weighting Coding. The probabilities in an arithmetic coding can be computed in different ways. Willems et al. in [14] proposed a universal compression algorithm denoted by Context Tree Weighting (CTW) method which has on average a good compression ratio for an unknown model. The CTW encoder consists of two parts: a source modeler which is the actual CTW algorithm, which receives the uncompressed data and estimates the probability of the next symbol and an arithmetic encoder which uses the estimated probabilities to compress the data.

One important concept in the the CTW algorithm is the context tree which is built dynamically during encoding/decoding process. All of the already visited substrings of shorter size than a fixed bound (the height of the tree), exist as a path in the tree. Each node of the tree contains a probability. In order to encode a given bit, the following steps are performed: the path in the context tree which coincides with the current context is searched and if needed extended. For every node in this context path, an estimated probability of the next symbol is computed using the data stored in the node. Then a weighted probability is computed using a weighting function on all the estimated probability values. The idea here is that if good coding distributions for two different texts are weighted then the weighted distribution is a good coding distribution for both sources. Finally the weighted probability is sent to the arithmetic encoder which encodes the symbol, and the encoder goes to the next symbol.

2.2 Encoding of Numbers

Different integer numbers have to be encoded in our algorithm. For example, the segments have not a fixed length, so this length has to be encoded. For any repeat segment, the position of the reference substring of the input, from which we copy this segment, should be encoded. When the copies are approximate (and not exact) the positions of the modifications should be encoded. There is no bound on any of these numbers, so these integers should be encoded in a self-delimited way rather than being encoded in a fix number of bits. For encoding the reference position, encoding the relative difference of position of the reference and the copy itself is preferable.

Fibonacci Encoding. An efficient self-delimited representation of arbitrary numbers is the Fibonacci encoding [1]. The Fibonacci encoding is based on the fact that any positive integer n can be uniquely expressed as the sum of distinct Fibonacci numbers, so that no two consecutive Fibonacci numbers are used in the representation. This means that if we use binary representation of a Fibonacci encoding of a number, there are no two consecutive 1 bits. So by adding a 1 after the 1 corresponding to the biggest Fibonacci number in the sum, the representation becomes self-delimited. The Fibonacci representation of some numbers are given in the Table 1.

Shifted Encoding. Although Fibonacci encoding is a good coder for an unknown set of numbers, one can construct better codes if we have some information about the numbers. For example, if there are many small numbers and not a lot of large numbers to encode, Fibonacci encoding can be improved by using a *shifted* version. We define a *k-shifted Fibonacci encoding* as a coding where all the numbers in the range $[1..2^k - 1]$ into their normal binary representation and codes all the other numbers 0^k followed by the Fibonacci encoding of $n - (2^k - 1)$. In Table 1, k-shifted representation of some numbers for $k = 1$ and $k = 3$ are given.

Table 1. Fibonacci and shifted fibonacci representation of some numbers; depending on the distribution of the numbers to be encoded one method can be preferred to the others.

	1	2	3	4	8	18
Fibonacci	11	011	0011	1011	000011	0001011
1-Shifted Fibonacci	1	011	0011	00011	001011	01010011
3-Shifted Fibonacci	001	010	011	100	00011	00001011

2.3   Hamming-Based Transcription

Suppose a substring v is an approximate repeat of substring u of the same size. To encode v, we first encode the relative position of its already visited repeat u (the pattern to be copied). Then we need to encode the *edit transcription* which transforms u to v. We use three types of instructions: the first instruction is $Copy(l)$ which indicates that the next l symbols of the two substrings are the same. $Replace(x)$ indicates that the symbol in the current position of u should be replaced by x in order to generate v. The last instruction is the $Finish$ instruction which indicates that v is completely generated. Using this termination instruction is a way to prevent encoding the size of the string v.

One important remark is that we use *Hamming* distance, i.e. approximation is done only by substitutions, whereas some other compressors use the *Edit* distance, where approximation can also be done by deletions and insertions. Although we didn't experiment with it, previously published results have shown that the benefit in compression ratio [3] is not worth the increased complexity and computation time.

3   The Algorithm

In this section firstly we explain our method which is based on dynamic programming. Then we comment about the optimizations which makes our algorithm working in a reasonably good time.

3.1   Dynamic Programming vs. Greedy Algorithms

DNACompress, *GenCompress* and *CTWLZ* obtain the best results among the existing algorithms. Both *GenCompress* and *DNACompress* use the greedy approach for selection of the repeat segments. *GenCompress* selects the best prefix of the region which is not yet encoded to be coded at the next step. As shown in figure 1(a), the greedy selection of the segment A, prevents the possibility of selecting the longer segment B. *DNACompress* has a different greedy scheme. In each step, it chooses the most profitable segment which does not intersect with the already chosen segments. Figure 1(b) shows how, by this greedy selection, the algorithm may be prevented from choosing the best set of segments.

CTW+LZ tries to solve the problem of *GenCompress* by using some heuristics which are unfortunately very time-consuming without yielding to real improvements. Moreover, they cannot be applied to long sequences, because of their time consumption.

In our algorithm, *DNAPack*, we use a dynamic programming approach for selection of the segments, therefore solving the problem of greedy selection. We use a set of optimizations which make the running time of our algorithm, reasonably small, so it can be applied to very long sequences.

Let s be the input DNA sequence. Let $BestComp[i]$ be the smallest compressed size of the prefix $s[1..i]$. The following simple recurrence is the general scheme of our dynamic programming.

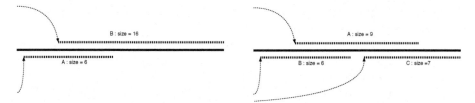

Fig. 1. (a) On the left-hand side, choosing the first segment as gencompress does is not optimal. (b) On the right-hand side, choosing the biggest segment and discarding overlapping segments is also non-optimal.

Initialization: $BestComp[0] = 0$
Recurrence:

$$\forall i > 0 \qquad BestComp[i] = \min \begin{cases} BestComp[j] + CopyCost(j,i,k) & \forall k \ \forall \, 0 < j < i \\ BestComp[j] + PalinCopyCost(j,i,k) & \forall k \ \forall \, 0 < j < i \\ BestCopy[j] + MinCost(j+1,i) & \forall \, 0 < j < i \end{cases}$$

Fig. 2. Dynamic Programming scheme for finding the best compression.

$CopyCost(j,i,k)$ is the number of bits needed to encode the substring of size k starting at position i if it is an approximate repeat of the substring of size k starting at j. The $PalinCost$ is similarly defined for reverse complementary substrings. The function $MinCost(j+1,i)$ is the number of bits needed for compression of the segment $s[j+1,i]$. It depends on the size of the substring (for the size of the Fibonacci encoding) as well as the compression ratio obtained for the algorithm by arithmetic coding or CTW. $MinCost$ allows us to create a repeat segment only if it would yield a benefit in the compression ratio. These three functions are estimations of the real cost, since the efficiency of some optimizations done during the encoding cannot be computed at this point.

3.2 Reducing Execution Time

A direct implementation of this algorithm has a complexity of $O(n^3)$, which is much too high for long DNA sequences. Therefore, we use several techniques to reduce the execution time in practice. First, we authorize only the repeats which have a common *seed*. The seed is a small string of size l (a parameter of our program), whose already found positions are stored in a hash table. To find a repeat, we need only to find the positions of its seed in the hash table, and try to increase their sizes.

In the third line of the recurrence, we do not really need to examine all the j's. A careful observation shows that we only need to compute $MinCost(j+1,i)$ for a j which is the end of a repeat segment, since there is no gain in creating two consecutive non-repeat segments: each non-repeat segment contains its size in Fibonacci encoding, and the size of two small encoded numbers is greater than the size of one big encoded number. In fact, we can even narrow this search among all of the j's which $BestComp[j+1]$ is not optimized by copying a segment from the same position as $BestComp[j]$.

In the case of repeats, if $s[i-1] = s[j-1]$ then there is no need to check the different values of k; one can verify that $BestComp[j-1] + CopyCost(j-1, i, k+1) \leq BestComp[j] + CopyCost(j, i, k)$.

Similar observation can be made for the case of the reverse repeat (2nd line of the recurrence). As a result of these optimizations, the number of possible j and k to search in our dynamic programming will be reduced enormously such that it is possible to execute the algorithm on large sequences in a few seconds (in our experimentations for example, $MinCost(j+1, i)$ is only computed for 2 or 3 different j for every i).

4   Practical Encoding

As written in the introduction, the encoding of bases on two bits already gives a good compression ratio, which can be hard to beat if we don't pay enough intention to the encoding scheme used for the approximate repeats. Indeed, previous compression algorithms for DNA in the literature mainly focus on the algorithm used to find the repeats, unfortunately forgetting to discuss the various ways of encoding them, and thus, leading the not so good compressors. As a consequence, we discuss here the choice we did in our implementation to efficiently encode the various compression operations.

The encoding function takes as input a sequence of segments, where each segment is either a sequence of bases, or a repeat of a preceding sequence of bases. It outputs a file containing the same data in a compact representation.

4.1   The Structure of the Compressed File

The compressed file consists of three different regions: HEADER, CODE and BASES.

The HEADER contains all the information that must be known to decode the CODE and BASES regions. For example, it contains:

- The type of compression used for sequences of bases (it is either Arithmetic-2 Coding, CTW or None), on 2 bits.
- The number of segments in the CODE part.
- The minimum size of the first Copy operation in the repeats.
- The most frequent base substituted for another base in a repeat substitution.

The CODE region consists of two different types of segments: repeats and non-repeats. For the non-repeats segments, the CODE region only contains the length of the segment, encoded in Fibonacci encoding, whereas all the bases are put in the BASES region. When all the non-repeats have been processed, the complete BASES region is compressed using either Arithmetic-2 Coding, Context-Tree Weighted Coding or 2-bits Coding, whichever gives the best compression ratio.

Since $|FibEncode(a + b)| \leq |FibEncode(a)| + |FibEncode(b)|$, the CODE region never contains two consecutive non-repeats segments, as they would more efficiently be encoded as a single segment. Consequently, we use the following encoding to describe the type of the segments:

- – - an empty code for the first segment of the gene, which is always a non-repeat.
- – 0 for a non-repeat segment after a repeat segment.
- – 1 for a repeat segment after a repeat segment.
- – - an empty code for a repeat segment after a non-repeat segment.

4.2   The Encoding of Repeats

A repeat segment must contain the following information:

- – The type of repeat: direct repeat or complement-palindrome repeat. We only need one bit for this information.
- – The offset to the origin of the repeat (increased by one for complement-palindrome repeats to avoid zeroes). We simply encode this offset in Fibonacci encoding.
- – The sequence of operations to repeat the segment, containing either copies or mutations.

In this first implementation, we force the sequence of operations to always finish with a Copy. Thanks to this simplification, a single bit can be used per operation to distinguish between copies and Replaces:

- – - an empty code for the first operation, which is always a Copy, since our algorithm to find repeats looks for repeats with at least l characters in common.
- – 0 for the end of the repeat after a Copy.
- – 1 for a Replace after a Copy.
- – 0 for a Copy after a Replace.
- – 1 for a Replace after a Replace.

4.3   The Encoding of Operations Arguments

A Copy operation requires only one argument, the number of bases to be copied from the original segment. Although we cannot optimize the representation of this length in the general case, our algorithm guarantees that at least the first l bases (called seed) will be similar between the two substrings. Thus, we compute the minimal length of the first Copy of each repeat-segment, and we always encode the first Copy of a segment after removing this minimum. With hundreds of repeats in each gene, 4 or 5 bits saved per repeat, this simple optimization finally saves a few thousands bits.

For each Replace operation, we need to supply the base to replace the former base of the original segment. However, since we know that former base, the new base can only be one of the 3 other bases. Therefore, we can represent it more efficiently:

– 0 for the most probable base.
– 10 and 11 for the two other bases.

Instead of using probabilities, our first implementation simply computes the most frequent substitution for every former base, and store it in the HEADER region of the file.

5   Experimental Results

To experiment our algorithm, we tried to compress a standard set of DNA sequences with our algorithm, and we compare with results published for other efficient DNA compressors. This standard test sequences contains different sequences of mithocondry DNA, viruses and parts of human genome. The results are displayed on table 2. The table shows that our program, DNAPack, performs slightly better than other programs, except DNACompress in a few cases.

During our experiments, we tried to compress all the sequences while varying a few parameters used by our algorithm:

– l, the size of the exact prefix that two repeats must have in common to be compared.
– compressions, the set of compressions algorithms used to compress BASES, ranging in $\{Arith - 2, CTW, 2 - Bits\}$.
– approx, the estimation of the compression ratio that will probably be obtained on the BASES region, used during the dynamic programming phase.

Due to space constraints, we cannot display all these results, but we can briefly summarize them[1]: a big l gives very short execution time, without decreasing too much the compression ratio (in the table we have considered only two different values for the value of l: the three first genes are compressed with l = 30 and for the others l = 8; all results are obtained in less than 15 seconds, except for MPOMTCG and VACCG which were produced in around 1 minutes). The two different compressions of BASES are also important: among the 11 genes compressed, 7 were compressed using CTW, 4 using Arith-2. For some genes, 2-Bits was more efficient than Arith-2. Finally, having the most accurate value of approx also impacts a lot on performances, especially for small values of l, where a lot of choices between small repeats and non-repeats must be done.

6   Conclusion

We have presented a new algorithm to compress DNA sequences. As most other DNA compressors, our algorithm works by finding approximate repeats and trying to optimally encode them. The first version of our implementation has results

---

[1] The best compressions ratios as well as the details of the effects of the different parameters on the compression ratios and the running times can be found on the DNAPack page at URL: http://yquem.inria.fr/~lefessan/src/dnapack/

Table 2. Comparison of compression ratios for different algorithms (bits/base).

sequence	length	BioCompress-2	GenCompress	CTW-LZ	DNACompress	DNAPack
CHMPXX	121024	1.6848	1.6730	1.6690	1.6716	**1.6602**
CHNTXX	155844	1.6172	1.6146	1.6120	1.6127	**1.6103**
HEHCMVCG	229354	1.8480	1.8470	1.8414	1.8492	**1.8346**
HUMDYSTROP	33770	1.9262	1.9231	1.9175	1.9116	**1.9088**
HUMGHCSA	66495	1.3074	1.0969	1.0972	**1.0272**	1.039
HUMHBB	73308	1.8800	1.8204	1.8082	1.7897	**1.7771**
HUMHDABCD	58864	1.8770	1.8192	1.8218	1.7951	**1.7394**
HUMHPRTB	56737	1.9066	1.8466	1.8433	1.8165	**1.7886**
MPOMTCG	186609	1.9378	1.9058	1.9000	**1.8920**	1.8932
PANMTPACGA	100314	1.8752	1.8624	1.8555	1.8556	**1.8535**
VACCG	191737	1.7614	1.7614	1.7616	**1.7580**	1.7583
Average	—	1.7837	1.7428	1.7389	1.7254	**1.7148**

which on average are slightly better than former algorithms. It is mainly due to the benefits of dynamic programming, and the careful choice of the encoding of the repeats. We are now working on different aspects of our compressor: first, we are tuning the different parameters to improve the compression ratio while decreasing the computation time; we are experimenting it on larger genes (chromosomes contain at least twenty million bases on average), and finally, we are trying to find a better compression method for some sequences, where approximate repeats are unfrequent (HUMDYSTROP for example), who failed to be compress efficiently by all the known compressors.

The future works will be more bioinformatics related. The reliability of measuring the relatedness of the different organisms by comparing their compresion ratios, the reason why the genes compress with different ratios are interesting questions to be studied.

References

1. Apostolico A. and Fraenkel A.S.: Robust transmission of unbounded strings using Fibonacci representations. IEEE trans. inform., 33(2), pp 238-245, 1987.
2. Apostolico A. and Lonardi S.: Compression of biological sequences by greedy offline textual substitution. Proc. DCC'00, 143-152, 2000.
3. Chen, X., Kwong, S., Li, M.: A compression Algorithm for DNA sequences and its applications in genome comparison. The 10th workshop on Genome Informtics (GIW'99), pp 51-61, Tokyo, Japan, 1999.
4. Chen, X., Kwong, S., Li, M.: A compression Algorithm for DNA sequences. IEEE Engineering in Medicine and Biolgoy Magazine, 20(4), 61-66, Jul/Aug 2001.
5. Chen, X., Li, M., Ma, B. and Tromp, J.: DNACompress: fast and effective DNA sequence compression. Bioinformatics, 18:1696-1698, 2002.
6. Chang C.-H.: DNAC: A Compression Algorithm for DNA Sequences by Nonoverlapping Approximate Repeats. Master Thesis, 2004.
7. Grumbach S. and Tahi F.: Compression of DNA Sequences. In Data compression conference, pp 340-350. IEEE Computer Society Press, 1993.

8. Grumbach S. and Tahi F.: A new Challenge for compression algorithms: genetic sequences. Journal of Information Processing and Management, 30, 875-866, 1994.

9. Li M., Badger J. H., Chen X., Kwong S., Kearney P., Zhang H.: An information based sequences distance and its application to whole motochondrial genome phylogeny," Bioinformatics, 17(2): 149-154, 2001.

10. Matsumuto T., Sadakane K.,Imai H.: Biological sequence compression algorithms. Genome Inform. Ser. Wokrshop Genome Inform. 11:43-52, 2000

11. Ma B., Tromp J. and Li M.: PatternHunter–faster and more sensitive homology search. Bioinformatics, 18, 440-445, 2002.

12. Manzini G. and Rastero M.: A simple and fast DNA compressor. Sofware: Practice and Experience, 34(14), 1397-1411, 2004.

13. Rivals E., Delahaye J.-P., Dauchet M., Delgrange O.: A Guaranteed Compression Scheme for Repetitive DNA Sequences. Data Compression Conference, 1996.

14. Willems F. M. J., Shtrakov Y. M. and Tjalkens T. J.: The Context Tree Weighting Method: Basic Properties. IEEE Trans. Inform. Theory, IT-41(3), pp 653-664, 1995.

On the Complexity of Sparse Exon Assembly

Carmel Kent[1,*], Gad M. Landau[1,2,*], and Michal Ziv-Ukelson[3,**]

[1] Dept. of Computer Science, Haifa University, Haifa 31905, Israel
{ckent,landau}@cs.haifa.ac.il

[2] Department of Computer and Information Science, Polytechnic University,
Brooklyn, NY 11201-3840, USA
landau@poly.edu

[3] Dept. of Computer Science, Technion – Israel Institute of Technology,
Haifa 32000, Israel
michalz@cs.technion.ac.il

Abstract. Gene structure prediction is one of the most important problems in computational molecular biology. A combinatorial approach to the problem, denoted *Gene Prediction via Spliced Alignment*, was introduced by Gelfand, Mironov and Pevzner [5]. The method works by finding a set of blocks in a source genomic sequence S whose concatenation (splicing) fits a target gene T belonging to a homologous species. Let S,T and the candidate exons be sequences of size $O(n)$. The innovative algorithm described in [5] yields an $O(n^3)$ result for spliced alignment, regardless of filtration mode.

In this paper we suggest a new algorithm which targets the case where filtering has been applied to the data, resulting in a set of $O(n)$ candidate exon blocks. Our algorithm yields an $O(n^2\sqrt{n})$ solution for this case.

1   Introduction

Recognition of genes in eukaryotic DNA is seriously complicated by noisy regions (*introns*) that interrupt the coding regions (*exons*) of genes. The *gene-prediction via spliced alignment* approach, due to Gelfand, Mironov and Pevzner [5, 15, 21] incorporates similarity analysis into gene prediction by attempting to find a set of potential exons in a genomic sequence whose concatenation is highly similar to one of the already known gene sequences in the database.

The task of gene prediction is generally divided into two stages. The first task is that of finding *candidate exons* in a long DNA sequence believed to contain a gene. A candidate exon is a sequence fragment whose left boundary is an *acceptor* site or a start codon, and the right boundary is a *donor* site or a stop codon. The nucleotide sequence in Figure 1 contains marked sites where a candidate exon may begin and end. Uppercase A-E mark identified sites where an exon is likely to begin (start/acceptor sites), and lowercase f-j mark sites where exons are likely to end (stop/donor sites). Candidate exons are A-f, A-g, A-h, A-i, A-j, B-f, B-g, B-h, B-i, B-j, C-g, etc.

* Research supported in part by by the Israel Science Foundation grant 282/01.
** Research supported in part by the Aly Kaufman Post Doctoral Fellowship.

A. Apostolico, M. Crochemore, and K. Park (Eds.): CPM 2005, LNCS 3537, pp. 201–218, 2005.

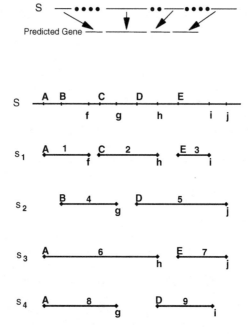

Fig. 1. A nucleotide sequence (S) and four of its derived candidate genes (s_1, s_2, s_3, s_4).

The second task is that of selecting the best subset of non overlapping candidate exons to cover the sequence of the predicted gene. (Four of the many possible assemblies of candidate exons as candidate genes are shown in the figure: $s_1 = \{A - f, C - h, E - i\}$, $s_2 = \{B - g, D - j\}$, $s_3 = \{A - h, E - j\}$ and $s_4 = \{A - g, D - i\}$.) Each candidate gene (a concatenation of non-intersecting candidate exons which satisfy some natural consistency conditions [20]) is compared against the target sequence, which is an already known gene from a homologous species.

An interesting combinatorial approach, using network dynamic programming, which explores all possible exon assemblies in polynomial time, is described in [5]. Assuming that S and T as well as the sizes of the candidate exons is $O(n)$, this algorithm yields an $O(n^3)$ solution for Sparse Spliced Alignment.

Good filtration is crucial for exon assembly, especially if targets from distant taxa are used. In [15], the authors studied the performance of the spliced alignment algorithm for different targets on a complete set of human genomic sequences with known relatives and demonstrated that the average performance of the method remains high even for distant targets. The authors analyzed several filtration procedures of varying strength and demonstrated that weak filtration provides better results with mammalian targets. In the case of distant targets, the stronger filtering was more useful than in the case of close targets, and sometimes it was shown to significantly improve the prediction quality. Furthermore, it was also explicitly shown (see *http://www-hto.usc.edu/software/procrustes-*

/#salign) that the number of candidate exons generated in either weak or moderate filtration modes is linear in the size of the genomic sequence: the default (weak) filter retained approximately 1 exon per 14 nucleotides on the average, while the moderate filter retained approximately 1 exon per 33 nucleotides.

Therefore, in this paper we re-address the spliced alignment problem for the linear-sized candidate exon-set case. More formally, for any two substrings B and B' of a genomic sequence S, we write $B \prec B'$ if B ends before B' starts. A sequence $\Gamma = (B_1 \ldots, B_n)$ of substrings of S is a *chain* if $B_1 \prec B_2 \prec \ldots \prec B_n$. We denote the concatenation of strings from the chain Γ by $\Gamma^* = B_1 * B_2 * \ldots * B_n$.

Definition 1. *Given two sequences, S and T, of size $O(n)$ each, and a set $\beta = \{B_1, \ldots B_b\}$ containing $O(n)$ blocks (substrings of S), of size $O(n)$ each. The* <u>Sparse Spliced Alignment Problem</u> *is to find a chain Γ of strings from β such that $score(\Gamma^*, T)$ is maximum among all chains of blocks from β.*

In this paper we suggest a new algorithm for *Sparse Spliced Alignment*. Our new approach is based in efficient elimination of redundancy due to candidate-exon overlaps. Note that dominant portions of each of the competing candidate gene assemblies in Figure 1 are segments common to other candidates, since the candidate exons overlap in the genomic source sequence. (For example, the two source strings S_1 and S_2 share the substrings B-f, C-g, D-h and E-i.) The authors of [5] indeed noticed this redundancy and utilized it to speed up the naive dynamic programming algorithm. When no filtration is applied, and the number of candidate exons generated is $O(n^2)$, their approach reduces the spliced alignment complexity from the naive $O(n^4)$ down to $O(n^3)$. However, when filtration is applied, and the number of candidate exons is $O(n)$, their algorithm still yields the same $O(n^3)$ result.

At first glance it may seem that the algorithm of [5] indeed exploits to its maximum the power of dynamic programming in utilizing such block overlaps. A second, more thorough examination of the problem leads to the conclusion that it is the dependency of traditional dynamic programming on the direction in which it is applied, as well as the fact that values in each dynamic programming table are sensitive to the content of preceding (or symmetrically following) chained blocks in the candidate solution, which stand in the way of further isolating the common denominator between blocks and exploiting the overlap redundancy.

1.1   The Results of This Paper

We describe an $O(n^2\sqrt{n})$ solution for Sparse Spliced Alignment, which improves upon the previous results by $O(\sqrt{n})$. Furthermore, the new algorithm degrades gracefully, so that even in the case when no filtration is applied to the exon set, and the number of candidate exons may be $O(n^2)$, our algorithm will yield an $O(n^3)$ complexity which is no worse than previous results. The efficiency improvement is based in a tighter, more sophisticated elimination of overlap redundancy among the candidate exons. The crux of the new algorithm is based in three components.

1. A Rectilinear Steiner Minimal Arborescence technique [6, 7, 13, 19] is applied to the analysis of the overlapping candidate exons. The Steiner technique is a well-practiced tool in both Computational Geometry and Graph Theory problems. Its importance stems from the fact that it has applications in as diverse areas as VLSI-layout and the study of phylogenetic trees. The application of the Steiner tool here to the parsing of overlapping candidate exons leads to efficient re-use of the substrings shared by multiple exon candidates and is key to the resulting efficiency gain. (See section 4.)

2. We replace the dynamic programming tables in the network graph with alternative $DIST$ data structures. (See Section 3.) This will allow us to focus on the local common denominator between overlapping blocks, and mask out the global information which varies for each considered chain in which the blocks are embedded.

3. In order to achieve direction flexibility in the alignment computation, a new key operation is introduced in this paper which supports both left-to-right and right-to-left computations. (See Section 5.) Note that related work on dynamic programming "against the grain" without the I/O independence feature can be found in [9–11].

The combination of the above three components enables the new algorithm to eliminate redundancy by applying the major part of the alignment work to multiple blocks in tandem, thus reducing the work associated with re-computation of segments shared by several blocks.

The results of this paper apply to all distance or similarity scoring schemes which use a scoring table with rational number values and employ a linear gap penalty. (Note that [5] also used linear gap penalty with indel score ranging from 3 to 1 and a PAM120 matrix whose entries are in fact integers in the range $-8\ldots12$.) The interested reader is referred to *http://www.nslij-genetics.org/ gene/* for a thorough "state-of-the-art" survey on the subject of computational gene recognition.

2   Gelfand, Mironov and Pevzner's Algorithm

The spliced alignment algorithm scans all candidate exon blocks in polynomial time and computes the optimal alignment, as follows. The exon assembly problem is first reduced to a search for the optimal path in a graph. Nodes in this graph correspond to candidate-exon blocks, arcs correspond to potential transitions between blocks, and the path weight is defined as the weight of the optimal alignment between the concatenated blocks of this path and the target sequence.

Figure 2 demonstrates the network alignment as suggested by [5]. Each of the $O(n)$ rectangles corresponds to the dynamic programming table for the alignment of a single candidate-exon substring S_i^j of S versus T. Clearly, each such table is of size $O(n^2)$. The first row in each such dynamic programming table is denoted I and the last row is denoted O. In addition, the algorithm uses a vector, denoted *the I/O vector*, to maintain global information regarding the various possible chainings of the dynamic programming tables for the exon-blocks.

I/O

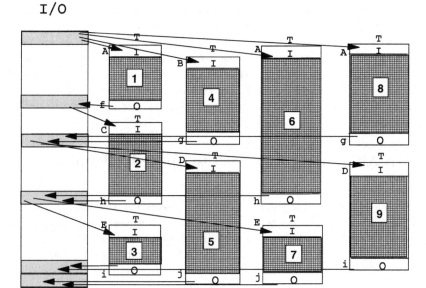

Fig. 2. A example of the basic network dynamic programming algorithm, showing the candidate exon block dynamic programming tables. Consecutive "state-shots" of the I/O vector at the stages when it is accessed also shown. This figure continues the example of Figure 1.

The I/O vector shown in the figures assists in the computation of the highest scoring path through the candidate exons by reflecting global updates.

The algorithm computes the values of rows in the dynamic programming tables in a top-to-bottom sweep-line of increasing row-index in S. Let $k = 1 \ldots n$ denote the running index of the computed rows.

At step k of the algorithm, the following work is done:

1. First, all dynamic programming tables whose I row is at index k will be initialized with the values of the I/O vector.

2. Then, the values of all rows internal to blocks (neither I nor O) which correspond to the character at index k of S, will be computed from their preceding row via dynamic programming.

3. Finally, for each dynamic programming table DP_i^k (corresponding to the alignment of candidate exon S_i^k versus T and whose O row is therefore at index k of S): the I/O vector will be updated with row O of DP_i^k, using the maximization $I/O[\ell] = max\{DP_i^k[k, \ell], I/O[\ell]\}$, for $\ell = 1 \ldots n$.

Time Complexity Analysis

In Sparse Spliced Alignment there are $O(n)$ candidate exon blocks. For each block, a dynamic programming table of size $O(n^2)$ is computed. Therefore, the complexity of the algorithm is $O(n^3)$.

We note that the algorithm is further enhanced in [5] to save the work spent on computing multiple dynamic programming tables for overlapping exon substrings which end in the same index of S. For lack of space, we do not describe this enhancement here. In the Dense Spliced Alignment case, when the number of candidate exons is $O(n^2)$, this enhancement reduces the complexity from $O(n^4)$ down to $O(n^3)$. However, in the case of Sparse Spliced Alignment, which is the subject of this paper, the enhanced algorithm still yields an $O(n^3)$ time complexity.

3   An Alternative Approach to Spliced Alignment

Our new algorithm for Sparse Spliced Alignment will maintain the main frame of the original algorithm and will similarly run a sweep-line, top-to-bottom traversal over the network graph of candidate exon blocks. However, the new approach will be based in replacing the dynamic programming tables for the blocks with an alternative data structure which analyzes the DP graph (see Figure 3,6 and 9), denoted $DIST$ [1, 3, 8, 18].

Definition 2. $\underline{DIST_B^A[0 \ldots n][0 \ldots n]}$- *given the DP Graph for the alignment of a sequence A of size m versus a sequence B of size n, $DIST_B^A[i,j]$ stores the weight of the highest scoring path from vertex $(0,i)$ in the first row of the DP graph to vertex (m,j) in the last row of the DP graph.*

In other words, $DIST_B^A[i,j]$ stores $score(A, B_i^j)$ (see Figure 3).

An $O(n)$ representation of $DIST$, which replaces the full $O(n^2)$ $DIST$, will be used in this paper and is explained in Section 5.1.

Consider the DP graph for the alignment of any candidate exon S_i^j with T in Figure 2. By replacing the dynamic programming table with a $DIST$ data structure, the alignment work involved in the computation of column O from column I can be greatly reduced, as follows. Given $DIST_{S_i^j}^T$ and input row I, the output row O can be computed in $O(n)$ time instead of $O(n^2)$, by employing the techniques from [4, 12].

Intuitively, the savings can be viewed as follows: for each block, the algorithm will eliminate the work which is invested by the original spliced alignment algorithm in the computation of all dynamic programming table rows between I and O (highlighted with dark squares in Figure 2). Clearly such an approach could lead to an $O(n^2)$ time complexity for the computation of the optimal path through the exon blocks, assuming that the $DIST$s for the comparison of each block with T are available.

However, note that computing a single $DIST$ for the comparison of two $O(n)$-sized sequences would naively take $O(n^3)$ time. Schmidt [18] shows how to compute such a $DIST$ in $O(n^2)$ time. Thus, the computation of $O(n)$ $DIST$s, where each $DIST$ represents two strings of size $O(n)$ each, can be done in $O(n^3)$ time. This creates a complexity bottleneck which overrides the speed-up which was obtained in reducing the work for the network dynamic programming graph to $O(n^2)$.

To:

From:

	1	2	3	4	5	6	7	8	9	10	11	12	13
1	8	7	7	6	5	5	5	4	5	4	5	6	7
2		8	7	6	5	5	5	4	4	3	4	5	6
3			8	7	6	6	5	4	3	2	3	4	5
4				8	7	6	5	4	3	2	3	4	5
5					8	7	6	5	4	3	4	5	6
6						8	7	6	5	4	5	5	5
7							8	7	6	5	6	6	6
8								8	7	6	6	6	5
9									8	7	7	6	5
10										8	7	6	5
11											8	7	6
12												8	7
13													8

Fig. 3. The full $DIST_B^A$ where $A = $ "$ACCADBAB$", $B = $ "$BBCAACABABCCB$", for the Edit Distance metric. Note that $\psi = 3$.

Therefore, in the rest of this paper we address the challenge of how to compute the $DIST$s for all blocks in an efficient manner that would reduce the $O(n^3)$ $DIST$-construction bottleneck to $O(n^2\sqrt{n})$.

4 Breaking the $O(n^3)$ Bottleneck with "Append-Prepend" Parsing

In Section 5, the following two incremental $DIST$ construction operations will be described. Both operations cost $O(n)$ time each, and will be used for efficient computations of all $DIST$s for β (Definition 1).

Definition 3. *DISTAppend - given a single input character a and $DIST_B^A$, computes $DIST_B^{Aa}$, where Aa is the concatenation of the character a to the end of string A.*

This operation will be based on the work of [18] and is surveyed in Section 5.2

Definition 4. *DISTPrepend - given a single input character a and $DIST_B^A$, computes $DIST_B^{aA}$, where aA is the concatenation of the character a to the beginning of string A.*

This operation will be based on a new technique, to be described in section 5.3.

Consider the candidate exons $1 \dots 9$ which are shown in Figure 4. Dotted vertical lines are used in this example to mark all start and end positions of

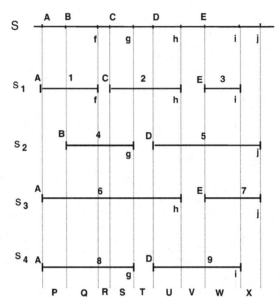

Fig. 4. An example of a set of candidate exon blocks. This figure continues the example of Figure 1. Let $|P| = 1$, $|Q| = 4$, $|R| = 1$, $|S| = 2$, $|T| = 3$, $|U| = 3$, $|V| = 3$, $|W| = 4$ and $|X| = 2$.

candidate-exons. Clearly, each such dotted line can be translated to at least one I/O-vector update. The letters $P, Q, \ldots T$ are used to mark *unit substrings* of S, which are uninterrupted by a beginning or end of a candidate exon.

Naively, the $DIST$ for each candidate-exon could be generated by a series of $O(n)$ $DISTAppend$ operations, or alternatively by a series of $O(n)$ consecutive $DISTPrepend$ operations. This would yield a total of $O(n^2)$ $DISTAppend$ and $DISTPrepend$ operations. Since the complexity of each $DISTAppend$ and $DISTPrepend$ operation is $O(n)$, the total work would amount to $O(n^3)$. However, a more careful construction scheme would try to order the $DIST$ increment operations in such a way as to minimize re-generation of unit-substrings that appear in more than one exon. For example, generating the two exons "PQ" (block 1 in Figure 4) and "QRS" (block 4) by a series of $DISTAppend$ operations would yield a total of 12 operations. Alternatively, suppose that the substring "Q", which is common to both exons, is first computed at the cost of 4 $DISTAppend$ operations, and then "PQ" is obtained from "Q" via a single $DISTPrepend$ while "QRS" is obtained from "Q" via 3 $DISTAppend$ operations. The total cost in this case would be 8 instead of 12, since "Q" is only generated once. From this example we conclude that an efficient construction of a set of $DISTs$ for overlapping substrings dictates the following optimization problem.

Definition 5. *The* Append-Prepend Parsing optimization problem: *Compute the minimal-cost series of $DISTAppend$ and $DISTPrepend$ operations that will generate the $DISTs$ for all the candidate exons in β.*

4.1   "Append-Prepend Parsing" Reduced to UTRSMA

In this section we show how to solve the "Append-Prepend Parsing" optimization problem by reducing it to a Steiner-Tree problem [7]. Furthermore, the special features of the problem will allow us to tightly map it to a special case of directed Steiner trees on a rectilinear grid. Such trees have the great advantage that their size has a proven bound - a feature which is key to the efficiency gain suggested by our algorithm.

The Rectilinear Steiner Minimal Arborescence (RSMA) is defined as follows [19]. (Note that an *arborescence* is a rooted tree with all edges directed away from the root.)

Definition 6. *Given a set N of nodes lying in the first quadrant of E^2 and assuming that distances are measured in the L_1 metric, the <u>Rectilinear Steiner Minimal Arborescence (RSMA)</u> is to find a minimum length directed tree rooted at the origin and containing all nodes in N, composed solely of horizontal and vertical arcs oriented only from left to right and from bottom to top.*

This problem, which is NP-Complete, was first studied by Ladeira de Matos [14]. He proposed an exponential time dynamic programming algorithm to solve the problem. Rao, Sadayappan, Hwang and Shor [19] have suggested a heuristic 2-approximation algorithm for the problem. Additional related work can be found in [6, 7, 13]. We observe that the "Append-Prepend Parsing problem" (Definition 5) reduces to the following variant of RSMA.

Claim. Append-Prepend Parsing can be reduced to an RSMA variant in which the weights of all edges in the lower-left triangle are set to zero. This problem variant will be denoted <u>UTRSMA (Upper-Triangular Rectilinear Steiner Minimal Arborescence)</u>.

Proof: Consider the following $n \times n$ directed grid graph G where edge direction is restricted to either north or east (see Figure 5). The origin of this graph is point $(0,0)$ in the lowest, leftmost corner of the grid. Let (x,y) denote a point in the grid with row number x in respect to the origin and column number y in respect to the origin. Each node in G corresponds to a unique substring of S: substring S_i^j is represented by node $(j, n-i)$ in G. This index-mapping could be more intuitively visualized as follows: the nodes in the main diagonal are assigned consecutive characters from S, such that node (i,j) on the diagonal corresponds the character i of S (starting with substring S_1^1 in vertex $(1,n)$ of the grid and up to substring S_n^n in vertex $(n,1)$ of the grid). For any other point p in the upper triangle, its substring can be realized by stretching a straight line south till it hits the main diagonal and a straight line west till it hits the main diagonal: the substring represented by p consists of the consecutive characters on the diagonal between the two hit-points.

Clearly, only nodes in the upper-triangle, where $i > n - j$, correspond to relevant substrings of S. Therefore, all edges in the upper triangle of the grid graph are assigned unit-weights and are directed, either north or east. An edge leaving a node in the northern direction corresponds to an extension of the substring represented by the node via a *DIST Append* operation. Similarly, an edge leaving a node in the eastern direction corresponds to an extension of the substring represented by the node via a *DIST Prepend* operation.

Let N be a set of $O(n)$ terminal nodes, such that each terminal node corresponds to a unique candidate-exon substring: candidate-exon S_i^j in β is represented by a terminal at index $(j, n - i)$ of G.

Consider a sequence of *DIST Append* and *DIST Prepend* operations, starting from a subset of single-character substrings of S, and generating all the candidate exon substrings. Clearly, such a sequence can be mapped to a forest which spans all the terminals in N, such that each tree in the forest is rooted in the main diagonal of G and grows in the north-east direction. A minimal-weight such forest would therefore yield a solution to the "Append-Prepend Parsing" optimization problem.

In order to apply known RSMA algorithms to the computation of such a minimum-weight forest in G we need to further adapt the problem to that of computing an arborescence rooted at the origin of a full grid. Therefore, the weights of all edges in the lower-left triangle of G are set to zero. An additional extra terminal, denoted z_1, is set at index $(0, 0)$ of the grid, and is the designated root. The UTRSMA problem is then to find a set of paths from z_1 to all terminals in $N - z_1$ such that the total weight of the edges in these paths is as small as possible (see Figure 5). $\square$

Lemma 1. *A 2-Approximation of a UTRSMA on G can be computed in $O(n \log n)$.*

Proof: Define $m(a, b)$ to be the point with coordinates $(min\{x_a, x_b\}, min\{y_a, y_b\})$. Hanan [6] proved that in an RSMA, if c has "children" a and b then c must be $m(a, b)$. Any point in the grid which the arborescence passes through is denoted a *steiner point*.

Rao *et al.* [19] presented a heuristic 2-Approximation scheme for RSMA. The basic step is: choose a pair of terminals a and b such that $c = m(a, b)$ is as far from the origin as possible, record connections from c to a and b, and replace a and b in N by a new terminal at c (unless c was already a terminal). Repeat the basic step until N is reduced to the origin. This algorithm can be implemented by a (diagonal) line sweep approach that maintains a priority queue of the distances from the origin to each $m(a, b)$, where a and b are adjacent (with respect to the sweep line). Therefore, it can be implemented in $O(n \log n)$ time. They prove that the heuristic produces a rectilinear Steiner arborescence with a total size which is at most twice that of the optimal solution.

We claim that running the very same algorithm on G would yield a 2-Approximation to UTRSMA. The only modification would be in the distance measurement, as follows.

In the original RSMA algorithm, the distance in L_1 of a point (x, y) from the origin, denoted $|(x, y)|$, is $x + y$. In the UTRSMA version, the weight $|(x, y)|$ will be computed as follows:

- If point (x, y) is in the upper-triangle of G, then $|(x, y)| = x + y - n$.
- If point (x, y) is in the lower-triangle of G, then $|(x, y)| = 0$.

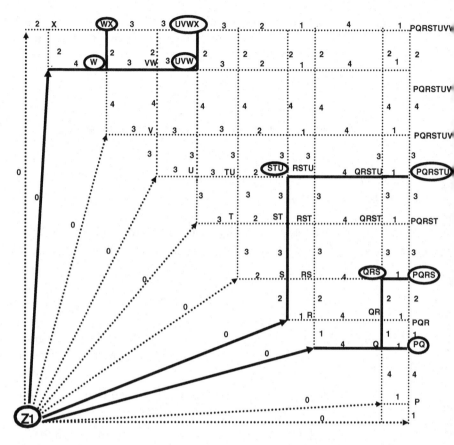

Fig. 5. Append-Prepend Parsing reduced to an Upper Triangular Minimal Stein Arborescence problem on a Rectilinear Grid. The terminal nodes, representing th candidate-exon substrings, are circled. The designated root z_1 is located at the orig $(0, 0)$. This figure continues the examples of Figures 1 and 4.

The distance of any point in the upper-triangle of G from the origin, in the L metric, is equivalent to its distance from the main diagonal plus n, since an point on the main diagonal $(x + y = n)$ is of distance n from the origin in L Furthermore, subtracting the same value of n from any two competing poin during a run of the diagonal sweep-line algorithm of [19] would clearly preser their original order. Thus, the order in which the terminals and steiner points a processed in the original algorithm remains correctly intact when transformin to the problem of UTRSMA on G.

As for steiner points in the lower-triangle, they can actually be selected i any arbitrary order since the parts of the paths in the lower-triangle of G do n contribute anything to the weight of the UTRSMA. Thus, applying the abov variant of [19] to G would yield a 2-approximation of the UTRSMA.

Let $\tau_G(N)$ denote the approximated UTRSMA obtained by running the algorithm of Lemma 1 on G. The next lemma, which is based on Rao *et al.* [19], defines a bound on the size of $\tau_G(N)$.

Lemma 2. $|\tau_G(N)| = O(n(\sqrt{n}))$

4.2   The New Sparse Spliced Alignment Algorithm

The new algorithm is given below.

Algorithm Sparse Spliced Alignment:

Input: a set β of $O(n)$ candidate-exon substrings of S and the homologous gene sequence T.

Output: the score of the best alignment of the graph of exons threaded with T.

1. Compute an approximation $\tau_G(N)$ of the UTRSMA of G as described in section 4.1.

2. Using $\tau_G(N)$, compute the linear encodings of the $DIST$s for all candidate exons in β, using the $DISTAppend$ and $DISTPrepend$ operations described in section 5.

3. Using the linear encodings of the $DIST$s, scan the network graph in a top-to-bottom sweepline of increasing row index, and for each scanned block S_i^j:

  3a. Initialize I with the I/O vector.

  3b. Compute O from I, applying the technique from [12] to the linear encoding of $DIST_{S_i^j}^T$ which was computed in Step 2.

  3c. Update the I/O vector with O, as described in section 2.

4. Upon completion, report the maximal value in the I/O vector.

Time Complexity Analysis

A 2-Approximation $\tau_G(N)$ of the UTRSMA for $O(n)$ points in an $n \times n$ grid can be computed in $O(n \log n)$ as explained in the proof of Lemma 1. By Lemma 2, the size of the obtained tree $\tau_G(N)$ is $O(n\sqrt{n})$.

Following the incremental order defined by $\tau_G(N)$, the linear encodings of the $DIST$s for all exons in B are computed in $O(n\sqrt{n})$ steps. Each step consists of either a single $DISTAppend$ or a single $DISTPrepend$ operation, each in $O(n)$ time (See Section 5). Altogether, the time invested in the construction of the $DIST$s is $O(n^2\sqrt{n})$.

Using the $O(n)$ linear encodings of the $DIST$s, the computation of I from O for each of the $O(n)$ blocks is done in $O(n)$ time using [12]. In addition, the I/O update work for initializing the I row for each block from the I/O vector and for updating the I/O vector with the resulting O row for each block is also $O(n)$ per block. Altogether, this stage contributes a term of $O(n^2)$ work to the total complexity.

Thus, the total time complexity of the new Sparse Spliced Alignment algorithm is $O(n^2\sqrt{n})$.

5   A DP Toolkit to Support Append-Prepend Parsing

In this section we describe the two $DIST$ construction operations, that will enable us to utilize the UTRSMA approximation $\tau_G(N)$, which was computed as a solution to the "Append-Prepend Parsing" of the exon-candidate set β, to efficiently construct the $DIST$ data structures which represent the alignments of all blocks in β with T. We will first explain the compressed, linear encoding representation of $DIST$, and then describe the $DISTAppend$ and $DISTPrepend$ construction operations on this data structure.

5.1   Properties of DIST That Enable Linear Encoding

For discrete scoring schemes, a more efficient encoding of high scoring paths in the DP Graph can be achieved, by utilizing the fact that, due to the Monge property [16] of $DIST$ [2], the number of relevant changes, from one column to the next, is constant. This property, also discussed in [12, 18], allows for a representation of $DIST$ via an $O(n)$ number of "relevant" points. The importance of this property will become clearer in subsection 5.2.

The $HDIFF$ matrix on columns of $DIST$ is defined as follows (see Figure 6).

Definition 7. $HDIFF_{colB}^{A}[i,j] = DIST_B^A[i,j] - DIST_B^A[i,j-1]$, for $i,j = 1\ldots n$.

The range of possible values for $HDIFF_{colB}^{A}[i,j]$ depends on the scoring scheme which is used for the string comparison, and is actually the upper bound for the value difference between two consecutive elements in the dynamic programming table. We will use the term ψ to denote the range bound for $HDIFF[i,j]$ values. As an example, if the similarity metric used is LCS, the only possible values for $HDIFF$ will be either 1 or 0, and ψ assumes a value of 1. For the Edit Distance metric, on the other hand, ψ is 2, since $HDIFF$ can only assume one of the 3 values: -1, 0, 1 [22]. Our algorithm applies to all scoring scheme metrics for which ψ is a constant. Masek and Paterson [17] observed that ψ is a constant for discrete scoring schemes (*i.e.* when the values of the applied scoring matrices are restricted to rational numbers).

Schmidt [18] showed that since, for discrete scoring schemes, the number of "steps" (row indices in which the series of column entries increases in value) in each column of $HDIFF$ is constant, each column $j = 1\ldots n$, can be encoded by a sorted list of $\psi = O(1)$ row indices i_k, where i_k is the highest row index in column j, such that $HDIFF_{colB}^{A}[i_k,j] = k$. Altogether, $HDIFF_{colB}^{A}$ can be encoded by its $O(n)$ "steps", using the data structure defined below (See Figure 6).

Definition 8. $HLIST_{colB}^{A}$ is the linear encoding of $HDIFF_{colB}^{A}$. i.e., $HLIST_{colB}^{A}[j,k]$ holds the value of the **highest** row index i in which $HDIFF_{colB}^{A}[i,j] = k$, for $j = 1\ldots n$, $k = 1\ldots\psi$.

	1	2	3	4	5	6	7	8	9	10	11	12	13
1	-	-1	0	-1	-1	0	0	-1	1	-1	1	1	1
2			-1	-1	-1	0	0	-1	0	-1	1	1	1
3				-1	-1	0	-1	-1	-1	-1	1	1	1
4					-1	-1	-1	-1	-1	-1	1	1	1
5						-1	-1	-1	-1	-1	1	1	1
6							-1	-1	-1	-1	1	0	0
7								-1	-1	-1	1	0	0
8									-1	-1	0	0	-1
9										-1	0	-1	-1
10											-1	-1	-1
11												-1	-1
12													-1
13													

column	Highest row for -1	Highest row for 0	Highest row for 1
1			
2	1		
3	2	1	
4	3		
5	4		
6	5	3	
7	6	2	
8	7		
9	8	2	1
10	9		
11	10	9	7
12	11	8	5
13	12	7	5

(a)   (b)

Fig. 6. The linear encoding compression of $DIST_B^A$ by columns, where $A =$ "$ACCADBAB$", $B =$ "$BBCAACABABCCB$", for the Edit Distance metric. (a) $HDIFF_{col\,B}^A$. (b) $HLIST_{col\,B}^A$. This Figure continues the example of Figure 3.

We have shown in [12] that the linear encoding of $DIST$ is sufficient to compute I from O, thus liberating the algorithm from the time and space overhead of maintaining the full $O(n^2)$ $DIST$ representation. In the following sections we will show that the linear representation of $DIST$ suffices for the computation of both $DISTAppend$ and $DISTPrepend$, thus allowing for the efficient $O(n)$ computation of these operations.

5.2   Schmidt's Algorithm for $DISTAppend$ on the Linear Encoding of DIST

In this section we will survey the work of [18] in describing the $DISTAppend$ operation. This is intended as a stepping-stone for the new $DISTPrepend$ operation which will be described in Section 5.3. Consider the DP graph for the alignment of Aa versus B. Note that column j in $DIST_B^A$ represents the j paths starting at row 0 of the DP graph for the alignment of A versus B, and ending at vertex (m, j). Thus, appending a single character to the end of sequence A corresponds to appending a new row to the last, bottom row of the DP graph (see Figure 7). The goal of the $DISTAppend$ operation is to compute the linear-encoded representation of $DIST_B^{Aa}$ from the linear-encoded representation of $DIST_B^A$, namely computing all the paths which end at vertices of row $m + 1$ of

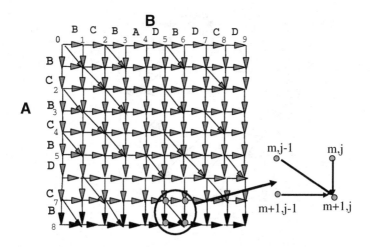

Fig. 7. The DP graph for computing the similarity between $A =$ "BCBCBDCB" and $B =$ "BCBADBDCD". The highlighted edges demonstrate the extension of the prefix "BCBCBDC" of A by appending the character 'B'.

the DP graph. More formally, the objective of the $DISTAppend$ algorithm is to compute $HLIST_{colB}^{Aa}$ from $HLIST_{colB}^{A}$ in a column-by column manner.

For each vertex in the newly appended row $(m + 1, j)$, $j = 1 \ldots n$, given the differences: $DIST_B^A[i, j] - DIST_B^A[i, j - 1]$ (i.e., entry j of $HLIST_{colB}^{A}$) and $DIST_B^A[i, j - 1] - DIST_B^{Aa}[i, j - 1]$, the algorithm computes, in $O(1)$, the differences: $DIST_B^{Aa}[i, j] - DIST_B^{Aa}[i, j - 1]$ (entry j of $HLIST_{colB}^{Aa}$) and $DIST_B^A[i, j] - DIST_B^{Aa}[i, j]$. The series of differences $DIST_B^A[i, j] - DIST_B^A[i, j - 1]$, for $j = 1 \ldots n$, are given as input to the algorithm in the form of $HLIST_{colB}^{A}$, while the "step" values of $DIST_B^A[i, j] - DIST_B^{Aa}[i, j]$ are computed incrementally from one vertex to the next. Due to lack of space, we refer the interested reader to [18] for the detailed description of this algorithm.

Time and Space Complexity Analysis of the $DISTAppend$ Operation: Given a string B of size $O(n)$, a character a, a discrete scoring table, and the linear encoding of $DIST_B^A$ ($HLIST_{colB}^{A}$) for a string A, the linear encoding of $DIST_B^{Aa}$ ($HLIST_{colB}^{Aa}$), can be computed in $O(n)$ time and space complexity.

5.3 $DISTPrepend$ on the Linear Encoding of DIST

Given $HLIST_{colB}^{A}$ and a single character a, in this section we will show how to compute the $DISTPrepend$ operation, i.e., compute the linear encoding of $DIST_B^{aA}$ ($HLIST_{colB}^{aA}$), where aA is the concatenation of the character a to the beginning of sequence A. Note that this simple technique is new.

Lets examine $DIST_B^A$'s rows and columns. Column j of this $DIST$ represents all the paths which originate in vertices 0 to j of the first row ℓ (note that we say "row ℓ" instead of "row 0" for the sake of notation clarity) of the DP graph for A versus B, and ending at vertex (m, j) of the graph (see Figure 8). Respectively,

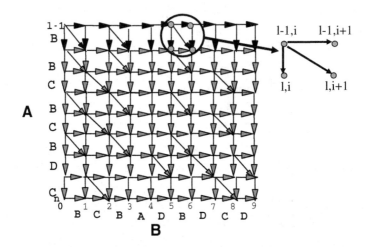

Fig. 8. The DP graph for computing the similarity between $A = BCBCBDC$ and $B = BCBADBDCD$. The highlighted edges demonstrate the extension of the suffix "BCBCBDDC" of A by prepending the character 'B'.

row i of $DIST_B^A$ represents all the paths originating in vertex (ℓ, i) and ending in vertices i to n of row m of the graph . Reversing the directed edges in the grid graph will enable us to view row i in $DIST_B^A$ as the paths ending (instead of originating) at vertex (ℓ, i) in the DP graph, while the values (the weights of the paths) remain the same. Therefore we can consider the paths as going now in the opposite direction: from right to left, bottom-up.

Appending a single character to the beginning of sequence A is equivalent to appending a new row (row $\ell - 1$ in Figure 8) to the top of the DP graph. In this case, in a symmetric manner to the way we viewed the *Append* operation in Section 5.2, every vertex (ℓ, i), which is the end-point of $n - i$ paths that originate the last row m of the DP graph, is represented as row i in $DIST_B^A$. Therefore, extending the DP graph by appending a row to its top end, requires extending some representation of $DIST_B^A$ by the differences between its **rows** instead of its columns. These are defined, symmetrically to the definitions of section 5.2, as $HDIFF_{row_B^A} = DIST_B^A[i, j] - DIST_B^A[i + 1, j]$ and $HLIST_{row_B^A}$. Given $HLIST_{row_B^A}$, $HLIST_{row_B^{aA}}$ could be computed in $O(n)$ time by using a similar, reversed variant of the algorithm described in section 5.2.

Thus, what is left to show in order to compute $DISTPrepend$ in $O(n)$ time and space complexity, is how to compute $HLIST_{row_B^A}$ from a given $HLIST_{col_B^A}$ in $O(n)$ time and space complexity. We will next show a simple technique which does that. The same technique can be applied in the opposite direction as well, computing $HLIST_{col_B^A}$ from a given $HLIST_{row_B^A}$, a fact which will enable us to prepend and append characters to $DIST$ alternately. The next claim can be demonstrated by comparing Figures 6 and 9.

(a)

	1	2	3	4	5	6	7	8	9	10	11	12	13
1	-	-1	0	0	0	0	0	0	1	1	1	1	1
2			-1	-1	-1	-1	0	0	1	1	1	1	1
3				-1	-1	0	0	0	0	0	0	0	0
4					-1	-1	-1	-1	-1	-1	-1	-1	-1
5						-1	-1	-1	-1	-1	-1	0	1
6							-1	-1	-1	-1	-1	-1	-1
7								-1	-1	-1	0	0	1
8									-1	-1	-1	0	0
9										-1	0	0	0
10											-1	-1	-1
11												-1	-1
12													-1
13													

(b)

row	Highest col for -1	Highest col for 0	Highest col for 1
1	2	3	9
2	3	7	9
3	4	6	
4	5		
5	6	12	13
6	7		
7	8	11	13
8	9	12	
9	10	11	
10	11		
11	12		
12	13		

Fig. 9. The linear encoding compression of $DIST_B^A$ by rows, where $A =$ "$ACCADBAB$", $B =$ "$BBCAACABABCCB$", for the Edit Distance metric. (a) $HDIFF_{row\,B}^A$. (b) $HLIST_{row\,B}^A$. This Figure continues the example of Figure 3.

Claim. Given any ordered pair (j, i) of $HLIST_{col\,B}^A$, the reversed ordered pair (i, j) will be listed in $HLIST_{row\,B}^A$ (i.e., index j will appear in one of the ψ "steps" at row i of $HLIST_{row\,B}^A$).

Using the above claim, $HLIST_{row\,B}^A$ can easily be computed from $HLIST_{col\,B}^A$ in $O(n)$ time and space via a single scan of its values.

Time and Space Complexity Analysis of the *DISTPrepend* Operation: Given string B of size $O(n)$, a character a, a discrete scoring table, and the linear encoding of $DIST_B^A$ ($HLIST_{col\,B}^A$) for a string A, the linear encoding of $DIST_B^{aA}$ ($HLIST_{col\,B}^{aA}$), can be computed as follows. First, $HLIST_{row\,B}^A$ is computed in $O(n)$ time and space complexity from $HLIST_{col\,B}^A$, as shown in this section. Then, an $O(n)$ "reversed" version of the *DISTAppend* described in Subsection 5.2 is applied to $HLIST_{row\,B}^A$, yielding $HLIST_{row\,B}^{aA}$. $HLIST_{col\,B}^{aA}$ can then be computed from $HLIST_{row\,B}^{aA}$ in $O(n)$ time, by a method which is symmetric to the one shown in this section. This yields a total of $O(n)$ time and space complexity for computing $HLIST_{col\,B}^{aA}$ from $HLIST_{col\,B}^A$.

Acknowledgments

Many thanks to Jeannette P. Schmidt for inspiration as well as very helpful discussions and comments, and in particular for pointing out to us that the number of filtered candidate exons is $O(n)$ in practice. Additional thanks to the anonymous CPM referees for their very helpful comments.

References

1. Apostolico, A., M. Atallah, L. Larmore, and S. McFaddin, Efficient parallel algorithms for string editing problems. *SIAM J. Comput.*, **19**, 968-998 (1990).
2. Aggarawal, A., and J. Park, Notes on Searching in Multidimensional Monotone Arrays, *Proc. 29th IEEE Symp. on Foundations of Computer Science*, 497–512 (1988).
3. Benson, G., A space efficient algorithm for finding the best nonoverlapping alignment score, *Theoretical Computer Science*, **145**, 357–369 (1995).
4. M. Crochemore, G. M. Landau, B. Schieber, and M. Ziv-Ukelson, Re-Use Dynamic Programming for Sequence Alignment: An Algorithmic Toolkit, *String Algorithmices*, NATO Book series, KCL Press, 2004.
5. Gelfand, M.S., A.A. Mironov, and P.A. Pevzner, Gene Recognition Via Spliced Sequence Alignment, *Proc. Natl. Acad. Sci. USA*, **93**, 9061–9066 (1996).
6. M. Hanan, On Steiner's problem with rectiliniar distance, *SIAM J. Appl. Match.* **14**(1966), 255–265(1966).
7. Hwang, F. K., D. S. Richards, and P. Winter, The Steiner Tree Problem, *Annals of Discrete Mathematics*, North-Holland Publisher (1992).
8. Kannan, S. K., and E. W. Myers, An Algorithm For Locating Non-Overlapping Regions of Maximum Alignment Score, *SIAM J. Comput.*, **25**(3), 648–662 (1996).
9. Kim, S., and K. Park, "A Dynamic Edit Distance Table.", *J. Discrete Algorithms*, **2**(2), 303–312 (2004).
10. Landau, G.M., E.W. Myers, and J.P. Schmidt, Incremental String Comparison, *SIAM J. Comput.*, **27**, 2, 557–582 (1998).
11. G.M Landau, E.W. Myers, and M. Ziv-Ukelson, Two Algorithms for LCS Consecutive Suffix Alignment, *15th Combinatorial Pattern Matching Conference*, 173–193 (2004).
12. Landau, G.M., and M. Ziv-Ukelson, On the Common Substring Alignment Problem, *Journal of Algorithms*, **41**(2), 338–359 (2001).
13. Bing Lu, Lu Ruan. Polynomial Time Approximation Scheme for the Rectilinear Steiner Arborescence Problem. *Journal of Combinatorial Optimization* **4** (3): 357-363 (2000).
14. Ladeira de Matos R. R., A Rectilinear Arborescence Problem, Dissertation, University of Alabama, 1979.
15. Mironov, A.A., M.A. Roytberg, P.A. Pevzner, and M.S. Gelfand, Performance-Guarantee Gene Predictions Via Spliced Alignemnt, *Genomics 51 A.N. GE985251*, 332–339 (1998).
16. Monge, G., Déblai et Remblai, *Mémoires de l'Academie des Sciences*, Paris (1781).
17. Masek, W. J. and M. S. Paterson, A faster algorithm computing string edit distances. *J. Comput. Syst. Sci.*, **20**, 18–31 (1980).
18. Schmidt, J.P., All Highest Scoring Paths In Weighted Grid Graphs and Their Application To Finding All Approximate Repeats In Strings, *SIAM J. Comput*, **27**(4), 972–992 (1998).
19. Rao, S. K., P. Sadayappan, F. K. Hwang, and P. W. Shor, The rectilinear Steiner arborescence problem. *Algorithmica*, **7**, 277–288 (1992).
20. Roytberg, M.A., T.V. Astakhova, and M.S. Gelfand, Combinatorial Approaches to Gene Recognition, *Computers Chemistry*, **21**, 4, 229–235 (1997).
21. Sze, S-H., and P.A. Pevzner, Las Vegas Algorithms for Gene Recognition: Suboptimal and Error-Tolerant Spliced Alignment, *J. Comp. Biol.* **4**, 3, 297–309 (1997).
22. Ukkonen, E., Finding Approximate Patterns in Strings, *J. Algorithms* **6**, 132–137 (1985).

An Upper Bound on the Hardness
of Exact Matrix Based Motif Discovery

Paul Horton and Wataru Fujibuchi

Computational Biology Research Center,
National Institute of Advanced Industrial Science, Japan
{horton-p,fujibuchi-wataru}@aist.go.jp

Abstract. Motif discovery is the problem of finding local patterns or *motifs* from a set of unlabeled sequences. One common representation of a motif is a Markov model known as a score matrix. Matrix based motif discovery has been extensively studied but no positive results have been known regarding its theoretical hardness. We present the first nontrivial upper bound on the complexity (worst-case computation time) of this problem. Other than linear terms, our bound depends only on the motif width w (which is typically 5-20) and is a dramatic improvement relative to previously known bounds.

We prove this bound by relating the motif discovery problem to a search problem over permutations of strings of length w, in which the permutations have a particular property. We give a constructive proof of an upper bound on the number of such permutations. For an alphabet size of σ (typically 4) the trivial bound is $n! \approx (\frac{n}{e})^n, n = \sigma^w$. Our bound is roughly $n(\sigma \log_\sigma n)^n$.

We relate this theoretical result to the exact motif discovery program, TsukubaBB, whose algorithm contains ideas which inspired the result. We describe a recent improvement to the TsukubaBB program which can give a speed up of nine or more and use a dataset of REB1 transcription factor binding sites to illustrate that exact methods can indeed be used in some practical situations.

1   Introduction

Position-specific score matrices (hereafter just *score matrices*) are routinely used in computational biology to characterize DNA and protein sequences. Many algorithms have been proposed for discovering motif score matrices from unlabeled sets of sequences which are thought to include one or more common motifs [2–11]. Except for the last three references, all of the above methods are heuristic algorithms which offer no guarantees regarding the quality of their solutions. One of the exact methods implemented with the TsukubaBB [8, 9] program can solve some problems of interest by utilizing bounding techniques which are effective for short motif widths. In this paper we formalize the effectiveness of focusing on motif width with a constructive proof which limits the number of solutions which an exact algorithm might have to examine to $O((w\sigma - w)^{(\sigma^w)}\sigma^w)$, *independent* of the length and number of input sequences. This is a very large (and

A. Apostolico, M. Crochemore, and K. Park (Eds.): CPM 2005, LNCS 3537, pp. 219–228, 2005.
© Springer-Verlag Berlin Heidelberg 2005

pessimistic) upper bound, but still a dramatic improvement over the previously best known upper bound of this sort, which is $O(\sigma^w!)$. Approximating $\sigma^w!$ with $(\frac{\sigma^w}{e})^{\sigma^w}$, the ratio of these two bounds is roughly $\left(\frac{e(\sigma-1)w}{\sigma^w}\right)^{\sigma^w}$.

We relate the proof result to TsukubaBB and report an improvement in the score based bound calculation used by the TsukubaBB algorithm. We close by showing that exact programs can process some real problems in a reasonable amount of time. We demonstrate this by measuring the running time of TsukubaBB with a dataset of REB1 transcription factor binding sites.

2   Motif Discovery and Consistent Permutations

Motif discovery is the task of finding meaningful *motif instances* of some motif (*i.e.* pattern) from longer unlabeled sequences. When applied to analyzing genomic sequences, this is typically simplified by fixing the motif width to be some small integer w.

The task is to find a set of length w substrings from the input sequences that are similar to each other. The motif is generally modeled as a w state Markov model M, which defines a probability distribution over strings of length w. M is a $\sigma \times w$ matrix in which $M(i,j)$ represents the log probability of character i occurring in position j of a motif instance.

For a user given parameter k (sometimes set to be the number of sequences), the task is to find k motif instances and a motif model M which assigns a maximal likelihood to the k instances.

Given a fixed set of k motif instances, it is easy to verify that to obtain the model M which gives the maximum likelihood, one simply sets $M(i,j)$ equal to the fraction of instances in which character i occurs at position j. Unfortunately simultaneously optimizing both M and the set of motif instances is difficult. Note however that if we could ask an oracle what the motif model M^* of the optimal scoring set of motif instances is, we could easily find the actual instances. The procedure would simply be to sort the length w substrings in the input by their likelihood assigned to by M^* and choose the first k substrings on this list. Note that this does not use all of the information in M^*, just the ordering of length w strings. Thus all that we need to ask the oracle for is a list $\mathbf{P}^*$ of all possible length w strings sorted in the order of the likelihood assigned to them by M^*. Our main result is an upper bound on the number of possible answers the oracle could give, *i.e.* the number of possible permutations of length w strings which could be in sorted order for some motif model.

3   Bound on Number of Consistent Permutations

3.1   Intuition

Suppose that the highest scoring string for a given score matrix M is "aaaa", could "acac" be the (unique) second highest string? The answer is no, the score for "acac" cannot exceed the scores of either "acaa" nor "aaac" because they both fix one mismatch between "acac" and the consensus "aaaa". Generalizing, one can see that the second string in an M consistent permutation can have no more than one mismatch to the first string and therefore there are exactly $w\sigma - w$ candidates for a second string once the first string is known. This kind of *ad hoc* reasoning gives a similar bound of $w\sigma - w - 1$ for the number of candidates for the third string given the first two. Continuing this reasoning in an informal way soon becomes unwieldy but this gives the basic intuition behind our proof.

3.2 Preliminaries

We consider the set of distinct strings of length w from an alphabet of size σ. There are $\sigma^w!$ permutations of this set. If we add some constraint to the permutations, that number will generally be reduced. In this paper we consider permutations that are *M consistent*, that is in best first score order relative to some $\sigma \times w$ score matrix M of real numbers. We use the term *M consistent partial permutation* to denote the first b, $1 \le b \le \sigma^w$ strings of some M consistent permutation. The element $M(i, j)$ of a scoring matrix represents the score of the ith character from the alphabet in column j. Let $t = t_1 t_2 \ldots t_w$ denote the character indices for a length w string t. In this paper we adopt the column independent additive score. The score $\mathcal{S}(M, t)$ of t for score matrix M is:

$$\mathcal{S}(M, t) = \sum_{i=1}^{w} M(t_i, i)$$

3.3 Proof Outline

We first give a brief, informal outline of the theorem and proof. We consider the set of all possible strings of length w from an alphabet of size σ. The main theorem states that if a permutation of those strings is constrained to be consistent with some score matrix then the number of possible permutations is drastically reduced. Consider the choice of the $b + 1$th string given the first b strings of a permutation. With no constraints the number of candidates for the next string is $\sigma^w - b$, however we prove that given the constraint that the ordering must be consistent with some scoring matrix, the number of candidates that need to be considered is no more than $w\sigma - w$. It is important to note at the onset that distinct strings can have the same score (indeed all strings may have the same score) for some score matrices and thus an M consistent permutation is not necessarily unique. With careful handling the possibility of score ties does not change the results presented here but does complicate the proof language somewhat. Therefore we present a simplified proof in which some statements may require further qualification if score ties are present.

3.4 Consistent Permutation Generator

In this section we present a non-deterministic algorithm, **CPG**, for generating consistent permutations.

Definition 1 *Let c_{ij} be the ith distinct character to appear in column j of some permutation $\mathbf{P}$. We use the term* rank *for i, i.e. we say the rank, $\mathcal{R}(\mathbf{P}, c_{ij}, j)$, of c_{ij} in column j (with respect to $\mathbf{P}$) is i. We refer to the string $c_{11} c_{12} \ldots c_{1w}$ as the* consensus string *of $\mathbf{P}$. (see Table 1.)*

Table 1. Character ranks for partial permutation "aa, ac, ca, cg" are shown.

$\mathbf{P}=$ aa	$\mathcal{R}(\mathbf{P},a,1)=1$	$\mathcal{R}(\mathbf{P},a,2)=1$
ac		$\mathcal{R}(\mathbf{P},c,2)=2$
ca	$\mathcal{R}(\mathbf{P},c,1)=2$	
cg		$\mathcal{R}(\mathbf{P},g,2)=3$

CPG extends an M consistent partial permutation $\mathbf{P}^b$ by adding one string, where $\mathbf{P}^b = P_1P_2\ldots P_b$ denotes the first b strings in some permutation. The procedure is repeated in an identical manner for each of the w columns. Without loss of generality, we describe the procedure when applied to some column d. Note that the characters from the alphabet can be categorized relative to information about M implicit in $\mathbf{P}^b$. Let k, $1 \leq k \leq \sigma$ be the number of distinct characters appearing in column d of $\mathbf{P}^b$. c_{1d} is the consensus character for column d and has the highest possible score of any character in column d. From these definitions, given $\mathbf{P}^b$ we know the rank of $c_{1d}, c_{2d}, \ldots c_{kd}$, in column d but not the rank of $c_{(k+1)d}c_{(k+2)d}\cdots c_{\sigma d}$.

If $\mathbf{P}^b$ is empty (base case) **CPG** returns all possible strings of length w, otherwise **CPG** can be broken into two cases:

1. For each character x of unknown rank in column d, **CPG** adds the string obtained by replacing c_{d1} with x in the consensus string P_1, or equivalently the string: $c_{11}c_{12}\ldots c_{1(d-1)}xc_{1(d+1)}c_{1(d+2)}\cdots c_{1w}$, to the set of candidates for P_{b+1}. (In the next iteration of **CPG** x will have rank 2 in column d.)
2. For each character of known rank c_{id}, $2 \leq i \leq k$ **CPG** considers the series of strings in $\mathbf{P}^b$ with character $c_{(i-1)d}$ in column d, ordered by their position in $\mathbf{P}^b$. **CPG** considers the string produced by substituting c_{id} for $c_{(i-1)d}$ in column d in each string in that series and adds the first one which is not in $\mathbf{P}^b$ (unless they are all in $\mathbf{P}^b$, in which case it adds nothing) to the set of candidates for P_{b+1}.

Except for the base case which has σ^w candidates, at most one candidate for each non-consensus character in each column is generated by **CPG**, so the number of candidates generated at one step is at most $w\sigma - w$. (In fact when applied to partial permutations of size two or more, the number of candidates never exceeds $w\sigma - w - 1$ (proof omitted)).

Theorem 1 *Let $\mathbf{P}^b$ be a partial permutation generated by **CPG**, which is consistent with some score matrix M. One of the·possible extensions of $\mathbf{P}^b$ obtained by applying **CPG** to $\mathbf{P}^b$ is consistent with M.*

Lemma 1 *Considering strings of length w. Let q, t, be strings with $\mathcal{S}(M,q) \geq \mathcal{S}(M,t)$ and Hamming distance $H(q,t) = d > 1$. At least one string r exists with Hamming distance $H(q,r) = 1$, such that $\mathcal{S}(M,r) \geq \mathcal{S}(M,t)$.*

Lemma 1. Proof: Let $r_1, r_2, \ldots r_d$ denote the set of d strings such that $\forall i \ H(q,r_i) = 1$, $H(r_i,t) = d - 1$. Omitting the M in $\mathcal{S}(M,q)$,

$$\mathcal{S}(q) - \mathcal{S}(t) = \frac{1}{d-1}\sum_{i=1}^{d}(\mathcal{S}(r_i) - \mathcal{S}(t))$$

(Note that each term in the sum will have $d-1$ non-zero terms while $\mathcal{S}(q) - \mathcal{S}(t)$ has d non-zero terms). $\mathcal{S}(q) \geq \mathcal{S}(t)$, so at least one term in the summation must be non-negative.   ◇

Lemma 2 *Let string q denote the highest scoring string not included in $\mathbf{P}^b$. If there are more than one with the same score arbitrarily pick one that has the minimum hamming distance from some string in $\mathbf{P}^b$. q has a hamming distance of one with at least one string in $\mathbf{P}^b$.*

Lemma 2 Proof: The proof (omitted for space) follows easily from Lemma 1. and the assumption that $\mathbf{P}^b$ is M consistent.   ◇

Lemma 3 *Let s be a string with a character of known rank c_{ij} in column j given $\mathbf{P}^b$. Let s' be the same as s except for substitution of the character of one smaller rank, $c_{(i-1)j}$ in column j. $\mathcal{S}(M, s') \geq \mathcal{S}(M, s)$.*

Lemma 3 Proof: The proof (sketched here) follows from the assumption that $\mathbf{P}^b$ is an M consistent partial permutation generated by **CPG** and therefore $c_{(i-1)j}$ and c_{ij} both first appeared in $\mathbf{P}^b$ via **CPG**'s case 1, with $c_{(i-1)j}$ appearing before c_{ij}.   ◇

Theorem 1. Proof: Consider the set of one or more highest scoring strings not in $\mathbf{P}^b$. Let q be one of those strings and t be the highest scoring string in $\mathbf{P}^b$ such that $H(q, t) = 1$. Lemma 2. guarantees that such a pair of strings exists. Without loss of generality assume that the column in which q and t differ is the first. Denote the candidate string produced by applying **CPG** to $\mathbf{P}^b$ for character q_1 in column 1 as u. (Note that this implies $u_1 = q_1$). For purposes of contradiction, assume that $u \neq q$. If q_1 is a character of unknown rank in $\mathbf{P}^b$ then u is the consensus sequence with q_1 substituted in column 1. Thus q cannot have a higher score than u in this case. So q_1 must be of known rank. Let x denote the character of one smaller rank than q_1 in column 1. By Lemma 3. we can assert that the string $xt_2t_3 \ldots t_w = xq_2q_3 \ldots q_w$ has a better score than q and therefore, by the assumed consistency of $\mathbf{P}^b$, is included in $\mathbf{P}^b$.

Since $xq_2q_3 \ldots q_w$ appears in $\mathbf{P}^b$, and q does not, **CPG** would only choose u over q if $\mathcal{S}(xu_2u_3 \ldots u_w) \geq \mathcal{S}(xq_2q_3 \ldots q_w)$. Since $q_1 = u_1$ this contradicts our assumption that $\mathcal{S}(q) > \mathcal{S}(u)$. and completes the proof.   ◇

3.5   Motif Discovery with CPG

The score matrix M found by (globally) optimizing a column independent score is a deterministic function of the input sequence and the exact scoring parameters, (*e.g.* motif width w, background model, pseudocounts, number of sites allowed per sequence, etc.). One can recover the best k scoring length w strings, *i.e.* the best k scoring instances by the motif represented by M, by using an M consistent partial permutation $\mathbf{P}$. Length w strings are simply chosen one by one according to $\mathbf{P}$ until a total of k strings are chosen. (The size of the partial permutation needed to do this may be more or less than k depending on whether strings in $\mathbf{P}$ appear more than once or not at all in the input sequences.) Note

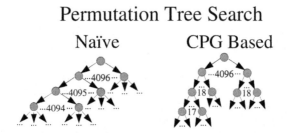

Fig. 1. Schematic picture of a naïve and **CPG** based tree search over permutations of strings of length 6 and all alphabet size of 4, showing the difference in branch factor.

that the score matrix is not necessary if the partial permutation **P** is known. An exhaustive search over possible partial permutations is guaranteed to include **P** and thus yields an exact algorithm. For partial permutations of size ≥ 2 **CPG** can be applied to greatly reduce the size of the search as shown in figure 1.

3.6 How Many Permutations Does CPG Really Generate?

The $O(\sigma w - w)$ bound on the branch factor of **CPG** is just an upper bound. We have implemented **CPG** to investigate the question of how many complete permutations **CPG** really generates. For $w = 2, \sigma = 4$ the answer is 533,224. Note that although large, this figure is significantly less than the theoretical upper bounds based on worst case branch factor. For $w \geq 3$ the number of complete permutations is too large for our program to compute in a reasonable amount of time. In motif discovery we are only interested in the high scoring candidates for motif occurrences and therefore only need the information contained in a relatively small partial permutation. Table 2 shows the number of partial permutations of size five and eight for various motif widths. Note that although empirically generated these numbers also represent a worst case analysis that is independent of the input sequences or details of the scoring parameters (other than motif width). Exact algorithms which use extra information can be expected to do better as discussed below.

Table 2. The number of partial permutations of size 5 and 8 generated by **CPG** are shown for various motif widths with an alphabet size of 4.

motif width	Perm. size 5	Perm. size 8
3	2.59×10^5	6.36×10^7
4	3.58×10^6	3.39×10^9
5	4.04×10^7	8.55×10^{10}
6	3.52×10^8	1.44×10^{12}
7	2.69×10^9	1.89×10^{13}
8	1.88×10^{10}	2.07×10^{14}

4   TsukubaBB

In the form described here **CPG** is primarily a vehicle for proving the upper bound on complexity. To be practically useful **CPG** will need to be combined with other bounds that are specific to the given input. This section describes a recent improvement to the TsukubaBB exact algorithm. We close by measuring the running time of TsukubaBB on two problems, the results of which support our claim that exact algorithms are not just of theoretical interest.

4.1   How TsukubaBB Relates to CPG

The TsukubaBB algorithm [8, 9] was the first algorithm to focus on the fact that the motif width is typically much smaller than the size of the input sequences. It is a branch and bound algorithm which uses a search tree similar to that discussed here in the context of **CPG** and also a concept of consistency. It is not, however, an implementation of **CPG**, which we have only recently discovered (in fact it could benefit from a redesign which incorporates the ideas in **CPG** more directly.) One important difference is that the nodes in the TsukubaBB search tree represent only strings of length w which appear in the input sequences instead of any possible string of length w. The consistency concept is similar but the implementation is quite different and will not be reviewed here.

4.2   Improvement to TsukubaBB Score Based Bound

TsukubaBB finds an optimal choice of k (a user specified parameter) length w strings from a set of input sequences. It does this with an exhaustive tree search but uses a few techniques to prune parts of the search tree where it can be guaranteed that such pruning cannot prevent the optimal alignment from being found. One bound TsukubaBB employs is a score based technique which depends on the input sequences. We briefly review this bound here in order to describe a recent improvement and further relate TsukubaBB to **CPG**. Let a sub-partition $\Pi = \Pi_1 \Pi_2 \ldots \Pi_h$ of a partial partition $\mathbf{P}$ be a subsequence of $\mathbf{P}$ (*i.e.* a subset of the strings in the same order as in $\mathbf{P}$). Consider the total score of a multiset (a set with possible repeats) of (length w) strings A with three components: A_1 contains only strings other than Π_h from Π, A_2 contains one or more instances of Π_h and A_3 contains enough instances of any strings not in $\mathbf{P}$ (and therefore not in Π either) for A to have a total of k strings, *i.e.* $|A_1| + |A_2| + |A_3| = k$. Let A_3' be some multiset of size $|A_3|$ consisting of strings found only in $A_1 \cup A_2$, and A' denote the union of A_1, A_2, and A_3'. If $\mathbf{P}$ is M consistent then for any choice of A_3 and A_3'.

$$\mathcal{S}(M, A') = \mathcal{S}(M, A_1) + \mathcal{S}(M, A_2) + \mathcal{S}(M, A_3')$$
$$\geq \mathcal{S}(M, A) = \mathcal{S}(M, A_1) + \mathcal{S}(M, A_2) + \mathcal{S}(M, A_3)$$

The score matrix we are interested in is the score matrix M^* which maximizes the score of the optimal alignment. We don't know the matrix M^* while we are searching but we can calculate the score matrix M' which maximizes the score of a given A'. TsukubaBB utilizes the fact that if $\mathbf{P}$ is M^* consistent the above equation also holds for $M = M'$. This follows from the convexity of the likelihood score function and is proved in [9]. In TsukubaBB, A is an alignment and $A_1 \cup A_2$ a partial alignment. Figure 2 illustrates the TsukubaBB score bound with a small example.

The improvement we report here is conceptually small. It is simply a better heuristic to quickly find a choice of A'_3 which gives a low upper bound. The heuristic is to first try setting A'_3 equal to Π_h (the string in A_2) repeated $|A_3|$ times and evaluate that bound. Then try all possible replacements of one string from A_1 into A'_3. If none yields a better bound quit, do the replacement in A'_3 that yielded the best bound and reiterate. Continue until either 1) a bound sufficiently high to prune is obtained, 2) the bound ceases to improve or 3) all occurrences of Π_h have been replaced. This heuristic is effective because while A_1 represents a parent node in the TsukubaBB search tree which has survived pruning attempts, the new string Π_h has not been tested and in most cases is not a good match for the strings in A_1. Thus adding all possible occurrences of Π_h tends to give a good starting point for greedy search. The original TsukubaBB also uses a greedy search but does not take advantage of the difference between Π_h and the strings in A_1 (the old heuristic is described in [9]). This simple improvement can lead to a significant speed up when k, the number of motif instances TsukubaBB is looking for, is large.

4.3   Example Running Times

A speed up of nine was obtained for a problem instance of finding 80 motif instances from 80 $E.\,coli$ promoter sequences with a motif width of five. Combined with hardware speed-up this allowed this problem instance which required 111 hours three years ago [9] to be solved in just 161 minutes on a 2.8GHz Pentium IV, 533MHz bus, commodity PC (running debian gnu linux). In a more realistic example we ran TsukubaBB with the new bound on a problem instance with 14 sequences (and their reverse complements) taken from the yeast promoter database SCPD [15] for REB1 transcription factor binding sites. The sequences were of length 250 to 900 with a harmonic mean of approximately 467. The consensus given in SCPD was of length 7 with 20 sites known. Using these parameters, pseudocounts of one for each base as a prior and the base composition of the input sequences (with their reverse complements added, so really just g+c content) as the background model TsukubaBB found the optimal scoring matrix in 574 minutes on a 2.8GHz Pentium linux machine. We have confirmed that most of the known sites found in SCPD closely match our results.

5   Discussion and Conclusion

We have presented the first positive theoretical result on the general complexity of matrix based motif discovery. The result is an efficient algorithm if the motif width w grows very slowly with the number of sequences n. On the other hand, Li *et al.* [12, 13] proved that this problem is NP-hard (and developed a polynomial time approximation scheme for a kind of column independent additive

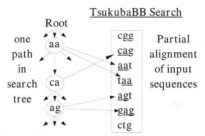

TsukubaBB Search

Score Bound, can ag be pruned?

$A_1 = \{aa, aa, ca\}$ $A_2 = \{ag, ag\}$ A_3=?

$A_3'=\{ag,ag\}$ or $\{ag,ca\}$ or $\{ag,aa\}$

or $\{ca,ca\}$ or $\{ca,aa\}$ or $\{aa, aa\}$

If A_1, A_2, on path to optimal alignment A^*:

$Score(A_1+A_2+A_3') > Score(A^*)$

Fig. 2. An example of the application of the TsukubaBB score bound is shown. The partial alignment of the input sequences (OOPS model) produced by TsukubaBB while descending a particular path in the search tree is shown on top, with lateral arrows indicating the correspondence between nodes in the search tree and strings chosen for the alignment. Unlike **CPG**, the TsukubaBB search tree does not include nodes for strings not found in the input such as "ac". The bound shown at bottom is valid for any choice shown for A_3'.

score). Akutsu *et al.* [1] show that the usual maximum likelihood score is hard to approximate (APX-hard) when the motif width is allowed to be as large as $\Omega(n^{25})$. This is of course an unrealistic situation. As those authors mention, a refinement of that proof could possibly reduce n^{25} to a smaller order polynomial but any reduction of the sort they use, in which each variable in an NP-hard problem is mapped to a separate column of an alignment, will only lead to hardness results for $w = \Omega(n)$ at best. In applications of interest how should w grow with n? In some sense it should not grow at all – the number of bases a DNA binding protein interacts with is determined by physics not statistics. In another sense, since more sequences give more information to estimate model parameters with, perhaps it should grow as a relatively slow function such as $\log(n)$. We pose an open question: what is the complexity of matrix based motif discovery for $w = O(\log n)$? Note that for DNA, even for $w = 20$, σ^w is not an impossible number for modern computers. Indeed $O(\sigma^w)$ time exact methods for consensus, rather than matrix based motif discovery, are easy to design (many references can be found in [14]) and are still a popular alternative despite the fact that the matrix methods have more expressive power.

Acknowledgments

We would like to thank Tim Bailey for careful reading of an earlier version of this manuscript.

References

1. Tatsuya Akutsu, Hiroki Arimura, and Shinichi Shimozono. On approximation algorithms for local multiple alignment. In *Proceedings of the fourth annual international conference on computational molecular biology (RECOMB2000)*, pages 1–7. ACM Press, 2000.

2. Tim Bailey and Charles Elkan. Unsupervised learning of multiple motifs in biopolymers. *Machine Learning*, 21:51–80, 1995.

3. Konstantinos Blekas, Dimitirios Fotiados, and Aristidis Likas. Greedy mixture learning for multiple motif discovery in biological sequences. *Bioinformatics*, 19(5):607–617, 2003.

4. Martin Frith, Ulla Hansen, John L. Spouge, and Zhiping Weng. Finding functional sequence elements by multiple local alignment. *Nucleic Acids Research*, 2004.

5. G. Z. Hertz, G. W. Hartzell III, and G. D. Stormo. Identification of consensus patterns in unaligned DNA sequences known to be functionally related. *CABIOS*, 6(2):81–92, 1990.

6. G. Z. Hertz and G. D. Stormo. Identifying DNA and protein patterns with statistically significant alignments of multiple sequences. *Bioinformatics*, 15:563–577, 1999.

7. Paul Horton. A branch and bound algorithm for local multiple alignment. In *Pacific Symposium on Biocomputing '96*, pages 368–383, 1996.

8. Paul Horton. Tsukuba BB: A branch and bound algorithm for local multiple sequence alignment. In *Proceedings of the 11th Annual Symposium on Combinatorial Pattern Matching*, pages 84–98. Springer-Verlag, 2000.

9. Paul Horton. Tsukuba BB: A branch and bound algorithm for local multiple alignment of DNA and protein sequences. *Journal of Computational Biology*, 8(3):249–282, 2001.

10. C. E. Lawrence, S. F. Altschul, M. B. Boguski, J. S. Liu, A. F. Neuwald, and J. C. Wootton. Detecting subtle sequence signals: A Gibbs sampling strategy for multiple alignment. *Science*, 262:208–214, 1993.

11. Charles E. Lawrence and Andrew A. Reilly. An expectation maximization (EM) algorithm for the identification and characterization of common sites in unaligned biopolymer sequences. *PROTEINS*, 7:41–51, 1990.

12. Ming Li, Bin Ma, and Lusheng Wang. Finding similar regions in many strings. In *Proceedings of the 32nd Annual ACM Symposium on the Theory of Computing (STOC)*, pages 425–434, 1999.

13. Ming Li, Bin Ma, and Lusheng Wang. Finding similar regions in many sequences. *Journal of Computer and System Sciences*, 65:73–96, 2002.

14. Gary D. Stormo. DNA binding sites: representation and discovery. *Bioinformatics*, 16:16–23, 2000.

15. Jian Zhu and Michael Q. Zhang. SCPD: a promoter database of the yeast saccharomyces cerevisiae. *Bioinformatics*, 15:607–611, 1999.

Incremental Inference of Relational Motifs with a Degenerate Alphabet

Nadia Pisanti[1,2,*], Henry Soldano[1,2], and Mathilde Carpentier[2]

[1] Laboratoire d'Informatique de l'Université Paris-Nord, UMR-CNRS 7030,
Av. J-B Clément, 93430 Villetaneuse, France
{nadia.pisanti,soldano}@lipn.univ-paris13.fr
[2] Atelier de BioInformatique, Université Paris 6, 12 rue cuvier 75005 Paris
{pisanti,soldano,mathilde}@abi.snv.jussieu.fr

Abstract. In this paper we define a new class of problems that generalizes that of finding repeated motifs. The novelty lies in the addition of constraints on the motifs in terms of relations that must hold between pairs of elements of the motifs. For this class of problems we give an algorithm that is a suitable extension of the KMR [3] paradigm and, in particular, of the KMRC [7] as it uses a degenerate alphabet. The algorithm contains several improvements with respect to [7] that result especially useful when – as it is required for relational motifs – the inference is made by partially overlapping shorter motifs. The efficiency, correctness and completeness of the algorithm is assured by several nontrivial properties. Finally, we list some possible applications and we focus on one of them: the study of 3D structures of proteins.

1 Introduction

In this paper we define a new class of problems that extends the traditional inference of repeated motifs. This latter is a well-known problem that consists of finding frequent patterns in a given input text. This problem has applications in several data mining tasks, where data can be represented by a text. For many such applications it is indispensable that a certain degree of approximation is allowed among different occurrences of the same motif. For a survey on combinatorial algorithms for finding approximate repeated motifs, see for example Chapter 5 of [4] or Chapter 4 of [2]. When approximate motifs are sought, the problem becomes computationally difficult in the worst case as there can be an exponential number of motifs satisfying the required frequency and properties. This can even lead to unfeasibility and, in "better" cases, to a very noisy output. For this reason there have been attempts in the literature to refine the query in the direction of specifying the *structure* of the motifs [5] or of defining slim *generators* for the motifs [6]. In this paper we introduce a new type of refinement which consists of requiring that also relations between pairs of positions in the motifs are conserved. This apparently complicates the problem, but we will

---

* Supported by the ACI IMPBio *Evolrep* project of the French Ministry of Research.

A. Apostolico, M. Crochemore, and K. Park (Eds.): CPM 2005, LNCS 3537, pp. 229–240, 2005.
© Springer-Verlag Berlin Heidelberg 2005

exhibit an algorithm that uses a very efficient representation of the motifs and which – thanks to some non-trivial properties – results in a relatively efficient inference. Indeed, refining the query on the motifs reduces the output size and thus also the explosion of candidates that often makes the problem unfeasible. Moreover, relations allow one to constraint the motifs so that more specific properties are satisfied and thus a more sensitive tool can be conceived. The inference of motifs with relations can find application in many tasks. We will focus our attention on yet another application in molecular biology using as relations the distances between the α-Carbons of protein 3D structures.

In this paper we will use two input-defined degenerate alphabets for the description of the motifs (one for the motif elements and one for the relations) thus allowing the maximum freedom of approximation. Given that we refer to the paradigm of the KMR algorithm [3], we will have to adapt to the degenerate alphabet as in KMRC [7]. In particular, we will restrict our attention to *maximal* motifs for a notion of maximality that we will define. The choice of dealing with relational motifs motivates the fact that motifs will be inferred by means of an incremental construction by partially overlapping two suitably selected shorter motifs. By doing so we substantially differ from [3] in the same direction as [1] where relations in motifs had been introduced for the first time. In [1], however, several properties were unnoticed and thus unbearable drawbacks introduced. In this paper we will prove some properties that will allow to improve the time and space complexity of [1] by avoiding to generate at each step an exponential number of candidates that we will prove to be redundant.

2   The Problem

Our goal is to find approximate motifs on a input text that is a sequence over an alphabet Σ. In this section we formalize the way we express the approximation, and the motifs we want to infer according to this. Let the input text be a sequence t over the alphabet Σ. We assume that it has length n and we denote this by $|t| = n$. The letter at position p in t is denoted by $t[p]$, and therefore we have that $t = t[1]t[2]\cdots t[n]$ where $t[i] \in \Sigma$ for all $1 \le i \le n$.

Definition 1. *Given the alphabet Σ, a* cover *on Σ is a set $G=\{G_1, G_2, ..., G_{|G|}\}$ with $G_i \subseteq \Sigma$ for $1 \le i \le |G|$, such that $\cup_i G_i = \Sigma$ and there are no $1 \le i, j \le |G|$ with $i \ne j$ such that $G_i \subseteq G_j$. The sets G_i's are said* groups.

The alphabet Σ of the input sequence is implicitly given by means of the sequence itself, while that of the motifs is explicitly given by a cover on Σ defined as above and the alphabet used is that of the groups of such cover.

Definition 2. *A k-pattern is a k-long sequence on the alphabet of the groups. A k-pattern $x = x[1]x[2]\cdots x[k]$ with $x[i] \in G$ for all $1 \le i \le n$ occurs in t at position p if $t[i + p - 1] \in x[i]$ for all $1 \le i \le k$. In this case p is said to be an* occurrence *of x. We will denote with* extent *the complete set of occurrences of a pattern.*

Notice that different patterns may occur at the same position and that, even more, two different patterns may have the very same extent (this is the case when the motifs differ in positions that in the occurrences correspond to letters that belong to the intersections of distinct groups).

Definition 3. *Let k, q be integers and t a sequence on Σ. A k-motif of t is a k-pattern that occurs in t at least q times. The number q is named* quorum.

When unnecessary or clear from the context, we will omit the k and simply talk about *pattern* and *motif.*

Definition 4. *A k-motif I of t is said to be* maximal *if its extent L_I is not a proper subset of L_J for any other k-motif J. It is* non maximal *otherwise.*

Example 1. Let us consider the input sequence $\tilde{t} = xbxcxaxbxc$ on $\Sigma = \{a, b, c, x\}$ and the cover $G = \{C_1 = \{a, b\}, C_2 = \{b, c\}, C_3 = \{x\}\}$. Assuming $q = 2$, we have that $C_3 C_3 C_3$, $C_1 C_3 C_1$ and $C_1 C_3 C_2$ are all 3-patterns. Nevertheless, the first never occurs in $\tilde{t}$, the second occurs only at position 6 and thus is not a motif either, while the third occurs in 2, 6 and 8 and hence it is a 3-motif. Moreover, the 3-motif $C_2 C_3 C_2$ with extent $\{2, 8\}$ is not maximal in $\tilde{t}$ because $C_1 C_3 C_2$ has extent $\{2, 6, 8\}$; this latter is maximal as well as $C_3 C_1 C_3$ with extent $\{1, 5, 7\}$.

We will say that a k-motif I is a *duplication* if $L_I = L_J$ for any other k-motif J with $J \neq I$. Notice that if I is a duplication of J, then J is a duplication of I, as the relation is symmetrical (and transitive). If a k-motif is maximal and it is a duplication, we will say that it is a *maximal duplication.*

The problem we address is to find all maximal k-motifs eliminating their duplications. As stated so far, the problem has been solved in [7] by extending the method of [3] to the case of maximal motifs which are approximate in that they are expressed using the alphabet of the groups. Basically, in [7], like in [3], maximal k-motifs are obtained in $O(\log k)$ steps where at each step the length of the motifs is doubled by means of concatenation of shorter motifs, with the difference that in [7] only maximal motifs are kept and hence, in particular, each step is concluded with an exhaustive search of extents included into others in order to eliminate them. The set inclusions detection results to be a sensible bottleneck of the algorithm. In other words, each step of [7] is different from that of [3] as it deals with approximate and maximal motifs, but the two algorithms share the fact that an ℓ-long motif is obtained by a concatenation of two $(\ell/2)$-long motifs that occur in the input sequences at distance $\ell/2$ and in the same relative order. Only if the length k of the sought motifs is not a power of two, there is a final step in [7] where the motif of length k are generated by overlapping two motifs of length k' such that $k' < k < 2k'$ and k' is a power of two. We call such a generation an *overlap step*, and the previous ones *concatenation steps*. If the size of an overlap (that is, the length of the string fragment that the two words share) is o, then we will talk about o-overlap.

The goal of this paper is to further extend the method of [7] to the case in which $O(k)$ steps are overlap steps. In particular, we are interested in overlaps of size $\Theta(\ell)$ length where ℓ is the length of the motifs involved. The need of this apparently useless drawback is motivated by the fact that we introduce relations. Indeed, it can be shown that in this case the overall time complexity is smaller when overlap steps are performed.

3   Properties of (Maximal) k-Motifs

In this section we prove some properties of maximal motifs that will result useful in the next sections in order to set an upper bound on the cardinality of candidate motifs we will have to deal with. Let us start by observing that, since several different patterns may share an occurrence, we have that in general there is not an unique motif that can be associated to a list of occurrences. Nevertheless, in what follows, we will often implicitly represent a motif using its extent. These actually represent a set of motifs. Formally, for the input sequence t, a cover G, and a length k, the extent L represents the following set of patterns of length k (k-motifs if $|L| \geq q$ where q is the quorum):

$$\{x = x[1]\ldots x[k] \mid x[i] \in G \text{ such that } t[p+i-1] \in x[i] \,\forall\, 1 \leq i \leq k \text{ and } \forall\, p \in L\}.$$

Example 2. In our running example $\tilde{t} = xbxcxaxbxc$ with $G = \{C_1 = \{a, b\}, C_2 = \{b, c\}, C_3 = \{x\}\}$ we have that for $k = 3$ the extent $\{2, 8\}$ (the substring bxc occurs at both positions) represents both $C_1 C_3 C_2$ and $C_2 C_3 C_2$.

Definition 5. *Given a cover $G = \{G_1, G_2, \ldots, G_{|G|}\}$ on Σ, the degeneracy g of G is the maximum number of distinct groups to which a same $\sigma \in \Sigma$ belongs to.*

In other words, g measures indeed how *degenerate* is the alphabet of the motifs. For exact motifs we have $G = \Sigma$ and $g = 1$, but when an approximation is sought, we have in general $g > 1$ which is somehow a measure of the degree of such approximation. In theory, g can be as big as $|G|$, but in practical cases it will not. Given that we deal with a degenerate alphabet like [7], it can be useful to view the upper bound on the number of k-motifs also in terms of g. In [7] it is proved the following[1].

Proposition 1. *In an input sequence in Σ^n, given a cover G of Σ having degeneracy g, for a fixed k the number of distinct k-motifs occurring in the sequence is bounded by $min(|G|^k, ng^k)$.*

We now show that, even when dealing with extents only and with fixed length, in general one can generate quite more candidates than *just* the $|G|^k$ different k-motifs. We will show why, and also that our algorithm avoids this drawback. Let us start again with a simple example.

Example 3. Let us consider again the running example $\tilde{t} = xbxcxaxbxc$, $q = 2$, and $G = \{C_1, C_2, C_3\}$ with $C_1 = \{a, b\}$, $C_2 = \{b, c\}$ and $C_3 = \{x\}$. Let us consider

---

[1] In [7] the result is stated for maximal motifs. However the very same proof works for motifs in general.

the extent $\{1,7\}$ and length $k = 3$, corresponding to the substring xbx. This latter is repeated 2 times as requested by the quorum and it corresponds to $C_3(C_1 \cap C_2)C_3$, which does not match our definition of pattern. Notice that its extent is different from that of $C_3C_1C_3$ (that is $\{1,5,7\}$) and $C_3C_2C_3$ (that is $\{1,3,7\}$) that are both maximal 3-motifs. On the other hand, $(C_1 \cap C_2)C_3C_2$, which also occurs twice (at 2 and at 8) and it is not a k-pattern, has the same occurrences as $C_2C_3C_2$.

Definition 6. *A* pseudopattern *is a k-long sequence on the alphabet of the subsets of the groups whose extent is not the extent of a k-pattern. We name it a k-pseudomotif if it occurs at least q times and we name* pseudo extent *its complete list of occurrences.*

In Example 3 for $k = 3$ we have that $\{1,7\}$ is a pseudo extent for the pseudomotif $C_3(C_1 \cap C_2)C_3$ while $(C_1 \cap C_2)C_3C_2$ is not a pseudomotif and thus $\{2,8\}$ is not a pseudo extent because $\{2,8\}$ is also the extent of the motif $C_2C_3C_2$. Our concern on pseudomotifs is motivated by the fact that, given a cover G, there are $O(2^{|G|k})$ distinct pseudomotifs of length k because there are as many pseudopatterns as the number of distinct k-long strings on the alphabet of the subsets of G, which are not k-patterns, that is $2^{|G|k} - |G|^k$. Notice, however, that a pseudo extent can never be an extent of a maximal motif because it is always included into the extent of a k-motif. Namely, if the pseudomotif is, say, $x = C_1 \cdots (C_i \cap C_j) \cdots C_k$ with extent L, then by definition the k-motif $m = C_1 \cdots C_i \cdots C_k$ has an extent which is different from L and it must necessarily include it because m occurs wherever x does. Since we infer motifs of growing length, it is useful to know that at each step we only need to store maximal motifs because these are enough to produce longer ones.

Lemma 1. *For each maximal k-motif, its ℓ-long prefix and its ℓ-long suffix ($\forall$ $0 < \ell < k$) are maximal ℓ-motifs.*

The result of Lemma 1 actually holds for any substring and not just for prefixes and suffixes as the proof does not depend at all from the fact that the substring is a prefix or a suffix. Given an extent L and an integer d, we denote with $L + d$ the set $\{x + d \mid \forall x \in L\}$. Lemma 1 has the following consequence.

Theorem 1. *The extents of all maximal k-motifs can be computed from the extents of maximal ℓ-motifs for a fixed ℓ such that $k/2 \le \ell < k$.*

As a consequence, the set of *all* maximal motifs of a fixed length ℓ is sufficient to generate any (hence possibly all of them) maximal motif of length $\ell + d$ provided $\ell > d$. Therefore, we have that in our incremental construction of motifs we only need to have maximal motifs of intermediate length. On the other hand, we show now with an example that the overlap of two maximal motifs can generate a pseudomotif.

Example 4. In our running example $L_1 = \{2,6,8\}$, $L_2 = \{2,4,8\}$, $L_3 = \{1,5,7\}$, and $L_4 = \{1,3,7,9\}$ are the extents of the maximal 2-motif (respectively) $m_1 =$

C_1C_3, $m_2 = C_2C_3$, $m_3 = C_3C_1$, and $m_4 = C_3C_2$. If we perform a 1-overlap of m_3 and m_2, we obtain the extent $\{1, 7\}$ corresponding exactly to the pseudomotif exhibited in Example 3. The same happens overlapping m_4 and m_1.

Hence, not only generating pseudo-motifs would be useless, but they would even introduce a serious drawback on the performance of the method. Indeed, given how many the pseudomotifs can be, generating them all could cause a memory problem and, moreover, postponing their detection to the exhaustive search of included extents would result very inefficient in terms of time complexity. We will see in Section 4 a necessary condition on motifs that will allow us to avoid to generate pseudomotifs.

4   The Algorithm

Depending from how close symbols for which we need to check relations have to be in our relational motifs, the parameter d will be input defined. After this, the first $O(\log d)$ steps are concatenation steps exactly like in [7]. After these, we have obtained the set of all maximal ℓ_0-motifs where ℓ_0 is the smallest power of two greater than d. Then $O(k/d)$ steps follow, where at step i ($i \geq 0$) we have the extents of all maximal ℓ_i-motifs with $\ell_i = \ell_0 + id$, with which we: (i) Perform all possible pairwise ($\ell_i - d$)-overlaps of two ℓ_i-motifs and compute the extent of the resulting ℓ_{i+1}-motifs, storing from which pair of ℓ_i-motifs they have been obtained. (ii) Keep only those whose extents have size at least q. (iii) Eliminate non-maximal and duplicated extents. After these three steps we are left with all maximal and non duplicated ℓ_{i+1}-motifs. This is iterated as long as $\ell_i < k$. After that, if $\ell_i = k$ then we have completed the task, and otherwise we perform a final ($2\ell_i - k$)-overlap. We now describe how we intend to minimize the amount of extents generated at step (i) and thus also to speed up the filtering of step (ii), and especially of step (iii) which otherwise would be an unbearable bottleneck. The idea is that for each ordered pair I and J of maximal ℓ_i-motifs the extent of the ℓ_{i+1} motif obtained by overlapping I and J is computed, and the fact that I is its prefix and J its suffix is stored. Later on, whenever a motif X' has to be eliminated because its extent is included into that of X, X' is eliminated and X adds the prefix(es) and suffix(es) of X' to its. If this is the case, we say that X *inherits* X'. This storage of data about which maximal prefixes and suffixes a motif comes from, and their inheritance for eliminated motifs is motivated by the fact that actually the generation of a new motif will be conditioned by whether or not a simple property concerning this data holds. This will actually allow us to be guaranteed not to generate any pseudomotif, as we will see in next section.

At step i an ℓ_i-motif I is described by the following data: the identifier $\#I$, the extent L_I, and a pair (P_I, S_I) of lists indicating the set P_I of prefixes in terms of identifiers used in step $i-1$ (omitting the $\#$), and the set S_I of suffixes in terms of identifiers used in step $i-1$. For an efficient computation and for ease of notation, we will also make use, at step i, of a vector V_i of length n such that $V_i[p] = \{\#I \mid p \in L_I \text{ at step } i\}$. The algorithm is the following.

```
   //  INITIAL  PHASE  //
1.    Create an identifier for each $G_i \in G$ occurring in $t$ and compute its extent;
2.    Compute $V_1$;
3.    $\ell_0 := 1$;
4.    while $\ell_0 \le d$ do begin
5.        for each maximal $\ell_0$-motif $I$ do for each $x \in L_I$ do
6.            for each $\#J \in V_1[x + \ell_0]$ do
7.                $L_{IJ} := L_{IJ} \cup x$;
8.        Eliminate nonmaximal and duplications;
9.        $\ell_0 := 2\ell_0$;    end
   //  OVERLAP  PHASE  //
      $i := 0$;
10. repeat
      begin
11.       Compute $V_i$;
12.       for each maximal $\ell_i$-motif $I$ do for each $x \in L_I$ do
13.           for each $\#J \in V_i[x + d]$ do
14.               if $S_I \cap P_J \ne \emptyset$ then begin $L_{IJ} := L_{IJ} \cup x$;  $P_{IJ} := I$;  $S_{IJ} := J$ end;
15.       Detect and discard extents below quorum, nonmaximal and duplications;
16.       for each eliminated nonmaximal or duplicated $I'$ do
          begin
17.           choose one $I$ such that $L_{I'} \subseteq L_I$ with $I$ maximal;
18.           $P_I := P_I \cup P_{I'}$;  $S_I := S_I \cup S_{I'}$
          end;
19.       $i := i + 1$;  $\ell_i := \ell_i + d$
      end
20. until $\ell_i > k - d$;
   //  FINAL  STEP  //
21. if $\ell_i < k$ then SAME AS LINES $11 - 15$ WITH $d = k - \ell_i$;
```

Notice that the pseudo-code could be written in a much more compact way grouping the three phases into a unique cycle parametrizing the size of the overlap. We chose to display it as it is for ease of exposition. We denote with L_{IJ} the set $L_I \cap (L_J - d)$ which is the extent which is possibly generated at lines 12-14 by overlapping the two maximal motifs I and J (in fact, lines 12-14 are executed for each $x \in (L_I \cap (L_J - d))$). Althought not explicitly processed (due to complexity reasons), it is clear that a motif IJ obtained by an $(\ell - d)$-overlap of I and J inherits their composition in the following way. If I (resp. J) was a duplication, it actually represents several motifs; let $G_1 \ldots G_d \ldots G_\ell$ (resp. $G'_1 \ldots G'_{\ell-d} \ldots G'_\ell$) be any representation of I (resp. J). We also denote this with $I[i] = G_i$ (resp. $J[i] = G'_i$). Then we have that $IJ = G_1 \ldots G_d(G_{d+1} \cap G'_1) \ldots (G_\ell \cap G'_{\ell-d})G'_{\ell-d+1} \ldots G'_\ell$. Therefore, IJ will be a motif only if for all such representations of I and J we will have that for all $1 \le d \le \ell - d$ the intersection $(G_{d+i} \cap G'_i)$ restricted to the set $L_{IJ} + d + i$ is equal to G_{d+i} or to G'_i. In other words, definitely $IJ[i] \in G$ for $1 \le i \le d$ and $(\ell + 1) \le i \le (\ell + d)$, but for all positions where the occurrences of I and J overlap, whether IJ is a motif is in general an open question whose answer is relevant in terms of complexity issues and it is addressed in the next section. The following three results guarantee correctness and completeness of the algorithm.

Theorem 2. *Let q be the quorum and let I and J be maximal ℓ-motifs such that $|L_{IJ}| = |L_I \cap (L_J - d)| \geq q$ and $S_I \cap P_J = \emptyset$. Then we have that L_{IJ} is either a pseudo extent or a duplication.*

Theorem 3. *Let $L_{M_1}, L_{M_2}, L_{M'}$ be three extents of ℓ-motifs generated at step $i > 2$ such that $L_{M'} \subseteq L_{M_1}$ and $L_{M'} \subseteq L_{M_2}$ and both M_1 and M_2 are maximal. If (wlog) M_1 inherits M' and M_2 does not, then completeness is preserved.*

Corollary 1. *At all steps $i > 2$, let $p + 1$ extents $L_{M_1}, L_{M_2}, ..., L_{M_p}$ and $L_{M'}$ of ℓ-motifs be generated such that $L_{M'} \subseteq L_{M_i}$ for $i = 1, 2, ..., p$. If only one of the p motifs inherits M', then the resulting set of maximal $(\ell + d)$-motifs is the same as if all of them (or a part of them) inherit M'.*   ●

No pseudomotifs are generated at lines 12-14 due to the following result.

Theorem 4. *Let IJ be a $(\ell + d)$-long pseudomotif that could be obtained by overlapping two maximal ℓ-motifs I and J. Then we have that $S_I \cap P_J = \emptyset$.*

Hence, at each step it is enough to store the extents of all generated motifs, and later on only those of all maximal motifs with their list of prefixes and suffixes (which are at worst as many, given that each eliminated motif leaves a constant size prefix and suffix information). Therefore, the space complexity is the size of the former for which Proposition 1 gave us an upper bound of $O(n \cdot g^k)$. Time complexity in the worst case coincides with the cost of the overlapping phase. The *repeat* starting at line 10 is done $O(k/d) = O(k)$ times and its dominant parts are the nested *for* cycles of lines $12 - 14$ and the inclusions detection of line 15. The former take $O(n \cdot g^k)$ because this is the maximum number of motifs it generates, and the latter takes $O(n \cdot g^{2k})$ assuming it is made like in [7]. Therefore, overall the time complexity is in $O(k(ng^k + ng^{2k})) = O(kng^{2k})$. Notice that it is at worst linear in the input size.

5   Relational Motifs

In this section we define at last the problem of inferring *relational* motifs that is what motivates the use of overlap steps rather than concatenations. The novelty starts with the fact that the input sequence is enriched with relations that hold between pair of distinct positions. For the relations we also have an alphabet and a cover on it that will allow a degree of approximation in terms of the relations as well. The problem introduced in Section 2 will be enriched and as a consequence its solution quite straightforwardly extended. This section will formalize this starting with some basic definitions that integrate those already given earlier in this paper. In particular we still assume there is an input string $t \in \Sigma^n$ whose p^{th} position is denoted by $t[p]$ and a cover G on Σ. On this string we seek k-motifs which – so far – are strings $x \in G^k$ represented by their complete extents $L_x \subseteq \{1, \ldots, n - k + 1\}$.

Definition 7. *Let* $R = \{r_1, \ldots, r_{|R|}\}$ *be the* relations alphabet *and* $r \in R$ *a relation. Let* $G_R = \{CR_1, \ldots, CR_{|G_R|}\}$ *with* $CR_i \subseteq R$ *for* $1 \leq i \leq |G_R|$ *be a relations cover* on R *where the* CR_i's *are denoted as* relations groups *and none of them is included into another.*

Similarly to the case of the cover on the alphabet Σ, a *relations degeneracy* g_R notion exists on G_R. The input sequence is no longer just $t \in \Sigma^n$, but also a set of relations $R = \{r_1, \ldots, r_{|R|}\}$ is given as well as for each pair (p_1, p_2) of positions in t, with $p_2 > p_1$, the unique relation $r \in R$ such that r holds between p_1 and p_2. We will also denote this with $r(p_1, p_2)$ and with $(p_1, p_2) \in r$. Note that when considering k-long *relational* motifs, we only need to verify relations between positions p_1 and p_2 for $p_2 < p_1 + k$. The notion of pattern is enriched and therefore that of motifs and occurrence as well. Formally:

Definition 8. *A relational k-pattern is a k-pattern plus a relation group per each pair of its distinct positions. A relational k-pattern x with relations groups $CR_1, \ldots, CR_{|G_R|}$ (where for each $CR_i \in G_R$ it is indicated the set of pairs (u, v) such that $(u, v) \in r \in CR_i$ for some $1 \leq i \leq |G_R|$) is said to occur in t at position p if the pattern x occurs at position p of t and for all pairs $(u, v) \in CR_i$ we have that $r(p+u, p+v)$ for $r \in CR_i$. Finally, given the quorum q, a relational k-motif is a relational k-pattern that occurs at least q times.*

We will still denote with *extent* the complete set of occurrences of a relational pattern and, moreover, a relational k-motif I_R is said to be *maximal* if its extent L_I is not a proper subset of L_J for any other relational k-motif J_R. Given that there is one (and only one) relation per each pair of positions of the pattern, an extent, together with the length k, denotes again a relational motif that would be unique if it weren't for the degenerate alphabet that holds for relations too. Finally, the notion of prefix and suffix of a relational pattern/motif is also straightforwardly extended as it will implicitly still represent relations.

Example 5. Let us consider as input sequence our running example of $\tilde{t} = xbxcxaxbxc$ with in addition the alphabet of relations $R = \{r_1, r_2, r_3\}$ with its cover $G_R = \{CR_1 = \{r_1, r_2\}, CR_2 = \{r_2, r_3\}\}$ having degeneracy $g_R = 2$ and such that $(\{(i, i+1) \mid 1 \leq i \leq k-1\} \cup \{(1, 4), (2, 5), (3, 6), (2, 6), (4, 8)\}) \in r_1$, $\{(1, 3), (3, 5), (5, 7), (7, 9), (4, 7), (7, 10), (1, 5), (3, 7), (5, 9), (6, 10)\} \in r_2$, and all other pairs $1 \leq i, j \leq k$ are in relation r_3. We have that all 2-motifs are relational 2-motifs because the relations between consecutive positions is always the same and thus definitely conserved. On the other hand, the 4-motif with extent $\{2, 6\}$ is not a relational motif because in its two occurrences the relations between the first and last positions are different and in different groups (because $(2, 5) \in r_1 \in (CR_1 \setminus CR_2)$ and $(6, 9) \in r_3 \in (CR_2 \setminus CR_1)$). Moreover, the maximal 4-motif with extent $\{1, 5, 7\}$ has two occurrences, 1 and 7, where the relation between the first and last positions is in CR_1 (respectively there are $(1, 4) \in r_1$ and $(7, 10) \in r_2$), and again two occurrences, namely 5 and 7, where such relation is in CR_2 because $(5, 8) \in r_3$ and again $(7, 10) \in r_2$. Hence, this 4-motif corresponds to two distinct relational 4-motifs.

The possibility to extend the algorithm of Section 4 to the case of relational motifs is based on the following result that is straightforward to verify.

Theorem 5. *A k-pattern is a relational k-motif if, for any $1 \leq d < k/2$:*

  (i) *Its $(k-d)$-long prefix I is a relational motif.*
 (ii) *Its $(k-d)$-long suffix J is a relational motif.*
(iii) *Its relations between all d^2 pairs of positions (l, r) with $1 \leq l \leq d$ and $(k-d+1) \leq r \leq k$ are conserved in at least q of its occurrences.*
(iv) *$S_I \cap P_J \neq \emptyset$.*

Moreover, the proofs of Lemma 1 and Theorem 1 can easily be extended to prove the following.

Theorem 6. *The extents of all maximal relational k-motifs can be computed from the extents of maximal relational ℓ-motifs for $k/2 \leq \ell < k$.*

We now show how the algorithm of Section 4 can be extended to take into account also relations and how its correctness and completeness is preserved. We name this new algorithm *KMRoverlapR*. The first new feature is that the extent of a motif now represents not just a repeated pattern, but rather a repeated relational pattern. The overlap of two relational *submotifs* of length ℓ that occur at distance d at least q times and in the same relative order necessarily results into a $(\ell+d)$-motif (as before) that also has conserved all relations between pairs of position that are at distance at most ℓ and that come from the same submotif. The only new relations that need to be checked are those between the positions that are the at the two d-long non overlapped ends of the new motif for a total of $O(d^2)$ checks to be done as shown in Theorem 5. Hence, at each step i, whenever the vector V_i is checked (at lines 6 and 13 that is, when the occurrences of two ℓ_i-patterns are detected at distance d so that their overlap is a $(\ell_i + d)$-pattern), these $O(d^2)$ comparisons are also made. In order to do so, we use a vector W_i that stores (e.g. for $d = 1$) in $W_i[j]$ the relation groups CR's whose relations hold between position j and position $j + \ell_i - 1$ of the input sequence. This is the only kind of relations to be checked at step i (for any $d > 1$, each position of W contains d values). There are two possible results of these $O(d^2)$ checks for the relations. In a first case we can have that in at least q occurrences of the motif the relations are conserved as well, and then a new extent is created per each distinct conserved relation group (this is the case of the 4-motif with extent $\{1, 5, 7\}$ in Example 5). In a second case, no relation is conserved at least q times and the motif is discarded (like the 4-motif with extent $\{2, 6\}$ in Example 5).

For all other features of the algorithm, everything can be left unchanged. In particular, all properties concerning pseudomotifs, maximality, and the inheritance of prefixes and suffixes hold in the very same way when an extent represents a relational motif rather than a "normal" one. Indeed, also the relations are implicitly stored with the extents, which in *KMRoverlapR* have the invariant to represent motifs (and not pseudomotifs) that are repeated *and* with conserved relations. The complexity of *KMRoverlapR* changes with respect to

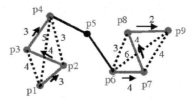

Fig. 1. A sequence of 3D points: subsequences are shown as sets of internal distances.

that of Section 4 because now also the degeneracy g_R of the relations has to be taken into account. Similarly to what proved in Proposition 1, we can say that there are at most $n(g^k + g_R^{k^2})$ relational motifs (counting both degeneracies and including the extents). Again, this is the only theoretical upper bound we can give, but it is far from being tight in practical cases. Then, assuming that d is a constant and thus the cost of the $O(d^2)$ relations tests is negligible, the time complexity of *KMRoverlapR* can be computed as in Section 4 and therefore it is in $O(kn(g^k + g_R^{k^2})^2)$. Notice that in *KMRoverlapR* the input size is no longer n but rather $n \cdot k$ because only relations between position at distance at most k are indicated, and hence the complexity is again linear in the input size.

6   Applications to 3D Protein Structures

A promising area of application of *KMRoverlapR* is the inference of repeated structures in R^d space. The relation between two points x_p and x_q can be discretized by the euclidian distance $d(x_q, x_p)$. We find then geometrical motifs in a multidimensional space, i.e. motifs whose occurrences are insensitive to translations and rotations. When considering only the α-Carbons in the 3D structure of the protein we obtain a sequence of points in the 3D space representing the α-Carbons backbone of the protein. Figure 1 describes the subsequences p1-p2-p3-p4 and p6-p7-p8-p9 in a 9-long sequence t. We consider a set of relational groups $\{R_j = \{j, ..., j + \delta\}\}$ where δ represents a tolerance level: two discretized distances $d(x_p, x_q)$ and $d(x_{p'}, x_{q'})$ belong to the same group whenever $|d(x_p, x_q) - d(x_{p'}, x_{q'})| \leq \delta$. Note that as a consequence we have $g_R = \delta + 1$. In the example of Figure 1, we consider $\delta = 1$ and so $g_R = 2$ and find occurrences of a 4-long relational pattern at positions 1 and 6 in t. Hereunder we give an example of the results obtained when searching a structural pattern repeated in the backbone of several proteins. Note that here we have to slightly adapt the algorithm in order to find patterns that occur at least q times in set of m protein structures. Here $m = q = 5$. The distances between α-Carbon are discretized using 0.5Å-long intervals, with a tolerance level $\delta = 2$ and so $g_R = 3$. Here k-motifs are obtained from $(k - 1)$-long motifs. The average length of the sequences considered is about 200. There are 10 relational groups (amongst 40) representing distances appearing in the sequences. We give for some overlap steps the number of generated k-motifs, avoided pseudomotifs and resulting maximal k-motifs:

$k-1 \to k$	generated motifs	avoided pseudomotifs	maximal motifs
$3 \to 4$	624	0	109
$4 \to 5$	33551	38567	1110
$5 \to 6$	448552	1778569	936
$6 \to 7$	356070	1739419	167
$7 \to 8$	7519	9263	27
$8 \to 9$	1093	2189	21

It is clear that the amount of pseudo-motifs is considerable and thus that the results of this paper are relevant for finding relational motifs by means of overlap steps. Moreover, these results also show that the number of maximal motifs is sensibly smaller than that of generated motifs. This motivates the validity of our choice to focus our attention on maximal motifs. Indeed, although in theory the upper bound on the number of maximal motifs in the worst case is the same as motifs (that is, they can all be maximal), in practice the difference is sensible.

References

1. N. El-Zant and H. Soldano. Finding repeated flexible relational words in sequences. *Journal of Systemics, Cybernetics and Informatics*, 2(4), 2004.
2. N. C. Jones and P. A. Pevzner. *An Introduction to Bioinformatics Algorithms*. The MIT Press, 2004.
3. R. Karp, R. Miller, and A. Rosenberg. Rapid identification of repeted patterns in strings, trees and arrays. In *Fourth ACM Symposium on Theory of Computing*, pages 125–136, 1972.
4. M. Lothaire. *Applied Combinatorics on words*. Cambridge University Press, 2005.
5. L. Marsan and M.-F. Sagot. Algorithms for extracting structured motifs using a suffix tree with application to promoter and regulatory consensus identification. *Journal of Computational Biology*, 7:345–360, 2001.
6. N. Pisanti, M. Crochemore, R. Grossi, and M.-F. Sagot. A basis of tiling motifs for generating repeated patterns and its complexity for higher quorum. In B.Rovan and P.Vojtás, editors, *Mathematical Foundations of Computer Science*, LNCS 2747, pages 622–631. Springer-Verlag, 2003.
7. H. Soldano, A. Viari, and M. Champesme. Searching for flexible repeated patterns using a non-transitive similarity relation. *Pattern Recognition Letters*, 16:243–246, 1995.

Speeding up Parsing
of Biological Context-Free Grammars

Daniel Fredouille and Christopher H. Bryant*

The Robert Gordon University, Aberdeen, UK
{chb,df}@comp.rgu.ac.uk
http://www.comp.rgu.ac.uk/research/cig

Abstract. Grammars have been shown to be a very useful way to model biological sequences families. As both the quantity of biological sequences and the complexity of the biological grammars increase, generic and efficient methods for parsing are needed. We consider two parsers for context-free grammars: depth-first top-down parser and chart parser; we analyse and compare them, both theoretically and empirically, with respect to biological data. The theoretical comparison is based on a common feature of biological grammars: the gap – a gap is an element of the grammars designed to match any subsequence of the parsed string. The empirical comparison is based on grammars and sequences used by the bioinformatics community. Our conclusions are that: (1) the chart parsing algorithm is significantly faster than the depth-first top-down algorithm, (2) designing special treatments in the algorithms for managing gaps is useful, and (3) the way the grammar encodes gaps has to be carefully chosen, when using parsers not optimised for managing gaps, to prevent important increases in running times.

1 Introduction

Among models used to represent sets of strings, *formal grammars* introduced by Chomsky [1] have been the subject of many studies. Searls [2] made the link between this formalism and structural phenomena found in biological sequences, showing the capabilities and limits of this formalism to represent biological sequences families. Numerous types of grammar formats are used for biological sequences analysis. Sub-regular patterns are used in PROSITE [3]; more complex patterns have been designed using Definite Clause Grammars (DCG) [4], String Variable Grammars (SVG) [5], PATSCAN patterns [6] or Basic Gene Grammars (BGG) [7]. For all but PATSCAN patterns, parsing is realised through algorithms available in the field of *context-free grammar parsing*: DCG and SVG with depth-first top-down parsing, and BGG with chart parsing. In this article, we focus on context-free grammars (CFG) parsers because they are generic[1],

---

* Contact author.

[1] CFGs can represent a wide range of grammatical constructs, and special treatments can be easily added to the parsers to take into account constructs beyond context-free.

A. Apostolico, M. Crochemore, and K. Park (Eds.): CPM 2005, LNCS 3537, pp. 241–256, 2005.

and are well studied[2]. However, to the best of our knowledge, they have never been analysed and compared when executed on biological data. Such a comparison has become important because there is a growing need for efficient parsers for biological grammars: the quantity of biological sequences is increasing daily and biological grammars are becomming more complex.

Our preliminary experiments made it clear to us that the respective performances of the considered parsers on biological data are closely related to a very common feature of biological grammars: the notion of *gap*. A gap is a rule designed to match any subsequence of the parsed string. This article compares the algorithms both theoretically (for grammars containing gaps) and empirically on biological strings and grammars. Our conclusions are: (1) the chart parser (CP) possesses a significant advantage in terms of running time over depth-first top-down parser (DFTDP), (2) designing special treatments for gaps in these parsers is useful, and (3), when using parsers not optimised for gaps, the gap rule design has to be carefully chosen to prevent important increases in running times.

After presenting the definitions (Section 2), we analyse the complexity of the DFTDP and the CP with respect to gaps (Sections 3 and 4). This analysis is then empirically validated on biological data (Section 5). The appendix contains the proofs (or sometimes hint of the proofs due to space restrictions) for the properties of the paper.

2   Definitions

Words, languages and grammars: For any finite set $\mathcal{S}$, we denote by $|\mathcal{S}|$ its cardinality and by $\mathcal{S}^*$ its free monoid, i.e., the set of all sequences made by concatenating 0 or more symbols of $\mathcal{S}$. An element of $\mathcal{S}^*$ is called a *word* over $\mathcal{S}$. The length of a word w is denoted by $|w|$, the word of length 0 or *empty word* is denoted by ϵ. Any set of words over $\mathcal{S}$ (i.e., any subset of $\mathcal{S}^*$) is called a *language* over $\mathcal{S}$. Languages can be represented by formal systems called *grammars*. The grammars we consider in this paper are *Context-Free*.

Definition 1. *A* Context-Free Grammar *(CFG) is a tuple* $\mathcal{G} = \langle \mathcal{T}, \mathcal{N}, S, \mathcal{R} \rangle$ *where* $\mathcal{T}$ *and* $\mathcal{N}$ *are finite sets of symbols called respectively* terminals *and* non-terminals. $\mathcal{T}$ *and* $\mathcal{N}$ *are disjoint and their union is denoted by* $\mathcal{V} = \mathcal{T} \cup \mathcal{N}$. S *is a nonterminal called the* start symbol *and* $\mathcal{R}$ *is the set of* production rules; *each rule in* $\mathcal{R}$ *is of the form* $A \twoheadrightarrow \alpha$ *where* $A \subset \mathcal{N}$ *is called the* left part *of the rule, and* $\alpha \in \mathcal{V}^*$. □

A CFG represents a language over $\mathcal{T}$ using the relation $\rightarrow$ defined by:

$$\forall u, v \in \mathcal{V}^* : \ u \rightarrow v \Leftrightarrow \exists \, (A \twoheadrightarrow \alpha) \in \mathcal{R}, \ \exists u_1, \, u_2 \in \mathcal{V}^*, \ u = u_1 A u_2, \ v = u_1 \alpha u_2.$$

We denote by $\rightarrow^*$ the transitive closure of $\rightarrow$; if $u \rightarrow^* v$, v is said to *derive* from u. The language $L(N)$ generated by a nonterminal N is the set of words over $\mathcal{T}$ derived from N, i.e., $L(N) \triangleq \{u \in \mathcal{T}^* : \ N \rightarrow^* u\}$. The language represented by a grammar $\mathcal{G} = \langle \mathcal{T}, \mathcal{N}, S, \mathcal{R} \rangle$ is $L(\mathcal{G}) \triangleq L(S)$.

---

[2] Among others, in the field of natural language processing.

Gaps rules: An *unlimited gap* is a nonterminal G such that $L(G) = T^*$. For fixed values $lo, up \in \mathbb{N}$, a *limited gap* is a nonterminal G such that $L(G) = \{u \in T^* : lo \leq |u| \leq up\}$. Numbers lo and up are respectively the *lower* and *upper* *bounds* of the limited gap, the value $ra = up - lo$ is its *range*.

Gaps can be implemented using different sets of grammar rules. To define these rules we use the following notation: N^i denotes nonterminal N repeated i times (e.g., $N^2 = NN$, and $N^0 = \epsilon$) and X is a nonterminal with rules $\{X \rightarrow t : t \in T\}$. We study the following unlimited gap implementations: the *left-recursive* gap G_l with rules $\{G_l \twoheadrightarrow \epsilon, G_l \twoheadrightarrow G_l\, X\}$, and the *right-recursive* gap G_r with rules $\{G_r \twoheadrightarrow \epsilon, G_r \twoheadrightarrow X\, G_r\}$. We study the following limited gap implementations, with bounds lo and up fixed, and range $ra = up - lo$: the *linear* gap $G_{1,lo,up}$, with rules $\{G_{1,lo,up} \twoheadrightarrow X^{lo}\, G'_{1,ra}, G'_{1,ra} \twoheadrightarrow X^{ra}_e, X_e \twoheadrightarrow X, X_e \twoheadrightarrow \epsilon\}$, and the *quadratic* gap $G_{2,lo,up}$, with rules $\{G_{2,lo,up} \twoheadrightarrow X^{lo}\, G'_{2,ra}\} \cup \{G'_{2,ra} \twoheadrightarrow X^i : i \in [0,ra]\}$. The linear and quadratic gaps are so called because they respectively need, to represent the gap, a linear or a quadratic number of symbols in function of ra. It can be checked that these implementations respect the gap definitions, i.e.: $L(G_l) = L(G_r) = T^*$ and $L(G_{1,lo,up}) = L(G_{2,lo,up}) = \{u \in T^* : lo \leq |u| \leq up\}$. We denote by $Gaps$ the set of nonterminals we use to implement gaps, i.e., $Gaps \triangleq \{G_l, G_r, X, X_e\} \cup \{G_{1,lo,up}, G_{2,lo,up}, G'_{1,ra}, G'_{2,ra} : lo, up, ra \in \mathbb{N}, lo \leq up\}$.

Other notations: In the remainder of this paper we consider that: a grammar $\mathcal{G} = \langle T, \mathcal{N}, S, \mathcal{R} \rangle$ is given, with $V = T \cup \mathcal{N}$; that lower case letters $u, v, w, \dots$ denote words over T with w being the word to parse by the grammar; that greek letters $\alpha, \beta, \dots$ denote words over V and that lower case letters $i, j, \dots$ denote natural numbers.

For a word u, $u[i{:}j]$ (with $i, j \in [0, |u|]$, $i \leq j$) denotes the subword of u starting at position i and ending at position j excluded (e.g. $abcd[0{:}1] = a$, $abcd[2{:}4] = cd$, $abcd[1{:}1] = \epsilon$). $u[i]$, $u[i{:}]$ and $u[{:}i]$ are respectively shortcuts for $u[i{:}i{+}1]$, $u[i{:}|u|]$ and $u[0{:}i]$.

3 Parsing Gaps Using Depth-First Top-Down Parsing

In this section we consider the study of the depth-first top-down parser (DFTDP) with respect to gaps. Subsection 3.1 describes the principle of the DFTDP, then, in Subsections 3.2 and 3.3 we study respectively the effect of the implementation of gap rules on the DFTDP and a way of speeding it up when extra information is available on which rules represent gaps.

3.1 The Depth-First Top-Down Parser

The DFTDP can parse words in any CFG which is not left-recursive, i.e. such that $\forall N \in \mathcal{N} : \neg(N \rightarrow \alpha \rightarrow^* N\beta)$. Its worst complexity is non polynomial $(O(|w|^{|\mathcal{G}|}))$, where $|\mathcal{G}|$ is the sum of the length of all rules in $\mathcal{G}$. However, this parser possesses the advantages of being very easy to implement, to need only $O(|\mathcal{G}| \times |w|)$ memory, and is considered to be fast for most grammars in practice.

Algorithm 1 Depth-first top-down parser, the initial call is DFTDP(w,S) with boolean *accepted* set to *false*.

1: **Function** DFTDP(u, α)
2: **if** $\alpha = \epsilon$ **then**{ **if** $u = \epsilon$ **then** {*accepted* $\leftarrow$ *true*; Stop algorithm}}
3: **else if** $\alpha[0] \in \mathcal{N}$ **then**{**for all** $\alpha[0] \twoheadrightarrow A_1 \ldots A_n \in \mathcal{R}$ **do** DFTDP($u, A_1 \ldots A_n\alpha[1:]$)}
4: **else if** $\alpha[0] \in \mathcal{T}$ **then**{**if** $u \neq \epsilon$ **and** $u[0] = \alpha[0]$ **then** DFTDP($u[1:], \alpha[1:]$)}

The DFTDP uses the $\rightarrow$ relation to explore the space of all possible derivations of S and tries to find one equal to the input word w. This space is explored in a depth-first manner, and is pruned as soon as an incompatibility between the input word and the derivation currently considered is found. It can be described in a simplified manner by Algorithm 1. The word w is accepted by Algorithm 1 iff boolean *accepted* is true after execution.

3.2 Complexity of Parsing Gaps with DFTDP

The worst case execution time for the DFTDP is when the whole space of derivations has to be explored in order to reject a word. As we focus on gaps, we consider this worst case arising from the presence of a gap.

Concerning unlimited gaps, the DFTDP does not work on left-recursive rules implying that the right-recursive gap implementation has to be used. Property 1 shows that the DFTDP has a reasonable linear behaviour in this case.

Property 1. For a call DFTDP($u, G_r a$), with $u[|u|-1] \neq a$, the number of recursive DFTDP calls is linear in $|u|$.

Concerning limited gaps, from Property 2 we can expect the quadratic implementation to be far more efficient than the linear one.

Property 2. For a call DFTDP($u, G_{1,lo,up}$) (resp. DFTDP($u, G_{2,lo,up}$)), with $|u| > up$, the number of recursive DFTDP calls is linear in lo and non polynomial (resp. quadratic) in $ra = up - lo$.

Conditions $u[|u| - 1] \neq a$ and $|u| > up$, respectively in Property 1 and 2, ensure the worst case complexity is reached by forcing the parsed word u to be rejected.

3.3 Adapting the Algorithm

We have seen in the previous subsection which rules are adequate to represent gaps when using the DFTDP. In this subsection, we consider the option of implementing an algorithm based on the DFTDP, but adapted to gap rules. The proposed adaptation consists in changing line 3 of Algorithm 1 to obtain a special treatment of gap rules as shown by Algorithm 2. Property 3 shows that this modification deals with any kind of gaps in linear time, compared to quadratic or exponential behaviour given by Property 2.

Algorithm 2 Line 3 of Algorithm 1 with gap optimisation.

1: **else if** $\alpha[0] \in \mathcal{N}$ **then**
2:     **if** $\alpha[0]$ is a gap **then if** $\alpha[0]$ is limited **then** let lo and up be its bounds
3:                              **else** let $lo \leftarrow 0$ and $up \leftarrow \infty$
4:                              **for all** $i \in [lo, \min(|u|, up)]$ **do** DFTDP$(u[i:], \alpha[1:])$
5:     **else for all** $\alpha[0] \twoheadrightarrow A_1 \ldots A_n \in \mathcal{R}$ **do** DFTDP$(u, A_1 \ldots A_n\alpha[1:])$

Property 3. We denote by DFTDP$'$ Algorithm 1 with modification of Algorithm 2, and by G a gap nonterminal with bounds lo and up (with $lo = 0$ and $up = \infty$ if the gap is unlimited). The call DFTDP$'(u, Gb)$, with $b \in \mathcal{T}$ and $u[|u| - 1] \neq b$ generates a number of recursive calls linear in $\min(|u|, up) - lo$.

4   Parsing Gaps Using Chart Parsing

We study in this section the behaviour of the chart parser (CP) when it encounters gaps. Subsection 4.1 describes the CP, Subsection 4.2 examines the effect of the gap implementation on it and Subsection 4.3 provides a way of speeding it up when it is provided with extra information on which rules represent gaps.

4.1   Chart-Parsing

The CP can parse any CFG (most CFG parsers are limited to subsets of CFG). Its worst complexity is polynomial, $O(|w|^3)$, and it has the advantage of representing all the alternative ways of parsing a sequence (potentially an exponential number) into a structure of polynomial size.

We will not detail the whole algorithm, only its main abstract data types and principles. For details on the algorithm, the interested reader can consult [8, 9]. The basic component of chart parsing is the *item*, this is a structure of the form: $R \twoheadrightarrow \alpha \bullet \beta @i, j$. Such an item means that the α part of rule $R \twoheadrightarrow \alpha\beta$ can derive $w[i, j]$, more formally:

$$\alpha \rightarrow^* w[i{:}j] \tag{1}$$

Symbols $\bullet$ and @ are separators between respectively α and β, and between β and the couple i, j. R is called the *left part* of the item, and indice j is called the *ending position* of the item. Items are stored in a set called *itemset*. From Equation 1, w is accepted by the grammar iff *itemset* contains an item of the form $S \rightarrow \alpha \bullet @0, |w|$.

In its most studied implementation due to Earley [10, 11], the CP first inserts (in *itemset*) items which end at position 0, and then iteratively fills *itemset* with items ending at position j (j being incremented from 1 to $|w|$) . The CP stops after inserting items for $j = |w|$. In the Earley implementation, items also respect the following equation:

$$\exists \gamma, \delta \in \mathcal{V}^* \text{ such that: } S \rightarrow^* \gamma R\delta \text{ and } \gamma \rightarrow^* w[:i] \tag{2}$$

Equation 2 represents the fact that items with a left part that cannot be reached from S at position i of w are useless to check the acceptance of w, and therefore do not need to be stored. The only items which the Earley implementation stores in *itemset* are those which satisfy both Equations 1 and 2.

4.2   Complexity of Parsing Gaps with Chart Parsing

We will compare the gap implementations by assessing their complexity using the number of items the CP stores in *itemset*. The fewer items we need to store, the more efficient is the CP.

Property 4. Let $G = G_r$ when considering right-recursive gaps and $G = G_l$ when considering left-recursive ones. For $l \in [0, |w|]$, let $\mathcal{P}_l = \{k \in [0, l] : \exists R \rightarrow \alpha \bullet G\beta@j, k \in itemset, R \neq G\}$, and $p_1 = \min(\mathcal{P}_{|w|} \cup \{|w| + 1\})$. Suppose $S \neq G$, the number of items in *itemset* with G as left part is S'_r for right recursive gaps, and S'_l for left-recursive gaps with: $S'_r = S'_l = 0$ iff $p_1 > |w|$; $S'_r = (1 - 5p_1/2 + p_1^2/2) + |w|(2.5 - p_1) + |w|^2/2$ and $S'_l \leq (2|w| + 1)|\mathcal{P}_{|w|}| \leq (2|w|^2 + |w|)|$ iff $p_1 \leq |w|$.

From Property 4, for right-recursive and left-recursive gaps, *itemset* can contain a number (resp. S'_r and S'_l) of items in the worst case quadratic in the size of the parsed word. However, in practice, $|\mathcal{P}_{|w|}|$ representing the number of positions where a gap is started in w, it can be supposed small compared to $|w|$. Moreover, biological grammars often model a pattern to be found somewhere in the parsed word, implying the use of unlimited gap before the pattern, and in this case $p_1 = 0$. Considering these points, the following approximations can be made: $S'_r \simeq \frac{5|w|}{2} + \frac{|w|^2}{2}$ and $S'_l \simeq 2 * K * |w|$ where K is small, showing that right-recursive gaps imply a better behaviour of the CP than left-recursive ones.

Property 5. For $l \in [0, |w|]$, let $\mathcal{I}_1(l, ra)$ (resp. $\mathcal{I}_2(l, ra)$) be the set of items in *itemset* having l as ending position and with $G'_{1,ra}$ or X_e (resp. $G'_{2,ra}$) as left part. We have: $|\mathcal{I}_1(l, ra)| > |\mathcal{I}_2(l, ra)| + 2ra$

From Property 5, we can see that we will always have more items in *itemset* when using linear limited gaps instead of quadratic limited gaps, the difference being proportional to the $ra = up - lo$ value of the gap for items ending at position l. Considering all items, the difference can therefore be quite large (in $O(|w| * ra)$) implying that the use of quadratic gaps is recommended for chart parsing.

4.3   Adapting the Algorithm

Some modifications of the CP have already been proposed to speed it up when encountering particular rules: [10] propose optimisations linked with rules of the form $A \rightarrow \epsilon$, and in [7] an optimisation for gap rules is briefly explained. We adapt this last one for the Earley implementation changing the algorithm the following way: (a) Items of the form $A \rightarrow \alpha \bullet \beta@i, j$ with $A \in Gaps$ are not introduced in *itemset*. (b) Each time an item of the form $R \twoheadrightarrow \alpha \bullet G\beta@i, j$, with G a gap nonterminal, is inserted into *itemset*, we store $R \twoheadrightarrow \alpha G \bullet \beta@i, j$ into a set called *gapset*. (c) Before the algorithm fills in *itemset* with items ending at position k, we insert items $R \twoheadrightarrow \alpha G \bullet \beta@i, k$ iff item $R \twoheadrightarrow \alpha G \bullet \beta@i, j$ is present in *gapset* and $k \in [lo + j, up + j]$, where lo and up are the bounds of the gap, or $0, \infty$ if the gap is unlimited.

With these modifications, no more item with $G \in Gaps$ as left part is inserted in *itemset*, but some items are inserted in *gapset*. The size of *gapset* is in the worst case of the order of $O(|w|^2)$ like the worst case given in Subsection 4.2. In practice, a quadratic behaviour is in fact very unlikely to happen since, as we already argued in Subsection 4.2, the number of position where a gap can start should be small for non artificial data (i.e., the number of possible k in items of the form $R \twoheadrightarrow \alpha \bullet G\beta@i, k$ is small).

5   Experimental Comparison

The material of the experiments is available at `http://www.comp.rgu.ac.uk/staff/chb/research/data_sets/cpm05/README.html`. Running times have been obtained on a SunBlade 2500 (under SunOS 5.8).

5.1   Parsing Protein Grammars and Sequences

Data: The first experimental comparison uses patterns of the PROSITE[3] database [3] as a source of grammars, and the UNIPROT[4] database [12] as source of sequences. We chose the PROSITE (resp. UNIPROT) database because it contains the largest collection of hand validated protein patterns (resp. protein sequences) in the world. PROSITE patterns can be seen as grammars with low expression power. (They represent a subset of regular languages). Their wide use by the bioinformatics community shows that they can be considered as potentially pertinent subparts of more complex biological grammars. Thus, their efficient parsing is a prerequisite to the efficient parsing of more complex grammars.

Experimental setting: For each one of a random sample of 500 PROSITE patterns, we sampled 1000 sequences from UNIPROT, and parsed these sequences with a grammar equivalent to the pattern. For each pattern-sequence couple, the parsing time has been stored.

Results: Table 1 gives the mean parsing times for pattern-sequence couples with the different parsers and gaps implementation. A particular event explained later made us separate one of the patterns from the others in the last column. The means are taken over the 499 reminding patterns and the 1000 sequences parsed in each pattern. Figure 1 presents these results graphically as a function of the length of the parsed word.

---

[3] `http://www.expasy.ch/prosite/`

[4] `http://www.expasy.uniprot.org/`

Table 1. Mean execution times per sequence on 499 PROSITE patterns and for the particular pattern PDOC00354.

Experiment		Mean	Standard	PDOC00354
Algo.	Gaps	time	deviation	mean time
CP	G_l, G_1	$4.37ms$	$81.4ms$	$32.0ms$
CP	G_l, G_2	$4.36ms$	$81.4ms$	$16.4ms$
CP optimised		$1.54ms$	$62.4ms$	$1.20ms$
CP	G_r, G_1	$1.88s$	$4.82s$	$32.0ms$
CP	G_r, G_2	$1.88s$	$4.81s$	$16.5ms$
DFTDP	G_r, G_1	$4.35ms$	$83.0ms$	$> 86.4s^*$
DFTDP	G_r, G_2	$4.31ms$	$82.4ms$	$53.2ms$
DFTDP optimised		$0.63ms$	$49.8ms$	$0.350ms$

$^*\ 86.4s = 24h * 60mn * 60s/1000$ sequences

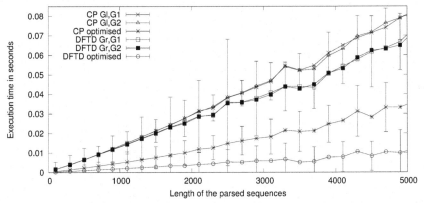

Fig. 1. Parsing time as a function of sequence length: each point is the mean parsing time for sequences with length ±100 around the value of the x-axis. Only a subset of the standard deviations bars were plotted to keep the graph readable. Times for sequences lengths greater than 5000 were removed because less than 20 sequences were available for each mean. The results of the CP with G_r gaps were removed due to their large running time.

Considering non optimised versions of the parsers, the CP with left-recursive gaps and the DFTDP with right-recursive gaps have similar running times. For the CP, the unlimited gap implementation has a strong affect on running time, confirming the recommendation of Section 4.3 to use left-recursive gaps. For both parsers, important improvments have been obtained by using the modifications described in Section 3.3 and 4.3 (speeding up the parsers by a factor larger than 6 for the DFTDP and 2 for the CP).

For all but one of the patterns, the experiments do not show any significative difference between the linear and the quadratic gap implementations. The exception is the pattern PDOC00354: `<x(10,115)[DENF][ST][LIVMF][LIVSTEQ]Vx[AGP][STANEQPK]`. This pattern comprises a limited gap with range 105, followed by alternative choices for each position. The differences between this pattern and

other PROSITE patterns are the position of the gap (at the beginning of the pattern) and its large range. This led to an important impact on the running time depending on the limited gap implementation. The DFTDP with linear gap had to be stopped on this pattern after 24 hours, showing the exponential blow-up predicted in Section 3.2. As a consequence, mean running times on this pattern have been separated from the 499 remaining in the last column of Table 1. From this column we see that, as predicted in Sections 3.2 and 4.2, using the quadratic gap implementation leads to better running times for all parsers, despite the fact that the grammar is described with more symbols.

5.2   Parsing DNA Grammars and Sequences

This subsection compares parsing times for DNA grammars. These grammars represent more elaborate concepts than those of PROSITE.

Data: Different formalisms exist to represent patterns in DNA or RNA sequences, the one proposed by PATSCAN [6] has been widely used by the DNA/ RNA modeling community. A collection of such patterns can be found on the UTRSITE[5] [13] which gives patterns modelling untranslated 3' and 5' regions of eukariotic mRNAs. This database is used to evaluate our approach for different reasons: (1) it is one of the rare places where a collection of patterns can be found, (2) the high degree of variation in the patterns gives rise to a wide variety of grammars providing a thorough test of the parsers, and (3) the patterns can generally be translated without too much difficulty into context-free grammars. The parsed sequences have been taken from UTRDB[6], the sequence database of UTRs associated with UTRSITE.

Experimental setting: PATSCAN patterns of UTRSITE were translated into a CFG[7]. Then, we randomly sampled 5000 sequences from the UTRDB database[8]. Finally we parsed the 5000 sequences in each CFG using those parsers which had a reasonable execution time on PROSITE patterns: DFTDP optimised, DFTDP with quadratic limited gaps, CP optimised, CP with left-recursive gaps and with either linear or quadratic limited gaps.

Results: Execution times for the different algorithms are given in Table 2.

The DFTDP had to be stopped for several grammars after running more than 24h to parse the 5000 sequences. A possible explanation of this is that there was an exponential blow-up for this parser due to features of PATSCAN patterns that were not present in PROSITE ones. This shows that the DFTDP is not adequate

---

[5] http://www2.ba.itb.cnr.it/UTRSite/

[6] http://www.ba.itb.cnr.it/srs7bin/cgi-bin/wgetz?-page+top

[7] An exact translation was not possible in all cases, so we sometimes modified the patterns to obtain a slightly more general form that could be translated. We also removed some patterns that were "too simple", for example if the pattern was just a subword to be found in the sequence. Also, as we do not study here parsing with error-correcting, error limits were removed.

[8] Because some of the sequences in the database are very short (some are only one nucleic acid), we considered only sequences of length larger than 100.

Table 2. Mean execution times per sequence on the 20 patterns of UTRDB.

Experiment		Mean	Standard
Algo.	Gaps	time	deviation
CP	G_l, G_1	40.3ms	423ms
CP	G_l, G_2	40.7ms	429ms
CP	optimised	27.8ms	321ms
DFTDP	G_r, G_2 [*]	832s	2.63s
DFTDP	optimised [*]	940s	2.84s

For experiments with the [*] symbol, 4 executions were stopped after running 24 hours.

to parse complex biological grammars (even if the results of Subsection 5.1 on simple grammars were very good).

The optimised version of the DFTDP was even slower than the one using G_r and $G_{2,lo,up}$ gaps. A likely explanation is based on the number $\mathcal{Z}$ of executions of line 2 of algorithm 2. A blow-up implies $\mathcal{Z}$ to be exponential in the pattern size, if the encountered nonterminals at line 2 are not often gaps, this line brings few speed-up while spending an amount of ressources proportional to $\mathcal{Z}$ (i.e., exponential) to be evaluated.

The CP, on the other hand, showed a very stable behaviour: even if it is slower than the DFTDP for simple grammars, it seems more suitable for complex ones. We also see that the optimisations we added to the CP can be useful but are not needed if a grammar contains well designed gap rules.

6 Conclusion

We have studied two context-free grammar parsing algorithms. We have shown that for both the original and optimised versions of parsers, the CP is faster with respect to experimental data than the DFTDP. Indeed, even if the DFTDP can run much faster than the chart parser on simple biological grammars, its complexity increases drastically when provided with more complex grammars.

For algorithms not optimized to manage gaps, both our theoretical study of complexity, and our empirical study conclude that rules representing gaps have to be carefully choosen such as to obtain reasonable parsing times. On the other hand, when optimised algorithms can be implemented, an interesting speed-up can be achieved: between a factor of $\frac{4}{3}$ to 6 depending on both the considered algorithms and data.

References

1. Chomsky, N.: Three models for the description of language. IRE Trans. on Information Theory **2** (1956)
2. Searls, D.B.: The linguistics of DNA. American Scientist **80** (1992) 579–591
3. Falquet, L. *et multi al..*: Protein data bank. Nucleic Acid Research **30** (2002) 235–238

4. Pereira, F., Warren, D.H.D.: Definite clause grammars for language analysis – a survey of the formalism and a comparison with augmented transition networks. Artificial Intelligence **13** (1980) 231–278
5. Searls, D.B.: String variable grammar: A logic grammar formalism for the biological language of DNA. Journal of logic Programming **12** (1993)
6. Dsouza, M., Larsen, N., Overbeek, R.: Searching for patterns in genomic data. Trends in Genetics **13** (1997) 497–498
7. Leung, S.w., Mellish, C., Robertson, D.: Basic Gene Grammars and DNA-ChartParser for language processing of Escherichia coli promoter DNA sequences. Bioinformatics **17** (2001) 226–236
8. Grune, D., Jacobs, C.J.: Parsing techniques – a practical guide. Ellis Horwood, Chichester, England (1990)
9. Gazdar, G., Mellish, C.: Natural Language Processing in Prolog. Addison Wesley (1989)
10. Aycock, J., Horspool, R.N.: Practical Earley parsing. The Computer Journal **45** (2002)
11. Jay, E.: An efficient context-free parsing algorithm. Commun. ACM **13** (1970) 94–102
12. Apweiler, R. *et multi al..*: UniProt: the universal protein knowledgebase. Nucl. Acids Res. **32** (2004) D115–119
13. Pesole, G., Liuni, S.: Internet resources for the functional analysis of 5' and 3' untranslated regions of eukaryotic mRNA. Trends in Genetics **15** (1999) 378

Proofs of Properties

Properties on the DFTDP

For properties 1 and 2, we denote by $|\text{DFTDP}(v, \alpha)|$ the number of DFTDP calls realised when executing the call $\text{DFTDP}(v, \alpha)$.

Property 1. The call of $\text{DFTDP}(u, G_r b)$, with $b \in \mathcal{T}$, $u[|u| - 1] \neq b$, generates a number of recursive DFTDP calls linear in $|u|$.

Proof. We consider the value of $|\text{DFTDP}(u, G_r b)|$ and proceed by induction. The base case is: $|\text{DFTDP}(\epsilon, G_r b)| = |\mathcal{T}| + 3$. Indeed:

$$
\begin{aligned}
|\text{DFTDP}(\epsilon, G_r b)| &= 1 + & |\text{DFTDP}(\epsilon, X G_r b)| & + |\text{DFTDP}(\epsilon, b)| \\
&= 1 + & |\text{DFTDP}(\epsilon, X G_r b)| & + 1 \\
&= 1 + 1 + \Sigma_{t \in \mathcal{T}} |\text{DFTDP}(\epsilon, t G_r b)| & + 1 & = |\mathcal{T}| + 3
\end{aligned}
$$

The induction step with $a \in \mathcal{T}$ is: $|\text{DFTDP}(au, G_r b)| = |\mathcal{T}| + 2 + |\text{DFTDP}(u, G_r b)| + |\text{DFTDP}(au, b)|$. Indeed:

$$
\begin{aligned}
|\text{DFTDP}(au, G_r b)| &= 1 + & |\text{DFTDP}(au, X G_r b)| & + |\text{DFTDP}(au, b)| \\
&= 1 + & (1 + \Sigma_{t \in |\mathcal{T}|} |\text{DFTDP}(au, t G_r b)|) & + |\text{DFTDP}(au, b)| \\
&= 1 + & (1 + |\text{DFTDP}(au, a G_r b)| + |\mathcal{T}| - 1) & + |\text{DFTDP}(au, b)| \\
&= 1 + & (1 + 1 + |\text{DFTDP}(u, G_r b)| + |\mathcal{T}| - 1) & + |\text{DFTDP}(au, b)|
\end{aligned}
$$

We have $|\text{DFTDP}(au, b)| = 1$ if $a \neq b$ and $|\text{DFTDP}(au, b)| = 1 + |\text{DFTDP}(u, \epsilon)| = 2$ if $a = b$. The induction step stays valid because the call $\text{DFTDP}(\epsilon, \epsilon)$ will never be considered due to the condition $u[|u| - 1] \neq b$ (the algorithm will not stop because of the condition of line 2, implying that all considered calls will be executed). Therefore, we have the following recursive equation:

$$\begin{cases} |\text{DFTDP}(\epsilon, G_r b)| = |T| + 3 \\ |\text{DFTDP}(au, G_r b)| = |T| + 2 + |\text{DFTDP}(u, G_r b)| + |\text{DFTDP}(au, b)| \end{cases}$$

which admit as solution:

$|\text{DFTDP}(u, G_r b)| = |T| + 3 + \Sigma_{1 \leq i \leq |u|}(|T| + 2 + |\text{DFTDP}(u, b)|)$
$= |T| + 3 + |u|(|T| + 2) + \Sigma_{1 \leq i \leq |u|}|\text{DFTDP}(u, b)|$
$= |T| + 3 + |u|(|T| + 2) + |u| + 1 + K$ where K is the number of letters equal to b in u
$= (|u| + 1)(|T| + 3) + K.$ □

Property 2. The call $\text{DFTDP}(u, G_{1,lo,up})$ (resp. $\text{DFTDP}(u, G_{2,lo,up})$), with $|u| > ra$ generates a number of recursive DFTDP calls linear in lo and non-polynomial (resp. quadratic) in $ra = up - lo$.

Proof. We first consider the calls $\text{DFTDP}(u, G_{1,lo,up})$ (resp. $\text{DFTDP}(u, G_{2,lo,up})$) generates a linear number of calls in function of lo, and then calls $\text{DFTDP}(u, G'_{1,ra})$ (resp. $\text{DFTDP}(u, G'_{2,ra})$), where the quadratic (resp. non-polynomial) complexity is observed. Depending on the gap implementation, let $G_{lo,up}$ denote $G_{1,lo,up}$ or $G_{2,lo,up}$, and G'_{ra} denote $G'_{1,ra}$ or $G'_{2,ra}$.

Call $\text{DFTDP}(u, G_{lo,up})$:

We have: $|\text{DFTDP}(u, G_{lo,up})| = 1 + \text{DFTDP}(u, X^{lo}G'_{ra})$ (rule $G_{lo,up} \rightarrow X^{lo}G'_{ra}$, and line 3 of algorithm 1). We show by induction that: $\text{DFTDP}(u, X^{lo}G'_{ra}) = (|T|+1)* lo + |\text{DFTDP}(u, X^{lo}G'_{ra})|$. The base case is: $|\text{DFTDP}(u, X^0 G'_{ra})| = |\text{DFTDP}(u, G'_{ra})|$. For $lo > 0$, the induction step is:

$|\text{DFTDP}(au, X^{lo}G'_{ra})| = 1 + \Sigma_{t \in T}|\text{DFTDP}(au, tX^{lo-1})|$
$= 1 + |T| - 1 + |\text{DFTDP}(au, aX^{lo-1})| = |T| + 1 + |\text{DFTDP}(u, X^{lo-1})|$

From the base case and the induction step, we have for $lo \geq 0$:

$|\text{DFTDP}(au, X^{lo}G'_{ra})| = |\text{DFTDP}(u, G'_{ra})| + \Sigma_{1 \leq i \leq lo}|T| + 1$
$= |\text{DFTDP}(u, G'_{ra})| + lo * (|T| + 1).$

We now consider separately the proof for the linear and quadratic gap implementation.

Call $\text{DFTDP}(u, G'_{1,ra})$:

We have $|\text{DFTDP}(u, G'_{1,ra})| = 1 + |\text{DFTDP}(u, X^{ra}_e)|$ (rule $G'_{1,ra} \rightarrow X^r_e$, line 3 of Algorithm 1).

We consider the value of $|\text{DFTDP}(u, X^{ra}_e)|$ and proceed by induction. The base case is: $|\text{DFTDP}(u, X^0_e)| = |\text{DFTDP}(u, \epsilon)| = 1$ due to line 2 of Algorithm 1. For $ra > 0$, the induction step is:

$|\text{DFTDP}(au, X_e^{ra})| = 1 + |\text{DFTDP}(au, XX_e^{ra-1})| + |\text{DFTDP}(au, X_e^{ra-1})|$
$= 1 + (1 + \Sigma_{t \in T}|\text{DFTDP}(au, tX_e^{ra-1})|) + |\text{DFTDP}(au, X_e^{ra-1})|$
$= 1 + (1 + |\text{DFTDP}(au, aX_e^{ra-1})| + |T| - 1) + |\text{DFTDP}(au, X_e^{ra-1})|$
$= 1 + (1 + 1 + |\text{DFTDP}(u, X_e^{ra-1})| + |T| - 1) + |\text{DFTDP}(au, X_e^{ra-1})|$
$= 2 + |T| + |\text{DFTDP}(u, X_e^{ra-1})| + |\text{DFTDP}(au, X_e^{ra-1})|$

We have $|\text{DFTDP}(u, X_e^{ra-1})| = |\text{DFTDP}(au, X_e^{ra-1})|$ due to the condition $|u| > ra$ and therefore: $|\text{DFTDP}(au, X_e^{ra})| = 2 + |T| + 2|\text{DFTDP}(u, X_e^{ra-1})|$

As $\forall i \geq 1$, $|\text{DFTDP}(u, X_e^{ra})| > f(|u|)$, where $f(0) = 1$ and $\forall i > 0$, $f(i) = 2f(i-1) = 2^i$, $|\text{DFTDP}(u, X_e^{ra})| > f(|u|)$ is not polynomial in i.

Call $\text{DFTDP}(u, G'_{2,ra})$:

We have $|\text{DFTDP}(u, G'_{2,ra})| = 1 + \Sigma_{0 \leq j \leq ra}|\text{DFTDP}(u, X^j)|$.

We consider the value of $|\text{DFTDP}(u, X^j)|$ ($\forall j \geq 0$) and proceed by induction. The base case is:$|\text{DFTDP}(u, X^0)| = |\text{DFTDP}(u, \epsilon)| = 1$ due to line 2 of Algorithm 1. The induction step is for $j > 0$:

$|\text{DFTDP}(au, X^j)| = 1 + \Sigma_{t \in T}|\text{DFTDP}(au, tX^{j-1})|$
$= 1 + |\text{DFTDP}(au, aX^{j-1})| + |T| - 1 = 1 + 1 + |\text{DFTDP}(u, X^{j-1})| + |T| - 1$
$= |T| + 1 + |\text{DFTDP}(u, X^{j-1})|$

From the base case and the induction step, we have $\forall j \geq 0$:

$|\text{DFTDP}(au, X^j)| = 1 + \Sigma_{1 \leq i \leq j}(|T| + 1) = 1 + j(|T| + 1)$

And therefore:

$|\text{DFTDP}(u, G'_{2,ra})| = 1 + \Sigma_{0 \leq j \leq ra}|\text{DFTDP}(u, X^j)| = 1 + \Sigma_{0 \leq j \leq ra}(1 + j(|T| + 1))$
$$= 1 + (ra + 1) + (|T| + 1) * \frac{ra(ra+1)}{2} \qquad \square$$

Proof of Property 3. We denotes by DFTDP' the algorithm 1 with modification of algorithm 2, and by G a gap nonterminal with bounds lo and up (with $lo = 0$ and $up = \infty$ if the gap is unlimited). The call $\text{DFTDP}'(u, Gb)$, with $b \in T$ and $u[|u| - 1] \neq b$ generates a number of recursive calls linear in $min(|u|, up) - lo$.

Proof. We consider the value of $|\text{DFTDP}'(u, Gb)|$. From line 4 of algorithm 2, this imply recursive calls of the form $|\text{DFTDP}'(u[i :], b)|$ for $i \in [lo, min(|u|, up)]$. Therefore:

$|\text{DFTDP}'(u, Gb)| = 1 + \Sigma_{i \in [lo, min(|u|, up)]}|\text{DFTDP}'(u[i :], b)|$
$\text{DFTDP}'(u[i :], b)$ calls imply a new call (and only one) iff $u[0] = b$, so if we denote by K the number of b in $u[lo : min(|u|, up) + 1]$, we have:
$|\text{DFTDP}'(u, Gb)| = 1 + (min(|u|, up) - lo) + K.$ $\qquad \square$

Properties on the CP

When evaluating the performances of the CP, we will not count items in *itemset* with X as left part neither those of the form $N \rightarrow \epsilon \bullet \epsilon @ i, j$. Indeed counting them would not realise a fair comparison between the gap implementations since optimisations of the CP exist that suppress (the vast majority of) these items from the *itemset*[9].

For the proofs of this section, we will use the following notations: The symbol G will represent $G = G_r$ when considering right-recursive gaps, $G = G_l$ when considering left-recursive gaps, $G = G'_{1,ra}$ for linear limited gaps and $G = \{G'_{2,ra}\}$ for quadratic limited gaps. For $l \in [0, |w|]$, let $\mathcal{P}_l = \{k \in [0, l] : \exists R \rightarrow \alpha \bullet G\beta@j, k \in itemset, R \neq G\}$, and $p_1 = \min(\mathcal{P}_{|w|} \cup \{|w| + 1\})$.

Intuitively, $\mathcal{P}_l$ is the set of positions in $w[0 : l+1]$ where an unlimited gap can be started, or where the range of a limited gap starts to influence the algorithm[10], and p_1 is the first of these positions for $w[0 : |w| + 1] = w$.

For these properties, we will also suppose that $S \notin Gaps)$, indeed, the case $S \in Gaps$ is not useful in practice (such grammars are too simple to be used in practice), and taking them into account complexify the proofs.

Proof of Property 4. In this subsection, for $l \in [0, |w|]$, the set of items in *itemset* with G as left part and ending at position l are denoted $\mathcal{I}_r(l)$ for right-recursive gaps and $\mathcal{I}_l(l)$ for left-recursive gaps.

Property 4 Suppose $S \neq G$, the number of items in *itemset* with G as left part is S'_r for right recursive gaps, and S'_l for left-recursive gaps with:

$S'_r = S'_l = 0$ iff $p_1 > |w|$
$S'_r = (1 - 5p_1/2 + p_1^2/2) + |w|(2.5 - p_1) + |w|^2/2$ and $S'_l \leq (2|w| + 1)|\mathcal{P}_{|w|}| \leq (2|w|^2 + |w|)|$ iff $p_1 \leq |w|$.

Proof. Let $l \in [0, |w|]$, from Lemma 1, *itemset* contains all and only items with ending position equal to l and with G as left part of rule that are present in the set $\mathcal{I}_r(l)$ for right-recursive gaps and $\mathcal{I}_l(l)$ for left-recursive gaps. The size of $\mathcal{I}_r(l)$ (resp. $\mathcal{I}_l(l)$) can be easily deduced from Lemma 1, we denote it $S_r(l)$ (resp. $S_l(l)$), with:

$$S_r(l) = \begin{cases} 2 + l - p_1 \text{ if } p_1 < l \\ 1 + l - p_1 \text{ if } p_1 = l \\ 0 \text{ if } p_1 > l \end{cases} \quad \text{and} \quad S_l(l) = \begin{cases} 2 * |\mathcal{P}_l| \text{ if } l \notin \mathcal{P}_l \\ 2 * |\mathcal{P}_l| + 1 \text{ if } l \in \mathcal{P}_l \end{cases}$$

If $p_1 = |w| + 1$, we have trivially $S'_r = S'_l = 0$, otherwise ($p_1 \leq |w| + 1$) we obtain values for S_r and S'_l by summing $S_r(l)$ and $S_r(l)$ for all possible l:

$$\begin{aligned} S'_r &= \Sigma_{l \in [0, |w|]} S_r(l) = \Sigma_{l \in [p_1, |w|]}(2 + l - p_1) - 1 \\ &= (1 - 5p_1/2 + p_1^2/2) + |w|(2.5 - p_1) + |w|^2/2 \\ S'_l &= \Sigma_{l \in [0, |w|]} S_l(l) = |\mathcal{P}_{|w|}| + \Sigma_{l \in [0, |w|]}(2 * |\mathcal{P}_l|) \\ \Rightarrow S'_l &\leq |\mathcal{P}_{|w|}| + 2 * |w| * |\mathcal{P}_{|w|}| \Rightarrow S'_l \leq |w| + 2 * |w|^2 \end{aligned} \qquad \square$$

---

[9] Optimisation known under the name of *look-ahead* implies that most items with X as left part do not have to be stored [8]; and an optimisation due to [10] implies that items of the form $N \rightarrow \epsilon \bullet \epsilon@i, j$ do not have to be stored either.

[10] For limited gaps, as the rules $G_{1,lo,up} \rightarrow X^{lo} G'_{1,up-lo}$ and $G_{2,lo,up} \rightarrow X^{lo} G'_{2,up-lo}$ are similar, they will not be useful to characterize the difference between the implementations, this is why we focus on rules $G'_{1,ra}$ and $G'_{2,ra}$.

Lemma 1. *Suppose $S \neq G$, then:*

$$\mathcal{I}_r(l) = \quad \{G_r \twoheadrightarrow \bullet X G_r @l, l : l \geq p_1\} \tag{r.1}$$
$$\cup \{G_r \twoheadrightarrow X \bullet G_r @l\text{-}1, l : l > p_1\} \tag{r.2}$$
$$\cup \{G_r \twoheadrightarrow X G_r \bullet @i, l : \; k \in \mathcal{P}_l, k \leq i < l\} \tag{r.3}$$

and

$$\mathcal{I}_l(l) = \quad \{G_l \twoheadrightarrow \bullet G_l X @l, l : \; l \in \mathcal{P}_l\} \tag{l.1}$$
$$\cup \{G_l \twoheadrightarrow G_l \bullet X @k, l : \; k \in \mathcal{P}_l\} \tag{l.2}$$
$$\cup \{G_l \twoheadrightarrow G_l X \bullet @k, l : \; k \in \mathcal{P}_l, k < l\} \tag{l.3}$$

Proof. We use equations 1 and 2 to show respectively that $G_l \twoheadrightarrow \bullet G_l X @i, l \in$ itemset $\wedge S \neq G_l$ is equivalent to $i = l \wedge l \in \mathcal{P}_l \wedge S \neq G_l$, and that $G_r \twoheadrightarrow \bullet X G_r @i, l \in$ itemset $\wedge S \neq G_l$ is equivalent to $i = l \wedge l \geq p_1 \wedge S \neq G_r$.

From this first step, which corresponds to the content of line respectively l.1 and r.1, we can show similar properties for lines r.2, r.3 and l.2, l.3. Due to space restrictions the full proof is not included in the paper.

Proof of Property 5. We use the following definitions in this subsection: let $\mathcal{I}_1(l, ra)$ be the set of items with $G'_{1,ra}$ or X_e as left part of rule and l as ending position present in *itemset*. Similarly, let $\mathcal{I}_2(l, ra)$ be the set of items with $G'_{2,ra}$ as left part of rule and l as ending position present in *itemset*.

Property 5 $|\mathcal{I}_1(l, ra)| > |\mathcal{I}_2(l, ra)| + 2ra$.

Proof. Lemma 2 shows which items are present in each of the $\mathcal{I}_1(l, ra)$ and $\mathcal{I}_2(l, ra)$ sets. From Lemma 2 equations, we can see that the part 4.1 of $\mathcal{I}_1$ is always larger than $\mathcal{I}_2$, and that parts 4.2 and 4.3 of $\mathcal{I}_1$ have size ra, showing that $|\mathcal{I}_1(l, ra)| > |\mathcal{I}_2(l, ra)| + 2ra$. □

Lemma 2. *The $\mathcal{I}_1(l, ra)$ and the $\mathcal{I}_2(l, ra)$ contents respects the following equations:*

$$\mathcal{I}_1(l, ra) \supseteq \{G'_{1,ra} \twoheadrightarrow X_e^{i+l-k} \bullet X_e^{ra-i-l+k} @k, l \; : \; k \in \mathcal{P}_l, i \in [0, ra+k-l]\} \tag{4.1}$$
$$\cup \{X_e \twoheadrightarrow \bullet X @l, l : \; k \in \mathcal{P}_l, \; l \in [k, k+ra[\} \tag{4.2}$$
$$\cup \{X_e \twoheadrightarrow X \bullet @l-1, l : \; k \in \mathcal{P}_l, \; l \in]k, k+ra]\} \tag{4.3}$$

And

$$\mathcal{I}_2(l, ra) = \{G \twoheadrightarrow X^{l-k} \bullet X^j @k, l \; : k \in \mathcal{P}_l, \; j \in [0, ra+k-l], \; l \neq k \vee j \neq 0\}.$$

Proof. For $\mathcal{I}_1(l, ra)$, the proof consists in first showing that $G'_{1,ra} \twoheadrightarrow X^j \bullet X_e^{ra-j} @k, l \in$ itemset $\wedge S \neq G'_{1,ra}$ is equivalent to $k \in \mathcal{P}_l \wedge i = k - l + j \wedge 0 \leq i \leq k - l + ra$ by using equations 1 and 2. Then it can be shown from this first result and some more use of equations 1 and 2 that this implies the presence of at least the items of line 4.2 and 4.3 (other items are the ones comming from different possible values for ra). For $\mathcal{I}_2(l, ra)$, the proof is:

$$\begin{cases} G'_{2,ra} \twoheadrightarrow X^i \bullet X^j @k, l \in itemset \\ S \neq G'_{2,ra} \end{cases} \Leftrightarrow \exists \gamma, \delta \in V^* \; : \begin{cases} X^i \twoheadrightarrow^* w[k, l] \\ S \twoheadrightarrow^* \gamma G'_{2,ra} \delta \\ \gamma \twoheadrightarrow^* w[0{:}k] \\ 0 < i + j \leq ra \\ S \neq G'_{2,ra} \end{cases}$$

$$\Leftrightarrow \begin{array}{l} \exists m \in \mathbb{N}, \\ \exists R \twoheadrightarrow \alpha G'_{2,ra}\beta \in \mathcal{R}, \\ \exists \gamma', \delta' \in \mathcal{V}^* \end{array} \quad : \begin{cases} i = l - k \\ S \twoheadrightarrow^* \gamma' R \delta' \rightarrow \gamma' \alpha G'_{2,ra} \beta \delta' \\ \gamma' \twoheadrightarrow^* w[0{:}m] \\ \alpha \twoheadrightarrow^* w[m{:}k] \\ 0 < i + j \leq ra \end{cases}$$

$$\Leftrightarrow \begin{array}{l} \exists m \in \mathbb{N}, \\ \exists R \twoheadrightarrow \alpha G'_{2,ra}\beta \in \mathcal{R} \end{array} \quad : \begin{cases} i = l - k \\ R \rightarrow \alpha \bullet \beta @ m, k \in itemset \\ -i < j \leq ra - i \end{cases}$$

$$\Leftrightarrow \begin{cases} i = l - k \\ k \in \mathcal{P}_l \\ -i < j \leq ra + k - l \end{cases} \Leftrightarrow \begin{cases} i = l - k \\ k \in \mathcal{P}_l \\ 0 \leq j \leq ra + k - l \\ i + j \neq 0 \end{cases} \Leftrightarrow \begin{cases} i = l - k \\ k \in \mathcal{P}_l \\ 0 \leq j \leq ra + k - l \\ l - k + j \neq 0 \end{cases}$$

$$\Leftrightarrow \begin{cases} i = l - k \\ k \in \mathcal{P}_l \\ 0 \leq j \leq ra + k - l \\ l \neq k \vee i \neq 0 \end{cases} \qquad\qquad \Box$$

A New Periodicity Lemma[*]

Kangmin Fan[1], William F. Smyth[1,2], and R.J. Simpson[3]

[1] Algorithms Research Group, Department of Computing & Software
McMaster University, Hamilton, Ontario, Canada L8S 4K1
fank@mcmaster.ca
www.cas.mcmaster.ca/cas/research/groups.shtml
[2] Department of Computing, Curtin University, GPO Box U1987
Perth WA 6845, Australia
smyth@computing.edu.au
[3] Department of Mathematics & Statistics, Curtin University
GPO Box U1987, Perth WA 6845, Australia
simpson@math.curtin.edu.au

Abstract. Given a string $x = x[1..n]$, a ***repetition*** of period p in x is a substring $u^r = x[i..i+rp-1]$, $p = |u|$, $r \geq 2$, where neither $u = x[i..i+p-1]$ nor $x[i..i+(r+1)p-1]$ is a repetition. The maximum number of repetitions in any string x is well known to be $\Theta(n \log n)$. A ***run*** or ***maximal periodicity*** of period p in x is a substring $u^r t = x[i..i+rp+|t|-1]$ of x, where u^r is a repetition, t a proper prefix of x, and no repetition of period p begins at position $i-1$ of x or ends at position $i+rp+|t|$. In 2000 Kolpakov and Kucherov showed that the maximum number $\rho(n)$ of runs in any string x is $O(n)$, but their proof was nonconstructive and provided no specific constant of proportionality. At the same time, they presented experimental data strongly suggesting that $\rho(n) < n$. In this paper, as a first step toward proving this conjecture, we present a periodicity lemma that establishes limitations on the number of squares, and their periods, that can occur over a specified range of positions in x. We then apply this result to specify corresponding limitations on the occurrence of runs.

1 Introduction

The study of strings began with an investigation of periodicity properties [15], and periodicity of various kinds still remains today a central theme, important both in theory and practice – for example, in data compression, pattern-matching, computational biology, and many other areas. In this paper we present results that specify restrictions on the nature and extent of periodic behaviour in strings. Although these results are theoretical, their importance is very much a product of their practical application, as we explain below.

It will be convenient throughout to represent strings in boldface (for example, $x = x[1..n]$) and their lengths in italics (for example, $x = |x|$).

[*] The work of the first and second authors was supported in part by grants from the Natural Sciences & Engineering Research Council of Canada.

A. Apostolico, M. Crochemore, and K. Park (Eds.): CPM 2005, LNCS 3537, pp. 257–265, 2005.
© Springer-Verlag Berlin Heidelberg 2005

A *repetition* in x is a substring $u^r = x[i..i+ru-1]$, $r \geq 2$, where neither $x[i..i+u-1]$ nor $x[i..i+(r+1)u-1]$ is a repetition. We call u the *generator* and u the *period* of the repetition, and we represent it economically by an integer triple (i, u, r). In the early 1980s three quite different $O(x \log x)$ algorithms were published [1, 2, 12] for the computation of all the repetitions in a given string x. In a sense these algorithms were all asymptotically optimal, since in [2] it was shown that in fact a Fibonacci string f_n contains $\Theta(f_n \log f_n)$ repetitions.

In [11] a more compact encoding of repetitions was introduced: a *run* or *maximal periodicity* of period u in x is a substring $u^r t = x[i..i+ru+t-1]$ of x, where u^r is a repetition, t a proper prefix of u, and no repetition of period u begins at position $i-1$ of x or ends at position $i+ru+t$. u is called the *generator* of the run, t its *tail*, and a run is economically represented by a 4-tuple (i, u, r, t). Computing all the runs in x permits all the repetitions in x to be listed in an obvious way. Main [11] showed how to compute all the "leftmost" runs in x in time $\Theta(x)$, provided that the suffix tree [13, 16] and the Lempel-Ziv factorization [9] of x were both available. In [3] it was shown that a suffix tree could be computed in linear time on an *indexed* (bounded integer) alphabet; since the LZ factorization is computable in linear time from the suffix tree, this meant that the overall worst-case time requirement of Main's algorithm was $\Theta(x)$ on an indexed alphabet. In [8] Kolpakov & Kucherov took matters a step further by extending Main's algorithm to also compute non-leftmost runs in x in time proportional to their number, and then by showing that the maximum number $\rho(x)$ of runs in any string x was at most

$$k_1 x - k_2 \log_2 x \sqrt{x}, \tag{1}$$

where k_1 and k_2 are positive constants. Thus, at least in principle, all the runs in x could be determined in linear time.

However, there is a problem with (1): the proof is nonconstructive and gives no information about the magnitude of the constants k_1 and k_2. Nevertheless Kolpakov & Kucherov provide convincing experimental evidence that

* $\rho(x) < x$;
* $\rho(x)$ is achieved by a cube-free string x on alphabet $\{a, b\}$;
* $\rho(x + 1) \leq \rho(x) + 2$.

As far as we know, the only published work that addresses these fundamental questions of periodicity is [5], where an infinite family of strings x is constructed that is conjectured for sufficiently large x to achieve $\rho(x) < x$.

In order to show that in general $\rho(x) < x$, it seems to be necessary to establish restrictions on the number of runs that can occur near a position in x at which one or two runs are already known to occur. Perhaps the most famous theoretical result available for such a purpose is the "periodicity lemma":

Lemma 1 [4] *Let p and q be two periods of x, and let $d = \gcd(p, q)$. If $p+q \leq x+d$, then d is also a period of x.* □

Unfortunately this lemma provides no special information about runs, or the squares with which runs must begin, and it places no restrictions on the positions at which periodic substrings may occur. To our knowledge the only result that provides such information is the following:

Lemma 2 [10, Lemma 8.1.14] *Let u^2 be a repetition, and suppose $w \neq u^k$ for any $k \geq 1$. If u^2 is a prefix of w^2, in turn a proper prefix of v^2, then $u+w \leq v$.*

Our main result in this paper is essentially a generalization of this result, that we call a "new periodicity lemma".

2   New Periodicity Lemma

In this section we prove results that establish restrictions on the squares that can occur in the neighbourhood of positions in a string at which one or two squares already appear. We begin with two simple definitions:

Definition 3 *A square u^2 is said to be **irreducible** if u is not a repetition.*

Definition 4 *A square u^2 is said to be **minimal** if no proper prefix of u^2 is a square.*

Lemma 5 *If u^2 is minimal, then u^2 is irreducible.*

Proof. By Definition 4, no proper prefix of u^2 is a square; thus, in particular, no prefix of u is a square. Therefore u cannot be a repetition, and so by Definition 3 u^2 is irreducible.   □

The existence of a minimal square already imposes significant limitations on the nature of other squares that can exist, as the following result shows:

Lemma 6 *If $x = u^2$ is minimal, then for all integers $k \geq 0$ and $w \in u/2..u-1$:*

(a) *if*

$$k + w \leq u, \quad k+3w \geq 2u, \tag{2}$$

$x[k+1..k+2w]$ *is not a square;*
(b) *if*

$$k + w > u, \quad k+2w \leq 2u, \tag{3}$$

either $x[k+1..k+2w]$ *is not a square* **or** $x[w'+1..w'+u]$ *has period $u-w$, where*

$$w' = (k+w)-u. \quad □$$

Proof. Suppose that for some pair of integers k and w satisfying either (2) or (3), $x[k+1..k+2w] = w^2$.

First assume that $k = 0$. Then if (2) holds, either $w = u$, a contradiction, or else $w < u$, contradicting the minimality of u^2. On the other hand, if (3) holds, then both $w > u$ and $w \leq u$ must hold, again a contradiction. Thus we can assume that $k \geq 1$.

(a) Suppose that (2) holds, let $w' = u-(k+w)$, and consider

$$\widehat{w} = x[1..w-w'] = x[k+w'+1..k+w].$$

Since by (2)

$$(w-w') - (k+w') = k+3w-2u \geq 0,$$

the substring $x[1..k+w]$ has period $k+w'$. Again by (2),

$$(k+w) - 2(k+w') = (k+w) - 2(u-w) \geq 0,$$

so that $x[1..k+w]$ has prefix $\big(x[1..k+w']\big)^2$, contradicting the minimality of u^2. Thus in case (a) no such k and w can exist.

(b) Next we suppose that (3) holds, so that $w < u$, hence that $k-w' = u-w > 0$. Consider

$$w = x[w'+1..w'+w] = x[k+1..u+w'].$$

Since by (3) $w'+w = k+(2w-u) \geq k$, the substring $x[w'+1..w'+u]$ of length u has period $k-w' = u-w$, as required.   □

To show that in case (a) of Lemma 6 the assumption that $k+3w \geq 2u$ (as well as the weaker condition $w \geq u/2$) is necessary, consider the example $u = 14, k = 6, w = 5$:

$$x = u^2 = abbaba(babab)(bab\|ab)(babab)ababbab.$$

Here $w = babab$ and w^3 is a substring of x.

To show that in case (b) of Lemma 6 the substring w^2 can in fact exist, consider the example $u = 11, k = 4, w = 8$ with $w' = 1$:

$$x = u^2 = babc(abcabca\|b)(abcabcab)ca.$$

The substring $x[2..12] = (abc)^3 ab$ has period $u-w = 3$.

We turn now to the situation in which a minimal square and an irreducible square occur at the same position. We first prove two basic lemmas that describe the relationship between minimality and irreducibility, then go on to prove our main result.

Lemma 7 *If v^2 is irreducible with minimal proper prefix u^2, then*

$$v > \max\{u+1, 3u/2\}.$$

Proof. Observe that $1 \leq u < v$, and observe further that $u+1 \geq 3u/2$ if and only if $u \leq 2$.

For $u = 1$, $u^2 = \lambda^2$ for some letter λ and the shortest irreducible square $v^2 = (\lambda^2\mu)^2$ for some letter $\mu \neq \lambda$. Thus for $u = 1$, $v \geq 3 > u+1$, as required.

For $u = 2$, since u^2 is minimal, $u^2 = (\lambda\mu)^2$ and the shortest irreducible square $v^2 = (\lambda\mu\lambda\mu\nu)^2$ for some letter ν. Thus for $u = 2$, $v \geq 5 > u+1$, as required.

Suppose therefore that $u \geq 3$, and suppose further, without loss of generality, that $v < 2u$. Then

$$v = uu[1..v-u] = u[v-u+1..u]v[2u-v+1..v],$$

where $y = u[1..v-u]$ of length $v-u$ is a prefix of u, hence of v, and $z = u[v-u+1..u]$ of length $2u-v$ is a prefix of v, hence of u. If now we assume $2v \leq 3u$, it follows that $v-u \leq 2u-v$, so that y is also a prefix of z. Thus u has prefix y^2 and so u^2 cannot be minimal, a contradiction. We conclude that $2v > 3u$, as required. □

Lemma 8 *If $x = v^2$ is irreducible with minimal proper prefix u^2, $v < 2u$, then*

$$x = u_1 u_2 u_1 u_1 u_2 u_1 u_2 u_1 u_1 u_2,$$

where $u_1 = 2u-v, u_2 = 2v-3u$.

Proof. Since $v < 2u$, $u \geq 3$ by Lemma 7. Since $u_1+u_2 = v-u < u$, u has proper prefix $u_1 u_2$. Since $u-(v-u) = 2u-v = u_1$, $u = u_1 u_2 u_1$. Since $v = uu[1..v-u] = uu_1 u_2$, the result follows. □

For the proof of our main result, the following definitions are helpful. A substring of a given string x is said to be ***internal*** if and only if it is neither a prefix nor a suffix of x. And if $x = x_1 x_2$, x_2 nonempty, then $x_2 x_1 = R_{x_1}(x)$ is said to be the x_1^{th} ***rotation*** of x.

We also make use of the following two well-known results::

Lemma 9 [14, p. 76] *Let x be a string of length n and minimum period p, and let $j \in 1..n-1$ be an integer. Then $R_j(x) = x$ if and only if x is a repetition and p divides j.* □

Lemma 10 [14, p. 76] *Let x be a string of length at least 3. If x is a repetition, then so is every rotation of x.* □

Lemma 11 (NPL) *If x has minimal prefix u^2 and irreducible prefix v^2, $u < v < 2u$, then for every $w \in u+1..v-1$ and for every $k \in 0..v-u-1$, $x[k+1..k+2w]$ is not a square.*

Proof. Suppose that for $0 \leq k < v-u$ and $u < w < v$, $w^2 = x[k+1..k+2w]$. For $k = 0$, Lemma 2 requires that $u+w \leq v$, hence that $2u < v$, a contradiction. Thus the lemma holds for $k = 0$, and so we assume $k \geq 1$. Making use of the notation of Lemma 8, we consider two main cases:

I $1 \leq k < u_1$ (k small)

Since $k+1 < u_1+1$ and $k+w \geq u+2 = 2u_1+u_2+2$, therefore $u_2 u_1 = x[u_1+1..2u_1+u_2]$ is an internal substring of $w = x[k+1..k+w]$. Then

$$u_2 u_1 = x[u_1+1+w..2u_1+u_2+w]$$

is also an internal substring of $w = x[k+1+w..k+2w]$. Further, since

$$u_1+1+w > u_1+1+u = 3u_1+u_2+1,$$
$$2u_1+u_2+w < 2u_1+u_2+v = 5u_1+3u_2,$$

therefore $u_2 u_1$ is an internal substring of $x[3u_1+u_2+1..5u_1+3u_2] = (u_2 u_1)^2$. Thus $u_2 u_1 = R_j(u_2 u_1)$ for some $j > 0$, and so by Lemma 9 $u_2 u_1$ is a repetition. Then by Lemma 10 $u_1 u_2$ is a repetition, contradicting the minimality of u^2. Hence $k \notin 1..u_1-1$.

II $u_1 \le k < v-u$ (k large)

This case divides into two subcases:

II.1 $k+w \ge v$ ($k+w$ large)

Observe that now $w_1 = x[k+1..k+w]$ must have prefix $R_{k-u_1}(u_2 u_1^2)$, while $w_2 = x[k+1+w..k+2w]$ must have prefix $R_j(u_2 u_1^2)$ for some j. In order that j should equal $k-u_1$, the beginning of w_2 would have to be offset by v from the beginning of w_1, implying that $w = v$, an impossibility. Therefore $j \ne k-u_1$.

We conclude that w has a prefix equal to two distinct rotations of $u_2 u_1^2$, so that by Lemma 9, $R_j(u_2 u_1^2)$ is a repetition. Hence by Lemma 10 so also is $u = u_1 u_2 u_1$, contradicting the minimality of u^2. Thus this subcase is impossible.

II.2 $k+w \le v-1$ ($k+w$ small)

Since $k \ge u_1$ and $w \ge u+1$, we may assume from now on that

$$u+u_1+1 \le k+w \le v-1. \tag{4}$$

Again we must divide into subcases:

II.2.1 $k+2w \ge u+v$ ($k+2w$ large)

Since $w \le v-1$, II.2 implies that

$$k+2w \le 2v-u_1-2,$$

so that $w_2 = x[k+1+w..k+2w]$ must have suffix $R_{j_2}(u_2 u_1^2)$ for some $j_2 \in 0..u_1+u_2$. At the same time, (4) implies that $w_1 = x[k+1..k+w]$ must have suffix $R_{j_1}(u_2 u_1^2)$ for some $j_1 \in 1..u_2-1$.

Suppose $j_1 = j_2$. Then since w_1 terminates at some position in the second occurrence of u_2 in x, so also must w_2 terminate at the same position in the fourth occurrence of u_2 in x. But this again requires that $w = v$, contradicting the assumption that $w \leq v-1$.

Hence $j_1 \neq j_2$ and so w has a suffix that is two distinct rotations of $u_2 u_1{}^2$. Again using Lemma 9 and Lemma 10, we argue that $u = u_1 u_2 u_1$ is a repetition, contradicting the minimality of u^2. Thus II.2.1 is impossible.

II.2.2 $k+2w < u+v$ $(k+2w$ small)

By (4) we can write

$$w_1 = u_2[k-u_1+1..u_2]u_1u_1u_2[1..K],$$

where $k-u_1+1 \leq K \leq u_2-1$. Setting

$$z = w[1..z] = u_2[k-u_1+1..K],$$

we may write $w = u+z$, where

$$z = K-(k-u_1). \tag{5}$$

Observe that w_1 has prefix $y = u_2[k-u_1+1..u_2]u_1$ of length $y = u-k$ that must also be a prefix of

$$w_2 = x[u+u_1+K+1..u+u_1+K+w].$$

Thus y has border $u_2[K+1..u_2]u_1$ of length u_1+u_2-K and therefore period

$$(u-k) - (u_1+u_2-K) = z.$$

Hence for some integer $q \geq 1$ and some proper prefix z^* of z,

$$w = w_1 = z^q z^* t \tag{6}$$
$$= w_2 = z^{q-1} z^* u_2[1..z]t, \tag{7}$$

where $u_2[1..z] = R_j(z)$ for some $j \in 0..z-1$, and because of (6),

$$t = u_1 u_2[1..K],$$

while as a consequence of (7),

$$t = u_2[z+1..z+u_1+K], \quad z+u_1+K \leq u_2;$$
$$= u_2[z+1..u_2]u_1[1..z+u_1+K-u_2], \quad \text{otherwise.}$$

Thus t is a border of $x_1 = x[v+1..k+2w] = x[1..k+2w-v]$, so that x_1-t is a period of x_1. Since $x_1 = k+2w-v = u_1+z+t$, it follows that u_1+z is a period of x_1. In other words, x has a prefix of length u_1+z+t of period u_1+z. Since

$$(u_1+z+t) - 2(u_1+z) = (u_1+K) - (u_1+z)$$
$$= K-z$$
$$= k-u_1, \quad \text{by (5)}$$
$$\geq 0, \quad \text{by II}$$

we conclude that x has prefix s^2, where $s = u_1u_2[1..z]$, in contradiction to the minimality of u^2. Therefore II.2.2 also is impossible. □

We can state an equivalent of Lemma 11 for runs. Observe first that by definition every run is irreducible. Observe also that if a run of period u and tail t occurs at position i in x, no run of the same period can occur at any position $j \in i..i+u+t$. Thus, if we define a **minimal run** to be a run of generator u where u^2 is a minimal square, we can state

Lemma 12 *Suppose x has a minimal run of period u as prefix and another run of period $v < 2u$ as prefix. Then for every positive integer $k < v-u$ and for every $w \in u..v$, no run of period w occurs at position $k+1$ of x.* □

3   Discussion

We have proved two main lemmas (6 and 11) that restrict the periods w of squares that can occur at positions $i+k$ in x when at position i either one (Lemma 6) or two (Lemma 11) squares are known to occur. It seems that, with the exception of [10, Lemma 8.1.14], such properties have not previously been studied. In particular, we hope that with the help of Lemma 11, it will be possible to establish, or at least make progress with, the three conjectures arising out of [8].

The Main/Kolpakov-Kucherov algorithm [8, 11] is the only known linear-time algorithm for computing all the runs in a given string x. It is complex and, until recently, depended for its worst-case linear behaviour on the use of Farach's algorithm [3], also complex and not space-efficient, for linear-time computation of suffix trees. Since 2003 two worst-case linear-time suffix array construction algorithms [6, 7] have been available for use in the computation of the LZ factorization, but even after the substitution of suffix arrays for suffix trees in the all-runs algorithm, significant complications remain. We expect that, with a more precise understanding of the periodicity of runs, it will become possible to design simpler algorithms that will compute all the runs in a string in a more direct and more space-efficient manner.

References

1. Alberto Apostolico & Franco P. Preparata, **Optimal off-line detection of repetitions in a string**, *Theoret. Comput. Sci. 22* (1983) 297–315.

2. Maxime Crochemore, **An optimal algorithm for computing the repetitions in a word**, *Inform. Process. Lett. 12–5* (1981) 244–250.
3. Martin Farach, **Optimal suffix tree construction with large alphabets**, *Proc.* 38th *IEEE Symp. Found. Computer Science* (1997) 137–143.
4. N. J. Fine & Herbert S. Wilf, **Uniqueness theorems for periodic functions**, *Proc. Amer. Math. Soc. 16* (1965) 109–114.
5. Frantisek Franek, R. J. Simpson & W. F. Smyth, **The maximum number of runs in a string**, *Proc.* 14th *Australasian Workshop on Combinatorial Algorithms*, Mirka Miller & Kunsoo Park (eds.) (2003) 26–35.
6. Juha Kärkkäinen & Peter Sanders, **Simple linear work suffix array construction**, *Proc.* 30th *Internat. Colloq. Automata, Languages & Programming* (2003) 943–955.
7. Pang Ko & Srinivas Aluru, **Space efficient linear time construction of suffix arrays**, *Proc.* 14th *Annual Symp. Combinatorial Pattern Matching*, R. Baeza-Yates, E. Chávez & M. Crochemore (eds.), LNCS 2676, Springer-Verlag (2003) 200–210.
8. Roman Kolpakov & Gregory Kucherov, **On maximal repetitions in words**, *J. Discrete Algs. 1* (2000) 159–186.
9. Abraham Lempel & Jacob Ziv, **On the complexity of finite sequences**, *IEEE Trans. Information Theory 22* (1976) 75–81.
10. M. Lothaire, *Algebraic Combinatorics on Words*, Cambridge University Press (2002) 504 pp.
11. Michael G. Main, **Detecting leftmost maximal periodicities**, *Discrete Applied Maths. 25* (1989) 145–153.
12. Michael G. Main & Richard J. Lorentz, **An $O(n \log n)$ algorithm for finding all repetitions in a string**, *J. Algs. 5* (1984) 422–432.
13. Edward M. McCreight, **A space-economical suffix tree construction algorithm**, *J. Assoc. Comput. Mach. 32–2* (1976) 262–272.
14. Bill Smyth, *Computing Patterns in Strings*, Pearson Addison-Wesley (2003) 423 pp.
15. Axel Thue, **Über unendliche zeichenreihen**, *Norske Vid. Selsk. Skr. I. Mat. Nat. Kl. Christiana 7* (1906) 1-22.
16. Peter Weiner, **Linear pattern matching algorithms**, *Proc. 14th Annual IEEE Symp. Switching & Automata Theory* (1973) 1–11.

Two Dimensional Parameterized Matching

Carmit Hazay[1], Moshe Lewenstein[1,*], and Dekel Tsur[2,**]

[1] Bar-Ilan University
{harelc,moshe}@cs.biu.ac.il
[2] University of California, San Diego
dtsur@cs.ucsd.edu

Abstract. Two equal length strings, or two equal sized two dimensional texts, *parameterize match (p-match)* if there is a one-one mapping (relative to the alphabet) of their characters. *Two dimensional parameterized matching* is the task of finding all $m \times m$ substrings of an $n \times n$ text that p-match to an $m \times m$ pattern. This models, for example, searching for color images with changing of color maps. We present an algorithm that solves the two dimensional parameterized matching problem in $O(n^2 + m^{2.5} \cdot \text{polylog}(m))$ time.

1 Introduction

Let S and S' be two equal length strings. We say that S and S' *parameterize match*, or *p-match* for short, if there is a bijection π from the alphabet of S to the alphabet of S' such that $S'[i] = \pi(S[i])$ for every index i. In the *parameterized matching problem*, introduced by Baker [9, 11], one is given a text T and pattern P and the goal is to find all the substrings of T of length $|P|$ that p-match to P. Baker introduced parameterized matching for applications that arise in software tools for analyzing source code. Other applications for parameterized matching arise in image processing and computational biology (see [2]).

In [9, 11], an optimal linear time algorithm was given for p-matching. However, it was assumed that the alphabet was of constant size. An optimal algorithm for p-matching in the presence of an unbounded size alphabet was given in [6]. In [10], a novel method was presented for parameterized matching by constructing *parameterized suffix trees*, which also allows for online p-matching. The parameterized suffix tree was further explored by Kosaraju [16] and faster constructions were given by Cole and Hariharan [12].

In [7], approximate parameterized matching was introduced and a solution for binary alphabets was given. In [15], an $O(nk^{1.5} + mk \log m)$ time algorithm was given for approximate parameterized matching with k mismatches, and a strong relation was shown between this problem and maximum matchings in bipartite graphs.

---

* The second author was supported by an IBM faculty award grant.
** The third author was a postdoc at Caesarea Rothschild Institute of Computer Science, University of Haifa during the research of these results.

A. Apostolico, M. Crochemore, and K. Park (Eds.): CPM 2005, LNCS 3537, pp. 266–279, 2005.

One of the interesting problems in web searching is searching for color images, see [4, 8, 17]. If the colors are fixed, this is exact two dimensional pattern matching [3]. However, images can appear under different color maps. The image is the same image however each color has been recolored with a unique color. Two-dimensional parameterized search is precisely what is needed. The fastest algorithm for solving the two dimensional parameterized matching problem was given in [2], and its time complexity is $O(n^2 \log^2 m)$.

It is an open question whether a linear time algorithm for the two dimensional parameterized matching problem exists. In this paper we show that it is possible to get an algorithm that is linear in the text size, but with a penalty in the preprocessing stage. More precisely, the time complexity of our algorithm is $O(n^2 + m^{2.5} \cdot \text{polylog}(m))$. For alphabets drawn from a large universe (larger than polynomial in n) the time complexity increases to $O(n^2 \log |\Sigma| + m^{2.5} \cdot \text{polylog}(m))$. However, this seems to be unavoidable as it was shown in [6] that the one-dimensional parameterized matching requires $\Omega(n \log |\Sigma|)$ time.

Due to lack of space, some proofs are omitted.

2   Preliminaries and Definitions

Let T and T' be two texts of size $k \times k$. We say that there is a *function matching* between T and T' if there is a mapping f from the alphabet of T to the alphabet of T' such that $T'[i, j] = f(T[i, j])$ for all i and j. If the mapping f is one-to-one, we say that T and T' *parameterize match*, or *p-match* for short. Note that the definition of function matching is asymmetric whereas the definition of parameterized matching is symmetric. The parameterized matching problem is defined as follows:

Input: An $n \times n$ text T and an $m \times m$ pattern P.
Output: All substrings of T of size $m \times m$ that p-match to P.

The algorithms for one dimensional parameterized matching are based on converting the pattern and text strings into predecessor strings. The *predecessor* of location i in a string S is the location containing the previous appearance of the symbol $S[i]$, if there is such a location. The *predecessor string* of S is obtained by replacing each character in S by the distance to its predecessor, or by 0 if the character does not have a predecessor. For example, the predecessor string of $aabbaba$ is $0, 1, 0, 1, 3, 2, 2$. A simple and well-known fact is that:

Observation 1 *S and S' p-match iff they have the same predecessor string.*

Observation 1 gives a handle on finding p-matches for 1-dimensional texts. We would like to use a similar observation for 2-dimensional texts as well. In order to do so we define the following.

Definition 1 (strip). *Let T be an $n \times n$ text. The i-th strip of T is the $n \times m$ substring $T[1 .. n, i .. i + m - 1]$.*

Let A be a $k \times l$ string. We define the *linearization* of A to be the one-dimensional string $A[1, 1], \ldots, A[1, l], A[2, 1], \ldots, A[2, l], \ldots, A[k, 1], \ldots, A[k, l]$.

Definition 2 (predecessor). *Let T be an $n \times n$ text, T' be a strip of T, and (i, j) be a location in T. The predecessor of (i, j) w.r.t. T' is the location (i', j') in T such that $(i' - 1)m + j'$ is the predecessor of location $(i - 1)m + j$ in the linearization of T'.*

A pair of a location in T and its predecessor will be called a *location-predecessor pair*.

3   Overview

We begin by giving an overview of the algorithm. As in many pattern matching algorithms, we assume w.l.o.g. that $n = 2m$. Larger texts can be cut into $2m \times 2m$ pieces which are handled separately.

The outline of the algorithm follows the "duel-and-sweep"-paradigm that appeared in [3] (there it is named "consistency and verification" and was used for 2-dimensional exact matching) and is based upon ideas of duelling techniques [18, 19]. The idea of the "duel-and-sweep"-paradigm is to maintain a list of $m \times m$ substrings of T, called *candidates*, that might match to P. Starting with all the $m \times m$ substrings of T, the list is pruned in two stages to a list of all the candidates which actually match. The two stages are called the *duelling stage* and the *sweeping stage*. However, exact matching turns out to be much simpler than parameterized matching. This is mainly because of the "witness" which is used in the duelling stage to differentiate between two pattern alignments. In exact matching a witness is simply one location with a mismatch between the two alignments. However, in parameterized matching one location is not sufficient to rule out a match. The following definition captures the concept of a witness in parameterized matching.

Definition 3 (witness). *Let P be a pattern of size $m \times m$. Consider an alignment of P with itself, starting at location $(a + 1, b + 1)$ (namely, $P[x, y]$ in the first copy of P is aligned with $P[x + a, y + b]$ in the second copy of P). A witness relative to the offset (a, b) is a pair of locations $(x, y), (x', y')$ such that one of the following holds:*

1. *$P[x, y] = P[x', y']$ and $P[x + a, y + b] \neq P[x' + a, y' + b]$.*
2. *$P[x, y] \neq P[x', y']$ and $P[x + a, y + b] = P[x' + a, y' + b]$.*

In the duelling stage, we use the fact that if two p-matches of P in T overlap, then there is a p-matching between the two substrings of P that correspond to the overlapping area of the two matches. Using a witness array for P, we can check pairs of overlapping candidates which do not agree on their overlapping area, and rule out at least one candidate from the pair in constant time per pair. After this stage we remain only with candidates that agree with each over.

In the sweeping stage, we need to check the remaining candidates. This is done by going over all the strips of T from left to right, and for each strip, checking the candidates that are contained in the current strip.

Suppose that the current strip starts at column y, and consider some candidate $T' = T[x \ldots x + m - 1, y \ldots y + m - 1]$ in the strip. Suppose that we know the predecessor for every location in the current strip of T.

Before we make the next observation, a central concept which has a similar flavor to the witness defined above is as follows.

Definition 4 (mismatch pair). *Let R and S be two equal sized 2-dimensional strings. A* mismatch pair *between R and S is a pair of locations $(i, j), (i', j')$ such that one of the following holds:*

1. *$R[i, j] = R[i', j']$ and $S[i, j] \neq S[i', j']$.*
2. *$R[i, j] \neq R[i', j']$ and $S[i, j] = S[i', j']$.*

We now observe that:

Observation 2   1. *If T' p-matches to P, then every location-predecessor pair inside T' (namely, both the location and its predecessor are in T') is not a mismatch pair for T' and P.*
2. *If there is no location-predecessor pair inside T' which is a mismatch pair for T' and P, then there is a function matching between T' and P.*
3. *If there is a function matching between T' and P, then there is a p-matching between T' and P if and only if the number of distinct characters in T' is equal to the number of distinct characters in P.*

By Observation 2, the algorithm for checking the candidates will have two steps: In the first step, we go over all the location-predecessor pairs inside the candidate, and check whether one of these pairs is a mismatch pair. In the second step we compute the number of distinct characters in each candidate and compare it to the number of distinct characters in P.

In order to implement the first step, we go over al strips of T (from left to right) while maintaining the predecessor of every location in the current strip. Computing the predecessor of every location in the first strip of T takes $O(m^2)$ time. When going from one strip to the next strip, only at most $6m$ predecessors are changed, and we will show how to do the update in $O(m)$ time.

Clearly, if we check each location-predecessor pair for each candidate separately, then the algorithm will not be efficient (the time complexity will be $\Theta(m^4)$ in the worst case). However, we can use the fact that after the duelling stage, all the remaining candidates agree with each other. Therefore, for each location-predecessor pair in T, the pair is either a mismatch pair for P and every candidate that contains the pair, or the pair is not a mismatch pair for any candidate. Thus, for each location-predecessor pair we need to check only two characters in P, and if there is a mismatch, we can rule out all the remaining candidates that contain the pair.

The second step is done by computing the number of distinct characters in every $m \times m$ substring of T. Amir et al. [4] gave an algorithm for this problem whose time complexity is $O(m^2 \log m)$. We can solve the problem in $O(m^2)$ time, but omit the details for space reasons. (Amir and Cole [5] also have solved the problem in the same time bounds).

4   Algorithm Details

From Observation 2, we need to check for each candidate whether the location-predecessor pairs inside it are mismatch pairs. As discussed in Section 3, we will check every location-predecessor pair only once during the entire algorithm.

The main idea is as follows: We go over the strips of T from left to right. When going from the $(y-1)$-th strip to the y-th strip, there are at most $3n = 6m$ new location-predecessor pairs: (1) Every location in column $y + m - 1$ and its predecessor form a new pair, (2) Every location in column $y+m-1$ may become the predecessor of some location in columns $y, \ldots, y + m - 2$, and (3) Every location in columns $y, \ldots, y + m - 2$ whose predecessor was in column $y - 1$ will form with its new predecessor a new pair. After a preprocessing step on T that will be described in Section 5, we can find all the new location-predecessor pairs in time $O(m)$.

Now, we only need to check whether there is a mismatch pair among the new location-predecessor pairs, as we already checked the old pairs in the previous iterations. Let $(r, c), (r', c')$ be some new location-predecessor pair for the y-th strip. All the candidates that contain the locations (r, c) and (r', c') agree with each other, so $(r, c), (r', c')$ is a mismatch pair for all of these candidate, or for none. Therefore, we only need to find one candidate (z, w) (with $w \geq y$) that contains both locations, and check whether $P[r - z + 1, c - w + 1] = P[r' - z + 1, c' - w + 1]$. If these two character are not equal, then (z, w) cannot be a match, and moreover, every candidate that contains (r, c) and (r', c') cannot be a match. In other words, we can rule out every candidate whose top-left corner is in the rectangle $\{r - m + 1, \ldots, r'\} \times \{y, \ldots, \min(c, c')\}$. Note that it is possible that the predecessor of (r, c) changes at some strip y' for $y < y' \leq \min(c, c')$, so $(r, c), (r', c')$ is not a location-predecessor pair for some of the candidates that we rule out. However, this does not affect the correctness of the algorithm.

We now need to handle two issues: How to find a candidate that contains the pair $(r, c), (r', c')$, and in a case of a mismatch, how to rule out the candidates in the corresponding rectangle.

We first deal with the first issue. Given a location-predecessor pair (r, c), (r', c'), we will find the highest candidate that can contain the pair $(r, c), (r', c')$, which will be denoted (z, w). More precisely, among all the candidates in $\{r - m + 1, \ldots, n\} \times \{y, \ldots, \min(c, c')\}$ (note that the rectangle here ends in row n), (z, w) is the candidate with smallest row number (ties are broken arbitrarily). Clearly, if (z, w) does not contain the pair $(r, c), (r', c')$ (that is, if $z > r'$), then there is no candidate (that begins in a column greater than y) that contains the pair $(r, c), (r', c')$.

We now describe how to find the highest candidate in constant time. To do that, we build an $n \times n$ array A, where $A[i, j]$ is the smallest row in which a candidate starts, among all the candidates with start row at least $i - m + 1$ and start column j. If there are no such candidates, then $A[i, j] = 2m$. The array A can be easily computed by scanning the text column by column, from bottom to top. Now, given a location-predecessor pair $(r, c), (r', c')$, in order to find the highest candidate that can contain the pair, we need to find the minimum value among the subrow $A[r, y], A[r, y+1], \ldots, A[r, \min(c, c')]$. This is the range minima problem [13], so after preprocessing each row of A in $O(m)$ time per row, we can find the minimum element in some subrow of A in constant time.

We now turn to the problem of eliminating candidates. As discussed above, during the algorithm we find rectangles that do not contain a match. Instead of eliminating the candidates at the time each rectangle is discovered, we store the rectangle in a list L, and after obtaining all the rectangles, we perform a candidates elimination stage.

In the candidates elimination stage, we need to remove each candidate whose top-left corner is in some rectangle of L. This is done by moving a vertical sweep line from left to right. We maintain two vectors V and B, where $V[i]$ (resp., $B[i]$) is the number of rectangles in L that intersect the current sweep line, and whose top (resp., bottom) row is i. Using these vectors, we can compute the number of rectangles that contain each point on the sweep line, and eliminate the candidates whose top-left corner is contained in at least one rectangle. The time complexity of this step is linear in the number of rectangles in L, which is at most $6m^2$.

5   Text Preprocessing

In this section, we show how to compute an array of pointers, which will be used to maintain the predecessors of the current strip.

Definition 5 (left predecessor). *For a location (i, j) in T with $j > m$, the left predecessor of (i, j) is the predecessor of location (i, j) w.r.t. the $(j-m+1)$-th strip of T.*

Given the left predecessors of all the locations in T, it is straightforward to maintain the predecessor of every location w.r.t. the current strip.

We now show how to compute the left predecessor of every location in T. We scan the entire text bottom-up left-to-right. For each symbol σ, we keep a list L_σ of all the locations (i, j) with $j > m$ and $T[i, j] = \sigma$ for which we haven't computed a left predecessor yet. The elements of L_σ are ordered according to their scan order. When the scan of T reaches a location (x, y), we need to check for which elements of $L_{T[x,y]}$ the left predecessor is (x, y), and these elements will be removed from $L_{T[x,y]}$. Moreover, if $y > m$ and the left predecessor of (x, y) is not in row x, then (x, y) is added to the end of $L_{T[x,y]}$. For efficient implementation of the algorithm above, we use the following properties of the L_σ lists.

Claim 1 *If (i, j) and (i', j') are two elements of some list L_σ, where (i, j) appears in the list before (i', j'), then $i > i'$ and $j < j'$.*

Claim 2 *Let $(i_1, j_1), \ldots, (i_s, j_s)$ be the locations in $L_{T[x,y]}$ according to their order. A location (x, y) is either the left predecessor of $(i_1, j_1), \ldots, (i_f, j_f)$ for some $1 \le f \le s$, the left predecessor of $(i_f, j_f), \ldots, (i_s, j_s)$ for some $1 < f \le s$, or the left predecessor of none of these locations.*

From Claim 2, the text preprocessing stage can be implemented in $O(n^2)$ time.

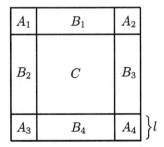

Fig. 1. The subsets of D.

6   Pattern Preprocessing

Let P be an $m \times m$ string. We will show how to compute a witness for every offset (a, b) that has a witness.

Let l be some integer that will be specified later. Consider an alignment of P against itself, with offset (a, b). We say that (a, b) is a *source* if there is a p-match between the overlapping areas in the two copies of P. If (a, b) is not a source, then a there is at least one witness for (a, b). A witness $(x, y), (x', y')$ is called a *witness of type 1* if it satisfies condition 1 in Definition 3, and otherwise, it is called a witness of type 2. There are four cases that we need to consider, according to the signs of a and b. In the following, we will handle the case when $a \geq 0$ and $b \geq 0$. The other cases are symmetrical, and thus omitted.

Let (a, b) be an offset which is not a source, and let $D = \{1, \ldots, m - a\} \times \{1, \ldots, m - b\}$ be the set of locations in the overlapping area of P when P is aligned against itself with offset (a, b). We partition D into subsets (see Figure 1): $A_1, \ldots, A_4$ are the $l \times l$ squares in the corners of D. $B_1, \ldots, B_4$ are rectangles of width or height l in the borders of D excluding the corners, and C is the remaining part of D (namely, $C = D \setminus (A_1 \cup \cdots \cup A_4 \cup B_1 \cup \cdots \cup B_4)$). Formally,

$$A_1 = \{(x, y) \in \mathbb{Z}^2 : 1 \leq x \leq l \text{ and } 1 \leq y \leq l\},$$
$$A_2 = \{(x, y) \in \mathbb{Z}^2 : 1 \leq x \leq l \text{ and } m - b - l + 1 \leq y \leq m - b\},$$

etc.

We say that a witness w for (a, b) is *simple* if it does not satisfy any of the following conditions:

1. w is of type 1, and one of the locations of w is in A_1.
2. w is of type 1, one of the locations of w is in $A_2 \cup B_3 \cup A_4$, and the other location is in $A_3 \cup B_4 \cup A_4$.
3. w is of type 2, and one of the locations of w is in A_4.
4. w is of type 2, one of the locations of w is in $A_1 \cup B_1 \cup A_2$, and the other location is in $A_1 \cup B_2 \cup A_3$.

The algorithm consists of three stages:

1. Find simple witnesses.
2. Find witnesses that satisfy conditions 1 or 3 above.
3. Find witnesses that satisfy conditions 2 or 4 above.

The three stages of the algorithm are described in the next sub-sections. In each stage, we will handle only offsets do not contain witnesses that were handled by the previous stages.

6.1   Stage 1

This stage is similar to the algorithm of Amir et al. [2]: We create new strings P_1 and P_2 by replacing every character $P[x, y]$ in P by $8\frac{m}{l} + 4$ characters, where each of these characters is either a pointer to some location (x', y') in P such that $P[x', y'] = P[x, y]$, or a null pointer.

For each location (x, y) in P, we define rectangles on the grid $\mathbb{Z}^2$ in following way: For $i = -\frac{m}{l}, \ldots, \frac{m}{l} - 1$, let

$$H_{i,(x,y)} = \{(x', y') \in \mathbb{Z}^2 : y' \le y \text{ and } x + il \le x' < x + (i+1)l\},$$

$$\hat{H}_{i,(x,y)} = \{(x', y') \in \mathbb{Z}^2 : y' \ge y \text{ and } x + il \le x' < x + (i+1)l\},$$

$$V_{i,(x,y)} = \{(x', y') \in \mathbb{Z}^2 : x' \le x \text{ and } y + il \le y' < y + (i+1)l\},$$

and

$$\hat{V}_{i,(x,y)} = \{(x', y') \in \mathbb{Z}^2 : x' \ge x \text{ and } y + il \ge y' < y + (i+1)l\}.$$

Furthermore, let $H_{(x,y)} = \{(x, y') \in \mathbb{Z}^2 : y' \le y\}$, and we similarly define the rectangles $\hat{H}_{(x,y)}$, $V_{(x,y)}$, and $\hat{V}_{(x,y)}$. We say that a rectangle $H_{i,(x,y)}$ (or other H rectangle) is *inside the square of P* if there is at least one column of $H_{i,(x,y)}$ that is contained in $\{1, \ldots, m\} \times \{1, \ldots, m\}$, namely, if $1 \le y + il$ and $y + (i-1)l - 1 \le m$. A V rectangle is inside the square of P if there is at least one row of the rectangle that is contained in $\{1, \ldots, m\} \times \{1, \ldots, m\}$.

The string P_1 is constructed by replacing every character $P[x, y]$ in P by the characters $c_1, \ldots, c_{8m/l+4}$ (P_1 is an $m \times ((8\frac{m}{l} + 4)m)$ string) which are defined as follows:

- For $i = -\frac{m}{l}, \ldots, \frac{m}{l} - 1$, if the rectangle $H_{i,(x,y)}$ is inside the square of P, traverse over the elements of $H_{i,(x,y)}$ in a column major order (from right to left), until reaching a location (x', y') for which $P[x', y'] = P[x, y]$, if there is such a location. If a location (x', y') was found, then set $c_{m/l+i+1} = (x - x', y - y')$, and we say in this case that $c_{m/l+i+1}$ *points to* (x', y'). Otherwise (namely, the rectangle $H_{i,(x,y)}$ does not contain a character equal to $P[x, y]$), set $c_{m/l+i+1} = \phi$.
  If the rectangle $H_{i,(x,y)}$ is not inside the square of P, then set $c_{m/l+i+1} = \phi$.
- For $i = -\frac{m}{l}, \ldots, \frac{m}{l} - 1$, the character $c_{3m/l+i+1}$ is built from the rectangle $\hat{H}_{i,(x,y)}$ in the same way described above, except that the rectangle is traversed from right to left, and furthermore, if the rectangle does not contain a character equal to $P[x, y]$, then $c_{3m/l+i+1} = 0$.

- For $i = -\frac{m}{l}, \ldots, \frac{m}{l} - 1$, the characters $c_{5m/l+i+1}$ and $c_{7m/l+i+1}$ are built from the rectangles $V_{i,(x,y)}$ and $\hat{V}_{i,(x,y)}$ the same as above, except that the rectangles are traversed in a row major order (if the corresponding rectangle does not contain a character equal to $P[x,y]$, we use ϕ for $c_{5m/l+i+1}$ and 0 for $c_{7m/l+i+1}$).
- The character $c_{8m/l+1}$ corresponds to the rectangle $H_{(x,y)}$, and it is handled the same as the characters $c_1, \ldots, c_{2m/l}$. Furthermore, the characters $c_{8m/l+2}$, $c_{8m/l+3}$, and $c_{8m/l+4}$ correspond to the rectangles $\hat{H}_{(x,y)}$, $V_{(x,y)}$, and $\hat{V}_{(x,y)}$, respectively.

The string P_2 is built in two steps. The first step is the same as building P_1, except that we replace the roles of ϕ and 0, that is, we use ϕ for characters that correspond to the rectangles $\hat{H}_{i,(x,y)}$ and $\hat{V}_{i,(x,y)}$, and 0 for characters that correspond to the rectangles $H_{i,(x,y)}$ and $V_{i,(x,y)}$. After the first step, P_2 is an $m \times ((8\frac{m}{l}+4)m)$ string. In the second step, we expand P_2 into a $2m \times 2((8\frac{m}{l}+4)m)$ string, where all the new characters are ϕ.

After building P_1 and P_2, we solve the (standard) matching problem with don't care symbols on P_1 and P_2, where P_1 is the pattern, P_2 is the text, and ϕ is the don't care symbol. Moreover, using the algorithm of Alon and Naor [1], we find witnesses for every mismatch between P_1 and P_2, namely, for every (a,b) such that P_1 does not match to $P_2[a+1..a+m, b+1..b+m]$, we find a location (x,y) such that $P_1[x,y] \neq P_2[x+a, y+b]$.

Consider some fixed pair (a,b), and define $P_2' = P_2[a+1..a+m, b+1..b+m]$.

Claim 3 *If P_1 does not match to P_2', then (a,b) is not a source. Moreover, from every witness to the mismatch of P_1 and P_2' we can obtain a witness for (a,b) in constant time.*

The converse of Claim 3 is not true. A weaker result is given in the following lemma.

Lemma 1. *If (a,b) has a simple witness then P_1 does not match to P_2'.*

Proof. Suppose that $w = \{(x,y),(x',y')\}$ is a simple witness for (a,b). W.l.o.g. we assume that $x \geq x'$, and moreover, if $x = x'$ we assume that $y > y'$. We will deal with the case when w is a witness of type 1, and omit the proof for the case when w is of type 2. We consider 3 cases.

Case 1. In the first case, suppose that either $x = x'$ or (x',y') is in $B_1 \cup C \cup B_4$, or in other words, $l + 1 \leq y' \leq m - b - l$. We prove the lemma using induction on $x - x'$.

If $x = x'$, we have that $(x,y') \in H_{(x,y)}$. Thus, the character of P_1 that corresponds to $H_{(x,y)}$ points to some location (x,y'') such that $y' \leq y'' < y$ and $P[x,y''] = P[x,y]$. If $P[x+a, y''+b] \neq P[x+a, y+b]$, then the character of P_2 that corresponds to $H_{(x+a,y+b)}$ either points to some location other than $(x+a, y''+b)$, or is equal to 0. In both cases, we conclude that P_1 does not match to P_2'. If $P[x+a, y''+b] = P[x+a, y+b]$, then $w' = \{(x,y''),(x,y')\}$ is a simple witness for (a, b) of type 1. We can now use the argument above on w' and either obtain that P_1 does not match to P_2', or obtain a new witness w''. We can continue this process until obtaining a mismatch between P_1 and P_2'.

Now, suppose that $x > x'$, and we proved case 1 of the lemma for every witness in which the difference between the rows in the two locations is less than $x - x'$. Since $l + 1 \leq y' \leq m - b - l$, it follows that the rectangle $V_{i,(x,y)}$ that contains the location (x', y') is inside the square of P. Therefore, the character of P_1 that corresponds to $V_{i,(x,y)}$ points to some location (x'', y''), where $x \leq x'' < x'$. If $P[x'' + a, y'' + b] \neq P[x + a, y + b]$ then we are done since the character of P_2 that corresponds to $V_{i,(x+a,y+b)}$ either points to some location other than $(x'' + a, y'' + b)$, or is equal to 0. Otherwise, we use the induction hypothesis on $w' = \{(x'', y''), (x', y')\}$. Note that it is possible that $(x'', y'') \in A_1$ and therefore w' is not simple. However, the arguments we used above still work on w', so we still obtain that P_1 does not match to P_2'.

Case 2. The second case is when either $y = y'$ or leftmost location among (x, y) and (x', y') is in $B_2 \cup C \cup B_3$. The proof for the case is symmetrical to the proof of case 1 (we use the rectangles $V_{(x^*, y^*)}$ and $H_{i,(x^*, y^*)}$ instead of $H_{(x,y)}$ and $V_{i,(x,y)}$, where (x^*, y^*) is the rightmost location).

Case 3. Assume that cases 1 and 2 do not occur. Since case 1 does not occur, we have that either $y' \leq l$ or $y' \geq m - b - l + 1$. We consider 4 sub-cases:

1. $y' \leq l$ and $y > y'$. Since (x', y') is the leftmost location and case 2 does not occur, we have that either $x' \leq l$ or $x' \geq m - a - l + 1$. If $x' \leq l$ then $(x', y') \in A_1$, and therefore w is not simple, a contradiction.
   If $x' \geq m - a - l + 1$, then the rectangle $H_{-1,(x,y)}$ is inside the square of P, and it contains the location (x', y'). Therefore, using the same arguments as in case 1, we obtain that P_1 does not match to P_2'.
2. $y' \leq l$ and $y < y'$. In this case, the rectangle $V_{0,(x,y)}$ is inside the square of P, and it contains the location (x', y'). Thus, P_1 does not match to P_2'.
3. $y' \geq m - b - l + 1$ and $y > y'$. The rectangle $V_{-1,(x,y)}$ is inside the square of P, and it contains the location (x', y'), so P_1 does not match to P_2'.
4. $y' \geq m - b - l + 1$ and $y < y'$. Since (x, y) is the leftmost location, it follows that either $x \leq l$ or $x \geq m - a - l + 1$. In the former case, the rectangle $H_{0,(x',y')}$ is inside the square of P, and it contains the location (x, y). It follows that P_1 does not match to P_2'. In the latter case, we obtain that w is not simple, a contradiction. $\square$

From Claim 3 and Lemma 1 we conclude that stage 1 of the algorithm correctly finds a witness for every offset (a, b) that has simple witnesses. The time complexity of this stage is $O(|P_2| \cdot \log^{4+o(1)} |P_1|) = O(\frac{m^3}{l} \cdot \log^{4+o(1)} m)$.

6.2   Stage 2

In the following stages, we will describe only how to find witnesses of type 1, as handling the witnesses of type 2 is symmetrical. The second stage is composed of four sub-stages. We will not give detailed proofs for the correctness of these steps, as the proofs are similar to the proof of Lemma 1.

Stage 2a. In this stage we find witnesses w such that the two locations of w are in A_1. For each location (x, y) in P, we define rectangles as follows:

$$H^2_{i,(x,y)} = \{(x + i, y') \in \mathbb{Z}^2 : y' \le y\}$$
$$V^2_{i,(x,y)} = \{(x', y + i) \in \mathbb{Z}^2 : x' \le x\}.$$

Using these rectangles, we build strings P^2_1 and P^2_2 by replacing each character $P[x, y]$ in P by $4l$ characters that correspond to the rectangles $H^2_{i,(x,y)}$ and $V^2_{i,(x,y)}$ for $i = -l+1, \ldots, l-1$. Each of the $4l$ characters is chosen by traversing the appropriate rectangle similarly to the construction of P_1 and P_2 in stage 1. Then, we solve the matching problem for P^2_1 and P^2_2 and find witnesses for the mismatches. The correctness of this sub-stage follows from the fact that for two locations in A_1, one of the locations is inside the rectangles of the other location.

Stage 2b. In this stage we find all the witnesses w such that one location of w is in A_1, and the other location is in $B_1 \cup B_2 \cup C \cup A_3 \cup B_4$.

As in the previous stages, we create new strings by replacing each character in P with pointers to other occurrences of the character. However, instead of creating one matching problem instance, we will create $O(m^2/l)$ instances. The main idea is to group the different offsets into set and build a matching problem instance for each set, and then use the instance to find witnesses for the offsets in the set. In each set, all the offsets are close to each other, and we use this fact in our construction.

Consider a set of offsets $(a, b), (a, b + 1), \ldots, (a, b + l/2 - 1)$ (we assume that l is even), where b is a multiple of l. Define the rectangles

$$H^{3,a,b}_{(x,y)} = \{(x', y') \in \mathbb{Z}^2 : y \le y' \le y + m - b - l \text{ and } 0 \le x' \le m - a\}$$
$$H^{4,a,b}_{(x,y)} = \{(x', y') \in \mathbb{Z}^2 : y' \le y \text{ and } x \le x' \le m - a\}$$
$$H^{5,a,b}_{(x,y)} = \{(x' + a, y') : (x', y') \in H^{3,a,b}_{(x,y)}\}$$

and

$$H^{6,a,b}_{(x,y)} = \{(x' + a, y') : (x', y') \in H^{4,a,b}_{(x,y)}\}.$$

Next, build the strings $P^{3,a,b}_1$ and $P^{3,a,b}_2$ as follows: For every location (x, y) with $1 \le x \le l$ and $1 \le y \le l/2$, the string $P^{3,a,b}_1$ contains two characters for $P[x, y]$ corresponding to the rectangles $H^{3,a,b}_{(x,y)}$ and $H^{4,a,b}_{(x,y)}$. For every location (x, y) with $a + 1 \le x \le a + l$ and $b + 1 \le y \le b + 3l/2$, the string $P^{3,a,b}_2$ contains two characters for $P[x, y]$ corresponding to the rectangles $H^{5,a,b}_{(x,y)}$ and $H^{6,a,b}_{(x,y)}$. Moreover, the string $P^{3,a,b}_2$ is padded with don't care symbols.

As in the previous stages, we solve the matching problem for $P_1^{3,a,b}$ and $P_2^{3,a,b}$ and find witnesses for the mismatches. If $\{(x,y),(x',y')\}$ is a witness for (a,b') where $b \leq b' \leq b + l/2$, $(x,y) \in \{1,\ldots,l\} \times \{1,\ldots,l/2\}$, and $(x',y') \in B_1 \cup B_2 \cup C \cup A_3 \cup B_4$, then one of the rectangles $H_{(x,y)}^{3,a,b'}$ and $H_{(x,y)}^{4,a,b'}$ contains the location (x',y'), and it follows that $P_1^{3,a,b'}$ does not match to $P_2^{3,a,b'}$. Moreover, from every witness to the mismatch of $P_1^{3,a,b'}$ and $P_2^{3,a,b'}$, we can obtain a witness for (a,b').

Finding witnesses with one location of the witness in $\{1,\ldots,l\} \times \{l/2 + 1,\ldots,l\}$ and the other in $B_1 \cup B_2 \cup C \cup A_3 \cup B_4$ is done in a similar way.

Stage 2c. This stage finds all the witnesses w such that one location of w is in A_1, and the other location is in $A_2 \cup B_3$. This stage is analogous to stage 2b, and we omit the details.

Stage 2d. In this final sub-stage, we find all the witnesses w such that one location of w is in A_1, and the other location is in A_4. Recall that

$$H_{i,(x,y)}^2 = \{(x+i,y') \in \mathbb{Z}^2 : y' \leq y\}.$$

For every set of offsets $\{(a+i,b+j) : i = 0,\ldots,l-1 \text{ and } j = 0,\ldots,l-1\}$ where a and b are multiples of l, build strings $P_1^{5,a,b}$ and $P_2^{5,a,b}$: For every location (x,y) with $m - a - 2l + 2 \leq x \leq m$ and $m - b - 2l + 2 \leq y \leq m$, $P_1^{5,a,b}$ contains $3l - 3$ characters for $P[x,y]$, corresponding to the rectangles $H_{i,(x,y)}^2$ for $i = m - a - 3l + 2,\ldots,m - a - 1$. Similarly, for every (x,y) with $1 \leq x \leq 2l - 1$ and $1 \leq y \leq 2l - 1$, $P_2^{5,a,b}$ contains $3l - 3$ characters for $P[x,y]$, corresponding to the rectangles $H_{i,(x,y)}^2$ for $i = m - a - 3l + 2,\ldots,m - a - 1$.

The total time complexity of stage 2 is $O(m^2 l \cdot \log^{4+o(1)} m)$.

6.3   Stage 3

Let (a,b) be some offset for which no witness was found during the previous stages. We first look for witnesses with one location in $B_3 \cup A_4$ and the other location in $A_3 \cup B_4 \cup A_4$. Define $D' = D \setminus (A_1 \cup B_1 \cup A_2)$. For a rectangle $D'' \subseteq D'$ define $D'' + (a,b) = \{(x + a, x + b) : (x,y) \in D''\}$. Since there are no simple witnesses for (a,b), and no witnesses that satisfy condition 3 in the definition of a simple witness, we conclude that there are no type 2 witnesses with both locations inside D'. Therefore, we make the following observation:

Claim 4 *For every rectangle $D'' \subseteq D'$, the number of distinct characters inside the region D'' of P is less than or equal to the number of distinct characters inside the region D'' of P, with equality if and only if there is no witness w for (a,b) whose both locations are in D''.*

From Claim 4, we devise the following algorithm for finding a witness in D': Check the number of distinct characters inside the regions D' and $D' + (a, b)$ of P. If these numbers are equal then stop (no witness was found). Otherwise, find a minimal rectangle D'' in D' for which the number of distinct characters in D'' is strictly less than the number of distinct characters in $D'' + (a, b)$. Then, one of the pairs of opposite corners of the rectangle D'' is a witness for (a, b). The problem with this algorithm is that we do not know how to efficiently find such a rectangle D''. Instead, we will find a rectangle D^* which will be approximately equal to D''.

In order to find D^*, consider the following intersection counting problem: Given a set S of points in the plane where each point has a color, preprocess S in order to answer efficiently queries of the form "what is the number of distinct color in the points inside the rectangle $(-\infty, b] \times [c, d]$?". Denote by n the number of points in S. Gupta et al. [14] showed a data-structure for this problem with preprocessing time $O(n \log^2 n)$ which answers queries in $O(\log^2 n)$ time. Using this result, we obtain the following lemma:

Lemma 2. *Let P be an $m \times m$ string, and let l be an integer. After preprocessing of P in $O(\frac{m^3}{l} \log^2 m)$ time, the following queries can be answered in $O(\log^2 m)$ time: "what is the number of distinct characters in the substring $P[a \mathinner{.\,.} b, c \mathinner{.\,.} d]$?", where at least one of a, b, c, d is either 1, m, or a multiple of l.*

We now return to the problem of finding the rectangle D^*. The algorithm is as follows: First, build the data-structure of Lemma 2 on P. Then, compute the number of distinct characters inside the regions D' and $D' + (a, b)$ of P. If these numbers are equal, stop. Otherwise, find a minimal rectangle $D^* = \{x, \ldots, m - a\} \times \{y, \ldots, z\} \subseteq D$ such that the number of distinct characters inside the regions D^* and $D^* + (a, b)$ of P are not equal, and x is a multiple of l. Finding D^* is is done using binary search and queries to the data-structure of Lemma 2 (note that the queries we make satisfy the conditions of Lemma 2).

Let X be the set of all locations (c, d) such that $c \in \{x, \ldots, x + l - 1\} \cup \{m - a - l + 1, \ldots, m - a\}$ and $d \in \{y, z\}$. From Claim 4 and the minimality of X, we obtain that there is a witness w for (a, b) of type 1 whose both locations are in X. We find such a witness as follows:

1. Initialize tables $V[1 \mathinner{.\,.} |\Sigma|]$ and $L[1 \mathinner{.\,.} |\Sigma|]$ to zeros.
2. Go over the locations in X in some order. For every location (c, d), if $V[P[c, d]] \notin \{0, P[c + a, d + b]\}$ output the witness $\{L[P[c, d]], (c, d)\}$. Otherwise, set $V[P[c, d]] \leftarrow P[c + a, d + b]$ and $L[P[c, d]] \leftarrow (c, d)$.

By Lemma 2, the time complexity of this stage is $O(\frac{m^3}{l} \log^2 m + m^2 \log^3 m + m^2 l)$ (note that the initialization of the tables V and L above takes $O(1)$ time). Therefore, the total time complexity for preprocessing the pattern is $O((\frac{m}{l} + l)m^2 \cdot \log^{4 + o(1)} m)$. The last expression is $O(m^{5/2} \cdot \log^{4 + o(1)} m)$ when $l = \Theta(\sqrt{m})$.

References

1. N. Alon and M. Naor. Derandomization, witnesses for boolean matrix multiplication and construction of perfect hash functions. *Algorithmica*, 16:434–449, 1996.
2. A. Amir, Y. Aumann, R. Cole, M. Lewenstein, and E. Porat. Function matching: Algorithms, applications and a lower bound. In *Proc. 30th International Colloquium on Automata, Languages and Programming (ICALP)*, pages 929–942, 2003.
3. A. Amir, G. Benson, and M. Farach. An alphabet independent approach to two dimensional pattern matching. *SIAM J. on Computing*, 23(2):313–323, 1994.
4. A. Amir, K. W. Church, and E. Dar. Separable attributes: a technique for solving the submatrices character count problem. In *Proc. 13th Symposium on Discrete Algorithms (SODA)*, pages 400–401, 2002.
5. A. Amir and R. Cole. Personal communications, 2004.
6. A. Amir, M. Farach, and S. Muthukrishnan. Alphabet dependence in parameterized matching. *Information Processing Letters*, 49:111–115, 1994.
7. A. Apostolico, P. Erdős, and M. Lewenstein. Parameterized matching with mismatches. *manuscript*.
8. G.P. Babu, B.M. Mehtre, and M.S. Kankanhalli. Color indexing for efficient image retrieval. *Multimedia Tools and Applications*, 1(4):327–348, 1995.
9. B. S. Baker. A theory of parameterized pattern matching: algorithms and applications. In *Proc. 25th ACM Symposium on the Theory of Computation (STOC)*, pages 71–80, 1993.
10. B. S. Baker. Parameterized string pattern matching. *J. Comput. Systems Sci.*, 52(1):28–42, 1996.
11. B. S. Baker. Parameterized duplication in strings: Algorithms and an application to software maintenance. *SIAM J. on Computing*, 26(5):1343–1362, 1997.
12. R. Cole and R. Hariharan. Faster suffix tree construction with missing suffix links. In *Proc. 32nd ACM Symposium on the Theory of Computation (STOC)*, pages 407–415, 2000.
13. H. N. Gabow, J. L. Bentley, and R. E. Tarjan. Scaling and related techniques for geometry problems. *Proc. 16th ACM Symposium on Theory of Computing (STOC)*, 67:135–143, 1984.
14. P. Gupta, R. Janardan, and M. Smid. Further results on generalized intersection searching problems: Counting, reporting, and dynamization. *J. of Algorithms*, 19(2):282–317, 1995.
15. C. Hazay, M. Lewenstein, and D. Sokol. Approximate parameterized matching. In *Proc. 12th European Symposium on Algorithms (ESA)*, pages 414–425, 2004.
16. S. R. Kosaraju. Faster algorithms for the construction of parameterized suffix trees. *Proc. 36th Symposium on Foundation of Computer Science (FOCS)*, pages 631–637, 1995.
17. M. Swain and D. Ballard. Color indexing. *International Journal of Computer Vision*, 7(1):11–32, 1991.
18. U. Vishkin. Optimal parallel pattern matching in strings. In *Proc. 12th International Colloquium on Automata, Languages and Programming (ICALP)*, pages 91–113, 1985.
19. U. Vishkin. Deterministic sampling — a new technique for fast pattern matching. *SIAM J. on Computing*, 20:303–314, 1991.

An Optimal Algorithm
for Online Square Detection

Gen-Huey Chen, Jin-Ju Hong, and Hsueh-I Lu[*]

Department of Computer Science and Information Engineering
National Taiwan University

Abstract. A *square* is the concatenation of two identical non-empty strings. Let S be the input string which is given character by character. Let m be the (unknown) smallest integer such that the m-th prefix of S contains a square. The *online square detection* problem is to determine m as soon as the m-th character of S is read. The best previously known algorithm of the online square detection problem, due to Leung, Peng, and Ting, runs in $O(m \log^2 m)$ time. We improve the time complexity to $O(m \log \beta)$, where β is the number of distinct characters in the m-th prefix of the input string. It is not difficult to implement our algorithm to run in expected $O(m)$ time.

1 Introduction

Let $X \circ Y$ denote the concatenation of strings X and Y. A *square* is a non-empty string of the form $X \circ X$. A string does not contain any square is *square free*. Let $S[i, j]$ denote the substring of string S starting from position i and ending at position j. If string X equals $S[i, j]$, we say that X *starts* (or *occurs*) at position i and *ends* at position j in S.

Let S be a length-n string. Observe that there could be $\Omega(n^2)$ squares in S, e.g., when S is an all-one string. There are several $O(n \log n)$-time algorithms for finding compact representations of all squares in S [1, 2, 8]. In particular, each of these algorithms outputs $O(n \log n)$ periodic substrings of S such that any square of S occurs in one or more of those $O(n \log n)$ periodic substrings of S. These algorithms are optimal with respect to the worst-case output size [2].

Whether S is square free or not can be determined in $O(n \log \alpha)$ time [3, 4, 9], where α is the number of distinct characters in S. For example, Crochemore's approach [3, 4] is based upon the following f-factorization (also known as s-factorization [3], which is a variant of LZSS factorization [10]) of S. Let $|S|$ denote the length of string S. The f-*factorization* of S, obtainable in $O(n \log \alpha)$ time, is a partition of S into disjoint segments $B_1, B_2, \ldots, B_p$ for some $p \geq 1$ such that the following conditions hold for each $i = 2, 3, \ldots, p$, where $j = |B_1| + |B_2| + \cdots + |B_{i-1}|$:

---

[*] Corresponding author. Address: 1 Roosevelt Road, Section 4, Taipei 106, Taiwan, R.O.C. http://www.csie.ntu.edu.tw/~hil/, hil@csie.ntu.edu.tw

A. Apostolico, M. Crochemore, and K. Park (Eds.): CPM 2005, LNCS 3537, pp. 280–287, 2005.

Condition 1 If $S[j+1]$ does not occur in $S[1,j]$ (i.e., $B_1 \circ B_2 \circ \cdots \circ B_{i-1}$), then $B_i = S[j+1]$;

Condition 2 Otherwise, B_i is the longest prefix of $S[j+1,n]$ that occurs in S before position $j+1$.

Suppose that $S[1,i]$ is known to the algorithm in $\Theta(i)$ time for each $i = 1,2,\ldots,n$ and the problem is to determine the smallest m such that $S[1,m]$ contains a square. (Once m is known, one can easily identify all squares of $S[1,m]$ in $O(m)$ time using longest common extensions.) Although there does not seem to be any previous work on this problem, it can be solved in $O(m \log \beta)$ time, where β is the number of distinct characters in $S[1,m]$. For example, we can resort to the f'-*factorization* of S, whose definition is the same as that of f-factorization except replacing its Condition 2 with the following.

Condition 2' Otherwise, B_i is the longest prefix of $S[j+1,n]$ that occurs in S and ends before position $j+1$.

Let $B'_1, B'_2, \ldots, B'_p$ be the f'-factorization of S. Suppose that i is the smallest index such that $|B'_1| + |B'_2| + \cdots + |B'_i| \geq m$. It is not difficult to see that the first i blocks of the f'-factorization of S as well as a square in $S[1,m]$ can be obtained in $O(m \log \beta)$ time.

Leung, Peng, and Ting [7] studied the square detection problem in a more restricted setting. Suppose that S is given to the algorithm character by character and the algorithm has to recognize m as soon as it reads $S[m]$. Leung, Peng, and Ting [7] gave an $O(m \log^2 m)$-time algorithm for the online square detection problem. Our contribution, summarized in Theorem 1, is to improve the running time to $O(m \log \beta)$. The $O(\log \beta)$ factor comes from the binary search required by the traversal of a suffix tree. Therefore, the expected running time of our algorithm can easily be reduced to $O(m)$ using hash tables. Our approach is inspired by Crochemore's algorithm [4] using the f-factorization of S.

Theorem 1. *The online detection problem for a string S can be solved in deterministic $O(m \log \beta)$ time, where $S[1,m]$ is the shortest prefix of S that contains a square and β is the number of distinct characters in $S[1,m]$.*

The rest of the paper is organized as follows. Section 2 describes our algorithm. Section 3 gives the implementation of our algorithm, whose time complexity is analyzed in Section 3.2. We conclude the paper with some open questions in Section 4.

2   Our Algorithm

A square $X \circ X$ is *centered* at position i in S if

$$S[i - |X| + 1, i + |X|] = X \circ X.$$

Let i_1, i_2, and i be positions in S with $i_1 < i_2 \leq i$. The following concept is crucial to our algorithm.

– An $L(i_1, i_2, i)$-*square* of S is a square of $S[i_1, i]$ that ends at position i and is centered at a position between i_1 and $i_2 - 1$ in S.
– An $R(i_1, i_2, i)$-*square* of S is a square of $S[i_1, i]$ that ends at position i and is centered at a position between i_2 and i in S.

See Figure 1 for an illustration.

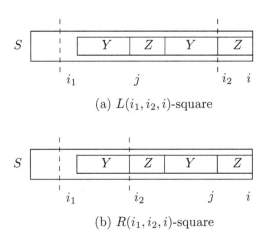

(a) $L(i_1, i_2, i)$-square

(b) $R(i_1, i_2, i)$-square

Fig. 1. $L(i_1, i_2, i)$-square and $R(i_1, i_2, i)$-square.

Our algorithm runs iteratively, where the i-th iteration receives $S[i]$ and detects whether there are squares in $S[1, i]$. More specifically, the i-th iteration obtains the f-factorization of $S[1, i]$ from that of $S[1, i-1]$. Suppose that $S[i]$ belongs to the k-th block of the f-factorization of $S[1, i]$. The algorithm then detects whether there are

– $L(b_{k-1}, b_k, i)$-squares,
– $R(b_{k-1}, b_k, i)$-squares, or
– $R(1, b_{k-1}, i)$-squares,

where for each $j = 1, 2, \ldots, k$, let b_j denote the starting position of the j-th block of the f-factorization of $S[1, i]$. If no square is detected, then the algorithm proceeds to the next iteration. Otherwise, the algorithm outputs i and halts.

Lemma 1. *If the input string S is not square free, then our algorithm correctly outputs the smallest index m such that $S[1, m]$ is not square free.*

Proof. Since $S[1, m-1]$ is square free, the algorithm does not halt before the m-th iteration. It suffices to show that a square of $S[1, m]$ has to be an $L(b_{k-1}, b_k, i)$-square, an $R(b_{k-1}, b_k, i)$-square, or an $R(1, b_{k-1}, i)$-square, where b_j is the starting position of the j-th block B_j in the f-factorization of $S[1, m]$ for each $j = 1, 2, \ldots, k$.

Since $S[b_k, m]$ is in B_k, by definition of f-factorization, $S[b_k, m]$ is a substring of $S[1, m-1]$. Since $S[1, m-1]$ is square free, so is $S[b_k, m]$. If a square of $S[1, m]$ occurs before b_{k-1}, then the square has to be an $R(1, b_{k-1}, m)$-square. If a square of $S[1, m]$ occurs at a position between b_{k-1} and $b_k - 1$, then the square has to be an $L(b_{k-1}, b_k, m)$-square or an $R(b_{k-1}, b_k, m)$-square.   □

Comment: Our proof of Lemma 1 is modified from that of Theorem 8.2 in [4].

3   Implementation

Longest common extensions [8] are crucial to the implementation of our algorithm. For positions $i \le j \le k$ in S,

- Let $X_R(i, j, k)$ denote the *longest common right extension* of positions i and j with boundaries k, i.e., the length of the longest common prefix of $S[i, k]$ and $S[j, k]$.
- Let $X_L(j, k, i)$ denote the *longest common left extension* of positions j and k with boundaries i, i.e., the length of the longest common suffix of $S[i, j]$ and $S[i, k]$.

It is not difficult to see the following lemma from Figure 1.

Lemma 2 (Main and Lorentz [8]).

1. *S has an $L(i_1, i_2, i)$-square if and only if there is an index j with $i_1 \le j < i_2$ such that $X_R(j, i_2, i) = |S[i_2, i]|$ and $X_L(j-1, i_2-1, i_1) + X_R(j, i_2, i) \ge |S[j, i_2 - 1]|$.*
2. *S has an $R(i_1, i_2, i)$-square if and only if there is an index j with $i_2 < j < i$ such that $X_R(i_2, j+1, i) = |S[j+1, i]|$ and $X_L(i_2-1, j, i_1) + X_R(i_2, j+1, i) \ge |S[i_2, j]|$.*

Our implementation uses several suffix trees [6, 11]. Let T' be the suffix tree of a string S'. If W' is a substring of S', then there is a unique path, denoted $P(T', W')$, in T' whose label spells out W'. Moreover, if S' contains β' distinct characters, then, given the ending position of $P(T', W')$ in T', it takes $O(|W''| \log \beta')$ time to determine whether $W' \circ W''$ is also a substring of S'.

3.1   Detecting $L(i_1, i_2, i)$-Squares

Let $i_1 < i_2 \le i_3$ be three given indices. Suppose that the number of distinct characters in $S[i_1, i_3]$ is $O(\beta)$. The following lemma is a key ingredient in the implementation of our algorithm.

Lemma 3. *Let i be the smallest index with $i_2 \le i \le i_3$ such that S has an $L(i_1, i_2, i)$-square. There is an algorithm $A_L(i_1, i_2, i_3)$ that*

- *either determines in $O((i_3 - i_1) \log \beta)$ time that i is undefined without reading any characters in $S[i_3 + 1, n]$*
- *or identifies i in $O((i - i_1) \log \beta)$ time without reading any character of $S[i + 1, n]$.*

The rest of the subsection proves Lemma 3.

The preprocessing. The first step is the $O(|S[i_1, i_2]|)$-time preprocessing with which the value of $X_L(j, i_2 - 1, i_1)$ for any index j with $i_1 \leq j < i_2$ can be determined in $O(1)$ time [5, 8]. We then build the suffix tree T_1 of $S[i_1, i_2 - 1] \circ \$$, where $\$$ is a character not in S [11]. One can easily verify that the preprocessing takes $O((i_2 - i_1) \log \beta)$ time.

Define $z(j) = |S[j, i_2 - 1]| - X_L(j - 1, i_2 - 1, i_1)$ for each index j with $i_1 \leq j < i_2$. Finally, for each node v of T_1, we store an index, denoted $j(v)$, at node v that minimizes $z(j)$ overall all indices j such that $P(T_1, S[j, i_2 - 1])$ passes v. The indices $j(v)$ for all nodes v of T_1 can be computed in $O(i_2 - i_1)$ time in a bottom-up manner.

The iterative procedure. For $i = i_2, i_2 + 1, \ldots, i_3$, the i-th iteration does the following. If $S[i_2, i]$ occurs in $S[i_1, i_2 - 1]$ and $|S[i_2, i]| \geq z(j(v))$, where v is the highest node in T_1 such that the path of T_1 between the root of T_1 and v contains $P(T_1, S[i_2, i])$, then the procedure reports i and halts. Otherwise, the procedure proceeds to the next iteration.

Correctness. The condition $X_R(j, i_2, i) = |S[i_2, i]|$ in Lemma 2(1) is equivalent to the condition that $S[i_2, i]$ is a prefix of $S[j, i_2 - 1]$, which is also equivalent to the condition that $P(T_1, S[j, i_2 - 1])$ contains $P(T_1, S[i_2, i])$. With $X_R(j, i_2, i) = |S[i_2, i]|$, the condition $X_L(j - 1, i_2 - 1, i_1) + X_R(j, i_2, i) \geq |S[j, i_2 - 1]|$ in Lemma 2(1) is equivalent to the condition

$$|S[i_2, i]| \geq |S[j, i_2 - 1]| - X_L(j - 1, i_2 - 1, i_1).$$

Let v be the highest node in T_1 such that the path of T_1 between v and the root of T_1 contains $P(T_1, S[i_2, i])$. By definition of $z(j(v))$, the above condition is equivalent to the condition

$$|S[i_2, i]| \geq z(j(v)).$$

Therefore, by Lemma 2(1), the above iterative procedure does report the smallest index i, if any, with $i_2 \leq i \leq i_3$ such that S has an $L(i_1, i_2, i)$-square.

Time complexity. Suppose that in the previous iteration we already have the ending position of $P(T_1, S[i_2, i - 1])$ in T_1. It takes $O(\log \beta)$ time to determine whether $S[i_2, i]$ is a substring of $S[i_1, i_2 - 1]$. If $S[i_2, i]$ does occur in $S[i_1, i_2 - 1]$, we also keep the ending position of $P(T_1, S[i_2, i])$ to be used in the next iteration. As a result, it is not difficult to verify that the time complexity described in Lemma 3 holds.

3.2   Detecting $R(i_1, i_2, i)$-Squares

Let $i_1 < i_2 < i_3$ be three given indices. Suppose that the number of distinct characters in $S[i_1, i_3]$ is $O(\beta)$. The following lemma is also a key ingredient in the implementation of our algorithm.

Lemma 4. *Let i be the smallest index with $i_2 < i \leq i_3$ such that S has an $R(i_1, i_2, i)$-square. There is an algorithm $A_R(i_1, i_2, i_3)$ such that*

- *if i is undefined, then $A_R(i_1, i_2, i_3)$ reports "i is undefined" in $O((i_3 - i_2) \log \beta)$ time without reading any character of $S[i_3 + 1, n]$;*
- *otherwise, if S has no $L(i_1, i_2, j)$-squares for any $j \in \{i_2, i_2 + 1, \ldots, i\}$, then algorithm $A_R(i_1, i_2, i_3)$ reports i in $O((i - i_2) \log \beta)$ time without reading any character of $S[i + 1, n]$.*

The rest of the subsection proves Lemma 4.

The iterative procedure. For each $i = i_2 + 1, i_2 + 2, \ldots, i_3$, the i-th iteration does the following.

- We first compute the index j_i in $O(1)$ time such that $|S[j_i, i_2 - 1]| = \min(|S[i_1, i_2 - 1]|, |S[i_2, i]|)$.
- We then compute the suffix tree T_2 of $S[j_i, i_2 - 1] \circ \$$ from that of $S[j_{i-1}, i_2 - 1] \circ \$$ in amortized $O(\log \beta)$ time using, e.g., Inenaga's algorithm [6].
- We maintain a data structure for $S[j_i, i_2 - 1]$ from which the value of $X_L(j, i_2 - 1, j_i)$ for any j with $j_i \leq j < i_2$ can be computed in $O(1)$ time. According to [5, 8], such a data structure for $S[j_i, i_2 - 1]$ can be obtained from that of $S[j_{i-1}, i_2 - 1]$ in amortized $O(1)$ time.
- We maintain a data structure for $S[i_2, i]$ from which the value of $X_R(i_2, j, i)$ for any j with $i_2 \leq j \leq i$ can be computed in $O(1)$ time. Similarly, according to [5, 8], such a data structure for $S[i_2, i]$ can be obtained from that of $S[i_2, i - 1]$ in amortized $O(1)$ time.
- Let $F(i)$ denote the longest suffix of $S[i_2, i]$ that is a substring of $S[j_i, i_2 - 1]$. We obtain the ending position of $P(T_2, F(i))$ in T_2 from the ending position of $P(T_2, F(i - 1))$ in amortized $O(\log \beta)$ time. It then takes $O(1)$ time to compute an index $y(i) \leq i_2 - 1$ such that an occurrence of $F(i)$ in $S[i_1, i_2 - 1]$ ends at position $y(i)$. We determine in $O(1)$ time

$$X_L(i_2 - 1, i, i_1) = \begin{cases} |F(i)| & \text{if } y(i) = i_2 - 1; \\ \min(|F(i)|, X_L(y(i), i_2 - 1, j_i)) & \text{otherwise.} \end{cases} \quad (1)$$

- Now we insert in $O(1)$ time the index i to the set $K(e(i))$, where

$$e(i) = i + |S[i_2, i]| - X_L(i_2 - 1, i, i_1).$$

- If there is an index j in $K(i)$, if

$$X_R(i_2, j + 1, i) = |S[j + 1, i]|,$$

then our procedure reports i; otherwise, the iterative procedure proceeds to the next iteration.

Correctness. First of all, one can see the correctness of Equation (1) by verifying that both sides of the equality are equal to $X_L(i_2 - 1, i, j_i)$. Observe that in the i-th iteration $K(i)$ has collected all the indices $j < i$ with $e(j) = i$. If $X_R(i_2, j + 1, i) = |S[j + 1, i]|$, then the condition

$$X_L(i_2 - 1, j, i_1) + X_R(i_2, j + 1, i) \geq |S[i_2, j]|$$

in Lemma 2(2) is equivalent to the condition $e(j) \leq i$. Moreover, the condition

$$X_L(i_2 - 1, j, i_1) + X_R(i_2, j + 1, i) > |S[i_2, j]|,$$

which is equivalent to the condition $e(j) < i$, implies that S has a square ending at position $i - X_L(i_2 - 1, j, i_1) + X_R(i_2, j + 1, i) + |S[i_2, j]|$. Therefore, by Lemma 2(2), our iterative procedure outputs i if and only if S has an $L(i_1, i_2, i)$-square.

Time complexity. According to the above explanation, it is not difficult to see that the time complexity of Lemma 4 holds.

3.3   The Implementation

With subroutines $A_L(i_1, i_2, i_3)$ and $A_R(i_1, i_2, i_3)$, we prove the following lemma.

Lemma 5. *Our algorithm described in Section 2 can be implemented to run in* $O(m \log \beta)$ *time.*

Proof. The implementation proceeds iteratively for $i = 1, 2, \ldots, n$, where the i-th iteration reads $S[i]$ and performs the following steps.

- We obtain the suffix tree T of $S[1, i]$ from the suffix tree of $S[1, i - 1]$ in amortized $O(\log \beta)$ time. We then determine the index k_i such that $S[i]$ is in the k_i-th block of the f-factorization of S. Observe that with the help of T, one can compute k_i from k_{i-1} in $O(\log \beta)$ time. If $k_i = 1$, we proceed to the next iteration.
- Knowing $k_i \geq 2$, we perform
  - the i-th iteration of $A_L(k_{i-1}, k_i, k_{i+1})$,
  - the i-th iteration of $A_R(k_{i-1}, k_i, k_{i+1})$, and
  - the i-th iteration of $A_R(1, k_{i-1}, k_{i+1})$
  in the above order. If any of these three i-th iterations reports i and halts, then our implementation also reports i and halts. Otherwise, our implementation proceeds to the next iteration.

The description of our implementation ignores on purpose the fact that we do not know the value of k_{i+1} in the i-iteration. However, one can verify that this abuse to the interface of subroutines $A_L()$ and $A_R()$ is all right, since each iteration of our implementation calls only the i-th iterations of subroutines $A_L()$ and $A_R()$. It follows from Lemmas 3 and 4 that our implementation correctly outputs m in $O(m \log \beta)$ time.   □

Now one can easily see that Theorem 1 is immediate from Lemmas 1 and 5.

4   Concluding Remarks

As we mentioned in the introduction, each of those $O(\log \beta)$ terms comes from the binary search required for choosing the right branch to go while traversing a suffix tree of a string with $O(\beta)$ distinct characters. Using hash tables, one can implement our algorithm to run in expected $O(m)$ time. An immediate open question is to see if it is possible to further reduce the required running time to worst-case $O(m)$ time. It would also be of interest to see if the technique of f-factorization can be extended to detect repeats of the form X^k with $k > 2$ in an online manner.

References

1. A. Apostolico and F. P. Preparata. Optimal off-line dection of repetitions in a string. *Theoretical Computer Science*, 22:294–315, 1983.
2. M. Crochemore. An optimal algorithm for computing the repetitions in a word. *Information Processing Letters*, 12(5):244–250, 1981.
3. M. Crochemore. Recherche linéaire d'un carré dans un mot. *Comptes Rendus des Séances de l'Académie des Sciences. Série I. Mathématique*, 296(18):781–784, 1983.
4. M. Crochemore. Transducers and repetitions. *Theoretical Computer Science*, 45(1):63–86, 1986.
5. D. Gusfield. *Algorithms on strings, trees, and sequences: computer science and computational biology*. Cambridge University Press, 1997.
6. S. Inenaga. Bidirectional construction of suffix trees. *Nordic Journal of Computing*, 10(1):52–67, 2003.
7. H.-F. Leung, Z. Peng, and H.-F. Ting. An efficient online algorithm for square detection. In K.-Y. Chwa and J. I. Munro, editors, *Proceedings of the 10th Annual International Conference*, Lecture Notes in Computer Science 3106, pages 432–439, Jeju Island, Korea, August 17-20 2004. Springer-Verlag.
8. M. G. Main and R. J. Lorentz. An $O(n \log n)$ algorithm for finding all repetitions in a string. *Journal of Algorithms*, 5(3):422–432, 1984.
9. M. G. Main and R. J. Lorentz. Linear time recognition of squarefree strings. In A. Apostolico and Z. Galil, editors, *Combinatorial Algorithms on Words*, volume F12 of *NATO ASI Series*, pages 271–278. Springer-Verlag, 1985.
10. J. A. Storer and T. G. Szymanski. Data compression via textual substitution. *Journal of the ACM*, 29(4):928–951, 1982.
11. E. Ukkonen. On-line construction of suffix trees. *Algorithmica*, 14(3):249–260, 1995.

A Simple Fast Hybrid
Pattern-Matching Algorithm*

Frantisek Franek[1], Christopher G. Jennings[2], and William F. Smyth[1,3]

[1] Algorithms Research Group, Department of Computing & Software
McMaster University, Hamilton ON L8S 4K1, Canada
franek@mcmaster.ca
www.cas.mcmaster.ca/cas/research/groups.shtml
[2] School of Computing Science, Simon Fraser University
8888 University Drive, Burnaby BC V5A 1S6, Canada
cjennings@acm.org
[3] School of Computing, Curtin University, GPO Box U1987
Perth WA 6845, Australia
smyth@computing.edu.au

Abstract. The Knuth-Morris-Pratt (KMP) pattern-matching algorithm guarantees both independence from alphabet size and worst-case execution time linear in the pattern length; on the other hand, the Boyer-Moore (BM) algorithm provides near-optimal average-case and best-case behaviour, as well as executing very fast in practice. We describe a simple algorithm that employs the main ideas of KMP and BM (with a little help from Sunday) in an effort to combine these desirable features. Experiments indicate that in practice the new algorithm is among the fastest exact pattern-matching algorithms discovered to date, perhaps dominant for alphabet size 8 or more.

1   Introduction

Since 1977, with the publication of both the Boyer-Moore [1] and Knuth-Morris-Pratt [16] pattern-matching algorithms, there have certainly been hundreds, if not thousands, of papers published that deal with exact pattern-matching, and in particular discuss and/or introduce variants of either BM or KMP. The literature has had two main foci:

- reducing the number of letter comparisons required in the worst/average case (for example, [3–5, 7, 10, 11]);
- reducing the time requirement in the worst/average case (for example, [6, 8, 13, 14, 21]).

This contribution resides in the second of these categories: in an effort to reduce processing time, we propose a mixture of Sunday's variant [21] of BM [1] with KMP [16, 19]. Our goal is to combine the best/average case advantages of Sunday's algorithm (BMS) with the worst case guarantees of KMP. Experiments

* Supported in part by grants from the Natural Sciences & Engineering Research Council of Canada.

A. Apostolico, M. Crochemore, and K. Park (Eds.): CPM 2005, LNCS 3537, pp. 288–297, 2005.

suggest that our new algorithm (FJS) is among the fastest in practice for computating all occurrences of a pattern $p = p[1..m]$ in a text string $x = x[1..n]$ on an alphabet Σ of size k. Based on $\Theta(m+k)$-time preprocessing, it also guarantees that matching requires at most $3n-2m$ letter comparisons and $O(n)$ time.

Several comparative surveys of pattern-matching algorithms have been published over the years [9, 14, 17, 18, 20] and a useful website [2] is maintained that gives C code for the main algorithms and describes their important features.

In this paper we first introduce, in Section 2, the new algorithm, establish its asymptotic time and space requirements in the worst case, and demonstrate its correctness. Then in Section 3 we describe experiments that compare Algorithm FJS with algorithms that, from the available literature, appear to provide the best competition in practice; specifically: Horspool's algorithm (BMH) [13], Sunday's algorithm (BMS) [21], Reverse Colussi (RC) [6], and Turbo-BM (TBM) [8]. Finally, in Section 4, we draw conclusions from our experiments.

2   The New Algorithm

Algorithm FJS combines two well-known pattern-matching ideas:

(1) In accordance with the BM approach, FJS first compares $p[m]$, the rightmost letter of the pattern, with the letter in the corresponding text position i'. If a mismatch occurs, a "Sunday shift" is implemented, moving p along x until the rightmost occurrence in p of the letter $h = x[i'+1]$ is positioned at $i'+1$. At this new location, the rightmost letter of p is again matched with the corresponding text position. Only when a match is found does FJS invoke the next (KMP) step; otherwise, another Sunday shift occurs.
(2) If $p[m] = x[i']$, KMP pattern-matching begins, starting (as KMP does) from the lefthand end $p[1]$ of the pattern and, if no mismatch occurs, extending as far as $p[m-1]$. Then, whether or not a match for p is found, a KMP shift is eventually performed, followed by a return to step (1).

The pseudocode for Algorithm FJS is shown in the figure below.

As discussed in [15], the real rationale for the algorithm lies in the avoidance of Markov effects combined with efficient shifting: a match of $p[m]$ with $x[i']$ can in most circumstances be regarded as independent of a match (or mismatch) with $p[1]$, where KMP matching begins; if $p[m] \neq x[i']$, then the Sunday shift provides an efficient mechanism for sliding p across x. Viewed from one perspective, FJS just performs KMP matching in a slightly different order: position m of p is compared first, followed by $1, 2, \ldots, m-1$. Indeed, since the KMP shift is also employed, the number of worst-case letter comparisons required for FJS is bounded above, as we show below, by $3n-2m$, compared with KMP's $2n-m$.

Preprocessing

The algorithm uses two arrays: Sunday's array $\Delta = \Delta[1..k]$ computable in $\Theta(m+k)$ time, and the KMP array $\beta' = \beta'[1..m+1]$, computable in $\Theta(m)$ time.

Algorithm 1 (Hybrid Matching)

Find all occurrences of $p = p[1..m]$ in $x = x[1..n]$

if $m < 1$ **then return**
$i' \leftarrow m$; $j \leftarrow 1$; $m' \leftarrow m-1$
while $i' \leq n$ **do**

    — *BM (Sunday) shift if $p[m]$ fails to match*
    if $p[m] \neq x[i']$ **then**
      repeat
        $i' \leftarrow i' + \Delta\big[x[i'+1]\big]$
        if $i' > n$ **then return**
      until $p[m] = x[i']$
      $j \leftarrow 1$

    — *KMP matching if $p[m]$ matches*
    if $j \leq 1$ **then**
      $i \leftarrow i' - m'$; $j \leftarrow 1$
    while $j < m$ **and** $x[i] = p[j]$ **do**
      $i \leftarrow i+1$; $j \leftarrow j+1$

    — *Restore invariant $i' = i+m-j$ for next shift*
    if $j = m$ **then**
      $i \leftarrow i+1$; $j \leftarrow j+1$; **output** $i-m$
    $j \leftarrow \beta'[j]$; $i' \leftarrow i+m-j$

The hth position in the Δ array is accessed directly by the letter h of the alphabet, and so we need to make the assumption required by all BM-type algorithms, that the alphabet is *indexed* [20] – essentially, that $\Sigma = \{1, 2, \cdots, k\}$ for some integer k fixed in advance. Then for every $h \in 1..k$, $\Delta[h] = m - j' + 1$, where j' is the position of rightmost occurrence of the letter h in p, if it exists; zero otherwise. Thus in case of a mismatch with $x[i']$, $\Delta\big[x[i' + 1]\big]$ computes a shift that places the rightmost occurrence j' of letter $x[i' + 1]$ in p opposite position $i'+1$ of x, whenever j' exists in p, and otherwise shifts p right past position $i'+1$.

To define the β' array, consider first an array $\beta[1..m+1]$ in which $\beta[1] = 0$ and for every $j \in 2..m+1$, $\beta[j]$ is one more than the length of the longest border of $p[1..j-1]$. Then $\beta'[j]$ is defined as follows:

If $j = m+1$, $\beta'[j] = \beta[j]$. Otherwise, for $j \in 1..m$, $\beta'[j] = j'$ where $j'-1$ is the length of the longest border of $p[1..j-1]$ such that $p[j'] \neq p[j]$; if no such border exists, $\beta'[j] = 0$.

See [2] for C code and [9, 20] for further discussion of the preprocessing arrays.

The Algorithm

The KMP part of the algorithm needs to compare position i of x with position j of p, where j may be the result of a partial match with $p[1..j-1]$ or of an assignment $j \leftarrow \beta'[j]$. On the other hand, the BMS part needs to compare position

$$i' = i + m - j \tag{1}$$

of x with position m of p. Thus (1) is maintained as an invariant by FJS. Since the assignment $j \leftarrow \beta'[j]$ may actually set j to zero, (1) may not hold if $j = 0$ and $p[m] = x[i']$ at the next match; it is for this reason that the assignment $j \leftarrow 1$ is made for $j \leq 1$ at the beginning of the KMP section.

Correctness

The correctness of Algorithm FJS is a consequence of the correctness of BMS and KMP. Note that a sentinel letter needs to be added at position $n+1$ of x to ensure that $\Delta\big[x[i'+1]\big]$ is well defined for $i' = n$. If this is undesirable, the final alignment at $x[n - m + 1..n]$ can be tested as a special case outside of the main loop.

Letter Comparisons

In the worst case there may be as many as $n-m+1$ executions of the BM-type match in Algorithm FJS. Then KMP-type letter comparisons could take place on the remaining $m-1$ positions of the pattern over a text string of length $n-1$ (the final letter of x would never be subject to KMP-type matching). It is well known (see, for example, [20]) that Algorithm KMP performs at most $2n'-m'$ letter comparisons to find matches for a pattern of length m' in a string of length n'. Substituting $n' = n-1$, $m' = m-1$, we find the largest possible number of letter comparisons by Algorithm FJS is

$$2(n-1) - (m-1) + (n-m+1) = 3n-2m.$$

It is straightforward to verify that this bound is in fact attained by $p = a^{m-2}ba$, $x = a^n$. Thus

Theorem 1 *Algorithm FJS requires at most $3n-2m$ letter comparisons in the worst case, a bound attained by $p = a^{m-2}ba$, $x = a^n$.* $\square$

We see that, in terms of worst-case letter comparisons, there is a slight price to be paid for the improved average-case efficiency of FJS.

3   Experimental Results

As mentioned in Section 1, we conducted a number of experiments to compare Algorithm FJS with four competitors (BMH, BMS, RC, TBM) known to be among the fastest in practice[1].

---

[1] Colussi presents two versions of RC. We used the first version, which is faster on average but requires $\Theta(mn)$ time in the worst case; a second version matches in worst-case $\Theta(n)$ time but is typically slower. Tests of the second version did not produce significantly different results relative to FJS.

Our implementations were adapted from [2], which provides well-tested C code for many pattern-matching algorithms. This gave us a standard to mimic for FJS, ensuring fairness and consistency. A significant change was the replacement of calls to the C library functions *memcmp()* and *memset()*, made by a few of the implementations, with equivalent loops. The library calls, which are optimized for large memory regions, were four to five times slower for our tests.

Timing made use of the high-frequency hardware clocks available on modern computers. Each test was repeated 20 times and the fastest time was kept. This is closest to a true minimum independent of external effects such as cache misses. All times include both preprocessing and matching.

The results presented here were taken from the test system with the most precise timing – an AMD Athlon 2500+ PC with 512MB RAM, running Windows 2000 (SP4) and using Microsoft C/C++ 12.00.8168. However, the resulting trends were highly stable across eight environments using a variety of hardware, operating system, and compiler vendor combinations.

Test Data

The primary corpus was drawn from a set of 1000 randomly selected texts from Project Gutenberg [12], an online source of public domain documents. The corpus contained a total of 446 504 073 letters, with individual texts ranging from 10 115 to 4 823 268 letters in length.

A second corpus was constructed using the Human Genome Project's map of the first human chromosome. A string of 210 992 564 nucleotides was transformed into a bit string by mapping A, T, C, and G to 00, 01, 10, and 11, respectively. Random substrings were then used to make texts of varying alphabet size.

Frequency of Occurrence

We constructed high- and moderate-frequency pattern sets to observe the effect of match frequency on performance. To obtain comparable results, we fixed the number and length of the patterns in both sets. As both values must be kept fairly small to construct a meaningful high-frequency pattern set, we settled on sets of seven patterns of length six.

The high-frequency set was selected by finding the seven most frequent length six substrings in a random sample of 200 texts from our primary corpus. The resulting set, with ␣ representing the space symbol, is as follows:

$$␣of␣th \quad of␣the \quad f␣the␣ \quad ␣that␣ \quad ,␣and␣ \quad ␣this␣ \quad n␣the␣$$

These patterns occur 3 366 899 times in the primary corpus. Figure 1 graphs performance on this set. The execution time for each text is the total time taken for all patterns, where the time for each pattern is determined as described above.

For the moderate frequency set, we constructed a set of 7 words of at least length six sharing an expected frequency of 4 instances per 10 000 words (long words were truncated to six letters). The actual match frequency may vary since patterns may occur often within other words, but this tends to occur in practice as well. After restricting all members to at most six letters the resulting set is:

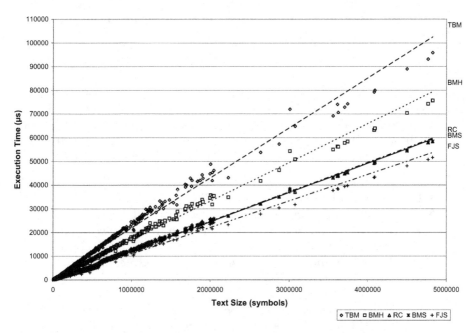

Fig. 1. Execution Time versus Text Length for High-frequency Pattern Set

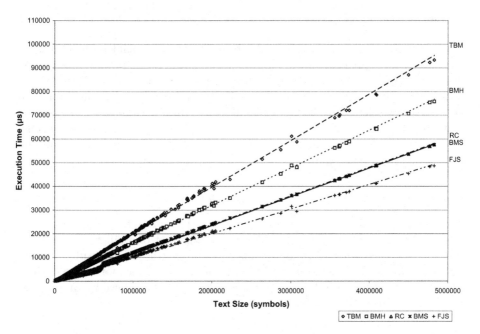

Fig. 2. Execution Time versus Text Length for Moderate-frequency Pattern Set

better   enough   govern   public   someth   system   though

These patterns occur 266 792 times in our corpus. Figure 2 graphs the results.

Pattern Length

Pattern sets were constructed consisting of nine patterns for each pattern length from three to nine. These were selected using a similar process to the one described above, but with an expected frequency of 2–3 times per 10 000 words. The reduced frequency was needed to allow sufficient candidates of each length.

Length	Matches	Pattern Set
3	586 198	*air, age, ago, boy, car, I'm, job, run, six*
4	346 355	*body, half, held, past, seem, seen, tell, week, word*
5	250 237	*death, field, money, quite, seems, shall, taken, whose, words*
6	182 353	*became, behind, cannot, having, making, moment, period, really, result*
7	99 109	*already, brought, college, control, federal, further, provide, society, special*
8	122 854	*anything, evidence, military, position, probably, problems, question, students, together*
9	71 371	*available, community, education, following, necessary, political, situation, sometimes, therefore*

Figure 3 graphs the results from this test. The time at each length is the total time for all nine patterns in the relevant set over the entire primary corpus. As the trends of FJS and BMS suggest that they are asymptotically the same, an additional experiment was performed testing 90 patterns with lengths from 25 to 175, randomly selected from the corpus. FJS and BMS became indistinguishable from about $m = 100$ onward. RC was burdened by its $O(m^2)$ preprocessing time, placing last from $m = 30$ on. At $m = 175$, it was more than an order of magnitude slower than its nearest competitor.

Alphabet Size

These tests used the secondary corpus of DNA-derived texts. This corpus contained 6 texts of 500 000 letters, each over an alphabet of a different size. Each text was searched with 20 random substrings of length 6. The results, seen in Figure 4, suggest that Algorithm FJS may be a poor choice for $k < 8$ – thus, perhaps, not optimal for DNA sequences ($|\Sigma| = 4$), but suitable for proteins composed of amino acids ($|\Sigma| = 20$).

Pathological Cases

Periodic strings can induce theoretical worst-case behaviour in pattern-matching algorithms. For FJS in particular, $x = a^n, p = aba$ maximizes the comparison

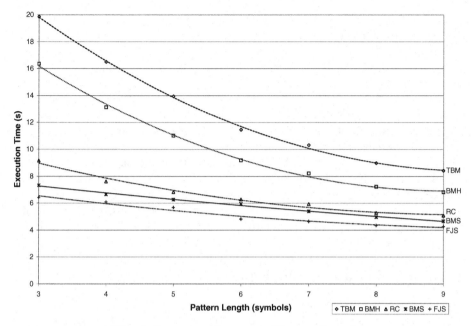

Fig. 3. Execution Time versus Pattern Length

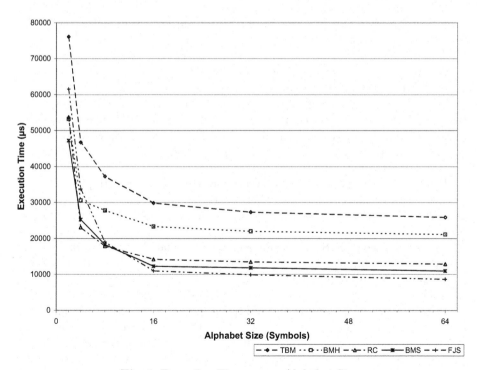

Fig. 4. Execution Time versus Alphabet Size

count. We compared performance on these strings for values of n from 10 000 to 100 000 at 10 000 letter intervals. The rank order, from fastest to slowest, was RC, BMH, BMS, FJS, TBM; RC timed 41% faster than FJS on average.

On the other hand, patterns of the form $\boldsymbol{x} = a^n, \boldsymbol{p} = a^m$ (and in particular, $m = \lceil n/2 \rceil$) maximize comparisons for many non-linear BM variants, including BMH and BMS. Fixing the text as $\boldsymbol{x} = a^{100000}$, we timed the five implementations for $\boldsymbol{p} = a^3$ through $\boldsymbol{p} = a^9$. The results showed FJS to be an average of 36% faster than second-place TBM, the only $\Theta(n)$ competitor.

The worst case for the original BM algorithm can be triggered with $\boldsymbol{x} = (a^k b)^r, \boldsymbol{p} = a^{k-1} b a^{k-1}$. As in the previous case, both the pattern and the text are highly repetitive. We performed two tests on string pairs of this kind. In the first test, we held r at 100 000 and varied k from 2 through 20. In the second test, we held k at 10 and varied r from 100 000 through 500 000. Both experiments indicated an advantage to FJS by 15–20% over BMS and RC and by a large margin over all others.

4 Discussion and Conclusion

We have tested FJS against four high-profile competitors (BMH, BMS, RC, TBM) over a range of contexts: pattern frequency (C1), pattern length (C2), alphabet size (C3), and pathological cases (C4).

Over contexts (C1) and (C2) for English text, FJS was uniformly 10% or so faster than BMS and RC, its closest adversaries. For very long patterns, the Sunday skip loop dominates and FJS and BMS are interchangeable.

In terms of (C3), for small alphabets the expected incidence of $\boldsymbol{p}[m] = \boldsymbol{x}[i']$ is high: KMP will be invoked often, slowing FJS with respect to BMS and RC. For $k \geq 8$, FJS regains its 10% or so advantage.

The overall speed advantage of FJS probably relates to its efficient average-case processing of the most common case (initial mismatch) resulting from the use of the skip loop to avoid repeated settings of $j = 1$ and Markov independence of position m and position j in the pattern $\boldsymbol{p}$. As discussed in [15], the first factor appears to be the more important.

For FJS the pathological cases (C4) are those in which the KMP part is forced to execute on prefixes of patterns where KMP has no advantage (no nonempty borders). On the other hand, FJS performs well on periodic patterns, precisely because of its KMP component.

The advantage of FJS over TBM seems to be related to the extra time involved in TBM's shift logic; while the advantage over BMH seems to be a compound of an improved shift methodology together with the effect of the KMP component.

In summary: we presented the hybrid algorithm FJS which combines the benefits of KMP and BMS. It requires $\Theta(m+k)$ time and space for preprocessing, and finds all matches in at most $3n - 2m$ letter comparisons. We also compared FJS with some of the fastest algorithms available. The results suggest that FJS is competitive with these algorithms in general, and that for $k \geq 8$ it is the algorithm of choice.

References

1. Robert S. Boyer & J. Strother Moore, **A fast string searching algorithm**, *Commun. Assoc. Comput. Mach. 20–10* (1977) 762–772.
2. Christian Charras & Thierry Lecroq, *Exact String Matching Algorithms*, Laboratoire d'Informatique, Université de Rouen (1997): http://www-igm.univ-mlv.fr/~lecroq/string/index.html.
3. Richard Cole & Ramesh Hariharan, **Tighter bounds on the exact complexity of string matching**, *Proc. 33rd IEEE Symp. Found. Comp. Sci.* (1992) 600–609.
4. Richard Cole, Ramesh Hariharan, Michael S. Paterson & Uri Zwick, **Tighter lower bounds on the exact complexity of string matching**, *SIAM J. Comput. 24–1* (1995) 30–45.
5. Livio Colussi, **Correctness and efficiency of pattern matching algorithms** *Information & Computation 95* (1991) 225–251.
6. Livio Colussi, **Fastest pattern matching in strings**, *J. Algs. 16–2* (1994) 163–189.
7. Livio Colussi, Zvi Galil & Raffaele Giancarlo, **On the exact complexity of string matching**, *Proc. 31st IEEE Symp. Found. Comp. Sci.* (vol. I) (1990) 135–143.
8. Maxime Crochemore, Artur Czumaj, Leszek Gąsieniec, Stefan Jarominek, Thierry Lecroq, Wojciech Plandowski & Wojciech Rytter, **Speeding up two string-matching algorithms**, *Algorithmica 12* (1994) 247–267.
9. Maxime Crochemore, Christophe Hancart & Thierry Lecroq, *Algorithmique du Texte*, Vuibert, Paris (2001).
10. Zvi Galil & Raffaele Giancarlo, **On the exact complexity of string matching: lower bounds**, *SIAM J. Comput. 20–6* (1991) 1008–1020.
11. Zvi Galil & Raffaele Giancarlo, **On the exact complexity of string matching: upper bounds**, *SIAM J. Comput. 21–3* (1992) 407–437.
12. Michael Hart, *Project Gutenberg*, Project Gutenberg Literary Archive Foundation (2004): http://www.gutenberg.net.
13. R. Nigel Horspool, **Practical fast searching in strings**, *Software – Practice & Experience 10–6* (1980) 501–506.
14. Andrew Hume & Daniel Sunday, **Fast string searching**, *Software – Practice & Experience 21–11* (1991) 1221–1248.
15. Christopher G. Jennings, *A Linear-Time Algorithm for Fast Exact Pattern Matching in Strings*, M. Sc. thesis, McMaster University (2002) 97 pp.
16. Donald E. Knuth, James H. Morris & Vaughan R. Pratt, **Fast pattern matching in strings**, *SIAM J. Comput. 6–2* (1977) 323–350.
17. Thierry Lecroq, **Experimental results on string matching algorithms**, *Software – Practice & Experience 25–7* (1995) 727–765.
18. Thierry Lecroq, *New Experimental Results on Exact String-Matching*, Rapport LIFAR 2000.03, Université de Rouen (2000).
19. James H. Morris & Vaughan R. Pratt, *A Linear Pattern-Matching Algorithm*, Tech. Rep. 40, University of California, Berkeley (1970).
20. Bill Smyth, *Computing Patterns in Strings*, Pearson Addison-Wesley (2003) 423 pp.
21. Daniel M. Sunday, **A very fast substring search algorithm**, *Commun. Assoc. Comput. Mach. 33–8* (1990) 132–142.

Prefix-Free Regular-Expression Matching*

Yo-Sub Han, Yajun Wang, and Derick Wood

Department of Computer Science
The Hong Kong University of Science and Technology
{emmous,yalding,dwood}@cs.ust.hk

Abstract. We explore the regular-expression matching problem with respect to prefix-freeness of the pattern. We show that the prefix-free regular expression gives only linear number of matching substrings in the size of a given text. Based on this observation, we propose an efficient algorithm for the prefix-free regular-expression matching problem. Furthermore, we suggest an algorithm to determine whether or not a given regular language is prefix-free.

1 Introduction

In 1968, Thompson [11] introduced what became a classical automaton construction, the Thompson construction. It was used to find all matching strings from a text with respect to a given regular expression in the unix editor, ed. Subsequently, Aho [1] investigated the regular-expression matching problem as an extension of the keyword pattern matching problem [2], where the set of keywords is represented by a regular expression. Regular-expression matching has been adopted in many applications such as grep, vi, emacs and perl. For instance, with grep, we search for the last position of a matching string since the command outputs the line that contains the matched string.

Prefix-freeness is fundamental in coding theory; for example, Huffman codes are prefix-free sets. The advantage of prefix-free codes is that we can decode a given encoded string deterministically. Since codes are languages and prefix-free codes are a proper subfamily of codes, prefix-free regular languages are a proper subfamily of regular languages. Prefix-free regular languages have already been used to define *determinism* for generalized automata [6] and for expression automata [7].

The regular-expression matching problem has been well studied in the literature. Given a regular expression E and a text T, Aho [1] showed that we can determine whether or not there is a substring of T that is in $L(E)$ in $O(mn)$ time using $O(m)$ space, where m is the size of E and n is the size of T. Recently, Crochemore and Hancart [5] presented an algorithm to find all end positions

* Han and Wood were supported under the Research Grants Council of Hong Kong Competitive Earmarked Research Grant HKUST6197/01E and Wang was supported under the Research Grants Council of Hong Kong Competitive Earmarked Research Grant HKUST6206/02E.

A. Apostolico, M. Crochemore, and K. Park (Eds.): CPM 2005, LNCS 3537, pp. 298–309, 2005.

of matching substrings of T with respect to $L(E)$ in $O(mn)$ time using $O(m)$ space. Myers et al. [10] solved the problem of identifying start positions and end positions of all matching substrings of T that belong to $L(E)$ in $O(mn \log n)$ time using $O(m \log n)$ space. Clarke and Cormack [4] considered an interesting problem, the *shortest-match substring search*. Given a finite-state automaton A and a text T, identify all substrings of T that are accepted by A and also form an *infix-free set*. They showed that there are at most n matching substrings in T and they suggested an $O(kmn)$ worst-case running time algorithm using $O(m)$ space, where k is the maximum number of out-transitions from a state in A, m is the number of states and n is the size of T. (If we assume that A is a Thompson automaton, then $k = 2$.) In the regular-expression matching problem, there are a quadratic number of matching substrings of a given text in the worst-case. On the other hand, Clarke and Cormack [4] hinted that if an input regular expression is infix-free, then there are at most a linear number of matching substrings and it ensures a faster running time. Since the family of prefix-free regular languages is a proper subfamily of regular languages and a proper superfamily of infix-free regular languages, it is natural to investigate the prefix-free regular-expression matching problem. As far as we are aware, there does not appear to have been any prior consolidated effort to study the prefix-free regular-expression matching problem.

We want to find all $(start, end)$ positions of matching substrings; similar to the work of Myers et al. [10] and Clarke and Cormack [4]. We reexamine the regular-expression matching problem with this requirement and investigate the prefix-free regular-expression matching problem. Moreover, we suggest an algorithm to determine whether or not a given regular language L is prefix-free, where L is described by a nondeterministic finite-state automaton or by a regular expression. If L is represented by a deterministic finite-state automaton, then L is prefix-free if and only if there are no out-transitions from any final state in the given automaton [7].

In Section 2, we define some basic notation. We then, in Section 3, present an algorithm to identify all matching substrings of T with respect to a regular expression E based on the algorithm by Crochemore and Hancart [5]. The worst-case running time for the algorithm is $O(mn^2)$ using $O(m)$ space, where m is the size of E and n is the size of T. We also study the infix-free regular expression matching problem motivated by the shortest-match substring search problem. In Section 4, we examine the prefix-free regular-expression matching problem and propose an $O(mn)$ worst-case running time algorithm using $O(m)$ space. It implies that if E is prefix-free, then we can improve the total running time for the matching problem. In Section 5, we present a polynomial-time algorithm to determine whether or not a given regular language is prefix-free.

2   Preliminaries

Let Σ denote a finite alphabet of characters and Σ^* denote the set of all strings over Σ. A language over Σ is any subset of Σ^*. The character $\emptyset$ denotes the empty language and the character λ denotes the null string. Given two strings x and y in Σ^*, x is said to be a *prefix* of y if there is a string w such that $xw = y$. Given a set X of strings over Σ, X is *prefix-free* if no string in X is a prefix of any other string in X. Given a string x, let x^R be the reversal of x, in which case $X^R = \{x^R \mid x \in X\}$.

A finite-state automaton A is specified by a tuple $(Q, \Sigma, \delta, s, F)$, where Q is a finite set of states, Σ is an input alphabet, $\delta \subseteq Q \times \Sigma \times Q$ is a (finite) set of transitions, $s \in Q$ is the start state and $F \subseteq Q$ is a set of final states. Let $|Q|$ be the number of states in Q and $|\delta|$ be the number of transitions in δ. Given a transition (p, a, q) in δ, where $p, q \in Q$ and $a \in \Sigma$, we say p has an *out-transition* and q has an *in-transition*. Furthermore, p is a *source state* of q and q is a *target state* of p. A string x over Σ is accepted by A if there is a labeled path from s to a final state in F that spells out x. Thus, the language $L(A)$ of a finite-state automaton A is the set of all strings spelled out by paths from s to a final state in F. We define A to be *non-returning* if the start state of A does not have any in-transitions and A to be *non-exiting* if a final state of A does not have any out-transitions. We assume that A has only *useful* states; that is, each state appears on some path from the start state to some final state.

We define a (regular) language L to be prefix-free if L is a prefix-free set. A regular expression E is prefix-free if $L(E)$ is prefix-free. In a similar way, we define suffix-free regular languages and regular expressions. We define L to be *infix-free* if, for all distinct strings x and y in L, x is not a substring of y and y is not a substring of x. Then, a regular expression E is infix-free if $L(E)$ is infix-free. The size $|E|$ of a regular expression E is the total number of character appearances.

3   Regular-Expression Matching

The regular-expression matching problem is an extension of the pattern matching problem, for which a pattern is given as a regular expression E. If $L(E)$ consists of a single string, then the problem is the string matching problem [3, 9] and if $L(E)$ is a finite language, then we obtain the multiple keyword matching problem [2].

Definition 1. *Given a regular expression E and a text $T = w_1 w_2 \cdots w_n$, the regular-expression matching problem is to identify all matching substrings of T that belong to $L(E)$.*

We answer the regular-expression matching problem by using Thompson automata [11]. We give the inductive construction of Thompson automata in Fig. 1. Note that a state q in a Thompson automaton has at most two in-transitions and at most two out-transitions. Furthermore, if q has a transition (q, a, r) and $a \in \Sigma$, then state r has at most two out-transitions that are null.

Given a regular expression E over Σ, we prepend Σ^* to E; thus, allowing matching to begin at any position in T. We construct the Thompson automaton A for $\Sigma^* E$ and process T using ExpressionMatching defined in Fig. 2.

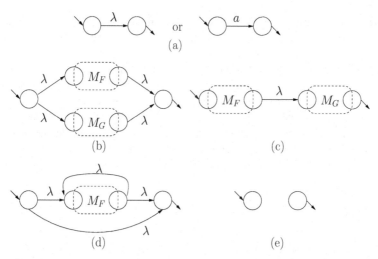

Fig. 1. The Thompson construction. Let E, F and G be regular expressions and M_F and M_G be the corresponding Thompson automata for F and G, respectively. (a) $E = a + \lambda$, (b) $E = F + G$, (c) $E = F \cdot G$, (d) $E = F^*$ and (e) $E = \emptyset$.

ExpressionMatching (A, T)

$Q = null(\{s\})$
if $f \in Q$ **then output** λ
for j=1 **to** n
    $Q = null(goto(Q, w_j))$
    if $f \in Q$ **then output** j

Fig. 2. A regular-expression matching procedure for a given Thompson automaton $A = (Q, \Sigma, \delta, s, f)$ and a text $T = w_1 \cdots w_n$. The procedure reports all the end positions of matching substrings of T.

Note that ExpressionMatching was already considered by Crochemore and Hancart [5], which is a modified version of Aho's algorithm [1].

ExpressionMatching (EM) in Fig. 2 has two sub-functions: $null(Q)$ and $goto(Q, w_j)$. The function $null(Q)$ computes all states in A that can be reached from a state in the set Q of states by null transitions. We use depth-first traversal to compute $null(Q)$ since A is essentially a graph. We traverse A using only null transitions. If we reach a state q that has already been visited by another null transition, then we stop exploring from q. Therefore, each state in A is visited at most twice since a state in a Thompson automaton has at most two in-transitions. Thus, the $null(Q)$ step takes $O(m)$ time in the worst-case, where m is the size of A. Now $goto(Q, w_j)$ gives all states that can be reached from a state in Q by a transition with w_j, the current input character. We only have to check whether a state in Q has an out-transition with w_j on it since the target state of the current state can have only null out-transitions. Therefore, the $goto(Q, w_j)$ step takes $O(|Q|)$ time, which is $O(m)$ in the worst-case. Overall, EM runs in $O(mn)$ worst-case time using $O(m)$ space.

Note that EM reports all the last positions of matching substrings of T with respect to A. It is, in some applications like grep, sufficient to have the end positions of matching substrings. However, if we want to report exact positions of matching strings, then we have to read T from right to left for each end position to find the corresponding start positions. For example, we need seven reverse scans of T to find all matching substrings in Fig. 3.

$E = a(a+b)^*a$

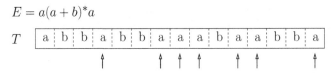

Fig. 3. An example of finding all end positions of T for a given regular expression E using EM. EM reports seven end positions indicated by "↑". There are, however, 28 matching substrings of T with respect to E and some matching substrings end at the same position.

We construct the Thompson automaton A' for E^R to find the start positions that correspond to the end positions we have already computed. For each end position j in T, we process $w_j \cdots w_2 w_1$ with respect to A' using EM to identify all corresponding start positions for j. In the worst-case, there are $O(n)$ end positions for matching substrings and we have to read T^R for each end position to find all corresponding start positions. A worst-case example is when $E = (a + b)^*$ and $T = abaaabababa \cdots aba$. Total running time for the regular-expression matching problem is $O(mn) + O(mn) \cdot O(n) = O(mn^2)$; that is (search all end positions) + [(find all corresponding start positions for each end position) × (the number of end positions)], using $O(m)$ space in the worst-case.

Theorem 1. *Given a regular expression E and a text T, we can identify all matching substrings of T that belong to $L(E)$ in $O(mn^2)$ worst-case time using $O(m)$ space, where m is the size of E and n is the size of T.*

Before we tackle the prefix-free regular-expression matching problem, we consider the simpler case of E being infix-free. Note that this problem is similar to, yet different from, the shortest-match substring search by Clarke and Cormack [4]. They were interested in reporting all matching substrings that form an infix-free set for a given (normal) regular expression and we are interested in the case when a given regular expression is strictly infix-free.

Theorem 2. *Given an infix-free regular expression E and a text T, we can identify all matching substrings of T that belong to $L(E)$ in $O(mn)$ worst-case time using $O(m)$ space, where m is the size of E and n is the size of T.*

A brief description of the algorithm for Theorem 2 is as follows: First, we find all end positions $P = \{p_1, p_2, \ldots, p_k\}$ of matching substrings in T using EM, where k is the number of matching substrings in T. Note that $k \leq n$ since $L(E)$ is infix-free[1]. Then, we construct the Thompson automaton A' for $\Sigma^* E^R$ and find all the end positions $P^R = \{q_1, q_2, \ldots, q_k\}$ of substrings of T^R with respect to A' using EM. Note that P^R also has k positions. We assume that both P and P^R are sorted in ascending order.

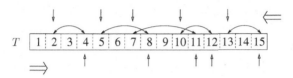

Fig. 4. An example of infix-free regular-expression matching. The upper arrows indicate P^R and the lower arrows indicate P. We output (2,4), (5,8), (7, 11), (10,12) and (13,15).

Since $L(E)$ is infix-free, no matching substring can be nested within any other matching substring. Therefore, once we have P^R and P, then we output (q_i, p_i) for $1 \leq i \leq k$, where $q_i \in P^R$ and $p_i \in P$. Fig. 4 illustrates this step when $P^R = \{2, 5, 7, 10, 13\}$ and $P = \{4, 8, 11, 12, 15\}$. Since we run EM twice to compute P and P^R and the output step from P and P^R takes only linear time in the size of P, which is $O(n)$ in the worst-case, the total complexity is $O(mn)$ time using $O(m)$ space.

Since all infix-free (regular) languages are prefix-free (regular) languages it is natural to investigate more general case, the prefix-free regular-expression matching problem.

4   The Prefix-Free Regular-Expression Matching Problem

We now consider the regular-expression matching problem for prefix-free regular expressions.

Lemma 1. *Given a prefix-free regular expression E and a text T, there are at most n matching substrings that belong to $L(E)$, where n is the size of T.*

Proof. Assume that the number of matching substrings is greater than n. Then, by the pigeonhole principle, there must be two distinct substrings s_1 and s_2 that start from the same position in T. We assume without loss of generality that s_1 is shorter than s_2, which, in turn, implies that s_1 is a prefix of s_2 — a contradiction. Therefore, there are at most n matching substrings. $\Box$

---

[1] This is a special case of Lemma 1 in Section 4 since an infix-free language is also a prefix-free language.

We design an algorithm for the prefix-free regular-expression matching problem. First, we find all end positions of matching substrings of $T = w_1 \cdots w_n$ using EM with respect to E. Let $P = \{p_1, p_2, \ldots, p_k\}$ be the set of end positions of matching substrings, where $k \leq n$ is the number of matching substrings. Then, we need to search for the corresponding start position of each end position in P. We construct the Thompson automaton $A' = (Q, \Sigma, \delta', s', f')$ for E^R and scan $T^R = w_n \cdots w_1$ starting from the last position p_k in P. Note that E^R is suffix-free.

Definition 2. *Given a position $j \in P$ and a current input position i in T^R in EM, where $i < j$, we define $\mathcal{Q}_j$ to be the set of states such that there is a path from s' to each state in $\mathcal{Q}_j$ that spells out the substring $w_j w_{j-1} \cdots w_i$ of T^R in A'.*

The notion of a set of reachable states in Definition 2 is not new. We already used it in EM in Fig. 2 implicitly. We now maintain sets of reachable states in A' for all end positions in P.

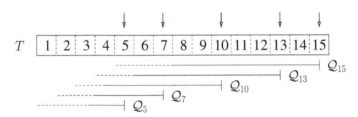

Fig. 5. Once we find the set P of all end positions, then we read T^R and maintain sets of reachable states for P in EM. For example, we have $\mathcal{Q}_{15}$, $\mathcal{Q}_{13}$ and $\mathcal{Q}_{10}$ when reading w_8 of T^R.

We process T^R from the last position in P with respect to A' using EM. If $\mathcal{Q}_j$, for some position $j \in P, 1 \leq j \leq n$, contains the final state f' of A' when reading w_i of T^R, where $i < j$, then we output the matching substring position (i, j) and continue to read the remaining input of T^R. Since each end position in P has exactly one corresponding start position, we can delete $\mathcal{Q}_j$ from our data structure after identifying a matching substring. However, we may meet another end position $j-1$ before finding the start position for $\mathcal{Q}_j$ and need to maintain another set $\mathcal{Q}_{j-1}$ of reachable states for position $j-1$ in P. For example, we may have sets $\mathcal{Q}_{15}$, $\mathcal{Q}_{13}$ and $\mathcal{Q}_{10}$ when we are reading w_8 of T^R in Fig. 5. We have to maintain k sets of reachable states and update k sets simultaneously while reading each character for T^R in the worst-case. As proved in Section 3, the size of each set of reachable states can be $O(m)$ in the worst-case. Therefore, we need $O(kmn)$ time and $O(km)$ space to answer the prefix-free regular-expression matching problem, which is $O(mn^2)$ time and $O(mn)$ space in the worst-case. We now show that we can reduce the complexity to $O(mn)$ time and $O(m)$ space because of prefix-freeness of E.

Lemma 2. *If a state r in A' is reached from two different states p and q, where $p \in Q_i$ and $q \in Q_j$, when reading a character w_h in EM, where $h \le i < j$, then both paths from p and q via r cannot reach f' by reading any prefix of the remaining input in EM.*

Proof. Note that it is not possible that one path reaches f' while the other path does not since both paths must share the same path after reading w_h and arriving at r. Assume that both paths reach f' after reading some prefix $w_{h-1} \cdots w_g$ of the remaining input from r, where $g < h$. It implies that both strings $w_i \cdots w_h \cdots w_g$ and $w_j \cdots w_h \cdots w_g$ belong to $L(E^R)$. Observe that $w_i \cdots w_g$ is a suffix of $w_j \cdots w_g$. It contradicts the suffix-freeness of E^R. Therefore, if r is reached by two states from different sets of reachable states, then both paths from p and q via r cannot reach f' by reading any prefix of the remaining input in EM. □

Lemma 2 demonstrates that if a state r in A' is reached from two different sets of reachable states when reading a character w_h in EM, then r should not belong to the both sets since both paths cannot reach the final state by reading any prefix of the remaining input. Therefore, each state in A' appears in at most one reachable set and any two sets of reachable states are disjoint from each other as a result of reading a character in T^R. Since any state r in a Thompson automaton has at most two in-transitions, r can be visited at most twice in EM and we need at most $O(m)$ time to update all sets of reachable states simultaneously at each step to read a character in EM. Note that we use only $O(m)$ space.

Theorem 3. *Given a prefix-free regular expression E and a text T, we can identify all matching substrings of T that belong to $L(E)$ in $O(mn)$ worst-case time using $O(m)$ space, where $m = |E|$ and $n = |T|$.*

5 Prefix-Free Regular Languages

A regular language is represented by a finite-state automaton or described by a regular expression. We present algorithms to determine whether or not a given regular language L is prefix-free based either on finite-state automata or on regular expressions. Note that if a finite-state automaton A is deterministic, then $L(A)$ is prefix-free if and only if A is non-exiting.

We first consider the representation of a regular language L by a nondeterministic finite-state automaton (NFA) A. If A has any out-transitions from a final state, then we immediately know that $L(A)$ is not prefix-free; A must be non-exiting to be prefix-free. If A is non-exiting and has several final states, then all final states are equivalent and, therefore, merged into a single final state.

Given an NFA $A = (Q, \Sigma, \delta, s, f)$, we assign a unique number for each state from 1 to m, where m is the number of states in Q. Assume 1 denotes s and m denotes f. We use q_i, for $1 \le i \le m$, to denote the corresponding state in A. If $L(A)$ is not prefix-free, then there are two strings s_1 and s_2 accepted by A and s_1

is a prefix of s_2. It implies that there are two distinct paths in A that spell out s_1 and s_2 and these two paths spell out the same prefix s_1. For example, in Fig. 6, two paths for $s_1 = abcbb$ and $s_2 = abcbbab$ are different although they have the same subpath for ab in common. If the path for s_1 is a subpath of the path for s_2, then it implies that there is another final state that has an out-transition. This contradicts that A is non-exiting.

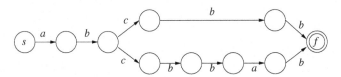

Fig. 6. Two distinct paths for $abcbb$ and $abcbbab$.

We introduce the *state-pair graph* to capture the situation when two distinct paths in A spell out s_1 and s_2 and s_1 is a prefix of s_2.

Definition 3. *Given a finite-state automaton $A = (Q, \Sigma, \delta, s, f)$, we define the state-pair graph $G_A = (V, E)$, where V is a set of nodes and E is a set of edges, as follows:*

$$V = \{(i, j) \mid q_i \text{ and } q_j \in Q\} \text{ and}$$
$$E = \{((i, j), a, (x, y)) \mid (q_i, a, q_x) \text{ and } (q_j, a, q_y) \in \delta \text{ and } a \in \Sigma\}.$$

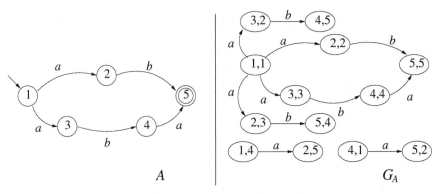

Fig. 7. An example of a state-pair graph G_A for a given finite-state automaton A. We omit all nodes that have no out-transitions in G_A.

Fig. 7 illustrates the state-pair graph for a given finite-state automaton A; $L(A) = \{ab, aba\}$ is not prefix-free because the prefix ab appears on the path from $(1, 1)$ to $(5, 4)$ in G_A.

Theorem 4. *Given a finite-state automaton A, $L(A)$ is prefix-free if and only if there is no path from $(1, 1)$ to (m, j), for any $j \neq m$, in G_A.*

Proof. $\Longrightarrow$ Assume that there is a path from $(1,1)$ to (m,j) that spells out a string x in G_A. Then, by the definition of state-pair graphs, there should be two distinct paths, one of which is from q_1 to q_m and the other is from q_1 to q_j in A, where $q_m = f$ and $q_j \neq f$. Note that both paths spell out x in A. Since A has only useful states, state q_j must have an out-transition (q_j, z_1, q_k), where $z_1 \in \Sigma$. Then, there is a transition sequence $(q_j, z_1, q_k), (q_k, z_2, q_{k+1}), \ldots, (q_{k+l-2}, z_l, q_m)$, for some $l \geq 1$, such that $z_1 \cdots z_l = z$. In other words, A accepts both x and xz — a contradiction. Therefore, if $L(A)$ is prefix-free, then there is no path from $(1,1)$ to (m,j) in G_A.

$\Longleftarrow$ Assume that $L(A)$ is not prefix-free. Then, there are two strings x and y and x is a prefix of y in $L(A)$. Since A is non-exiting, there should be two distinct paths that spell out x and y in A. Since x is a prefix of y, these two paths in A make a path from $(1,1)$ to (m,j), where $j \neq m$ in G_A — a contradiction. Thus, if there is no path from $(1,1)$ to (m,j) for any $j \neq m$ in G_A, then $L(A)$ is prefix-free. $\qquad\square$

Let us consider the complexity of the state-pair graph $G_A = (V,E)$ for a given finite-state automaton $A = (Q, \Sigma, \delta, s, f)$. It is clear that $V = |Q|^2$ from Definition 3. Let δ_i denote the set of out-transitions from state q_i in A. Then, $|\delta| = \sum_{i=1}^{m} |\delta_i|$, where $m = |Q|$. Since a node (i,j) in G_A can have at most $|\delta_i| \times |\delta_j|$ out-transitions, $|E| = \sum_{i,j=1}^{m} |\delta_i| \times |\delta_j| \leq |\delta|^2$. Therefore, the complexity of G_A is $|Q|^2$ nodes and $|\delta|^2$ edges.

Prefix-Freeness$(A = (Q, \Sigma, \delta, s, f))$

if A is not non-exiting
    then return no
Construct $G_A = (V, E)$ from A

DFS$((1,1))$ in G_A
if we meet a node (m,j) for some j, $j \neq m$
    then return no

return yes

Fig. 8. A prefix-freeness checking algorithm for a given automaton.

The sub-function DFS$((1,1))$ in Prefix-Freeness (PF) in Fig. 8 is a depth-first search that starts at node $(1,1)$ in G_A. The construction $G_A = (V, E)$ from A takes $O(|Q|^2 + |\delta|^2)$ time in the worst-case and DFS takes $(|V| + |E|)$ time. Therefore, the total running time for PF is $O(|Q|^2 + |\delta|^2)$.

Theorem 5. *Given a finite-state automaton* $A = (Q, \Sigma, \delta, s, f)$, *we can determine whether or not* $L(A)$ *is prefix-free in* $O(|Q|^2 + |\delta|^2)$ *worst-case time using* PF.

Since $O(|\delta|) = O(|Q|^2)$ in the worst-case for NFAs, the running time of PF is $O(|Q|^4)$ in the worst-case. On the other hand, if a language is described by a regular expression, then we can choose a construction for finite-state automata that improves the worst-case running time. Since the complexity of the state-pair graph depends on the number of states and the number of transitions of a given automaton, we need a finite-state automata construction that results in fewer states and transitions. One possibility is to use the Thompson construction [11].

Given a regular expression E for L, the Thompson construction shown in Fig. 1 takes $O(|E|)$ time and the resulting Thompson automaton has $O(|E|)$ states and $O(|E|)$ transitions [8]; namely, $|Q| = |\delta| = O(|E|)$. Even though Thompson automata are a subfamily of NFAs, they define all regular languages. Therefore, we can use Thompson automata to determine prefix-freeness of a regular language given by a regular expression. Since Thompson automata have null transitions, we include the null transition case to construct the edges for a state-pair graph as follows:

$$V = \{(i,j) \mid q_i \text{ and } q_j \in Q\} \text{ and}$$
$$E = \{((i,j), a, (x,y)) \mid (q_i, a, q_x) \text{ and } (q_j, a, q_y) \in \delta \text{ and } a \in \Sigma \cup \{\lambda\}\}.$$

The complexity of the state-pair graph based on this new construction is the same as before; namely, $O(|Q|^2 + |\delta|^2)$. Therefore, we have the following result when checking regular expression prefix-freeness.

Theorem 6. *Given a regular expression E, we can determine whether or not $L(E)$ is prefix-free in $O(|E|^2)$ worst-case time.*

Proof. We construct the Thompson automaton A_T for E. Hopcroft and Ullman [8] showed that the number of states in A_T is $O(|E|)$ and also the number of transitions, $|Q| = |\delta| = O(|E|)$. Thus, we construct the state-pair graph based on the new construction that includes null transitions and determine whether or not there is a path from $(1,1)$ to (m,j) for some $j \neq m$ in $O(|E|^2)$ time using PF. □

6   Conclusions

We have investigated the regular-expression, the infix-free regular-expression and the prefix-free regular-expression matching problems. We have shown that the regular-expression matching problem can be solved in $O(mn^2)$ time using $O(m)$ space based on the algorithm of Crochemore and Hancart [5]. Whereas, we observed that the infix-free regular-expression matching problem can be solved in $O(mn)$ time using $O(m)$ space. We have extended the matching problem for a more general case, the prefix-free regular-expression matching problem and proved that the prefix-free regular-expression matching problem can also be solved in $O(mn)$ worst-case time using $O(m)$ space.

Furthermore, we have shown that we can determine whether or not $L(A)$ is prefix-free for a given NFA $A = (Q, \Sigma, \delta, s, f)$ in $O(|Q|^2 + |\delta|^2)$ worst-case time based on the state-pair graph defined in Section 5. Finally, if a language L is described by a regular expression E, then we can improve the running time to $O(|E|^2)$ using the Thompson construction [11].

References

1. A. Aho. Algorithms for finding patterns in strings. In J. van Leeuwen, editor, *Algorithms and Complexity*, volume A of *Handbook of Theoretical Computer Science*, 255–300. The MIT Press, Cambridge, MA, 1990.
2. A. Aho and M. Corasick. Efficient string matching: An aid to bibliographic search. *Communications of the ACM*, 18:333–340, 1975.
3. R. S. Boyer and J. S. Moore. A fast string searching algorithm. *Communications of the ACM*, 20(10):762–772, 1977.
4. C. L. A. Clarke and G. V. Cormack. On the use of regular expressions for searching text. *ACM Transactions on Programming Languages and Systems*, 19(3):413–426, 1997.
5. M. Crochemore and C. Hancart. Automata for matching patterns. In G. Rozenberg and A. Salomaa, editors, *Linear modeling: background and application*, volume 2 of *Handbook of Formal Languages*, 399–462. Springer-Verlag, 1997.
6. D. Giammarresi and R. Montalbano. Deterministic generalized automata. *Theoretical Computer Science*, 215:191–208, 1999.
7. Y.-S. Han and D. Wood. The generalization of generalized automata: Expression automata. In *Proceedings of CIAA'04*, 156–166. Springer-Verlag, 2004. Lecture Notes in Computer Science 3317.
8. J. Hopcroft and J. Ullman. *Formal Languages and Their Relationship to Automata*. Addison-Wesley, Reading, MA, 1969.
9. D. Knuth, J. Morris, Jr., and V. Pratt. Fast pattern matching in strings. *SIAM Journal on Computing*, 6:323–350, 1977.
10. E. W. Myers, P. Oliva, and K. S. Guimãraes. Reporting exact and approximate regular expression matches. In *Proceedings of CPM'98*, 91–103. Springer-Verlag, 1998. Lecture Notes in Computer Science 1448.
11. K. Thompson. Regular expression search algorithm. *Communications of the ACM*, 11:419–422, 1968.

Reducing the Size of NFAs
by Using Equivalences and Preorders

Lucian Ilie*,**, Roberto Solis-Oba***, and Sheng Yu**

Department of Computer Science, University of Western Ontario
London, Ontario, N6A 5B7, Canada
{ilie,solis,syu}@csd.uwo.ca

Abstract. The efficiency of regular expression matching algorithms depends very much on the size of the nondeterministic finite automata (NFA) obtained from regular expressions. Reducing the size of these automata by using equivalences has been shown to reduce significantly the search time. We consider the problem of reducing the size of arbitrary NFAs using equivalences and preorders. For equivalences, we give an algorithm to optimally combine equivalent states for reducing the size of the automata. We also show that the problem of optimally using preorders to reduce the size of an automaton is NP-hard.

Keywords: regular expression matching, finite automata, state complexity, equivalences, preorders

1 Introduction

Regular expressions lie at the heart of many applications, such as linguistics, computational biology, pattern recognition, text retrieval, and so on. A powerful and elegant theory provides tools to easily and efficiently solve many complex problems by mapping them to regular expressions, then obtaining nondeterministic finite automata (NFA) that recognize them, and finally constructing deterministic finite automata (DFA). However, a severe obstacle in any real implementation of the above scheme is the size of the DFA, which can be exponential in the length of the original regular expression. A simple algorithm for minimizing DFAs exists [7], but it has the drawback of requiring first the construction of the DFA to later minimize it. This might not be practical because of memory requirements and construction cost of the DFA.

A more promising (and more challenging) alternative is directly reducing the NFA before converting it into a DFA. This has the advantage of working over a much smaller structure (of size polynomial in the length of the regular expression) and of building the smaller DFA without the need to go through a larger one first. However, the NFA state minimization problem is hard (PSPACE-complete, [14]) and, therefore, algorithms such as [15–17] cannot be used in practice. There

---

* Corresponding author.
** Research partially supported by NSERC.
*** Research partially supported by NSERC grant 227829-04.

A. Apostolico, M. Crochemore, and K. Park (Eds.): CPM 2005, LNCS 3537, pp. 310–321, 2005.
© Springer-Verlag Berlin Heidelberg 2005

are also algorithms which build small NFAs from regular expressions, see [6, 10]. These algorithms consider the total size of NFAs, that is, they count both states and transitions, and they increase artificially the number of states to reduce the number of transitions. As the implementation crucially depends on the number of states, such algorithms may not help.

The idea of reducing the size of NFAs by merging states was first introduced by Ilie and Yu [12] who used left and right equivalence relations. Later, Champarnaud and Coulon [2] modified the idea to work for preorders. An algorithm to compute the equivalences in $O(m \log n)$ time on an NFA with n states and m transitions and an $O(mn)$ algorithm for computing preorders are presented in [11].

The above mentioned algorithms identify sets of states that could be merged without modifying the language accepted by the automaton. The number of states of the resulting NFA depends on the order in which the states are merged. Randomly choosing the order in which these mergings take place, as used so far, does not guarantee that the smallest NFAs that can be built with these techniques are produced.

In this paper we investigate optimal ways to use the information in equivalences and preorders to reduce NFAs. We first give an efficient algorithm for optimally combining the left and right equivalences for achieving the maximum reduction in the size of an NFA. We show that the same problem for preorders, however, is NP-hard. Since, potentially, preorders could produce a better reduction, a number of open problems remain, such as looking for alternative ways, e.g., approximation algorithms, to reduce NFAs using preorders.

Notice that we do not claim that the above techniques achieve optimal reduction in the size of nondeterministic finite automata, as this problem is PSPACE-complete. Rather, we use the adjective "optimal" to refer to the maximum reduction in size that these techniques can achieve. We will explain this more precisely in the following sections.

We expect our results to have applications to regular expression matching. A single equivalence was shown by Ilie et al. [11] to reduce significantly the search time, more so than the special properties of the Glushkov automaton (see [18, 19]). It remains to be tested how much we can further speed up regular expression search using the present reduction algorithms. Several important research directions are mentioned in the conclusions section.

2   Basic Notions

We recall here the basic definitions we need throughout the paper. For further details we refer to [9] or [21].

Let A be an alphabet of constant size and A^* be the set of all words over A; ε denotes the empty word. A *language* over A is a subset of A^*. A *nondeterministic finite automaton* (*NFA*) is a tuple $M = (Q, A, \delta, I, F)$, where Q is the set of states, $I \subseteq Q$ is the set of initial states, $F \subseteq Q$ is the set of final states, and $\delta : Q \times A \to 2^Q$ is the transition mapping; δ is extended to $\delta : 2^Q \times A^* \to 2^Q$

by $\delta(S, a) = \bigcup_{q \in S} \delta(q, a)$, $\delta(S, \varepsilon) = S$, and $\delta(S, aw) = \delta(\delta(S, a), w)$, for $S \subseteq Q$, $w \in A^*$. The *language* recognized by M is

$$\mathcal{L}(M) = \{w \in A^* \mid \delta(I, w) \cap F \neq \emptyset\}.$$

For $p, q \in Q$, we denote

$$\begin{aligned}
\mathcal{L}_L(M, p) &= \{w \in A^* \mid p \in \delta(I, w)\}, \\
\mathcal{L}_R(M, p) &= \{w \in A^* \mid \delta(p, w) \cap F \neq \emptyset\}, \\
\mathcal{L}(M, p, q) &= \{w \in A^* \mid q \in \delta(p, w)\};
\end{aligned}$$

when M is understood, we simply write $\mathcal{L}_L(p)$, $\mathcal{L}_R(p)$, and $\mathcal{L}(p, q)$, respectively. The *reversed* automaton of M is $M^r = (Q, A, \delta^r, F, I)$, where $q \in \delta^r(p, a)$ iff $p \in \delta(q, a)$.

3   NFA Reduction with Equivalences

The idea of reducing the size of NFAs by merging states was investigated first by Ilie and Yu [12]; see also [13]. We describe it briefly in this section.

Let $M = (Q, A, \delta, I, F)$ be an NFA. We define $\equiv_R$ as the coarsest equivalence relation over Q that satisfies:

$(\mathcal{P}_1)$ $\equiv_R \cap (F \times (Q - F)) = \emptyset$,
$(\mathcal{P}_2)$ $\forall p, q \in Q, \forall a \in A, \ (p \equiv_R q \Rightarrow \forall q' \in \delta(q, a), \exists p' \in \delta(p, a), q' \equiv_R p')$.

The equivalence $\equiv_R$ is the largest equivalence over Q which is right-invariant with respect to M; see [12, 13]. Given $\equiv_R$, the algorithm to reduce the automaton M is simple: while there are non-trivial equivalence classes, merge all states in a non-trivial equivalence class and modify the transitions accordingly.

Symmetrically, the relation $\equiv_L$ can be defined using the reversed automaton. An automaton M can be reduced according to either equivalence.

Example 1. Consider, for example, the automaton in Figure 1(a) where the equivalence classes are also shown. States 1, 2, and 3 belong to the same equivalence class of $\equiv_R$, and so they would be merged into a single state as shown in Fig 1(b). As Figure 1(c) shows, there are NFAs that can be reduced more by simultaneously using both equivalences.

Furthermore, there might not be a unique way to use optimally both $\equiv_R$ and $\equiv_L$ as the following example (from [13]) shows.

Example 2. In Figure 2, the automaton from the left has only two pairs of equivalent states: $1 \equiv_R 3$ and $1 \equiv_L 2$. We may either merge 1 with 3 or 1 with 2 but not both, since merging all three states into one introduces the word bd which is not in the language. Therefore, we have two different optimal ways of reducing the automaton.

Classes of $\equiv_R$: $\{0\}$
$\{1,2,3\}$
$\{4\}, \{5\}$
$\{6\}, \{7\}$

Classes of $\equiv_L$: $\{0\}, \{1\}$
$\{2\}, \{3\}$
$\{4,5,6\}$
$\{7\}$

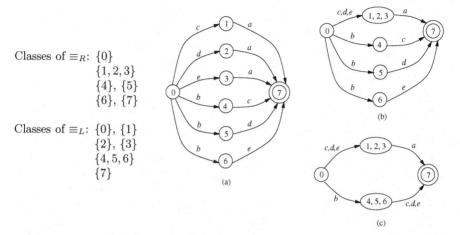

Fig. 1. (a) An NFA. (b) Its reduced version using $\equiv_R$. (c) Its reduced version using $\equiv_R$ and $\equiv_L$.

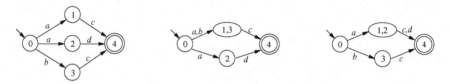

Fig. 2. An NFA, and its reduced versions using $\equiv_R$ and $\equiv_L$.

In [13] it is posed as an open problem to find a best way to do the reduction using both equivalences. In Section 4 we give an efficient algorithm for solving this problem.

A classical algorithm of Paige and Tarjan [20] was used in [11] to compute the equivalences fast. Given an automaton with n states and m transitions, the algorithm of [11] runs in time $\mathcal{O}(m \log n)$ and space $\mathcal{O}(m + n)$.

4   Efficient Use of Equivalences

We describe now an efficient algorithm for reducing the size of an NFA $M = (Q, A, \delta, I, F)$ by merging states according to the equivalence classes $\equiv_R$ and $\equiv_L$. In a certain sense, to be made precise below, we use the information in the two equivalences optimally.

Each of the two equivalences $\equiv_R$ and $\equiv_L$ defines a partition of the set Q of states. Let these partitions be

$$\Pi_R = \{X_1, X_2, \ldots, X_r\}$$
$$\Pi_L = \{X_{r+1}, X_{r+2}, \ldots, X_{r+s}\},$$

respectively. Two states p, q belong to the same set X_i, $i \le r$ ($i > r$), if and only if $p \equiv_R q$ ($p \equiv_L q$).

A reduction merges states belonging to the same equivalence class into a single state. Let a reduction be $X^* = \{X_1^*, X_2^*, \ldots, X_\ell^*\}$, where each X_i^* represents a set of equivalent states that is merged into a single state in the reduced automaton. The reduced NFA has, then, ℓ states. Observe that each set X_i^* is a subset of at least one of the sets X_j. Let $X_i^* \subseteq X_{\pi(i)}$, where $1 \leq \pi(i) \leq r + s$. Clearly, $\ell \leq \min\{r, s\}$.

Note that $\cup_{i=1}^\ell X_i^* = Q$, where Q is the set of states of the NFA. Then, $\cup_{i=1}^\ell X_{\pi(i)} = Q$, and so $\{X_{\pi(1)}, X_{\pi(2)}, \ldots, X_{\pi(\ell)}\}$ is a *set cover* for Q from the family of sets $X = \Pi_R \cup \Pi_L$.

We can identify optimal use of the equivalences by finding an optimal solution for the instance $\langle Q, X = \Pi_R \cup \Pi_L \rangle$ of the *set covering problem*. In the set covering problem, given a finite set Q and a family X of subsets of Q, the goal is to find the smallest subset of X that includes all elements in Q. Any subset of X that includes all elements in Q is called a *set cover* for Q.

Let S^* be a smallest set cover for $\langle Q, X \rangle$. To achieve the maximum possible reduction in the size of the NFA that can be obtained with the equivalences, we first remove duplicated occurrences of the same state from the sets in S^*; i.e., if state p belongs to two subsets $S_i^*, S_j^* \in S^*$, then we remove p from either S_i^* or S_j^* so that p appears in only one subset of S^*. Then, all the states in the same subset $S_i^* \in S^*$ are merged into a single state in the reduced NFA. The reduced NFA will be called the EQ-*reduced NFA*.

The set covering problem is NP-hard, so the above algorithm for reducing NFAs might not be practical. Fortunately, the instance $\langle Q, X \rangle$ of the set covering problem defined by $\equiv_R$ and $\equiv_L$ is not an arbitrary one, but it has a very special structure. In particular, every state $p \in Q$ belongs to at most two of the subsets of X. Therefore, the algorithm of Bar-Yehuda end Even [1] gives a 2-approximate solution for this problem.

We can do better than this, though. Let us model the set covering problem as a bipartite graph $G_B = (L \cup R, E)$. Each set X_i is a vertex in this graph. Put vertices $X_1, \ldots, X_r$ in L and the rest in R. Every edge $p \in E$ corresponds to a state p of the NFA and it joins the two sets containing it (see Figure 3).

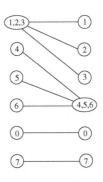

Fig. 3. Bipartite graph G_B for the NFA of Figure 1(a).

An optimal set cover for $\langle Q, X \rangle$ corresponds to a minimum *vertex cover* for G_B (a vertex cover for G_B is a subset of vertices incident on all edges). Since the graph G_B is bipartite, a minimum vertex cover can be easily derived from a maximum matching, which can be computed in $O(m'\sqrt{n}) = O(n^{3/2})$ time using the algorithm of Hopcroft and Karp [8], where m' is the number of edges in the bipartite graph and n is the number of vertices. The number of edges is equal to the number n of states in the NFA, and the number of vertices is the number of equivalence classes in $\equiv_R$ and $\equiv_L$, which is at most n.

The problem of computing a minimum vertex cover for a bipartite graph has been widely studied in the literature. For completeness, we present a simple algorithm for finding a minimum vertex cover for G_B from a maximum matching M^* of G_B. First, build the *residual network* G_{M^*} corresponding to the matching:

- Add a source node n_s to G_B and connect it to every vertex in L.
- Add a sink node n_t to G_B and connect it to every vertex in R.
- Direct every edge in the matching from R to L. Direct every edge (n_s, u), where u is incident to an edge in the matching, from u to n_s. Direct every edge (v, n_t) incident on the matching from n_t to v.
- All other edges are directed from left to right.

Do a depth first search traversal on this graph starting at vertex n_s, marking every vertex that can be reached from n_s. A minimum vertex cover C^* is formed by all marked vertices in R plus all un-marked vertices in L. Every marked vertex $v \in R$ is incident on an edge of the matching, because otherwise the path n_s, u, v used to reach v would include an edge (u, v) not incident on M^*, contradicting that M^* is maximum. Also, every un-marked vertex $u \in L$ must be incident on M^* since the edge between s and u must be directed from u to s. Hence, $|C^*| \leq |M^*|$. This procedure requires linear time.

Lemma 1. *C^* is a minimum vertex cover for the bipartite graph G_B, and the size of C^* is equal to the size of M^*.*

Proof. The above algorithm simply finds a cut of capacity C^* for a flow network G that has the same topology as G_{M^*}, but in which all edges (of unit capacity) are directed from left to right. By the max-flow min-cut theorem, we know that the size of M^* is equal to the capacity of a minimum cut, and thus, that the size of M^* is equal to the size of C^*. To see that C^* is a vertex cover, note that a minimum cut of G intersects every path from n_s to n_t. Therefore, for every edge (u, v) of G, the path n_s, u, v, n_t is intersected by a minimum cut and, thus, in the residual network G_{M^*} either v (but not n_t) is reachable from n_s or u is not reachable from n_s. This implies that either u or v belong to C^*, so edge (u, v) is covered by C^*.

We have proved the following result.

Theorem 1. *Given an NFA with n states and m transitions, there is an algorithm that computes the corresponding EQ-reduced automaton in $O(n^{3/2} + m \log n)$ time.*

5   NFA Reduction with Preorders

Champarnaud and Coulon [2] noticed that a better reduction can be obtained if the axioms $(\mathcal{P}_1)$ and $(\mathcal{P}_2)$ above are used to construct a preorder relation instead of an equivalence. Let us denote the largest (w.r.t. inclusion) preorder which satisfies $(\mathcal{P}_1)$ and $(\mathcal{P}_2)$ by $\subseteq_R$. It is then immediate that $p \subseteq_R q$ implies $\mathcal{L}_R(p) \subseteq \mathcal{L}_R(q)$.

As in the case of equivalences, the relation $\subseteq_L$ is symmetrically defined using the reversed automaton. Then, $p \subseteq_L q$ implies $\mathcal{L}_L(p) \subseteq \mathcal{L}_L(q)$.

The reduction with preorders is more complicated than with equivalences. We can merge two states p and q as soon as any of the following conditions is met:

(i) $p \subseteq_R q$ and $q \subseteq_R p$,
(ii) $p \subseteq_L q$ and $q \subseteq_L p$,
(iii) $p \subseteq_R q$, $p \subseteq_L q$, and $\mathcal{L}(p,p) = \{\varepsilon\}$.

However, after merging two states, the preorders $\subseteq_R$ and $\subseteq_L$ must be updated such that their relation with the languages $\mathcal{L}_R$ and $\mathcal{L}_L$ (see above) is preserved. For instance, in the case (i), assuming the merged state of p and q is denoted q, the update amounts to removing from $\subseteq_L$ all pairs (q, s) for which $p \not\subseteq_L s$. Case (ii) is handled similarly and (iii) does not need any update.

The condition (iii) appears in [2, 3] without the requirement $\mathcal{L}(p,p) = \{\varepsilon\}$ and, as noticed by [4], it is incorrect. In fact [4] removes this condition because its proof is incorrect. We give below a counterexample showing that, indeed, condition (iii) without the requirement $\mathcal{L}(p,p) = \{\varepsilon\}$ does not work.

Example 3. Consider the automaton in Figure 4. We have $\mathcal{L}_L(1) = ab^* \subseteq ab^* \cup \{x\} = \mathcal{L}_L(2)$ and $\mathcal{L}_R(1) = b^*c \subseteq b^*c \cup \{y\} = \mathcal{L}_R(2)$, but we cannot merge states 1 and 2 as this would add xb^*y to the language.

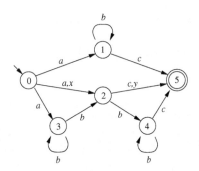

Fig. 4. The condition (iii) without $\mathcal{L}(p,p) = \{\varepsilon\}$; 1 and 2 cannot be merged.

Let us prove that our condition (iii) as stated above is correct. Denote the initial automaton by M and the one obtained after merging p and q by M'.

Denote also the merged state in M' by q. We need to prove that $\mathcal{L}(M') \subseteq \mathcal{L}(M)$. The only problem might come from a word $w \in \mathcal{L}(M')$ such that $w_1 \in \mathcal{L}_L(M',q)$ for some prefix w_1 of w. This word w can be decomposed as $w = w_1 w_2 w_3$ such that: there is a path labelled w_1 in M' from an initial state to q which does not pass through q twice; there is a path labelled w_3 in M' from q to a final state which does not pass through q twice; and, there is a path labelled w_2 in M' which starts and ends in q. We have then

$$w_1 \in \mathcal{L}_L(M,p) \cup \mathcal{L}_L(M,q) = \mathcal{L}_L(M,q),$$
$$w_3 \in \mathcal{L}_R(M,p) \cup \mathcal{L}_R(M,q) = \mathcal{L}_R(M,q), \text{ and}$$
$$w_2 \in (\mathcal{L}(M,p,p) \cup \mathcal{L}(M,p,q) \cup \mathcal{L}(M,q,p) \cup \mathcal{L}(M,q,q))^*.$$

Since $\mathcal{L}(M,p,p) = \{\varepsilon\}$, at least one of $\mathcal{L}(M,q,p)$ and $\mathcal{L}(M,p,q)$ must be empty. Assume $\mathcal{L}(M,q,p)$ is empty. (The other case is similarly proved.) Then, using

$$\mathcal{L}(M,q,q)\mathcal{L}_R(M,q) \subseteq \mathcal{L}_R(M,q) \text{ and}$$
$$\mathcal{L}(M,p,q)\mathcal{L}_R(M,q) \subseteq \mathcal{L}_R(M,p) \subseteq \mathcal{L}_R(M,q),$$

we obtain $w \in \mathcal{L}_L(M,q)\mathcal{L}_R(M,q) \subseteq \mathcal{L}(M)$, as claimed.

Since the preorder requirement is weaker than the equivalence requirement, $p \equiv_R q$ implies that $p \subseteq_R q$ and $q \subseteq_R p$. The converse is not true in general (see [2] for an example). Therefore, using preorders we have a chance to obtain a better reduction of the NFA. It remains to investigate how much better. Notice that the experiments in [3] are no longer valid since one of the conditions they used in the reduction was invalid. The preorders $\subseteq_R$ and $\subseteq_L$ can be computed in time $\mathcal{O}(mn)$ and space $\mathcal{O}(n^2)$; see [11] and [3].

6   Optimal Use of Preorders Is Hard

Contrary to the case of equivalences, it is hard to find the optimal way to use preorders to achieve best possible reductions. Again, what we mean by "optimal" is precisely defined below. All proofs in this section will be omitted due to lack of space.

As mentioned above, two states p, q of an automaton M can be merged into a unique state if any of the conditions (i)-(iii) is satisfied. Given the preorders $\subseteq_R$ and $\subseteq_L$, we let

$$p \cong_R q \quad \text{iff} \quad p \subseteq_R q \text{ and } q \subseteq_R p, \text{ and}$$
$$p \cong_L q \quad \text{iff} \quad p \subseteq_L q \text{ and } q \subseteq_L p.$$

These new equivalences, $\cong_R$ and $\cong_L$, are coarser than $\equiv_R$ and $\equiv_L$, and they induce two partitions π_R and π_L of the set of states of M. Condition (iii) induces a partial order $\preceq$ on the set of states, where

$$p \preceq q \quad \text{iff} \quad p \subseteq_R q, \ p \subseteq_L q \text{ and } \mathcal{L}(p,p) = \{\varepsilon\}.$$

This partial order induces a family π_P of state subsets $P_1, P_2, \ldots, P_k$, $k \leq n$, where each P_i has a unique maximal element m_i, and two sets p, q belong to the same set P_i iff $p \preceq m_i$ and $q \preceq m_i$. Note that sets P_i cover all sates of M, but they are not necessarily a partition of Q.

We formulate the "optimal" use of preorders $\subseteq_R$ and $\subseteq_L$ for merging the states of M as an instance $\langle Q, \pi \rangle$ of the set covering problem: given a set Q of states and a family of state subsets $\pi = \pi_R \cup \pi_L \cup \pi_P$, the goal is to find the smallest subset S^* of π that includes all states of Q.

Consider an optimal solution S^* for the above set covering problem. Let $S^* = \{S_1^*, S_2^*, \ldots, S_\ell^*\}$; we reduce the automaton by merging all states in each set S_i^* into a unique state. Care must be taken that a state $p \in Q$ belonging to two different sets S_i^*, S_j^* is not merged twice. To ensure this, the sets S^* are considered in order. First, the set S_1^* is contracted to a single new state, and all states that belong to S_1^* are removed from the remaining sets $S_2^*, \ldots, S_\ell^*$. Then, S_2^* is contracted and all states in S_2^* are discarded from the remaining sets $S_3^*, \ldots, S_\ell^*$, and so on. The number of states in the final NFA M^* is ℓ; we call this automaton the PRE-*reduced NFA*.

The PRE-reduced NFA M^* has minimum size among those obtained by reducing M using preorders as explained above. This is because if there were another NFA, say M' with $\ell' < \ell$ states, that could be obtained from M by merging states as indicated by (i)-(iii), then the way in which the states are merged to produce M' defines a solution for the set covering problem $\langle Q, \pi \rangle$ of size $\ell' < \ell$, contradicting the optimality of S^*.

Observe that $\langle Q, \pi \rangle$ is a restricted instance of the set covering problem and, thus, the problem of optimally using preorders for reducing the number of states of a NFA might be simpler to solve than the general set covering problem. We show now that despite its restricted structure the set covering problem $\langle Q, \pi \rangle$ is still NP-hard. In fact, we show that an even more restricted version of the problem is NP-hard.

Let us consider only instances $\langle Q, \pi \rangle$, $\pi = \pi_R \cup \pi_L \cup \pi_P$, where the family π_P is a partition of Q. For these instances each state p appears in precisely 3 sets of π (one set belonging to each of π_R, π_L, and π_P). This particular class of instances of the set covering problem can be modeled as *3-partite hypergraphs* $H_M = (V_\pi, E_Q)$, where each vertex $v \in V_\pi$ corresponds to a subset in π and each hyperedge $e_p \in E_Q$ is incident on the vertices corresponding to the three sets $A_p \in \pi_R$, $B_p \in \pi_L$, and $C_p \in \pi_P$ containing p. A hypergraph is said to be 3-partite if its vertices can be partitioned into 3 disjoint sets such that every hyperedge is incident on exactly one vertex from each partition.

Note that every set cover of $\langle Q, \pi \rangle$ corresponds to a vertex cover (set of vertices incident on all hyperedges) of H_M. The vertex covering problem on 3-partite hypergraphs can be shown to be NP-hard via a reduction from the 3-SAT problem. We explain very briefly the idea.

Recall the 3-SAT problem. Given a boolean formula $f(x_1, \ldots, x_n) = C_1 \wedge C_2 \wedge \cdots \wedge C_m$, where each clause C_i contains exactly 3 literals (a literal is either a variable x_i or its negation $\bar{x}_i$), the problem is to decide whether there is an assignment of values to the variables that satisfies all clauses. The 3-SAT problem is known to be NP-hard [5].

Given a boolean formula $f(x_1, \ldots, x_n)$ we build a 3-partite hypergraph $H_f = (V_f, E_f)$ as follows. Let n_i be the number of occurrences of x_i (either as x_i or as $\bar{x}_i$) in f. For each variable x_i we create $8n_i$ nodes: $x_{i1}, \ldots, x_{in_i}, \bar{x}_{i1}, \ldots, \bar{x}_{in_i}$, $d_{i1}, \ldots, d_{in_i}, \bar{d}_{i1}, \ldots, \bar{d}_{in_i}, s_{i1}, \ldots, s_{i\,4n_i}$. Nodes $x_{ij}, \bar{x}_{ij}$ represent the j-th occurrence of the variable x_i (in its j-th occurrence x_i can be either negated or not). Dummy nodes $d_{ij}, \bar{d}_{ij}$, and s_{ij} are used to ensure that the resulting hypergraph is 3-partite. These nodes are connected forming a cycle. Each hyperedge spans 3 nodes.

Furthermore, for each clause $C_k = \ell_{k1} \vee \ell_{k2} \vee \ell_{k3}$, we add a hyperedge incident on the 3 nodes corresponding to the literals ℓ_{ki} (note that different occurrences of the same variable are represented by different nodes). A very simple hypergraph, for the formula $f(x_1, x_2, x_3) = x_1 \vee \bar{x}_2 \vee x_3$, is shown in Fig. 5.

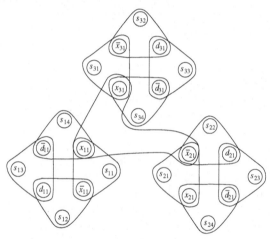

Fig. 5. Hypergraph corresponding to formula $f(x_1, x_2, x_3) = x_1 \vee \bar{x}_2 \vee x_3$.

The next step is to consider those 3-partite graphs as described above, which we call *3-SAT hypergraphs*, and show that the vertex cover problem on 3-SAT hypergraphs reduces to the problem of optimally using preorders for NFA reduction.

Consider a hypergraph H_f built from a boolean formula f. We construct an automaton M_f for which its preorders $\subseteq'_R$ and $\subseteq'_L$ define a hypergraph identical to H_f, but for 2 additional, isolated hyperedges. Denote the 3 partitions of the vertices of H_f by R_f, L_f, P_f. Let $\cong'_R, \cong'_L$, and $\preceq'$ be the equivalence relations and partial order, respectively, defined by the preorders $\subseteq'_R$ and $\subseteq'_L$.

The idea of the construction is as follows. The automaton is built so that each node of H_f corresponds to a set of states of M_f. Specifically, a vertex $u \in R_f$ defines a set of states that are equivalent under $\cong'_R$, a vertex $v \in L_f$ corresponds to an equivalence class under $\cong'_L$, and a vertex $w \in P_f$ corresponds to a member of the family of state subsets induced by the partial order $\preceq'$. Furthermore, each hyperedge of H_f incident on vertices u, v, and w, corresponds to a state of the automaton that belongs to classes u, v, and w of R_f, L_f, and P_f, respectively. The details of the construction are omitted due to lack of space.

The main result of this section is

Theorem 2. *Given an NFA, the problem of computing the corresponding* PRE-*reduced automaton is NP-hard.*

7   Conclusions and Further Research

We wish to point out that our algorithm for computing the EQ-reduced NFA only finds the best way of merging states with respect to the equivalence classes Π_R and Π_L. It is possible to reduce the size of an NFA by first merging some equivalent states in $\Pi_R \cup \Pi_L$ to get a new NFA and new equivalence classes Π'_R and Π'_L. Then, some equivalent states in $\Pi'_L \cup \Pi'_R$ could be merged to produce new equivalence classes, and so on. It is an open problem to find the best way of reducing an NFA by using this method.

We note that our algorithm for equivalences can be iterated for better results, but this does not solve the above problem. After reducing the size of an NFA using the equivalences, we can compute the new right and left equivalences $\tilde{\Pi}_R$ and $\tilde{\Pi}_L$ for the reduced automaton. Then, we apply the algorithm to $\tilde{\Pi}_R$ and $\tilde{\Pi}_L$. We can continue this process until no further reduction is achieved.

For preorders, we proved that the problem of optimally (as defined above) using them to attain the maximum possible reduction in the size of the automaton is NP-hard. Therefore, reductions with preorders, potentially more powerful than those with equivalences, might be too expensive to compute. This opens a new research topic: designing efficient approximation algorithms for using preorders in reducing NFAs, and testing their performance in practice.

More theoretical and experimental work is needed to determine which of the two relations, equivalences or preorders, is better in practice and which approach achieves greatest speedup for regular expression matching.

References

1. Bar-Yehuda, R., and Even, S., A linear-time approximation algorithm for the weighted vertex cover problem, *Journal of Algorithms* **2**, 1981, 198–203.
2. Champarnaud, J.-M., and Coulon, F., NFA reduction algorithms by means of regular inequalities, in: Z. Ésik, Z. Fülöp, eds., *Proc. of DLT 2003* (Szeged, 2003), Lecture Notes in Comput. Sci. **2710**, Springer-Verlag, Berlin, Heidelberg, 2003, 194–205.
3. Champarnaud, J.-M., and Coulon, F., NFA reduction algorithms by means of regular inequalities, *Theoret. Comput. Sci.* **327**(3) 241–253.
4. Champarnaud, J.-M., and Coulon, F., NFA reduction algorithms by means of regular inequalities – correction, *Theoret. Comput. Sci.*, to appear.
5. Garey M.R. and Johnson D.S., *Computers and intractability: a guide to the theory of NP-completeness*, W.H. Freeman and Company, New York, 1979.

6. Hagenah, C., and Muscholl, A., Computing ϵ-free NFA from regular expressions in $O(n\log^2(n))$ time, *Theor. Inform. Appl.* **34** (4) (2000) 257–277.
7. Hopcroft, J., An $n\log n$ algorithm for minimizing states in a finite automaton, *Proc. Internat. Sympos. Theory of machines and computations*, Technion, Haifa, 1971, Academic Press, New York, 1971, 189–196.
8. Hopcroft, J.E., and Karp, R., An $n^{5/2}$ algorithm for maximum matchings in bipartite graphs, *SIAM Journal on Computing*, bf 2(4) (1973), 225–231.
9. Hopcroft, J.E., and Ullman, J.D., *Introduction to Automata Theory, Languages, and Computation*, Addison-Wesley, Reading, Mass., 1979.
10. Hromkovic, J., Seibert, S., and Wilke, T., Translating regular expressions into small ϵ-free nondeterministic finite automata, *J. Comput. System Sci.* **62** (4) (2001) 565–588.
11. Ilie, L., Navarro, G., and Yu, S., On NFA reductions, in: J. Karhumaki, H. Maurer, G. Paun, G. Rozenberg, eds., *Theory is Forever* (Salomaa Festschrift), Lecture Notes in Comput. Sci. 3113, Springer-Verlag, Berlin, Heidelberg, 2004, 112–124.
12. Ilie, L., and Yu, S., Algorithms for computing small NFAs, in: K. Diks, W. Rytter, eds., *Proc. of the 27th MFCS*, (Warszawa, 2002), Lecture Notes in Comput. Sci., **2420**, Springer-Verlag, Berlin, Heidelberg, 2002, 328–340.
13. Ilie, L., and Yu, S., Reducing NFAs by invariant equivalences, *Theoret. Comput. Sci.* **306** (2003) 373–390.
14. Jiang, T., and Ravikumar, B., Minimal NFA problems are hard, *SIAM J. Comput.* **22**(6) (1993), 1117–1141.
15. Kameda, T., and Weiner, P., On the state minimization of nondeterministic finite automata, *IEEE Trans. Computers* **C-19**(7) (1970) 617–627.
16. Melnikov, B. F., A new algorithm of the state-minimization for the nondeterministic finite automata, *Korean J. Comput. Appl. Math.* **6**(2) (1999) 277–290.
17. Melnikov, B. F., Once more about the state-minimization of the nondeterministic finite automata, *Korean J. Comput. Appl. Math.* **7**(3) (2000) 655–662.
18. Navarro, G., and Raffinot, M., Compact DFA Representation for Fast Regular Expression Search, *Proc. WAE'01*, Lecture Notes Comput. Sci. **2141**, Springer-Verlag, Berlin, Heidelberg, 2001, 1–12.
19. Navarro, G., and Raffinot, M., *Flexible Pattern Matching in Strings. Practical On-Line Search Algorithms for Texts and Biological Sequences*, Cambridge University Press, Cambridge, 2002.
20. Paige, R., and Tarjan, R.E, Three Partition Refinement Algorithms, *SIAM J. Comput.* (1987) **16**(6) 973–989.
21. Yu, S., Regular Languages, in: G. Rozenberg, A. Salomaa, *Handbook of Formal Languages, Vol. I*, Springer-Verlag, Berlin, 1997, 41–110.

Regular Expression Constrained
Sequence Alignment

Abdullah N. Arslan

Department of Computer Science
The University of Vermont
Burlington, VT 05405, USA
aarslan@cs.uvm.edu

Abstract. Given strings S_1, S_2, and a regular expression R, we introduce *regular expression constrained sequence alignment* as the problem of finding the maximum alignment score between S_1 and S_2 over all alignments such that in these alignments there exists a segment where some substring s_1 of S_1 is aligned with some substring s_2 of S_2, and both s_1 and s_2 match R, i.e. $s_1, s_2 \in L(R)$ where $L(R)$ is the regular language described by R. A motivation for the problem is that protein sequences can be aligned in a way that known motifs guide the alignments. We present an $O(nmr)$ time algorithm for the regular expression constrained sequence alignment problem where n, and m are the lengths of S_1, and S_2, respectively, and r is in the order of the size of the transition function of a finite automaton M that we create from a nondeterministic finite automaton N accepting $L(R)$. M contains $O(t^2)$ states if N has t states.

Keywords: Regular expression, sequence alignment, dynamic programming, pattern matching, finite automaton.

1 Introduction

We introduce *regular expression constrained sequence alignment (RECSA)* as the following problem: given strings S_1, S_2, and a regular expression R, find the maximum alignment score between S_1 and S_2 over all alignments that satisfy a *regular expression constraint*. An alignment satisfies the constraint if it includes a segment in which a substring s_1 of S_1 is *aligned with* a substring s_2 of S_2, and both s_1 and s_2 match R where a string s is said to match a regular expression R if $s \in L(R)$, i.e. s is a string in the language described by R. We precisely explain what we mean by "substring s_1 is aligned with substring s_2" when we define alignment paths in Section 3. In a simple case, if s_1, and s_2 are of the same length then we say that s_1 is aligned with s_2 if they appear in the same window of columns in the alignment matrix as shown in Figure 1.

Figure 1 illustrates an example in which sequences $S_1 = $ TGFPSVGKTKDDA, and $S_2 = $ TFSVAKDDDGKSA are aligned in a way to maximize the number of matches (this is the *longest common subsequence* problem). An optimal alignment with 8 matches is shown in part (a). For the regular expression constrained sequence

A. Apostolico, M. Crochemore, and K. Park (Eds.): CPM 2005, LNCS 3537, pp. 322–333, 2005.

```
T  G  F  P  S  V  G  K  T  K  D  D  -  -  -  -  A
|     |     |  |     |  |                          |
T  -  F  -  S  V  A  -  -  K  D  D  D  G  K  S  A
```

(a)

```
T  -  -  -  G  F  P  S  V  G  K  T  K  D  D  A
|                          |  |                 |
T  F  S  V  A  K  D  D  D  G  K  S  -  -  -  A
```

(b)

Fig. 1. For strings S_1 = TGFPSVGKTKDDA and S_2 = TFSVAKDDDGKSA: (a) An alignment with maximum number of matches, 8. (b) An alignment in which substring GFPSVGKT of S_1 is aligned with substring AKDDDGKS of S_2, and both match $R = (\text{G} + \text{A})\Sigma\Sigma\Sigma\Sigma\text{GK}(\text{S} + \text{T})$ where Σ is a fixed alphabet on which the sequences are defined. This alignment has 4 matches, and it satisfies the regular expression constraint.

alignment problem with $R = (\text{G} + \text{A})\Sigma\Sigma\Sigma\Sigma\text{GK}(\text{S} + \text{T})$, where Σ denotes a fixed alphabet over which sequences are defined, the alignments sought change. The alignment in part (a) does not satisfy the regular expression constraint. Part (b) shows an alignment with which the constraint is satisfied. The alignment includes a region (shown with a rectangle drawn in dashed lines in the figure) where the substring GFPSVGKT of S_1 is aligned with substring AKDDDGKS of S_2, and both substrings match R. In this case, optimal number of matches achievable with the constraint decreases to 4.

The motivation for the problem is that when computing the homology of two protein sequences it may be important to take into account a common specific or putative structure. Family of similar protein sequences include a conserved region. Such conserved amino acid residues associated with a particular function is called a sequence motif. Typically, motifs span 10 to 30 amino acid residues. The notion of a motif was first explicitly introduced by Russell Doolittle in 1981 [5]. Discovery of sequence motifs related to a vast variety of enzymatic and binding activities of proteins has continued at a steady rate [2], and the motifs, in the form of amino acid patterns, were incorporated by Amos Bairoch in the PROSITE database. PROSITE (http://www.expasy.org/prosite, mirrored in the US at http://us.expasy.org/prosite) is maintained by Amos Bairoch and tightly integrated with SWISS-PROT [8]. For many years, PROSITE has been a collection of sequence motifs, which were represented and stored as regular expressions. For example, the motif in Figure 1 is the famous P-loop motif, first described in 1982 by John Walker and colleagues as "Motif A" and found later in many ATP- and GTP-binding proteins, corresponds to a flexible loop, sandwiched between a b-strand and an a-helix and interacting with b- and g-phosphates of ATP or GTP [12]. In PROSITE database it is represented as [GA]-X(4)-G-K-[ST] (ATP/GTP-binding site motif A (P-loop) (PS00017)) which means that the first position of the motif can be occupied by either Ala or Gly, the second, third, fourth, and fifth positions can be occupied by any amino acid residue, and the sixth and seventh positions have to be Gly and Lys, respectively, followed by either Ser or Thr.

The regular expression constraint can guide the alignments. As we observe in Figure 1 the regular expression constraint change the optimality of the alignments. If the sequences contain the same motif then it is more meaningful to seek an alignment that contains the motif (i.e. that satisfies the corresponding regular expression constraint) over those that do not because the motif should be part of the true alignment. In Figure 1 strings S_1, and S_2 are not real protein sequences. We use them to present the advantage of using the regular expression constraint in a simple setting with short strings.

In this paper we present an algorithm for the $RECSA$ problem whose time complexity is $O(nmr)$ where r is the size of the finite automaton M we create. M is a weighted automaton that accepts alignments that satisfy the regular expression constraint where the weights of the states in M correspond to optimum constrained alignment scores. The algorithm is based on a given dynamic programming formulation for sequence alignment. Instead of computing optimum scores, it uses the dynamic programming solution to compute weights for automaton M. M has $O(t^2)$ states if N has t states where N is an automaton that accepts the language described by the regular expression R.

The outline of this paper is as follows. In Section 2 we summarize the previous related work, and results. In Section 3 we describe a framework for sequence alignment. In Section 4 we describe how we create the finite automaton that we use in our algorithm for the $RECSA$ problem we present in Section 5. In Section 6 we include our concluding remarks, and pointers for future work.

2   Previous Related Work

Given two sequences S_1 and S_2 the *pairwise sequence alignment* [13] problem is to compute the maximum score over all possible alignment matrixes for these sequences. In an alignment matrix we insert special symbols $'-'$ in S_1, and S_2, generating respectively, sequences S_1^*, and S_2^* with equal length, and align the symbols of S_1^*, and S_2^* by placing symbols at the same positions in the same column. In an alignment matrix, a given scoring scheme assigns a score to each column corresponding to the symbols appearing in the column. The score of an alignment matrix is the sum of its column-scores. The *multiple sequence alignment* is the generalization of this problem for multiple sequences.

The constrained versions of the sequence alignment problems have been studied in the literature extensively [1, 3, 4, 7, 9–11].

Tang et al. [9] introduces the *constrained multiple sequence alignment (CM SA)* problem in which we are given k sequences $S_1, S_2, \ldots, S_k$ with maximum length n, and a pattern P with length r, and the solution of the problem is an alignment with optimal score such that each $P[i]$ appears in an entire column of the multiple sequence alignment matrix. A motivation for the problem is the alignment of RNase sequences. Such sequences are all known to contain three active residues His(H), Lyn(K), His(H) that are essential for RNA degrading.

Therefore, it is natural to expect that in an alignment of RNA sequences, each of these residues should be aligned in the same column, i.e. alignment satisfies the constrained sequence "HKH". The $CMSA$ problem when $k = 2$ is called the *constrained pairwise sequence alignment (CPSA) problem* [3, 9]. Solutions for $CPSA$ can be used to solve the $CMSA$ problem. We can progressively align the sequences into a multiple alignment by using a minimum spanning tree obtained from a pairwise distance matrix of the sequences [3, 9, 11]. Tang et al. [9] introduces the $CPSA$ problem, and presents an algorithm whose both time and space requirements are $O(rn^4)$. For the $CPSA$ problem, Chin et al. [3], and Tang et al. [11] present improved algorithms with time complexity $O(nmr)$ where n, and m are the lengths of the sequences compared, and r is the length of the pattern P.

The longest common subsequence (LCS) problem for two strings is to find a common subsequence in both strings having maximum length. The LCS problem has many applications, and it has been studied extensively. Tsai [10] introduces the *constrained longest common subsequence* problem, and gives a dynamic programming solution whose time complexity is $O(rn^2m^2)$. For given strings S_1, S_2, and pattern P whose lengths are n, m, and r respectively, the longest common subsequence problem is to find a longest common subsequence lcs of S_1 and S_2 such that P is a subsequence of this lcs. Chin et al. [7], and Arslan and Eğecioğlu [1] give different dynamic programming solutions for the constrained LCS problem with time complexity $O(nmr)$. Chin et. al [7] also shows that the constrained LCS problem is a special case of the *multiple sequence alignment* problem. Arslan and Eğecioğlu [1] introduces the *edit distance constrained LCS* problem as a generalization of the constrained LCS problem. The edit distance constrained LCS problem is, given strings S_1, S_2, P, and distance d, to find a longest common subsequence lcs of S_1 and S_2 such that this lcs has a subsequence whose simple edit distance from P is smaller than d. Simple edit distance between two strings is the minimum number of edit operations required to transform one string into the other where the edit operations are insert, delete, and substitute. Arslan and Eğecioğlu [1] present an $O(dnmr)$-time algorithm for this problem.

Using edit distances as a constraint in the alignments is a step toward allowing patterns that may slightly differ in each sequence. Another approach proposed by Comet and Henry [4] uses a method that rewards alignments containing motifs. From the motif database the method first finds a known motif (or motifs) in each sequence separately to determine a common motif (or motifs). Next, it extends the dynamic programming sequence alignment solution by reconsidering each region where the motif appears in each sequence simultaneously. In this paper we continue in this direction. Protein sequences contain motifs that are described in PROSITE format (http://www.expasy.org/txt/prosuser.txt) that can be translated into simple regular expressions. Our main contribution in this paper is that we present an algorithm for the $RECSA$ problem where the constraint is a regular expression. This makes it possible to restrict the alignment of protein sequences to contain a given motif.

3   Framework

Given two strings S_1 and S_2, the global pairwise sequence alignment of S_1, and S_2 is to find an alignment path with the maximum score.

Given two strings $S_1[1..n]$ and $S_2[1..m]$ with $n \geq m$, we use the *alignment graph* G_{S_1,S_2} to analyze *alignments* between all substrings of S_1, and S_2. The alignment graph is a directed acyclic graph having $(n+1)(m+1)$ lattice points (u,v) as vertices for $0 \leq u \leq n$, and $0 \leq v \leq m$ (Figure 2). An *alignment path* for substrings S_1 and S_2 is a directed path from the vertex $(0,0)$ to (n,m) in G_{S_1,S_2}. To each vertex there is an incoming arc from each neighbor if it exists. Horizontal and vertical arcs correspond to insert and delete operations respectively. The diagonal arcs correspond to substitutions which are either matching (if the corresponding symbols are the same), or mismatching (otherwise). If we trace the arcs of an alignment path, and perform the indicated edit operations on S_1 in the order of the arcs in the alignment then we obtain S_2. Blocks of insertions and deletions are referred to as *gaps*.

The objective of sequence alignment is to quantify the similarity between S_1 and S_2 under a given *scoring scheme*. In the *simple scoring scheme*, the arcs of G_{S_1,S_2} are assigned weights determined by some real function γ.

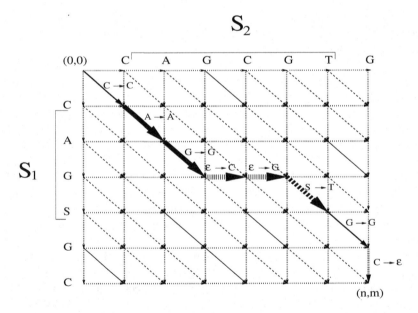

Fig. 2. Alignment graph G_{S_1,S_2} where S_1 = CAGSGC and S_2 = CAGCGTG. Matching diagonal arcs are drawn as solid lines while mismatching diagonal arcs are shown by dashed lines. Dotted lines are used for horizontal and vertical arcs. An example alignment path is shown. Labels of the arcs on this path are the corresponding edit operations where ϵ denotes the null string.

The following is the classical dynamic programming formulation [13] to compute the maximum global alignment score $\mathcal{H}_{i,j}$ achieved by an optimal alignment ending at each vertex (i, j):

$$\mathcal{H}_{i,j} = \max\{ \ \mathcal{H}_{i-1,j} + \gamma(S_1[i] \to \epsilon), \ \mathcal{H}_{i-1,j-1} + \gamma(S_1[i] \to S_2[j]), \atop \mathcal{H}_{i,j-1} + \gamma(\epsilon \to S_2[j]) \ \} \tag{1}$$

for $1 \leq i \leq n$, $1 \leq j \leq m$, with the boundary conditions $\mathcal{H}_{i,j} = -\infty$ whenever $i = 0$ or $j = 0$ except for $\mathcal{H}_{0,0} = 0$. Then $\mathcal{H}_{n,m}$ is the global alignment score between S_1, and S_2. The global alignment score can be computed in time $O(nm)$ using $O(m)$ space because only $O(m)$ entries of the dynamic programming matrix need to be stored at any given time [13].

We say that substring s_1 of S_1 is *aligned with* substring s_2 of S_2 in a given alignment if there exists in the alignment a segment whose projection on S_1 is s_1, and whose projection on S_2 is s_2. In the alignment shown in Figure 2, $s_1 = $ AGS is aligned with $s_2 = $ AGCGT. The corresponding segment of the alignment is shown in thick lines in the figure.

In our algorithm for the $RECSA$ problem we use the dynamic programming formulation in (1) but instead of scores we compute finite automata that we describe next.

4   Weighted Finite Automaton

We imagine alignments as strings of edit operations, and we construct an automaton M that moves on edit operations. M changes states as the alignments are formed. M accepts those alignments in which the regular expression constraint is satisfied. An alignment satisfies a given regular expression constraint if M enters a final state after reading the edit operations in the alignment. That is, M must remember if the regular expression constraint is partially or completely satisfied by substrings s_1 of S_1, and s_2 of S_2 that are aligned together. Since there may be many alignments accepted by M and we are interested in finding the maximum alignment score, we assign weights to the states, and as the alignments are formed the weights will be updated after each move.

We construct M from a given regular expression R in several steps. We first construct a nondeterministic finite automaton A from R such that they are equivalent, i.e. $L(A) = L(R)$ [6]. A possibly have ϵ-moves. Then we construct an equivalent nondeterministic finite automaton $N = (Q, \Sigma, \delta, q_0, F)$ with no ϵ-moves as described in [6]. N has the same number of states as A. To summarize, N accepts the set of strings described by the regular expression R.

We define a *weighted $N \times N$ automaton* as the finite automaton $M = (Q^M, W^M, \Sigma^M, q_0^M, F^M)$ which we construct as follows:

- $Q^M = Q \times Q$ is the set of states. Each state of M corresponds to a pair of states in N. M remembers in each state what part of the regular expression has been seen in S_1, and S_2.

- $W^M : Q^M \to \mathbb{R}$ is a function that assigns real weights to each state in Q^M, and initially all weights are $-\infty$. We determine the active set of states of M by examining their weights. The active states of M have weights different than $-\infty$.
- $\Sigma^M = (\Sigma \times \Sigma) - \{\epsilon \to \epsilon\}$. The alphabet for M is the set of edit operations which does not include $\epsilon \to \epsilon$.
- $\delta^M : Q^M \times \Sigma^M \to Q^M$. M moves on edit operations:
  - For $x \neq \epsilon$, $\delta^M((p,q), x \to \epsilon) = \{(p',q) \mid p' \in \delta(p,x)\}$.
  - For $y \neq \epsilon$, $\delta^M((p,q), \epsilon \to y) = \{(p,q') \mid q' \in \delta(q,y)\}$.
  - For $x \neq \epsilon, y \neq \epsilon$, $\delta^M((p,q), x \to y) = \{(p',q') \mid p' \in \delta(p,x), \ q' \in \delta(q,y)\}$.
  Once an alignment satisfies the regular expression constraint, i.e. once a final state is reached in M, the rest of the alignment does not alter the satisfaction of the constraint. Therefore, M has the option of staying in a final state on any input after that final state is reached. Thus, for all $x \to y \in \Sigma^M$, and $q_f \in F^M$, we also add q_f to $\delta^M(q_f, x \to y)$.
- $q_0^M = (q_0, q_0)$ is the start state whose weight is 0, and stays as 0 always.
- $F^M = F \times F$ is the set of final states. If M is in a final state then M has processed an alignment that satisfies the regular expression constraint. That is, there are substrings s_1 of S_1 and s_2 of S_2 that are aligned together in an alignment, and both s_1, and s_2 take N to final states.

Figure 3 includes an example weighted $N \times N$ automaton in part (b) for the finite automaton N shown in part (a) that is equivalent to regular expression $R = A(C + G)^*(S + T)$. For clarity, we choose as an example a simple regular expression, and we do not show the weights of the $N \times N$ automaton in part (b).

The active states (the states with non $-\infty$ weights) of the automaton M makes the following moves in two steps on input $x \to y \in \Sigma^M$:

Step 1. For all (p,q), if there exists (p',q') such that $(p,q) \in \delta^M((p',q'), x \to y)$ and $W^M(p',q') \neq -\infty$ then $W^M(p,q) = \max\{W^M(p',q') + \gamma(x \to y) \mid (p,q) \in \delta^M((p',q'), x \to y)\}$. New active states are those that are reachable from the active states on input $x \to y$. The weights of the active states are updated using the weight $\gamma(x \to y)$ of the edit operation $x \to y$, and the weights of the states through which new states are reached.

Step 2. For all (p,q), if there does not exist (p',q') such that $(p,q) \in \delta^M((p', q'), x \to y)$ and $W^M(p',q') \neq -\infty$ then $W^M(p,q) = -\infty$. After the move some previously active states may become inactive. This occurs when a suffix of S_1 (or S_2) partially matching the regular expression R no longer partially matches R when the suffix is extended with x (or y). If a state is no longer active then its weight is set to $-\infty$.

It is important that M makes its move in these two steps, first Step 1, and then Step 2, because otherwise, the newly reachable states (new active states), and their weights may not be updated correctly.

For any given weighted $N \times N$ automaton M we denote by $M^{x \to y}$ for any $x \to y \in \Sigma^M$ a copy of the automaton M after making the move on $x \to y$.

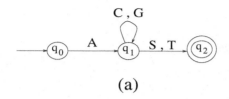

(a)

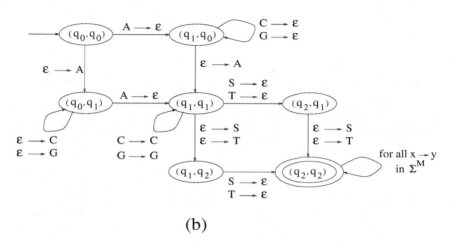

(b)

Fig. 3. (a) Finite automaton N equivalent to $R = A(C + G)^*(S + T)$. (b) Weighted $N \times N$ automaton M.

We will use multiple copies of the same weighted $N \times N$ automaton M. The weights will be updated as the alignment computations progress. At any given time the set of weights determine the current context in that copy of the automaton M. Otherwise all copies are identical.

Given two weighted $N \times N$ automata M_1 and M_2, we define a commutative and associative operation max_M such that $max_M\{M_1, M_2\}$ is a weighted $N \times N$ automaton M with state weights calculated as follows:

$$\text{for all } (p, q) \in Q^M, W^M(p, q) = \max\{W^{M_1}(p, q), W^{M_2}(p, q)\}.$$

5 Algorithm

Let $|S_1| = n$, $|S_2| = m$ with $n \geq m$, and let N be a nondeterministic automaton with no ϵ-moves equivalent to regular expression R, and let M be a weighted $N \times N$ automaton constructed from N as we describe in Section 4.

We denote by $S[i..j]$ the substring of S from positions i to j, $i \leq j$. Let $S[i]$ denote the ith symbol of string S.

We say that a substring s matches a regular expression R if $s \in L(R)$.

Instead of optimal alignment scores in the classical dynamic programming solution we will compute *optimal finite automata*. A weighted $N \times N$ automaton

$M_{i,j}$ is optimally weighted for $S[1..i]$, and $S_2[1..j]$ (or we simply say that $M_{i,j}$ is optimal since $S_1[1..i]$ and $S_2[1..j]$ are implied by the indices i and j in $M_{i,j}$) if the following two properties hold:

Property 1: For all final states $(p,q) \in F^{M_{i,j}}$, $W^{M_{i,j}}(p,q)$ is the maximum alignment score between $S_1[1..i]$ and $S_2[1..j]$ over all alignments that include a region in which substring s_1 of $S_1[1..i]$ is aligned with substring s_2 of $S_2[1..j]$, and $s_1, s_2 \in L(R)$, i.e. N on input s_1 enters final state $p \in F$, and on input s_2 enters final state $q \in F$. If there do not exists such s_1 and s_2 then $W^{M_{i,j}}(p,q)$ is $-\infty$ ((p,q) is an inactive state in $M_{i,j}$).

Property 2: For all states $(p,q) \notin F^{M_{i,j}}$, $W^{M_{i,j}}(p,q)$ is the maximum alignment score between $S_1[1..i]$ and $S_2[1..j]$ over all alignments that include a region in which s_1 is aligned with s_2, and s_1 is a suffix of S_1, and s_2 is a suffix of S_2, and N on input s_1 enters state $p \in Q$, and on input s_2 enters state $q \in Q$. If there do not exists such s_1 and s_2 then $W^{M_{i,j}}(p,q)$ is $-\infty$ ((p,q) is an inactive state in $M_{i,j}$).

We compute all optimal $M_{i,j}$, and output the weight $\max\{W^{M_{n,m}}(p,q) \mid (p,q) \in F^{M_{n,m}}\}$. That is, the maximum regular expression constrained alignment score is the maximum weight of the final states in the optimal automaton $M_{n,m}$.

For all i,j, $0 \leq i \leq n$, $0 \leq j \leq m$, both $M_{i,0}$ and $M_{0,j}$ are identical weighted $N \times N$ automaton whose state-weights are all $-\infty$ (except for the weight of the start state (q_0, q_0) which is always 0).

For all i,j, $1 \leq i \leq n$, $1 \leq j \leq m$

$$M_{i,j} = max_M \left\{ M_{i-1,j}^{S_1[i] \to \epsilon}, \ M_{i-1,j-1}^{S_1[i] \to S_2[j]}, \ M_{i,j-1}^{\epsilon \to S_2[j]} \right\} \qquad (2)$$

Figure 4 schematically describes the computations of $M_{i,j}$. We claim that for all i,j, $M_{i,j}$ computed in (2) is optimal. The correctness can be proved by induction on nodes (i,j). We consider an ordering for the nodes in which (i,j) comes after its neighbors $(i-1,j)$, $(i,j-1)$, and $(i-1,j-1)$ if they exist. This ordering can be generated by two nested loops: the outer loop $i = 0$ to n, and the inner loop $j = 0$ to m. The base case is when $i = 0$ for all j in which all weights are $-\infty$ in $M_{0,j}$, and the claim is true. Assuming that the claim is true for $M_{i-1,j}$, $M_{i,j-1}$, and $M_{i-1,j-1}$ we will show that each of the following automata is optimally weighted for $S_1[1..i]$, and $S_2[1..j]$ when the alignments are constrained to use the indicated arc:

1. $M_{i-1,j}^{S_1[i] \to \epsilon}$ when $((i-1,j),(i,j))$ is a required arc for the alignments,
2. $M_{i,j-1}^{\epsilon \to S_2[j]}$ when $((i,j-1),(i,j))$ is a required arc for the alignments,
3. $M_{i-1,j-1}^{S_1[i] \to S_2[j]}$ when $((i-1,j-1),(i,j))$ is a required arc for the alignments.

Optimality of $M_{i,j}$ will follow from these results since an optimal constrained alignment at node (i,j) uses one of these arcs, and we compute maximum scores for all possible optimal alignments (as state-weights) which partially or completely satisfy the regular expression constraint in the resulting optimal automaton in (2).

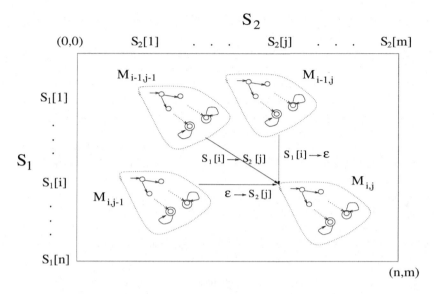

Fig. 4. Computations of weighted $N \times N$ automata.

To show that $M_{i-1,j}^{S_1[i] \to \epsilon}$ is optimally weighted for $S_1[1..i]$ and $S_2[1..j]$ when the alignments are constrained to use the arc $((i-1,j),(i,j))$, we need to show that Property 1 and Property 2 hold for $M_{i-1,j}^{S_1[i] \to \epsilon}$ with the given requirement. In this case, we consider only the alignments that include the arc $((i-1,j),(i,j))$. An optimal regular expression constrained score with this requirement is obtained from an optimal score obtained at node $(i-1,j)$ by adding to it the score $\gamma(S_1[i] \to \epsilon)$. For Property 1 consider final states $(p,q) \in F_{M_{i,j}}$. There are two cases to consider: 1) If a final state (p,q) was already an active state in $M_{i-1,j}$ then the optimality of the weight $W^{M_{i,j}}$ is followed from Property 1 of $M_{i-1,j}$, and the fact that all optimal alignment scores in this case are constrained to include the score $\gamma(S_1[i] \to \epsilon)$. 2) If a final state (p,q) is entered newly, i.e. (p,q) is an active state in $M_{i,j}$ but not an active state in $M_{i-1,j}$ then the optimality is obtained in this case from the optimality of the weights of all non-final states in $M_{i-1,j}$ (Property 2), the fact that all optimal alignment scores in this case are constrained to include the score $\gamma(S_1[i] \to \epsilon)$, and the regular expression match is obtained through one of these non-final states. For Property 2, the optimality is followed from the fact that all optimal alignments in this case use the same arc, $((i-1,j),(i,j))$.

Proving the case for $M_{i,j-1}^{S_1[i] \to \epsilon}$ with the constraint that the alignments are required to use the arc $((i,j-1),(i,j))$ is very similar to the case for $M_{i,j-1}^{S_1[i] \to \epsilon}$ and arc $((i-1,j),(i,j))$ because these two cases are symmetric.

The proof of the case for $M_{i-1,j-1}^{S_1[i] \to S_2[j]}$ with the required arc $((i-1,j-1),(i,j))$ is also similar. In this case, 1) If a final state (p,q) was already an active state in $M_{i-1,j-1}$ then the optimality of the weight $W^{M_{i,j}}$ is followed from Property

1 of $M_{i-1,j-1}$, and the fact that all optimal alignment scores in this case are constrained to include the score $\gamma(S_1[i] \rightarrow S_2[j])$. 2) If a final state (p,q) is entered newly, i.e. (p,q) is an active state in $M_{i,j}$ but not in $M_{i-1,j-1}$ then the optimality is obtained in this case from the optimality of the weights of all non-final states in $M_{i-1,j-1}$ (Property 2), and the fact that all alignment scores in this case are constrained to include the score $\gamma(S_1[i] \rightarrow S_2[j])$. Property 2 holds because of the fact that all optimal alignments in this case use the same arc, $((i-1, j-1), (i,j))$. This concludes the proof.

Computing each $M_{i,j}$ in formulation (2) takes time $O(r)$ where r is the size of the transition function of M since each transition needs to be examined a constant number of times for each move on an edit operation as well as in each execution of max_M. Therefore, all $M_{i,j}$ can be computed, and the regular expression constrained maximum alignment score can be calculated, and returned in time $O(nmr)$ using $O(rm)$ space. We note that $r = O(t^4)$ where t is the number of states in automaton N accepting the language $L(R)$.

6   Concluding Remarks and Future Work

We formally introduce the regular expression constrained sequence alignment problem, and present an algorithm for it.

It is possible to adapt the algorithm to use in computing regular expression constrained local alignments based on the Smith-Waterman dynamic programming solution [13]: let $\mathcal{H}_{i,j} = 0$ when i or j is 0, and define

$$\mathcal{H}_{i,j} = \max\{\, 0, \mathcal{H}_{i-1,j} + \gamma(S_1[i] \rightarrow \epsilon),\ \mathcal{H}_{i-1,j-1} + \gamma(S_1[i] \rightarrow S_2[j]), \atop \mathcal{H}_{i,j-1} + \gamma(\epsilon \rightarrow S_2[j])\, \} \tag{3}$$

and the maximum local alignment score is $\max_{i,j} \mathcal{H}_{i,j}$.

It is also possible to modify our algorithm for other scoring schemes. For example, affine gap penalties is another common scoring scheme in which the total penalty for a gap of size k, i.e. a block of k insertions (or deletions), is $\alpha + (k-1)\mu$ where α is the gap open penalty, and μ is called the gap extension penalty. The dynamic programming formulation for local alignment in this case can be described as follows ([13]): let $\mathcal{E}_{i,j} = \mathcal{F}_{i,j} = \mathcal{H}_{i,j} = 0$ when i or j is 0, and define

$$\mathcal{E}_{i,j} = \max\{\mathcal{H}_{i,j-1} - \alpha,\ \mathcal{E}_{i,j-1} - \mu\}, \qquad \mathcal{F}_{i,j} = \max\{\mathcal{H}_{i-1,j} - \alpha,\ \mathcal{F}_{i-1,j} - \mu\}, \atop \mathcal{H}_{i,j} = \max\{0,\ \mathcal{H}_{i-1,j-1} + s(x_i, y_j),\ \mathcal{E}_{i,j},\ \mathcal{F}_{i,j}\} \tag{4}$$

Affine gap penalties do not increase the asymptotic complexity of the local alignment problem.

It is easy to see that the technique we develop in this paper is applicable to both formulations in (3) and (4). The idea of constructing a weighted finite automaton can be generalized to the problems in which we consider a regular expression composed of given regular expressions. For example, we can locate known motifs in each sequence separately, and find alignments containing these motifs in some order by creating, and using an automaton that combines the automata for these motifs. We can also create, and use a weighted automaton to align multiple sequences with a given regular expression constraint.

Our algorithm guides the alignments by forcing them to contain a pattern which is described as a regular expression. A very important application is the alignment of protein sequences that include a given motif.

Acknowledgement

We thank an anonymous referee for bringing Reference [4] into our attention.

References

1. A. N. Arslan and Ö. Eğecioğlu. Algorithms for the constrained common sequence problem. *Proc. Prague Stringology Conference 2004, (Eds. M. Simanek and J. Holub)*, pp. 24-32, Prague August 2004.
2. P. Bork and E. V. Koonin. Protein sequence motifs. *Curr. Opin. Struct. Biol.*, 6:366-376, 1996.
3. F. Y. L. Chin, N. L. Ho, T. W. Lam, P. W. H. Wong, M. Y. Chan. Efficient constrained multiple sequence alignment with performance guarantee. *Proc. IEEE Computational Systems Bioinformatics (CSB 2003)*, pp. 337-346, 2003.
4. J.-P. Comet and J. Henry. Pairwise sequence alignment using a PROSITE pattern-derived similarity score. *Computers and Chemistry*, 26, pp. 421-436, 2002.
5. R. F. Doolittle. Similar amino acid sequences: chance or common ancestry. *Science*, 214:149-159, 1981.
6. J. E. Hopcroft and J. D. Ullman. Introduction to automata theory, languages, and computation. *Addison-Wesley Publishing Company*, 1979.
7. F. Y.L. Chin, A. D. Santis, A. L. Ferrara, N. L. Ho, S. K. Kim. A simple algorithm for the constrained sequence problems. *Information Processing Letters* Vol. 90, pp. 175-179, 2004.
8. L. Falquet, M. Pagni, P. Bucher, N. Hulo, C. J. Sigrist, K. Hofmann, A. Bairoch. The PROSITE database, its status in 2002. *Nucleic Acids Res.*, 30:235-238, 2002.
9. C. Y. Tang, C. L. Lu, M. D.-T. Chang, Y.-T. Tsai, Y.-J. Sun, K.-M. Chao, J.-M. Chang, Y.-H. Chiou, C.-M. Wu, H.-T. Chang, and W.-I. Chou. Constrained multiple sequence alignment tool development and its applications to rnase family alignment. *Proceeding of the 1st IEEE Computer Society Bioinformatics Conference (CSB 2002)*, pp. 127-137, 2002.
10. Y.-T. Tsai. The constrained common sequence problem. *Information Processing Letters*, 88:173-176, 2003.
11. Y.-T. Tsai, C. L. Lu, C. T. Yu, and Y. P. Huang. MuSiC: A tool for multiple sequence alignment with constraint. *Bioinformatics*, 20(14):2309-2311, 2004.
12. J. E. Walker, M. Saraste, M. J. Runswick, N. J. Gay. Distantly related sequences in the alpha- and beta-subunits of ATP synthase, myosin, kinases and other ATP-requiring enzymes and a common nucleotide binding fold. *EMBO J.*, 1:945-951, 1982.
13. M. S. Waterman. *Introduction to computational biology*. Chapman & Hall, 1995.

A Linear Tree Edit Distance Algorithm
for Similar Ordered Trees

Hélène Touzet

LIFL – UMR CNRS 8022 – Université Lille 1
59 655 Villeneuve d'Ascq cedex, France
Helene.Touzet@lifl.fr

Abstract. We describe a linear algorithm for comparing two similar ordered rooted trees with node labels. The method for comparing trees is the usual tree edit distance. We show that an optimal mapping which uses at most k insertions or deletions can then be constructed in $O(nk^3)$ where n is the size of the trees. The approach is inspired by the Zhang-Shasha algorithm for tree edit distance in combination with an adequate pruning of the search space.

1 Introduction

The problem of determining the similarity between two labeled ordered trees occurs in several areas of computer science: hierarchically structured data, image decomposition, RNA secondary structures in computational biology ...

There are at least two paradigms to compare ordered trees: edit distance and alignment. The original edit distance is based on three edit operations on nodes – insertion, deletion and substitution – and operations can apply without any restriction in any order. Tai [10] introduced a first solution for this problem. Zhang and Shasha [12] gave a faster dynamic programming algorithm. The time required is $O(n^2 collapsed\_depth^2)$ where n is the size of the trees and *collapsed_depth* is a parameter that depends of the shape of the tree. The value of *collapsed_depth* is in $O(n)$, but it is bounded by the depth and by the number of leaves of the trees, which makes it smaller in average. Klein [8] proposed an improved algorithm in $O(n^3 \log(n))$. Further analyses of Zhang-Shasha and Klein approaches can be found in [2, 3].

Alignment has been introduced by Jiang *et al.* [7] as an alternative to tree edit. All insertions should be performed before deletions. In other words, an alignment between two trees is obtained by applying insert operations on the two trees so they become isomorphic when labels are ignored. Alignment is less expressive than the edit distance approach. Figure 1 provides a typical example where the alignment requires more edition operations than the edit distance. Moreover, figure 2 shows that there is no bounded ratio between the scores of the distance and the alignment. The best known algorithm for alignment runs in $O(n^2 d^2)$ where d is the maximal degree of the trees. So for trees with bounded degrees, the alignment algorithm turned to be quadratic. Recent results dealing with local and gapped alignments have been proposed in [4, 5].

A. Apostolico, M. Crochemore, and K. Park (Eds.): CPM 2005, LNCS 3537, pp. 334–345, 2005.
© Springer-Verlag Berlin Heidelberg 2005

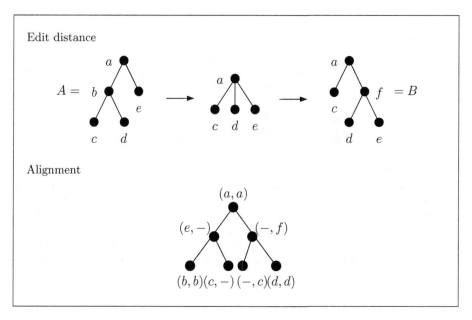

Edit distance

$$A = \ldots$$

Alignment

(a, a)

$(e, -)$ $(-, f)$

$(b, b)(c, -)(-, c)(d, d)$

Fig. 1. Edit distance versus alignment 1 (borrowed from [7]). The first picture shows the optimal mapping for the two trees A and B with the edit distance: the mapping contains a deletion and an insertion. That makes two errors. With the alignment, the optimal mapping involves four errors. The cost of the edit operations is defined as follows: `sub = ins = del = 1`.

In this article, we address the problem of comparing similar trees. We assume that the number of errors between the two input trees can be bounded in advance by a positive integer k. Errors are edit operations that affect the skeleton of the tree: insertions or deletions. This question of comparing similar trees occurs when comparing functionnaly related RNA secondary structures for instance. A fast algorithm has been proposed for tree alignment with k errors [6]: in this context, the method can construct an optimal alignment in $O(n \log(n) d^3 k^2)$ time. In particular, if both trees are of bounded degree the running time reduces to $O(n \log(n) k^2)$.

We focus here on the tree edit distance paradigm with k errors. The good news is that it is then possible to convert the $O(n^4)$ method of Zhang-Shasha into a linear algorithm. The approach is inspired by the known k-band method for an optimal alignment between similar strings and uses a graph-theoretical formalisation called *edit graph*. We show that if there is an optimal mapping between the two input trees which uses at most k errors, then the edit distance can be computed in $O(nk^3)$.

2   Graph Representation for the Tree Edit Problem

Definition 1 (Tree). *A tree is a node (called the root) connected to an ordered sequence of disjoint trees. Each node is assigned a label. ε denotes the empty tree.*

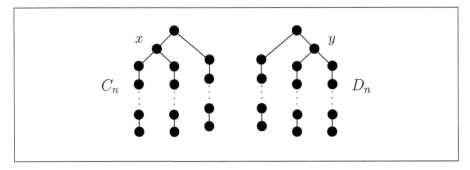

Fig. 2. Edit distance versus alignment 2. For each natural number n, define the trees C_n and D_n of height $n + 1$ and of size $3n + 2$ as displayed above. This family of trees shows that the difference between the distance and the optimal alignment can be linear in the size of the trees. The value of the edit distance between C_n and D_n does not depend of n: the optimal mapping is composed of the deletion of x followed by the insertion of y. As for the optimal alignment, the cost is in $O(n)$, since it involves at least $n - 1$ deletions.

In the sequel, we shall use the following notations.

Notation 1 *Let A be a tree.*

- *given a node x of A, $A(x)$ denotes the subtree of A rooted at x,*
- size(A) *denotes the number of nodes of the tree A, and* size(x) *is the size of $A(x)$,*
- depth(x) *is the length of the path from the root of A to x,*
- height(x) *is the length of the longest path originated from x. The height of a leaf is 0.*

As usual, the edit distance relies on three elementary edit operations: the *substitution*, which consists in replacing a label of a node by another label, the *insertion* of a node, and the *deletion* of a node. Each edit operation is assigned a cost: sub, ins and del denote the costs for respectively substituting, inserting and deleting a node.

Definition 2 (Edit distance). *Let A and B be two trees. The* tree edit distance *between A and B, denoted* td(A, B), *is the minimal cost of edit operations needed to transform A into B. For each pair of nodes (x, y) in $A \times B$, we write* td(x, y) *for the distance between the two subtrees $A(x)$ and $B(y)$.*

As mentioned in the introduction section, Zhang-Shasha and Klein proposed efficient algorithms for this problem. Both methods use dynamic programming decompositions on the input trees. We introduce an alternative formulation that is based on a graph-theoretical representation. It is known that the alignment of two strings can be reduced to the question of searching for an optimal path in a grid. Let u and v be two strings of length m and n respectively. The construction of the optimal alignment is based on a bidimensional array that can be represented as a weighted directed graph. Vertices are in $0..m \times 0..n$. Three arcs are originated from each vertex (x, y):

$$(x, y) \rightsquigarrow (x - 1, y) \qquad \text{labeled by del}$$
$$(x, y) \rightsquigarrow (x, y - 1) \qquad \text{labeled by ins}$$
$$(x, y) \rightsquigarrow (x - 1, y - 1) \text{ labeled by } \text{sub}(x, y)$$

The set of paths from the node (m, n) to the node $(0, 0)$ is exactly the set of all possible alignments between the two strings. The optimal alignment is the path of smallest weight. One can adapt this point of view to the problem of the edit distance for trees. This has been done in [1] or [11] for a restrained version of the edit distance: substitution can occurs only between nodes with the same depth. We make it more general here and apply the construction to the full tree edit distance. The motivating idea is that a mapping between two trees induces a sequence alignment between the two associated postorder traversal: enumerating the nodes of the subtrees and then the root. Of course every possible path in the grid does not lead to a correct tree mapping. The mapping should be consistent with the structures of the trees. If the node x of A is matched with the node y of B, then the subtrees $A(x)$ and $B(y)$ should be matched together too. Concerning the graph representation, it means that every path containing the diagonal arc $(x, y) \rightsquigarrow (x - 1, y - 1)$ should visit the vertex $(x - \text{size}(x), y - \text{size}(y))$. We take into account this constraint and modify the edit graph consequently. The set of vertices constituting the grid is identical, as well as arcs for insertions and deletions. Only arcs corresponding to substitution operations are modified.

Definition 3 (Tree edit graph). *Let A and B be two trees of size m and n respectively. Nodes of A and B are enumerated in the postorder notation, indices starting at 1. The tree edit graph of A and B is a weighted directed graph composed by nodes in $0..m \times 0..n$ whose incident arcs are defined as follows:*

$$\text{deletion arc} : (x, y) \rightsquigarrow (x - 1, y) \text{ labeled by } \text{del}$$
$$\text{insertion arc} : (x, y) \rightsquigarrow (x, y - 1) \text{ labeled by } \text{ins}$$
$$\text{substitution arc} : (x, y) \rightsquigarrow (x - \text{size}(x), y - \text{size}(y)) \text{ labeled by } \text{td}(x, y)$$

Figure 3 gives an example of a tree edit graph. Before explaining how to compute the labels td of the substitution arcs, we establish briefly that this construction is correct. This is the purpose of Lemmas 1 and 2.

Definition 4 (Subgraph and top-level path). *Let A and B be two trees and let (x, y) be a pair of nodes of $A \times B$. We write G for the edit graph of A and B. The subgraph $G(x, y)$ associated to $A(x)$ and $B(y)$ is the restriction of G to nodes and arcs in $\{\text{size}(x) - x..x\} \times \{\text{size}(y) - y..y\}$ without the substitution arc $(x, y) \rightsquigarrow (x - \text{size}(x), y - \text{size}(y))$ and with an extra arc $(x, y) \rightsquigarrow (x - 1, y - 1)$ labeled by $\text{sub}(x, y)$. A top-level path of $A(x)$ and $B(y)$ is an optimal path in $G(x, y)$ from the bottom-right corner to the upper-left corner.*

Given a path P in the edit graph, define $M(P)$ as the set of vertices that are the origin of a diagonal arc:

$$M(P) = \{(x, y) \in A \times B, \ (x, y) \rightsquigarrow (x - \text{size}(x), y - \text{size}(y)) \in P\}$$

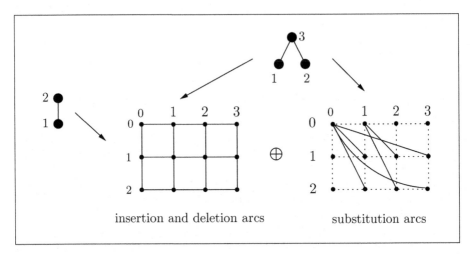

Fig. 3. Edit graph. For clarity's sake, the insertion and deletion arcs and the substitution arcs are drawned on two separate grids. The edit graph is obtained by overlaying the two grids. All arcs are oriented from the bottom-right node to the upper-left node.

Lemma 1. *Let A and B be two trees and P a path for A and B. Then $M(P)$ is a mapping of A to B. Conversely, let M be a mapping of A to B such that*

$$(x, y) \in M \wedge (x', y') \in M \;\Rightarrow\; x \notin A(x') \wedge x' \notin A(x)$$

Then there is a path P in the edit graph from $(\mathtt{size}(A), \mathtt{size}(B))$ to $(0, 0)$ such that $M = M(P)$.

How to derive an optimal mapping from the edit graph ? The mapping is no longer obtained with a single path, but with a serie of top-level paths.

Lemma 2. *Let A and B be two trees. An optimal mapping can be built up recursively as follows.*

$$\begin{aligned}
\mathtt{Mapping}(A, \varepsilon) &= \emptyset \\
\mathtt{Mapping}(\varepsilon, B) &= \emptyset \\
\mathtt{Mapping}(A, B) &= M(P) \cup_{(x,y) \in M(P)} \mathtt{Mapping}(A(x), B(y))
\end{aligned}$$

where P is an optimal path for A and B in the associated edit graph. The cost of the mapping is the weight of the top-level path for A and B.

At each step, the time needed to compute the top-level path for (x, y) is in $O(\mathtt{size}(x) \times \mathtt{size}(y))$. Since a mapping contains only a linear number of matching pairs, the overall computation time is $O(n^3)$.

We now come to the problem of determining the labels of the substitution edges in the edit graph. $td(x, y)$ is obtained as the weight of a top-level path for $A(x)$ and $B(y)$. Let (h, l) be the coordinates of the first node of $G(x, y)$: $h = x - \mathtt{size}(x)$, $l = y - \mathtt{size}(y)$. For each (i, j) in $G(x, y)$ distinct from (x, y), we denote $fd(i, j, h, l)$ the cost of an optimal path from (k, l) to (i, j). The usual dynamic programming algorithm for an optimal in a graph gives the following equations for fd.

$$fd(h, l, h, l) = 0$$
$$fd(i, l, h, l) = fd(i - 1, l, h, l) + \texttt{del}$$
$$fd(h, j, h, l) = fd(h, j - 1, h, l) + \texttt{ins}$$

$$fd(i, j, h, l) = \min \begin{cases} fd(i - 1, j, h, l) + \texttt{del} \\ fd(i, j - 1, h, l) + \texttt{ins} \\ fd(i - \texttt{size}(i), j - \texttt{size}(j), h, l) + td(i, j) \end{cases}$$

(1)

Readers that are familiar with the original formulation of Zhang-Shasha algorithm may note that Equation 1 is the main recurrence formulas for the computation of the tree edit distance (lemmas 3 and 4 in [12]). The value of $fd(i, j, h, l)$ is exactly the distance between the subforest $[h..i]$ of A and the subforest $[l..j]$ in B, denoted $\texttt{forestdist}(h..i, l..j)$ in the Zhang-Shasha article.

From Equation 1, we can deduce the distance $td(x, y)$ for $A(x)$ and $B(y)$. This is

$$td(x, y) = \min \begin{cases} fd(x - 1, y, h, l) + \texttt{del} \\ fd(x, y - 1, h, l) + \texttt{ins} \\ fd(x - 1, y - 1, h, l) + \texttt{sub}(x, y) \end{cases}$$

(2)

Klein's algorithm is based on another strategy for the traversal of the grid for finding optimal paths. For the problem of the edit distance with k errors, we shall focus on the direct strategy of Zhang-Shasha.

3   Tree Edit Distance with k Errors

The general idea of the algorithm with k errors is to prune the edit graph to keep only relevant vertices and arcs. For that we implement three optimisations, that are given by lemmas 3, 4 and 5. The first property is analogous to the k-band alignment algorithm for strings of [9]. If the trees are similar, then the best mappings have their paths near the main diagonal in the edit graph. It means that is is not necessary to build the entire graph.

Definition 5 (k-strip). *Let k be a positive integer. For two trees A and B, we define the set of pairs of nodes k-strip(A, B) as*

$$k\text{-strip}(A, B) = \{(x, y) \in G(A, B), \ |x - y| \leq k\}$$

where $G(A, B)$ is the tree edit graph of A and B. We write k-strip(x, y) for k-strip$(A(x), B(y))$.

Lemma 3. *Let A and B be two trees and let x and y be two nodes in A and B respectively. If there is a mapping between A and B which uses at most k errors and that visits the vertex (x, y), then $(x, y) \in k$-strip(A, B).*

Definition 6 (k-relevant). *Let k be a positive integer. Given two trees A and B and a pair of nodes (x, y) in k-strip(A, B), the pair (x, y) is called k-relevant if*

$$|\texttt{size}(A) - x - \texttt{size}(B) + y| + |\texttt{size}(x) - \texttt{size}(y)| + |x - \texttt{size}(x) - y + \texttt{size}(y)| \le k.$$

Furthermore, we define the maximal number of errors $e(x, y)$ *for* $A(x)$ *and* $B(y)$ *as*

$$e(x, y) = k - |x - \texttt{size}(x) - y + \texttt{size}(y)| - |\texttt{size}(A) - x - \texttt{size}(B) + y|.$$

Lemma 4. *Let A and B be two trees and let x and y be two nodes in A and B respectively. If there is a mapping between A and B which uses at most k errors so that $A(x)$ is mapped to $B(y)$, then (x, y) is k-relevant and the number of errors to compare $A(x)$ and $B(y)$ is bounded by $e(x, y)$.*

Proof. If $A(x)$ is mapped to $B(y)$, then it implies that the path should visit four vertices in the edit graph: $(\texttt{size}(A), \texttt{size}(B))$, (x, y), $(x - \texttt{size}(x), y - \texttt{size}(y))$ and finally $(0, 0)$. The total amount of errors along this path is greater than $|\texttt{size}(A) - x - \texttt{size}(B) + y| + |\texttt{size}(x) - \texttt{size}(y)| + |x - \texttt{size}(x) - y + \texttt{size}(y)|$. In particular, the number of errors outside $A(x) \times B(y)$ is greater than $|x - \texttt{size}(x) - y + \texttt{size}(y)| + |\texttt{size}(A) - x - \texttt{size}(B) + y|$. If the total number of errors should be bounded by k, it remains $e(x, y)$ errors for $A(x)$ and $B(y)$. □

Lemmas 3 and 4 lead to the following outline for the computation of the distance with k errors.

Procedure *Distance*

Input: two trees A and B, integer k
Output: fills up the array td. For each (x, y) of $A \times B \cap k$-strip(A, B), $td(x, y)$ is the distance between $A(x)$ and $B(y)$. The whole distance is $td(\texttt{size}(A), \texttt{size}(B))$.
for $(x, y) \in A \times B \cap k$-strip$(A, B)$ **do**
    if not k-relevant(x, y)
        then $td(x, y) \leftarrow +\infty$
        else $e \leftarrow |x - \texttt{size}(x) - y + \texttt{size}(y)| + |\texttt{size}(A) - x - \texttt{size}(B) + y|$
               compute $td(x, y)$ with e errors with Equations 1 and 2

Equations 1 and 2 of the previous section have to be adapted to compute $td(x, y)$ for paths in k-strip(A, B) and fd for paths k-strip$(A, B) \cap e$-strip(x, y). In each case, borders of the search space have to be delineated explicitly. This gives two functions **ForestDist1**, for fd, and **TreeDist1**, for td.

Function *ForestDist1*

Input: $i \in A(x)$, $j \in B(y)$, integers e, k
Output: compute the weight $fd(i, j)$ of an optimal path from (i, j) to $(x - \texttt{size}(x), y - \texttt{size}(y))$

($\star$ *initial cases* $\star$)
if $i = x - \texttt{size}(x)$ and $j = y - \texttt{size}(y)$ **then return** 0
if $i = x - \texttt{size}(x)$ **then return** $f(i, j - 1) + \texttt{ins}$
if $j = y - \texttt{size}(y)$ **then return** $f(i - 1, j) + \texttt{del}$
($\star$ *general case* $\star$)
$fd(i, j) \leftarrow +\infty$
if $(i - \texttt{size}(i), j - \texttt{size}(j)) \in k\text{-}strip(A, B) \cap e\text{-}strip(x, y)$ ($\star$ *substitution* $\star$)
    then $r \leftarrow td(i, j) + fd(i - \texttt{size}(i), j - \texttt{size}(j))$
if $(i - 1, j) \in k\text{-}strip(A, B) \cap e\text{-}strip(x, y)$ ($\star$ *deletion* $\star$)
    then $r \leftarrow \min(r, fd(i - 1, j)) + \texttt{del}$
if $(i, j - 1) \in k\text{-}strip(A, B) \cap e\text{-}strip(x, y)$ ($\star$ *insertion* $\star$)
    then $r \leftarrow \min(r, fd(i, j - 1)) + \texttt{ins}$
return r

Note that the two last parameters for fd in Equation 1 are omitted. $fd(i, j)$ stands here for $fd(i, j, x - \texttt{size}(x), y - \texttt{size}(y))$.

Function *TreeDist1*

Input: $x \in A$, $y \in B$, integers e, k
Output: compute the distance $td(x, y)$ between $A(x)$ and $B(y)$ with e errors
for $i \in x - \texttt{size}(x)..x$ **do**
    for $j \in y - \texttt{size}(y)..y$ such that $(i, j) \in k\text{-}strip(A, B) \cap e\text{-}strip(x, y)$ **do**
        compute $fd(i, j)$ with function ForestDist1
return $\min\{fd(x - 1, y) + \texttt{del}, fd(x, y - 1) + \texttt{ins}, fd(x - 1, y - 1) + \texttt{sub}(x, y)\}$

It gives raise to a algorithm in $O(n^2 k^2)$ that can be further improved with the following lemma.

Lemma 5. *Let A and B be two trees. Let x and i be two nodes in A, such that i is a descendant of x. If there exists a mapping between $A(x)$ and B which uses at most e errors and such that the associated top-level path contains a vertex of the form (i, j) with j in B, then* $\texttt{depth}(i) \leq \texttt{depth}(x) + e + 1$.

Proof. If (i, j) belongs to a top-level path for $A(x)$ and B, then no node along the path from x (x excluded) to i is involved in a substitution. So the top-level path contains at least $\texttt{depth}(i) - \texttt{depth}(x) - 1$ deletions. $\square$

This lemma ensures that when calculating $td(x, y)$ with at most e errors for $A(x)$ and $B(y)$, then it is not necessary to inspect pairs (i, j) where $\texttt{depth}(i) > \texttt{depth}(x) + e + 1$.

Definition 7 (Truncated tree). *Let A be a tree, x be a node in A. Let e be a natural number. The* truncated tree $A(x, e)$ *is defined in a unique way as the largest subtree of A whose root is x and whose height is e. We write* $\texttt{size}(A, x, e)$ *for the size of $A(x, e)$*

The functions `ForestDist1` and `TreeDist1` should be modified to take into account this new property.

Function *ForestDist2*

Input: $i \in A(x)$, $j \in B(y)$, integers e, k
Output: compute the weight $fd(i,j)$ of an optimal path from (i,j) to $(x - \text{size}(x), y - \text{size}(y))$

($\star$ *initial cases* $\star$)
if $i = x - \text{size}(x)$ and $j = y - \text{size}(y)$ **then return** 0
if $i = x - \text{size}(x)$ **then return** $f(i, j - 1) + \text{ins}$
if $j = y - \text{size}(y)$ **then return** $f(i - 1, j) + \text{del}$
($\star$ *general case* $\star$)
$fd(i,j) \leftarrow +\infty$
if $(i - \text{size}(i), j - \text{size}(j)) \in k\text{-}strip(A, B) \cap e\text{-}strip(x, y)$ ($\star$ *substitution* $\star$)
    then $r \leftarrow td(i,j) + fd(i - \text{size}(i), j - \text{size}(j))$
if $\text{depth}(i - 1) - \text{depth}(x) \le e + 1$ and $(i - 1, j) \in k\text{-}strip(A, B) \cap e\text{-}strip(x, y)$
($\star$ *deletion* $\star$)
    then $r \leftarrow \min(r, fd(i - 1, j)) + \text{del}$
if $(i, j - 1) \in k\text{-}strip(A, B) \cap e\text{-}strip(x, y)$ ($\star$ *insertion* $\star$)
    then $r \leftarrow \min(r, fd(i, j - 1)) + \text{ins}$
return r

Function *TreeDist2*

Input: $x \in A$, $y \in B$, integers e, k
Output: compute the distance $td(x,y)$ between $A(x)$ and $B(y)$ with e errors, with optimization of Lemma 5

($\star$ *traversal of* $A(x,e)$ $\star$)
for $i \in x - \text{size}(x)..x$ such that $\text{depth}(i) - \text{depth}(x) \le e + 1$ **do**
    for $j \in y - \text{size}(y)..y$ such that $(i, j) \in k\text{-}strip(A, B) \cap e\text{-}strip(x, y)$ **do**
        compute $fd(i, j)$ with function ForestDist2
return $\min\{fd(x - 1, y) + \text{del}, fd(x, y - 1) + \text{ins}, fd(x - 1, y - 1) + \text{sub}(x, y)\}$

The time for the computation of $td(x,y)$ with `TreeDist2` is $O(\text{size}(A, x, k)k)$, instead of $O(\text{size}(x)k)$ for the function `TreeDist1`. It remains one question to be answered: how to implement it in a effective way. The tricky point is the traversal of the truncated tree $A(x,e)$. So far, nodes of A have always been ranked and visited in postorder. We now have to be able to skip all nodes whose depth is greather than $e + 1$ in $A(x)$. For that, we combine postorder and bottom-up traversals. We introduce two arrays that allow to translate the index of a node from the postorder notation to the bottom-up notation, and vice-versa: for each $i \in \{1..\text{size}(A)\}$, define

- `bottom_up`(i) as the index in the bottom-up notation of the node of rank i in the postorder notation,
- `post_order`(i) as the index in the postorder notation of the node of rank i in the bottom-up notation.

These two attributes may be computed with a linear time pre-processing. The function `TreeDist3` is a new version of `TreeDist2` with full details.

Function *TreeDist3*

Input: $x \in A$, $y \in B$, integers e,k
Output: compute the distance $td(x,y)$ between $A(x)$ and $B(y)$ with e errors, using the optimization of lemma 5 – full details.

($\star$ *initialisation of i and nextnode* $\star$)
$i \leftarrow x - \texttt{size}(x)+$
$nextnode \leftarrow$ first node of depth $\texttt{depth}(x) + e + 1$ in $A(x)$
($\star$ *traversal of* $A(x,e)$ $\star$)
while $i \leq x$ **do**
      for $j \in y - \texttt{size}(y)..y$ such that $(i,j) \in k\text{-}strip(A,B) \cap e\text{-}strip(x,y)$ **do**
          compute $fd(i,j)$ with function ForestDist2
      ($\star$ *computation of the index i of the next node of A to be visited* $\star$)
      if $\texttt{depth}(i) - \texttt{depth}(x) = e + 1$
          then $nextnode \leftarrow \texttt{post\_order}(\texttt{bottom\_up}(i) + 1)$
      if $\texttt{depth}(i + 1) - \texttt{depth}(x) > e + 1$
          then $i \leftarrow nextnode$
          else $i \leftarrow i + 1$
return $\min\{fd(x - 1, y) + \texttt{del}, fd(x, y - 1) + \texttt{ins}, fd(x - 1, y - 1) + \texttt{sub}(x,y)\}$

The variable *nextnode* is introduced to perform the traversal of $A(x,e)$. The initialisation of *nextnode* is done in $O(A(x,e))$ using the \texttt{height} attribute: if the height of x is smaller than $e + 1$, then *nextnode* is not usefull. Otherwise pick up the first child z of x whose height is at least e, and repeat this process from z and its first child of height at least $e - 1$ until a node of depth $\texttt{depth}(x) + e + 1$ is reached. So it does not affect the total complexity of \texttt{TreeDist3}.

Procedure *FinalDistance*

Input: two trees A and B, integer k
Output: fills up the array td. For each (x,y) of $A \times B \cap k\text{-}strip(A,B)$, $td(x,y)$ is the distance between $A(x)$ and $B(y)$. The whole distance is $td(\texttt{size}(A), \texttt{size}(B))$.

for $(x,y) \in A \times B \cap k\text{-}strip(A,B)$ **do**
    if not $k\text{-}relevant(x,y)$
        then $td(x,y) \leftarrow +\infty$
        else $e \leftarrow |x - \texttt{size}(x) - y + \texttt{size}(y)| + |\texttt{size}(A) - x - \texttt{size}(B) + y|$
          compute $td(x,y)$ with function TreeDist3

We conclude with the complexity analysis of the procedure **FinalDistance**, that is based on the size of $A(x,e)$.

Lemma 6. *Let A be a tree. Let e be a positive integer.*

$$\sum_{x \in A} \texttt{size}(A, x, e) \leq (e + 1) \texttt{size}(A).$$

Proof. The proof is by induction on e and on the size of A. $\qquad\square$

Theorem 1. *The procedure* FinalDistance *computes the tree edit distance with* k *errors in* $O(nk^3)$ *time and* $O(kn)$ *space. Moreover it is then possible to reconstruct an optimal mapping in* $O(nk^2)$.

Proof. The implementation of FinalDistance uses two bidimensional arrays td and fd. Both are indexed by $\{0..\texttt{size}(A)\} \times \{-k..k\}$:

- td stores the values $td(x, y)$ of the distance between $A(x)$ and $B(y)$ for (x, y) in k-strip(A, B). More precisely, td[x,y-x] equals $td(x, y)$.
- fd is a permanent array with temporary values. At each call of TreeDist3 with parameters x and y, fd stores the values for optimal intermediate paths in $G(x, y)$. More precisely, fd[i,j-i] equals $fd(i, j)$, the weight of an optimal path from (i, j) to $(x - \texttt{size}(x), y - \texttt{size}(y))$.

The size of each array is $(2k + 1)n$. As noticed previously, the run time of TreeDist3 for (x, y) is in $O(\texttt{size}(A, x, k)k)$. So the whole algorithm is in

$$\sum_{(x,y)\in k\text{-}strip(A,B)} \texttt{size}(A, x, k)k.$$

Lemma 6 yields the following bound:

$$(2k + 1)^2 \sum_{x\in A} \texttt{size}(A, x, k) \leq (k + 1)(2k + 1)k^2 \, \texttt{size}(A).$$

Concerning the construction of an underlying optimal mapping, as for the full edit distance, we have to consider all successive top-level paths for matching pairs of nodes x and y (Lemma 2). A property worth to notice is that the top-level path for $A(x)$ and $B(y)$ can be obtained in restricting the search to vertices in $A(x, k) \times B(y) \cap k\text{-}strip(A, B)$. It can be done in $O(k \, \texttt{size}(A, x, k))$. So the whole trace back needs only $O(nk^2)$ time. $\qquad\square$

4   Final Comment

Our algorithm can construct an optimal mapping for two trees A and B in $O(nk^3)$ time if the number of errors can be bounded in advance by k. When taking the trivial bound $k = \texttt{size}(A) + \texttt{size}(B)$, this leads to the same asymptotic complexity $O(n^4)$ as Zhang-Shasha algorithm. However the average complexity would be worse, because we do not use the optimization of Zhang-Shasha that consists in eliminating redundant computations between a pair of nodes and the pair of their leftmost children.

If k is not specified in advance, it is also possible to apply the same scheme as in [6, 9]. The idea goes as follows. It uses iterated application of the distance with k errors with increasing values of k. The starting value for k is $|\texttt{size}(A) - \texttt{size}(B)|$ and then k is doubled at each step. The stopping condition for k is given by a relationship between the score and the number of errors.

References

1. S. Chawathe. Comparing hierarchical data in external memory. In *Twenty-fifth International Conference on Very Large Data Bases*, pages 90–101, 1999.
2. S. Dulucq and L. Tichit. RNA secondary structure comparison: exact analysis of the Zhang-Shasha tree edit algorithm. *Theoretical Computer Science*, 306(1-3):471–484, 2003.
3. S. Dulucq and H. Touzet. Analysis of tree edit distance algorithms. In *Combinatorial Pattern Matching*, volume 2676, pages 83–95. Lecture Notes in Computer Science, 2003.
4. M. Höchsmann, T. Töller, R. Giegerich, and S. Kurtz. Local similarity in RNA secondary structures. In *IEEE Bioinformatics Conference*, pages 159–168, 2003.
5. J. Jansson, N. Trung Hieu, and W.-K. Sung. Local gapped subforest alignment and its application in finding RNA structural motifs. In *ISAAC*, volume 3341, pages 569–580. Lecture Notes in Computer Science, 2004.
6. J. Jansson and A. Lingas. A fast algorithm for optimal alignment between similar ordered trees. *Fundamenta Informaticae*, 56(1,2):105 – 120, 2003.
7. T. Jiang, L. Wang, and K. Zhang. Alignment of trees - an alternative to tree edit. *Theoretical Computer Science*, 143(1):137–148, 1995.
8. P. Klein. Computing the edit-distance between unrooted ordered trees. In *6th European Symposium on Algorithms*, pages 91–102, 1998.
9. J. Setubal and J. Meidanis. *Introduction to computational biology*, chapter Sequence Comparison and Database Search. International Thomson Publishing Company, 1997.
10. K.C. Tai. The tree-to-tree correction problem. *Journal of the Association for Comput. Machi.*, 26:422–433, 1979.
11. G. Valiente. *Algorithms on Trees and Graphs*. Springer, 2002.
12. K. Zhang and D. Shasha. Simple fast algorithms for the editing distance between trees and related problems. *SIAM Journal of Computing*, 18(6):1245–1262, 1989.

A Polynomial Time Matching Algorithm
of Ordered Tree Patterns
Having Height-Constrained Variables

Kazuhide Aikou[1], Yusuke Suzuki[1,2], Takayoshi Shoudai[1],
Tomoyuki Uchida[2], and Tetsuhiro Miyahara[2]

[1] Department of Informatics, Kyushu University, Kasuga 816-8580, Japan
{k-aikou,y-suzuki,shoudai}@i.kyushu-u.ac.jp
[2] Faculty of Information Sciences,
Hiroshima City University, Hiroshima 731-3194, Japan
uchida@cs.hiroshima-cu.ac.jp, miyahara@its.hiroshima-cu.ac.jp

Abstract. Tree structured data such as HTML/XML files are represented by rooted trees with ordered children and edge labels. Knowledge representations for tree structured data are quite important to discover interesting features which such tree structured data have. In order to represent tree structured patterns with rich structural features, we introduce a new type of structured variables, called height-constrained variables. An (i, j)-height-constrained variable can be replaced with any tree such that the trunk length of the tree is at least i and the height of the tree is at most j. Then, we define a term tree as a rooted tree structured pattern with ordered children and height-constrained variables. In this paper, given a term tree t and an ordered tree T, we present an $O(N \max\{nD_{\max}, \mathcal{S}\})$ time algorithm of deciding whether or not t matches T, where $D_{\max}$ is the maximum number of the children of an internal vertex in T, $\mathcal{S}$ is the sum of all trunk length constraints i of all (i, j)-height-constrained variables in t, and n and N are the numbers of vertices of t and T, respectively.

1 Introduction

Due to the rapid growth of Internet usage, semistructured data such as Web documents have been rapidly increasing. Since such data have tree structures, they are called tree structured data and represented by rooted trees with ordered children and edge labels, according to Object Exchange Model [1]. In the field of data mining, many researches of extracting frequent substructures from tree structured data have been proposed [3–6, 14]. Moreover, in order to clarify not only associations but also structural relations between substructures common to tree structured data, some types of tree structured patterns have been proposed [4, 7, 11, 12]. In order to directly represent such relations among tree structured data, we propose an *ordered term tree*, simply called a *term tree*, as a tree structured pattern with ordered children and structured variables. We call an ordered tree a tree simply. A variable consists of two vertices, called the parent port and

A. Apostolico, M. Crochemore, and K. Park (Eds.): CPM 2005, LNCS 3537, pp. 346–357, 2005.

the child port. A variable is replaced with any tree T by identifying the parent
port with the root of T and the child port with a distinguished leaf of T. We call
the distance between the root and the distinguished leaf *the trunk length* of T.
For example, in Fig. 1, both trees T_1 and T_2 can be obtained from a term tree s
by replacing variables having labels "x", "y" and "z" with appropriate trees. In
this paper, we introduce a new kind of variables, called *height-constrained variables* (abbreviated to HC-variables), in order to present a tree structured pattern
which can also have distance relations between substructures common to tree
structured data. An (i, j)-*height-constrained variable* (abbreviated to (i, j)-HC-
variable) is replaced with any tree T such that the trunk length of T is at least
i and the height of T is at most j. For example, in Fig.1, T_2 is obtained from
t by replacing the $(1,1)$-HC-variable "$x(1, 1)$", the $(2,3)$-HC-variable "$y(2, 3)$"
and the $(2,2)$-HC-variable "$z(2, 2)$" with g_1, g_2 and g_3, respectively. However, T_1
cannot be obtained from t.

A term tree t is said to be *linear* (or *regular*) if all variable labels in t are
mutually distinct. We consider a problem of deciding whether or not a linear
term tree t having HC-variables matches a tree T, that is, T is obtained from
t by substituting some trees for all HC-variables in t. Efficient algorithms for
solving matching problems are necessary for designing useful data mining tools
of extracting linear term trees having HC-variables from tree structured data.
In this paper, we present an $O(N \max\{nD_{\max}, \mathcal{S}\})$ time algorithm of solving the
matching problem for a given linear term tree t and a given tree T, where $D_{\max}$
is the maximum number of the children of an internal vertex in T, $\mathcal{S}$ is the sum of
all trunk length constraints i of all (i, j)-HC-variables in t, and n and N are the
numbers of vertices of t and T, respectively. Algorithms of solving a matching
problem govern the efficiency and usefulness of data mining tools having term
trees as knowledge representations.

A term tree is different from other representations of tree structured patterns
such as in [3, 4, 6, 14] in that a term tree has structured variables which can be
substituted by trees and a term tree represents not a substructure but a whole
tree structure. In [7, 13], we have considered matching problems for different
types of term trees from term trees in this paper. From the viewpoint of computational learning theory, some fundamental sets of linear ordered or unordered
term trees whose languages are polynomial time inductively inferable from positive data have been given in [7, 10–12]. Moreover, learning of term trees with
height-bounded variables from queries has been considered in [8]. Data mining
tools having term trees with erasing variables have been proposed in [9].

2 Preliminaries

We give the definition of ordered term trees with two-port variables. The general
definition of ordered term trees with multiple-port variables are given in [12].
For a set S, the number of elements in S is denoted by $|S|$.

Let $T = (V_T, E_T)$ be a rooted tree with ordered children, called an *ordered
tree*, or a *tree* simply, where V_T is a set of vertices and E_T is a set of edges.

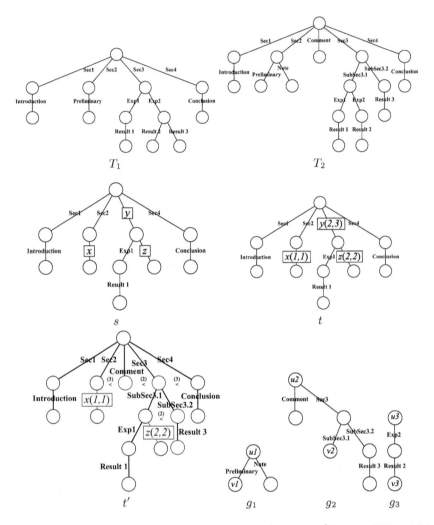

Fig. 1. Trees T_1, T_2, a term tree s, and term trees t and t' having HC-variables. Variables are denoted by squares each of which connects to the parent port and the child port of the variable. A square with x shows a variable labeled with a variable label x, and a square with $x(i, j)$ shows an (i, j)-HC-variable with a variable label x. The term tree t' is obtained from t by replacing the $(2, 3)$-HC-variable with the variable label y with the tree g_2 and updating the ordering of each internal vertex in t'.

Let E_g and H_g be a partition of E_T, i.e., $E_g \cup H_g = E_T$ and $E_g \cap H_g = \emptyset$. And let $V_g = V_T$. A triplet $g = (V_g, E_g, H_g)$ is called an *ordered term tree*, or a *term tree* simply. And elements in V_g, E_g and H_g are called a *vertex*, an *edge* and a *variable*, respectively. The root of g is the root of T and the leaves of g are the leaves of T. The *height* of a term tree g is the length of the longest path from the root to a leaf. We denote by $[v, v']$ a variable in H_g such that v

is the parent of v'. We call v the *parent port* of $[v, v']$ and v' the *child port* of $[v, v']$. For a term tree g, all children of every internal vertex u in g have a total ordering on all children of u. The ordering on the children of u is denoted by $<_u^g$. We assume that every edge and variable of a term tree is labeled with some words from specified languages. A label of a variable is called a *variable label*. Λ and X denote a set of edge labels and a set of variable labels, respectively, where $\Lambda \cap X = \phi$. A term tree $g = (V_g, E_g, H_g)$ is called *linear* (or *regular*) if all variables in H_g have mutually distinct variable labels in X. In this paper, we deal with linear term trees only. Thus we assume that all term trees in this paper are linear.

Definition 1 (Height-constrained variables). Let $X^{\mathcal{H}}$ be an infinite subset of a variable label set X. For two integers $1 \leq i \leq j$, let $X^{\mathcal{H}(i,j)}$ be an infinite subset of $X^{\mathcal{H}}$. We assume that $X^{\mathcal{H}} = \bigcup_{1 \leq i \leq j} X^{\mathcal{H}(i,j)}$ and $X^{\mathcal{H}(i,j)} \cap X^{\mathcal{H}(i',j')} = \emptyset$ for $(i,j) \neq (i',j')$. A variable label in $X^{\mathcal{H}(i,j)}$ is called an (i,j)-*height-constrained variable label* for any $1 \leq i \leq j$. A variable $[u,v]$ of a term tree is said to be an (i,j)-*height-constrained variable* (abbreviated to (i,j)-HC-variable) if the variable has an (i,j)-height-constrained variable label, and denoted by $[u,v]^{\mathcal{H}(i,j)}$.

Let f and g be term trees with at least two vertices, and x a variable label in $X^{\mathcal{H}(i,j)}$ for $1 \leq i \leq j$. Let $\sigma = [u, u']$ be a list of two vertices in g where u is the root of g and u' is a leaf of g. The length of the path between u and u' is called the *trunk length* of σ. The form $x := [g, \sigma]$ is called a *binding* for x if (i) the trunk length of σ is at least i, and (ii) the height of g is at most j.

For a variable label $x \in X$, a new term tree $f\{x := [g, \sigma]\}$ is obtained by applying the binding $x := [g, \sigma]$ to f in the following way. Let $e = [v, v']$ be a variable in f with the variable label x. Let g' be one copy of g and w, w' the vertices of g' corresponding to u, u' of g, respectively. For the variable $e = [v, v']$, we attach g' to f by removing the variable e from H_f and by identifying the vertices v, v' with the vertices w, w' of g', respectively. A *substitution* θ is a finite collection of bindings $\{x_1 := [g_1, \sigma_1], \cdots, x_n := [g_n, \sigma_n]\}$, where x_i are mutually distinct variable labels in X and g_i are trees $(1 \leq i \leq n)$. The term tree $f\theta$, called the *instance* of f by θ, is obtained by applying the all bindings $x_i := [g_i, \sigma_i]$ on f simultaneously. The root of the resulting term tree $f\theta$ is the root of f. Moreover, we define the new ordering of children of an internal vertex v of $f\theta$ in the natural way. The precise definition of the new ordering is found in [12]. For example, let t be a term tree in Fig. 1 and $\theta = \{x := [g_1, [u_1, v_1]], y := [g_2, [u_2, v_2]], z := [g_3, [u_3, v_3]]\}$ a substitution, where g_1, g_2 and g_3 are trees in Fig. 1. Then the instance $t\theta$ of t by θ is the tree T_2 in Fig. 1. The term tree t' in Fig. 1 is the instance $t\{y := [g_2, [u_2, v_2]]\}$. The number drawn between siblings of t' indicates the applied case [12] in updating the ordering on vertices in t'.

We say that two term trees $f = (V_f, E_f, H_f)$ and $g = (V_g, E_g, H_g)$ are *isomorphic*, denoted by $f \equiv g$, if there is a bijection φ from V_f to V_g such that (i) the root of f is mapped to the root of g by φ, (ii) $\{u, v\} \in E_f$ if and only if $\{\varphi(u), \varphi(v)\} \in E_g$, (iii) $[u, v]^{\mathcal{H}(i,j)} \in H_f$ if and only if $[\varphi(u), \varphi(v)]^{\mathcal{H}(i,j)} \in H_g$ for $1 \leq i \leq j$, and (iv) for any internal vertex u in f which has more than one child, and for any two children u' and u'' of u, $u' <_u^f u''$ if and only if $\varphi(u') <_{\varphi(u)}^g \varphi(u'')$. Let Λ be a set of edge labels. We denote by $\mathcal{OT}_\Lambda$ the set of all edge-labeled ordered trees whose labels are in Λ. For a term tree t, the *term tree language* $L_\Lambda(t)$ of a term tree t is defined as $\{s \in \mathcal{OT}_\Lambda \mid s \equiv t\theta \text{ for a substitution } \theta\}$. $\mathcal{OTT}_\Lambda^{\mathcal{H}}$ denotes the set of all term trees such that all variable labels are in $X^{\mathcal{H}}$ and all edge labels are in Λ.

3   A Polynomial Time Matching Algorithm for $\mathcal{OTT}_\Lambda^{\mathcal{H}}$

3.1   Algorithm MATCHING

We proposed polynomial time algorithms for solving the matching problems for term trees with general variables [13]. These algorithms are based on dynamic programming and run in $O(nN)$ time where n and N are numbers of vertices of a given term tree t and a given tree T, respectively. For a term tree with HC-variables, we need more time to check whether or not there exists a binding satisfying the constraints of a couple of HC-variables. In this section, we give a polynomial time algorithm for the matching problem for $\mathcal{OTT}_\Lambda^{\mathcal{H}}$ where $|\Lambda| = 1$. We can easily modify it to give a polynomial time algorithm for $|\Lambda| \geq 2$.

Let $T = (V_T, E_T)$ and $t = (V_t, E_t, H_t)$ be a tree in $L_\Lambda(t)$ and a term tree in $\mathcal{OTT}_\Lambda^{\mathcal{H}}$, respectively. A term tree t is said to *match* a tree T if T is included in $L_\Lambda(t)$. For a vertex u' of a term tree t, we denote by $t[u']$ the term tree consisting of u' and all descendants of u'. We use the same notation for a tree T. For a vertex u of a tree T and its descendant v, we denote by $T[u] - T[v]$ the tree consisting of u and all descendants of u except for all proper descendants of v. We note that v is a vertex in $T[u] - T[v]$. For a tree T and a vertex u of T, the height of T, the height of $T[u]$, and the height of $T - T[u]$ are denoted by $height(T)$, $height_T(u)$, and $\overline{height}_T(u)$, respectively. For two vertices u and v of a tree or a term tree, we denote by $dist(u, v)$ the distance between u and v.

First, we give all the vertices in t the sequential numbers from 1 to $|V_t|$ by the breadth-first search method. We call these numbers *vertex identifiers* (VIDs for short). The VID of the root of t is 1 and for any internal vertex u the children of u have consecutive VIDs. Below we identify a vertex with its VID. A *correspondence-set* (C-set for short) of a vertex $u \in V_T$, denoted by $CS(u)$, is a subset of $V_t \times \mathcal{N} \times \mathcal{N}$, where $\mathcal{N}$ is the set of all nonnegative integers. The main algorithm is described in Fig. 2. The algorithm proceeds by constructing C-sets for each vertex of a given tree T in the bottom-up manner. After the algorithm terminates, all C-sets satisfy the following lemma.

Lemma 1. *Let u' be the child port of an (i, j)-HC-variable of t and u a vertex of T. After Algorithm MATCHING terminates, $(u', 0, 0) \in CS(u)$ if and only if $t[u']$ matches the subtree $T[u]$.*

3.2   Procedure VID-INHERITING

Lemma 2. *Let u' be the child port of an (i, j)-HC-variable of t and u a vertex of T. After Algorithm MATCHING terminates, the following two statements hold.*

Algorithm MATCHING(t, T);
input t : a term tree in $\mathcal{OTT}_\Lambda^{\mathcal{H}}$ with the root r; T : a tree in $\mathcal{OT}_\Lambda$ with the root R;
begin
    Let $Rule(t)$ be the set of C-set-attaching rules of t;
    foreach leaf ℓ of T **do begin**
        $CS(\ell) = \{(\ell', 0, 0) \mid \ell' \text{ is a leaf of } t\}$; $height_T(\ell) := 0$
    end;
    while there is an internal vertex u of T such that
        u has no C-set and all children of u have C-sets **do begin**
        $CS(u) :=$ VID-INHERITING$(u, H_t) \cup$ C-SET-ATTACHING$(u, Rule(t))$;
        $height_T(u) := \max\{height_T(v) \mid v \text{ is a child of } u\}$
    end;
    if $(r, 0, 0) \in CS(R)$ **then** t matches T **else** t does not match T
end.

Fig. 2. Algorithm MATCHING: The procedures VID-INHERITING and C-SET-ATTACHING play important roles in the algorithm to construct C-sets.

1. For any i' $(0 \le i' < i-1)$, if there is a descendant v of u such that $(u', 0, 0) \in CS(v)$, $dist(u, v) = i'$, and $\overline{height}_{T[u]}(v) \le j$ then there is an integer j' $(0 \le j' \le \overline{height}_{T[u]}(v))$ such that $(u', i', j') \in CS(u)$. Conversely, if $(u', i', j') \in CS(u)$ $(0 \le i' < i-1, 0 \le j')$ then there is a descendant v of u such that $(u', 0, 0) \in CS(v)$, $dist(u, v) = i'$ and $\overline{height}_{T[u]}(v) = j' \le j$.

2. For any i' $(i' \ge i-1)$, if there is a descendant v of u such that $(u', 0, 0) \in CS(v)$, $dist(u, v) = i'$ and $\overline{height}_{T[u]}(v) \le j$, then there is an integer j' $(0 \le j' \le \overline{height}_{T[u]}(v))$ such that $(u', i-1, j') \in CS(u)$. Conversely, if $(u', i-1, j') \in CS(u)$ then there is a descendant v of u such that $(u', 0, 0) \in CS(v)$, $dist(u, v) \ge i-1$ and $\overline{height}_{T[u]}(v) = j' \le j$.

We give an example in Fig. 3. $CS(c_1)$ has $(5, 2, 3)$, which means that there is a descendant d_1 of c_1 such that $(5, 0, 0) \in CS(d_1)$, $dist(c_1, d_1) = 2$ and $\overline{height}_{T[c_1]}(d_1) = 3$. Similarly, $(5, 2, 2) \in CS(c_3)$ and $(5, 2, 3) \in CS(c_4)$ imply that there are d_3 and d_4 which are descendants of c_3 and c_4, respectively, such that both $CS(d_3)$ and $CS(d_4)$ include $(5, 0, 0)$, $dist(c_3, d_3) = dist(c_4, d_4) = 2$, and $\overline{height}_{T[c_3]}(d_3) = 2$ and $\overline{height}_{T[c_4]}(d_4) = 3$. It is easy to see that $\overline{height}_{T[u]}(d_1) = 7$, $\overline{height}_{T[u]}(d_3) = 5$, and $\overline{height}_{T[u]}(d_4) = 7$. Since the smallest number among them is $\overline{height}_{T[u]}(d_3)$, we add $(5, 2+1, \overline{height}_{T[u]}(d_3)) = (5, 3, 5)$ to $CS(u)$.

Formally we describe the computation as follows. Let u be an internal vertex of T and $c_1, \ldots, c_m$ be all children of u. Let u' be the child port of an (i, j)-HC-variable of t. For all i' $(0 \le i' \le i-1)$, let $c_{m_1}, \ldots, c_{m_k}$ be all children of u such that $(u', i', j'_\ell) \in CS(c_{m_\ell})$ for some j'_ℓ $(0 \le j'_\ell \le j, 1 \le \ell \le k)$. M_1 and M_2 are the indices $(1 \le M_1, M_2 \le m)$ such that the tree $T[c_{M_1}]$ has the maximum height over $\{T[c_1], \ldots, T[c_m]\}$ and the tree $T[c_{M_2}]$ has the maximum

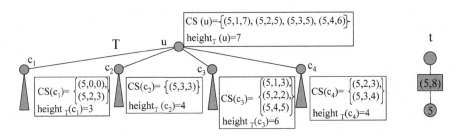

Fig. 3. An example of VID-INHERITING.

height over $\{T[c_1], \ldots, T[c_m]\} - \{T[c_{M_1}]\}$. Then, there is a descendant v of u such that $(u', 0, 0) \in CS(v)$, $dist(u, v) = i' + 1$ and $\overline{height}_{T[u]}(v) = j(i')$ where

$$j(i') = \begin{cases} \min\{height_{T[u]}(c_{M_1}), \max\{j_{M_1}, height_{T[u]}(c_{M_2})\}\} + 1 \\ \qquad\qquad\qquad\qquad\qquad\qquad\qquad\qquad \text{if } M_1 \in \{m_1, \ldots, m_k\}, \\ height_{T[u]}(c_{M_1}) + 1 \qquad\qquad\qquad\quad \text{otherwise.} \end{cases}$$

For all i' ($0 \leq i' < i - 2$), if $j(i') \leq j$ then we add $(u', i' + 1, j(i'))$ to $CS(u)$. And if $\min\{j(i-2), j(i-1)\} \leq j$ then we add $(u', i-1, \min\{j(i-2), j(i-1)\})$ to $CS(u)$. Procedure VID-INHERITING for an internal vertex u of T is defined as all the above computations of the vertex u for all child ports u' of t.

Let $\mathcal{S} = \sum_{[v', u']^{\mathcal{H}(i,j)} \in H_t} i$. Let u' be a child port of an (i, j)-HC-variable. For any vertex u of T, $CS(u)$ contains i elements of the form (u', i', j') since $0 \leq i' \leq i - 1$. Then for all child ports in H_t, $CS(u)$ contains $\mathcal{S}$ elements. Then the total time complexity of VID-INHERITING is $O(\mathcal{S}m)$.

3.3   Procedure C-SET-ATTACHING

Procedure C-SET-ATTACHING adds an element of the form $(u', 0, 0)$ to $CS(u)$. At first, we construct the *C-set-attaching rule* of a vertex u' of t as follows.

Definition 2 (C-set-attaching rules). Let u' be a vertex of a term tree t and $c'_1, \ldots, c'_{m'}$ all children of u'. We assume that c'_ℓ is smaller than $c'_{\ell'}$ for any $\ell < \ell'$ with respect to their VIDs. The *C-set-attaching rule* of u' is of the form $u' \leftarrow J(c'_1), \ldots, J(c'_{m'})$ where for $\ell = 1, \ldots, m'$,

$$J(c'_\ell) = \begin{cases} c'_\ell & \text{if } c'_\ell \text{ is not a child port,} \\ (c'_\ell, i, j) & \text{if } c'_\ell \text{ is a child port of an } (i, j)\text{-HC-variable.} \end{cases}$$

The *C-set-attaching rule* of a term tree t, denoted by $Rule(t)$, is the set of all *C-set-attaching rules* of internal vertices of t.

Let t be a term tree and T a tree. Let u and u' be internal vertices of T and t, respectively. Procedure C-SET-ATTACHING works so that $(u', 0, 0) \in CS(u)$ if and only if $t[u']$ matches the subtree $T[u]$ of T (Lemma 1). Let $c_1, \ldots, c_m$ be all the children of u with C-sets $CS(c_1), \ldots, CS(c_m)$ and $c_p \ldots, c_q$ consecutive children of u ($1 \leq p \leq q \leq m$). Let $c'_1, \cdots, c'_{m'}$ be all the children of u' and $c'_{p'}, \cdots, c'_{q'}$

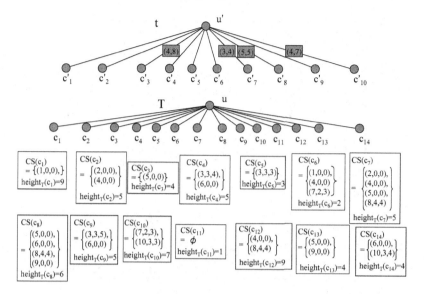

Fig. 4. An example of C-SET-ATTACHING.

consecutive children of u' $(1 \leq p' \leq q' \leq m')$. We denote by $t[u', c'_{p'}, \cdots, c'_{q'}]$ the term tree consisting of u' and all descendants of $c'_{p'}, \cdots, c'_{q'}$. Similarly we denote by $T[u, c_p, \cdots, c_q]$ the tree consisting of u and all descendants of $c_p, \cdots, c_q$. We assume that for all $c_1, \ldots, c_m$, Lemma 1 holds.

Let us consider an example in Fig. 4. We obtain from t a *C-set-attaching rule* $u' \leftarrow c'_1, c'_2, (c'_3, 4, 8), c'_4, c'_5, c'_6, (c'_7, 3, 4), (c'_8, 5, 5), c'_9, (c'_{10}, 4, 7)$. This rule can be applied to the vertex u of T in the following way. $t[c'_1]$ matches $T[c_1]$, $t[c'_2]$ matches $T[c_2]$, $t[u', c'_3]$ matches $T[u, c_3, c_4, c_5, c_6]$, $t[c'_4]$ matches $T[c_7]$, $t[c'_5]$ matches $T[c_8]$, $t[c'_6]$ matches $T[c_9]$, $t[u', c'_7, c'_8]$ matches $T[u, c_{10}, c_{11}, c_{12}]$, $t[c'_9]$ matches $T[c_{13}]$, $t[u', c'_{10}]$ matches $T[u, c_{14}]$. Then we can add $(u', 0, 0)$ to $CS(u)$. We reduce the problem which decides whether or not $t[u']$ matches $T[u]$ to a directed graph reachability problem.

Let $c'_{p'}, \cdots, c'_{q'}$ be consecutive children of u' $(1 \leq p' \leq q' \leq m')$ such that all $[u, c'_{\ell'}]$ $(p' \leq \ell' \leq q')$ are HC-variables and neither $c'_{p'-1}$ nor $c'_{q'+1}$ is a child port. We suppose that $c'_{\ell'}$ $(p' \leq \ell' \leq q')$ is a child port of an $(i_{\ell'}, j_{\ell'})$-HC-variable. Let $N_D = \{(c'_{\ell'}, c_\ell) \mid p' \leq \ell' \leq q', 1 \leq \ell \leq m\}$. Each vertex $(c'_{\ell'}, c_\ell) \in N_D$ has an interval $[r_{(\ell', \ell)}, s_{(\ell', \ell)}] \subseteq [1, m]$ as a vertex label which is the maximal interval such that $\ell \in [r_{(\ell', \ell)}, s_{(\ell', \ell)}]$, $height_T(c_k) < j_{\ell'}$ for all $r_{(\ell', \ell)} \leq k \leq s_{(\ell', \ell)}(k \neq \ell)$, and there exists a nonnegative integer $\gamma < j_{\ell'}$ such that $(\ell', i_{\ell'}, \gamma) \in CS(\ell)$. Let $A_D = \{((c'_{x'}, c_y), (c'_{x'+1}, c_z)) \mid y < z$ and $r_{(x'+1, z)} \leq s_{(x', y)} + 1\}$. Then let $D[(c'_{p'}, \ldots, c'_{q'}), (c_1, \ldots, c_m)]$ be an auxiliary directed graph (N_D, A_D). It is easy to see the following lemma.

Lemma 3. *There exists a directed path from $(c'_{p'}, c_p)$ to $(c'_{q'}, c_q)$ in the auxiliary directed graph $D[(c'_{p'}, \ldots, c'_{q'}), (c_p, \ldots, c_q)]$ if and only if $t[u', c'_{p'}, \ldots, c'_{q'}]$ matches $T[u, c_p, \ldots, c_q]$.*

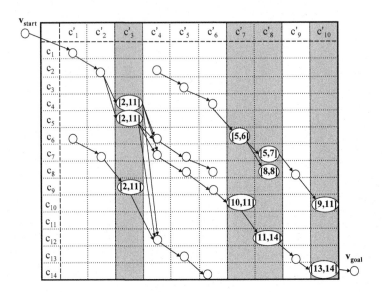

Fig. 5. A final directed graph D obtained from t and T (Fig. 4).

The construction of an auxiliary directed graph contains two steps. The first step is to compute each interval of all vertices. The second step is to decide whether or not there is a directed edge between any two vertices. Therefore the total time complexity is $O((q' - p' + 1)m^2)$ time.

We obtain a new auxiliary directed graph by connecting two auxiliary directed graphs. We suppose that $c'_{p'_1} \ldots, c'_{q'_1}$ are consecutive children of u' ($1 \leq p'_1 \leq q'_1 < m' - 1$) and $c'_{p'_2} \ldots, c'_{q'_2}$ are consecutive children of u' ($q'_1 + 1 < p'_2 \leq q'_2 \leq m'$) such that both $c'_{q'_1}, c'_{p'_2}$ are child ports of HC-variables and neither of $c'_{q'_1+1}, \ldots, c'_{p'_2-1}$ is a child port. Let $D[(c'_{p'_1}, \ldots, c'_{q'_1}), (c_1, \ldots, c_m)] = (N_{D_1}, A_{D_1})$ and $D[(c'_{p'_2}, \ldots, c'_{q'_2}), (c_1, \ldots, c_m)] = (N_{D_2}, A_{D_2})$ be two auxiliary directed graphs. Let $N_D = \{(c'_{\ell'}, c_\ell) \mid p'_1 \leq \ell' \leq q'_2, p \leq \ell \leq q\}$ and $A_D = A_{D_1} \cup A_{D_2} \cup A'$. A' is the set of all directed edges obtained by the following way. Let SC be the set of all intervals $[\ell, \ell + p'_2 - q'_1 - 2]$ ($p \leq \ell \leq q$) such that $c'_{q'_1+1} \in CS(c_\ell), c'_{q'_1+2} \in CS(c_{\ell+1}), \ldots, c'_{p'_2-1} \in CS(c_{\ell+p'_2-q'_1-2})$. For two vertices $(c'_{q'_1}, c_y) \in N_{D_1}$ with a label $[r_{(q'_1,y)}, s_{(q'_1,y)}]$ and $(c'_{p'_2}, c_z) \in N_{D_2}$ with a label $[r_{(p'_2,z)}, s_{(p'_2,z)}]$, we make $p'_2 - q'_1$ directed edges $((c'_{q'_1}, c_y), (c'_{q'_1+1}, c_\ell))$, $((c'_{q'_1+1}, c_\ell), (c'_{q'_1+2}, c_{\ell+1})), \ldots, ((c'_{p'_2-1}, c_{\ell+p'_2-q'_1-2}), (c'_{p'_2}, c_z))$ if there is an interval $[r, s] \in SC$ satisfying the following three conditions: (i) $[r, s] \subseteq [y + 1, z - 1]$, (ii) $r \leq s_{(q'_1,y)} + 1$, and (iii) $r_{(p'_2,z)} - 1 \leq s$. Then we obtain a new auxiliary directed graph $D[(c'_{p'_1}, \ldots, c'_{q'_2}), (c_1, \ldots, c_m)] = (N_D, A_D)$. We denote this graph by $D[(c'_{p'_1}, \ldots, c'_{q'_1}), (c_1, \ldots, c_m)] * D[(c'_{p'_2}, \ldots, c'_{q'_2}), (c_1, \ldots, c_m)]$. For example, we give the final directed graph of t and T in Fig. 5 obtained from a term tree t and a tree T in Fig. 4. Since the number of pairs of vertices which we have to

Procedure RULE-MATCHING$((c_1, \ldots, c_m), u' \leftarrow J(c'_1), \ldots, J(c'_{m'}))$;
input: the children $c_1, \ldots, c_m$ of an internal vertex and
      a C-set-attaching rule $u' \leftarrow J(c'_1), \ldots, J(c'_{m'})$;
begin

Step 1. At first, we divide the body of the rule $u' \leftarrow J(c'_1), \ldots, J(c'_{m'})$ into several
pieces in the following way. We find intervals $[p'_1, q'_1], [p'_2, q'_2], \ldots, [p'_{k'}, q'_{k'}]$ such that
for all ℓ' $(1 \leq \ell' \leq k')$,
(i) all of $c'_{p'_{\ell'}}, \ldots, c'_{q'_{\ell'}}$ are child ports of HC-variables,
(ii) neither of $c'_{q'_{\ell'}+1}, \ldots, c'_{p'_{\ell'+1}-1}$ is not a child port,
(iii) if $p'_1 > 1$ then neither of $c'_1, \ldots, c'_{p'_1-1}$ is not a child port, and
(iv) if $q'_{k'} < m'$ then neither of $c'_{q'_{k'}+1}, \ldots, c'_{m'}$ is not a child port.

Step 2. If neither of $c'_1, \ldots, c'_{p'_1-1}$ is not a child port and $c'_{i'} \in CS(c_{i'})$ for all i'
$(1 \leq i' \leq p'_1 - 1)$ then
      RULE-MATCHING$((c_{p'_1}, \ldots, c_m), u' \leftarrow J(c'_{p'_1}), \ldots, J(c'_{m'}))$,
else return *no*.

Step 3. If neither of $c'_{q'_{k'}+1}, \ldots, c'_{m'}$ is not a child port and $c'_{i'} \in CS(c_{m-m'+i'})$ for all
i' $(q'_{k'} + 1 \leq i' \leq m')$ then
      RULE-MATCHING$((c_1, \ldots, c_{m-m'+q'_{k'}}), u' \leftarrow J(c'_1), \ldots, J(c'_{q'_{k'}}))$,
else return *no*.

Step 4. Construct k' auxiliary directed graphs:
$D[(c'_{p'_1}, \ldots, c'_{q'_1}), (c_1, \ldots, c_m)], \ldots, D[(c'_{p'_{k'}}, \ldots, c'_{q'_{k'}}), (c_1, \ldots, c_m)]$.

Step 5. Connect the k' auxiliary directed graphs into one directed graph D:
$D := D[(c'_{p'_1}, \ldots, c'_{q'_1}), (c_1, \ldots, c_m)] * \cdots * D[(c'_{p'_{k'}}, \ldots, c'_{q'_{k'}}), (c_1, \ldots, c_m)]$.

Step 6. Let v_{start} and v_{goal} are two new vertices. Let $E_{start} := \{(v_{start}, (c'_1, c_x)) \mid c_1 \in [r_{(1,x)}, s_{(1,x)}]\}$ and $E_{goal} := \{((c'_{m'}, c_x), v_{goal}) \mid c_m \in [r_{(m',x)}, s_{(m',x)}]\}$. Add
two vertices v_{start} and v_{goal}, and two edge sets E_{start} and E_{goal} to D.

Step 7. If v_{goal} is reachable from v_{start} then return *yes* else return *no*.
end;

Procedure C-SET-ATTACHING$(u, Rule(t))$;
input: an internal vertex u of T and the C-set-attaching rule $Rule(t)$ of t;
begin

   Let $c_1, \ldots, c_m$ be the children of u;
   $CS := \emptyset$;
   forall $u' \leftarrow J(c'_1), \ldots, J(c'_{m'}) \in Rule(t)$ **do**
      if RULE-MATCHING$((c_1, \ldots, c_m), u' \leftarrow J(c'_1), \ldots, J(c'_{m'}))$ returns *yes* **then**
         $CS := CS \cup \{(u', 0, 0)\}$;
   return CS
end;

Fig. 6. Procedures RULE-MATCHING and C-SET-ATTACHING.

decide the existence of a directed edge is $O(m^2)$, this work consumes $O(m^2)$ time. We give the formal description of Procedure RULE-MATCHING in Fig. 6. We have the following lemma. The correctness follows from Lemma 3 and the construction of the final auxiliary directed graph.

Lemma 4. *Let $c_1, \ldots, c_m$ be the children of an internal vertex u in T and $u' \leftarrow J(c'_1), \ldots, J(c'_{m'})$ a C-set-attaching rule of t. Procedure RULE-MATCHING for $c_1, \ldots, c_m$ and $u' \leftarrow J(c'_1), \ldots, J(c'_{m'})$ decides whether or not $t[u']$ matches $T[u]$ in $O(m'm^2)$ time.*

Procedure C-SET-ATTACHING for an internal vertex u of T is defined as all procedure calls for RULE-MATCHING for the vertex u and all C-set-attaching rules of t (Fig. 6). From Lemma 4, it is easy to see that C-SET-ATTACHING needs $O(NnD_{\max})$ time where $D_{\max}$ is the maximum number of the children of an internal vertex of T and N is the number of vertices of T. Finally we have the following theorem.

Theorem 1. *For any set of edge labels Λ, the matching problem for $OTT_\Lambda^{\mathcal{H}}$ is solvable in $O(N \max\{nD_{\max}, \mathcal{S}\})$ time, where n and N are the numbers of vertices of t and T, respectively, $\mathcal{S} = \sum_{[v', u']^{\mathcal{H}(i,j)} \in H_t} i$, and $D_{\max}$ the maximum number of the children of an internal vertex in T.*

4   Concluding Remarks

In order to represent tree structured patterns with rich structural features, we proposed term trees having height-constrained variables as new ordered tree structured patterns and gave a polynomial time matching algorithm for them. As an application of term trees having height-constrained variables, we presented a metasearch system in [2], which provides an effective unified access to multiple existing search sites.

In a similar way to height-constrained variables, we can define (i, j)-width-constrained variables which can be replaced with any tree T such that the width of T is at least i and at most j. As future works, we will consider a tree structured pattern which can give precious knowledge to us, by combining two constraints with respect to *height* and *width*. Then, for tree structured data, we will also present data mining tools having such tree structured patterns as knowledge representations.

References

1. S. Abiteboul, P. Buneman, and D. Suciu. *Data on the Web: From Relations to Semistructured Data and XML*. Morgan Kaufmann, 2000.
2. K. Aikou, Y. Suzuki, T. Shoudai, and T. Miyahara. Automatic Wrapper Generation for Metasearch using Ordered Tree Structured Patterns. *Proc. AI-2004, Springer-Verlag, LNAI 3339*, pages 1030–1035, 2004.

3. T. R. Amoth, P. Cull, and P. Tadepalli, On exact learning of unordered tree patterns, *Machine Learning*, **44**, pp. 211–243, 2001.
4. H. Arimura, H. Sakamoto, and S. Arikawa. Efficient learning of semi-structured data from queries. *Proc. ALT-2001, Springer-Verlag, LNAI 2225*, pages 315–331, 2001.
5. T. Asai, H. Arimura, T. Uno, and S. Nakano. Discovery of frequent substructures in large unordered trees. *Proc. DS-2003, Springer-Verlag, LNAI 2843*, pages 47–61, 2003.
6. M. Fernandez and D. Suciu. Optimizing regular path expressions using graph schemas. *Proceedings of the 14th International Conference on Data Engineering (ICDE-98), IEEE Computer Society*, pages 14–23, 1998.
7. S. Matsumoto, Y. Hayashi, and T. Shoudai. Polynomial time inductive inference of regular term tree languages from positive data. *Proc. ALT-97, Springer-Verlag, LNAI 1316*, pages 212–227, 1997.
8. S. Matsumoto and T. Shoudai. Learning of Ordered Tree Languages with Height-Bounded Variables Using Queries. *Proc. ALT-2004, Springer-Verlag, LNAI 3244*, pages 425–439, 2004.
9. T. Miyahara, Y. Suzuki, T. Shoudai, T. Uchida, K. Takahashi, and H. Ueda. Discovery of Maximally Frequent Tag Tree Patterns with Contractible Variables from Semistructured Documents. *Proc. PAKDD-2004, Springer-Verlag, LNAI 3056*, pages 133–144, 2004.
10. T. Shoudai, T. Uchida, and T. Miyahara. Polynomial time algorithms for finding unordered term tree patterns with internal variables. *Proc. FCT-2001, Springer-Verlag, LNCS 2138*, pages 335–346, 2001.
11. Y. Suzuki, R. Akanuma, T. Shoudai, T. Miyahara, and T. Uchida. Polynomial time inductive inference of ordered tree patterns with internal structured variables from positive data. *Proc. COLT-2002, Springer-Verlag, LNAI 2375*, pages 169–184, 2002.
12. Y. Suzuki, T. Shoudai, T. Miyahara, and T. Uchida. Ordered Term Tree Languages Which Are Polynomial Time Inductively Inferable from Positive Data. *Proc. ALT-2002, Springer-Verlag, LNAI 2533*, pp.188–202, 2002.
13. Y. Suzuki, K. Inomae, T. Shoudai, T. Miyahara, and T. Uchida, A Polynomial Time Matching Algorithm of Structured Ordered Tree Patterns for Data Mining from Semistructured Data, *Proc. ILP-2002, Springer-Verlag, LNAI 2583*, pp. 270–284, 2003.
14. K. Wang and H. Liu. Discovering structural association of semistructured data. *IEEE Trans. Knowledge and Data Engineering*, 12:353–371, 2000.

Assessing the Significance of Sets of Words

Valentina Boeva[1], Julien Clément[2],
Mireille Régnier[3], and Mathias Vandenbogaert[4]

[1] Moscow State University, Vorob'evy Gory, Russia
valeyo@mail333.com
[2] IGM, Université de Marne-la-Vallée, France
Julien.Clement@univ-mlv.fr
[3] INRIA, 78153 Le Chesnay, France
Mireille.Regnier@inria.fr
[4] Biozentrum, Basel Universitat, Switzerland
mathias.vandenbogaert@unibas.ch

Abstract. Various criteria have been defined to evaluate the significance of sets of words, the computation of them often being difficult. We provide explicit expressions for the waiting time in such a context. In order to assess the significance of a cluster of potential binding sites, we extend them to the co-occurrence problem. We point out that these criteria values depend on a few fundamental parameters. We provide efficient algorithms to compute them, that rely on a combinatorial interpretation of the formulae. We show that our results are very tight in the so-called twilight zone and improve on previous rough approximations. One assumes that the text is generated according to a Markov stationary process. These results are developed for an extended model of consensus.

1 Introduction

Many statistical softwares have been designed in the last decade to search for exceptional words and predict biological functions *In silico*. Using some pattern matching algorithms to detect some candidates, one assesses their biological significance by comparing the observed number and the expected number. The main differences between softwares are the underlying probability models, the searching algorithms and the comparison criteria. One common underlying assumption is that the genome is randomly generated according to some probability model. In this paper, the model can be either Bernoulli or Markov. The comparison criteria depend on the applications and the parameters of the problem. One first classification arises from the *size* of the problem, that is to say the number of word occurrences and the text size. A typical application with large texts is the search of recognition sites for Restriction Modification Systems in a genome. It is shown in [1, 2] that these sites are avoided words. Symmetrically, it is proved in [3] that the *Chi*-motif is overrepresented in *E. Coli*. One may also search for common words in a set of (small) sequences. A typical application is the search of regulatory signals in upstream sequences of genes that are either orthologous or coregulated. When the signal is degenerated, each signal can be represented

A. Apostolico, M. Crochemore, and K. Park (Eds.): CPM 2005, LNCS 3537, pp. 358–370, 2005.
© Springer-Verlag Berlin Heidelberg 2005

by a set $\mathcal{H}_1$ or $\mathcal{H}_2$. This set is defined from experimental data, as a consensus or a position matrix (PSSM, PWM...).

Word counting results have been derived by several authors for a single word H or a set of words $\mathcal{H}$. Recently, special attention has been paid to the simultaneous occurrence of different binding sites in upstream sequences. Indeed, it has been observed [4] in eucaryotes that multiple transcription factors binding to the same transcription control region are often involved in the same transcriptional regulation. Hence, the co-occurrence and spatial relationships of individual binding sites provides a better understanding of regulation and of multifactorial control of gene expression. Therefore, we formalize below the co-occurrence problem and extend previous exact formulae in this case. A second aim of this paper is the rewriting of exact matricial expressions [5, 6] or induction algorithms [7, 8] in a suitable form. Indeed, we define a few fundamental parameters and show that tight numerical computations depend on these parameters. Third, simple combinatorial interpretations as overlapping sequences are provided for exact expressions or fundamental parameters. We provide efficient algorithms to compute them. In passing, we define an extended consensus model that is close to PSSM (Positional Specific Scoring Matrix) and suitable for the search of regulatory signals.

2   Main Steps and Results

Distribution formulae or algorithms always involve the possible overlaps of the words to be counted [5, 6, 9, 10]. The correlation sets were introduced in the seed paper [11]. We define the notion of *complement* and *minimal complement*.

Definition 1. *Given two strings* F *and* G, *the* overlap set *of* F *and* G *is the set of suffixes of* F *that are proper prefixes of* G. *Any suffix of* G *in the associated factorizations of* G *is named a* right complement *of* F *in* G. *The set of right complements of* F *in* G *is called the* correlation set *of* F *and* G *and denoted* $C_{F,G}$. *When* F $=$ G, *the* autocorrelation set *is* $A_F = C_{F,F} + \varepsilon$ *with* ε *the empty word.*

Given a set $\mathcal{H}$, *a* right complement *of a word* F *in* $\mathcal{H}$ *is any right complement of* F *in a word* G *in* $\mathcal{H}$. *A right complement* w *of* F *is* minimal *iff no proper prefix of* w *is a right complement of* F *in* $\mathcal{H}$. *The set of minimal right complements of* F *that belong to* $C_{F,G}$ *is denoted* $\widetilde{C}_{F,G}$.

We assume below that all words have the same size m. The next definition provides tools for word counting.

Definition 2. *Given a set of* q *words* $\mathcal{H} = (H_i)_{1 \le i \le q}$, *one denotes* $H(z) = (P(H_1)z^m, \ldots, P(H_q)z^m)$. *The* probability matrix $\mathbb{H}(z)$ *is the* $q \times q$ *matrix with* q *rows equal to* $H(z)$. *Given two words* H_i *and* H_j, *the* complement polynomial *(resp.* complement minimal polynomial*) is*

$$C_{i,j}(z) = \sum_{w \in C_{H_i,H_j}} P(w)z^{|w|} \quad (resp. \ \widetilde{C}_{i,j}(z) = \sum_{w \in \widetilde{C}_{H_i,H_j}} P(w)z^{|w|}).$$

The complement matrix *(resp.* complement minimal matrix*) is the* $q \times q$ *matrix* $\mathbb{C}(z) = (C_{i,j}(z))_{1 \leq i,j \leq q}$ *(resp.* $\widetilde{\mathbb{C}}(z) = (\widetilde{C}_{i,j}(z))_{1 \leq i,j \leq q}$*) and the* correlation matrix *is* $\mathbb{A}(z) = \mathbb{I} + \mathbb{C}(z)$. *The* fundamental counting matrix *is*

$$\mathbb{D}(z) = (1 - z)\mathbb{A}(z) + \mathbb{H}(z).$$

When one counts a single word, $\mathbb{D}(z)$ reduces to a polynomial $D(z)$ in the Bernoulli case [11] or a series in a Markov model [5]. The following theorem, where the *fundamental counting matrix* plays a central rôle, is stated for the Bernoulli case in [5, 12] and for the Markov case in [6].

Theorem 1. *Let* $R(z) = \sum_n R_n(\mathcal{H})z^n$ *with* $R_n(\mathcal{H})$ *the probability that the first occurrence of a word from* $\mathcal{H}$ *ends at position* n. *The generating function satisfies*

$$R(z) = H(z)\ \mathbb{D}(z)^{-1}\ \mathbf{1}_q{}^\mathrm{t}, \tag{1}$$

where $\mathbf{1}_q$ *a row vector with* q *columns equal to 1. Let* $t_n^k(\mathcal{H})$ *be the probability that* k *occurrences of a word from a set* $\mathcal{H}$ *occur in a text of size* n. *The generating function* $T_k(z) = \sum_{n \geq 0} t_n^k(\mathcal{H})z^n$ *satisfies*

$$T_k(z) = H(z)\mathbb{D}(z)^{-1}\mathbb{M}(z)^{k-1}\mathbb{D}(z)^{-1}\mathbf{1}_q{}^\mathrm{t},$$

where $\mathbb{M}(z)$ *is the* minimal matrix *defined as* $\mathbb{M}(z) = \mathbb{I} + (z - 1)\mathbb{D}(z)^{-1}$.

Here, we unify the two definitions of the polynomial $D(z)$ and the fundamental counting matrix. Indeed, the waiting time depends on a *fundamental multioccurrence series*, that we define below.

Definition 3. *The* fundamental multioccurrence series *of a set* $\mathcal{H}$ *is*

$$Q_\mathcal{H}(z) = \mathrm{Trace}\left(\mathbb{H}(z)\mathbb{A}^{-1}(z)\right).$$

When $\mathcal{H}$ reduces to a single word H, one has $D(z) = (1 - z + Q(z))A(z)$.

In this paper, we first extend Theorem 1 for several sets of words, in order to address the co-occurrence problem. Counting results are also rewritten as some functions of the fundamental multioccurrence series. Simple combinatorial interpretations as overlapping sequences are provided for these functions. Hence, it turns out that the so-called z-scores, and our tight numerical approximations for the waiting time as well, depend on a few fundamental parameters. Namely,

Definition 4. *Given a set of words* $\mathcal{H}$, *one denotes* $P(\mathcal{H}) = \sum_{F \in \mathcal{H}} P(F)$,

$$C(\mathcal{H}) = \sum_{F,G \in \mathcal{H}} \sum_{w \in C_{F,G}} P(Fw), \quad \widetilde{C}(\mathcal{H}) = \sum_{F,G \in \mathcal{H}} \sum_{w \in \widetilde{C}_{F,G}} P(Fw).$$

where $P(\mathcal{H})$ *is called the* occurrence probability, $C(\mathcal{H})$ *is called the* overlap factor *of* $\mathcal{H}$ *and* $\widetilde{C}(\mathcal{H})$ *is called the* minimal overlap factor.

Note that $P(\mathcal{H}) = \mathrm{Trace}(\mathbb{H}(1))$. Overlap factors $C(\mathcal{H})$ and $\widetilde{C}(\mathcal{H})$ are the sum of the coefficients of $\mathbb{H}(1)\mathbb{C}(1)$ and $\mathbb{H}(1)\widetilde{\mathbb{C}}(1)$, respectively.

Statistical criteria in computational biology can be expressed as simple functions of parameters $P(\mathcal{H})$ and $C(\mathcal{H})$. Let $O_n(\mathcal{H})$ be the number of occurrences of words with overlap from $\mathcal{H}$ in a random text of size n under a Bernoulli model. The mean $\mathrm{E}[O_n(\mathcal{H})]$ and the variance $\mathrm{Var}[O_n(\mathcal{H})]$ satisfy [13]

$$\mathrm{E}[O_n(\mathcal{H})] = (n - m + 1)\, P(\mathcal{H}),$$
$$\mathrm{Var}[O_n(\mathcal{H})] = (n - m + 1)\big(P(\mathcal{H}) + (1 - 2m)\, P(\mathcal{H})^2 + 2C(\mathcal{H})\big)$$
$$+ m(m - 1)\, P(\mathcal{H})^2 - 2\widehat{C}(\mathcal{H}),$$

where $\widehat{C}(\mathcal{H}) = \sum_{F,G \in \mathcal{H}} \sum_{w \in A_{F,G}} |w| \times P(Fw)$ is a slight modification of $C(\mathcal{H})$. We will show in Section 4 how to compute these quantities in an efficient way.

A correcting factor is derived for a single pattern in the Markov model in [5] and extended for a set of patterns in [6]. As this factor mainly depends on the stationary distribution, it can be viewed as a *preprocessing*.

These results allow for an efficient computation of the z-score in computational biology. When k occurrences of $\mathcal{H}$ are observed in a sequence of length n, the z-score is $Z(\mathcal{H}) = \frac{k - \mathrm{E}[O_n(\mathcal{H})]}{\sqrt{\mathrm{Var}[O_n(\mathcal{H})]}}$. This is an empirical measure of the departure from the normal distribution. High values of $|Z(\mathcal{H})|$ indicate an over representation (positive values) or an underrepresentation (negative values).

3   Waiting Time

We address below different variants of the waiting time problem. Indeed, the meaningful event may be the apparition – or not – of a word in the sequence under study. We consider also the co-occurrence problem.

3.1   Waiting Time Generating Functions

An analytic expression of the probability of first occurrence is derived in [11] for the uniform model, in [13] to the biased model and in [6] to the Markov model. Nevertheless, the results are expressed through a generating function, which yields two problems: the *computational complexity* and the *numerical stability*. Clearly, when the size of the set $\mathcal{H}$ or/and the sequence become large, a naive computation for a given n – such as the computation by induction [7] – is computationally expensive. The computation also turns out to be quickly untractable with the improved implementation based on the symbolic system *Combstruct*. Moreover, numerical instability appears that can only be avoided with a careful and tricky implementation [14]. The same problems arise with the software *RegExpCount*. The set $\mathcal{H}$ is viewed as a regular expression, the associated automaton is built and the generating function follows [15]. Our first result in this section is a further writing of the generating function in a more explicit form.

Theorem 2. *Let $\mathcal{H}$ be a set of q words and $F_n(\mathcal{H})$ be the probability that at least one word in $\mathcal{H}$ occurs in a random sequence of size n. The generating function $F_{\mathcal{H}}(z) = \sum_{n \geq 0} F_n(\mathcal{H}) z^n$ satisfies*

$$F_{\mathcal{H}}(z) = \frac{1}{1 - z} - \frac{1}{1 - z + Q_{\mathcal{H}}(z)}. \tag{2}$$

Proof. Our proof relies on new expressions for matrices $\mathbb{D}(z)$ and $\mathbb{M}(z)$ in the Bernoulli model that extend to the Markov model.

Proposition 1. *The inverse matrix of the fundamental counting matrix satisfies*

$$\mathbb{D}(z)^{-1} = \frac{\mathbb{A}^{-1}(z)}{1-z}\left(\mathbb{I} - \frac{\mathbb{H}(z)\mathbb{A}^{-1}(z)}{1-z+\mathrm{Trace}(\mathbb{H}(z)\mathbb{A}^{-1}(z))}\right). \tag{3}$$

The minimal matrix $\mathbb{M}(z)$ satisfies

$$\mathbb{M}(z) = \mathbb{I} - \mathbb{A}^{-1}(z)\left(\mathbb{I} - \frac{\mathbb{H}(z)\mathbb{A}^{-1}(z)}{1-z+\mathrm{Trace}(\mathbb{H}(z)\mathbb{A}^{-1}(z))}\right).$$

Proof. Let us call a 1-*matrix* any matrix whose rows are all equal. One has that any 1-matrix $\mathbb{B}$ satisfies $(\mathbb{I}+\mathbb{B})^{-1} = \mathbb{I} - (1+\mathrm{Trace}(\mathbb{B}))^{-1}\mathbb{B}$. The main arguments for the proof of Prop. 1 are that $\mathbb{A}(z)$ can be inverted in some disc around 0 and that, for any integer $i \geq 0$, $\mathbb{H}(z)\mathbb{A}(z)^{-i}$ is a 1-matrix (details are omitted).

Let us return to the proof of Theorem 2. Let $R_q(\mathcal{H})$ be the probability that the first occurrence of a word from set $\mathcal{H}$ ends at position q. It follows from the definition that $F_n(\mathcal{H}) = \sum_{q \leq n} R_q(\mathcal{H})$. Hence, $F_{\mathcal{H}}(z) = \frac{1}{1-z}\sum_n R_n(\mathcal{H})z^n = \frac{R(z)}{1-z}$. Using Eq. (3), we rewrite $\mathbb{H}\mathbb{D}(z)^{-1} = \frac{\mathbb{B}}{1-z}[\mathbb{I} - \frac{\mathbb{B}}{1-z+\mathrm{Trace}(\mathbb{B})}]$ with $\mathbb{B} = \mathbb{H}(z)\mathbb{A}^{-1}(z)$. As $\mathbb{B}^2 = \mathrm{Trace}(\mathbb{B})\mathbb{B}$ and $\mathrm{Trace}(\mathbb{B}) = Q_{\mathcal{H}}(z)$, we get $\mathbb{H}\mathbb{D}(z)^{-1} = \frac{\mathbb{B}}{1-z+Q_{\mathcal{H}}(z)}$. One rewrites $H(z) = (\,1\ 0\ \cdots\ 0\,)\mathbb{H}(z)$. Then, Eq. (1) yields $R(z) = (\,1\ 0\ \cdots\ 0\,)\mathbb{H}(z)\mathbb{D}(z)^{-1}\mathbf{1}_q{}^t$, and finally $R(z) = \frac{1}{1-z+Q_{\mathcal{H}}(z)}(\,1\ 0\ \cdots\ 0\,)\mathbb{B}\mathbf{1}_q{}^t$. For any matrix $\mathbb{M}$, the product $(\,1\ 0\ \cdots\ 0\,)\mathbb{M}\mathbf{1}_q{}^t$ is the sum of all coefficients in the first row. For a 1-matrix, this sum is equal to the trace. It follows that $R(z) = \frac{Q_{\mathcal{H}}(z)}{1-z+Q_{\mathcal{H}}(z)}$ and decomposition $\frac{Q_{\mathcal{H}}(z)}{(1-z)(1-z+Q_{\mathcal{H}}(z))} = \frac{1}{1-z} - \frac{1}{1-z+Q_{\mathcal{H}}(z)}$ yields Eq. (2).

Our second result deals with the *co-occurrences* of two signals. Given two sets $\mathcal{H}_1$ and $\mathcal{H}_2$, one studies the probability to have one occurrence from each set in a given short sequence. Typically, each set represents potential binding sites for a regulatory protein.

Theorem 3. *Let $\mathcal{H}_1$ and $\mathcal{H}_2$ be two disjoint sets of words of size m. Denote $\mathcal{H} = \mathcal{H}_1 \cup \mathcal{H}_2$. Let $F_n^{[1,1]}(\mathcal{H}_1, \mathcal{H}_2)$ be the probability that at least one word in $\mathcal{H}_1$ and one word in $\mathcal{H}_2$ occur in a random sequence of size n. The generating function $F_{\mathcal{H}_1,\mathcal{H}_2}^{[1,1]}(z) = \sum_n F_n^{[1,1]}(\mathcal{H}_1, \mathcal{H}_2)z^n$ satisfies*

$$F_{\mathcal{H}_1,\mathcal{H}_2}^{[1,1]}(z) = \frac{1}{1-z} - \frac{1}{1-z+Q_{\mathcal{H}_1}(z)} - \frac{1}{1-z+Q_{\mathcal{H}_2}(z)} + \frac{1}{1-z+Q_{\mathcal{H}}(z)}, \tag{4}$$

where $Q_{\mathcal{H}}(z), Q_{\mathcal{H}_1}(z)$ and $Q_{\mathcal{H}_2}(z)$ are the fundamental multioccurrence series of $\mathcal{H}$, $\mathcal{H}_1$ and $\mathcal{H}_2$ respectively.

Proof. Let us consider a text of length n with n_1 $\mathcal{H}_1$-occurrences and n_2 $\mathcal{H}_2$-occurrences. The total number of $\mathcal{H}$-occurrences is $n_1 + n_2$ and we have

$$P((n_1 > 0) \cap (n_2 > 0)) = 1 - P(n_1 = 0) - P(n_2 = 0) + P(n_1 + n_2 = 0).$$

Since by Theorem 2, $[z^n]\frac{1}{1-z+Q_{\mathcal{H}}(z)}$ is the probability that there is no word from $\mathcal{H}$ in a text of size n, this equality translates to Eq. (4).

Remark. These results generalize to a Markov process. As for the mean and variance [5], the two contributions due to the overlapping structure of $\mathcal{H}$ and the Markovian process are almost independent. Indeed, it turns out that the results are some functions of the *sum* of $\mathbb{A}(z)$ and $\mathbb{N}(z)$, that represent the dependency to the overlapping structure and the dependency to the Markov process characteristics, respectively. An induction approach [16, 17] does not achieve such a separation. A complexity improvement follows.

3.2   Practical Computation

Our practical results rely on simple observations. When the size of the text increases, the probability to find at least one occurrence increases from 0 to 1. Indeed, for small (respectively large) n, $F_n(\mathcal{H})$ is exponentially close to 0 (respectively 1). Hence, the range where $F_n(\mathcal{H})$ is a meaningful criteria and worth study is in between. The location and size of this "twilight zone" depend on the expected value of $O_n(\mathcal{H})$, e.g. $P(\mathcal{H})$, *and* the number of sequences where the set $\mathcal{H}$ is searched for. Therefore, we assume below that $nP(\mathcal{H})$ is smaller than 1. In this range, an asymptotic expansion turns out to be very tight. More details on the relationship between this bound and the number of sequences will be given in an extended paper.

Theorem 4. *When $nP(\mathcal{H})$ is upper bounded by 1, one has*

$$F_n(\mathcal{H}) = 1 - \left(1 + P(\mathcal{H}) - \widetilde{C}(\mathcal{H})\right)^{-n} \left(1 + O\left(\tfrac{1}{n}\right)\right). \tag{5}$$

The co-occurrence probability satisfies

$$F_n^{[1,1]}(\mathcal{H}_1, \mathcal{H}_2) \sim 1 + e^{-n\log(1+P(\mathcal{H})-C(\mathcal{H}))}$$
$$- e^{-n\log(1+P(\mathcal{H}_1)-C(\mathcal{H}_1))} - e^{-n\log(1+P(\mathcal{H}_2)-C(\mathcal{H}_2))}.$$

Remarks. Numerical evaluation shows that these formulae are very tight. Due to the simplicity of its computation, our formulae favorably compare to intricate and unstable computation by induction. Expansion (5) also is an improvement on a common numerical approximation [18, 19]

$$F_n(\mathcal{H}) = 1 - (1 - P(\mathrm{H}))^{n-m+1}.$$

Unfortunately, this approximation does not take the words overlaps into account, although they do induce a significant change [20]. Moreover, it is not valid in the finite range. When $\mathcal{H}$ reduces to a single pattern H, a tighter approximation holds in both cases. Namely $\frac{P(\mathrm{H})}{A_{\mathrm{H}}(1)}$ is slightly more accurate than $P(\mathcal{H}) - \widetilde{C}(\mathcal{H})$.

Proof. Generating functions in Eq. (2) and Eq. (4) depend on the *fundamental multioccurrence series* properties. Lemma below provides a uniform approximation for the fundamental multioccurrence series.

Lemma 1. *The fundamental multioccurrence series of a set $\mathcal{H}$ satisfies*

$$Q_{\mathcal{H}}(z) = P(\mathcal{H})z^m - \sum_{H,F \in \mathcal{H}} \sum_{w \in \tilde{C}_{H,F}} P(Hw)z^{|Hw|} + O\left(m\,P(\mathcal{H})^2\right). \tag{6}$$

The root of smallest modulus of $1 - z + Q_{\mathcal{H}}(z)$ is a real positive number ρ that is greater than 1 and satisfies

$$\rho - (1 + P(\mathcal{H}) - \tilde{C}(\mathcal{H})) = O(mP(\mathcal{H})^2)\ . \tag{7}$$

Proof. We first prove that

$$\sum_{j=1}^{m}[z^{m+j}]\,\mathrm{Trace}(\mathbb{H}\mathbb{A}^{-1}(z)) = \sum_{j=1}^{m}[z^{m+j}]Q_{\mathcal{H}}(z) = \sum_{\substack{H,F \in \mathcal{H} \\ w \in \tilde{C}_{H,F}}} P(Hw)z^{|Hw|}. \tag{8}$$

One has $\mathbb{A}^{-1}(z) = \mathbb{I} + \sum_{k \geq 1}(-1)^k\mathbb{C}^k$. A non-zero term in $[z^\ell]\mathbb{H}\mathbb{C}^k$ is mapped to a word of length ℓ which is an overlapping chain of words from $\mathcal{H}$. The weight of each chain is its probability. Such a word w can be decomposed unambiguously as a product $H \cdot \tilde{c}_1 \cdots \tilde{c}_j$ of one word $H \in \mathcal{H}$ and a product of j *minimal right complements*. Assume now that $m < |w| < 2m$. There are $\binom{j-1}{r-1}$ choices of grouping consecutive words among the $\tilde{c}_i$'s in order to get a valid decomposition $w = Hc_1 \cdots c_r$ where the c_i's are right complements. Therefore, the contribution of w to $\mathrm{Trace}(\mathbb{H}(\mathbb{I} + \sum_{k \geq 1}(-1)^k\mathbb{C}^k))$ is $z^\ell\,P(w)\sum_{r=1}^{j-1}\binom{j-1}{r-1}(-1)^r$. This sum is $z^\ell\,P(w)$ if $j = 1$ (which means $w = H\tilde{c}$ with $\tilde{c}$ a minimal right complement) and 0 otherwise. Eq. (8) is established.

A simple combinatorial argument provides for $\sum_{\ell \geq 2m}[z^\ell]\,\mathrm{Trace}(\mathbb{H}\mathbb{A}^{-1}(z))$ the upper bound $O(mP(\mathcal{H})^2)$. Indeed, each monomial in the sum is associated to an overlapping chain w of $\mathcal{H}$-words. Chain w rewrites unambiguously $H_1w_1H_2w_2$ where H_1 its prefix in $\mathcal{H}$ and H_2 the first $\mathcal{H}$-word that goes beyond position $2m$. The overall probability of such events is trivially upper bounded by $P(\mathcal{H})mP(\mathcal{H})$.

We study now the zeros of the equation $g(z) = 1 - z + Q_{\mathcal{H}}(z)$. For small values of $P(\mathcal{H})$, a *bootstrapping* approach [21, 22] allows for a derivation of the local development of ρ given in Eq. (7).

The Darboux theorem for the series $\phi(z)/g(z)$ implies that the n-th coefficient of this series satisfies $p_n \sim \frac{\phi(\rho)}{\rho g'(\rho)}\rho^{-n}$. General and detailed results on its use on rational series can be found in [23]. Using Eq. (7) for sets $\mathcal{H}$, $\mathcal{H}_1$ and $\mathcal{H}_2$ yields Theorem 4. As $P(\mathcal{H}) = O(\frac{1}{n})$ in this range, we get the approximation order.

4   Efficient Computation of Fundamental Parameters

To put formulae into effect, one needs to compute efficiently for a set of words $\mathcal{H}$ the fundamental quantities of Definition 4. First we present a general method for an arbitrary set $\mathcal{H}$ based on a classical algorithm. If $\mathcal{H}$ has a particular structure (i.e. consists of approximate words), a more efficient way is available.

4.1   Correlation for an Arbitrary Set of Words

We resort in this section to the well-known Aho-Corasick algorithm [24, 25] which builds from a finite set of words $\mathcal{H}$ a deterministic complete automaton (not necessarily minimal) recognizing the language $\Sigma^*\mathcal{H}$ where Σ is the (finite) alphabet. This automaton is the basis of many efficient algorithms on string matching problems and is often called the *string matching automaton*. We use a variant represented as a trie together with a failure function. Let $\mathcal{T}_{\mathcal{H}}$ be the ordinary trie representing $\mathcal{H}$, seen as a finite deterministic automaton $(Q, \delta, \varepsilon, T)$ where the set of states is $Q = \mathit{Pref}(\mathcal{H})$ (prefixes of words in $\mathcal{H}$), the initial state is ε, the set of final states is $T = \Sigma^*\mathcal{H} \cap \mathit{Pref}(\mathcal{H})$ and the incomplete transition function δ is defined by $\delta(p, a) = pa$ if $pa \in \mathit{Pref}(\mathcal{H})$ and undefined otherwise. For a word $u \in \mathit{Pref}(\mathcal{H})$, the failure function Border associates

$$\mathit{Border}(u) = \text{the longest proper suffix of } u \text{ which belongs to } \mathit{Pref}(\mathcal{H}).$$

In the following we identify a word $u \in \mathit{Pref}(\mathcal{H})$ with the node at the end of the branch labelled by u, so that Border defines also a map on the nodes of the tree. There are efficient $O(|\mathcal{H}|)$ algorithms [24, 25] linear both in time and space building such a tree structure together with the auxiliary Border function.

For any set $\mathcal{H}$ and $w \in \mathcal{H}$, one can compute $C_{w,\mathcal{H}}$ and $\widetilde{C}_{w,\mathcal{H}}$ using this structure. Indeed, we associate to $w \in \mathcal{H}$ a suffix chain of nonempty words $(u_1, \ldots, u_k)$ obtained by successive application of the failure function before getting ε. Then the trie $\mathcal{T}$ of the right complements of H in $\mathcal{H}$ is obtained by merging all the subtries rooted at the nodes labelled by the u_i's. The trie $\widetilde{\mathcal{T}}$ of the minimal complements of H in $\mathcal{H}$ corresponds to the pruning of $\mathcal{T}$ where, along any branch, we only keep the nodes from the root to the first terminal node (see Fig. 1). One can easily compute the quantities $C(\mathcal{H})$ and $\widetilde{C}(\mathcal{H})$ (or $P(\mathcal{H})$) along the construction of these trees.

4.2   Approximate Words and Generalized Consensus

In this section, we present algorithms to compute the occurrence probability and the correlation factor (but due to limitations of our approach not the minimal correlation factor) for a certain kind of set of words.

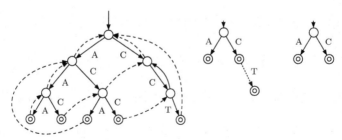

Fig. 1. For the set $\mathcal{H} = \{\text{AAA}, \text{AAC}, \text{ACA}, \text{ACC}, \text{CCT}\}$: The trie $\mathcal{T}_{\mathcal{H}}$ with (dashed) links Border (left), the trie of the right complements of AAC in $\mathcal{H}$ (middle) and the trie of the minimal right complements of AAC in $\mathcal{H}$.

Definition 5. *A positional pattern of length m is a sequence of sets of letters $(\mathcal{H}_i)_{i=1}^m$. Each set $\mathcal{H}_i \subseteq \Sigma$ is the set of symbols permitted at position i among symbols of the alphabet Σ.*

Hereafter we identify a positional pattern and the set of words it represents. For instance, the pattern $\mathcal{H} = (\{A, C\}, \{T\}, \{A, T\})$ is the set $\{ATA, ATT, CTA, CTT\}$. To define a neighborhood, we will use in this section the *Hamming distance d*.

Definition 6. *A neighborhood of $\mathcal{H} = (\mathcal{H}_i)_{i=1}^m$ is a set of words $\mathcal{N} = (\mathcal{N}_i)_{i=1}^m$ such that $\mathcal{H} \subseteq \mathcal{N}$ (i.e. $\mathcal{H}_i \subseteq \mathcal{N}_i$ for $i = 1..m$). The k-neighborhood (relative to $\mathcal{N}$) $B_k(\mathcal{H})$ of center $\mathcal{H}$ and radius k is $B_k(\mathcal{H}) = \{w \in \mathcal{N} \mid d(\mathcal{H}, w) \leq k\}$.*

The most natural example consists in a center $\mathcal{H}$ reduced to one word of length m and a neighborhood $\mathcal{N} = \Sigma^m$ where all letters are allowed. However our model enables us to consider words with some forbidden errors at specific positions.

The set of words $\mathcal{H}$ is called below the *center* of the neighbourhood. It is the so-called *consensus* of the biologists. The motifs in the neighbourhood are the *approximate words*, also called *spurious motifs* [18]. They appear in the extraction of regulatory signals. Our definition – and our algorithms as well – covers the case where the substitutions occur at some specific positions. It also covers the case of an extended alphabet, for instance the fifteen IUPAC ambiguity code [26]. Symmetric structures can also be addressed, as in the special case of palindromes, where the errors must maintain the palindromic structure. This case is of interest for the study of restriction-modification systems [2].

Note that when k errors are allowed, the number of words in the neighborhood is $O(m^k)$. Therefore, a naive algorithm that examines all the words of the neighborhood is an exponential algorithm with respect to k. Our algorithm is polynomial in m and k for both Bernoulli and Markov models. The key idea is to consider a word or a set of words as a formal series. One knows [23] that given a rational language, substituting probabilities to symbols yields in the Bernoulli model the probability occurrence. Finally if we know in advance the number of errors allowed, we can use truncated expansion of the series.

Occurrence probability for approximate words. In this section, we compute the occurrence probability of the neighborhood $B_k(\mathcal{H})$.

Definition 7. *For a pattern $\mathcal{H}$ of length m and a neighborhood $\mathcal{N}$, let us define the generating function*

$$F_{\mathcal{H}}(u) = \sum_{w \in \mathcal{N}} P(w) u^{d(\mathcal{H}, w)}. \tag{9}$$

The occurrence probability of $B_k(\mathcal{H})$ is $P(B_k(\mathcal{H})) = \sum_{i=0}^k [u^i] F_{\mathcal{H}}(u)$.

Bernoulli model. In this model, Eq. (9) rewrites $F_{\mathcal{H}}(u) = \prod_{i=1}^m (P(\mathcal{H}_i) + u\, P(\mathcal{N}_i \setminus \mathcal{H}_i))$. Since we are only interested in coefficient degree less than k, it is enough to compute the truncated expansion up to degree k. Remark that k is known in advance and usually small in applications.

PROBABILITYBERNOULLI($k, \mathcal{H}, \mathcal{N}$)

```
1   f(u) ← 1
2   for i ← 1 to m do
3       f(u) ← f(u) × (P(Hᵢ) + u P(Nᵢ \ Hᵢ))
4   return Σᵏᵢ₌₀[uⁱ]f(u)
```

Proposition 2. *The algorithm* PROBABILITYBERNOULLI(), *for a Bernoulli model, computes the probability* $P(B_k(\mathcal{H}))$ *with* $O(mk)$ *time complexity and* $O(k)$ *space complexity.*

One needs only to store one polynomial $f(u)$ of degree k at a time. Moreover the iterative step 3, updating $f(u)$, can be computed *in place* so no extra storage is needed and requires only $O(k)$ operations since we need to multiply a polynomial of degree k with a polynomial of degree at most 1.

Markov model. For a Markov model of order $p > 0$, the stationary probability of w is $P(w) = \sum_{c \in \Sigma^p} \pi_c P(w|c)$, with $P(w|c)$ the probability that H occurs after c, and π_c the stationary probability of c. So in this context, Eq. (9) rewrites

$$F_{\mathcal{H}}(u) = \sum_{c \in \Sigma^p} \pi_c f_{\mathcal{H},c}(u), \quad \text{where } f_{\mathcal{H},c}(u) = \sum_{w \in \mathcal{N}} P(w|c) u^{d(w,\mathcal{H})}.$$

In the following algorithm we will need two notations. For a set S, $\delta_S(j) = 1$ if $j \in S$ and 0 otherwise. For a word $c \in \Sigma^p$ and a symbol $j \in \Sigma$, the *j-shift* $\sigma_j(c)$ of the word c by j is the word of length p obtained by erasing the first letter of c and adding the symbol j at the end. For instance, $\sigma_G(\text{ATC}) = \text{TCG}$.

PROBABILITYMARKOV($k, \mathcal{H}, \mathcal{N}$)

```
1    for c ∈ Σᵖ do
2        f_c(u) ← 1
3    for i ← m downto 1 do
4        for c ∈ Σᵖ do
5            f'_c(u) ← 0
6            for j ∈ Σ do
7                c' ← σⱼ(c)
8                f'_c(u) ← f_{c'}(u) × P(j|c) × δ_{Nᵣ}(j)u^{1-δ_{Hᵢ}(j)}
9        for c ∈ Σᵖ do
10           f_c(u) ← f'_c(u)
11   ▷ Use the stationary distribution π to obtain the result
12   F(u) ← 0
13   for c ∈ Σᵖ do
14       F(u) ← F(u) + π_c × f_c(u)
15   return Σᵏᵢ₌₀[uⁱ]F(u)
```

Without proof, let us state the complexity of this algorithm.

Proposition 3. *The algorithm* PROBABILITYMARKOV() *computes for a Markov model of order* p, *the probability* $P(B_k(\mathcal{H}))$ *with* $O(mV^{p+1}k)$ *time complexity and* $O(V^pk)$ *space complexity where* V *is the cardinal of the alphabet, k is the number of errors and $\mathcal{H}$ is of length m.*

Overlap factor for approximate words. Our aim here is to provide a symbolic computation of the *overlap factor* $C(B_k(\mathcal{H}))$. Similarly to Section 4.2, for each consecutive possible overlap position i, we consider a bivariate polynomial with the Hamming distance d where u marks the number of errors relatively to a prefix of length m and v marks the numbers of errors relatively to a suffix of size m

$$D_{i,\mathcal{H}}(u,v) = \sum_{\substack{F,G \in \mathcal{N} \\ \text{overlapping at } i}} P(F\, G^m_{m-i+1}) u^{d(\mathcal{H},F)} v^{d(\mathcal{H},G)}.$$

The following algorithm computes $C(B_k(\mathcal{H}))$ and has $O(m^2 k^2)$ time complexity and $O(k^2)$ space complexity. Note also that this algorithm can be readily extended as in Section 4.2 to a Markov model of order p with alphabet of cardinality V with a time complexity $O(m^2 V^{p+1} k^2)$.

OVERLAPFACTORBERNOULLI$(k, \mathcal{H}, \mathcal{N})$

1 $D(u,v) \leftarrow 0$
2 **for** $i \leftarrow 2$ **to** $m-1$ **do**
3      $f(u,v) \leftarrow 1$
4   **for** $j \leftarrow m+i-1$ **to** m **do**
5          $f(u,v) \leftarrow f(u,v) \times \big(P(\mathcal{H}_j) + v\, P(\mathcal{N}_j \setminus \mathcal{H}_j) \big)$
6   **for** $j \leftarrow m$ **to** i **do**
7          $f(u,v) \leftarrow f(u,v) \times \big(P(\mathcal{H}_j \cap \mathcal{H}_{j-i+1})$
                      $+ u\, P((\mathcal{N}_j \setminus \mathcal{H}_j) \cap \mathcal{H}_{j-i+1}) + v\, P((\mathcal{N}_{j-i+1} \setminus \mathcal{H}_{j-i+1}) \cap \mathcal{H}_j)$
                      $+ uv\, P((\mathcal{N}_j \setminus \mathcal{H}_j) \cap (\mathcal{N}_{j-i+1} \setminus \mathcal{H}_{j-i+1})))$
8   **for** $j \leftarrow i-1$ **to** 1 **do**
9          $f(u,v) \leftarrow f(u,v) \times \big(P(\mathcal{H}_j) + u\, P(\mathcal{N}_j \setminus \mathcal{H}_j) \big)$
10     $D(u,v) \leftarrow d(u,v) + f(u,v)$
11 **return** $\sum_{0 \leq i,j \leq k} [u^i v^j] D(u,v)$

5   Conclusion

We provided efficient algorithms to assess the significance of exceptional words in a long sequence – typically a whole genome – or a set of small sequences. While the approaches to word counting through recurrences suffer from a combinatorial explosion when the text is Markovian or when the signal is strongly degenerated, our formulae or algorithms allow for a fast (polynomial) computation. We are currently working on a possible extension to structured motifs or dyads [8]. Among the possible applications, it might be interesting to compile regulatory motifs in eucaryotic genomes, possibly the human genome, and to evaluate their significance.

References

1. Panina, E., Mironov, A., Gelfand, M.: Statistical analysis of complete bacterial genomes:Avoidance of palindromes and restriction-modification systems. Mol. Biol. **34** (2000) 215–221

2. Vandenbogaert, M., Makeev, V.: Analysis of bacterial RM-systems through genome-scale analysis and related taxonomic issues. In Silico Biol. **3** (2003) 12

3. Robin, S., Schbath, S.: Numerical comparison of several approximations on the word count distribution in random sequences. J. Comput. Biol. **8** (2001) 349–359

4. Chiang, D., Moses, A., Kellis, M., Lander, E., Eisen, M.: Phylogenetically and spatially conserved word pairs associated with gene-expression in yeasts. Genome Biol. **4:R43** (2003)

5. Régnier, M., Szpankowski, W.: On pattern frequency occurrences in a Markovian sequence. Algorithmica **22** (1997) 631–649

6. Régnier, M.: A unified approach to word occurrences probabilities. Discrete Appl. Math. **104** (2000) 259–280 Special issue on Computational Biology.

7. Robin, S., Daudin, J.J.: Exact distribution of word occurrences in a random sequence of letters. J. Appl. Prob. **36** (1999) 179–193

8. Robin, S., Daudin, J.J., Richard, H., Sagot, M., Schbath, S.: Occurrence probability of structured motifs in random sequences. J. Comput. Biol. **9** (2001) 761–773

9. Pevzner, P., Borodovski, M., Mironov, A.: Linguistics of nucleotide sequences i: the significance of deviations from mean statistical characteristics and prediction of the frequencies of occurrence of words. J. Biomol. Struct. Dynam. **6** (1989) 1013–1026

10. Bender, E.A., Kochman, F.: The Distribution of Subwords Counts is Usually Normal. European J. Combin. **14** (1993) 265–275

11. Guibas, L., Odlyzko, A.: String Overlaps, Pattern Matching and Nontransitive Games. J. Combin. Theory Ser. A **30** (1981) 183–208

12. Tanushev, M., Arratia, R.: Central limit theorem for renewal theory for several patterns. J. Comput. Biol. **4** (1997) 35–44

13. Régnier, M., Szpankowski, W.: On the approximate pattern occurrences in a text. In: Compression and Complexity of SEQUENCES, IEEE Computer Society (1997) 253–264

14. Klaerr-Blanchard, M., Chiapello, H., Coward, E.: Detecting localized repeats in genomic sequences: A new strategy and its application to *B. subtilis* and *A. thaliana* sequences. Comput. Chem. **24** (2000) 57–70

15. Nicodème, P., Salvy, B., Flajolet, P.: Motif statistics. Theoret. Comput. Sci **287** (2002) 593–618

16. Chrysaphinou, C., Papastavridis, S.: The occurrence of sequence of patterns in repeated dependent experiments. Theory Probab. App. **79** (1990) 167–173

17. Szpankowski, W.: Average Case Analysis of Algorithms on Sequences. John Wiley and Sons, New York (2001)

18. Buhler, J., Tompa, M.: Finding Motifs Using Random Projections. In: RE-COMB'01, ACM (2001) 69–76

19. Beaudoing, E., Freier, S., Wyatt, J., Claverie, J., Gautheret, D.: Patterns of Variant Polyadenylation Signal Usage in Human Genes. Genome Res. **10** (2000) 1001–1010

20. van Helden, J., André, B., Collado-Vides, J.: Extracting regulatory sites from the upstream region of yeast genes by computational analysis of oligonucleotide frequencies. J. Mol. Biol. **281** (1998) 827–842 http://rsat.ulb.ac.be/rsat/.

21. Knuth, D.: The average time for carry propagation. Indag. Math. **40** (1978) 238–242

22. Régnier, M.: Mathematical tools for regulatory signals extraction. In Kolchanov, N., Hofestaedt, R., eds.: Bioinformatics of Genome Regulation and Structure, Kluwer Academic Publisher (2004) 61–70

23. Flajolet, P., Sedgewick, R.: Analysis of Algorithms. Addison-Wesley (1996)

24. Aho, A.V., Corasick, M.J.: Efficient string matching: an aid to bibliographic search. Commun. ACM **18** (1975) 333–340
25. Crochemore, M., Rytter, W.: Jewels of Stringology. World Scientific Publishing, Hong-Kong (2002) 310 pages.
26. Blanchette, M., Sinha, S.: Separating real motifs from their artifacts. Bioinformatics (ISMB special issue) **817** (2001) 30–38

Inferring a Graph from Path Frequency

Tatsuya Akutsu[1,*] and Daiji Fukagawa[2]

[1] Bioinformatics Center, Institute for Chemical Research, Kyoto University
Gokasho, Uji, Kyoto 611-0011, Japan
takutsu@kuicr.kyoto-u.ac.jp
[2] Graduate School of Informatics, Kyoto University
Yoshida-Honmachi, Sakyo-ku, Kyoto 606-8501, Japan
daiji@kuicr.kyoto-u.ac.jp

Abstract. We consider the problem of inferring a graph (and a sequence) from the numbers of occurrences of vertex-labeled paths, which
is closely related to the pre-image problem for graphs in machine learning: to reconstruct a graph from its feature space representation. We
show that this problem can be solved in polynomial time in the size of
an output graph if graphs are trees of bounded degree and the lengths
of given paths are bounded by a constant. On the other hand, we show
that this problem is strongly NP-hard even for planar graphs of bounded
degree.

1 Introduction

In the past decade, there has been significant progress in *kernel methods* [5],
which include *support vector machines* [4]. In particular, kernel methods have
been applied to various classification problems in bioinformatics [16], which is
one of the main target areas of combinatorial pattern matching. In order to apply
kernel methods to bioinformatics problems, it is usually required to develop a
mapping from the set of objects in the target problem to a *feature space* (i.e.,
each object is transformed to a vector of reals) and a kernel function is defined
as an inner product between two *feature vectors*. For instance, in the *spectrum
kernel* method [10], each sequence is mapped to a frequency vector of fixed length
substrings (i.e. frequency of n-grams). In some cases, a feature space can be an
infinite dimensional space (Hilbert space) and some kernel trick is developed to
compute the value of a kernel function efficiently without explicitly computing
feature vectors [5].

Recently, a new approach was proposed for designing and/or optimizing objects using kernel methods [2, 3]. In this approach, a desired object is computed
as a point in the feature space using suitable objective function and optimization technique and then the point is mapped back to the input space, where this
mapped back object is called a *pre-image*. Let ϕ be a mapping from an input

* Supported in part by Grant-in-Aid for Scientific Research on Priority Areas (C) for
"Genome Information Science" and Grant-in-Aid #16300092 from the Ministry of
Education, Culture, Sports, Science and Technology (MEXT) of Japan.

A. Apostolico, M. Crochemore, and K. Park (Eds.): CPM 2005, LNCS 3537, pp. 371–382, 2005.

372   Tatsuya Akutsu and Daiji Fukagawa

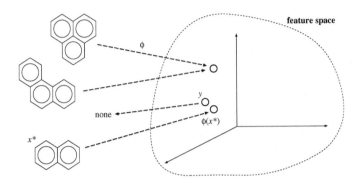

Fig. 1. Inference of a graph from a feature vector. Multiple objects may be mapped to the same point in a feature space. If there does not exist $\phi^{-1}(y)$, it is required to find x^* such that $dist(y, \phi(x^*))$ is the minimum

space $\mathcal{G}$ to a feature space $\mathcal{F}$. Then, the problem is, given a point y in $\mathcal{F}$, to find a pre-image x in $\mathcal{G}$ such that $y = \phi(x)$. It should be noted that ϕ is not necessarily injective or surjective. If ϕ is not surjective, we need to compute the approximate pre-image x^* for which distance of y and $\phi(x)$ is minimized (see Fig. 1): $x^* = \arg\min_x dist(y, \phi(x))$.   Bakir, Weston and Scölkopf proposed a method to find pre-images in a general setting by using Kernel Principal Component Analysis and regression [2]. Bakir, Zien and Tsuda developed a stochastic search algorithm to find pre-images for graphs [3]. It should be noted that the pre-image problem for graphs is very important from a practical viewpoint because it has potential application to drug design [3] by using a suitable objective function reflecting desired properties. Indeed, several studies have been done for designing molecules with optimal values using heuristic methods (genetic algorithms) [13, 17] though they did not use kernel methods. However, all of the above approaches are statistical, stochastic or heuristic. Thus, it seems that these do not lead to polynomial time algorithms for solving pre-image problems exactly.

In this paper, we study algorithmic aspects of this pre-image problem. Moreover, we focus on pre-image problems for feature spaces defined by frequency of distinct vertex-labeled paths because this type of feature space has been successfully used for classification of both biological sequences [10] and chemical compounds [8, 11]. As mentioned in the above, each sequence is transformed to a frequency vector of n-grams in the spectrum kernel [10] where each n-gram corresponds to a path of fixed length. In the *marginalized graph kernel* [8], each graph is transformed to a vector of probabilities of vertex-labeled paths. Though some kernel trick was developed for handling unbounded length paths efficiently, it is known that the marginalized kernel works well even if bounded length paths are used [8]. Thus, we only consider the case of bounded length paths. Moreover, we do not consider the probabilities; instead we consider for simplicity the number of occurrences of labeled paths as in the case of the spectrum kernel (probability corresponds to the number of occurrences if we consider regular graphs).

We first show that the exact pre-image problem for sequences can be solved in polynomial time in the length of the sequence to be inferred. For that purpose, we employ the *Eulerian path approach* which was originally developed for *sequencing by hybridization* [14]. Next, we present dynamic programming algorithms for both exact and approximate pre-image problems for trees of bounded degree, which work in polynomial time in the size of an output graph when a feature vector is defined by frequency of bounded length paths over a finite set of labels. On the other hand, we show that the pre-image problem is strongly NP-hard even for planar graphs of bounded degree. Though the algorithms proposed for graphs are not practical and the gaps between the positive and negative results are not small, these results provide new insights on the pre-image problem.

Several related problems have been studied in theoretical computer science. As mentioned above, sequencing by hybridization and the shortest common superstring problem [14] are close to the pre-image problem for sequences. Graphical degree sequence problems [1], graph inference from walks [12, 15] and the graph reconstruction problem [9] are related to the pre-image problem for graphs. However, to our knowledge, results on these three graph problems are not directly applicable to the pre-image problem for graphs.

2   Problem Definitions

In this section, we define the problems formally.

First, we define the pre-image problem for sequences. We use feature vectors in the spectrum kernel [10]. Let Σ be an alphabet and Σ^K be the set of strings with length K over Σ. For two strings t and s, $occ(t, s)$ denotes the number of occurrences of substring t in s. Then, the feature vector $\boldsymbol{f}_K(s)$ of level K for s is a $|\Sigma^K|$-dimensional integer vector such that the coordinate indexed by $t \in \Sigma^K$ is $occ(t, s)$. That is, $\boldsymbol{f}_K(s)$ is defined by $\boldsymbol{f}_K(s) = (occ(t, s))_{t \in \Sigma^K}$. For example, consider string 00101111 over $\Sigma = \{0, 1\}$. Then, $\boldsymbol{f}_2(s) = (1, 2, 1, 3)$ because $occ(00, s) = 1$, $occ(01, s) = 2$, $occ(10, s) = 1$ and $occ(11, s) = 3$.

If K is large, the number of dimensions of a feature vector will be large (exponential of K). In such a case, many coordinates will have value 0. Thus, when K is not a constant, we assume that a vector is represented in an appropriate way (linear size of a target sequence) so that the coordinates having value 0 are not included in the data structures.

Definition 1. (SISF: Sequence Inference from Spectrum Feature) *Given a feature vector $\boldsymbol{v}$ of level K, output a string s satisfying $\boldsymbol{f}_K(s) = \boldsymbol{v}$. If there does not exist such s, output "no solution".*

The above definition can be extended for the case of finding the sequence nearest to a given feature vector. Though we consider Hamming distances in this paper, the results in this paper may be extended for the Euclidean distance and other appropriate distances.

Definition 2. (SISF-M: Sequence Inference from Spectrum Feature with Minimum Error) *Given a feature vector $\boldsymbol{v}$ of level K, output a string s such that $dist(\boldsymbol{f}_K(s), \boldsymbol{v})$ is the minimum.*

Next, we define pre-image problems for graphs. Let $G(V, E)$ be an undirected vertex-labeled graph and Σ be a set of vertex labels. A sequence of vertices $(v_0, v_1, \ldots, v_h)$ of G is called a *path* of length h ($h \geq 0$) if $\{v_i, v_{i+1}\} \in E$ holds for $i = 0, \ldots, h-1$. It should be noted that the same vertex (and the same edge) can appear more than once in the above definition. Since most papers on marginalized graph kernels [8, 11, 16] use this notation, we employ this definition of a path. Let $\Sigma^{\leq k}$ be the set of label sequences (i.e., the set of strings) over Σ whose lengths are between 1 and k. Let $l(v)$ be the label of vertex v. For a path $P = (v_0, \ldots, v_h)$ of G, $l(P)$ denotes the label sequence of P (i.e., $l(P) = l(v_0)l(v_1)\ldots l(v_h)$). It should be noted that the length of $l(P)$ is the length of P plus one. For graph G and label sequence t, $occ(t, G)$ denotes the number of paths P in G such that $l(P) = t$. Then, the feature vector $\boldsymbol{f}_K(G)$ of level K for $G(V, E)$ is an integer vector such that the coordinate index by $t \in \Sigma^{\leq K+1}$ is $occ(t, G)$. That is, $\boldsymbol{f}_K(G)$ is defined by $\boldsymbol{f}_K(G) = (occ(t, G))_{t \in \Sigma^{\leq K+1}}$. For example, consider a star $G(V, E)$ consisting of four vertices where the center vertex has label 0 and the other three vertices have label 1. Then, $\boldsymbol{f}_1(G) = (1, 3, 0, 3, 3, 0)$ because $occ(0, G) = 1$, $occ(1, G) = 3$, $occ(00, G) = 0$, $occ(01, G) = 3$, $occ(10, G) = 3$ and $occ(11, G) = 0$.

It should be noted that, different from the case of the spectrum kernel, various length paths are considered in the above definition and in the marginalized kernel [8]. In this paper, we assume for simplicity that *tottering paths* (paths for which there exists some i such that $v_i = v_{i+2}$) are not counted in feature vectors because removal of tottering paths does not decrease the prediction accuracy [11]. However, all the results on graphs in this paper are also valid even if tottering paths are not removed.

Definition 3. (**GIPF**: Graph Inference from Path Frequency) *Given a feature vector $\boldsymbol{v}$ of level K, output a graph $G(V, E)$ satisfying $\boldsymbol{f}_K(G) = \boldsymbol{v}$. If there does not exist such $G(V, E)$, output "no solution".*

The above definition can be extended for the case of finding the graph nearest to a given feature vector as in Definition 2.

Definition 4. (**GIPF-M**: Graph Inference from Path Frequency with Minimum Error) *Given a feature vector $\boldsymbol{v}$ of level K, output a graph $G(V, E)$ such that $dist(\boldsymbol{f}_K(G), \boldsymbol{v})$ is the minimum.*

It is worthy to note that both the number of dimensions of the feature vector and the maximum coordinate value of the feature vector are bounded by a polynomial in the size of the graph if we consider constant K.

3   Algorithms for Sequences

We can easily develop an efficient algorithm for SISF by employing Eulerian path approach for sequencing by hybridization [14].

Suppose that a feature vector $\boldsymbol{v}$ of level K over Σ is given for the SISF problem (i.e., $occ(t, s)$ is given). We construct a directed multi graph $G'(V, E)$

such that $V = \Sigma^{K-1}$ and for each $t \in \Sigma^K$ there exist directed edges (t', t'') with multiplicity $occ(t, s)$, where t' and t'' are the prefix and suffix of t with length $K-1$, respectively. Then, we can see that there exists an Eulerian path in $G'(V, E)$ iff. there is a solution for the SISF problem. It should be noted that we need not create vertices which are neither prefix or suffix of substrings such that $occ(t, s) = 0$. Let n be the length of the target sequence (i.e., $n = K - 1 + \sum_t occ(t, s)$). Using the result on sequencing by hybridization [14], we have:

Proposition 1. *SISF is solved in $O(n)$ time.*

For the SISF-M problem, we may construct graph $G'(V, E)$ in the same way. But, $G'(V, E)$ does not necessarily have an Eulerian path. Thus, we should add or delete edges (using the minimum number of additions/deletions) so that the resulting graph has an Eulerian path. Though it is unclear whether or not this can be done in polynomial time, we can solve SISF-M in polynomial time in n if K and Σ are fixed by using a dynamic programming algorithm similar to that in the next section (details are omitted in this version).

Proposition 2. *SISF-M is solved in polynomial time in n if K and Σ are fixed.*

4   Algorithms for Trees

In this section, we present dynamic programming algorithms for inference of trees from feature vectors of constant levels. It should be noted that these do not work in polynomial time with respect to the size of a feature vector because a feature vector may be represented in $O(\log n)$ size, where n is the number of vertices of the graph (i.e., n is the sum of frequencies of paths of length 0). But, these work in pseudo polynomial time (i.e., these work in polynomial time in n). Considering such algorithms is quite reasonable because these work in polynomial time with respect to the size of an output graph. First, we consider the case of inference of trees of level 1. Though the following result is very simple and may be improved, we present it because it is useful for understanding the algorithm for a more general case (to be shown in Theorem 2).

Theorem 1. *GIPF for trees is solved in polynomial time in n for $K = 1$ and a fixed alphabet.*

Proof. We only show the algorithm for the case of the binary alphabet (i.e., $\Sigma = \{0, 1\}$), where extension to an arbitrary fixed alphabet is straight-forward. We construct the table $D(\ldots)$ defined by

$$D(n_0, n_1, n_{00}, n_{01}, n_{10}, n_{11}) =$$
$$\begin{cases} 1, & \text{if there exists tree } T \text{ such that } \boldsymbol{f}_1(T) = (n_0, n_1, n_{00}, n_{01}, n_{10}, n_{11}), \\ 0, & \text{otherwise.} \end{cases}$$

This table can be constructed by the following dynamic programming procedure where the initialization part is straight-forward.

$$D(n_0, n_1, n_{00}, n_{01}, n_{10}, n_{11}) = 1 \textbf{ iff.}$$
$$D(n_0 - 1, n_1, n_{00} - 2, n_{01}, n_{10}, n_{11}) = 1 \quad \textbf{or}$$
$$D(n_0 - 1, n_1, n_{00}, n_{01} - 1, n_{10} - 1, n_{11}) = 1 \quad \textbf{or}$$
$$D(n_0, n_1 - 1, n_{00}, n_{01} - 1, n_{10} - 1, n_{11}) = 1 \quad \textbf{or}$$
$$D(n_0, n_1 - 1, n_{00}, n_{01}, n_{10}, n_{11} - 2) = 1.$$

The correctness of the algorithm follows from the fact that any tree can be constructed incrementally by adding a vertex (leaf) one by one. The required tree (if exists) can be obtained by means of a *traceback* procedure as in many dynamic programming algorithms. Since the value of each element of the feature vector is $O(n)$ where $n = n_0 + n_1$, the table size is $O(n^6)$ and thus the computation time is $O(n^6)$. □

It is worthy to note that a generate-and-test approach (enumerating all trees of size n and checking whether each tree T satisfies $\boldsymbol{f}_K(T) = \boldsymbol{v}$) does not yield a (pseudo) polynomial time algorithm because the number of possible trees is not bounded by a polynomial in n.

The algorithm above can be modified for GIPF-M. We only need to consider the table such that each coordinate value is $O(n)$ because each tree of size $O(n)$ can correspond to some element in that table. Therefore, we can find the feature vector $\boldsymbol{f}_K(T)$ closest to $\boldsymbol{v}$ in polynomial time by examining each vector in the table of polynomial size.

Corollary 1. *GIPF-M for trees is solved in polynomial time in n for $K = 1$ and a fixed alphabet.*

The above algorithm can be modified for SISF-M (see Proposition 2). For that purpose, we construct a table $D(\boldsymbol{v})$ incrementally according to increasing order of n, where $D(\boldsymbol{v}) = 1$ iff. there exists a sequence s such that $\boldsymbol{f}_K(s) = \boldsymbol{v}$.

Next, we extend the algorithm for cases of $K > 1$, where K is a constant and we only consider trees of bounded degree and of fixed Σ. Extension is not straight-forward and is somewhat involved. We explain the algorithm for trees of bounded degree 3, where it is not difficult to extend the algorithm for higher (but bounded) degree cases.

Though we do not consider directed trees, we will treat an undirected tree as if it were a rooted tree. Let r be the root of a tree T. The *depth* (denoted by $d(v)$) of a vertex $v \in T$ is the length of the (shortest) path from r to v. The *depth of a tree* ($d(T)$) is the depth of the deepest vertex.

For each vertex $v \in T$, $T_K(v)$ denotes the subtree of T induced by the vertex set $\{v\} \cup \{w | w$ is a descendant of $v, |P(v, w)| \le K\}$, where $P(v, w)$ denotes the (shortest) path from v to w.

$ID(v)$ denotes the signature (i.e., canonical labeling in [6]) of v where the signature is an integer number of value $O(n)$ such that $ID(v) = ID(v')$ iff. $T_K(v)$ is isomorphic to $T'_K(v')$. Since we consider constant K and trees of bounded degree, $ID(v)$ can be computed in $O(1)$ time for each v.

Each vertex v maintains the set of paths which contain v as the shallowest vertex. It should be noted that each vertex needs to maintain $O(1)$ paths since we consider constant K and trees of bounded degree 3. It should also be noted that each path is maintained by exactly one vertex.

For each tree T, we associate a table $E(d, id)$ where $E(d, id)$ denotes the number of vertices v such that $d(v) = d$ and $ID(v) = id$. Since there are $O(1)$ different signatures, $E(d, id)$ consists of $O(d(T))$ elements.

Let e denotes the vector consisting of $E(d, id)$ for $d = d(T), d(T) - 1, d(T) - 2, \ldots, d(T) - K$. Let $g_K(T)$ denotes e for T. It should be noted that the number of dimensions of e is bounded by a constant.

Then, we construct table $D(v, e, d)$ defined by: $D(v, e, d) = 1$ iff. there exists a tree T such that $f_K(T) = v$, $g_K(T) = e$ and $d(T) = d$. Let $\hat{D}(v, e, d)$ be the size of such tree T. It should be noted that the size of trees is uniquely determined from (v, e, d) though trees may not be uniquely determined (note that we can not maintain the whole structure of a tree). Construction of the table is done in an incremental manner as in the case of $K = 1$. We only add a new vertex at depth either d or $d + 1$. It should be noted that any tree can be constructed in this manner.

First we consider the case of adding a new vertex at depth $d = d(T)$ to a tree T of size n (see Fig. 2). For each (v, e, d) such that $D(v, e, d) = 1$ and $\hat{D}(v, e, d) = n$, we consider all ways of appending a new vertex w having label $l \in \Sigma$ to each subtree $T(v)$ such that $d(v) = d - K$ and $E(d - K, id(v)) > 0$. We need to consider one subtree with the same signature in the case of $E(d - K, id(v)) > 1$. Then, it is easy to see that the number of ways of appending a new vertex is bounded by a constant per (v, e, d) because the numbers of dimensions of v and e are bounded by constants. Moreover, addition of w affects signatures of $O(1)$ vertices because only signatures of vertices in $T(v)$ can change. Suppose that (v, e, d) changes to (v', e', d) by addition of w to some position of $T(v)$. Then, $D(v', e', d)$ is set to 1 (initially, all entries of the table are set to 0). It is not difficult to see that this update of the table can be done in constant time per (v, e, d).

Next we consider the case of adding a new vertex at depth $d(T) + 1$ to a tree T of size n. As in the above, we consider all ways of appending a new vertex. In this case, we need to take care so that e' consists of signatures of vertices of depth between $d(T) - K + 1$ and $d(T) + 1$. But, update of the table can still be done in constant time per (v, e, d).

By scheduling the above two types of operations adequately, we can have the algorithm for computing the table $D(v, e, d)$. The correctness of the algorithm can be seen from the following facts: any tree can be constructed by adding a vertex one by one in the increasing order of depth, addition of a new vertex only affects signatures of vertices in $T(v)$, and addition of a new vertex only affects paths (of length at most K) inside $T(v)$. Since the size of table $D(v, e, d)$ is bounded by a polynomial in n and constant time is required per entry of the table, the algorithm works in polynomial time in n. The required tree can be obtained by using the traceback technique.

Theorem 2. *GIPF for trees of bounded degree is solved in polynomial time in n if K and Σ are fixed.*

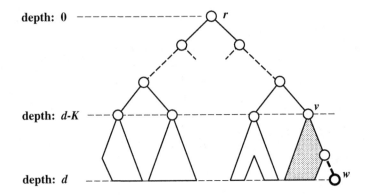

Fig. 2. Addition of a new vertex w to tree T. Vector e consists of signatures of vertices with depth between $d - K$ and d. Addition of w only affects signatures of vertices and paths (of length at most K) in the gray part (i.e., $T(v)$)

As in Corollary 1, we can extend this result for GIPF-M.

Corollary 2. *GIPF-M for trees of bounded degree is solved in polynomial time in n if K and Σ are fixed.*

5   Hardness of Graph Inference

In this section, we prove that GIPF is strongly NP-hard, from which strong NP-hardness of GIPF-M follows.

Theorem 3. *GIPF is strongly NP-hard even for planar graphs and $K = 4$.*

Proof. We use a *pseudo polynomial time transformation* [7] from 3-PARTITION, which is known to be strongly NP-complete. Recall that 3-PARTITION is defined as follows [7]: given a set X which consists of $3m$ elements x_i along with their integer weights $w(x_i)$ and a positive integer B where each $w(x_i)$ satisfies $B/4 < w(x_i) < B/2$, find a partition of X into $A_1, A_2, \ldots, A_m$ such that each A_i consists of 3 elements and $\sum_{x_j \in A_i} w(x_j) = B$ holds for each A_i.

We construct a feature vector of level 4 (i.e., $K = 4$), which is to be constructed from subgraphs of the target (planar) graph $G(V, E)$, where $G(V, E)$ corresponds to a solution to 3-PARTITION.

We let $\Sigma = X \cup \{a_i | i = 1, \ldots, m\} \cup \{a, b, c, c', d\}$. We identify a vertex with its label if the vertex with the same label appears only once in a graph. For each x_i, we construct a subgraph $G(x_i)$ shown in Fig. 3. Each $G(x_i)$ is called a *block*. Note that there are $w(x_i)$ vertices with label a in $G(x_i)$. Note also that three blocks will be connected to the same vertex labeled a_h though it is not specified by the feature vector which blocks are connected to the same vertex.

Next, we connect vertex d to m vertices with labels a_h's as in Fig. 3, where three paths of the form c'-c-b are also connected to each a_h. We call the subgraph

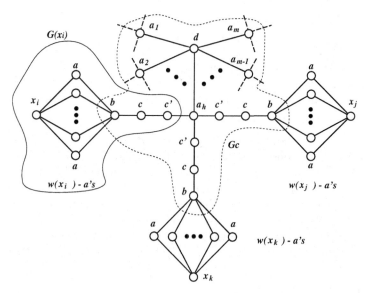

Fig. 3. Reduction from 3-PARTITION to GIPF, where a_h corresponds to set $A_h = \{x_i, x_j, x_k\}$

consisting of vertices with labels d, a_h's, b, c and c' the *center graph* (denoted by G_c in Fig. 3).

The feature vector $\boldsymbol{v}$ is constructed from the following paths:

PATHS-A: all paths at most length 4 in each block or in the center graph,
PATHS-B: for each a_h, we construct B paths of the form of a_h-c'-c-b-a and the corresponding B paths in the reverse direction.

Now, we show that there exists a graph $G(V, E)$ such that $\boldsymbol{f}_K(G) = \boldsymbol{v}$ if and only if there exists a solution for 3-PARTITION.

Suppose that there exists a solution $A_1, \ldots, A_m$ for 3-PARTITION. Then, we construct blocks $G(x_i)$ for $i = 1, \ldots, 3m$. We also construct a star which consists of the center vertex with label d and vertices with labels $a_1, \ldots, a_m$. For each $A_h = \{x_i, x_j, x_k\}$, we connect $G(x_i)$, $G(x_j)$ and $G(x_k)$ to a_h as in Fig. 3 (we connect each vertex with label c' in $G(\ldots)$ to a_h). Let the resulting graph be $G(V, E)$. Here, we show that $\boldsymbol{f}_K(G)$ corresponds to the union of PATHS-A and PATHS-B. First, note that $G(V, E)$ contains all the blocks and the center graph. Therefore, the multiset of paths corresponding to $\boldsymbol{f}_K(G)$ contains all paths in PATHS-A. Next, note that B paths of the form of a_h-c'-c-b-a start from each a_h in $G(V, E)$. Therefore, the multiset of paths corresponding to $\boldsymbol{f}_K(G)$ contains all paths in PATHS-B. Since each path of length at most three is contained in a block or in the center graph, the multiset of paths corresponding to $\boldsymbol{f}_K(G)$ is equivalent to the union of PATHS-A and PATHS-B. Therefore, we have $\boldsymbol{f}_K(G) = \boldsymbol{v}$.

Suppose that there exists a graph $G(V, E)$ such that $\boldsymbol{f}_K(G) = \boldsymbol{v}$. Then, the graph must contain all blocks and the center graph as subgraphs because of the following reasons:

- x_i appears exactly once in $G(V, E)$,
- Paths including x_i and paths including b uniquely define the structure of block $G(x_i)$,
- Paths including d uniquely define the star consisting of d and a_h's,
- Each a_h appears exactly once in $G(V, E)$,
- Paths including a_h's uniquely define the structure of the center graph along with the above information on paths,

where information about absence of some kinds of paths is also utilized. It is also seen from the constraint on $w(x_i)$'s that exactly 3 blocks can connect to each a_h. From these, we can see that $G(V, E)$ must have the structure shown in Fig. 3. Let $G(x_i)$, $G(x_j)$ and $G(x_k)$ be the blocks connected to a_h. Then, $w(x_i) + w(x_j) + w(x_k) = B$ must hold because v contains B paths of the form of a_h-c'-c-b-a. Therefore, there exists a solution for 3-PARTITION.

It is straight-forward to see that the reduction satisfies the conditions for a pseudo polynomial time transformation [7], from which we can see that GIPF is strongly NP-hard.   □

It follows from Theorem 3 that there does not exist a pseudo polynomial time algorithm for GIPF unless P=NP.

In the above reduction, the maximum degree of graph $G(V, E)$ or the size of Σ was not bounded. But, we can modify the above reduction for graphs of bounded degree 4 and of fixed Σ, where details of construction and proofs are omitted in this version. Let $L = \lceil \log \max(B, m) \rceil$. Then, we transform blocks and the center graph as in Fig. 4, where labels of vertices should be defined by using a kind of binary-codes. Recall that uniqueness of x_i's and a_h's plays an important role in the proof of Theorem 3, and we use binary-codes to guarantee the uniqueness of paths corresponding to x_i's and a_h's. It should be noted that the maximum degree of the constructed graph is 4.

In this reduction, we use a feature vector of level $8L$. It can be seen that both the number of dimensions of a feature vector and the size of $G(V, E)$ are bounded by polynomials in B and m. Moreover, each coordinate value of a feature vector is bounded by a polynomial in B and m. From these, we can see that the reduction satisfies the conditions of a pseudo polynomial time transformation.

Theorem 4. *GIPF is strongly NP-hard even for planar graphs of bounded degree 4 and of fixed Σ.*

6   Concluding Remarks

We have presented polynomial time algorithms for inferring sequences and trees from path frequency. We have also proven that this inference problem is strongly NP-hard even for planar graphs of bounded degree.

From a theoretical viewpoint, large complexity gaps remain between the positive and negative results. For example, the complexity (polynomial or NP-hard) of the following cases should be studied:

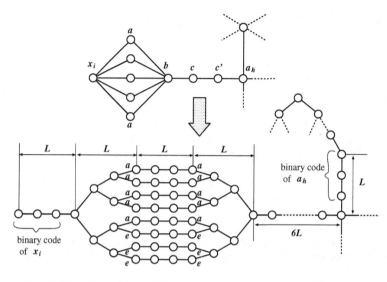

Fig. 4. Transformation of blocks and the center star in Theorem 4

- inference of trees from paths with non-constant K,
- inference of graphs of bounded degree from paths with constant K.

Another interesting future work is to develop approximation algorithms for NP-hard cases.

From a practical viewpoint, the proposed algorithms for trees are not useful because constant factors depending on K and Σ will be very large. Therefore, faster algorithms should be developed. Algorithms for more general classes of graphs should also be developed although algorithms for trees may still be useful since some heuristic methods have been developed for representing chemical structures using trees [13]. In this paper, we consider feature vectors defined by path frequency. However, probabilities of paths are used in the marginalized graphs kernels. Therefore, extensions for such cases should be studied.

Acknowledgements

We would like to thank Pierre Mahé, Nobuhisa Ueda, Jean-Luc Perret and Jean-Philippe Vert for collaboration on graph kernels, which motivated this work.

References

1. Asano, T.: An $O(n \log \log n)$ time algorithm for constructing a graph of maximum connectivity with prescribed degrees. J. Computer and System Sciences **51** (1995) 503–510
2. Bakir, G.H., Weston, J., Schölkopf, B.: Learning to find pre-images. Advances in Neural Information Processing Systems **16** (2004) 449–456

3. Bakir, G.H., Zien, A., Tsuda, K.: Learning to find graph pre-images. In Proc. the 26th DAGM Symposium. Volume 3175 of Lecture Notes in Computer Science, Springer (2004) 253–261

4. Cortes, C., Vapnik, V.: Support vector networks. Machine Learning **20** (1995) 273–297

5. Cristianini, N., Shawe-Taylor, J.: An Introduction to Support Vector Machines and Other Kernel-based Learning Methods. Cambridge Univ. Press (2000)

6. Dinitz, Y., Itai, A., Rodeh, M.: On an algorithm of Zemlyachenko for subtree isomorphism. Information Processing Letters **70** (1999) 141–146

7. Garey, M.R., Johnson, D.S.: Computers and Intractability. A Guide to the Theory of NP-Completeness. W.H. Freeman and Co. (1979)

8. Kashima, H., Tsuda, K., Inokuchi, A.: Marginalized kernels between labeled graphs. In Proc. 20th Int. Conf. Machine Learning (2003) 321–328

9. Lauri, J., Scapellato, R.: Topics in Graph Automorphisms and Reconstruction. Cambridge Univ. Press (2003)

10. Leslie, C., Eskin, E., Noble, W.S.: The spectrum kernel: a string kernel for SVM protein classification. In Proc. Pacific Symposium on Biocomputing **7** (2002) 564–575

11. Mahé, P., Ueda, N., Akutsu, T., Perret, J-L., Vert, J-P.: Extensions of marginalized graph kernels. In Proc. 21st Int. Conf. Machine Learning (2004) 552–559

12. Maruyama, O., Miyano, S.: Inferring a tree from walks. Theoretical Computer Science **161** (1996) 289–300

13. Nachbar, R.B.: Molecular evolution: automated manipulation of hierarchical chemical topology and its application to average molecular structures. Genetic Programming and Evolvable Machines **1** (2000) 57–94

14. Pevzner, P.A.: Computational Molecular Biology. An Algorithmic Approach. The MIT Press (2000)

15. Raghavan, V.: Bounded degree graph inference from walks. J. Computer and System Sciences **49** (1994) 108–132

16. Schölkopf, B., Tsuda, K., Vert, J-P. (eds.): Kernel Methods in Computational Biology. The MIT Press (2004)

17. Vinkers, H.M., de Jonge, M.R., Daeyaert, F.F.D., Heeres, J., Koymans, L.M.H., van Lenthe, J.H., Lewi, P.J., Timmerman, H., van Aken, K., Janssen, P.A.J.: Synopsis: synthesize and optimize system in silico. Journal of Medical Chemistry **46** (2003) 2765–2773

Exact and Approximation Algorithms for DNA Tag Set Design[*]

Ion I. Măndoiu and Dragoş Trincă

CSE Department, University of Connecticut
371 Fairfield Rd., Unit 2155, Storrs, CT 06269-2155
{ion.mandoiu,dragos.trinca}@uconn.edu

Abstract. In this paper we propose new solution methods for design-ing tag sets for use in universal DNA arrays. First, we give integer linear programming formulations for two previous formalizations of the tag set design problem, and show that these formulations can be solved to op-timality for instance sizes of practical interest by using general purpose optimization packages. Second, we note the benefits of periodic tags, and establish an interesting connection between the tag design problem and the problem of packing the maximum number of vertex-disjoint directed cycles in a given graph. We show that combining a simple greedy cy-cle packing algorithm with a previously proposed alphabetic tree search strategy yields an increase of over 40% in the number of tags compared to previous methods.

1 Introduction

Recently developed *universal DNA tag arrays* [5, 11, 14] offer a flexible and cost-effective alternative to custom-designed DNA arrays for performing a wide range of genomic analyses. A universal tag array consists of a set of DNA strings called *tags*, designed such that each tag hybridizes strongly to its own *antitag* (Watson-Crick complement), but to no other antitag. A typical assay based on universal tag arrays performs Single Nucleotide Polymorphism (SNP) genotyp-ing using the following steps [3, 7]: (1) A set of *reporter oligonucleotide probes* is synthesized by ligating antitags to the 5′ end of primers complementing the genomic sequence immediately preceding the SNP. (2) Reporter probes are hy-bridized in solution with the genomic DNA under study. (3) Hybridization of the primer part (3′ end) of a reporter probe is detected by a single-base extension reaction using the polymerase enzyme and dideoxynucleotides fluorescently la-beled with 4 different dyes. (4) Reporter probes are separated from the template DNA and hybridized to the universal array. (5) Finally, fluorescence levels are used to determine which primers have been extended and learn the identity of the extending dideoxynucleotides.

---

[*] Work supported in part by a Large Grant from the University of Connecticut's Research Foundation.

A. Apostolico, M. Crochemore, and K. Park (Eds.): CPM 2005, LNCS 3537, pp. 383–393, 2005.

Tag set design involves balancing two conflicting requirements: on one hand we would like a large number of tags to allow assaying a large number of biochemical reactions, on the other hand we would like the tags to work well for a wide range of assay types and experimental conditions.

Ben Dor et al. [2] have previously formalized the problem by imposing constraints on antitag-to-tag hybridization specificity under a hybridization model based on the classical 2-4 rule, and have proposed near-optimal heuristics. In Section 3 we give an integer linear programming (ILP) formulation for this problem and its variant in which tags are required to have equal length [12]. Empirical results in Section 5 show that these ILP formulations have extremely small integrality gap, and can be solved to optimality for instance sizes of practical interest by using general purpose optimization packages.

Previous works on tag set design [2, 12] require for substrings that may form a nucleation complex and initiate cross hybridization not to be repeated within any selected tag. This constraint simplifies analysis, but is *not* required for ensuring correct tag functionality – what is required is for such substrings not to appear simultaneously in two different tags. To our knowledge, no previous work has assessed the impact that adding this constraint has on tag set size. In this paper we propose two algorithms for designing tag sets while relaxing this constraint. The first one is a modification of the alphabetic tree search strategy in [11, 12], The second algorithm stems from the observation that periodic tags, particularly those with a short period, use the least amount of "resources" and lead to larger tag sets, where the limited resources are in this case minimal substrings that can form nucleation complexes (for formal models see Section 2). In Section 4 we establish an interesting connection between the tag design problem and the problem of packing the maximum number of vertex-disjoint directed cycles in a given graph, and propose a simple greedy algorithm for the latter one. Results in Section 5 show that combining the greedy cycle packing algorithm with alphabetic tree search strategy yields an increase of over 40% in the number of tags compared to previous methods.

2   Problem Formulations and Previous Work

A main objective of universal array designers is to maximize the number of tags, which directly determines the number of reactions that can multiplexed using a single array. At the same time, tag sets must satisfy a number of *stability* and *non-interaction* constraints [4]. The set of constraints depends on factors such as the array manufacturing technology and the intended application. In this section we formalize the most important stability and non-interaction constraints using the hybridization model in [2].

Hybridization model. Hybridization affinity between two oligonucleotides is commonly characterized using the *melting temperature*, defined as the temperature at which half of the duplexes are in hybridized state and the other half are in melted state. However, accurate melting temperature estimation is computationally expensive, e.g., estimating the melting temperature between two non-complementary oligonucleotides using the near-neighbor model of SantaLucia [16] is an NP-hard problem [8]. Ben-Dor et al. [2, 3] formalized a conservative hybridization model based on the observation that stable hybridization requires the formation of an initial *nucleation complex* between two perfectly complementary substrings of the two oligonucleotides. For nucleation complexes, hybridization affinity is modeled using the classical *2-4 rule* [17], which estimates the melting temperature of the duplex formed by an oligonucleotide with its complement as the sum between the number of *weak* bases (i.e., A and T) and twice the number of *strong* bases (i.e., G and C).

The *weight* $w(x)$ of a DNA string $x = a_1 a_2 \ldots a_k$ is defined as $w(x) = \sum_{i=1}^{k} w(a_i)$, where $w(\texttt{A}) = w(\texttt{T}) = 1$ and $w(\texttt{C}) = w(\texttt{G}) = 2$. Throughout this paper we assume the following *c-token hybridization model* [2]: hybridization between two oligonucleotides takes place only if one oligo contains as substring the complement of a substring of weight c or more of the other, where c is a given constant. The *complement* of a string $x = a_1 a_2 \ldots a_k$ over the DNA alphabet $\{\texttt{A}, \texttt{C}, \texttt{T}, \texttt{G}\}$ is defined as $\bar{x} = b_1 b_2 \ldots b_k$, where b_i is the Watson-Crick complement of a_{k-i+1}.

Hybridization stability. Current industry designs require a predetermined tag length l, e.g., GenFlex tag arrays manufactured by Affymetrix use $l = 20$ [1]. The model proposed in [2] allows tags of unequal length and instead require a minimum tag weight of h, for a given constant h. In this paper we consider both types of stability constraints, and use the parameter $\alpha \in \{l, h\}$ to denote the specific model used for hybridization stability.

Pairwise non-interaction constraints. A basic constraint in this category is for every antitag not to hybridize to non-complementary tags [2]. For a DNA string x and a set of tags $\mathcal{T}$, let $N_{\mathcal{T}}(x)$ denote the number of tags in $\mathcal{T}$ that contain x as a substring. Using the c-token hybridization model, the antitag-to-tag hybridization constraint is formalized as follows:

(C) For every feasible tag set $\mathcal{T}$, $N_{\mathcal{T}}(x) \leq 1$ for every DNA string x of weight c or more.

In many assays based on universal tag arrays it is also required to prevent antitag-to-antitag hybridization, since the formation of such antitag-to-antitag duplexes or antitag hair-pin structures prevents reporter probes from performing their function in the solution-based hybridization steps [4, 12]. The combined constraints on antitag hybridization are formalized as follows

($\bar{C}$) For every feasible tag set $\mathcal{T}$, $N_{\mathcal{T}}(x) + N_{\mathcal{T}}(\bar{x}) \leq 1$ for every DNA string x of weight c or more.

In the following we use the parameter $\beta \in \{C, \bar{C}\}$ to specify the type of pairwise hybridization constraints.

Substring occurrences within a tag. Previous works on DNA tag set design [2, 12] have imposed the following *c-token uniqueness constraint* in addition to constraints (C) and ($\bar{C}$): a DNA string of weight c or more can appear as a substring of a feasible tag at most once. This uniqueness constraint has been added purely for ease of analysis (e.g., it is the key property enabling the De-Bruijn sequence based heuristics in [2]), and is *not* required for ensuring correct assay functionality. To our knowledge, no previous work has assessed the impact that adding this constraint has on tag set size. In the following we will use the parameter $\gamma \in \{1, multiple\}$ to specify whether or not the c-token uniqueness constraint is enforced.

For every $\alpha \in \{l, h\}$, $\beta \in \{C, \bar{C}\}$, and $\gamma \in \{1, multiple\}$, the maximum tag set design problem with constraints α, β, γ, denoted MTSDP($\alpha|\beta|\gamma$), is the following: given constants c and l/h, find a tag set of maximum cardinality satisfying the constraints.

Previous work on tag set design. Ben-Dor et al. [2] formalized the c-token model for oligonucleotide hybridization and studied the MTSDP($h|C|1$) problem. They established a constructive upperbound on the optimal number of tags for this formulation, and gave a nearly optimal tag selection algorithm based on DeBruijn sequences. Similar upper bounds are established for the MTSDP($l|C|1$) and MTSDP($*|\bar{C}|1$) problems in [12], which also extends a simple alphabetic tree search strategy originally proposed in [11] to handle all considered problem variants.

For a comprehensive survey of hybridization models, results on the associated formulations for the tag set design problem, and further motivating applications in the area of DNA computing, we direct the reader to [4].

3   Integer Linear Programming Formulations for MTSDP($*|C|1$)

Before stating our integer linear program formulation, we introduce some additional notations.

Following [2], a DNA string x of weight c or more is called a *c-token* if all its proper suffixes have weight strictly less than c. Clearly, it suffices to enforce constraint (C) for all c-tokens x. Let N denote the number of c-tokens, and $\mathcal{C} = \{c_1, \ldots, c_N\}$ denote the set of all c-tokens. The results in [2] imply that $N = \Theta((1 + \sqrt{3})^c)$. Note that the weight of a c-token can be either c or $c + 1$, the latter case being possible only if the c-token starts with a strong base (G or C). We let $\mathcal{C}_0 \subseteq \mathcal{C}$ denote the set of c-tokens of weight $c+1$ that end with a weak base, i.e., c-tokens of the form $S<c-2>W$, where W (S) denote a weak (strong) base, and $<c-2>$ denotes an arbitrary string of weight $c-2$. We also let $\mathcal{C}_2 \subseteq \mathcal{C}$ denote the set of c-tokens of weight c that end with a strong base, i.e., c-tokens of the form $<c-2>S$.

Clearly, there is at most one c-token ending at every letter of a tag. It is easy to see that each c-token $x \in \mathcal{C}_0$ contains a proper prefix which is itself a c-token, and therefore x cannot be the first c-token of a tag, i.e., cannot be the c-token with the leftmost ending. All other c-tokens can appear as first c-tokens. When a c-token in $C \setminus (\mathcal{C}_0 \cup \mathcal{C}_2)$ is the first in a tag, then it must be a prefix of the tag. On the other hand, tokens in $\mathcal{C}_2$ can be the first both in tags that they prefix and in tags in which they are preceded by a weak base not covered by any c-token.

The ILP formulation for MTSDP($l|C|1$) uses an auxiliary directed graph $G = (V, E)$ with $V = \{s, t\} \cup \bigcup_{1 \leq i \leq N} V_i$, where $V_i = \{v_i^k \mid |c_i| \leq k \leq l\}$. G has a directed arc from v_i^k to v_j^{k+1} for every triple i, j, k such that $|c_i| \leq k \leq l - 1$ and c_j is obtained from c_i by appending a single nucleotide and removing the maximal prefix that still leaves a valid c-token. Finally, G has an arc from s to every $v \in V_{first}$, where $V_{first} = \{v_i^{|c_i|} \mid c_i \in \mathcal{C} \setminus \mathcal{C}_0\} \cup \{v_i^{|c_i|+1} \mid c_i \in \mathcal{C}_2\}$, and an arc from v_i^l to t for every $1 \leq i \leq N$.

We claim that, for $c \leq l$, MTSDP($l|C|1$) can be reformulated as the problem of finding the maximum number of s-t paths in G that collectively visit at most one vertex v_i^k for every i. Indeed, let P be an s-t path and v_i^k be the vertex following s in P. If $k = |c_i|$, we associate to P the tag obtained by concatenating c_i with the last letters of the c-tokens corresponding to the subsequently visited vertices, until reaching t. Otherwise, if $k = |c_i|+1$ (which implies that $c_i \in \mathcal{C}_2$) we associate to P the two tags obtained by concatenating either A or T with c_i and the last letters of subsequently visited c-tokens. The claim follows by observing that at most one of the tags associated with each path can be used in a feasible solution.

Our ILP formulation can be viewed as a generalized version of the integer maximum flow problem in which unit capacity constraints are imposed on *sets of vertices* of G instead of individual vertices. The formulation uses $0/1$ variables x_v and y_e for every every vertex $v \in V \setminus \{s, t\}$, respectively arc $e \in E$. These variables are set to 1 if the corresponding vertex or arc is visited by an s-t path corresponding to a selected tag. Let $in(v)$ and $out(v)$ denote the set of arcs entering, respectively leaving vertex v. The integer program can then be written as follows:

$$\text{maximize} \quad \sum_{v \in V_{first}} x_v \tag{1}$$

$$\text{subject to}$$

$$x_v = \sum_{e \in in(v)} y_e = \sum_{e \in out(v)} y_e, \quad v \in V \setminus \{s, t\} \tag{2}$$

$$\sum_{v \in V_i} x_v \leq 1, \quad 1 \leq i \leq N \tag{3}$$

$$x_v, y_e \in \{0, 1\}, \quad v \in V \setminus \{s, t\}, e \in E \tag{4}$$

Constraints (2) ensure that variables y_e set to 1 correspond to a set of s-t paths, and that a variable x_v is set to 1 if and only if one of these paths passes through v [1]. Antitag-to-tag hybridization constraints (C) and c-token uniqueness are enforced by (3). Finally, the objective (1) corresponds to maximizing the number of selected tags, since the shortest prefix of a tag that is a c-token must belong to $\mathcal{C} \setminus \mathcal{C}_0$.

---

[1] Variables x_v can be eliminated by replacing them with the corresponding sums of x_e's; we use them here merely for improving readability. ILP sizes reported in Section 5 refer to the equivalent reduced formulations obtained by eliminating these variables.

For a token $c_i = c_j X \in \mathcal{C}_0$, where $X \in \{\mathtt{A}, \mathtt{T}\}$, let $\widehat{c_i} = c_j \bar{a}$. Since both c_i and $\widehat{c_i}$ contain c_j as a prefix, and c_j can appear at most once in a feasible tag set $\mathcal{T}$, it follows that at most one of them can appear in $\mathcal{T}$. Therefore, the following valid inequality can be added to the the ILP formulation (1)–(4) to improve its integrality gap (i.e., the gap between the value of the optimum integer solution and that of the optimal fractional relaxation):

$$\sum_{v \in V_i \cup V_j} x_v \leq 1, \qquad c_i \in \mathcal{C}_0, \ c_j = \widehat{c_i}, \ i < j \qquad (5)$$

The formulation of MTSDP($l|C|1$) has exactly the same objective and constraints for a slightly different graph G. Let us define the *tail weight* of a c-token C, denoted $tail(C)$, as the weight of C's last letter. Also, let $h_i = h$ if c_i has a tail weight of 1 and $h_i = h + 1$ if c_i has a tail weight of 2. We will require that every tag ending with token c_i has total weight of at most h_i; it is easy to see that this constraint is not affecting the size of the optimum tag set. We now define the graph $G = (V, E)$ with $V = \{s, t\} \cup \bigcup_{1 \leq i \leq N} V_i$, where $V_i = \{v_i^k \mid w(c_i) \leq k \leq h_i\}$. G contains a directed arc from v_i^k to $v_j^{k+tail(i)}$ for every triple i, j, k such that $|c_i| \leq k \leq h_i - tail(c_i)$ and c_j is obtained from c_i by appending a single nucleotide and removing the maximal prefix that still leaves a valid c-token. Finally, G contains arcs from s to every $v \in V_{first}$, where V_{first} is now equal to $\{v_i^{w(c_i)} \mid c_i \in \mathcal{C} \setminus \mathcal{C}_0\} \cup \{v_i^{w(c_i)+1} \mid c_i \in \mathcal{C}_2\}$, plus arcs from every v_i^k to t for every $1 \leq i \leq N$ and $h_i - tail(c_i) < k \leq h_i$.

4   Algorithms for MTSDP($*| *|multiple$)

In the following we describe two algorithms for MTSDP($l|C|multiple$); both algorithms can be easily adjusted to handle the other MTSDP($*| *|multiple$) variants. The first algorithm (see [13] for a detailed pseudocode) is similar to the alphabetic tree search algorithms proposed for MTSDP($l|C|1$) in [12]. The algorithm performs an alphabetical traversal of a 4-ary tree representing all 4^l possible tags, skipping over subtrees rooted at internal vertices that correspond to tag prefixes including unavailable c-tokens. The difference from the MTSDP($l|C|1$) algorithm in [12] lies in the strategy used to mark c-tokens as unavailable. While the algorithm in [12] marks a c-token C as unavailable as soon as it incorporates it in the current tag prefix (changing C's status back to "available" when forced to backtrack past C's tail), our algorithm marks a c-token as unavailable only when a complete tag is found.

Note that the alphabetic tree search algorithm produces a *maximal* feasible set of tags $\mathcal{T}$, i.e., there is no tag t such that $\mathcal{T} \cup \{t\}$ remains feasible for MTSDP($l|C|multiple$). Hence, every tag of an optimal solution must share at least one c-token with tags in $\mathcal{T}$. Since every tag of $\mathcal{T}$ has at most $l - c/2 + 1$ c-tokens, it follows that the alphabetic tree algorithm (and indeed, every algorithm that produces a maximal feasible set of tags) has an approximation factor of $l - c/2 + 1$.

We call a tag t *periodic* if t is the length l prefix of an infinite string x^∞, where x is a DNA string with $|x| < |t|$. (Note that a periodic tag t is not necessarily the concatenation of an integer number of copies of its period x as in the standard definition of string periodicity [10].)

The following lemma shows that tag set design algorithms can restrict the search to two simple classes of tags.

Lemma 1. *For every c and l, there exists an optimal tag set $\mathcal{T}$ in which every tag has the uniqueness property or is periodic[2].*

Proof. Let $\mathcal{T}$ be an optimal tag set. Assume that $\mathcal{T}$ contains a tag t that does not have the uniqueness property, and let $c_{i_1}, \ldots, c_{i_k}$ be the sequence of c-tokens occurring in t, in left to right order. Since t does not have the uniqueness property, there exist indices $1 \le j < j' \le i_k$ such that $c_{i_j} = c_{i_{j'}}$. Let t' be the tag formed by taking the first l letters of the infinite string with c-token sequence $(c_{i_j}, \ldots, c_{i_{j'-1}})^\infty$; note that t' is a periodic tag. Since c-tokens $c_{i_j}, \ldots, c_{i_{j'-1}}$ do not appear in the tags of $\mathcal{T} \setminus \{t\}$, it follows that $(\mathcal{T} \setminus \{t\}) \cup \{t'\}$ is also optimal. Repeated application of this operation yields the lemma. □

Note that a periodic tag whose shortest period has length p contains as substrings exactly p c-tokens, while tags with the uniqueness property contain between $l - c + 1$ and $l - c/2 + 1$ c-tokens. Therefore, of the two classes of tags in Lemma 1, periodic tags (particularly those with short periods) make better use of the limited number of available c-tokens.

Each periodic tag corresponds to a directed cycle in the graph H_c which has $\mathcal{C}$ as its vertex set, and in which a token c_i is connected by an arc to token c_j iff c_i and c_j can appear consecutively in a tag, i.e., iff c_j is obtained from c_i by appending a single nucleotide and removing the maximal prefix that still leaves a valid c-token. Clearly, a vertex-disjoint packing of n cycles in H_c yields a feasible solution for MTSDP($l|\mathcal{C}|multiple$) consisting of n tags, since we can extract at least one tag of length l from each cycle, and tags extracted from different cycles do not have common c-tokens. This motivates the following:

MAXIMUM VERTEX-DISJOINT DIRECTED CYCLE PACKING Problem: Given a directed graph G, find a maximum number of vertex-disjoint directed cycles in G.

The next theorem shows that MAXIMUM VERTEX-DISJOINT DIRECTED CYCLE PACKING in arbitrary graphs is unlikely to admit a polynomial approximation scheme.

Theorem 1. MAXIMUM VERTEX-DISJOINT DIRECTED CYCLE PACKING *is APX-hard even for regular directed graphs with in-degree and out-degree of 2.*

The proof of Theorem 1, which uses a reduction from the MAX-2-SAT-3 problem similar to the one in [6], can be found in [13]. A stronger inapproximability results was recently established for arbitrary graphs by Salavatipour

---

[2] Note that the two classes of tags are not disjoint, since there exist periodic tags that have the uniqueness property.

and Verstraete [15], who proved that there is no $O(\log^{1-\varepsilon} n)$-approximation for MAXIMUM VERTEX-DISJOINT DIRECTED CYCLE PACKING unless $NP \subseteq DTIME(2^{polylogn})$. On the positive side, Salavatipour and Verstraete showed that MAXIMUM VERTEX-DISJOINT DIRECTED CYCLE PACKING can be approximated within a factor of $O(\sqrt{n})$ via linear programming techniques, matching the best approximation factor known for the edge-disjoint version of the problem [9].

We use a simple greedy algorithm to solve MAXIMUM VERTEX-DISJOINT DIRECTED CYCLE PACKING for the graph H_c: we enumerate possible tag periods in pseudo-lexicographic order, and check for each period if all c-tokens are available for the resulting tag. We refer to this algorithm as the *greedy cycle packing algorithm*, since it is equivalent to packing cycles greedily in order of length.

5   Experimental Results

Tables 1 and 2 give ILP statistics (number of constraints, number of variables, and number of non-zero coefficients), LP and ILP runtime, and LP and ILP solution values for MTSDP($l|C|1$) and MTSDP($h|C|1$). We also include the upper bounds established in [12] and [2] for these problems, and the number of tags found by using the alphabetic tree search algorithm in [12]. We solved all integer programs and their fractional relaxations using the CPLEX 9.0 commercial solver with default parameters run using a single CPU on a dual 2.8 GHz Dell PowerEdge 2600 Linux server. Missing entries did not complete in 10 hours.

The ILP solutions can be found in practical time for small values of c, which are appropriate for universal tag array applications, such as the emerging microfluidics-based labs-on-a-chip, where moderate multiplexing rates are sufficient and ensuring high hybridization stringency is costly. For all cases where the optimum could be computed, the difference between the optimal fractional and integer solution values was smaller than 1, indicating why CPLEX can solve to optimality these ILPs despite their size. Furthermore, ILP results confirm the

Table 1. ILP results for MTSDP($l|C|1$), i.e., tag set design with specified tag length l, antitag-to-tag hybridization constraints, and a unique copy of each c-token allowed in a tag.

l	c	#tags		Upper Bounds		LP/ILP statistics				
		[12]	ILP	LP	[12]	#constr	#vars	#non-zero	LP time	ILP time
10	4	7	8	8.57	9	406	1878	6004	0.13	0.71
10	5	23	28	28.00	29	1008	4600	14596	2.27	5.85
10	6	67	85	85.60	96	2434	10940	34470	11.40	98.25
10	7	196	259	259.67	328	5808	25422	79274	86.70	586.67
10	8	655	–	853.33	1194	13554	57138	175492	552.74	–
20	4	3	3	3.53	3	926	4638	15244	1.05	58.46
20	5	9	10	10.50	11	2448	12240	40076	13.72	381.33
20	6	26	29	29.87	32	6354	31860	104270	182.96	12448.61
20	7	75	–	88.00	93	16528	82662	270194	2675.68	–
20	8	213	–	257.23	275	42834	213578	697292	134525.81	–

Table 2. ILP results for MTSDP($h|C|1$), i.e., tag set design with specified minimum tag weight h, antitag-to-tag hybridization constraints, and a unique copy of each c-token allowed in a tag.

h	c	#tags [12]	ILP	Upper Bounds LP	[2]	#constr	#vars	#non-zero	LP time	ILP time
15	4	6	7	7.00	7	610	2966	9612	0.45	9.04
15	5	18	21	21.09	21	1550	7456	23998	5.66	117.62
15	6	47	63	63.20	63	3830	18322	58752	54.43	2665.39
15	7	149	192	192.00	192	9406	44416	141638	544.95	3644.85
15	8	460	–	588.00	590	22766	105746	334904	7153.87	–
28	4	3	3	3.30	3	1286	6554	21624	1.88	132.78
28	5	8	9	9.67	9	3422	17388	57122	34.66	1137.21
28	6	22	27	27.48	27	8926	45518	149492	392.42	18987.09
28	7	64	–	78.55	78	23342	118828	389834	7711.41	–
28	8	175	–	–	224	60830	309118	1013244	–	–

extremely high quality of the upperbound established for MTSDP($h|C|1$) in [2]; the upperbound established in [12] for MTSDP($l|C|1$) appears to be somehow weaker.

Tables 3 and 4 give the results obtained for MTSDP($*|*|multiple$) by the alphabetic tree search algorithm described in Section 4, respectively by the greedy cycle packing algorithm (in our implementation, we impose an upper bound of 15 on the length of the cycles that we try to pack) followed by running the alphabetic tree search algorithm with the c-tokens occurring in the selected cycles

Table 3. Results for MTSDP($*|C|multiple$), i.e., tag set design with antitag-to-tag hybridization constraints and multiple copies of a c-token allowed in a tag.

l/h	c	One c-token copy Algorithm in [12]		Multiple c-token copies Tree search		Cycle packing + Tree search		
		tags	c-tokens	tags	c-tokens	tags	c-tokens	% cyclic
	4	3	51	14	59	17	40	100.0
	5	9	146	31	165	40	140	100.0
	6	26	404	53	433	72	293	98.6
$l = 20$	7	75	1100	124	1179	178	928	99.4
	8	213	2976	281	3095	383	2411	97.1
	9	600	7931	711	8230	961	7102	96.9
	10	1667	20771	1835	21400	2344	19691	95.1
	4	3	58	14	61	17	40	100.0
	5	8	150	32	174	40	140	100.0
	6	22	398	44	432	72	300	98.6
$h \geq 28$	7	64	1119	118	1200	178	934	99.4
	8	175	2918	239	3037	379	2405	96.6
	9	531	8431	632	8622	943	6969	96.5
	10	1428	21707	1570	22145	2260	19270	94.1

Table 4. Results for MTSDP($*|\bar{C}|multiple$), i.e., tag set design with both antitag-to-tag and antitag-to-antitag hybridization constraints and multiple copies of a c-token allowed in a tag.

l/h	c	One c-token copy		Multiple c-token copies			
		Algorithm in [12]		Tree search		Cycle packing + Tree search		
		tags	c-tokens	tags	c-tokens	tags	c-tokens	% cyclic
	4	1	17	10	35	10	25	100.0
	5	4	65	17	83	23	85	100.0
	6	13	200	30	241	41	171	97.6
$l = 20$	7	37	537	68	585	97	512	99.0
	8	107	1480	147	1619	202	1268	98.0
	9	300	3939	362	4124	512	3799	96.3
	10	844	10411	934	10869	1204	10089	95.8
	4	1	22	10	36	10	25	100.0
	5	4	74	17	84	23	85	100.0
	6	12	213	29	238	41	178	97.6
$h \geq 28$	7	32	559	64	586	97	518	99.0
	8	90	1489	135	1632	199	1238	98.0
	9	263	4158	329	4314	504	3760	95.8
	10	714	10837	809	11250	1163	9937	93.6

already marked as unavailable. Performing cycle packing significantly improves the results compared to running the alphabetic tree search algorithm alone; as shown in the tables, most of the resulting tags are found in the cycle packing phase of the combined algorithm.

Across all instances, the combined algorithm increases the number of tags by at least 40% compared to the MTSDP($*|*|1$) algorithm in [12]; the improvement is much higher for smaller values of c. Quite notably, although the number of tags is increased, the tag sets found by the combined algorithm use a *smaller* total number of c-tokens. Thus, these tag sets are less likely to cross-hybridize to the primers used in the reporter probes, enabling higher tag utilization rates during tag assignment [3, 12].

6   Conclusions

In this paper we proposed new solution methods for designing tag sets for universal DNA arrays. We have shown that optimal solutions can be found in practical time for moderate problem sizes by using integer linear programming, and that the use of periodic tags leads to increases of over 40% in the number of tags, with simultaneous increases in effective tag utilization rates during tag assignment. Our algorithms use simple greedy strategies, and can be easily modified to incorporate additional practical design constraints, such as preventing the formation of hairpin secondary structures, or disallowing specific nucleotide sequences such as runs of 4 identical nucleotides [11].

An interesting open problem is to find tight upper bounds and exact methods for the MTSDP($*|$ $*$ $|multiple$) formulations. Settling the approximation complexity of MAXIMUM VERTEX-DISJOINT DIRECTED CYCLE PACKING is another interesting problem.

References

1. Affymetrix, Inc. Geneflex tag array technical note no. 1, available online at http://www.affymetrix.com/support/technical/technotes/genflex_technote.pdf.
2. A. Ben-Dor, R. Karp, B. Schwikowski, and Z. Yakhini. Universal DNA tag systems: a combinatorial design scheme. *Journal of Computational Biology*, 7(3-4):503–519, 2000.
3. A. BenDor, T. Hartman, B. Schwikowski, R. Sharan, and Z. Yakhini. Towards optimally multiplexed applications of universal DNA tag systems. In *Proc. 7th Annual International Conference on Research in Computational Molecular Biology*, pages 48–56, 2003.
4. A. Brenneman and A. Condon. Strand design for biomolecular computation. *Theor. Comput. Sci.*, 287(1):39–58, 2002.
5. S. Brenner. Methods for sorting polynucleotides using oligonucleotide tags. *US Patent 5,604,097*, 1997.
6. A. Caprara, A. Panconesi, and R. Rizzi. Packing cycles in undirected graphs. *Journal of Algorithms*, 48(1):239–256, 2003.
7. J.N. Hirschhorn et al. SBE-TAGS: An array-based method for efficient single-nucleotide polymorphism genotyping. *PNAS*, 97(22):12164–12169, 2000.
8. L. Kaderali. *Selecting Target Specific Probes for DNA Arrays*. PhD thesis, Köln University, 2001.
9. M. Krivelevich, Z. Nutov, and R. Yuster. Approximation algorithms for cycle packing problems. In *Proc. ACM-SIAM Annual Symposium on Discrete Algorithms*, pages 556–561, 2005.
10. M. Lothaire. *Combinatorics on Words*, volume 17 of *Encylopedia of Mathematics and Its Applications*, pages xix+238. Addison-Wesley, 1983.
11. M.S. Morris, D.D. Shoemaker, R.W. Davis, and M.P. Mittmann. Selecting tag nucleic acids. *U.S. Patent 6,458,530 B1*, 2002.
12. I.I. Măndoiu, C. Prăjescu, and D. Trincă. Improved tag set design and multiplexing algorithms for universal arrays. In *Proc. 1st International Workshop on Bioinformatics Research and Applications (IWBRA)*, 2005 (to appear).
13. I.I. Măndoiu and D. Trincă. Exact and approximation algorithms for DNA tag set design. ACM Computing Research Repository, cs.DS/0503057, 2005.
14. N.P. Gerry et al. Universal DNA microarray method for multiplex detection of low abundance point mutations. *J. Mol. Biol.*, 292(2):251–262, 1999.
15. M.R. Salavatipour and J. Verstraete. Disjoint cycles: Integrality gap, hardness, and approximation. In *Proc. 11th Conference on Integer Programming and Combinatorial Optimization (IPCO)*, 2005 (to appear).
16. J. SantaLucia. A unified view of polymer, dumbbell, and oligonucleotide DNA nearest-neighbor thermodynamics. *Proc. Natl. Acad. Sci. USA*, 95:1460–1465, 1998.
17. R.B. Wallace, J. Shaffer, R.F. Murphy, J. Bonner, T. Hirose, and K. Itakura. Hybridization of synthetic oligodeoxyribonucleotides to phi chi 174 DNA: the effect of single base pair mismatch. *Nucleic Acids Res.*, 6(11):6353–6357, 1979.

Parametric Analysis for Ungapped Markov Models of Evolution*

David Fernández-Baca[1] and Balaji Venkatachalam[1]

Department of Computer Science, Iowa State University, Ames, IA 50011, USA
{fernande,balaji}@cs.iastate.edu

Abstract. We present efficient sensitivity-analysis algorithms for two problems involving Markov models of sequence evolution: ancestral reconstruction in evolutionary trees and local ungapped alignment under log-odds scoring. Our algorithms generate complete descriptions of the optimum solutions for all possible values of the evolutionary distance. The running time for the parametric ancestral reconstruction problem under the Kimura 2-parameter model is $O(kn + kn^{2/3} \log k)$, where n is the number of sequences and k is their length, assuming all edges have the same length. For the parametric gapless alignment problem under the Jukes-Cantor model, the running time is $O(mn + mn^{2/3} \log m)$, where m and n are the sequence lengths and $n \leq m$.

1 Introduction

Understanding the evolution of biological sequences is one of the basic problems in biology. In this paper we consider a simple but widely-used Markov model, where sequences evolve only through random mutation. The goal is to find the most likely explanation for the input data, given the model. Our work is motivated by the observation that the answer provided by any such model is highly sensitive to the model parameters; that is, the mutation probabilities. Slight variations in these values can result in completely different answers. Mutation probabilities are themselves non-linear functions of evolutionary distance (or time). Our main results are algorithms that compute the solution at *all* possible evolutionary distances, while incurring only a slight overhead relative to the effort needed to compute the answer for any *fixed* distance. In the process, we gain some insight into the structure of these problems.

Markov models of evolution are the basis for many of the scoring schemes used in sequence comparison. Sensitivity analysis is especially relevant in these applications, since several scoring schemes implicitly assume knowledge of the evolutionary distance between the sequences being compared. There is a certain circularity in this, since sequences are compared to determine their similarity, which allows one to infer something about the evolutionary distance between them. Parametric analysis, which considers *all* possible evolutionary distances between a pair of sequences, is a means to partially break out of this vicious cycle, allowing us to identify similarities between sequences that would be missed if a single distance were assumed in comparing them.

---

* Research partially supported by grants CCR-9988348 and EF-0334832 from the National Science Foundation.

A. Apostolico, M. Crochemore, and K. Park (Eds.): CPM 2005, LNCS 3537, pp. 394–405, 2005.

Background. In the Markov model of DNA evolution considered here, sites evolve independently according to identical random processes. The model is *gapless* in that insertion and deletion events are not allowed. Mutation probabilities for one unit of evolutionary time are given in the form of a 4×4 matrix M. By the Markov property, the mutation probability matrix $M^{(t)}$ for t time units is simply M^t (that is, M raised to the power t). Parametric problems arise from the attempt to understand the sensitivity of the model to changes in the entries of M and the value of t. The nature of this dependence is clearly non-linear.

The Markov model of mutation is the basis for the two problems considered here: phylogeny construction and local alignment. Let S be a set of species, each represented by a sequence of the same length. An *evolutionary tree* or *phylogeny* is a rooted tree T whose leaves are labeled by the elements of S. Tree T is a representation of the evolutionary history of S; its internal nodes represent ancestral species. An *internal labeling* for T is an assignment of sequences to the internal nodes of T, representing a set of hypothetical ancestors for S. Each edge of T has a length, which is the evolutionary distance (time) between its two endpoints. The *ancestral reconstruction problem* is to find the most probable internal labeling for the tree. The probability of this optimum reconstruction is a function of the edge lengths, with different lengths possibly leading to different reconstructions. The probability of the most likely labeling is a measure of the likelihood of the tree [17]. An alternative measure of likelihood is the *total probability* of the tree, which is the sum of the probabilities of all possible all internal labelings for the tree. While the second notion of likelihood also depends on edge lengths, the dependency is more complex than for the first notion [3, 12, 13, 16]. We shall not consider this approach further here.

Markov models are also used to identify contiguous regions of high similarity between two sequences. Similarity in this case is measured using *log-odds* scoring [6], which is computed as the logarithm of the ratio of the probability that the similarity occurred by evolution (according to a Markov model) to the probability that this was a purely random event. The underlying mechanism exhibits the same kind of time-dependency as the phylogeny problem described above.

Our contributions. We present fast algorithms for computing the optimum solution to parametric ancestral reconstruction and local ungapped alignment for all possible evolutionary distances. Their running times are comparable to those of the algorithms to find optimum solutions for fixed distance. For the parametric ancestral reconstruction problem under the uniform Kimura 2-parameter model (where all edge lengths are equal), we achieve a running time of $O(kn + kn^{2/3} \log k)$, where n is the number of sequences and k is their length. This is comparable to the running time for the fixed-parameter problem. In contrast, typical approaches are slower by a factor at least equal to the number of distinct optima. For the parametric gapless alignment problem under the Jukes-Cantor model, we achieve a running time of $O(mn + mn^{2/3} \log m)$, where m and n are the sequence lengths and $n \leq m$. This is comparable to the time needed to solve the fixed-parameter problem by dynamic programming.

The algorithms are based on two ideas, which may be useful in solving other problems. The first is that, despite the non-linearity of the time dependency, the well-known *log-transform* allows us to view the problems as linear ones, at the expense of increasing the number of parameters. The second idea takes advantage of the independence between the positions. We use the idea of "lifting" the execution of a fixed-parameter algorithm so that it computes the optimum solution at all evolutionary distances. Implemented in the obvious way, this results in a slowdown proportional to the number of different optimum solutions. We avoid this overhead because the problems we study are amenable to divide-and-conquer.

Related work. Our work is closely related to *parametric sequence alignment*, which explores the effect of parameter variation on the optimum solution to sequence alignment problems over a *range* of parameter values. The goal is to build a decomposition of the parameter space into *optimality regions*, that is, maximal connected regions within which the optimum alignment is unique. Parametric pairwise alignment was first considered by Fitch and Smith [10]. Waterman et al. [18] proposed a systematic way of finding the optimality regions. Gusfield et al. [11] gave the first bounds on the number of regions. Fernández-Baca et al. [8] extended Gusfield et al.'s work to a broader class of problems characterized by their scoring system; these problems include parametric multiple sequence alignment and phylogeny construction.

The importance of parameter choice in stochastic models of sequence evolution has been known for some time (see [1] and the references cited therein). Agarwal and States [1] give an example of a pair of sequences for which local ungapped alignment varies as the distance increases. In two companion papers [12, 13], Pachter and Sturmfels show the connection between parameter choice in statistical models and parametric problems with feature-based scoring schemes. Among other contributions, they give general bounds on the number of optimality regions and describe how dynamic programming algorithms for the fixed-parameter versions of these problems can be "lifted" to solve these same problems parametrically. Their method – the *polytope propagation algorithm* – is closely related to the approach used here.

Organization of the paper. Section 2 reviews Markov models of sequence evolution and their application to phylogenetics. Section 3 studies the effect of parameter variation on these models, relying on the notion of linearization. Algorithms for sensitivity analysis are presented in Section 4. Section 5 discusses open problems.

2   Models of Sequence Evolution

We now review the simple model of DNA sequence evolution studied here. Details can be found in [6, 7, 14, 15]. Similar models exist for amino acid sequences [5, 6].

2.1   A Markov Model for Substitution

The basis for the model of sequence evolution is a 4×4 *substitution* matrix $M = [m_{ab}]$, where m_{ab} is the probability that nucleotide a is substituted by nucleotide b in one unit of evolutionary time. Let $M^{(t)} = [m_{ab}^{(t)}]$ be the matrix where $m_{ab}^{(t)}$ is the probability that nucleotide a is substituted by nucleotide b in t units of time. By the Markov property, $M^{(t)} = M^t$.

We consider two important cases where the elements of $M^{(t)}$ can be expressed in closed form. In the *Jukes-Cantor (JC)* model, $m_{ab}^{(t)} = r(t)$ when $a = b$ (a *match*) and $m_{ab}^{(t)} = s(t)$ when $a \neq b$ (a *mismatch*). Functions $r(t)$ and $s(t)$ are given by

$$r(t) = \frac{1}{4}\left(1 + 3e^{-4\alpha t}\right) \qquad \text{and} \qquad s(t) = \frac{1}{4}\left(1 - e^{-4\alpha t}\right), \tag{1}$$

where α is a rate parameter (see [6]). Thus, mismatches have a certain probability and matches have another (lower) one, but these probabilities are independent of the nucleotides involved.

A *transition* is a substitution of a purine (A or G) by a different purine or a pyrimidine (C or T) by a different pyrimidine. A *transversion* is a substitution of a purine by a pyrimidine or vice versa. The *Kimura 2-parameter (K2P)* model allows for different probabilities for transitions and transversions (the former being more likely than the latter). The entries of the K2P substitution matrix are given by $m_{ab}^{(t)} = r(t)$ when $a = b$, $m_{ab}^{(t)} = s(t)$ when $a \to b$ is a transversion, and $m_{ab}^{(t)} = u(t)$ when $a \to b$ is a transition. Functions $r(t)$, $s(t)$, and $u(t)$ are given by

$$s(t) = \frac{1}{4}\left(1 - e^{-4\beta t}\right), \tag{2}$$

$$u(t) = \frac{1}{4}\left(1 + e^{-4\beta t} - 2e^{-2(\alpha+\beta)t}\right), \tag{3}$$

$$r(t) = 1 - 2s(t) - u(t), \tag{4}$$

where α, β are transition and transversion rate parameters [6].

We often work with logarithms (here assumed to be base 2) of probabilities rather than with the probabilities themselves, since, as explained below, this yields linear expressions. For the JC and K2P models, it is convenient to use the following notation

$$\kappa(t) = \log r(t) \qquad \lambda(t) = \log s(t) \qquad \mu(t) = \log u(t). \tag{5}$$

Let $A = a_1 a_2 \ldots a_k$ and $B = b_1 b_2 \ldots b_k$ be two sequences. For each $i \in \{1, \ldots, k\}$, a_i (b_i) is referred to as *position i* or *site i* of A (B). Assume that site i of B evolved from site i of A through substitution, independently of and at the same rate as the other positions according to the Markov model just described. Then, the probability that B evolved from sequence A in t time units is given by

$$h_{AB}(t) = \prod_{i=1}^{k} m_{a_i b_i}^{(t)} \tag{6}$$

This expression can be simplified for the JC and K2P models. For the JC model, taking logarithms and using (5), we have

$$\log h_{AB}(t) = \kappa(t) \cdot x + \lambda(t) \cdot y, \tag{7}$$

where x is the number of matches and y is the number of mismatches. Similarly, for the K2P model, we have

$$\log h_{AB}(t) = \kappa(t) \cdot x + \lambda(t) \cdot y + \mu(t) \cdot z, \tag{8}$$

where x, y, z are the number of matches, transversions and transitions, respectively.

2.2   Phylogenies for Molecular Sequences

Let S be a multiset $\{A_1, \dots, A_n\}$ of DNA sequences of length k. An *evolutionary tree* or *phylogeny* for S is a rooted tree T whose leaves are labeled by S. Each edge e of T has a *length* l_e that gives the evolutionary distance between its two endpoints.

The internal nodes of a phylogeny T for S represent unknown ancestral sequences. An *internal labeling* for T is a mapping X that assigns a sequence X_v of length k to each node v of T. For each leaf w, X_w must equal the sequence from S that labels w.

Assume that evolution along the edges of T obeys a Markov process, as described in the previous section. Let $r(T)$ denote the root of T; for every $v \in T - r(T)$, $p(v)$ denotes the parent of v and $e(v)$ is the edge $(p(v), v)$. The *likelihood* of an internal labeling X for T is

$$L_X = \prod_{v \in T - r(T)} h_{X_{p(v)} X_v}(l_{e(v)}) \tag{9}$$

The *score* of an internal labeling X for T is the logarithm of the L_X. The score is clearly a function of the edge lengths. Here we consider only the simplest case, the *uniform* model, where all edges have the same length t. In this case, if evolution proceeds according to the JC model, the score of an internal labeling X is

$$score(X, t) = \kappa(t) \cdot x + \lambda(t) \cdot y, \tag{10}$$

where x and y are the number of matches and mismatches in X, respectively. Under the K2P model, the score becomes

$$score(X, t) = \kappa(t) \cdot x + \lambda(t) \cdot y + \mu(t) \cdot z, \tag{11}$$

where x, y, and z are the number of matches, transitions, and transversions in X.

Given a phylogeny T and a set of transition probabilities, the *ancestral reconstruction problem* is to find the most likely (that is, highest-scoring) internal labeling for T. The problem can be solved in $O(nk)$ time using the *Viterbi algorithm* [6].

2.3   Log-Odds Scoring and Gapless Local Alignment

Let s be a function that assigns a real-valued score $s(a, b)$ to every pair a, b of characters. A *gapless local alignment* (or simply an *alignment* for short) of two sequences $A = a_1 a_2 \dots a_n$ and $B = b_1 b_2 \dots b_m$ is a pair of equal-length consecutive subsequences $a_i a_{i+1} \dots a_{i+l-1}$ and $b_j b_{j+1} \dots b_{j+l-1}$ from A and B; its *score* is $\sum_{r=0}^{l-1} s(a_{i+r}, b_{j+r})$. The *optimum gapless alignment problem* is to find a maximum-score gapless alignment. Intuitively, the goal is to identify highly-related subsequences of two given sequences. The optimum gapless local alignment can be solved in $O(nm)$ time by dynamic programming.

Log-odds scoring schemes are based on the Markov model of Section 2.1. The log-odds score of the pair a, b is the logarithm of the ratio of the probability that a and b are related through evolution and the probability that they are aligned by pure chance. Thus, if the evolutionary distance between the two sequences is t, the log-odds score for a, b is $s(a, b) = \log m_{ab}^{(t)}/q_a q_b$, where q_a, and q_b are the probabilities that bases a and b appear in any position of a sequence.

The actual values of the $s(a, b)$'s depend on t and the model of evolution. We again consider the JC and K2P models, both of which have $q_a = 1/4$ for all a [6]. Let

$$\tilde{\kappa}(t) = \kappa(t) + 4 \qquad \tilde{\lambda}(t) = \lambda(t) + 4 \qquad \tilde{\mu}(t) = \mu(t) + 4. \tag{12}$$

Thus, for the JC model, the score of an alignment $\mathcal{A}$ is given by

$$score(\mathcal{A}, t) = \tilde{\kappa}(t) \cdot x + \tilde{\lambda}(t) \cdot y, \tag{13}$$

where x and y are the number of matches and mismatches. For the K2P model, the score is

$$score(\mathcal{A}, t) = \tilde{\kappa}(t) \cdot x + \tilde{\lambda}(t) \cdot y + \tilde{\mu}(t) \cdot z, \tag{14}$$

where x, y, and z are the number of matches, transitions, and transversions in $\mathcal{A}$.

3   Parametric Problems in Sequence Evolution

The problems introduced in the previous section involve finding a maximum-score feasible solution. In each case, this solution depends on t. Our ultimate goal is to partition the positive time axis into *intervals of optimality*; that is, into maximal intervals of time within which a single solution is optimum. This partition, along with the optimum solution within each interval, gives a complete description of the score of the optimum solution as a function of t, for all $t \geq 0$. Building this parameter space decomposition is what we call the *construction problem*. While the dependence of the optimum score on time is non-linear, by working in the log domain and temporarily ignoring certain aspects of this dependency, we obtain a *linearized problem*. The auxiliary problem is easier to analyze, but nevertheless still contains all the information needed to solve the construction problem. We now study linearization and its implications.

3.1   Linearization

The optimization problems encountered in Section 2 have the following form. Let $\mathcal{F}$ denote a (finite) set of feasible solutions. Each $X \in \mathcal{F}$ has a *feature vector* $p(X) = (p_1(X), \ldots, p_d(X)) \in \mathbb{Z}^d$; each coordinate of $p(X)$ is called a *feature*. The features are weighted according to a *parameter vector* $\gamma(t) = (\gamma_1(t), \ldots, \gamma_d(t))$ to yield the *score* of X as follows:

$$score(X, t) = p(X) \cdot \gamma(t), \tag{15}$$

where "$\cdot$" denotes the dot product. The problem is to find the highest-scoring feasible solution. Its score is given by the *optimum score function*,

$$Z(t) = \max_{X \in \mathcal{F}} score(X, t). \tag{16}$$

If we ignore the constraints imposed by the dependence on t, we obtain a *linearized* problem. Abusing notation, the score function for $x \in \mathcal{F}$ in this problem is

$$score(X, \gamma) = p(X) \cdot \gamma, \tag{17}$$

and the optimum score function is

$$Z(\gamma) = \max_{X \in \mathcal{F}} score(X, \gamma). \tag{18}$$

By its definition, the Z function for the linearized problem is the *upper envelope* (that is, the point-wise maximum) of a set of linear functions [2]. Therefore, Z induces a decomposition of the parameter space, $\mathbb{R}^d$, into convex polyhedral *optimality regions*, each of which is the maximal connected set of points for which a particular feasible solution has maximum score. Since $score(X, \mathbf{0}) = 0$ for all X, the optimality regions are cones that meet at the origin. Furthermore, the following result is known.

Theorem 1 (Pachter and Sturmfels [13]). *Let A be d-parameter linearized problem whose set of feasible solutions is $\mathcal{F}$ and let $\mathcal{P} = \{p(x) : x \in \mathcal{F}\}$. Suppose that there exist integers $n_1, \ldots, n_d$ such that $\mathcal{P} \subseteq [0, n_1] \times \cdots \times [0, n_d]$. Then the optimum score function of A induces $O\left(\left(\prod_{i=1}^d n_i \right)^{(d-1)/(d+1)} \right)$ optimality regions.*

The decomposition induced by Z contains all the information needed to solve the original parametric problem in t: As t varies from 0 to $+\infty$, $\gamma(t)$ traces a curve through the parameter space defined by a set of non-linear parametric equations in t. To solve the parametric construction problem, we must identify the regions in the linearized problem that are traversed by this curve.

3.2   Parametric Ancestral Reconstruction

As seen in Section 2, under the K2P model, the score of an internal labeling X for a phylogeny T is a function of three parameters, which weigh the number of matches, transitions, and transversions in X. While we can apply Theorem 1 directly to the linearized problem, we get a better bound by reducing the number of parameters as follows. Let m denote the number of edges in T. Then, $x + y + z = km$ where k, as before, is the sequence length. Therefore, the linearized version of equation (11) for the score can be reexpressed as

$$score(\mathcal{A}, \kappa, \lambda, \mu) = \kappa \cdot km + (\lambda - \kappa) \cdot y + (\mu - \kappa) \cdot z. \qquad (19)$$

Since the term $\kappa \cdot km$ is common to all internal labelings, we can eliminate it from the score. Define $\lambda' = \lambda - \kappa$ and $\mu' = \mu - \kappa$. Then, the score function can be redefined as

$$score'(\mathcal{A}, \lambda', \mu') = \lambda' \cdot y + \mu' \cdot z. \qquad (20)$$

Note that $y, z \leq mk$ and that $m = O(n)$, where n is the number of sequences. Thus, Theorem 1 implies that the number of regions induced by Z is $O(k^{2/3}n^{2/3})$. In fact, it is convenient to examine each position's contribution to the total score of T. Denote position i's contribution by Z_i. By independence, $Z = \sum_i Z_i$. Then, by arguments similar to the one just given, Z_i induces $O(n^{2/3})$ optimality regions.

Now consider the role of t. By Equations (2), (3), (4), (12), and (13), as t varies from 0 to $+\infty$, $(\lambda'(t), \mu'(t))$ traces a monotonically increasing curve on the negative quadrant that goes from $(-\infty, -\infty)$ to $(0, 0)$. The derivative of this curve is a continuously decreasing function of t that goes from 1 to 0 (Fig. 1). On the other hand, by the structure of the linearized score function, the boundaries between optimality regions in the linearized problem are straight line segments that meet at $(0, 0)$. Therefore, the

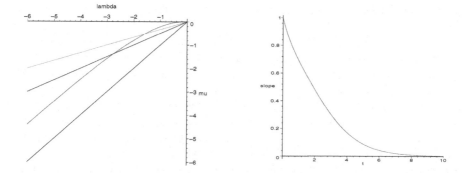

Fig. 1. Left: λ as a function of μ. The straight lines represent boundaries between regions of the decomposition. Right: Derivative of the λ-μ curve as a function of t.

curve intersects every region lying within the cone $\lambda' \leq \mu' \leq 0$ exactly once. Thus, given the space decomposition induced by the linearized problem, one can easily solve the parametric problem relative to t.

The Jukes-Cantor model only counts matches and mismatches. As we did for K2P, we can obtain a redefined score function $score'(\mathcal{A}, \lambda') = \lambda' \cdot y$, where y is the number of mismatches. Hence, for all $\lambda' < 0$, the problem is to minimize the number of mismatches; the value of λ', and thus t, is unimportant. Therefore, there is no parametric problem to study in this case.

3.3   Parametric Ungapped Alignment

Consider ungapped local alignment with log-odds scoring under the JC model. There are two parameters: the weight $\tilde{\kappa}(t)$ of the matches and the weight $\tilde{\lambda}(t)$ of the mismatches. The linearized score of an alignment $\mathcal{A}$ is $score(\mathcal{A}, \tilde{\kappa}, \tilde{\lambda}) = \tilde{\kappa} \cdot x + \tilde{\lambda} \cdot y$, where x and y are the number of matches and mismatches. Unlike the case for phylogenies, it is not possible to establish a linear relationship between x and y, so we cannot eliminate parameters. Since $0 \leq x, y \leq n$, where $n \leq m$, Theorem 1 implies that the number of optimality regions is $O(n^{2/3})$. Note that, as for the ancestral reconstruction problem, all optimality regions meet at $(0, 0)$; the boundary lines between them are rays emanating from this point.

Now consider the original non-linear problem in t. By Equations (1), (12), and (13), as t is increased from 0 to $+\infty$, $(\tilde{\kappa}(t), \tilde{\lambda}(t))$ traces a curve that goes from $(+4, -\infty)$ to $(2, 2)$, crossing the $\tilde{\lambda}$-axis at $t = (1/4\alpha) \ln(4/3)$. In the process, since $\tilde{\lambda}(t)$ is monotonically increasing, the curve intersects every optimality region of the linearized problem in the $(+, -)$ quadrant exactly once. In the positive quadrant, this curve intersects every optimality region that lies below the line $\tilde{\lambda} = \tilde{\kappa}$.

4   Algorithms for Parametric Analysis

Here we present algorithms for parametric phylogenetic analysis and parametric ungapped alignment. Both procedures are based on the same technique. The first step is to build the parameter-space decomposition induced by the linearized version of the problem. Recall that this problem ignores the constraints that probabilities must satisfy and thus considers a larger set of parameter values than actually needed. In the second step, these constraints are re-introduced. The parameters in the linearized problem are expressed as parametric equations in t. These equations define a curve that intersects with successive regions of the decomposition as t is varied from 0 to $+\infty$. To solve the parametric construction problem, we simply find these regions. Due to space limitations, we restrict our attention to the first step.

We construct the space decomposition induced by the linearized parametric problems by relying on dynamic programming algorithms for their fixed-parameter versions. These algorithms use two operations on real numbers: addition and finding the maximum. Instead of running the algorithms for a single parameter, we execute them for *all* parameter values. Instead of manipulating real numbers, the parametric algorithms work with piecewise linear convex functions. Instead of addition of real numbers, the modified algorithms add piecewise linear convex functions of the parameters, and instead of taking maxima of numbers, they compute upper envelopes of piecewise linear convex functions. This is similar to Pachter and Sturmfels' polytope propagation method [12, 13], with two differences. A minor one is that polytope propagation works in the dual space of convex hulls, while our method works in the original space of upper envelopes. A more significant difference is that the absence of gaps allows us to use divide-and-conquer. This leads to algorithms that solve optimization problems for all evolutionary distances in time that closely matches that needed to solve them for a fixed distance.

4.1   Parametric Ancestral Reconstruction

Our main result is the following.

Theorem 2. *The parametric ancestral reconstruction problem under the uniform Kimura 2-parameter model can be solved in time* $O(kn + kn^{2/3} \log k)$.

Exploiting the independence assumption, our algorithm processes each position separately. For each $i \in \{1, \ldots, k\}$, it constructs a function $Z_i(\lambda, \mu)$ that gives the optimum score for position i as a function of λ and μ. As noted in Section 3, we are only interested in the negative quadrant of the λ–μ plane. Furthermore, observe that, since the score of any internal labeling is 0 at $(0, 0)$, all optimality regions are cones that meet at the origin. This implies that to determine all the optimality regions in the quadrant of interest, we can fix one of the parameters, say λ, at any negative value, say -1, while varying the other. This reduces the dimensionality of the problem by one, and leaves us with convex piecewise linear functions of one parameter. Such functions consist of a succession of line segments that meet at *breakpoints*. The projection of these breakpoints onto the μ axis partitions it into a sequence of intervals. An important property of convex piecewise linear functions of one parameter is that the upper envelope and the sum of two such functions can be computed in time linear in their total number of breakpoints. Suppose we have $Z_i(\lambda, \mu)$ for each i. Then, the optimum score function is $Z(\lambda, \mu) = \sum_i Z_i(\lambda, \mu)$. As seen in Section 3, the number of optimality regions induced by Z_i is $O(n^{2/3})$. We can compute the sum of the Z_i's by a process similar to merging. We pair the functions arbitrarily and the sum of each pair is computed. The resulting functions are paired again and their sum computed. The pairing and adding process is repeated until a single function remains. There $\log k$ iterations of pairing and adding; there are $k/2^{j-1}$ functions at the jth iteration, each with $O(2^{j-1}n^{2/3})$ breakpoints. Thus, the total time to compute Z in this way is $O(kn^{2/3}\log k)$.

We claim that each Z_i can be constructed in $O(n)$ time. Due to space limitations, we illustrate the main ideas of the algorithm by considering the special case where the phylogeny T is a perfectly balanced, rooted binary tree. We traverse T in post-order. Thus, when processing a vertex v of T, each of its children u and w have already been processed. To process v means to obtain, for each possible base $a \in \{A, C, T, G\}$, the function $Z_{v,a}(\lambda, \mu)$ giving the score of the optimum internal labeling for the subtree rooted at v, given that position i of the sequence labeling v has base a. Denote this by $Z_i^{(v)}(a, \lambda, \mu)$. It is well known (see, e.g., [7]) that for each fixed choice of λ and μ,

$$Z_i^{(v)}(a, \lambda, \mu) = \max_b \left(\delta_{ab} + Z_i^{(u)}(b, \lambda, \mu) \right) + \max_b \left(\delta_{ab} + Z_i^{(w)}(b, \lambda, \mu) \right), \quad (21)$$

where δ_{ab} equals 0 if $a = b$, μ if $a \to b$ is a transition, and λ if $a \to b$ is a transversion.

Function $Z_i^{(v)}(b, \lambda, \mu)$ has the same properties as $Z_i(\lambda, \mu)$. If n denotes the number of nodes in the subtree rooted at v, $Z_i^{(v)}(b, \lambda, \mu)$ induces $O(n^{2/3})$ optimality regions. Also, to construct the function, it suffices to fix λ at any negative value and treat it as a one-parameter function of μ. Since we assume that T is balanced, there are approximately $n/2$ nodes in each of the subtrees rooted at u and w, respectively. Thus, for every choice of b, functions $Z_i^{(u)}(b, \lambda, \mu)$ and $Z_i^{(w)}(b, \lambda, \mu)$ induce $O(n^{2/3})$ optimality regions. We can use Equation (21) to obtain $Z_i^{(v)}(a, \lambda, \mu)$, by replacing the addition operator for real numbers with the addition operator for functions, and the max operator for reals with the upper envelope operator for functions. The total time to construct $\max_b(\delta_{ab} + Z_i^{(u)}(b, \lambda, \mu))$ is $O(n^{2/3})$, since there are only 4 choices for b. (Note that δ_{ab} is itself λ, μ, or 0 adding it to $Z_i^{(u)}$ only takes time $O(n^{2/3})$.) Similarly, the time to build $\max_b(\delta_{ab} + Z_i^{(w)}(b, \lambda, \mu))$ is $O(n^{2/3})$. The number of regions in each of these upper envelopes is $O(n^{2/3})$. Thus, computing their sum takes time $O(n^{2/3})$. Since we assume the tree is balanced, the time $T(n)$ needed to process the subtree rooted at v satisfies the recurrence $T(n) = 2T(n/2) + O(n^{2/3})$. The solution is $T(n) = O(n)$. Since the same procedure must be applied for all positions, the total time is $O(kn)$, which proves the theorem.

The result can be extended to trees that are not balanced using *centroid decomposition*, a technique used to evaluate expressions in trees [4] and which has been applied to other parametric problems [9]. Details are omitted for lack of space.

4.2 Parametric Local Alignment

Our main result is the following.

Theorem 3. *The parametric gapless alignment problem under the Jukes-Cantor model can be solved in $O(mn + mn^{2/3}\log m)$ time.*

We only sketch the proof of this result. Let $A = a_1 \ldots a_n$ and $B = b_1 \ldots b_m$ be the input sequences, where $n \le m$. As noted in Section 3, the number of regions induced by the linearized problem is $O(n^{2/3})$. Construct the usual $(n+1) \times (m+1)$ dynamic programming matrix $C = [c_{ij}]$ for the problem. Entry c_{ij} stores the cost of the optimum local alignment ending at a_i and b_j. Since no gaps are allowed, the value of any entry depends only on the entries along its same diagonal. Hence, we can consider the diagonals independently. Let $Z_i(\kappa, \lambda)$ be the optimum score function of diagonal i. It can be shown that this function induces $O(n^{2/3})$ regions. The optimum score function $Z(\kappa, \lambda)$ is given by $\max_i Z_i(\kappa, \lambda)$. We have $(m + n + 1)$ diagonals, with $O(n^{2/3})$ breakpoints along each diagonal. Therefore, by a process of pairing and taking upper envelopes (similar to the pairing and adding of the previous section), we can compute Z in time $O(m \cdot n^{2/3} \log m)$.

We compute each $Z_i(\kappa, \lambda)$ using divide-and-conquer. We split diagonal i into two equal parts, recursively find an optimum local alignment for each half, and then merge the results. This must be done with some care, since an optimal alignment for the diagonal might straddle both halves. For this reason, we obtain two alignments for each half. One of them is the best alignment that contains the common entry between the two halves; the other is the best alignment that does not contain the common entry. To combine the answers, we consider the three possible ways in which the optimum could arise (either in the first half, the second half, or straddling the two) and choose the one with maximum score. To build $Z_i(\kappa, \lambda)$, this computation must be done parametrically; that is, by adding and taking upper envelopes of piecewise linear functions. Since each of the functions involved has $O(n^{2/3})$ regions and there is only a constant number of cases, the combination can be done in $O(n^{2/3})$ time. Note that the length of a diagonal is at most $n + 1$. Thus, the recurrence for the total running time for each diagonal has the form $T(n) = 2T(n/2) + O(n^{2/3})$, which solves to $O(n)$. (Note that the recursion must be handled with care, since a subdiagonal at deeper level in the recursion may share its two endpoints in with other subdiagonals. This only increases the number of cases by a constant and does not affect the overall running time.) The total time over all diagonals is therefore $O(nm)$.

5   Discussion

Several open problems remain. First, there is the question of the parametric behavior of other Markov models of DNA evolution (for example, the Tamura-Nei model [7]) whose substitution matrices have more complex structures than those of JC and K2P. Also of interest are the various models of protein evolution. Of course, the number of distinct entries in the unit-time substitution matrices for these models is a limiting factor. Another problem is handling non-uniform edge lengths. While linearization can be applied here, the parameter dependence seems complex. One could also attempt to extend our results to models with varying rates of evolution between positions or where there are dependencies among sites. Finally, an important open problem is allowing gaps. While, at least for pairwise alignment, these can be handled by polytope propagation [13], it does not appear to be easy to attain the same efficiency as for gapless models.

References

1. P. Agarwal and D. States. A Bayesian evolutionary distance for parametrically aligned sequences. *Journal of Computational Biology*, 3:1–17, 1996.
2. P. K. Agarwal and M. Sharir. *Davenport-Schinzel Sequences and their Geometric Applications*. Cambridge University Press, Cambridge–New York–Melbourne, 1995.
3. B. Chor, A. Khetan, and S. Snir. Maximum likelihood on four taxa phylogenetic trees: analytic solutions. In *RECOMB '03: Proceedings of the seventh annual international conference on Computational molecular biology*, pages 76–83. ACM Press, 2003.
4. R. F. Cohen and R. Tamassia. Dynamic expression trees. *Algorithmica*, 13(3):245–265, 1995.
5. M. Dayhoff, R. Schwartz, and B. Orcutt. A model of evolutionary change in proteins. *Atlas of Protein Sequence and Structure*, 5:345–352, 1978.
6. R. Durbin, S. Eddy, A. Krogh, and G. Mitchison. *Biological Sequence Analysis: Probabilistic Models of Proteins and Nucleic Acids*. Cambridge University Press, 1998.
7. J. Felsenstein. *Inferring Phylogenies*. Sinauer Assoc., Sunderland, Mass, 2003.
8. D. Fernández-Baca, T. Seppäläinen, and G. Slutzki. Parametric multiple sequence alignment and phylogeny construction. *Journal of Discrete Algorithms*, 2:271–287, 2004. Special issue on Combinatorial Pattern Matching, R. Giancarlo and D. Sankoff, eds.
9. D. Fernández-Baca and G. Slutzki. Optimal parametric search on graphs of bounded treewidth. *Journal of Algorithms*, 22:212–240, 1997.
10. W. M. Fitch and T. F. Smith. Optimal sequence alignments. *Proc. Natl. Acad. Sci. USA*, 80:1382–1386, 1983.
11. D. Gusfield, K. Balasubramanian, and D. Naor. Parametric optimization of sequence alignment. *Algorithmica*, 12:312–326, 1994.
12. L. Pachter and B. Sturmfels. Parametric inference for biological sequence analysis. *Proc. Natl. Acad. Sci. USA*, 101(46):16138–16143, 2004.
13. L. Pachter and B. Sturmfels. Tropical geometry of statistical models. *Proc. Natl. Acad. Sci. USA*, 101(46):16132–16137, 2004.
14. C. Semple and M. Steel. *Phylogenetics*. Oxford Lecture Series in Mathematics. Oxford University Press, Oxford, 2003.
15. D. States, W. Gish, and S. Altschul. Improved sensitivity of nucleic acid database searches using application-specific scoring matrices. *Methods in Enzymology*, 3:66–70, 1991.
16. M. A. Steel. The maximum likelihood point for a phylogenetic tree is not unique. *Syst. Biology*, 43(4):560–564, 1994.
17. M. A. Steel and D. Penny. Parsimony, likelihood, and the role of models in molecular phylogenetics. *Molecular Biology and Evolution*, 17:839–850, 2000.
18. M. S. Waterman, M. Eggert, and E. Lander. Parametric sequence comparisons. *Proc. Natl. Acad. Sci. USA*, 89:6090–6093, 1992.

Linear Programming for Phylogenetic Reconstruction Based on Gene Rearrangements

Jijun Tang[1,*] and Bernard M.E. Moret[2]

[1] Dept. of Computer Science & Engineering, U. of South Carolina, Columbia, SC 29208
jtang@cse.sc.edu
[2] Dept. of Computer Science, U. of New Mexico, Albuquerque, NM 87131

Abstract. Phylogenetic reconstruction from gene rearrangements has attracted increasing attention from biologists and computer scientists over the last few years. Methods used in reconstruction include distance-based methods, parsimony methods using sequence-based encodings, and direct optimization. The latter, pioneered by Sankoff and extended by us with the software suite GRAPPA, is the most accurate approach, but has been limited to small genomes because the running time of its scoring algorithm grows exponentially with the number of genes in the genome. We report here on a new method to compute a tight lower bound on the score of a given tree, using a set of linear constraints generated through selective applications of the triangle inequality (in the spirit of GESTALT). Our method generates an integer linear program with a carefully limited number of constraints, rapidly solves its relaxed version, and uses the result to provide a tight lower bound. Since this bound is very close to the optimal tree score, it can be used directly as a selection criterion, thereby enabling us to bypass entirely the expensive scoring procedure. We have implemented this method within our GRAPPA software and run several series of experiments on both biological and simulated datasets to assess its accuracy. Our results show that using the bound as a selection criterion yields excellent trees, with error rates below 5% up to very large evolutionary distances, consistently beating the baseline Neighbor-Joining. Our new method enables us to extend the range of applicability of the direct optimization method to chromosomes of size comparable to those of bacteria, as well as to datasets with complex combinations of evolutionary events.

1 Introduction

Biologists can infer the ordering and strandedness of genes on a chromosome and thus represent each chromosome by an ordering of signed genes (where the sign indicates the strand). These gene orders can be rearranged by evolutionary events such as inversions and transpositions and, because they evolve slowly, give biologists an important new source of data for phylogeny reconstruction [8, 16, 18]. Appropriate tools for analyzing such data may help resolve some difficult phylogenetic reconstruction problems. Developing such tools is thus an important area of research: the recent DCAF symposium [22] was devoted to this topic, while results are rapidly accumulating [14].

---

* Contact author

A. Apostolico, M. Crochemore, and K. Park (Eds.): CPM 2005, LNCS 3537, pp. 406–416, 2005.

A natural optimization problem for phylogeny reconstruction from gene-order data is to reconstruct a tree that minimizes the total number of evolutionary events. This problem is NP-hard for most criteria – even the very simple problem of computing the median of just *three* genomes (the median of k genomes is a genome that minimizes the sum of the pairwise distances between itself and each of the k given genomes) under such models was proved NP-hard [4, 17].

For some datasets (e.g., chloroplast genomes of land plants), biologists conjecture that rearrangement events are predominantly *inversions* (also called reversals) [6]. In other datasets (e.g., mitochondrial genomes), transpositions are viewed as more likely, but their relative preponderance with respect to inversions is unknown. Sankoff proposed the *breakpoint* distance (the number of pairwise gene adjacencies present in one genome but absent in the other) as a measure of distance between genomes that is independent of any particular mechanism of rearrangement. The *breakpoint phylogeny* [1] is then the most parsimonious tree with respect to breakpoint distances. By analogy, the *inversion phylogeny* is the most parsimonious tree with respect to inversion distances.

The main software package for reconstructing the inversion (or breakpoint) phylogeny is our GRAPPA [15]. Its basic optimization tool is an algorithm for computing the inversion (or breakpoint) median of three genomes. Extensive testing has shown that the trees returned by GRAPPA are superior to those returned by other methods used in phylogenetic reconstruction based on gene orders, such as distance-based methods and parsimony based on encodings [13, 14, 29]. The closely related software of Pevzner's group, MGR [3], is the only method that approaches its accuracy. Moreover, our extension using disk-covering, DCM-GRAPPA [27], runs quickly on large datasets – indeed, the number of taxa in the dataset is no longer the main issue.

Two serious issues remain, however. Handling genomes with unequal gene content (i.e., involving duplications, insertions, and deletions of genes) remains largely unsolved, although some progress has been made in computing pairwise distances in such cases [9, 10, 25, 28]. Handling large genomes within GRAPPA is very expensive, because the median computation takes time exponential in the size of the genomes; this problem prevents its application to organismal genomes with thousands of genes. It is this second problem that we tackle here.

2   Definitions

A *phylogeny* for a set S of N genomes is a (preferably) binary tree with N leaves, with each leaf labeled by a distinct element of S. Let G be the genome with signed ordering of $g_1, g_2, \ldots, g_n$. An *inversion* between indices i and j $(i \leq j)$, produces the genome with linear ordering

$$g_1, g_2, \ldots, g_{i-1}, -g_j, -g_{j-1}, \ldots, -g_i, g_{j+1}, \ldots, g_n$$

A *transposition* on genome G acts on three indices i, j, k, with $i \leq j$ and $k \notin [i, j]$, picking up the interval $g_i, g_{i+1}, \ldots, g_j$ and inserting it immediately after g_k. Thus genome G is replaced by (assume $k > j$):

$$g_1, \ldots, g_{i-1}, g_{j+1}, \ldots, g_k, g_i, g_{i+1}, \ldots, g_j, g_{k+1}, \ldots, g_n$$

The *edit distance* between two genomes is the minimum number of evolutionary events required to transform one genome into the other. When only inversions are al-

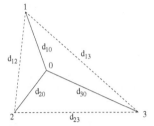

Fig. 1. The median problem: given gene orders 1, 2, and 3, find a gene-order 0 that minimizes $\sum_{i=1}^{3} d_{0,i}$.

lowed, the edit distance is the *inversion distance*. The *score* of a tree is the sum of the costs of its edges, where the cost of an edge is the distance (breakpoint or edit distance) between the two genomes that label the endpoints of the edge.

For N genomes $\{G_1, G_2, \ldots, G_N\}$, each with identical set of genes, the *median problem* is to find a signed gene order G_0 that minimizes $\sum_{i=1}^{N} d_{0,i}$, where $d_{0,i}$ is the distance between G_0 and G_i. Because our various genomic distances are all metrics, we must have

$$\sum_{i=1}^{N} d_{0,i} \geq \frac{1}{2} \left(d_{N,1} + \sum_{i=1}^{N-1} d_{i,i+1} \right)$$

When this inequality is an equality, we call the corresponding median a *perfect median*. Finding the gene order G_0 is NP-hard even for the case $N = 3$, the case (illustrated in Fig. 1) of most use in phylogenetic reconstruction [4, 17].

In the following, we will consider only genomes with *equal gene content*, that is, with the same number of genes and where each gene appears exactly once. Clearly, this restriction is unrealistic in biological practice; however, we use it here mostly for clarity of exposition: all results presented in this paper can be readily applied to genomes with unequal gene contents as long as a pairwise distance between such genomes can be computed, as in [9, 25].

3   GRAPPA

GRAPPA is based on the approach pioneered by Sankoff and Blanchette in the software package BPAnalysis [21], but uses various algorithmic techniques to improve its accuracy and speed. GRAPPA is an exhaustive search method, moving systematically through the space of all $(2N - 5)!!$ possible trees on N genomes. For each tree, the program tests a lower bound to determine whether the tree is worth scoring; if so, then the program will iteratively solve the median problems at internal nodes until convergence, as outlined in Fig. 2. Since the scoring procedure of GRAPPA involves solving numerous instances of median problems, a fast median solver is crucial. Two inversion median solvers are available, both using a branch-and-bound strategy. Caprara's solver [5] is based on an extension of the breakpoint graph; that developed by Siepel and Moret [24] runs a direct search. Although they are both fast when the pairwise distances among

```
Initially label all internal nodes with gene orders
Repeat
      For each internal node v, with neighbors A, B and C, do
      Solve median problem on A, B, C to yield m
      If relabeling v with m improves the tree score, then do it
Until no change occurs
```

Fig. 2. The GRAPPA scoring procedure.

the three given genomes are relatively small, they can become extremely slow when the distances become larger. For example, in the worst case, Siepel's algorithm needs to check n^d gene orders, where d is $min(d_{12}+d_{13},d_{21}+d_{23},d_{13}+d_{23})$ and n is the number of genes (see Fig. 1). Indeed, for large genomes, a single median problem can take anywhere from seconds to days of computation. It is thus crucial to avoid scoring trees unnecessarily and thus to use tight lower bounds.

4   Lower Bounding with Perfect Medians

Siepel and Moret [24] reported that almost all medians found by their algorithms were perfect medians, i.e., they obeyed

$$\sum_{i=1}^{3} d_{0,i} = \frac{d_{1,2}+d_{1,3}+d_{2,3}}{2}$$

When the pairwise distances were about $0.1n$, all medians were perfect; as the distances increased, the proportion of perfect medians decreased slowly – for instance, over 97% of the medians remained perfect with pairwise distances around $0.3n$ [23]. Moreover, even when the medians were not perfect, their scores exceeded the lower bound by only one inversion. These findings indicate that an assumption that all medians are perfect may lead to a tight lower bound.

Label a phylogenetic tree with N leaves as follows; the leaves are labeled from the set $\{1,2,\ldots,N\}$, while the internal nodes (of which there are at most $N-2$) are labeled from the set $\{N+1,N+2,\ldots,2N-2\}$; we number the edges from 1 to $2N-3$ and denote the length of edge i by d_i, as illustrated in Fig. 3.

Theorem 1. *The sum of the perfect median scores (over all internal tree nodes) is a lower bound on the tree score; that is, we have (see Fig. 3):*

$$w(T) = \sum_{i=1}^{2N-3} d_i \geq \frac{(d_{1,2}+d_{1,N+2}+d_{2,N+2})+\ldots+(d_{N-1,N}+d_{2N-3,N-1}+d_{2N-3,N})}{2}$$

Because most medians are perfect, this lower bound is very close – or perhaps even equal – to the tree score. Of course, we cannot compute this lower bound exactly without first solving the median problems, which would defeat the entire purpose of bounding. So we settle for a close approximation of that bound through mathematical programming.

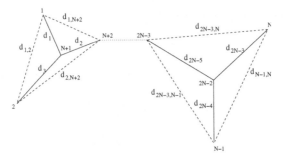

Fig. 3. Perfect medians for internal nodes.

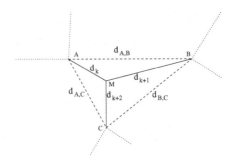

Fig. 4. Equation setup for any internal nodes.

5   Setting up the Integer Linear Program

An integer linear program is composed of a linear objective function and of a collection of constraints, most taking the form of linear equations or inequations and some requiring that certain variables assume only integer values. The scoring function for our method is just the length of the tree; that is, our objective is to minimize the sum of the tree edge lengths:

$$\min \sum_{i=1}^{2N-3} d_i \tag{1}$$

This function introduces a total of $2N - 3$ variables.

Given any internal node M, its three neighbors A, B. and C, and their associated tree edges k, $k+1$, and $k+2$ (see Fig. 4), we can write (if M is a perfect median):

$$d_k + d_{k+1} + d_{k+2} = \frac{d_{A,B} + d_{A,C} + d_{B,C}}{2} \tag{2}$$

Each of the $N - 2$ internal nodes gives rise to one such equation, which we use as an equality constraint in the integer linear program. (This approach was previously used in the sequence alignment program GESTALT [12] to help in deriving good sequence assignments for internal nodes.) Equation 2 introduces three new variables per node (the pairwise distances $d_{A,B}$, $d_{A,C}$, and $d_{B,C}$), unless two of the node's neighbors are leaves, in which case only two new variables are introduced (because one of the pairwise distances is then known). Thus, overall, Equations 1 and 2 (the latter applied at each internal node) introduce from $4N$ to $5N$ variables, depending on the tree shape. Therefore we must add many constraints (beyond our $N-2$ equalities) in order to obtain a solution.

A good selection of constraints derived from triangle inequalities in the tree should meet the following criteria:

- Since the only available data are in the distance matrix, we should use every pairwise distance in the set of constraints.
- Because LP solvers take more time when the number of constraints increases and because many constraints will be redundant, the number of constraints should be kept as small as possible.
- In order to obtain robust solutions, every variable added by Equations 1 and 2 should appear in at least one constraint.

Consider again Fig. 4: in addition to the edges of the tree (drawn with uninterrupted lines), we have shown the pairwise connections among the three neighbors of an internal node (drawn with dashed lines). By considering the graph resulting from the addition of these edges connecting neighbors of internal nodes to the the set of edges of the original tree, we get a graph with many alternate paths. We base our additional constraints on the distances between pairs of tree leaves, as measured directly and as measured along paths in the extended graph. Specifically, for each pair (i, j) of leaves, we can write the inequality

$$d_{i,j} \leq \sum_{e \in \text{path}} d(e)$$

where $d_{i,j}$ is the genomic distance between the two gene orders i and j and $d(e)$ is the length of edge e on the selected path from leaf i to leaf j in the graph. Since there are $\binom{n}{2}$ pairs of leaves, we immediately get a large number of constraints.

However, a number of edges in the extended graph may remain unused in any constraint; to remedy this problem, we generate *two* inequalities for each pair of leaves that are not siblings: one each for the two paths between these leaves with fewest edges. Finding the k shortest paths between two vertices in a graph is a thoroughly studied problem [11] and is easily done, especially when the length is just the number of edges. Using the two shortest paths will produce $N(N-2)$ inequality constraints, which works well in our context, for three reasons:

- Each pairwise distance shows up in at least one inequality constraints.
- For 20 genomes (the largest problem size we need to solve within the DCM approach), we get on the order of 100 variables and 400 constraints, an instance of quite modest size for a modern LP solver.
- There are roughly N^2 constraints and at most $5N$ variables, so that, on average, a variable will appear in $\frac{N}{5}$ constraints. Thus the probability that a variable does not appear in any constraint is very small.

6   Implementation Details

We implemented this bounding computation within our GRAPPA platform. We do not solve the integer linear program, but only its linear programming relaxation: the ILP itself is already an approximation and would take too long to solve exactly and many techniques (such as randomized rounding) are readily available to use LP solutions in order to obtain a good integer solution. We used a standard non-commercial package for linear programming, lp_solve (version 4.0).

The new bound can be used in two different contexts: (i) we can use it to improve the pruning rate of GRAPPA; or (ii) we can use it directly as a selection criterion. The current version of GRAPPA (2.0) already has very fast and strong pruning (often eliminating 99.9999% of the candidate trees); the LP bound, which is noticeably more expensive to compute than the bounds currently used in GRAPPA, can be used to filter the remaining trees in order further to reduce the number of trees that must be scored.

The LP bound offers (so far) no help in scoring a tree: the problem with medians of large genomes remains unaffected. Thus, while the first application of the LP bound does provide additional speedup for GRAPPA, it does not yet enable us to handle large genomes. The second application enables us to process trees quickly: we retain the pruning strategy of GRAPPA and simply compute a "score" (the LP lower bound) for each remaining tree, retaining those trees with the best score. With this approach, the size of the genomes no longer presents any computational problem, so that we can handle datasets of up to 16 arbitrarily large genomes with GRAPPA and much larger datasets with DCM-GRAPPA.

7   Experimental Results

We set out to test the accuracy of the second approach described above: using the LP bound as a direct selection criterion to choose among the trees not pruned away by GRAPPA. For this purpose, we generated datasets of 12 genomes each (datasets of that size form the bulk of the subproblems solved in the DCM approach to reconstruction from gene-order data when working on datasets of 1,000 genomes [27]) and chose genomes of 200, 500, and 1,000 genes, spanning the range from large organelles (such as plant mitochondria) to small bacteria (such as symbiotic bacteria). Our model trees are birth-death trees, but the number of evolutionary events along an edge is set independently of the birth-death process to avoid any semblance of a molecular clock. We used a large range of evolutionary rates, including very high rates: letting r denote the expected number of evolutionary events along an edge of the model tree, we used values of r in the range of 5% to 15% of the number of genes. The actual number of events along each edge is sampled from a uniform distribution on the set $\{1, 2, \ldots, 2r\}$. While all our distance computations are based on inversion distances, we generated the data with a deliberate model mismatch to test the robustness of our bounding, using a mix of 80% inversions and 20% transpositions. For each combination of parameter settings, we ran 10 datasets and averaged the results.

Given an inferred tree (reconstructed phylogeny), we can assess the topological accuracy in terms of *false positives* and *false negatives* [19] with respect to the true tree. If an edge in the true tree is missing in the inferred tree, this edge is then called a *false negative* (FN). Similarly, a *false positive* edge (FP) is an edge in the inferred tree but not in the true tree. The FP and FN rates are the number of false positives (resp., false negatives) divided by the number of edges (of non-zero length) in the true tree.

Our baseline is the basic neighbor-joining (NJ) method [20]. We considered all trees given the minimum score by our LP procedure and took their strict consensus. Therefore, the trees returned by our procedure need not be fully resolved and will tend to have somewhat better rates for false positives (FP) than for false negatives (FN). Thus we report FP and FN rates separately rather than as a single Robinson-Foulds score. We attempted to run GRAPPA on these datasets, but, for all but the lowest of the r values, some median computations took days or weeks. In consequence, we could not complete the runs, so that our comparisons are limited to NJ and our new LP-based method.

Fig. 5 shows our results for each genome size; we placed a line at the 5% error level, the typical threshold of acceptability for accuracy in phylogenetic reconstruction [26]. Note that, while the NJ trees almost always exceed the 5% error rate in both FP and FN, our LP-based method only exceeds that threshold for very large evolutionary rates; for instance, with 200 genes and $r = 28$, some edges will have up to 56 inversions and

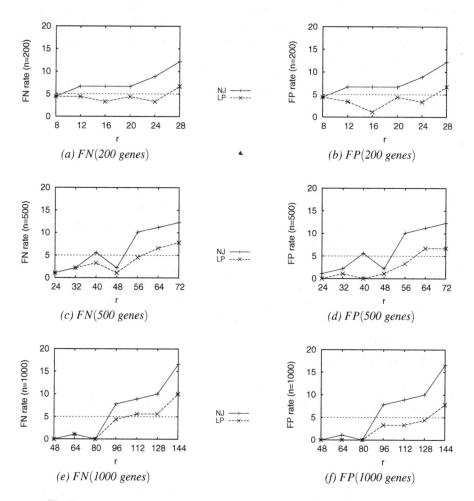

(a) FN(200 genes)   *(b) FP(200 genes)*

(c) FN(500 genes)   *(d) FP(500 genes)*

(e) FN(1000 genes)   *(f) FP(1000 genes)*

Fig. 5. Average FN and FP rates as a function of r for 200, 500, and 1,000 genes.

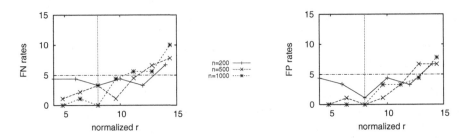

Fig. 6. Average FN (left) and FP (right) rates as a function of the normalized $\frac{r}{n}$ (the vertical line indicates when LP becomes significantly better than NJ).

transpositions, resulting in well over 100 breakpoints. In Fig. 6, we show the FP and FN rates for all three genome sizes, as a function of the ratio $\frac{r}{n}$ – the expected percentage of events per edge in terms of genome size. Again, note that, when the normalized r is 15%, the breakpoint distance could reach 70% of the genome size – values at which all past reconstruction methods based on distance fail as badly as NJ; in contrast, our new LP bound still selects good trees at that rate.

We also ran our procedure on small chloroplast datasets that we have used in the past (the Campanulaceae [7] and some land plants and algae [28]), with similar results.

8   Conclusions

We have used mathematical programming techniques to derive tight bounds on the total length (score) of a phylogenetic tree and have used these bounds as a selection crite- rion to reconstruct small phylogenies based on gene-order data for genomic sizes that had been out of reach of existing reconstruction tools. Our experiments show that the method works well, returning trees with accurate (better than 95%) topologies up to very large evolutionary rates. While we have not applied the method to the reconstruc- tion of ancestral genomes (and the solution of the median problem for genomes), we expect that knowledge of the edge lengths (provided by the LP solution) will enable us to speed up such reconstruction dramatically, thereby removing the last scaling problem left in phylogenetic reconstruction from gene-order data.

Acknowledgments

This work is supported by the US National Science Foundation under grants ANI 02- 03584, EF 03-31654, IIS 01-13095, IIS 01-21377, and DEB 01-20709, and by the Dept. of Computer Science and Engineering at U. of South Carolina.

References

1. M. Blanchette, G. Bourque, and D. Sankoff. Breakpoint phylogenies. In S. Miyano and T. Takagi, editors, *Genome Informatics 1997*, pages 25–34. Univ. Academy Press, 1997.

2. M. Berkelaar, K. Eikland, and P. Notebaert. lp_solve Available at www.geocities.com/lpsolve/.

3. G. Bourque and P. Pevzner. Genome-scale evolution: reconstructing gene orders in the ancestral species. *Genome Research*, 12:26–36, 2002.

4. A. Caprara. Formulations and hardness of multiple sorting by reversals. In *Proc. 3rd Ann. Int'l Conf. Comput. Mol. Biol. (RECOMB'99)*, pages 84–93. ACM Press, New York, 1999.

5. A. Caprara. On the practical solution of the reversal median problem. In *Proc. 1st Int'l Workshop Algs. in Bioinformatics (WABI'01)*, volume 2149 of *Lecture Notes in Computer Science*, pages 238–251. Springer Verlag, 2001.

6. Cosner, M.E., R.K. Jansen, J.D. Palmer and S.R. Downie SR (1997)   The highly rearranged chloroplast genome of Trachelium caeruleum (Campanulaceae): multiple inversions, inverted repeat expansion and contraction, transposition, insertions/deletions, and several repeat families. *Curr Genet 1997*, 31:419-429.

7. M.E. Cosner, R.K. Jansen, B.M.E. Moret, L.A. Raubeson, L. Wang, T. Warnow, and S.K. Wyman.   A new fast heuristic for computing the breakpoint phylogeny and experimental phylogenetic analyses of real and synthetic data. In *Proc. 8th Int'l Conf. on Intelligent Systems for Mol. Biol. (ISMB'00)*, pages 104–115, 2000.

8. S.R. Downie and J.D. Palmer.   Use of chloroplast DNA rearrangements in reconstructing plant phylogeny. In P. Soltis, D. Soltis, and J.J. Doyle, editors, *Plant Molecular Systematics*, pages 14–35. Chapman and Hall, 1992.

9. J. Earnest-DeYoung, E. Lerat, and B.M.E. Moret.   Reversing gene erosion: reconstructing ancestral bacterial genomes from gene-content and gene-order data. In *Proc. 4th Int'l Workshop Algs. in Bioinformatics (WABI'04)*, volume 3240 of *Lecture Notes in Computer Science*, pages 1–13. Springer Verlag, 2004.

10. N. El-Mabrouk. Genome rearrangement by reversals and insertions/deletions of contiguous segments. In *Proc. 11th Ann. Symp. Combin. Pattern Matching (CPM'00)*, volume 1848 of *Lecture Notes in Computer Science*, pages 222–234. Springer Verlag, 2000.

11. D. Eppstein. Finding the k shortest paths. *SIAM J. on Computing*, 28(2):652–673, 1998.

12. G. Lancia and R. Ravi, GESTALT: GEnomic STeiner ALignmenTs. In *Proc. 10th Ann. Symp. Combin. Pattern Matching (CPM'99)*, volume 1645 of *Lecture Notes in Computer Science*, pages 101–114. Springer Verlag, 1999.

13. B.M.E. Moret, J. Tang, L.-S. Wang, and T. Warnow. Steps toward accurate reconstructions of phylogenies from gene-order data. *J. Comput. Syst. Sci.*, 65(3):508–525, 2002.

14. B.M.E. Moret, J. Tang, and T. Warnow. Reconstructing phylogenies from gene-content and gene-order data. In O. Gascuel, editor, *Mathematics of Evolution and Phylogeny*, pages 321–352. Oxford University Press, 2005.

15. B.M.E. Moret, S.K. Wyman, D.A. Bader, T. Warnow, and M. Yan. A new implementation and detailed study of breakpoint analysis. In *Proc. 6th Pacific Symp. on Biocomputing (PSB'01)*, pages 583–594. World Scientific Pub., 2001.

16. J.D. Palmer. Chloroplast and mitochondrial genome evolution in land plants. In R. Herrmann, editor, *Cell Organelles*, pages 99–133. Springer Verlag, 1992.

17. I. Pe'er and R. Shamir. The median problems for breakpoints are NP-complete. *Elec. Colloq. on Comput. Complexity*, 71, 1998.

18. L.A. Raubeson and R.K. Jansen. Chloroplast DNA evidence on the ancient evolutionary split in vascular land plants. *Science*, 255:1697–1699, 1992.

19. D.R. Robinson and L.R. Foulds. Comparison of phylogenetic trees. *Mathematical Biosciences*, 53:131–147, 1981.

20. N. Saitou and M. Nei. The neighbor-joining method: A new method for reconstructing phylogenetic trees. *Mol. Biol. Evol.*, 4:406–425, 1987.

21. D. Sankoff and M. Blanchette. Multiple genome rearrangement and breakpoint phylogeny. *J. Comput. Biol.*, 5:555–570, 1998.

22. D. Sankoff and J. Nadeau, editors. *Comparative Genomics.* Kluwer Academic Pubs., Dordrecht, Netherlands, 2000.
23. A.C. Siepel. Exact algorithms for the reversal median problem. Master's thesis, U. New Mexico, Albuquerque, NM, 2001. Available at www.cs.unm.edu/~acs/thesis.html.
24. A.C. Siepel and B.M.E. Moret. Finding an optimal inversion median: experimental results. In *Proc. 1st Int'l Workshop Algs. in Bioinformatics (WABI'01)*, volume 2149 of *Lecture Notes in Computer Science*, pages 189–203. Springer Verlag, 2001.
25. K.M. Swenson, M. Marron, J.V. Earnest-DeYoung, and B.M.E. Moret. Approximating the true evolutionary distance between two genomes. In *Proc. 7th Workshop on Alg. Engineering & Experiments (ALENEX'05)*, Vancouver (2005), SIAM Press.
26. D.L. Swofford, G. Olson, P. Waddell, and D.M. Hillis. Phylogenetic inference. In D.M. Hillis, C. Moritz, and B. Mable, editors, *Molecular Systematics, 2nd ed.*, chapter 11. Sinauer Associates, 1996.
27. J. Tang and B.M.E. Moret. Scaling up accurate phylogenetic reconstruction from gene-order data. In *Proc. 11th Int'l Conf. on Intelligent Systems for Mol. Biol. (ISMB'03)*, volume 19 of *Bioinformatics*, pages i305–i312. Oxford U. Press, 2003.
28. J. Tang, B.M.E. Moret, L. Cui, and C.W. dePamphilis. Phylogenetic reconstruction from arbitrary gene-order data. In *Proc. 4th IEEE Symp. on Bioinformatics and Bioengineering BIBE'04*, pages 592–599. IEEE Press, Piscataway, NJ, 2004.
29. L.-S. Wang, R.K. Jansen, B.M.E. Moret, L.A. Raubeson, and T. Warnow. Fast phylogenetic methods for genome rearrangement evolution: An empirical study. In *Proc. 7th Pacific Symp. on Biocomputing (PSB'02)*, pages 524–535. World Scientific Pub., 2002.

Identifying Similar Surface Patches on Proteins Using a Spin-Image Surface Representation

Mary Ellen Bock[1], Guido M. Cortelazzo[2],
Carlo Ferrari[2], and Concettina Guerra[2]

[1] Department of Statistics, Purdue University, USA
mbock@stat.purdue.edu
[2] Department of Information Engineering, University of Padova, Italy
{corte,carlo,guerra}@dei.unipd.it

Abstract. We apply a spin image representation for 3D objects used in computer vision to the problem of comparing protein surfaces. Due to the irregularities of the protein surfaces, this is a much more complex problem than comparing regular and smooth surfaces. The spin images capture local features in a way that is useful for finding related active sites on the surface of two proteins. They reduce the three-dimensional local information to two dimensions which is a significant computational advantage.

We try to find a collection of pairs of points on the two proteins such that the corresponding members of the pairs for one of the proteins form a surface patch for which the corresponding spin images are a "match". Preliminary results are presented which demonstrate the feasibility of the method.

1   Introduction

We propose a solution to the problem of matching protein surfaces based on a protein surface representation as a set of two-dimensional (2D) images thus transforming the problem of matching 3D surfaces into that of matching sets of 2D images. This method can detect similar binding sites in proteins and is particularly useful when the proteins are unrelated by sequence or overall fold. It does not look for a predefined template of a binding site, rather it identifies similar spatial arrangements in proteins without any prior knowledge. We try to find a collection of pairs of points on the two proteins such that the corresponding members of the pairs for one of the proteins form a surface patch for which the corresponding spin images are a "match". Our approach is purely geometrical. At the present we do not take into consideration other physico-chemical properties of the atoms. These will be integrated later in the matching strategy to help eliminate unlikely solutions.

Spin images were introduced in the area of computer vision by [6] as an efficient way of solving the object recognition and reconstruction problems. The main contribution of this paper is the adaptation of the spin image technique

A. Apostolico, M. Crochemore, and K. Park (Eds.): CPM 2005, LNCS 3537, pp. 417–428, 2005.

to the problem of protein surface matching. Molecular surfaces have very complicated shapes and are not as smooth as the objects generally considered in computer vision. Thus the use of spin images for molecular recognition requires significant variations of the original matching strategy.

There are several methods for recognizing spatial motifs in proteins, that mostly deal with the problem of detecting a given template for a predefined cluster of atoms in a protein structure. Good surveys are [1] and [13]. Geometric hashing has been applied to molecular recognition by [12] and by [14]. The method by [10] looks for spatial arrangements of atoms that can be superimposed by a rigid transformation. A database for molecular surfaces of protein's functional sites is by [7]. An application of the search method to protein kinases and to phosphate binding sites is presented in [8]. Other tools for searching for predefined motifs consisting of constellations of atoms are SPASM and RIGOR ([9]).

The organization of the paper is the following. Section 2 contains a short review of the spin image concept. Section 3 presents a new way of labeling protein surface points based on certain features of their associated spin images. This labeling captures important geometric information thus allowing to significantly reduce the amount of computation needed to identify matching points. Furthermore, based on this labeling, a filtering operation can be applied to the spin images to eliminate redundant information.

Collections of matched points are obtained from individual good matches if some geometric consistency criteria are satisfied by nearby points on the surfaces. To facilitate the grouping of points into surface patches, all input surface points are mapped into a 3D matrix or grid and the matching restricted to points within cells of the grids. The grouping and matching is described in section 4. Finally, section 5 reports on preliminary results of the matching strategy applied to known examples from the literature.

2   Spin Images

The concept of spin images, due to [6], will be recalled here. Consider a three-dimensional point P on the protein surface and its normal $\mathbf{n}$ oriented to the outside of the protein surface; introduce a local coordinate system or two dimensional basis (P, n) with origin in P and axis $\mathbf{n}$. In this system, for every other surface point Q define two coordinates (α, β) as follows: α is the perpendicular distance of Q to $\mathbf{n}$, and β the signed perpendicular distance of Q to the plane $\mathbf{T}$ through P perpendicular to $\mathbf{n}$. The two coordinates are called spin coordinates because of the cylindrical symmetry about the normal axis of the system: the basis can spin about its axis $\mathbf{n}$ with no effect on the coordinates of points with respect to the basis itself.

For a given reference point P, the spin coordinates of all other surface points are discretized in a two dimensional array called spin image. The array is an accumulator of the pairs of values (α, β) relative to the surface points. Each cell of the array or image pixel contains the number of surface points whose coordinates provide indexes to that cell.

The spin image of point P is created by the following simple procedure (see [6]). For each point Q on the surface, its spin coordinates (α, β) in the local reference frame of P are determined as follows:

$$\alpha = \sqrt{\|Q - P\|^2 - (n \cdot (Q - P))^2}$$
$$\beta = n \cdot (Q - P)$$

If the point Q satisfies some requirements to be described later, the values (α, β) are discretized to produce two integers that are used as indexes to a 2D spin image array, where the corresponding image pixel or cell is incremented by one. Figure 1 shows examples of spin images, where (α_i, β_j) are the column index and row index, respectively, and the origin O is the cell (0,0). The images are displayed with darker pixels corresponding to higher accumulator value.

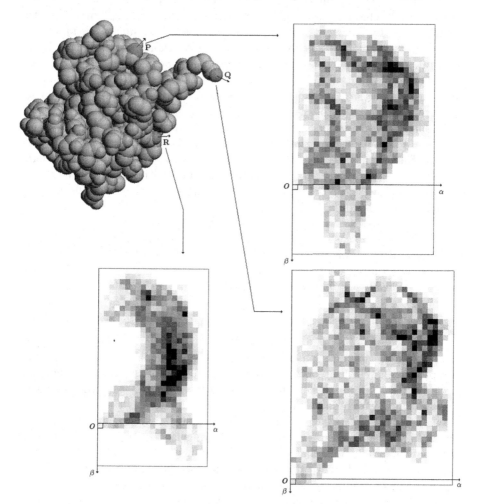

Fig. 1. Examples of spin images

The spin image dimensions depend on the point P and its corresponding tangent plane and corresponding normal $\mathbf{n}$ to its tangent plane T. The number of columns depends on the maximum distance α_{max} from $\mathbf{n}$ of other points on the surface of the object. The number of rows depends on the difference between the maximum β_{max} and minimum β_{min} heights of other points on the surface. Another important parameter which determines the spin image dimension, that is the number h of its rows and k of columns of the spin image, is the pixel size ϵ. If $\beta_r = \beta_{max} - \beta_{min}$ then,

$$h = \lfloor \frac{\beta_r}{\epsilon} \rfloor; k = \lfloor \frac{\alpha_{max}}{\epsilon} \rfloor \tag{1}$$

We choose ϵ equal the water molecule radius, i.e. 1.5 Å.

To control the amount of information contained in a spin image, some restriction is introduced on the portion of space swept out by a spin image. In the original paper by Johnson, two parameters are used, the *support distance* that limits the max value for the coordinate of any point represented in a spin image and the *support angle* that is the maximum angle between n and the surface normal of points that are allowed to contribute to the spin image. By changing the values of the control parameters, the information represented in a spin image can vary from global to local.

In our approach, all surface points that lie above the tangent plane T in the direction of $\mathbf{n}$ contribute to the spin image of P. Those are the points with positive β values in the reference frame of P. Points with negative β are considered only when $\beta > TB$ where TB is a threshold set to -8 Å in our experiments. No limitation is imposed on α that is by definition positive. Thus the spin image is defined for $\alpha \geq 0$ and $\beta \geq TB$.

As a last note, the use of a 2D rather than a complete 3D coordinate system is motivated by the ease and robustness of the computation. Systems based on 3D frames, defined, for instance, by the three axes of principal curvature, have also been used for matching purposes, however since the determination of the axes is not always possible they are not very robust.

3   Matching Surface Points

Protein surface computation is performed using Connolly's method [3], based on a probe sphere rolling on the VanDerWaal surface of the protein. The lower envelope of the probe is then the protein surface. Among the various formats of the output, we chose the dots format, that describes the external surface as a cloud of 3D points each with its associated surface normal. The number of generated points (and hence the accuracy of the surface description) is dependent on the sphere radius: the larger the probe radius the lower the accuracy. We decided to use a probe with the dimension almost like that of a water molecule, with a radius of around 1.5 Å, as the default in Connolly's method.

The first step of our matching procedure consists of matching individual points on the two surfaces based on their associated spin images. Points on two surfaces with similar shape tend to have similar spin images. [6] introduced a method of measuring the similarity between two 2D spin images based on the linear correlation coefficient. Given two images each with $N = n \times m$ pixels, R is defined to be the linear correlation coefficient for the two sets of pixels. The non independence of the pixels on the same spin image does not appear to cause a serious problem for the matching when the filtering methods given below are used. A high value of R indicates similarity of the two spin images.

Because our generated spin images may have different sizes, the correlation value is computed on the two sub-images that overlap. More precisely, if the two spin images have size $n_1 \times m_1$ and $n_2 \times m_2$, then the correlation is determined on the two sub-images with dimensions $n = \min\{n_1, n_2\}$ and $m = \min\{m_1, m_2\}$.

The number of pairwise image comparison to identify corresponding points based on the correlation of their spin images is $O(s * t)$, where s and t are the number of points that describe the two protein surfaces, respectively. This product is usually very large even for small protein sizes. For instance for the two proteins 1CYN (cyclophilin B) and 1BCK (cyclophiln A) considered in the section 5 with surfaces represented by about 10,000 dots each, the number of image comparisons would be about 10^8.

To speed up the computation, we apply two levels of filtering. The first level uses a labeling of surface points into *shadowed, blocked* or *clear*, based on certain features of their associated spin images. This labeling is fast and furthermore captures important geometric information that is relevant to the matching process. Thus we can restrict correspondences to points with the same label, a significant computational advantage.

To further reduce the computation time we do some pruning on the spin image list generated for the two proteins. For each atom on a protein surface there are typically several surface dots associated to it in the Connolly's representation. We try to limit the number of such dots again exploiting the similarity of their spin images. These two steps are described next.

3.1   Labeling Protein Surface Points

We label the protein surface points as *shadowed, blocked* or *clear* and restrict the correspondences in the matching process to points with the same label. As we will see this labeling can be easily obtained from the spin images.

First, a surface point P with normal **n** is labeled *unblocked* if **n** does not intersect the surface at any other point lying above the tangent plane T at P perpendicular to **n**. Because of discretization of spin coordinates, defining a point P as an unblocked point means that the normal **n** is at a distance greater than ϵ, the spin image pixel size, from any other surface point lying above the tangent plane T. This implies that in the reference frame for the spin image there should not be other surface points with coordinates $\beta > 0$ and $\alpha = 0$. A point is *blocked* if it is not unblocked. Our labeling scheme is different from previously used surface point classifications based on identifying geometric convexity. In fact, an unblocked point can belong either to a convex region on the surface or to a concave one.

Among the unblocked points we select those that belong to the convex hull of the protein surface. These are labeled *clear* points. If P is a *clear* point, then all other surface points are either on the tangent plane T or on the same side of the tangent plane, opposite to $\mathbf{n}$. Thus $h = 0$, where h is the number of rows of the spin image corresponding to $\beta \geq 0$ (in practice, $h \geq 2$).

Unblocked points which are not clear are labeled *shadowed*. Examples of shadowed, blocked and their corresponding spin images are shown in figures 2.

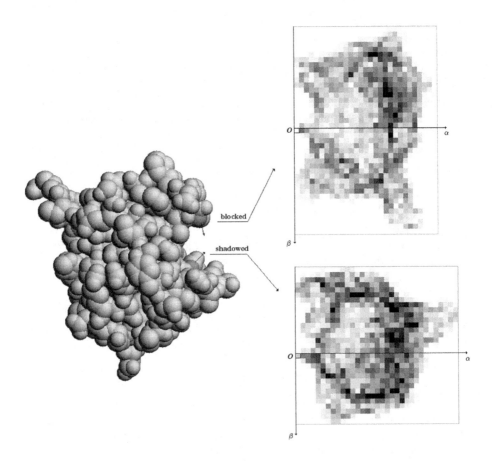

Fig. 2. Shadowed and blocked points

Once all spin images of a protein surface are created, labeling the points as shadowed, blocked or clear is computationally very simple since at most the pixels of one column of the spin image have to be examined.

An important attribute we compute for each spin image is the *visible area* defined as the number of pixels of the maximal compact connected region of 0-pixels with a border on the positive part of column 0 and contained in rows 0 through $c-1$, where $(c, 0)$ is the first non zero pixel of column 0. For a shadowed point $c-1$ is assumed to be h, the number of rows of the spin image with $\beta > 0$, since all pixels $(\beta, 0)$ with $\beta > 0$ are 0. The visible area of a shadowed point is shown in figure 3. For a blocked point P, c can be interpreted as follows. By definition, the normal $\mathbf{n}$ through a blocked point P intersects (or is close to) the protein surface at one or more other points: c is the smallest positive β of all such points. The procedure that computes the visible area is very simple since it scans all rows 0 trough $c-1$, and counts on each the number of 0-pixels until the first non zero pixel. The visible area of a clear point is assumed to be infinity.

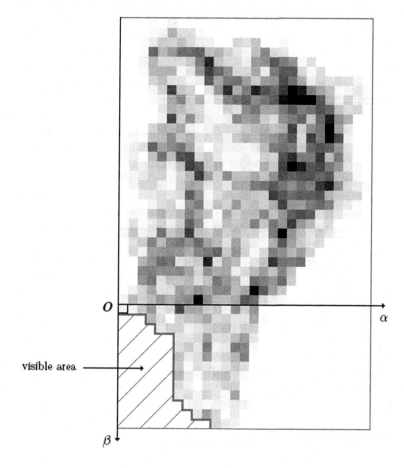

Fig. 3. The visible area for a spin image

For the proteins considered in our tests generally the number of *shadowed* points on a protein surface is bigger than that of *blocked* points, and only a small number of points is labeled *clear*.

3.2   Filtering the Spin Image List

As already observed, the number of spin images may be very large even for a protein of small size. This number depends on the number of dots on Connolly's surface and typically for a protein of about three thousand atoms may be above 10,000 with the default parameter values of 1.5 $\mathring{A}$ of Connolly procedure. Thus we apply a filtering procedure to significantly reduce the number of spin images while at the same time trying to keep an accurate surface representation. First we eliminate spin images of *blocked* points with small visible area since they may not be very reliable in surface comparison. If the visible area is below a given threshold TC then the spin image is removed from the spin image list. TC is set to 5 in our experiments. This is done because typically in this case the tangent plane at P crosses a significant part of the interior of the molecule and consequently the spin image may be too much affected by global shape information.

Second, we examine the spin images of Connolly's dots close to the same protein atom in an attempt to eliminate redundancy among them. Often the spin images associated to points close in space are very similar and it makes sense to keep only a few of them in a fast search for candidate matching regions on the two protein surfaces. The complete spin image list might be used for instance only to locally improve the fit between the two surface patches. Of the several surface dots that are typically found in the vicinity of same atom, we keep only the ones that are the most discriminative in the matching. More specifically, if atom A is close to a dot labeled *clear*, only its associated spin image is kept and all spin images of other points close to A are removed. Otherwise, if two points close to A have the same label (either *shadowed* or *blocked*) then the correlation value of their spin images is computed to measure the 2D spin image similarity; if such value is above a given threshold TS, only one of the two images is kept. More specifically, we keep the one the with larger visible area. We recall that such area is given by the size of the connected region of 0 pixels that starts at column 0. This region is contained in rows 0 through c if the point is *blocked* (see above) or through h if the point is *shadowed*, where h is the number of rows of the spin image.

At the end of this step, after all surface atoms and surface points of the protein have been considered, the number of surviving spin images is a significantly down, typically to less than 1/3 of the original number.

4   Finding Similar Surface Patches

This section describes how we group surface points of two proteins into corresponding surface patches. As we described in the previous section, point correspondences are established by comparing their associated spin images: the higher the correlation of the spin images, the better the matching between the points.

Since we are interested in local surface similarity, we concentrate our search of groups of corresponding points to nearby points. To this end, we use a simple data structure for storing all surface points, i.e. a three-dimensional matrix or grid. Given a grid cell resolution r, a surface point with coordinates (x, y, z) is mapped into the cell $(\lfloor x/r \rfloor, \lfloor y/r \rfloor, \lfloor z/r \rfloor)$. Thus points that map into the same cell are within $r\sqrt{3}$ distance from each other.

Let 3DGrid1 and 3DGrid2 be the grids associated to the sets of points of two protein surfaces. The grouping algorithm iterates over all the non-empty grid cells of 3DGrid1 and, for each such cell, over all the non-empty cells of 3DGrid2. For any pair of cells, one on each protein, we look for groups of corresponding points of the two cells, as follows. First, the spin-images are generated for all points in the two cells; then for each pair of points, one one in each cell, if their associated spin images have the same label their correlation value is determined. Pairs of points with a correlation value of their spin images less than some threshold are discarded, since the points are unlikely to be on similar patches. In our test the threshold TC is set to 0.5. The remaining pairs of points, ranked according to their correlation value, are added to the correspondence list L associated to the two cells.

The next step is to find subsets of correspondences from the list L based on a grouping criterion that is the geometric consistency of distances and angles between corresponding points and normals. More specifically, a correspondence $C = (P, P')$ between two points P and P' on the two protein surfaces is defined to be geometrically consistent with a group of already established correspondences $\{C_1 = (Q_1, Q_1'), ..., C_i = (Q_i, Q_i'), ..., C_n = (Q_n, Q_n')\}$ if the following criteria are satisfied: 1) the spin images of P and P' are highly correlated, 2) for every $i = 1, ..., n$, the distances between P and Q_i and between P' and Q_i' are within some user-defined tolerance, 3) for every $i = 1, ..., n$, the angle between the normals at P and Q_i is the same as the angle between the normals at P' and Q_i' within some user-defined tolerance.

The grouping algorithm proceeds as follows. The top element of the list L, i.e. the correspondence with the highest correlation value, is used to form the seed of the group under construction. It is also removed from the list L. Then the algorithm scans the list L in decreasing order with respect to the correlation values; if a correspondence is found that is geometrically consistent with those already in the group, then it is added to group and removed from L. When no more correspondences can be added, but the list L is not empty, the process starts over again with the reduced correspondence list to create a new group. In this way we generate several solutions. They are ranked according to the number of points within a group. Groups with fewer than a threshold number of elements are discarded.

There is obviously a limitation in using a grid representation of surface points and restricting matches only within cells. This scheme in fact may miss good solutions that cross the cell boundaries. The idea of simply shifting the boundaries of cells by half the size of a cell and repeat the matching algorithm is not feasible due to the high computational cost. Thus, we have resorted to a simple strategy. Once an initial set of good matches are obtained within any two given cells, they are used to derive a rigid transformation that superimposes the proteins. The initial solution can then be expanded to nearby points corresponding to superimposed points with high spin similarity.

5   Experimental Results

Our preliminary tests concentrate on known examples to evaluate both the parameter values and the methodology. In all considered cases, we found the correct solution, i.e. the one corresponding to the binding site reported by the PDB, among the top ranked solutions. For instance, in the case of proteins 1CYN and 1BCK (cyclophilin B and A respectively), that both bind with cyclosporins, the first ranked solution corresponds to 12 over 13 residues as they are listed in the PDB files. One residue is missing because no point of the computed protein surface is near enough to its atoms. This fact means there is a small concavity that was not detected while computing the external protein surface.

The 3D structure of the two input proteins is available from the PDB as a list of 3D coordinates. The input to the algorithm is a set of 3D points or dots from Connollys representation of the proteins. Typically, with the default parameter of 1.5 Å for Connolly's representation, the number of such dots is very high. For the proteins 1CYN and 1BCK consisting of 1430 and 1559 atoms the dots are 9183 and 9403, respectively.

Figure 4 displays with RASMOL proteins 1CYN and 1BCK and highligths in pink the atoms close to the collection of surface points corresponding to the solution with rank 1 reported by our algorithm. Figure 5 displays in yellow the binding sites of 1CYN and 1BCK derived from the record SITE contained in their PDB file. Looking at the visual representation of the two sites, we can conclude that our top solution correctly identifies atoms belonging to the active site.

As already mentioned, further processing can be used to extend the obtained surface patches to close atoms thus filling the gaps in the patches.

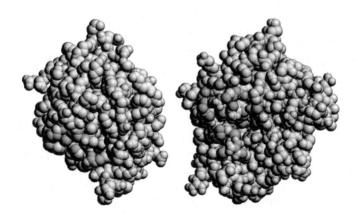

Fig. 4. Proteins 1CYN and 1BCK. The atoms close to the surface dots of the top solution are in pink

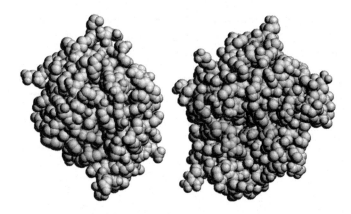

Fig. 5. Proteins 1CYN and 1BCK. The atoms of the SITE record of the PDB

References

1. Bartlett G.J., Todd A.E., Thornton J.M. (2003) Inferring protein function from structure. In *Structural Bioinformatics*, (Bourne P.E. and Weissig H. eds), Wiley-Liss.
2. Chua C., Jarvis R. (1996) 3D free form surface registration and object recognition, *Int. Journal of Computer Vision*, **17**, 77-99.
3. Connolly M.L. (1983) Solvent-accessible surfaces of proteins and nucleic acids. *Science* **221**,708-713.
4. Jones S., Thornton J.M. (1997) Analysis of protein-protein interaction sites using surface patches, *Journal of Molecular Biology*, **272**, 121-132.
5. Johnson A., and Hebert M. (1999) Using Spin-Images for efficient multiple model recognition in cluttered 3-D scenes. *IEEE Transactions on Pattern Analysis and Machine Intelligence*, **21(5)**, 433-449.
6. Johnson A., and Hebert M. (1998) Surface matching for object recognition in complex three-dimensional scenes. *Image and Vision Computing*, **16**, 635-651.
7. Kinoshita N., Furui J., Nakamura H. (2001) Identification of protein functions from a molecular surface database. eF-site. *J. Struct. Funct. Genomics*, **2**, 9-22.
8. Kinoshita N., Sadanami K., Kidera A., Go N. (1999) Structural motif pf phosphate-binding site common to various protein superfamilies: all-against-all structural comparison of protein mononucleotide complexes. *Protein Engineering*, **12**, 11-14.
9. Kleywegt G. (1999) Recognition of spatial motifs in protein structures. *Journal of Molecular Biology*, **285**, 1887-12897.
10. Kobayashi N., Go N. (1997) A method to search for similar protein local structures at ligand binding sites and its application to adenine recognition. *Eur Biophys Journal*, **26**, 135-144.
11. Lo Conte L., Chothia C., Janin J. (1999) The atomic structure of protein-protein interaction sites. *Journal of Molecular Biology*, **285**, 1021-1031.
12. Norel S. L., Fischer D., Wolfson, H. J., Nussinov R. (1994) Molecular surface recognition by a computer vision based technique. *Protein Eng.* , **7**, 39-46.
13. Via A., Ferre' F., Branetti B., Helmer Citterich M. (2000) Protein surface similarities: a survey of methods to describe and compare protein surfaces. Cell: Mol. Life Sci., **57**, 1970-1977.

14. Wallace A., Borkakoti N., Thornton J. (1997) TESS: a geometric hashing algorithm for deriving 3D coordinate templates for searching structural databases. Application to enzyme active sites. *Protein Science*, **6 (11)**, 2008-2023.
15. Zhang B., Rychlewski L., Pawlowski K., Fetrow J., Skolnick J., Godzik A. (1999) From fold predictions to function prediction: automation of functional site conservation analysis for functional genome predictions. *Protein Science*, **8 (5)**, 1104-1115.

Mass Spectra Alignments and Their Significance

Sebastian Böcker and Hans-Michael Kaltenbach

AG Genominformatik, Technische Fakultät
Universität Bielefeld
PF 100 131
33501 Bielefeld, Germany
{boecker,michael}@CeBiTec.uni-bielefeld.de

Abstract. Mass Spectrometry has become one of the most popular analysis techniques in Genomics and Systems Biology. We investigate a general framework that allows the alignment (or matching) of any two mass spectra. In particular, we examine the alignment of a reference mass spectrum generated *in silico* from a database, with a measured sample mass spectrum. In this context, we assess the significance of alignment scores for character-specific cleavage experiments, such as tryptic digestion of amino acids. We present an efficient approach to estimate this significance, with runtime linear in the number of detected peaks. In this context, we investigate the probability that a random string over a weighted alphabet contains a substring of some given weight.

1 Introduction

Mass Spectrometry is one of the most popular analysis techniques in the emerging field of Systems Biology [1]: The analysis of peptide fingerprints and tandem mass spectra for protein identification and de novo sequencing is performed daily in thousands of laboratories around the world. The efficiency of this analysis technique is mainly due to its unique accuracy: Masses of sample molecules can be determined with an accuracy of parts of a neutron mass.

One central problem in the interpretation of mass spectrometry data is the matching of mass spectra: Usually, we are given some sample mass spectrum and a set of reference mass spectra (typically generated *in silico* from a sequence database), and we want to know which of the reference mass spectra fits best to the sample mass spectrum. To compute such peak matchings, we investigate a general framework that allows to *align* any two spectra and give examples on how to score such alignments.

As the other main contribution of this paper, we assess the quality of such an alignment: We develop a framework for efficiently computing p-values for restriction-type experiments, such as tryptic digestion of amino acids also known as peptide mass fingerprinting [2]. We also report preliminary results for tandem mass spectrometry data [3].

In particular, we are interested in the question whether a random string over a weighted alphabet contains a (certain) substring of given weight. This

A. Apostolico, M. Crochemore, and K. Park (Eds.): CPM 2005, LNCS 3537, pp. 429–441, 2005.

question has been frequently addressed using heuristics and approximations [4, 5] in order to analyze mass spectrometry data. Here, we present a surprisingly simple recurrence relation that allows exact and efficient computation of these probabilities.

We believe that the two-step process of first aligning spectra, then assessing the significance of the alignment – which has proven useful in the context of string alignments – is also beneficial for the analysis of mass spectrometry data. First, the flexibility of scoring schemes allows to adjust to an application's peculiarities with a maximal degree of freedom. Second, certain scoring schemes emerge quite naturally in a statistical context. Third, alignment scores themselves are often quite useless for protein identification, because long proteins usually achieve better scores than short ones. Our approach allows an efficient estimation of the p-value of an alignment score taking into account protein lengths, and therefore combines the advantages of alignments and stochastical analysis. Note that MASCOT [4, 6], the most popular program for peptide mass fingerprinting, approaches this problem by a heuristical estimation of such p-values.

The problem of aligning mass spectra is clearly related to the well-known Longest Common Subsequence Problem. Similar approaches were used for physical map comparison [7] and aligning gel electrophoresis patterns [8, 9].

The significance or probability of mass spectrum matchings has been considered by [10] using a two-step stochastic process, by [11] using a hypothesis testing formulation, and by [12] using empirical statistics.

2   Definition of the Model

Solely for readability, we limit our attention to masses of molecules and ignore multiple charge states in the following. We can compute the mass of a biomolecule *in silico*, simply summing up the masses of its atoms. Mass spectrometry allows to estimate molecule masses with an exceptionally high accuracy such as 0.1 Dalton (Da), about one tenth the mass of a neutron. Still and all, measured masses usually differ from those theoretically predicted.

When comparing simulated and measured mass spectra, we have to take into account the *resolution* constraint of mass spectrometers: If two molecules have almost identical masses, the corresponding peaks may overlap in the measured mass spectrum, and ultimately create a joint peak with mass somewhere in-between the two original masses. This effect is hard to predict *in silico*, and one usually predicts the reference spectrum ignoring this effect. We have to take it into account when matching measured masses with those predicted, see Section 4.

In the following, we simplify matters by assuming that a *mass spectrum* is a set of peaks $\{1, \dots, n\}$. Every peak i has a *mass* m_i, and eventually other attributes such as *intensity* or signal-to-noise ratio. We require here and in the following that peaks are ordered with respect to mass, that is, $m_i < m_j$ holds for $1 \leq i < j \leq n$. Due to the imperfection of mass spectrometry and biochemistry, a sample mass spectrum may differ from an ideal mass spectrum and show *additional* and *missing* peaks.

Mass spectrometry measures the masses of sample molecules. For peptides as well as nucleotides, these molecules can be viewed as strings over the (amino acid or nucleic acid) alphabet, and the weight of a string is simply the sum of weights of its characters: For the alphabet Σ we are given a *weight function* $\mu : \Sigma \to \mathbb{R}$, and we can extend the domain of μ to strings $s = s_1 \ldots s_n \in \Sigma^*$ by defining $\mu(s) := \sum_{i=1}^n \mu(s_i)$. We set $\mu_{\min} := \min_{\sigma \in \Sigma} \mu(\sigma)$ and $\mu_{\max} := \max_{\sigma \in \Sigma} \mu(\sigma)$. Depending on the experimental settings, there exists a maximal mass $m_{\max} \in \mathbb{R}$ such that no masses above $m_{\max}$ are present in any mass spectrum: for example, $m_{\max} \approx 3000$ for tryptic digestion experiments. Then, $\mathcal{M} := [0, m_{\max}]$ is the *mass range* of interest, and $l_{\max} := \lfloor m_{\max}/\mu_{\min} \rfloor$ is the maximal length of a fragment that we can detect.

We will sometimes require that all masses are natural numbers. To this end, we round the true masses to integers using some mass accuracy $\Delta \in \mathbb{R}$: Above we have denoted integer masses for $\Delta = 0.1$. In this *discrete* case, $\mathcal{M} := \{0, \ldots, m_{\max}\}$ is the mass range of interest, for example $\mathcal{M} = \{0, 1, \ldots, 30\,000\}$ for tryptic digestion and accuracy $\Delta = 0.1$.

In Section 5, we investigate mass spectra that come from biochemical experiments involving character-specific cleavage, such as tryptic digestion of amino acids. A mathematical formalism for such cleavage was introduced in [13]. We are given a *sample string* $s \in \Sigma^*$ and a *cleavage character* $x \in \Sigma$ over the alphabet Σ. Then, $y \in (\Sigma - \{x\})^*$ is a *fragment* of s, x if xyx is a substring of xsx. Given a reference string, it is straightforward how to compute all masses in the corresponding reference spectrum [4, 13]. We do not go into the details here and refer the reader to the literature.

The utilized biochemistry sometimes leads to mass modifications of fragment masses, such as $+16$ Da for an additional H_2O group. We will ignore all mass modifications for the sake of readability, for they can easily be incorporated.

In Section 7, we confine our analysis to collision-induced dissociation by tandem mass spectrometry. There, we break the peptide string s into all prefixes and suffixes of s.

3   Spectrum Alignment

Let $\mathcal{S}, \mathcal{S}'$ be the two spectra that we want to match. We want to construct a peak matching, that is: a bijective map $\pi : \mathcal{S}_* \to \mathcal{S}'_*$ where $\mathcal{S}_* \subseteq \mathcal{S}$ and $\mathcal{S}'_* \subseteq \mathcal{S}'$ are the matched peaks, while all other peaks remain unmatched. We assume that the map π is a bijection, but we describe below how to deal with many-to-one matchings.

To find the optimal matching of $\mathcal{S} = \{1, \ldots, n\}$ and $\mathcal{S}' = \{1, \ldots, n'\}$, we have to assign scores to any possible matching using a scoring function *score* for single peak matching:

$$score : \left(\mathcal{S} \cup \{\varepsilon\}\right) \times \left(\mathcal{S}' \cup \{\varepsilon\}\right) \to \mathbb{R}$$

where ε denotes a special "gap" character and $score(\varepsilon, \varepsilon) := -\infty$. If we align some reference spectrum $\mathcal{S}$ with a sample mass spectrum $\mathcal{S}'$, then we will talk about *missing* peak scores $score(i, \varepsilon)$ and *additional* peak scores $score(\varepsilon, j)$.

In the following, we do not make any assumptions regarding the peak scoring function *score*. It is clear that such a scoring function must be based on the peaks attributes, such as mass or intensity: for example, if m_i is the mass of peak $i \in \mathcal{S}$ and m'_j the mass of peak $j \in \mathcal{S}'$, then $score(i, j)$ should be the higher, the smaller the mass difference $|m_i - m'_j|$ is. Solely for simplicity, we will often limit our attention to "masses" as the unique peak attributes in the following. The presented framework allows us to mimic *any* additive or multiplicative scoring scheme, such as that used by MASCOT [4] or log likelihood peak scoring [14]. We will discuss the details of useful scoring schemes in the next section.

Now, the score of the matching $\pi : \mathcal{S}_* \to \mathcal{S}'_*$ is the sum of scores of the peak matchings:

$$score(\pi) = \sum_{i \in \mathcal{S}_*} score(i, \pi(i)) + \sum_{i \in \mathcal{S} \setminus \mathcal{S}_*} score(i, \varepsilon) + \sum_{j \in \mathcal{S}' \setminus \mathcal{S}'_*} score(\varepsilon, j).$$

We are searching for a maximal score among all matchings. As an example using only peak masses, we define for all $i \in \mathcal{S}$ and $j \in \mathcal{S}'$: $score(i, j) = 1$ if $|m_i - m'_j| \leq \delta$ and $score(i, j) = 0$ otherwise; and $score(i, \varepsilon) = score(\varepsilon, j) = 0$. Here m_i is the mass of peak $i \in \mathcal{S}$, m'_j is the mass of peak $j \in \mathcal{S}'$, and $\delta \in \mathbb{R}$ is some constant mass difference. Using this peak scoring, we count the number of peaks we can match with a mass difference of at most δ.

From the fact that peak matchings should not cross, we can easily infer that we are searching for an *alignment* between the spectra $\mathcal{S}$ and $\mathcal{S}'$: This can be efficiently done using Dynamic Programming, and we define the (well-known) recurrence relation for the $(n + 1) \times (n' + 1)$ matrix E by

$$E[i + 1, j + 1] = \max\{E[i, j + 1] + score(i + 1, \varepsilon), E[i + 1, j] + score(\varepsilon, j + 1),$$
$$E[i, j] + score(i + 1, j + 1)\}$$

$$(1)$$

using the familiar boundary conditions. Now, $score(\mathcal{S}, \mathcal{S}') = E[n, n']$ holds the score of an optimal alignment between $\mathcal{S}, \mathcal{S}'$, and we can find all such optimal alignments by backtracking through the matrix E.

We can easily incorporate peak attributes such as peak mass differences, intensities, or others into this model, using the same recurrence relation which is of particular importance when scoring missing peaks and additional peaks: For missing peaks, recall that we have transformed the raw data of the mass spectrum into a peak list discarding candidates whose intensity falls below a given threshold. Hence, slight changes of this threshold can dramatically change scores that do not take into account peak intensities. For additional peaks, similar arguments apply.

It should be understood that for reasonable peak scorings, we do not have to fill in the complete matrix E: We can expect that $score(i, j)$ decreases as the mass difference between peaks i and j increases. In particular, $score(i, j)$ will be very small for high mass differences, because there is no reason to match two peaks that are, say, 1000 Da apart. On the contrary, scores $score(i, \varepsilon)$ and $score(\varepsilon, j)$ are mostly independent of peak masses. So, it suffices to fill in only those parts of the matrix E where $score(i,j)$ is not too small. Hence, the optimal alignment can be calculated by sparse dynamic programming in time $O(|C| + n + n')$ where $C := \{(i,j) : score(i,j) \geq score(i,\varepsilon) + score(\varepsilon,j)\}$ is the set of potential matches.

4   Many-to-One Peak Matchings and Scoring Functions

In the previous section, we have introduced a general setting that allow to align *any* two mass spectra. In the following, we concentrate on matching a single sample mass spectrum to a multitude of reference spectra generated *in silico*. We limit our attention to mass as the unique peak attribute, and ignore peak intensities and other peak attributes. This is done solely for the sake of readability, and generalization to other attributes is obligatory for applications.

Above, we have talked about peak scores $score(\cdot,\cdot)$ but so far, we have not elaborated on how to choose such scores. To this end, we define a *global peak scoring function* $\Psi : \mathcal{M} \times \mathcal{M} \to \mathbb{R}$ that maps a sample peak with mass $m' \in \mathcal{M}$ and a reference peak with mass $m \in \mathcal{M}$, to a peak score $\Psi(m, m')$. This map is independent of an actual reference or sample spectrum, and even actual peaks. Now, we can define $score(i,j) := \Psi(m_i, m'_j)$.

A sensible global peak scoring function is as follows: We assume that sample peak masses are normally distributed around the ideal peak mass m. The variance of this distribution may also depend on m, since large mass errors appear more often in high mass regions, but here we concentrate on a constant variance $\bar{\sigma}^2$ for the sake of simplicity. If we want to positively score, say, 95% of all sample peaks (so, the mass difference must be smaller than approximately $2\bar{\sigma}$) then we can define

$$\Psi(m, m') := 1 - \mathbb{P}(Z > -z \text{ and } Z < z)$$

where $z := |m - m'|/\bar{\sigma}$ and $Z \sim \mathcal{N}(0,1)$. Clearly, $\Psi(m,m) = 1$ and $\Psi(m,m') \approx 0$ holds for $|m - m'| = 2\bar{\sigma}$. Choosing a "good" peak scoring function highly depends on the underlying application, and surely is a problem of its own; we shall not go into the details here for the sake of brevity, but note that research on this problem is in progress.

We also have to score additional peaks $score(\varepsilon, j)$ and missing peaks $score(i, \varepsilon)$. To this end, let $\bar{\Psi} : \mathcal{M} \to \mathbb{R}$ and $\Phi : \mathcal{M} \to \mathbb{R}$ be two functions that score a missing peak with mass $m \in \mathcal{M}$, or an additional peak with mass $m' \in \mathcal{M}$. These functions can be defined constant, but it is also reasonable to take into account peak intensities as well as experiences about experimental settings, to allow more fine-grained evaluation of these events.

We introduce some notations that will be of use when calculating the significance of an alignment score. Given a fixed sample spectrum $\mathcal{S}'$, we concentrate on a single sample peak $j \in \mathcal{S}'$ with mass m'_j: We define a *peak scoring functions* ψ_j by

$$\psi_j : \mathcal{M} \to \mathbb{R}, \quad \psi_j(m) := \Psi(m, m'_j) \quad \text{for all } m \in \mathcal{M}.$$

Set $\bar{\psi}_j := \bar{\Psi}(m'_j) \in \mathbb{R}$ for additional peaks. To simplify computations, we postulate that every peak scoring function has finite and compact *support*: That is, $\psi_j(m)$ is above a certain threshold if and only if $m \in [m_1, m_2]$ for masses m_1, m_2. In the discrete case, the support $\{m_1, \ldots, m_2\}$ of ψ_j is denoted $\mathcal{U}_j$, and reference peaks with mass $m \notin \mathcal{U}_j$ will never be matched to sample peak j. We further require that the support of two peaks $j, j+1 \in \mathcal{S}'$ does not intersect, and we can achieve this by shrinking overlapping support.

As noted above, we may want to match a single sample peak to one $or\ more$ reference peaks. The simplest incorporation of such many-to-one peak matchings is as follows: We simply add scores of matching a sample peak j to all reference peaks i with mass $m_i \in \mathcal{U}_j$, and if there is no such reference peak, we score peak j by $\bar{\psi}_j$. Now,

$$score_{\mathrm{m2o}}(\mathcal{S}, \mathcal{S}') := \sum_{j \in \mathcal{S}'} \sum_{i \in \mathcal{S}, m_i \in \mathcal{U}_j} \psi_j(m_i) + \sum_{j \text{ additional}} \bar{\psi}_j + \sum_{i \text{ missing}} \varPhi(m_i) \quad (2)$$

where "j additional" runs over those $j \in \mathcal{S}'$ where there is no $i \in \mathcal{S}$ with $m_i \in \mathcal{U}_j$; and "i missing" runs over those $i \in \mathcal{S}$ where there is no $j \in \mathcal{S}'$ with $m_i \in \mathcal{U}_j$. We can compute $score_{\mathrm{m2o}}$ in time $O(n\,n')$, or $O(|C| + n + n')$ where C is again the set of potential matches.

The above score does not take into account any "interference" between reference peaks. For a particular reference spectrum $\mathcal{S}$ it is useful to take into account such interferences if additional peak attributes such as intensity are known: Peak intensities are mostly additive, and a sample peak that is matched to two or more reference peaks should show an intensity that is the sum of intensities of the reference peaks. We can modify the spectrum alignment of Section 3 to take into account multiple matches, by trying to align a single sample peak to more than only the last reference peaks in the dynamic programming recurrence (1). Such $merging\ alignment$ can be computed in time $O(n\,n'\,k)$ where k denotes the maximal number of reference peaks with masses that fall into the support of any single sample peak. Again, computations are usually faster than this worst-case runtime suggests. We omit the details for the sake of brevity.

5   Character-Specific Cleavage of Random Strings

We now concentrate on the case that the measured mass spectra come from biochemical experiments involving character-specific cleavage, such as tryptic digestion of amino acids. Recall that given a cleavage character $x \in \Sigma$, then $y \in (\Sigma - \{x\})^*$ is a $fragment$ of some string $s \in \Sigma^*$ if and only if xyx is a substring of xsx.

In the following, we ignore peak intensities in the reference spectrum for the sake of simplicity. Also, we assume that we can map a single reference peak to multiple sample peaks, as described in the previous section. We premise all masses to be natural numbers, as indicated in Section 2.

We concentrate on a single peak in the mass spectrum with mass m. To estimate the score contributed by this peak (see the next section), we must know what theoretical fragments y have mass m, and what strings s will generate y as a fragment. Let $x \in \Sigma$ be the fixed cleavage character, and suppose that the string s of fixed length $|s| = L$ was randomly drawn from Σ^L, where we assume for simplicity that all characters have identical probability $1/|\Sigma|$ – generalization to other character distributions is straightforward. What is the probability that xsx contains at least one substring xyx, for $y \in \Sigma_x^*$ and $\Sigma_x := \Sigma \setminus \{x\}$, such that $\mu(y) = m$ holds?

First, we want to calculate the number $d[m]$ of fragments $y \in \Sigma_x^*$ that have mass m. It is computer science folklore that we can compute this number using the simple recurrence relation $d[0] := 1$ and

$$d[m] = \sum_{\sigma \in \Sigma, \mu(\sigma) \leq m} d[m - \mu(\sigma)] \qquad \text{for } m \geq 0. \qquad (3)$$

Computing $d[\cdot]$ takes $O(|\Sigma| m_{\max})$ time, and storing it requires $O(m_{\max})$ space.

Here we also want to distinguish fragments of different lengths. For $l, m \in \mathbb{N}$ let $c[l, m]$ denote the number of strings $y \in \Sigma_x^l$ such that $\mu(y) = m$. We can easily calculate $c[\cdot, \cdot]$ by initializing $c[0, 0] := 1$, $c[0, m] := 0$ for all $m > 0$, and the recurrence relation

$$c[l, m] = \sum_{\sigma \in \Sigma_x, \mu(\sigma) \leq m} c[l - 1, m - \mu(\sigma)] \quad \text{for } l \geq 1 \text{ and } m \geq 0.$$

Note that $c[l, m] = 0$ for $l < m/\mu_{\max}$ as well as for $l > m/\mu_{\min}$. Computing $c[\cdot, \cdot]$ takes $O(|\Sigma| l_{\max} m_{\max})$ time, and storing it requires $O(l_{\max} m_{\max})$ space.

For fixed $m \in \mathbb{N}$ and $L \in \mathbb{N}$ we define the set of strings of length L which do have at least one fragment of mass m as

$$S_{L,m} := \left\{ s \in \Sigma^L : xsx \text{ contains substring } xyx \text{ with } y \in \Sigma_x^* \text{ and } \mu(y) = m \right\} \qquad (4)$$

and for readability, we define $r[l, m] := \mathbb{P}\big(y \in \Sigma_x^l, \mu(y) \neq m\big) = 1 - c[l, m]/(|\Sigma| - 1)^l$.

Theorem 1. *Suppose that the string s was uniformly drawn from Σ^L for some $L \in \mathbb{N}$. For a fixed mass m we define $\bar{p}[\cdot, m]$ using the initial value $\bar{p}[0, m] = 1$ and the recurrence relation*

$$\bar{p}[L, m] = r[L, m]\left(1 - \frac{1}{|\Sigma|}\right)^L + \sum_{l=1}^{L} \bar{p}[L - l, m]\, r[l - 1, m] \frac{1}{|\Sigma|}\left(1 - \frac{1}{|\Sigma|}\right)^{l-1} \qquad (5)$$

for $L > 0$. Then, $p[L, m] := 1 - \bar{p}[L, m]$ is the probability that s generates a fragment of mass m, that is, $p[L, m] = \mathbb{P}(s \in S_{L,m})$ holds.

Lemma 1. *With the notations of Theorem 1, the probability that xsx contains a substring xyx with $y \in \Sigma_x^*$ and $\mu(y) = m$ can be estimated as*

$$p[L, m] \approx 1 - \prod_{l}\left(1 - \frac{c[l, m]}{|\Sigma|^{l+1}}\right)^2 \cdot \left(1 - \frac{c[l, m]}{|\Sigma|^{l+2}}\right)^{L-l-1}.$$

The computations of Theorem 1 are *independent of the actual sample mass spectrum and the reference spectra*, and we can compute $p[L, m]$ during pre-processing for the relevant mass range $m = 1, \ldots, m_{\max}$ and string lengths $L = 1, \ldots, L_{\max}$. For any mass m, we can compute recurrence relation (5) in $O(l_{\max} L_{\max})$ time using one-dimensional dynamic programming, but we need $O(m_{\max} L_{\max})$ space to store p. For applications such as protein identification it is feasible to do exact computations and store p in memory. Clearly, we can leave out those rows $p[\cdot, m]$ where m has no decomposition as a fragment $y \in \Sigma_x^*$ with $\mu(y) = m$.

If memory limitations become an issue, we use Lemma 1 to estimate $p[L, m]$ for large L, m.

For the tryptic digestion of amino acids, the enzyme cleaves after the C-terminus of both lysine (K) and arginine (R) *except* before proline (P). We can achieve this by a recurrence similar to (5), we omit the details for the sake of brevity.

Example 1. We consider the alphabet $\Sigma := \{A, B, C, D\}$ with cleavage character $x := D$, and masses $\mu(A) = 3$, $\mu(B) = 5$, and $\mu(C) = 6$. Computation of $c[\cdot, \cdot]$ is straightforward, for example $c[5, 20] = c[4, 14] + c[4, 15] + c[4, 17] = 4 + 4 + 12 = 20$. For $m := 20$, the complete column $c[l, 20]$ reads:

l	0	1	2	3	4	5	6	7+
$c[l, 20]$	0	0	0	0	13	20	6	0

For computing $p[L, m]$ we use the recurrence of Theorem 1:

L	0	1	2	3	4	5	6	7	8	9	10
$p[L, m]$	0	0	0	0	$\frac{13}{256}$	$\frac{46}{1024}$	$\frac{163}{4096}$	$\frac{712}{16384}$	$\frac{3142}{65536}$	$\frac{13575}{262144}$	$\frac{58653}{1048576}$

So, $p[10, 20] = \frac{58653}{1048576} = 0.05593\ldots$ is the probability to draw a string $s \in \Sigma^{10}$ that generates a fragment of mass $m = 20$. Using Lemma 1 we estimate $p[10, 20] \approx 0.0555\ldots$ with a relative error of less than 1 %.

6   Significance of Alignment Scores

Using alignment scores as introduced above allows us to select a best-scoring simulated reference spectrum from, say, a database of sequences. But what are the chances that this score can be achieved by chance alone? Clearly, we cannot estimate this probability using only the scores obtained by aligning the sample spectrum to all reference spectra from the protein database.

Consider peak $j \in \mathcal{S}'$ of the sample mass spectrum $\mathcal{S}' = \{1, \ldots, n'\}$; we want to compute its contribution to the total score. We analyze many-to-one peak matching for the sake of simplicity, because this allows us to model alignment scores by independent random variables. See Section 4 for the definitions of ψ_j, $\mathcal{U}_j$, $\bar{\psi}_j$, and Φ.

Consider the set of outcomes $\Omega := \Sigma^L$ to be all reference strings of given length L. Recall that $p[L, m]$ is the probability that the random string s generates a fragment y with mass $\mu(y) = m$. Our goal is to define a random variable as the score of matching sample peak j to all "adequate" peaks of the reference spectrum.

First, let $\tilde{X}_j$ be the random variable that sums the scores over all peaks in the reference spectrum that we can match with peak j: For $m \in \mathcal{U}_j$ we use $S_{L,m}$ from (4) and define

$$\tilde{X}_j(s) := \sum_{m \in \mathcal{U}_j} \psi_j(m) \cdot \mathbb{1}(s \in S_{L,m})$$

where $\mathbb{1}(\cdot)$ denotes the indicator function. Assuming independence, we can easily see

$$\mathbb{E}(\tilde{X}_j) = \sum_{m \in \mathcal{U}_j} p[L, m]\, \psi_j(m), \operatorname{Var}(\tilde{X}_j) = \sum_{m \in \mathcal{U}_j} p[L, m]\, \psi_j(m)^2 - (\mathbb{E}(\tilde{X}_j))^2. \quad (6)$$

Second, if there is no peak in the reference spectrum with mass $m \in \mathcal{U}_j$, then the sample peak j is an additional peak and must be penalized by adding $\bar{\psi}_j = score(\varepsilon, j)$ to the spectrum score. We define the random variable

$$\bar{X}_j(s) := \bar{\psi}_j \cdot \mathbb{1}\left(s \notin \bigcup_{m \in \mathcal{U}_j} S_{L,m}\right)$$

for the "additional peak score". To simplify computations, we assume independence of the events that s generates fragments of distinct masses. Then, the probability that $\bar{X}_j(s) = \bar{\psi}_j$ holds, is

$$\mathbb{P}\left(\bar{X}_j(s) = \bar{\psi}_j\right) \approx \bar{p}_j := \prod_{m \in \mathcal{U}_j} \left(1 - p[L, m]\right). \quad (7)$$

We may use the estimation $\ln(1 - x) = -x - \frac{1}{2}x^2 - \frac{1}{3}x^3 - \dots$ for $0 \leq x < 1$ to compute $\bar{p}_j$ with high accuracy in time $O(|\mathcal{U}_j|)$. Now,

$$\mathbb{E}(\bar{X}_j) = \bar{p}_j\, \bar{\psi}_j, \operatorname{Var}(\bar{X}_j) = \bar{p}_j\, \bar{\psi}_j^2 - (\mathbb{E}(\bar{X}_j))^2.$$

We estimate expected value and variance of the random variable $X_j := \tilde{X}_j + \bar{X}_j$ as

$$\mathbb{E}(X_j) = \mathbb{E}(\tilde{X}_j) + \mathbb{E}(\bar{X}_j), \operatorname{Var}(X_j) = \operatorname{Var}(\tilde{X}_j) + \operatorname{Var}(\bar{X}_j) - 2\,\mathbb{E}(\tilde{X}_j) \cdot \mathbb{E}(\bar{X}_j) \quad (8)$$

in view of

$$\operatorname{Cov}(\tilde{X}_j, \bar{X}_j) = \mathbb{E}(\tilde{X}_j \cdot \bar{X}_j) - \mathbb{E}(\tilde{X}_j) \cdot \mathbb{E}(\bar{X}_j) = -\mathbb{E}(\tilde{X}_j) \cdot \mathbb{E}(\bar{X}_j)$$

because either $\tilde{X}_j(s) = 0$ or $\bar{X}_j(s) = 0$ holds for all $s \in S_{L,m}$.

Now, we consider peaks in the reference spectrum that we cannot match to a peak of the sample spectrum. Define $\mathcal{M}^+ := \bigcup_{j=1}^{n'} \mathcal{U}_j$ as the support of all peak scoring functions, then $\mathcal{M}^- := \mathcal{M} \setminus \mathcal{M}^+$ is the set of reference masses that cannot be matched with any sample peak. Any reference peak $m \in \mathcal{M}^-$ is therefore a missing peak, and must be penalized by $\Phi(m)$. We define random variables Y_m for $m \in \mathcal{M}^-$ by $Y_m(s) := \Phi(m)$ if the reference string s generates a fragment of mass m, and $Y_m(s) := 0$ otherwise. We easily calculate

$$\mathbb{E}(Y_m) = p[L, m]\,\Phi(m) \quad \text{and} \quad \text{Var}(Y_m) = p[L, m]\,\Phi(m)^2 - (\mathbb{E}(Y_m))^2. \quad (9)$$

We can compute $\sum_{m \in \mathcal{M}} p[L, m]\Phi(m)$ and $\sum_{m \in \mathcal{M}} p[L, m]\Phi(m)^2$ during preprocessing, what allows us to limit computations to masses $m \in \mathcal{M}^+$ in (10).

Finally, the random variable X is the total score of aligning the reference spectrum of a string $s \in \Sigma^L$ to the sample mass spectrum $\mathcal{S}' = \{1, \ldots, n'\}$, see (2). From the above,

$$X = \sum_{j=1}^{n'} X_j + \sum_{m \in \mathcal{M}^-} Y_m$$

and if we assume that these random variables are independent, we infer:

$$\mathbb{E}(X) = \sum_{j=1}^{n'} \mathbb{E}(X_j) + \sum_{m \in \mathcal{M}^-} \mathbb{E}(Y_m), \text{Var}(X) = \sum_{j=1}^{n'} \text{Var}(X_j) + \sum_{m \in \mathcal{M}^-} \text{Var}(Y_m)$$

$$(10)$$

Also, X is the sum of many nearly independent random variables, so X can be approximated by a *normal distribution* $\mathcal{N}(\bar{\mu}, \bar{\sigma}^2)$ with mean $\bar{\mu} := \mathbb{E}(X)$ and variance $\bar{\sigma}^2 := \text{Var}(X)$ using the central limit theorem.

In the above calculations, we had to assume independence of random variables though these variables are slightly correlated. To show that our estimations are accurate in application settings we have performed simulations, see Section 8.

Suppose we have computed an alignment score $sc := score(\mathcal{S}, \mathcal{S}')$ for a sample mass spectrum $\mathcal{S}'$ and a reference mass spectrum $\mathcal{S}$ generated *in silico* from a string s. This was done using either the simple many-to-one alignment of Section 4, or the more elaborate merging alignment. We can assess the probability that a score greater or equal sc is achieved by a random string of length $L := |s|$ by chance: We compute $\bar{\mu} := \mathbb{E}(X)$ and $\bar{\sigma}^2 := \text{Var}(X)$ as described above, what can be done in constant space and time $O(|\mathcal{M}^+|) = O(n'\,u)$, where u denotes the maximal width of any support $\mathcal{U}_j$. Finally, for $Z \sim \mathcal{N}(0, 1)$ we estimate the p-value

$$\mathbb{P}(X \geq sc) \approx \mathbb{P}\Big(Z \geq \frac{sc - \bar{\mu}}{\bar{\sigma}}\Big).$$

7   Collision-Induced Dissociation of Random Strings

Now, let us focus on collision induced dissociation of peptides by tandem mass spectrometry. Here, we break the peptide string s of known *parent mass* M into all prefixes and suffixes of s. We concentrate on the main ion series (b/y-ions) and ignore mass modifications of b/y-ions (addition H group for b-ions, additional H_3O group for y-ions) for the sake of readability. Again, we can easily incorporate these mass modifications as well as other ion series.

We require all masses to be natural numbers. The peaks detected in the sample mass spectrum correspond to prefixes and suffixes of the amino acid string s. Regarding s, we know its *parent mass* $M := \mu(s)$. So, we want to uniformly sample from the set $S[M] := \{s \in \Sigma^* : \mu(s) = M\}$. What is the probability that any such string has a prefix or suffix y of mass $\mu(y) = m$? Recall that we can easily compute the number of strings $s \in S[M]$ with $\mu(s) = m$ using (3).

The surprisingly simple result of this section is:

Theorem 2. *Let* $d[m]$ *denote the number of strings* $s \in \Sigma^*$ *with* $\mu(s) = m$. *For parent mass* $M \in \mathbb{N}$, *let* s *be a string uniformly drawn from the set of strings* $S[M]$ *with mass* M. *The probability that* s *has a prefix of mass* $m \in \{1, \ldots, M\}$, *is*

$$\tilde{q}[M, m] := \frac{1}{d[M]} d[m]\, d[M - m].$$

Set $\bar{m} := \min\{m, M - m\}$, *then the probability that* s *has a prefix or suffix of mass* m, *is*

$$q[M, m] := \frac{1}{d[M]} \Big(2d[\bar{m}]\, d[M - \bar{m}] - d[\bar{m}]^2\, d[M - 2\bar{m}] \Big).$$

Theorem 2 allows us to compute $q[M, m]$ in constant time, if $d[\cdot]$ is known.

Analogously to Section 5, we can define random variables $\tilde{X}_j$, $\bar{X}_j$, and Y_m to estimate mean and variance of alignment scores. Again, we must assume that these random variables are independent, what is less correct than in the previous section, because peaks with mass differences of character masses are clearly correlated. Such dependencies are not taken into account in Theorem 2, but it is straightforward how to generalize the theorem for dependencies of first or even higher order. Work on this topic is currently in progress.

8   Results

We want to asses the quality of our estimations for tryptic digestion of amino acids as described above. We use integer masses with accuracy $\Delta = 0.1$, and the following scoring scheme: Additional and missing peaks are penalized with score -0.2, matched peaks are given the Gaussian score described in section 4 using a standard deviation of 2 Da and a threshold of 95%. We do the following for $L = 350, 500$: We draw a random sample string of length L and simulate its cleavage pattern under tryptic digestion. Then, we draw 250000 random strings of length L and compute the alignment score for the respective mass spectra. Finally, we estimate mean and variance of a normal distribution using the method of Section 5. To demonstrate the correctness of the normal distribution assumption, quantile-quantile-plots are provided for each stringlength. The plots in Figure 1 clearly show that our approach allows quite accurate estimation of the distribution of scores.

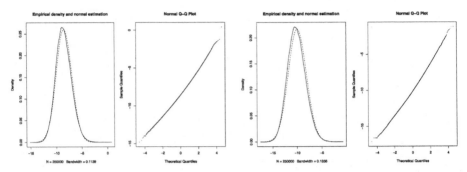

Fig. 1. Simulation results: Distribution of scores for randomly drawn strings (solid line) and normal distribution estimated using the method of Section 5 (dashed line) as well as quantile-quantile-plot for normal distribution for length $L = 350$ (left) and $L = 500$ (right).

9   Discussion and Improvements

We have presented a general approach for aligning two mass spectra and, in particular, aligning a sample spectrum and a (theoretically predicted) reference spectrum. For the latter, we show that the distribution of scores can be approximated by a normal distribution for restriction type experiments. We present a method that allows to compute the parameters of this distribution in linear time, and therefore allows an estimation of the significance of alignment scores. Doing so, we have combined the freedom of choosing a scoring scheme tuned for a particular application, with the rigid estimation of p-values for obtained scores.

Regarding substrings of a certain mass in random strings, we have presented efficient analytical methods to compute appearance probabilities. We think that our approach may allow for generalizations to related questions in the context of weighted strings.

In the future, we want to further evaluate spectrum alignments of tryptic digestion data using protein databases. In particular, scoring schemes are tested for their discriminative power. We will perform similar experiments for simulated mass spectra from collision-induced dissociation: As indicated in Section 7, the dependency among random variables makes it necessary to correct the estimated variance. We are currently applying our approach to mass spectrometry data and comparing its resolving power to existing approaches such as MASCOT, but this is beyond the scope of this paper to provide a rigid theoretical framework for estimating the significance mass spectra alignments, and will be reported elsewhere. We will integrate our algorithms into the PRODB system [15].

Acknowledgments

Sebastian Böcker is supported by "Deutsche Forschungsgemeinschaft" (BO 1910/ 1-1) within the Computer Science Action Program. Hans-Michael Kaltenbach is supported by the "International NRW Graduate School in Bioinformatics and Genome Research." The authors want to thank Sven Rahmann for helpful discussions.

References

1. Aebersold, R., Mann, M.: Mass spectrometry-based proteomics. Nature **422** (2003) 198–207
2. Patterson, S.D., Aebersold, R.: Mass spectrometric approaches for the identification of gel-separated proteins. Electrophoresis **16** (1995) 1791–1814
3. Cooks, R.G., ed.: Collision spectroscopy. Plenum Press, New York, NY (1978)
4. Pappin, D.J., Hojrup, P., Bleasby, A.: Rapid identification of proteins by peptide-mass fingerprinting. Curr. Biol. **3** (1993) 327–332
5. Wang, I.J., Diehl, C.P., Pineda, F.J.: A statistical model of proteolytic digestion. In: Proceedings of IEEE CSB 2003, Stanford, California (2003) 506–508
6. Perkins, D.N., Pappin, D.J., Creasy, D.M., Cottrell, J.S.: Probability-based protein identification by searching sequence databases using mass spectrometry data. Electrophoresis **20** (1999) 3551–3567
7. Huang, X., Waterman, M.S.: Dynamic programming algorithms for restriction map comparison. Comput. Appl. Biosci. **8** (1992) 511–520
8. Hermjakob, H., Giegerich, R., Arnold, W.: RIFLE: Rapid identification of microorganisms by fragment length evaluation. In: Proceedings of ISMB 1997, Halkidiki, Greece (1997) 131–139
9. Aittokallio, T., Ojala, P., Nevalainen, T.J., Nevalainen, O.: Automated detection of differently expressed fragments in mRNA differential display. Electrophoresis **22** (2001) 1935–45
10. Bafna, V., Edwards, N.: SCOPE: A probabilistic model for scoring tandem mass spectra against a peptide database. Bioinformatics **17** (2001) S13–S21
11. Colinge, J., Masselot, A., Magnin, J.: A systematic statistical analysis of ion trap tandem mass spectra in view of peptide scoring. In: Proc. of WABI 2003, Budapest, Hungary. Volume 2812 of Lect. Notes Comput. Sc., Springer (2003) 25–38
12. Keller, A., Nesvizhskii, A.I., Kolker, E., Aebersold, R.: Empirical statistical model to estimate the accuracy of peptide identifications made by MS/MS and database search. Anal. Chem. **74** (2002) 5383–5392
13. Böcker, S.: Sequencing from compomers: Using mass spectrometry for DNA de-novo sequencing of 200+ nt. J. Comput. Biol. **11** (2004) 1110–1134
14. Dančik, V., Addona, T.A., Clauser, K.R., Vath, J.E., Pevzner, P.A.: De novo peptide sequencing via tandem mass spectrometry. J. Comput. Biol. **6** (1999) 327–342
15. Wilke, A., Rückert, C., Bartels, D., Dondrup, M., Goesmann, A., Hüser, A.T., Kespohl, S., Linke, B., Mahne, M., McHardy, A.C., Pühler, A., Meyer, F.: Bioinformatics support for high-throughput proteomics. J. Biotechnol. **106** (2003) 147–56

Author Index

Lecture Notes in Computer Science

For information about Vols. 1–3431

please contact your bookseller or Springer